Hillman
Hunter
Owners
Workshop
Manual

by J H Haynes
Member of the Guild of Motoring Writers
and D H Stead

Models covered:

Hillman Minx Saloon, Estate and Automatic	January 1967 to October 1970
Hillman Hunter Saloon, Estate and Automatic, De-luxe, Super, GL, GLS and GT	October 1966 onwards
Singer Gazelle Saloon and Automatic	January 1967 to February 1970
Singer Vogue Saloon, Estate and Automatic	October 1966 to February 1970
Sunbeam Vogue Saloon, Estate and Automatic	February 1970 to October 1970
Humber Sceptre Saloon and Automatic	September 1967 onwards
Sunbeam Arrow (supplied for North American market)	

ISBN 0 900550 33 3

© Haynes Publishing Group 1977

ABCDE
FGHIJ
KLMNO
PQRS

Printed in England

HAYNES PUBLISHING GROUP
SPARKFORD YEOVIL SOMERSET ENGLAND
distributed in the USA by
HAYNES PUBLICATIONS INC
861 LAWRENCE DRIVE
NEWBURY PARK
CALIFORNIA 91320
USA

Acknowledgements

Thanks are due to Chrysler UK Ltd for their assistance with technical material and illustrations and to Castrol for lubrication details. Invaluable assistance from R.T. Grainger in preparing the engine photographs and L.Tooze for those of the gearbox must not be forgotten. Lastly, thanks are extended to all of those people at Sparkford who helped in the production of this manual, particularly Peter Ward and John Rose for bringing the manual up to date, and again to John for planning the layout of the new material.

About this manual

The aim of this book is to help you get the best value from your car. It can do so in two ways. First it can help you decide what work must be done, even should you choose to get it done by a garage, and secondly the routine maintenance and the diagnosis and course of action when random faults occur. But it is hoped that you will also use the second and fuller purpose by tackling the work yourself. On the simpler jobs, it may even be quicker than booking the car into a garage and going there twice, to leave and collect it. Perhaps most important, much money can be saved by avoiding the costs a garage must charge to cover their labour and overheads.

The book has drawings and descriptions to show the function of the various components so that their layout can be understood. Then the tasks are described and photographed in a step by step sequence so that even a novice can cope with complicated work. Such a person is the very one to buy a car needing repair yet be unable to afford garage costs.

The jobs are described assuming only normal tools are possible. Many special workshop tools produced by the makers merely speed the work, and in these cases guidance is given as to how to do the job without them, the often quoted example being the use of a large hose clip to compress the piston rings for insertion in the cylinder. But on a very few occasions the special tool is essential to prevent damage to components; then their use is described. Though it might be possible to borrow the tool, such work may have to be entrusted to the official agent.

To avoid labour costs a garage will often give a cheaper repair by fitting a reconditioned assembly. The home mechanic can be helped by this book to diagnose the fault and make a repair using only a minor spare part.

The manufacturer's official workshop manuals are written for their trained staff, and so assume special knowledge; detail is left out. This book is written for the owner, and so goes into detail.

The book is divided into thirteen Chapters. Each Chapter is divided into numbered sections which are headed in bold type between horizontal lines. Each section consists of serially numbered paragraphs.

There are two types of illustration: (1) Figures which are numbered according to Chapter and sequence of occurrence in that Chapter. (2) Photographs which have a reference number on their caption. All photographs apply to the Chapter in which they occur so that the reference figure pinpoints the pertinent section.

Procedures, once described in the text, are not normally repeated. If it is necessary to refer to another Chapter, the reference will be given.

When the left or right side of the car is mentioned, it is as if looking forward from the rear of the car.

Great effort has been made to ensure that this book is complete and up to date. The manufacturers continually modify their cars, even in retrospect.

Introduction

Since the introduction of the Hillman Hunter in 1966 there has been a profusion and confusion of models, all the same shape with different names and engines covering the Sunbeam and Singer marques as well. When the export names of Sunbeam Arrow and Sunbeam Minx are considered the permutation of names is mind-boggling and one can only commend Chrysler's rationalisation of the whole assortment in 1970. The words Singer, Vogue, Gazelle and Minx have now disappeared.

The older a car gets the more attention it will need as normal wear and tear takes its toll. Thus the buyer of a cheaper, older model is faced with the need for more attention to his vehicle in order to enable it to run safely and pass the tests required by law every twelve months. As the purchase of a cheaper car is usually due to economic necessity it follows that garage bills are equally to be avoided.

This manual is the **only** one written which is based on the author's personal experiences. The hands in most of the photographs are those of the person who has written the book. Manufacturers' own official workshop manuals are all very well for those whose knowledge on certain basic terminology and methods is assumed. For the rest, this manual provides clear illustrations and descriptions of the order and method for the jobs to be done, step-by-step.

It must be assumed that a range of tools is available to the do-it-yourself owner. The accumulation of good tools is normally done over a period of time and this is the one expense that the do-it-yourself man must be prepared for. Never buy cheap tools. Be discreet in borrowing tools and do not be annoyed if someone refuses to lend them. Appreciate how much they cost if lost or damaged.

Certain jobs require specialised tools and where these are essential this manual will say so. Otherwise alternative means are given. Much of the work involved in looking after a car and carrying out repairs depends on accurate diagnosis in the first place. Where possible, therefore, a methodical and progressive way of diagnosis is presented. The time that can be wasted in hopping from one possible source of trouble to another suggested at random quite often by self styled 'experts' must have been experienced by many people. It is best to say at the start therefore, 'This could be one of several things - let's get the book out'.

Hillman Hunter GL

Hillman Hunter DL Estate

Hillman Hunter GT

Humber Sceptre

Contents

Routine maintenance

Maintenance is essential for ensuring safety and desirable for the purpose of getting the best in terms of performance and economy from the car. Over the years the need for periodic lubrication - oiling, greasing and so on - has been drastically reduced if not totally eliminated. This has unfortunately tended to lead some owners to think that because no such action is required the items either no longer exist or will last for ever. This is a serious delusion. If anything, there are now more places, particularly in the steering, and suspension where joints and pivots are fitted. Although you do not grease them any more you still have to look at them - and look at them just as often as you may previously have had to grease them. It follows therefore that the largest initial element of maintenance is visual examination. This may lead to repairs or renewals.

At the beginning of each chapter in the manual the routine maintenance details covering that chapter are given.

In the summary given here the 'essential for safety' items are shown in **bold type.** These **must** be attended to at the regular frequencies shown in order to avoid the possibility of accidents and loss of life. Other neglect results in unreliability, increased running costs, more rapid wear and more rapid depreciation of the vehicle in general.

Every 250 miles (400 km) or weekly

STEERING
> **Check the tyre pressures.**
> **Examine tyres for wear or damage.**
> **Is steering smooth and accurate?**

BRAKES
> **Is there any fall off in braking efficiency?**
> **Try an emergency stop. Is adjustment necessary?**

LIGHTS, WIPERS & HORNS
> **Do all bulbs work at the front and rear?**
> **Are the headlamp beams aligned properly?**
> **Do wipers and horns work?**

ENGINE
> Check the sump oil level and top up if required?
> Check the radiator coolant level and top up if required.
> Check the battery electrolyte level and top up to the level of the plates with distilled water as needed.

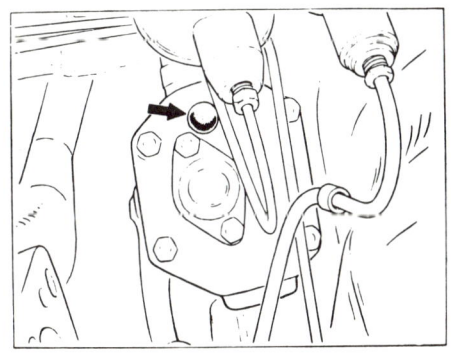

Steering box filler and level plug.

Every 1,000 miles (1,600 km) or monthly

!f there are indications that safety items are not functioning correctly, they must be attended to earlier.

STEERING
    Is there any free play between the steering wheel and the roadwheels?

BRAKES
    Check the fluid reservoir (hydraulic) level. If significantly lower examine the system immediately for signs of leaks.

Every 5,000 miles (8,000 km) or 6 monthly

If there are indications that safety items are not functioning correctly, they must be attended to earlier.

STEERING
    Examine all steering linkage rods, joints and bushes for signs of wear or damage.
    Check front wheel hub bearings and adjust if necessary.
    Check tightness of steering box mounting bolts.
    Check the steering box oil level.

BRAKES
    Examine disc pads and drum shoes to determine the amount of friction material left. Renew if necessary.
    Examine all hydraulic pipes, cylinders and unions for signs of chafing, corrosion, dents or any other form or deterioration or leaks.
    Lubricate the handbrake pull off springs.

SUSPENSION
    Examine all nuts, bolts and shackles securing the suspension units, front and rear. Tighten if necessary.
    Examine the rubber bushes for signs of wear and play.

ENGINE
    Change oil and filter element.
    Check valve clearances and adjust if necessary (aluminium head only).
    Check distributor contacts gap and lubricate the spindle and cam.
    Check fan belt tension.
    Check spark plug gaps.
    Lubricate the generator, rear bearing (not on alternators).
    Top up the carburettor damper oil.
    Top up the gearbox or automatic transmission (if fitted).
    Clean the air cleaner element and casing.
    Clean the crankcase breather valve and flame trap.

CLUTCH
    Check and top up if necessary the hydraulic fluid reservoir.
    Examine for any signs of leaks if the level has dropped significantly.

AUTOMATIC TRANSMISSION
    Check the fluid level, and clean off any mud, etc, from the cooling ducts and fluid pan.

BODY
    See that the water drain holes at the bottom of all doors are clear and that the drain tube from the heater air intake box is clear.

Every 10,000 miles (16,000 km) or yearly

If there are indications that safety items are not functioning correctly, they must be attended to earlier.

BODYWORK
    Examine the underbody for signs of rust, particularly where the rear suspension is anchored.
    Check the condition of the body frame mounting for the upper end of the front suspension units.

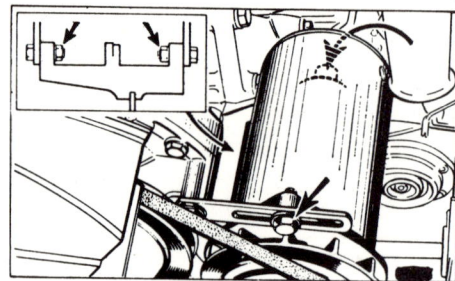

Adjustment bolts for fan belt tension with dynamo (top) and alternator (bottom.

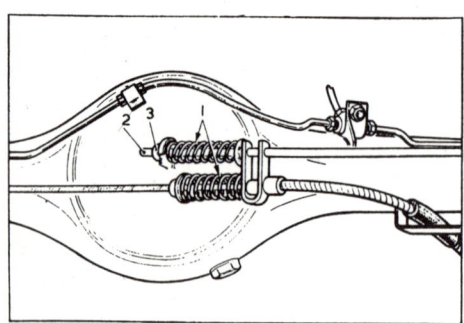

Greasing points of handbrake pull-off springs, rod and bush.

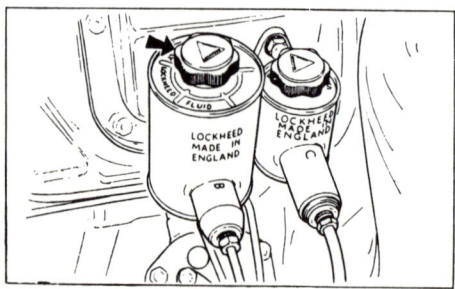

Hydraulic fluid reservoirs - (brake system arrowed).

ENGINE
Fit new distributor contact points.
Fit new spark plugs.
Fit new carburettor air cleaner element.
Flush out the cooling system.
Clean fuel pump sediment bowl and filter gauze.

GEARBOX
Check and top up oil level.

REAR AXLE
Check the oil level and top up as necessary.

STEERING
Remove front wheel hubs, flush out bearings, inspect and repack with grease.

BRAKES
Renew servo air filter element (if fitted).

Every 30,000 miles (48,000 km) or 2½ years

GEARBOX
Drain and refill with fresh oil.
Clean overdrive filter (if fitted).

REAR AXLE
Drain and refill with fresh oil.

In addition, time should be spent on the following:

CLEANING
The best way to examine a car and know what sort of a state it is in, is to thoroughly clean it, inside and out. One of the principal results of this, which is not covered by other maintenance operations, is the finding of any traces of rust in the body panels. If rust is allowed to go unchecked it could affect certain structural panels which may make the car unsafe and keep it off the road.

EXHAUST SYSTEM
An exhaust system must be leakproof and keep engine noise below a level of 86 decibels. Leaks may cause dangerous fumes to enter the interior and affect the driver and passengers - thus having an adverse effect on the driver's capabilities. Excessive noise constitutes a public nuisance. Both these faults can result in the vehicle being declared unfit for use.

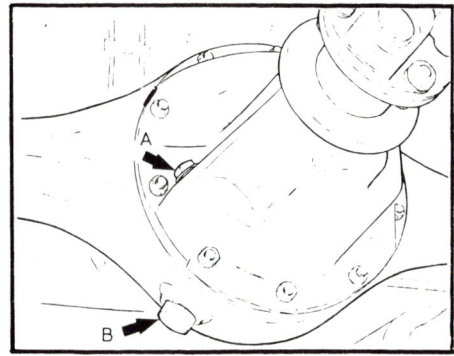

Rear axle filler/level plug (A) and drain plug (B)

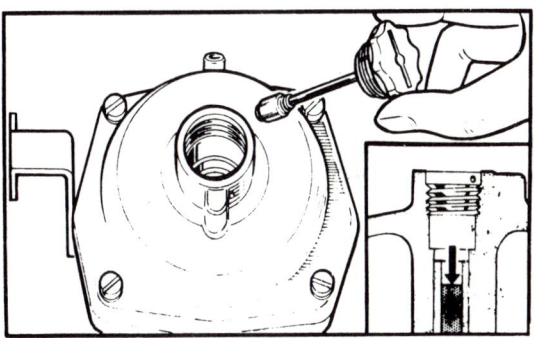

Carburettor dashpot damper removed and (inset) oil level height

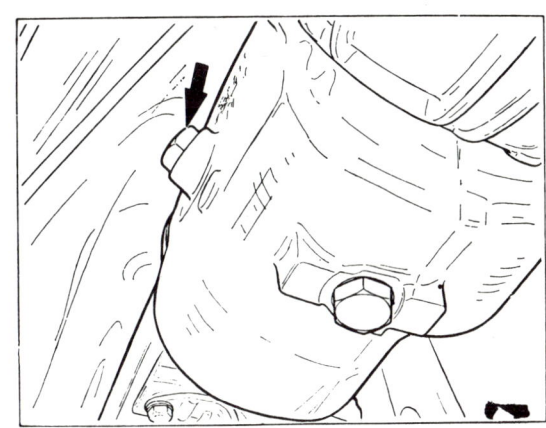

Gearbox filler/level plug

Buying spare parts

Spare parts are available from many sources, for example: Chrysler garages, other garages and accessory shops, and motor factors. Our advice regarding spare part sources is as follows:

Officially appointed Chrysler garages - This is the best source of parts which are peculiar to your vehicle or are otherwise not generally available (eg: complete cylinder heads, internal transmission components, badges, interior trim etc). It is also the only place at which you should buy parts if your car is still under warranty. To be sure of obtaining the correct parts it will always be necessary to give the storeman your car's engine and chassis number, and if possible, to take the 'old' part along for positive identification. Remember that many parts are available on a factory exchange scheme - any parts returned should always be clean! It obviously makes good sense to go straight to the specialists on your car for this type of part for they are best

equipped to supply you.

Other garages and accessory shops - These are often very good places to buy materials and components needed for the maintenance of your car (eg. oil filters, spark plugs, bulbs, fan belts, oils and greases, touch-up paint, filler paste etc). They also sell general accessories, usually have convenient opening hours, charge lower prices and can often be found not far from home.

Motor factors - Good factors will stock all of the more important components which wear out relatively quickly (eg; clutch components, pistons, valves, exhaust system, brake cylinder/pipes/hoses/seals/shoes and pads etc). Motor factors will often provide new or reconditioned components on a part exchange basis - this can save a considerable amount of money.

The *vehicle serial number and suffix letters* are stamped on a plate which is fixed to the bonnet lock platform.

General specifications

Dimensions

	Minx, Hunter Gazelle, Vogue	Hunter De-Luxe Super and GL	Hunter GLS and GT	Sceptre
Wheelbase	8' 2½'' (250.2 cm)	8' 2½'' (250.2 cm)	8' 2½'' (250.2 cm)	8' 2½'' (250.2 cm)
Track (front and rear)	4' 4'' (132 cm)	4' 4'' (132 cm)	4' 4½'' GLS (133 cm) 4' 4¾'' (134 cm) (Later cars) 4' 3¾'' GT (131 cm) 4' 4½'' (133 cm)	4' 4'' (132 cm) †4' 3¾'' (131 cm)
Overall length	14' 0'' (426.7 cm) Minx/Gazelle 14' 1½'' (430.5 cm) Hunter & Vogue 14' 4'' (436.9 cm) (Estate cars)	14' 0'' (426.7 cm) 14' 3'' (434.3 cm) (Later cars) 14' 2¾'' (433.7 cm) (Estate cars) 14' 5'' (439.4 cm) (Later Estate cars)	14' 0'' (426.7 cm) 14' 3'' (434.3 cm) (Later cars)	14' 1½'' (430.5 cm) 14' 3'' (434.3 cm) (Later cars) 14' 5'' (439.4 cm) (Estate cars)
Overall height (at kerb weight)	4' 8'' (142.2 cm)	4' 8'' (142.2 cm) 4' 8½'' (143.5 cm) (Later cars) 4' 7¾'' (141.6 cm) (Later Estate cars)	4' 8'' (142.2 cm) 4' 7¾'' (141.6 cm) (Later GT) 4' 8¼'' (142.9 cm) (Later GLS)	4' 8'' (142.2 cm) 4' 7½'' (141.0 cm) (Later cars) 4' 10'' (147.3 cm) (Estate car) **
Overall width	5' 3½'' (161.3 cm)	5' 3½'' (161.3 cm)	5' 3½'' (161.3 cm)	5' 4¾'' (164.5 cm) 5' 3½'' (161.3 cm) (Later cars and all Estate cars)
Minimum ground clearance	6¾'' (16.8 cm)	6½'' (16.5 cm)	6½'' (16.5 cm) 5½'' (14.0 cm) (Later GLS) 5¾'' (14.6 cm) (Later GT)	6¾'' (16.8 cm) 5½'' (14.0 cm) (Later cars and all Estate cars)
Turning circle	33' 6'' (10.2 m)	34' 0'' (10.36 m)	34' 0'' (10.36 m) 34' 2'' (10.40 m) (Later cars)	33' 6'' (10.2 m)
Towing capacity (max.)	17 cwt (864 kg)	17 cwt (864 kg)	17 cwt (864 kg)	17 cwt (864 kg)
Roof rack load (max.)	100 lb (45 kg)	100 lb (45 kg)	100 lb (45 kg)	100 lb (45 kg)

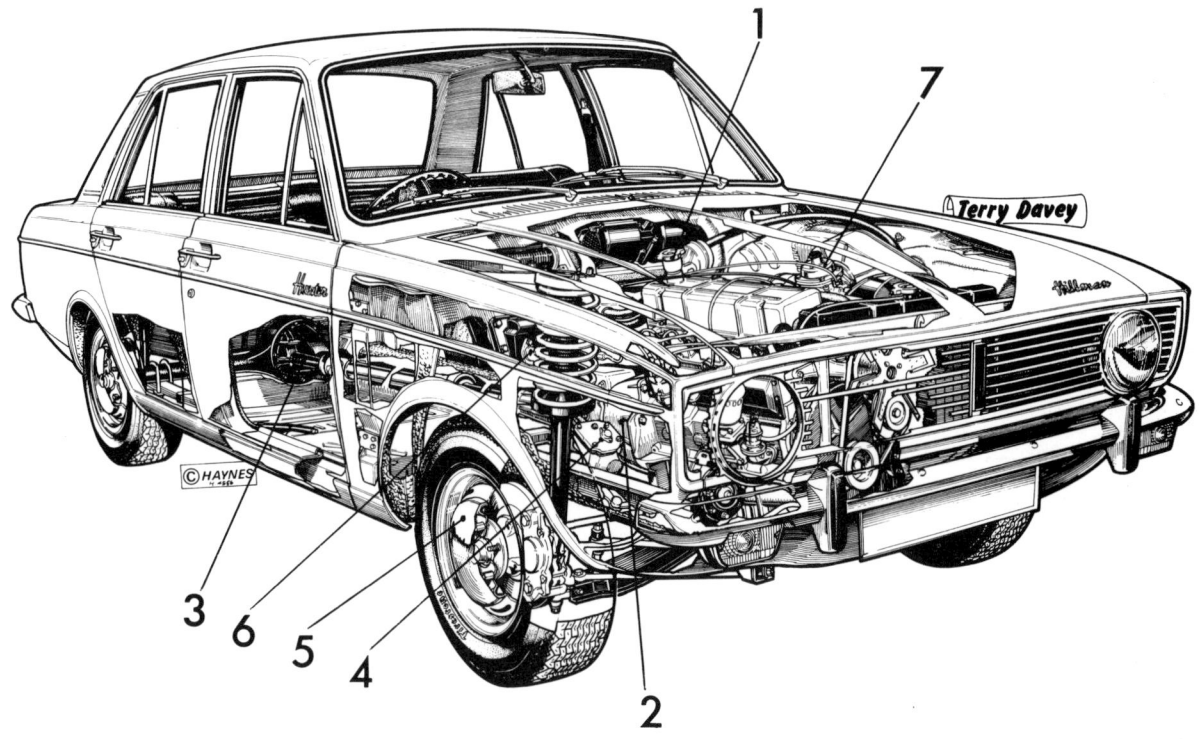

Recommended lubricants

Component		Lubricant
1	Engine	**Castrol GTX**
2	Gearbox	
	Manual and overdrive	**Castrol GTX**
	Automatic	**Castrol TQF**
3	Rear axle	**Castrol Hypoy**
4	Steering box	**Castrol Hypoy**
5	Wheel bearings	**Castrol LM Grease**
6	Brake system	**Castrol Girling Universal Brake and Clutch Fluid**
7	Carburettor damper	**Castrol GTX**

Castrol Everyman can be used to lubricate the distributor, dynamo bushes, doors, locks and catches

These are general recommendations only. Different operating conditions require different lubricants. Consult the handbook supplied with the car

Chapter 1 Engine

Contents

Specifications

Covers the 1500 and 1725 cc engines - the latter with either a cast iron or aluminium head. A high or low compression head is available for both size engines in cast iron only. For engine performance and valve timing tables, torque wrench settings and Holbay engine specifications, refer to Chapter 13.

Engine - general

Type		4 cylinder in-line OHV pushrod operated
Bore:		
Grade A		3.2102 - 3.2106 in (81.539 - 81.549 mm)
Grade B		3.2106 - 3.2110 in (81.549 - 81.559 mm)
Grade C		3.2110 - 3.2114 in (81.559 - 81.569 mm)
Grade D		3.2114 - 3.2118 in (81.569 - 81.579 mm)

	1725	**1500**
Stroke	3.25 (82.55 mm)	2.82 (71.8 mm)
Capacity (standard bore)	1724 cc (105.1 in^3)	1496 cc (91.28 in^3)
Firing order	1, 3, 4, 2	
No 1 cylinder position	Front of engine	

Cylinder block

Material	Cast iron
Max. oversize (with or without liners)	0.030 in (0.76 mm)

Camshaft

Bearings ...	3: steel shell lined with white metal
Journal diameter ...	1.7477 - 1.7470 in (44.39 - 44.37 mm)
Bearing internal diameter ...	1.7500 - 1.7490 in (44.45 - 44.51 mm)
Bearing running clearance ...	0.003 - 0.0013 in (0.07 - 0.03 mm)
Endfloat ...	0.002 - 0.003 in (0.05 - 0.07 mm)

Crankshaft

Throw -	
1275 engine ...	1.625 in (41.28 mm)
1500 engine ...	1.410 in (35.81 mm)
Bearings ...	5, steel shell lined with white metal
Journal diameter (A) ...	2.3745 - 2.3740 in (60.312 - 60.299 mm)
Journal diameter (B) ...	2.365 in (60.071 mm)
Maximum re-grinding undersize ...	-0.040 in (1.01 mm)
Crankpin diameter (A) ...	2.1260 - 2.1255 in (54.000 - 53.987 mm)
Crankpin diameter (B) ...	2.115 in (53.721 mm)
Endfloat thrust washers ...	2; semi-circular - copper lead face
Endfloat ...	0.002 - 0.008 in (0.05 - 0.20 mm)
Main bearing running clearance ...	0.0025 - 0.0010 in (0.063 - 0.025 mm)

Connecting rods

Type ...	'H' section steel forging
Distance between centres	
1725 engine ...	5.625 in (14.28 cms)
1500 engine ...	5.845 in (14.84 cms)
Big end bore (no bearings) ...	2.2715 - 2.2710 in (57.69 - 57.68 mm)
Big end running clearance ...	0.002 - 0.0015 in (0.05 - 0.03 mm)
Later models ...	0.0022 - 0.0055 in (0.056 - 0.013 mm)
Big end endfloat ...	0.0125 - 0.0075 in (0.32 - 0.19 mm)
Big end bearings ...	Steel shell aluminium/tin or copper/lead indium coated
Small end bore (with bush)	
White - High grade ...	0.9378 - 0.9377 in (23.820 - 23.817 mm)
Green - Med. grade ...	0.9377 - 0.9376 in (23.817 - 23.815 mm)
Yellow - Low grade ...	0.9376 - 0.9375 in (23.815 - 23.812 mm)

Gudgeon pins

Type ...	Fully floating with circlip location
Fit in piston ...	Push fit at 68°F (20°C)
Diameter:	
Service grade (blue) ...	0.9378 - 0.9377 in (23.82 - 23.817 mm)
High grade (white) ...	0.9377 - 0.9386 in (23.817 - 23.815 mm)
Med. grade (green) ...	0.9386 - 0.9375 in (23.815 - 23.812 mm)
Low grade (yellow) ...	0.9375 - 0.9374 in (23.812 - 23.809 mm)

Pistons

Type ...	Aluminium alloy, tin plated with slotted skirt	
Length ...	3.25 in (82.57 mm)	
Rings fitted ...	2 compression, 1 scraper	
Diameter:		
Grade A* ...	3.2096 - 3.2092 in (81.524 - 81.514 mm)	
Grade B* ...	3.2100 - 3.2096 in (81.534 - 81.524 mm)	
Grade C ...	3.2104 - 3.2100 in (81.544 - 81.534 mm)	
Grade D ...	3.2108 - 3.2104 in (81.555 - 81.544 mm)	
Grade E ...	3.2112 - 3.2108 in (81.565 - 81.555 mm)	
Oversize available above standard size (C, D or E) ...	0.030 in (0.76 mm)	
Clearance at skirt in cylinder measured at right angles to gudgeon pin axis ...	0.0006 - 0.0014 in (0.015 - 0.035 mm)	
Ring gap (Grade A bore) Top ring ...	0.032 - 0.024 in (0.81 - 0.60 mm)	
Ring gap - Second and scraper ...	0.014 - 0.009 in (0.35 - 0.22 mm)	
Piston bowl volume	*1725*	*1500*
High compression ...	6.9 - 7.5 cc	Flat top
Low compression ...	15.3 - 15.7 cc	6.9 - 7.5 cc
Maximum weight variation per set ...	3.55 grams (2 drams)	
Compression identification marks:		
HC ...	High compression	
△ ...	High compression, 1500	
LC ...	Low compression	
O ...	Low compression, 1725	
◇ ...	Low compression, 1500 and High compression, 1725 in	

Grades A and B are not available for service use

Cylinder head

Material	Aluminium
Gasket type	Steel, copper, asbestos (aluminium head) or varnished steel pressing (cast iron head)
Valve position	Overhead with rockers and pushrods

Valve clearances (hot):

255, 260 and 298 camshafts*	Inlet 0.012 in (0.30 mm), Exhaust 0.014 in (0.35 mm)
295 and 320 camshafts*	Inlet and exhaust 0.013 in (0.33 mm)
Valve seat and face angle	45°

Valve stem diameter:

Inlet	0.3110 - 0.3105 in (7.90 - 7.89 mm)
Exhaust	0.3100 - 0.3095 in (7.87 - 7.86 mm)

Valve stem to guide clearance:

Inlet

Early models	0.0015 - 0.003 in (0.038 - 0.076 mm)
Later models	0.001 - 0.0025 in (0.025 - 0.063 mm)
Exhaust	0.0025 - 0.004 in (0.63 - 0.102 mm)
Valve length	4.66 in (118.3 mm)

Valve guides:

O.D.	0.5640 - 0.5635 in (14.30 - 14.27 mm)
Interference fit	0.0025 - 0.0045 in (0.063 - 0.114 mm)

Length:

Inlet	2.0 in (50.8 mm)
Exhaust	2.15 in (54.6 mm)
Fitted height above head	0.50 in (12.7 mm)

	Aluminium head		Iron head (1725 and 1500)
Valve head diameter:			
Inlet	1.503 in (38.17 mm)		1.434 in (36.42 mm)
Exhaust	1.204 in (30.58 mm)		1.174 in (29.81 mm)
Valve springs:			
Type	Single	Dual	Single
Length fitted:			
inner	—	1.28 in (32.5 mm)	—
outer	1.48 in (37.6 mm)	1.40 in (35.6 mm)	1.58 in (40.1 mm)
Load fitted:			
inner	—	21.2 lb (9.6 kg)	—
	—	Later models	—
	—	28.3 lb (12.8 kg)	—
outer	75.2 lb (34.0 kg)	50.5 lb (22.9 kg)	83 lb (37.6 kg)
	—	Later models	—
	—	52 lb (23.6 kg)	—

Lubrication

Engine sump capacity (incl. filter)	7½ pints (9 US pints, 4.2 litres)
Filter capacity	1 pint (1.2 US pints, 0.56 litres)
Oil pump type	Eccentric lobe
Pump drive	Skew gear from camshaft
Normal pressure (hot engine new)	41 - 45 lb/in^2 (2.9 - 3.2 kg/cm^2)
Oil filter type	Full flow - disposable

For camshaft application see 'Engine performance' page 202.

1. General Description

The range of cars to which this manual refers is fitted with a 1500 cc or 1725 cc version of the Chrysler engine. Both versions are very similar, the main differences being that the 1725 cc engine has a cylinder head made of aluminium for the high performance high compression versions of the range. The increase in capacity for the 1725 cc engine is achieved by lengthening the stroke which means also that the throw of the crankshaft is different. The 1725 cc engine is, in fact, almost exactly a 'square' engine in that the bore and stroke are almost exactly the same, whereas the 1500 cc engine is quite noticeably over-square, the stroke being less than that of the larger capacity motor. Engines are all four cylinder, fitted with two valves per cylinder which are operated by overhead rockers and pushrods from a single camshaft mounted in the right-hand side of the engine block.

The crankshaft runs in five main bearings and the endfloat is controlled by a pair of semi-circular thrust washers located in the upper half of the centre main bearing journal. The camshaft is driven by a duplex chain from a sprocket on forward end of the crankshaft and this chain is tensioned by a hard rubber slipper supported on a steel leaf pivoting inside the cover. The camshaft, in turn, drives the oil pump through a skew gear and the oil pump drive shaft also drives the distributor.

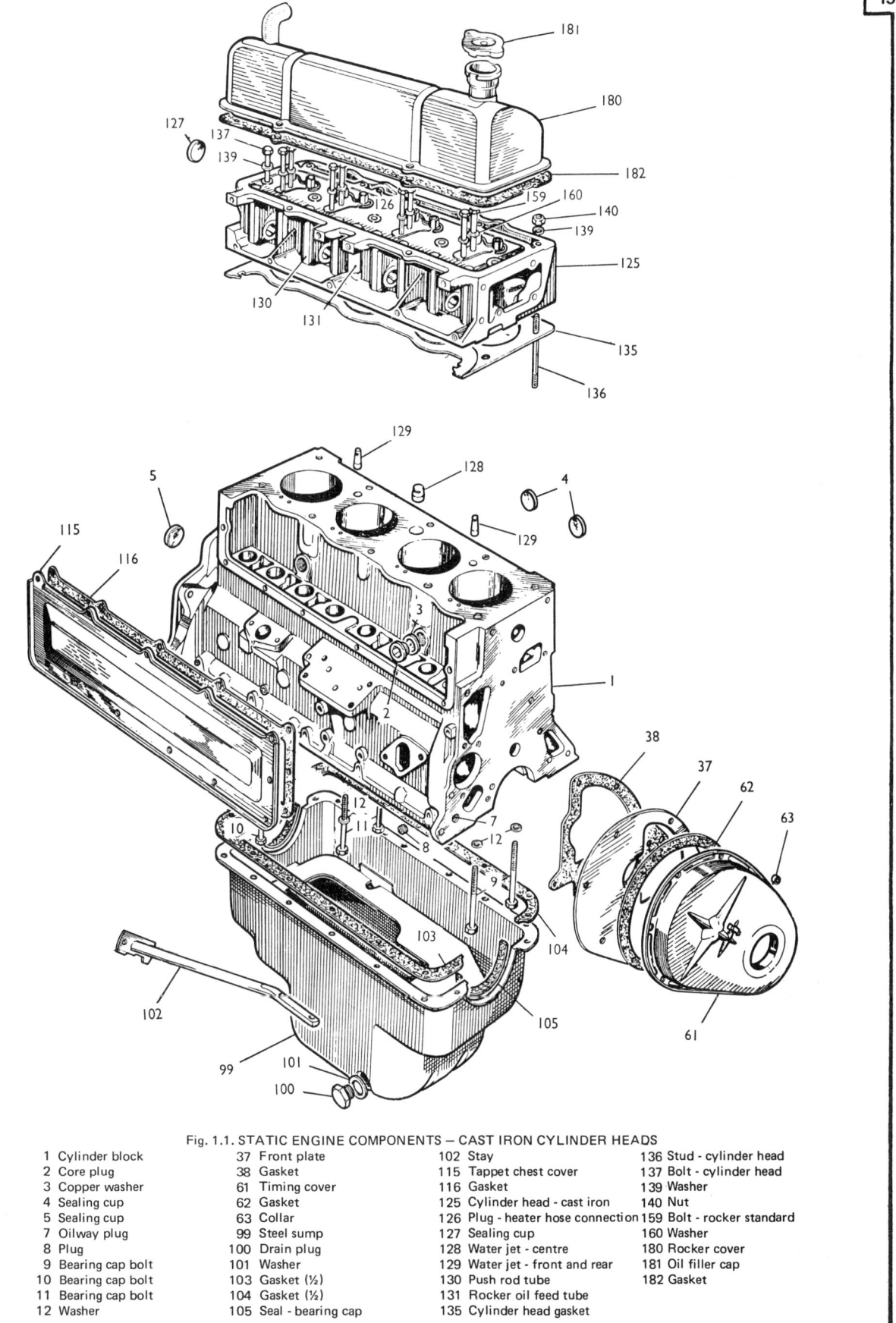

Fig. 1.1. STATIC ENGINE COMPONENTS — CAST IRON CYLINDER HEADS

1 Cylinder block	37 Front plate	102 Stay	136 Stud - cylinder head
2 Core plug	38 Gasket	115 Tappet chest cover	137 Bolt - cylinder head
3 Copper washer	61 Timing cover	116 Gasket	139 Washer
4 Sealing cup	62 Gasket	125 Cylinder head - cast iron	140 Nut
5 Sealing cup	63 Collar	126 Plug - heater hose connection	159 Bolt - rocker standard
7 Oilway plug	99 Steel sump	127 Sealing cup	160 Washer
8 Plug	100 Drain plug	128 Water jet - centre	180 Rocker cover
9 Bearing cap bolt	101 Washer	129 Water jet - front and rear	181 Oil filler cap
10 Bearing cap bolt	103 Gasket (½)	130 Push rod tube	182 Gasket
11 Bearing cap bolt	104 Gasket (½)	131 Rocker oil feed tube	
12 Washer	105 Seal - bearing cap	135 Cylinder head gasket	

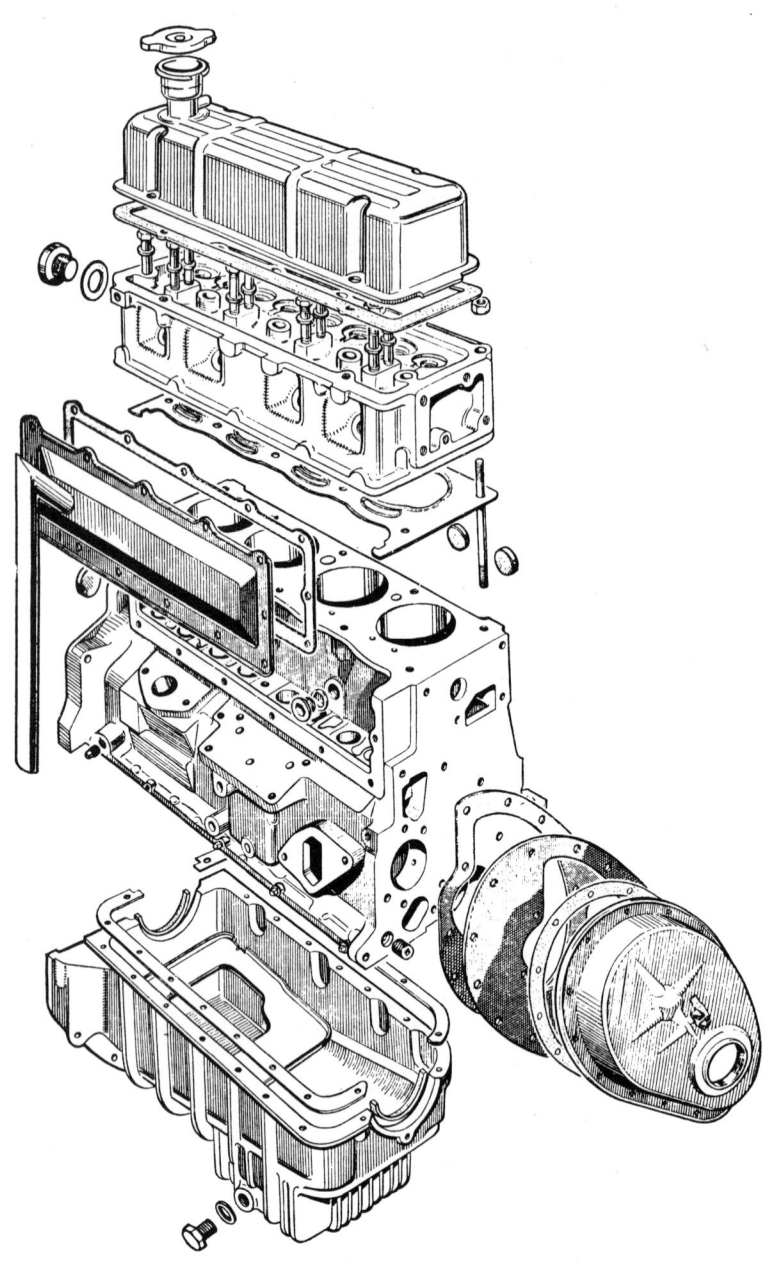

Fig. 1.2. Static engine components; engines with aluminium cylinder heads.

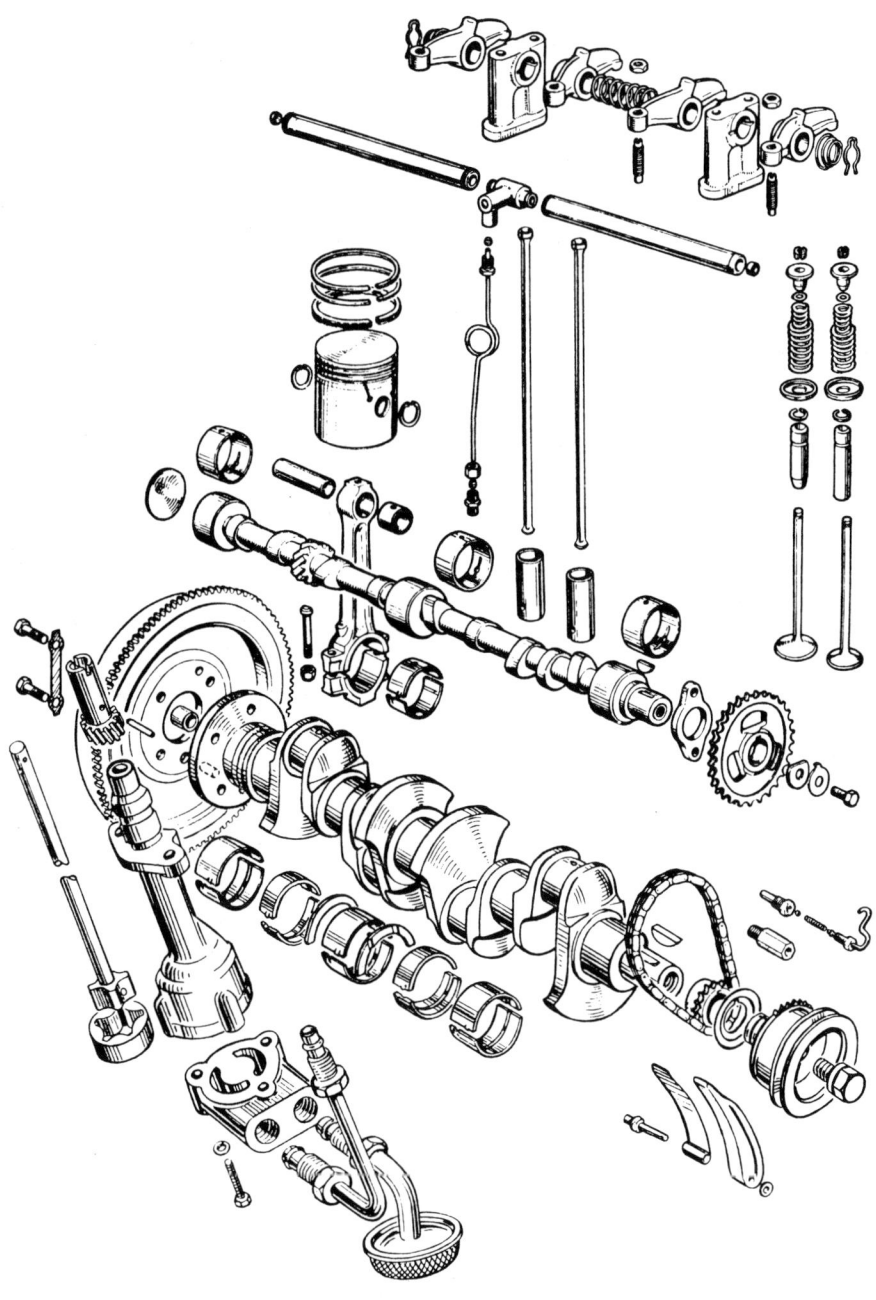

Fig.1.3. Moving engine components; engines with aluminium cylinder heads.

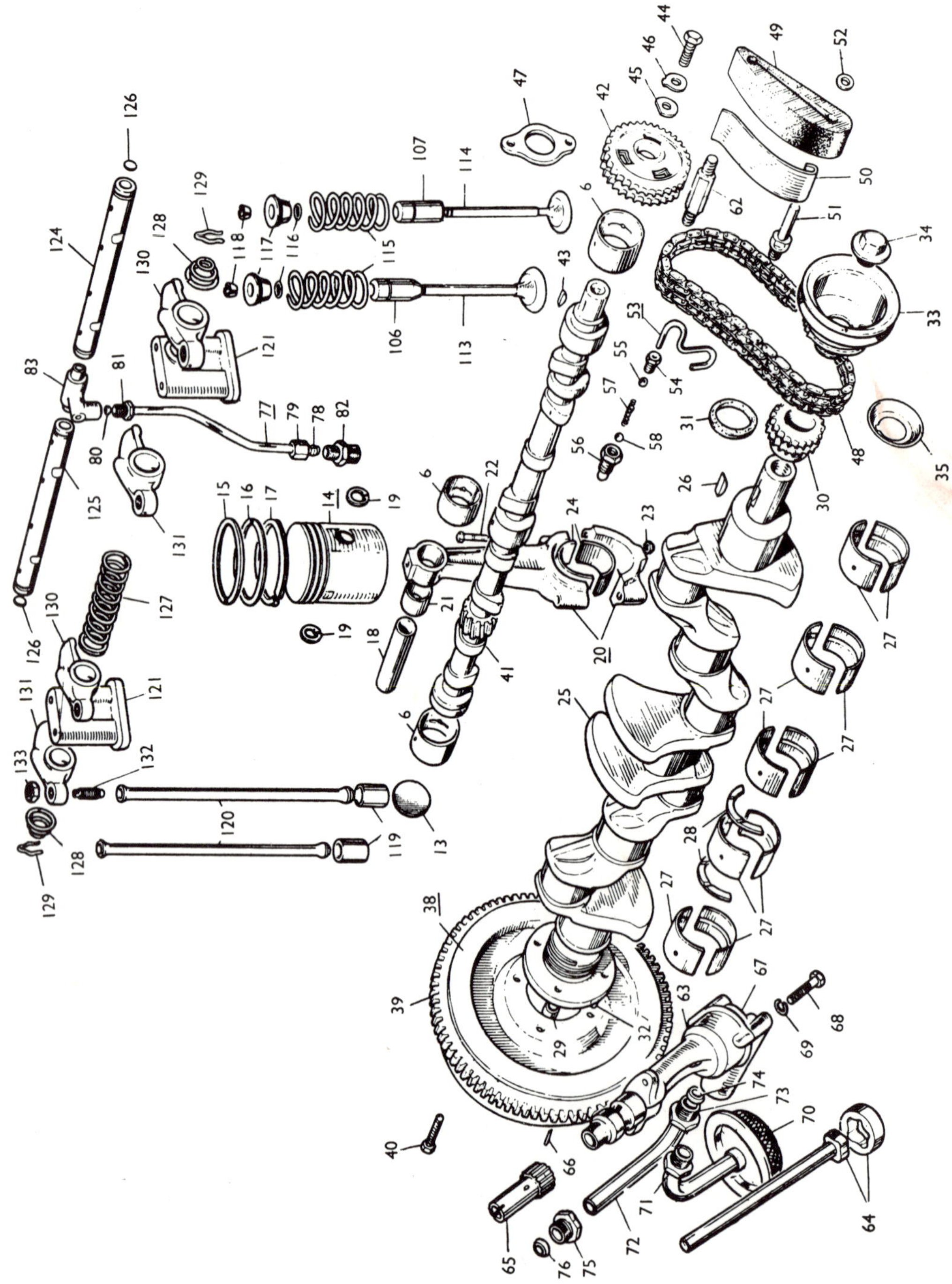

126
124
129
128
118
117
116
107
114
47
42
45
46
44
49
52
130
121
115
106
113
6
43
62
50
51
34
33
83
81
77
79
78
82
80
125
131
53
55
57
54
58
56
31
48
35
15
16
17
14
19
6
22
24
23
26
30
127
126
130
21
18
41
20
27
121
131
25
133
132
120
119
13
128
129
28
38
39
29
32
63
67
68
69
74
73
70
40
66
65
76
75
72
71
64

Fig. 1.4. MOVING ENGINE COMPONENTS – CAST IRON CYLINDER HEAD

6 Bearing - camshaft	34 Pulley bolt	58 Ball	83 Adaptor
13 Camshaft sealing disc	35 Oil thrower	62 Stud	106 Valve guide - inlet
14 Piston assembly	38 Flywheel	63 Oil pump body	107 Valve guide - exhaust
15 Top ring - compression	39 Starter ring	64 Oil pump shaft and rotor	113 Inlet valve
16 Lower ring - compression	40 Flywheel bolt	65 Drive gear	114 Exhaust valve
17 Scraper ring	41 Camshaft	66 Dowel pin	115 Valve spring
18 Gudgeon pin	42 Timing sprocket	67 End cover	116 Sealing ring
19 Circlip	43 Woodruff key	68 Cover screw	117 Cup
20 Connecting rod	44 Bolt	69 Spring washer	118 Cotter (collets)
21 Small end bush	45 Retaining washer	70 Strainer	119 Tappet
22 Connecting rod cap bolt	46 Tab washer	71 Locknut	120 Push rod
23 Nut	47 Thrust plate	72 Delivery pipe	121 Rocker shaft - standard
24 Big end bearing shells	48 Timing chain	73 Nut - pipe to pump	124 Rocker shaft - front
25 Crankshaft	49 Tensioner pad	74 Olive	125 Rocker shaft - rear
26 Woodruff key	50 Tensioner blade	75 Nut - pipe to block	126 Plug
27 Main bearing shells	51 Pivot pin	76 Olive	127 Inner spring
28 End float thrust washers	52 Washer	77 Pipe - rocker oil feed	128 Outer spring
29 Bush - input shaft	53 Oil pipe	78 Olive	129 Retaining clip
30 Timing sprocket	54 Nut	79 Nut	130 Rocker (Nos. 1, 3, 5 & 7)
31 Damper ring	55 Olive	80 Olive	131 Rocker (Nos. 2, 4, 6 & 8)
32 Flywheel dowel	56 Adaptor	81 Nut	132 Adjusting screw
33 Pulley wheel	57 Spring	82 Union	133 Locknut

The pistons are a fully floating fit to the connecting rods and the gudgeon pins are retained in the piston with circlips. The connecting rod small end bush is renewable and gudgeon pins are available in different sizes as required for the fit of the piston to the small end of the connecting rod. The lubrication system is of the forced feed type through a full flow oil filter to the crankshaft main bearings, connecting rod big end bearings, camshaft bearings and valve rocker gear. The oil pump is fully submersed and is of the eccentric lobe twin rotor type.

The engine is flexibly mounted into the body frame at three points. There is one mounting bracket fitted to each side of the engine block, centrally, and the third suspension point is onto a cross-member which runs underneath the gearbox. It will be appreciated, therefore, that neither the engine nor the gearbox is fully supported when either one is removed.

2. Routine Maintenance

1. Once a week or more often if high mileages are being driven, remove the oil level dipstick and check the level of the oil in the sump which should be at the full mark. Top up the level with the recommended grade of oil (see page 11 for details). If an engine appears to be using oil at a rate of more than 1 pint per 500 miles it should be considered as excessive and steps should be taken to discover whether there is a leak in the system or whether the oil is being consumed due to excessive wear in the engine.

2. Every 5,000 miles run the engine until it is hot. Then place a container with a minimum capacity of one gallon under the drain plug in the sump, undo the drain plug and allow the old oil to drain out for at least ten minutes. The oil filter cartridge should also be unscrewed and a new one fitted as described in Section 20 of this Chapter.

3. Carefully clean the drain plug and make sure that the washer is clean and intact and replace the plug in the sump tightening it firmly. Then refill the sump with 7½ pints of Castrol GTX oil and run the engine and recheck the level on the dipstick. Examine the point where the new filter cartridge has been screwed in to make sure that there are no oil leaks of any sort.

4. If the car is regularly used in extreme conditions of heat, cold or excessively dusty atmospheres, it is advantageous to change the engine oil more often. In such circumstances a frequency of 3,000 miles between changes is recommended.

3. Major Operations which may be carried out with the Engine in Place

1. The following work may be conveniently carried out with the engine in place:-

1) Removal and replacement of the cylinder head assembly.
2) Removal and replacement of the clutch assembly.
3) Removal and replacement of the engine front mountings.
4) Removal and replacement of the timing chain cover, timing chain and timing chain sprockets.

2. The following work can be carried out with the engine still mounted in the car but it is preferable, if possible, to remove the engine from the car. If the engine is left in position great care must be taken to ensure that all the parts removed and replaced are kept scrupulously clean. It is very easy for extraneous dirt to find its way where it should not be when the engine is still in situ in the car frame.

1) Removal and replacement of the sump.
2) Removal and replacement of the oil pump.
3) Removal and replacement of the connecting rod big end bearings.
4) Removal and replacement of pistons and connecting rods (after

the removal of the cylinder head and sump).
5) Removal and replacement of the camshaft.
6) Removal and replacement of the flywheel (after removing the gearbox and clutch).
7) Removal and replacement of the crankshaft main bearing shells.

4. Major Operations for which the Engine must be Removed from the Car

1. Removal and replacement of the crankshaft.
2. Renewal of the camshaft bearings.

5. Engine - Removal

1. The description which follows will assume that the engine is being removed from the car by itself, that is, with the gearbox left in the car. For occasions when it is required to remove the engine and gearbox together as one unit from the car the necessary information is given towards the end of this Section. As it is necessary to disconnect and remove several items from the engine before it can be lifted from the car, this Chapter will only indicate what has to be removed. Details of individual items which have to be removed will be found under their appropriate Chapter headings. For example, where an instruction to 'remove carburettor' is given, the full implication of this removal will be given in Chapter 3. Before starting work on the actual removal of the engine, it is well worth while to spend some time in getting the engine thoroughly cleaned off away from the area where the actual removal and subsequent dismantling may be taking place. If this cleaning can be done at a service station which may be equipped with pressure cleaning equipment, so much the better. Otherwise one should use paraffin and stiff brushes and scrapers to remove the bulk of the caked on dirt before removing the engine. The final thorough cleaning of the exterior of the engine may be left until it is removed from the car. Decide whether you are going to jack up the car and support it on axle stands or raise the front end of the car onto wheel ramps. If the latter method, run the car up now (and chock the rear wheels) whilst you still have engine power available. Remember that with the front wheels supported on ramps the working height and engine lifting height is going to be increased. If stands are to be used the front of the car can be jacked up later when ready.

2. Once you are sure that the car is in the correct position, which should be on level ground or level floor, the work of removing the engine may begin.

3. Open the bonnet and disconnect the battery leads and after having unscrewed the battery clamp, remove the battery from the car.

4. With the bonnet propped open, mark the position of the bonnet hinges, preparatory to removing the hinge clamping bolts. It is easier if you have somebody to help you at the next stage, to lift the bonnet off. Care is required if damage is to be avoided to the surrounding paintwork as the bonnet is quite heavy and it could easily slip and scratch the paint nearby. It can be done single-handed, however, by supporting the rear of the bonnet corners by blocks of wood. Full details can be found in Chapter 12. When the bonnet is finally removed place it somewhere where it cannot be damaged and where the edges will not be scratched or chipped by hard surfaces.

5. Drain the oil from the sump of the engine.

6. Drain the liquid from the cooling system.

7. Detach both hose pipes from the top and bottom of the radiator by slackening the hose clips and carefully pulling the pipes from the radiator shell. Detach the heater water hoses from their connections on the water pump body at the front of the engine. Also unclip the two hoses from the top of the cylinder head. When this has been done both of these hoses may be put to one side clear of the engine.

8. Undo the four bolts which secure the radiator to the front body panel of the car and holding the radiator vertical to prevent it being

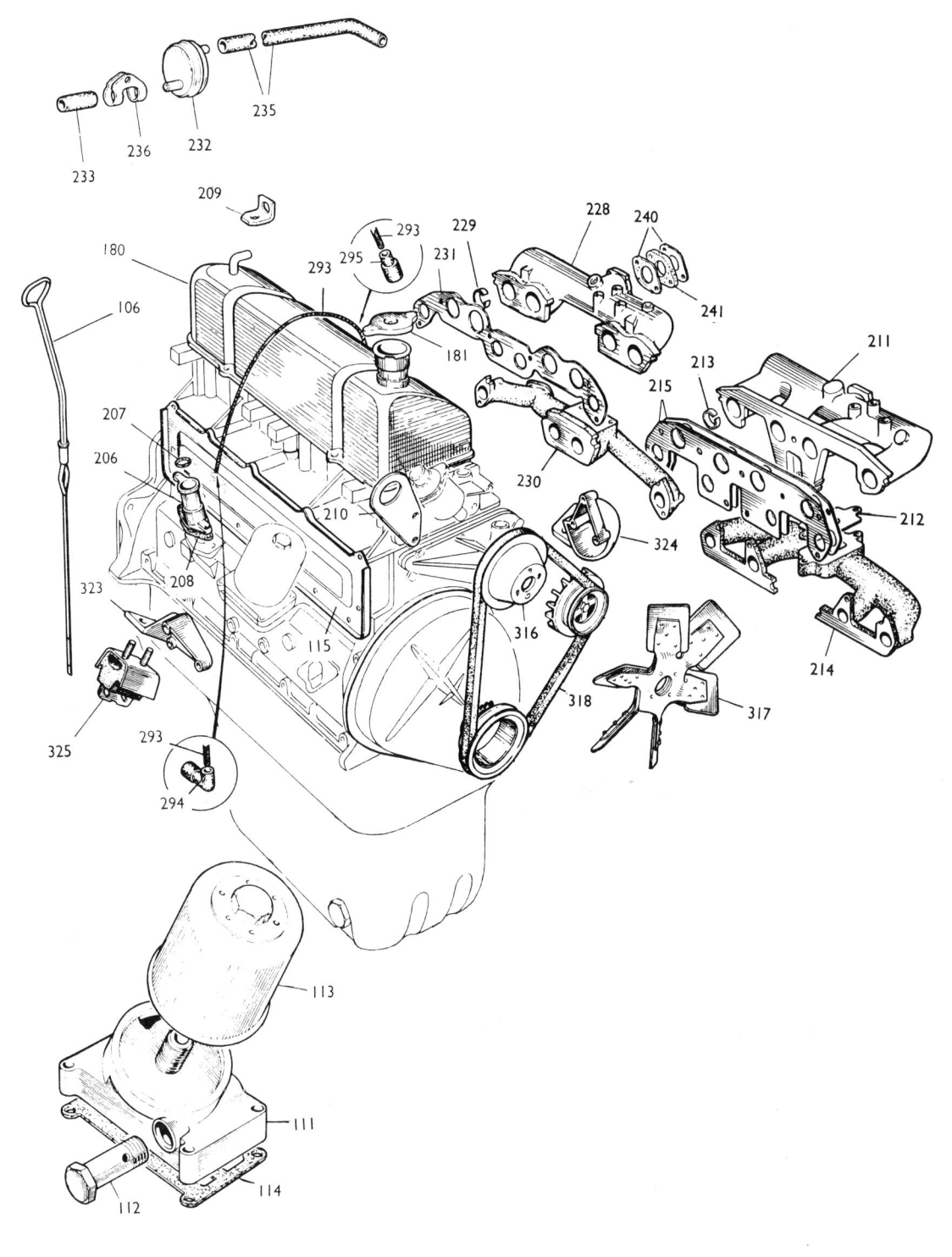

Fig. 1.5. ENGINE – ANCILLARY ATTACHMENTS

106 Dipstick	210 Slinging eye	231 Manifold gaskets C.I. head	294 Elbow
114 Gasket	211 Inlet manifold Al. head	232 Flame trap	295 Sleeve
118 Tappet cover	212 Hot spot plate	233 Breather hose	316 Fan pulley
180 Rocker cover	213 Locating ring	235 Breather hose	317 Fan
181 Filler cap (oil)	214 Exhaust manifold Al. head	236 Support sleeve	318 Fan belt
206 Distributor drive bracket	215 Manifold gaskets Al. head	237 Hose clip	323 Right hand) Engine
207 Oil seal	228 Inlet manifold C.I. head	240 Carburettor gaskets	324 Left hand) mounting
208 Gasket	229 Locating ring	241 Insulating washer	brackets
209 Lifting bracket	230 Exhaust manifold C.I. head	293 Suction pipe	325 Mounting rubber

damaged on the fan blades lift it out carefully.

9. Detaoh the high tension lead from the centre of the coil by simply pulling it out and then pull off all the high tension leads from the sparking plugs. After unclipping the distributor cap, the cap and leads may be lifted away. Disconnect both leads from the terminals at the end of the dynamo.

10 Disconnect the low tension lead from one of the coil terminals to the distributor.

11 Disconnect the lead wire from the terminal on the thermostat sender unit which is mounted in the water pump housing.

12 Disconnect the wire lead attached to the oil pressure gauge sender unit underneath the distributor in the side of the block.

13 Remove the carburettor. Although not essential, this is done for safety's sake. Disconnect the earthing cable strip which is attached to one of the bolts securing the timing cover case to the front of the engine. The other end of the cable is attached to the body frame nearby. Undo the union connecting the fuel pipe to the inlet side of the fuel pump on the right hand side of the engine.

14 Remove the nut on the terminal of the starter motor securing the lead from the battery.

15 Detach the exhaust pipe from the exhaust manifold by unscrewing the two nuts which hold the flange of the pipe to the manifold.

16 Remove the two bolts and the nuts holding the starter motor to the clutch flywheel bellhousing and remove the starter motor.

17 It is now time to go underneath the car so if it has not already been put up on wheel ramps and it is necessary to support it and raise it at the front on stands, do so now. It is best if the stands are placed underneath the side frame members in a position just behind the anti-roll bar clamps. It is most important that the car is properly and firmly supported because there are some bolts to be undone which may be quite stiff and the force required to turn them could well move the car off a shaky form of support.

18 Undo the nuts and bolts securing the clutch hydraulic slave cylinder to the bellhousing and lift it to one side. It is not necessary to disconnect any of the hydraulic lines for this, but ensure that nobody inadvertently puts his foot on the clutch pedal otherwise the piston will blow out of the cylinder and deposit hydraulic oil either over your floor or somebody underneath the car.

19 Remove the two clamps which hold the centre of the anti-roll bar to the side frame members. Each clamp is held by two bolts which locate into captive nuts in the side frame members. It is necessary to do this in order to enable the torsion bar to drop down a few inches. This will permit the sump of the engine to clear the torsion bar when the engine is drawn forward eventually to detach it from the gearbox input shaft.

20 Remove the four bolts which hold the two stays from the sump to the bellhousing. These stays act as stiffeners for the whole engine and gearbox assembly. The forward ends of the stays may next be detached from the side of the sump. Note that each stay is held by a bolt and a nut over a stud at the forward end. Do not lose the specially shaped nut as this is required in order to exactly line up the stay on assembly.

21 If everything has been done correctly, the engine is now attached to the car at only three positions, namely, the left and right hand side engine mountings and by the top bolts onto the gearbox bellhousing. Before proceeding further it will be necessary to provide support underneath the gearbox so that it will not tip right forward when the engine is taken away from it. This should now be done either using a jack or supporting the gearbox under the drain plug with suitable stand or wooden blocks. This must be done before any attempt is made to detach the engine from its mountings.

22 The engine should now be supported by the hoist of whichever type is being used, so that the weight of it may be taken before disconnecting the mounting brackets. On the left hand side of the cylinder head at the front and rear, are two holding down studs each with two nuts. In addition to the hose clips which are attached to them the rear stud also has a strong lifting bracket fitted to it. It is desirable to obtain another bracket exactly the same as this which should then be fitted underneath the top nut of the forward stud. A sling between these two brackets is the best means of lifting the

engine out. It is possible to use the eye of the large plate bracket attached to the front right hand side of the engine block, but this would impart a slight twist when the engine is lifted and this makes it difficult to draw the engine forward off the gearbox input shaft. This twist causes even greater problems when the engine is being fitted back.

23 Once the sling has been satisfactorily attached the strain should be taken on it sufficiently to permit the engine mounting bracket bolts to be removed without undue strain or without allowing the engine to drop.

24 The engine mountings should be undone by using the two bolts which attach the lower part of the flexible mounting to the chassis frame. Do not detach the bracket on the engine from the top of the mounting by undoing the two uppermost nuts. If the latter method is used it means that it is very difficult, if not impossible, to lift the engine vertically upwards as the mounting studs will be inclined at an angle of 45º.

25 The remainder of the bolts holding the gearbox bellhousing to the engine should now be removed. It should be noted that one of the long bolts on the lower left hand side of the bellhousing is, in fact, a dowel pin and once the nut has been removed it is not necessary to attempt to remove it as it will remain where it is when the engine is drawn away.

26 With all attachments now removed, other than the connection between the engine and gearbox input shaft, the whole engine should be drawn forward in order to disengage it from the gearbox. This normally presents no difficulties but in case the two are reluctant to part it will be necessary, perhaps, to do a bit of rocking in order to get it to come forward. It is very important to remember that the engine should not be raised or lowered at this stage in an attempt to separate it from the gearbox. Until it is clear of the gearbox input shaft any upwards or downwards strain could cause severe damage to the clutch or the gearbox.

27 Once the engine has been drawn forward from the gearbox, it may be lifted straight up and clear of the car without any tilting whatsoever.

28 If the engine is being removed together with the gearbox the procedures are exactly the same except that the bolts which join the engine and gearbox together at the bellhousing do not have to be removed. The starter motor may also remain in place.

29 In addition, however, it is necessary to remove the gearbox supporting crossmember in order that the rear end of the gearbox may be allowed to drop down sufficiently far for the engine to be tilted up to clear it through the engine compartment on the way out. Details of removal of the crossmember may be found in Chapter 6 under the Section concerned with gearbox removal. It will also be necessary to remove the gear change lever from inside the car as also described in Chapter 6.

30 The gearbox crossmember should only be removed after the full weight of the engine has been supported at the front and the engine mountings have been unbolted. As soon as this situation is reached, a support in the form of a jack or suitable blocks should be placed under the gearbox and the gearbox crossmember support detached from the bodywork of the car and then from the bottom of the gearbox itself.

31 Detach the speedometer cable from the side of the gearbox by unscrewing the milled retaining screw.

32 Without moving the support immediately from under the gearbox start to lift the engine forward and up. It will immediately be noted that the propeller shaft will have to be carefully lowered before it drops out of the tail end of the gearbox and also the gearbox itself will have to be lowered which will mean gradual or total removal of the support which has been placed underneath it. Prepare to collect any oil which may drop from the gearbox rear extension cover. It is in order to let the gearbox come to rest on the floor, but do not let it drop or scrape along the floor. By a gradual process of lifting and moving forward on the hoist the whole assembly can be drawn up through the engine compartment, but it will be considerably more difficult than lifting out the engine by itself and additional help will certainly be necessary if damage or accidents are to be avoided for

  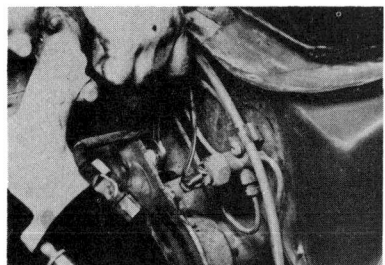

ENGINE REMOVAL — SECTION 5. Remove stay braces, and bellhousing bolts to separate engine from gearbox.

ENGINE REMOVAL — SECTION 5. Remove anti-roll bar clamps, to lower bar and clear sump.

ENGINE REMOVAL — SECTION 5. Detach mounting bolts and earth cable. Draw engine off gearbox before lifting up and out.

sure.

33 Once the engine is clear of the car, either with or without the gearbox attached, lower it as soon as possible to the ground or area where it is to be externally cleaned. It is better if this place is not right close to where the engine is going to be dismantled. Further cleaning at this stage is well worth the time spent on it as the risk of filth and grit getting into the engine later on is greatly reduced. Be careful not to let paraffin or cleaning fluids of any kind contaminate the clutch friction disc during this process. Once the engine is cleaned put it in the position where it is to be dismantled and prop it securely to prevent any damage either to itself or the people.

6. Engine Dismantling - General

1. Owners who have dismantled engines will know the need for a strong work bench and many tools and pieces of equipment, which make their life much easier when going through the process of dismantling an engine. For those who are doing a dismantling job for the first time, there are a few 'musts' in the way of preparation which, if not acquired, will only cause frustration and long delays in the job in the long run. It is essential to have sufficient space in which to work. Dismantling and reassembly is not going to be completed all in one go and it is therefore absolutely essential that you have sufficient area to leave things as they are when necessary. A strong work bench is also necessary together with a good engineer's vice. If you have no alternative other than to work at ground level, make sure that the floor is at least level and covered with a suitable wooden or wood composition material on which to work. If dirt and grit are allowed to get into any of the component parts all work which you carry out may be completely wasted. Before actually placing the engine wherever it is that you may be carrying out the dismantling, make sure that the exterior is now completely and thoroughly cleaned.

2. Once dismantling begins it is advisable to clean the parts as they are removed. A small bath of paraffin is about the best thing to use for this, but do not let parts which have oilways in them become immersed in paraffin otherwise there may be a residue which could cause harmful effects later on. If paraffin does get into oilways every effort should be made to blow it out. For this it may be necessary to carry the particular part to a garage fitted with a high pressure air hose. Short oilways such as there are in the crankshaft can be cleared easily with pipe cleaners.

3. Always obtain a complete set of gaskets when the engine is being dismantled - no gaskets on an engine are normally re-usable and any attempt to do so is quite unjustified in view of the relatively small cost involved. Before throwing any gaskets away, however, make sure that you have the replacements to hand. If, for example, a particular gasket cannot be obtained it may be necessary to make one, and the pattern of the old one is useful in such cases.

4. Generally speaking, it is best to start dismantling the engine from the top downwards. In any case, make sure it is firmly supported at all times so that it does not topple over whilst you are undoing the very tight nuts and bolts which will be encountered. Always replace nuts and bolts into their locations once the particular part has been removed, if possible. Otherwise keep them in convenient tins or pots in their groups, so that when the time comes to reassemble there is the minimum of confusion.

7. Engine Dismantling - Ancillaries

1. If you are intending to obtain an exchange engine complete, or what is called a half engine, which is basically the cylinder block, crankshaft and pistons, it will be necessary first of all to remove all those parts of the engine which are not included in the exchange. If you are stripping the engine completely yourself with the likelihood of some outside work to be done by specialists, all these items will be taken off anyway.

2. It is as well to check with whoever may be supplying the replacement exchange unit what is necessary to remove, but as a general guide the following items will have to be taken off. Reference is given to the appropriate Chapter for details of removal of each of these items:-

Dynamo or alternator - Chapter 10.
Distributor - Chapter 4.
Thermostat and housing - Chapter 2.
Oil filter (expendable) - Chapter 1.
Carburettor(s) - Chapter 3.
Inlet manifold - Chapter 1.
Exhaust manifold - Chapter 1.
Water pump - Chapter 2.
Fuel pump - Chapter 3.
Engine mounting brackets - Chapter 1.

3. If a half engine only is being obtained on a replacement exchange basis, the following items in addition to those already removed will have to be taken off:-

Cylinder head complete with valve rocker gear.
Flywheel.
Sump.
Oil pump.

8. Valve Rocker Gear - Removal

1. The valve rocker gear will need to be removed if it is desired to remove the cylinder head, either with the engine out of the car or in the car.

2. Remove the four screws which secure the rocker box cover to the cylinder head. It will be necessary to disconnect the breather pipe which goes into the cover and also to unclip the high tension plug leads from the rear end of the car in order to remove it.

3. The rocker gear may be removed as an assembly complete. The shaft and rocker arms are mounted on four standards, each of which is held to the head by two long bolts. All eight bolts should be undone evenly so as to permit any springs which may be in compression to ease themselves into their free state without unduly distorting the rocker shaft during the process of removing it. Undo the small brass union which connects the oil feed pipe to the T-piece in the centre of the rocker shaft assembly. By gripping the assembly with a hand at each end, it may now be lifted straight up off the head. Be careful not to let it separate in the centre as it will come apart quite easily, and the T-piece may drop somewhere difficult to reach.

9. Inlet and Exhaust Manifold - Removal

1. If the engine is being completely dismantled or if the cylinder head is being removed, it is not necessary to detach either the inlet or exhaust manifold, prior to carrying out this work.

2. The only occasions when one would expect to have to remove either of the manifolds would be to renew a suspected leaking gasket or, of course, a cracked or damaged manifold.

3. Both manifolds have to be removed together as they are bolted together and are mounted to the engine on a common gasket.

4. First of all disconnect all the carburettor controls and fuel pipe connections to the carburettor and remove the carburettor together with its air cleaner from the inlet manifold flange. Details are given in Chapter 3. Next disconnect the exhaust pipe from the flange on the exhaust manifold by undoing the two nuts securing it. Now remove the six nuts and three bolts which hold the manifolds to the cylinder head. The manifolds may then be lifted off together.

5. If the two manifolds are to be separated, the two bolts holding them together should be removed. Between the two manifolds there is a heat deflector plate. This has a hole in the centre which is normally positioned centrally above the aperture in the flange on the exhaust manifold.

For removal of twin carburettor manifold, see Chapter 13.

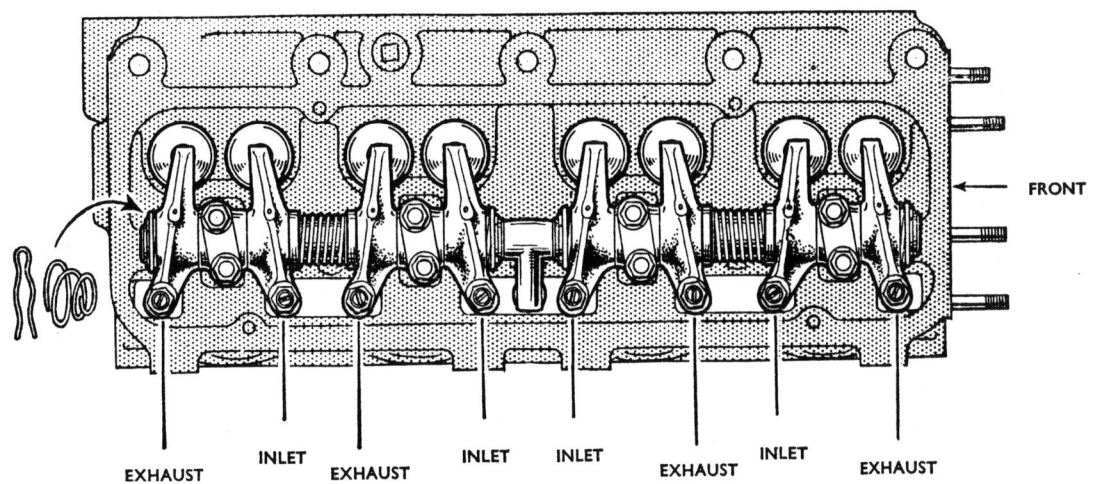

FRONT

EXHAUST INLET EXHAUST INLET INLET EXHAUST INLET EXHAUST

Fig. 1.6. Valve and rocker gear layout; aluminium cylinder heads

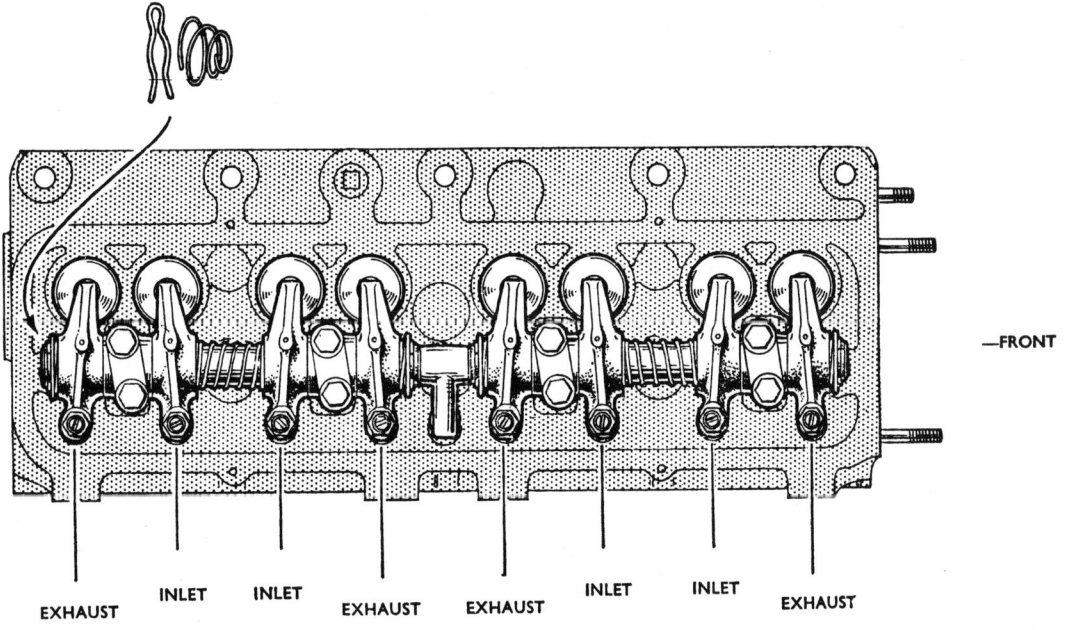

—FRONT

EXHAUST INLET INLET EXHAUST EXHAUST INLET INLET EXHAUST

Fig. 1.7. Valve and rocker gear layout; cast iron heads

10. Cylinder Head - Removal

1. The cylinder head may be removed with the engine either in or out of the car.
2. If the engine is to remain in the car, the following must be done first:-

a) Drain the cooling system.
b) Remove the air cleaner from the carburettor and preferably remove the carburettor also as a safety precaution.
c) Disconnect the top radiator hose from either the radiator or the cylinder head.
d) Remove the electrical lead from the water temperature gauge sender unit at the front of the cylinder head.
e) Disconnect all the leads from the sparking plugs.
f) Disconnect the heater water pipes from the water pump housing at the front of the cylinder head and also unclip them from the two clips mounted onto the cylinder head studs.
g) Disconnect the fuel feed pipe union from the outlet side of the fuel pump and also detach it from its clip bolted to the front of the cylinder head.
h) Disconnect the exhaust pipe from the exhaust manifold by unscrewing the nuts underneath the flange.

3. With the foregoing completed, removal of the cylinder head is now the same whether the engine is in or out of the car. Remove the screws which hold the top edge of the rocker cover to the cylinder head and slacken the other screws which hold the bottom edge of the rocker cover to the cylinder block. Remove the rocker cover and valve rocker gear assembly.
4. Next carefully remove all the pushrods. When lifting them out, make sure that they are not still attached to the tappets. If the tappets are inadvertently lifted up they could become dislodged inside the tappet chest involving a lot of extra work when the head is replaced. This, of course, applies only when the engine is in the car. Keep the pushrods in the same order and the same way up as they were removed from the engine. This can be done by putting them through a piece of pierced cardboard to arrange them in order. The head is held in position by eight bolts and two nuts on studs, one at the front and one at the rear on the left hand side of the head. These bolts and nuts should be slackened off in the reverse order of the tightening sequence which is indicated in fig. 1.17 in Section 47 'Cylinder Head - Replacement'.
5. It should now be possible to lift the head straight off the top of the cylinder block complete with the manifolds which provide a useful hand-hold when lifting the head.
6. Should there be any difficulty in removing the head, under no circumstances should any attempt be made to force any form of lever into the space between the head and cylinder block. This could cause damage to the finely machined surfaces of the two parts. With the engine still in the car, it is possible to use the piston compression in order to help lift the head and break the tight joint. The engine can be turned by either putting the car in gear and moving it forwards or backwards, or re-connecting the battery, and giving the engine a quick turn on the starter motor. With the engine out of the car, it may be necessary to strike against the side of the head with a wooden block or soft faced mallet. When the head has been satisfactorily lifted off remove also the old cylinder head gasket.

11. Sump - Removal

1. Removal of the sump with the engine in the car is possible, but not easy. The engine will need to be removed from its forward mountings and for those engines fitted with an aluminium cylinder head (and therefore an aluminium sump) it will be necessary to drop the front axle crossmember away from the bodywork side frame.
2. First of all disconnect the battery, and drain the sump of oil.
3. Next, raise the car sufficiently high so that it is possible to work underneath it comfortably. If working with the car over a pit or on a ramp, it should also be raised sufficiently to allow the wheels to clear the ground. The car must then be supported on proper body stands.
4. The weight of the engine must be supported during the sump removal operation, and this can be done by using a conventional hoist and supporting the engine as would be done for removing it.
5. For those engines with pressed steel sumps the engine can be raised sufficiently with the lifting tackle, after removing the engine mounting brackets, to permit the sump to be unbolted and dropped down sufficiently to remove it. When lifting the engine care should be taken to watch that none of the controls or wires connecting the engine is damaged. It will also be necessary to completely remove the anti-roll bar which runs across the front of the sump. In addition to drawing the sump forward, it has to be lowered considerably, of course, in order to clear the oil pump screen filter inside. After removing the sump face to bellhousing stay brackets, the remainder of the sump bolts may be removed and the sump itself lowered and drawn forward away from the engine. Aluminium sumps are much deeper than the pressed steel variety, and consequently the suspension crossmember has to be detached from the main body and lowered, in order to permit the sump to be dropped down and brought forward. There are four $5/8$ inch AF bolts which hold the front crossmember to the underframe. Once these have been removed the whole of the crossmember and front suspension can be pulled down against the springs and held down by putting suitable blocks of wood between the end of the crossmember and the side frames. Once this has been done the sump can be unbolted from both the cylinder block and the bellhousing, lowered, and removed.
6. With the engine on the bench, sump removal is perfectly straight-forward, although it is much better if the cylinder head is also removed so that the engine can be stood inverted. Before the engine is inverted see precautions under the Section headed 'Tappets'.

12. Crankshaft Pulley, Timing Gear Cover and Timing Gear - Removal

1. Removal of the crankshaft pulley, timing gear cover and timing gear will be necessary if the timing chain should be slack and noisy, or the tensioner needs attention. It is possible to carry out this work with the engine in the car. If the engine is in the car, first of all remove the radiator completely as described in Chapter 2.
2. Slacken the generator or alternator mounting bolts so as to slacken the fan belt and then remove the fan belt. For details see Chapter 2. The crankshaft pulley is held into position by a large bolt through the centre boss, and this must be undone using a suitable socket wrench. With the engine in the car a gear should be engaged to prevent the engine from turning when the bolt is being undone. If the engine is out of the car it will be necessary to hold the flywheel ring with a suitable lever engaged in the ring gear teeth.
3. The crankshaft pulley is keyed onto the end of the crankshaft and under normal circumstances it should be possible to pull it straight off. If some resistance is met, it is in order to lever it from behind equally on each side simultaneously but if reasonable pressure still fails to dislodge it, it may be necessary to obtain the services of a hub puller in order to draw it off properly without damaging anything.
4. Once the crankshaft pulley wheel has been removed the bolts which hold the timing case cover to the front of the engine block should next be taken out. The cover can then be removed and when this is done the timing chain tensioner, which is held in position by the cover, will fall down and hang on its pivot.
5. To remove the timing chain and sprockets, first take out the split pin from the tensioner pivot and remove the tensioner from the pivot.
6. The timing chain and the two sprockets on which it runs have all to be removed together. First remove the screw, tab washer and plain washer from the front of the camshaft tab. Take off the oil thrower which is mounted on the crankshaft in front of the crankshaft sprocket.
7. The crankshaft sprocket is a tight fit onto the keyed end of the

Fig. 1.8. Part of crossmember lowered to facilitate removal of aluminium sump

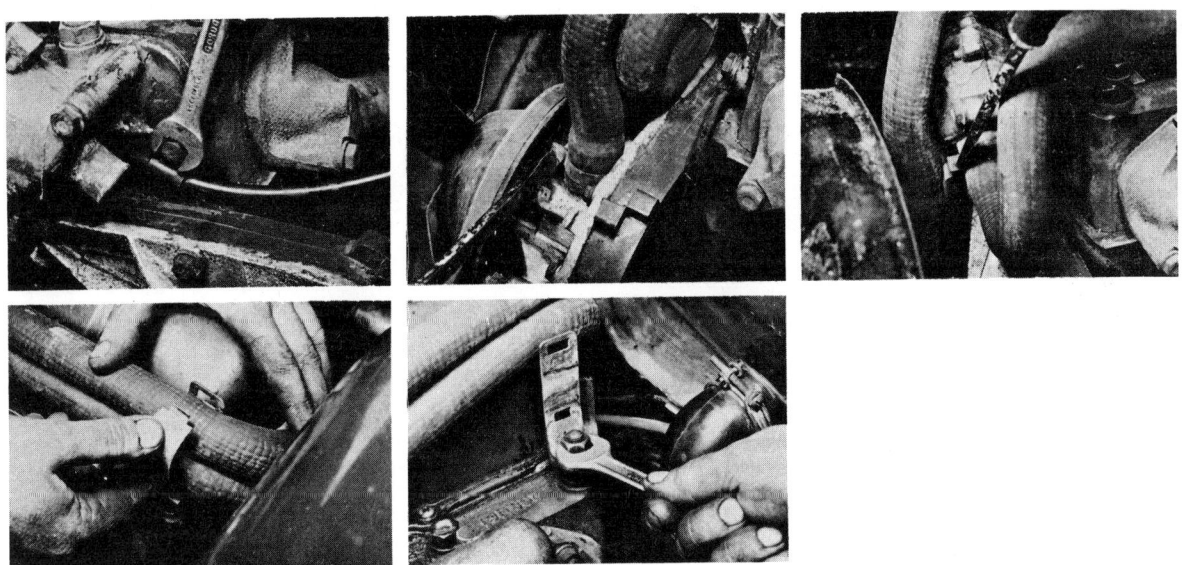

CYLINDER HEAD REMOVAL — SECTION 10. Detach the fuel feed pipe clip at the front of the head and unclip the heater hoses.

crankshaft and will most probably require the services of a puller in order to draw it off. Once the puller is in position and ready to move the sprocket the camshaft sprocket should also be moved forward with the aid of suitable levers at the same time as the other sprocket is being moved forward. Both sprockets and the chain can then be drawn off together.

13. Pistons, Connecting Rods and Big End Bearings - Removal

1. It is possible to remove the pistons, connecting rods and big end bearings from the engine with the engine still in the car provided that the cylinder head and sump are also removed first. With the engine removed from the car, the task is much easier and generally cleaner, but, of course, it is understood that if a quick emergency repair job is to be done and speed is of the essence, then it would be in order to do any work with the engine still in the car. With the sump removed and the crankshaft exposed, each of the big end bearing caps can be detached after removing the two self locking nuts which hold each cap to the connecting rod stud. Rotate the engine to bring each connecting rod cap suitably into position for unscrewing the nuts.

2. With the nuts removed, each big end bearing cap can be pulled off. It must be noted that the connecting rods and big end caps are not marked in any way, other than with a small forging flash on the side of the connecting rod and cap, which matches up on each one. It is, nevertheless, wise to make a mark of your own if the same connecting rods and caps are to be re-used, as they must be replaced exactly as they came out. The same applies to the big end bearing shells which will be released as soon as the connecting rods are detached from the crankshaft. It is inadvisable to re-use these shells anyway, but if they are not renewed they must be put back in exactly the same location from which they came.

3. If any difficulty is experienced in removing the big end bearing caps from the studs of the connecting rods, it will help if the crankshaft is revolved in order to dislodge them. If this is done, however, care must be taken to ensure that nothing gets jammed when the connecting rod comes away from the crankshaft at the top of its stroke. Once released, the connecting rods and pistons can be pushed up through the cylinder bores and out of the top of the block. Make sure that the pistons are kept in such a way that they can be easily identified and replaced into the same bore, if necessary.

4 The self-locking nuts securing the big-end bearing caps must **not** be reused. The bolts may only be reused if they have not been subject to abnormal strain imposed by a run big-end or a seizure.

14. Gudgeon Pins - Removal

The gudgeon pins will be removed if it is desired to fit new pistons to the existing connecting rods or vice versa. The gudgeon pins are held in position by a circlip in each side of the piston and after this is removed any carbon should be cleaned away. Warm the piston and connecting rod assemblies, preferably in warm oil, when the gudgeon pin can be pushed out with the finger. If the piston is cold and the gudgeon pin is tight, it should not be forced out.

15. Flywheel - Removal

1. The flywheel may be removed with the engine in the car provided that the gearbox and clutch assemblies are both removed first. The flywheel would normally be removed in these circumstances for purposes of renewing the starter ring, which may have damaged teeth, or because of a badly scored face due to a badly worn clutch friction disc.

2. With the gearbox and clutch removed as described in Chapters 6 and 5 respectively, the five bolt heads which secure the flywheel to the crankshaft flange will come into view. These bolts are locked into position by tab washers. Knock back the tabs and then undo and remove the five securing bolts. The flywheel is located to the crankshaft flange on a register and is positioned by a dowel pin. It

will be necessary to use a little leverage in order to draw the flywheel off and great care should be taken that it does not come off with a sudden jerk and fall down. One way of preventing this is by putting a stud another, longer bolt with the head sawn off, into one of the bolt holes so that when the flywheel comes free, the end of the stud will support it. If the dowel comes out together with the flywheel it should be remembered that the dowel should be removed from the flywheel and replaced in the crankshaft flange before the flywheel is replaced.

16. Oil Pump - Removal

1. The oil pump may be removed from the engine whilst the engine is still in the car. It is necessary first of all to remove the sump. As the oil pump drive spindle also drives the distributor, care must be taken to ensure that the ignition timing is not lost when the oil pump is removed and eventually replaced. It is, therefore, necessary also to remove the distributor cap and turn the engine until the rotor is in line with the number one plug high tension lead contact. The timing marker on the crankshaft pulley wheel must then also be set against the top dead centre position. For full details of engine timing refer to Chapter 4.

2. Once the crankshaft has been set to the correct position the distributor should be removed. By looking down into the distributor mounting opening it will be possible to see the top of the oil pump spindle and the position of the offset slot. Take a careful note of this position.

3. Disconnect the oil delivery pipe union from the pump and also at the other end from inside the crankcase. The two bolts holding the pump to the crankcase can then be removed and the pump drawn out.

17. Camshaft - Removal

Although it is possible to remove the camshaft from the engine whilst the engine is still in the car, it is not recommended. The occasions when it is necessary to remove the camshaft other than during the course of a complete engine overhaul must be so few that it is considered unnecessary to go into the details of how to set about removing it in this fashion. One other point that must be remembered about the camshaft is that they are not interchangeable between engines fitted with cast iron and aluminium cylinder heads. This is due to the different valve arrangements between the two engines. With the engine inverted on the bench (before inverting the engine, take the precaution as noted under the Section heading 'Tappets') and the timing sprockets and timing chain removed, all that is required is to undo the two bolts holding the camshaft thrust plate to the front of the block. When these are taken out the thrust plate may be taken off and the camshaft is then ready to be drawn out. Make sure that the tappets are all clear of the cam lobes. When withdrawing the camshaft from the block care should be taken to avoid chipping the camshaft shell bearings with the sharp hardened edges of the cam lobes. It is quite easy to gouge a deep line out of the shell bearing with one of the cam lobes, and if this is done, the bearing will possibly be damaged seriously enough to warrant replacement, and this is a specialist task. When taken out, put the camshaft where it cannot drop or be damaged as it is of a hard and brittle nature and could easily be cracked or chipped.

18. Tappets - Removal

It should always be remembered when the engine is removed from the car and the valve rocker gear detached, that if the engine is inverted, the tappets are liable to fall out of their bores. If it is not intended to remove the tappets, then this can be a nuisance as they should normally only be refitted into the bores from which they have come. It is, therefore, desirable to remove the tappet chest cover plate at an early stage in engine dismantling and lift the tappets from their bores and mark them with a pencil accordingly so that they may be returned to the same bore. Normally it is not necessary

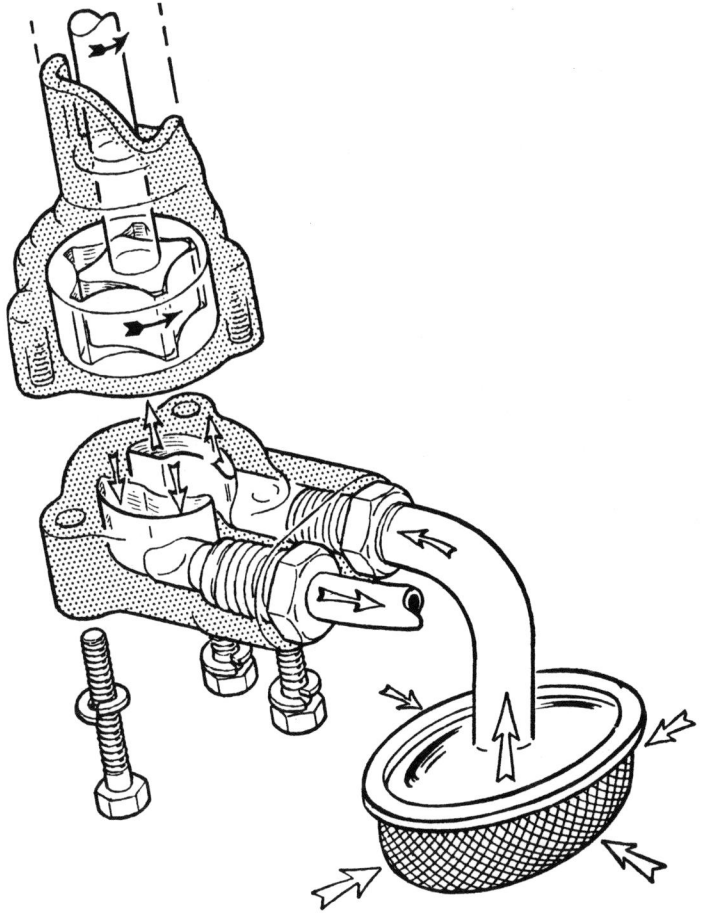

Fig. 1.9. Cut-away drawing of oil pump showing internal flow lines

to renew tappets unless they are severely scored or badly worn, and this is a feature which is normally associated with a damaged camshaft. Certainly if one or the other is badly damaged it is advisable to renew both. If it is wished to invert the engine, yet retain the tappets in position, (for example, when removing the camshaft for examination) then it is simple enough to remove the tappet chest cover, and stuff rags inside sufficient to prevent the tappets from dropping down. However, it must be remembered that they must be permitted to drop down far enough to clear the lobes of the camshaft when it is withdrawn from the engine block.

19. Crankshaft and Main Bearings - Removal

1. It is possible to examine the crankshaft and the crankshaft shell bearings without removing the engine from the car. It is also possible to replace the shell bearings with new ones if required, also without removing the engine from the car. However, as crankshaft shell bearings are not items which are replaced as a matter of routine other than doing a complete engine overhaul, we do not recommend this practice as it may very well be as a result of a wrong diagnosis of some engine fault. If the main bearing shells should appear as though they are in need of renewal, it is more than likely that all the other bearings are in a similar state and that the crankshaft itself needs regrinding.

2. With the engine removed from the car it is necessary for the sump, oil pump, timing chain and sprockets to be removed, together with the flywheel. It is also desirable that the cylinder head should have been removed so that the engine may be stood inverted. The front plate will also have to come off. This is held by the two bolts near the camshaft thrust plate; and the timing cover mounting stud.

3. The connecting rod bearing caps should all have been removed and, of course, this will have been done if the pistons are being removed from the engine as well.

4. Using a good quality socket spanner remove the two bolts from each of the three main bearing caps, Then lift off each of the caps.

5. Note that the front cap has the timing chain tensioner pivot pin screwed into it. With the three main bearing caps removed the crankshaft may be carefully lifted out of the block and it should then be placed somewhere safe where it cannot fall or be damaged. The upper half main bearing shells may then be removed from the crankcase.

20. Oil Filter Element - Removal and Replacement

The oil filter element is a throw-away disposable cartridge which is screwed into an adaptor casting bolted to the right hand side of the engine block. This casting comprises the inlet and outlet passages from the filter and also the oil pressure release valve and it can be detached for further investigation if necessary. The rubber jointing ring on the base of the filter cartridge has a tendency to stick and the cartridge therefore can be very difficult to turn. In such cases it will be necessary to fit some form of a strap around the cartridge with a suitable lever to apply sufficient pressure to turn it. Some versions have a hexagon on the top face and with these, of course, a spanner can be used. When refitting a new element make sure first of all that the jointing faces of the element and the casting are perfectly clean and lightly smeared with engine oil. Then screw in the cartridge by hand, making sure that the screw threads are running true until the mating faces just touch. Then screw the cartridge by hand another two-thirds of a revolution only. Do not overtighten otherwise it will be difficult to unscrew later. After fitting a new element the engine should always be run and a check made for signs of any leakage. Filters with a hexagon on their top face must not be tightened with a spanner.

21. Engine - Examination - General

1. Examination of an engine runs in two phases. The first is a visual

and aural examination when it is running and in the car, and the second is when it is out of the car, having decided that something is wrong and needs repairing. It is not difficult for any owner to find garages, friends and relatives all willing to tell him precisely what is wrong with his engine as they listen to it turning in his car! It is a different matter altogether to decide when to take the car off the road, and do something about putting right whatever faults there may be. In general, if the oil and fuel consumption are perfectly reasonable, the performance is satisfactory, and it is not suffering from overheating, underheating, or any other fault which causes aggravation and irritation on the road to a large degree, it is best left alone. Provided the regular maintenance requirements are carried out there is no need to take it to pieces.

2. The first indications of an engine becoming worn (if one has not been able to get the exact mileage that the engine has travelled) are an increase in oil consumption and possibly a corresponding increase in fuel consumption. This may also be accompanied by a falling off in performance. On an average family saloon car it is not always easy to detect a falling off in performance and it is quite a good idea to drive another car of the same type, which is known to be in very good condition, to make a comparison. If the signs are that the engine is performing poorly, using too much petrol and beginning to burn oil, then one of the first things to do is to test the compression in each cylinder with a proper compression testing gauge. This will indicate whether the pistons are leaking in the cylinders or the valves are leaking in the head. Depending on the results, the cylinder head may be removed and further examinations carried out to the bores and head as described in subsequent sections. Early action at this stage could well restore the engine to a satisfactory condition. Furthermore, such action would not call for a great deal of expense of either money or time. If the condition is left, however, it will get progressively worse until such time as the simple repairs which would have been needed earlier have reached the stage where more major operations are necessary. This will be proportionately much more expensive and time consuming.

22. Crankshaft and Crankshaft Main Bearings - Examination and Renovation

1. With the crankshaft removed examine all the crankpins and main bearing journals for signs of scoring or scratches. If all the surfaces of the bearing journals are obviously undamaged, check next that all the journals are round. This can be done with a micrometer or caliper gauge, taking readings across the diameter of each journal at six or seven points. If you do not own a micrometer or know how to use one, you should have little difficulty at any garage that has good mechanics to get someone to measure it for you.

2. If the crankshaft has ridges or severe score marks in it, it must be reground. The manufacturers of the Hillman Minx/Hunter series go further and say that a crankshaft in this condition should be renewed but as this can be a very expensive procedure, it is felt that regrinding should suffice in all but the most extraordinary situations. If there are no signs of ridging or severe scoring of the journals, it may be that the measurements indicate that the journals are not round. If the amount of ovality exceeds .002 inch it is possible that regrinding may be necessary. Certainly if it is more than this figure it is necessary. Here again it is best to get the advice of someone who is experienced and familiar with crankshafts and regrinding crankshafts to give an opinion.

3. The main bearing shells themselves are normally a matt grey in colour all over and should have no signs of pitting or ridging or discolouration usually indicates that the surface bearing metal has worn away and the backing material is showing through. It is worthwhile renewing the main bearing shells anyway if you have gone to the trouble of removing the crankshaft, but they must, of course, be renewed if there is any sign of damage to them or if the crankshaft has been reground. When the crankshaft is reground the diameter is reduced and consequently one must obtain the proper sized bearing shells to fit. These will normally be supplied by the firm

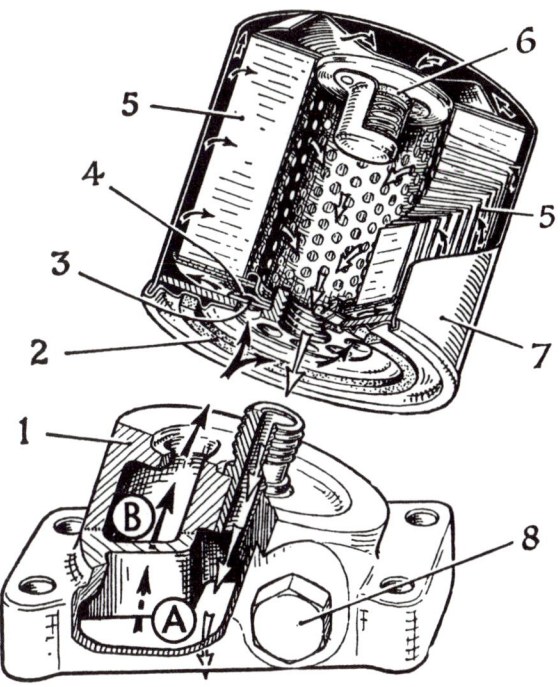

Fig. 1.10. CUT-AWAY DRAWING OF OIL
FILTER SHOWING FLOW LINES

1 Adaptor plate   5 Filter media
2 Cartridge sealing ring   6 Bypass valve
3, 4 Anti-drain valve   7 Cartridge case
              8 Pressure relief valve

*The oil passes through compartment 'B'
into the filter and returns to the engine
oil galleries via compartment 'A'*

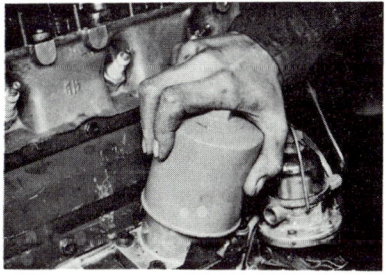

OIL FILTER ELEMENT — REMOVAL & REPLACEMENT — SECTION 20. Fitting the oil filter cartridge.

which has reground the crankshaft. Regrinding is normally done in multiples of .010 inch as necessary and bearing shells are obtainable to suit these standard regrinding sizes. If the crankshaft is not being reground, yet bearing shells are being renewed, make sure that you check whether or not the crankshaft has been reground once before. This will be indicated by looking at the back of the bearing shell and this will indicate whether or not it is minus .010 inch or more. The same version of shell bearing must be used when they are renewed.

23. Big End (Connecting Rod) Bearings - Examination and Renovation

The connecting rod, or big end, bearings as they are more commonly known are subject to wear at a greater rate than those for the crankshaft. Signs that one or more big end bearings is getting badly worn are a pronounced knocking noise from the engine, accompanied by a significant drop in oil pressure due to the increased clearance between the bearing and the journal permitting oil to flow more freely through the resultantly larger space. If this should happen quite suddenly and action is taken immediately, and by immediately is meant within a few miles, then it is possible that the bearing shell may be replaced without any further work needing to be done. If this happens in an engine which has been neglected and oil changes and oil filter changes have not been carried out as they should have been it is most likely that the rest of the engine is in a pretty terrible state anyway. If it occurs in an engine which has been recently overhauled, then it is almost certainly due to a piece of grit or swarf which has got into the oil circulation system and finally come to rest in the bearing shell and scored it. It is in these instances where a replacement of the shell alone accompanied by a thorough flush out of the lubrication system may be all that is required.

24. Cylinder Bores - Examination and Renovation

1. The cylinder bores may be examined for wear with the engine in the car once the cylinder head has been removed. Each bore may be examined in turn with the piston at the bottom of its stroke. A perfect cylinder is, as its name implies, perfectly cylindrical in shape. That is, the sides are parallel and a cross section is perfectly circular.
2. First of all, examine the top of the cylinder about a quarter of an inch below the surface of the block and with the finger feel if there is any ridge running round the circumference of the bore. In a worn cylinder bore a ridge will develop at the point where the top ring on the piston comes to the uppermost limit of its stroke. An excessive ridge indicates that the bore below the ridge is worn. If there is no ridge it is reasonable to assume that the cylinder is not badly worn. Measurement of the diameter of the cylinder bore both in line with the piston gudgeon pin and at right angles to it, at the top and bottom of the cylinder is also another check to be made. A cylinder is expected to wear at the sides where the thrust of the piston presses against it. In time this causes the cylinder to assume an oval shape. Furthermore, the top of the cylinder is likely to wear more than the bottom of the cylinder. It will be necessary to use a proper bore measuring instrument in order to measure the differences in bore diameter across the cylinder and variations between the top and bottom ends of the cylinder. As a general guide it may be assumed that any variations more than .010 inch indicate that the cylinders need re-boring. Provided all variations are less than .010 inch it is probable that the fitting of new piston rings will cure the problems of piston to cylinder bore clearances. Once again it is difficult to give a firm ruling on this as so much depends on the amount of time and effort which the individual owner is prepared or wishes to spend on the task. Certainly, if the cylinder bores are obviously deeply grooved or scored, they must be re-bored regardless of any measurement differences in the cylinder diameter. If the engine has been removed from the car for overhaul anyway, any cylinder bore wear in excess of .005 inch certainly qualifies it for a re-bore, to do otherwise would be a waste of time and effort. However,

one must bear in mind again the fact that a re-bore will require the fitment of new pistons and the expense of this once again, could affect the owner's decision.

25. Connecting Rods, Pistons and Piston Rings - Examination and Renovation

1. Pistons and rings are normally examined in relation to the cylinder bores. With the cylinder head removed it is possible to check the amount of movement between the piston and the wall, both visually and with the aid of a feeler gauge. If the condition of the bore seems to be satisfactory, any excessive clearance between piston and bore (.010 inch and upwards) could be due to wear on the piston itself. Piston ring wear is almost certain to have taken place also if this is the case, and will necessitate removal of the pistons for further examination. First of all, look for signs of damage to the piston ring grooves, and to the sides of the piston where scoring may be apparent. Any deep scoring or any obvious breakage between the piston ring grooves and the top of the piston will, of course, call for a new piston. If the pistons do not appear worn or damaged, next check the clearance between the piston rings and the piston ring grooves. This can be done with a feeler gauge and if it is in excess of the specified clearance the pistons should be renewed. Excessive clearance between the rings and the grooves allows the rings to chatter and they will break very easily. Unfortunately, the wear usually occurs on the piston rather than on the piston rings, although new rings should be used as a check before condemning the pistons.
2. To check the condition of the rings it will be necessary to remove them from the piston. Only the top ring on each piston need be checked and, in fact, if one of the four piston rings is bad it is reasonable to assume that the others will be similar and the whole lot should be replaced. Remove the top piston ring by spreading the ends apart sufficiently to enable it to be pulled out of the groove and over the top of the piston. Care must be taken not to twist the ring or draw it off unevenly, otherwise it could easily break. The ring should then be placed inside the cylinder bore from which it came and pressed down approximately two inches. It should lie perfectly horizontal across the bore and this can be achieved by using a piston from which all the rings have been removed to press it down square. Then the gap between the ends of the piston rings should be measured with a feeler gauge, if the piston ring gap exceeds that specified then the piston ring is worn out and should be replaced. If the top ring is worn it is reasonable to assume that the other two are worn on the same piston as well. Rings are normally only obtainable in sets anyway so any thoughts of economy by renewing one or two rings on a set of four pistons are really not worthwhile.
3. Provided the engine has not seized up or had some other calamitous damage caused to it, it is most unlikely that the connecting rods are in need of renewal at any time. In cases of seizure one or more could have become bent and to check this they will need setting up on a special jig. This is normally only within the competence of a specialist engineering organisation.
4. The small end bush of the connecting rod is a floating fit on the gudgeon pin. This means, therefore, that if new pistons are to be fitted, and new pistons come supplied with new gudgeon pins as a matter of course, the new gudgeon pin will need to be fitted correctly to the existing bush. The correct fit of a connecting rod small end to the gudgeon pin is when the connecting rod will fall under its own weight if the piston is held horizontal. At the same time there must be no play or rocking movement possible between the rod and the gudgeon pin. If the small end bush does not fit correctly onto the gudgeon pin it will need renewal and reaming out to fit. This, once again, is a tricky specialist task which must be left to people who have got the proper jig equipment. If it is decided to re-use the same pistons and the gudgeon pin is a slack fit in both the piston boss and the connecting rod small end bush, it is possible for oversize gudgeon pins to be fitted to the existing pistons and connecting rods. Here again, specialist facilities will be necessary in order that this work can be carried out.

26. Valve Rocker Gear - Examination and Renovation

1. Each rocker should move freely on the rocker shaft without any signs of looseness or slackness. If any slackness is apparent it will be necessary to dismantle the assembly as follows:-
2. Remove the spring clip from one end of each half of the complete assembly and remove the rockers, spacers, standards and springs, one at a time, laying them out carefully and noting the order in which they were removed. If either the rocker bushes or the rocker shaft are obviously scored and worn at those points where the rockers are pivoting then they should be renewed. The rockers themselves should also be examined on the faces where they bear onto the top of the valve stems and if signs of wear are excessive they should also be renewed.

27. Cylinder Head and Valves and Valve Springs - Examination and Renovation

1. Once the cylinder head has been removed, it should be placed upon a work bench so that a thorough examination can be carried out.
2. First of all, all the valves should be removed. The valves are located by a collar on a compressed spring which grips two collets (or a split collar) into a groove in the stem of the valve. The spring must be compressed with a special 'G' clamp in order to release the collets and then the valve. Place the specially shaped end of the clamp over the spring collar with the end of the screw squarely on the face of the valve. Screw up the clamp to compress the spring and expose the collet from the valve stem. Sometimes the spring collar sticks and the clamp screw cannot be turned. In such instances, with the clamp pressure still on, give the head of the clamp (over the spring) a tap with a hammer at the same time gripping the clamp frame firmly to prevent it slipping off the valve.
3. Take off the two collets, release the clamp, and the collar and spring can be lifted off. The valve can then be pushed out through its guide and removed. Make sure that each valve is kept in such a way that its position is known for eventual replacement. Unless new valves are being fitted, each valve must go back where it came from. The springs, collars and the collets should also be kept with their respective valves. A piece of card with eight holes punched in it is a good way to keep the valves in order.
4. The valves should be examined for signs of pitting or burning, particularly around their edges and where they seat into the cylinder head. If the valves are very much contaminated with carbon, this should first of all be removed with a wire brush. Very hard spots of carbon may need chipping off with the edge of a very hard blade or tool. Exhaust valves are the ones most likely to suffer from burning and if this is apparently quite severe, then the valves should be discarded. Next replace each valve into its own guide, after thoroughly cleaning the guide and valve stem, and check to see that there is no sideways movement of the valve in the guide. A very small amount of play is permissible but if it is very considerable, then it means that oil and exhaust gases can all make their way past the stem of the valve and this is not conducive to good performance. If the guides are obviously badly worn, then it will be necessary to have new ones fitted, together with new valves. The fitting of valve guides on this engine is a specialist task as they have to be reamed out to give a very close tolerance after fitting. If it is thought that the wear is on the valve stem rather than in the guide, the best way to check is to obtain a new valve and try it in position. If the valves are apparently in good general condition the next thing to do is to examine the valve seats themselves in the cylinder head. Here again, there should be no signs of pitting or burning. The valve seats should also be checked to make sure there are no cracks. If there are signs of damage to the seat in any way, then the head itself may need fitting with new valve seat inserts. Possibly, the existing valve seats may be recut; if you have the special tools for recutting valve seats, then these can be done by the owner but otherwise it is recommended that the job is given to a specialist. Provided the valves and seats are in good condition, then it is possible to re-seat them by grinding in position using a carborundum paste. This grinding-in process should also be carried out when a new valve is being fitted.
5. The carborundum paste used for this job is normally supplied in a double ended tin with coarse paste at one end and fine paste at the other. In addition, a suction tool for holding the valve head so that it may be rotated is also required. To grind in a valve, first smear a trace of the coarse paste onto the seat face and fit the suction grinder to the valve head. Then with a semi-rotary motion grind the valve head into its seat, lifting the valve occasionally to re-distribute the grinding paste. When a dull matt continuous line is produced on both the valve seat and the valve then the paste can be wiped off. Apply a little fine paste and finish off the grinding process. If a light spring is placed over the valve stem behind the head this can often be of assistance in raising the valve from time to time against the pressure of the grinding tool so as to re-distribute the paste evenly round the job. The width of the line which is produced after grinding should not be more than .07 inch (1.8 mm). If after a moderate amount of grinding it is apparent that the seating line is much wider than this then it means that the seat has already probably been cut back once or more times previously, or else the valve has been ground in several times. Here again, specialist advice is best sought on occasions such as this.
6. After each valve has been ground in the traces of carborundum paste which will remain in the area of the seat and inlet port must be thoroughly flushed away with paraffin. If possible, a high pressure air line should be used to blow away the final traces. Obviously, particles of carborundum grit are not wanted anywhere inside the engine.
7. Before the valves are finally replaced, all traces of carbon should be cleaned from them and also from the cylinder head itself. A wire cup brush and an electric drill are very useful in doing this work in the head. The face of the cylinder head should also be scraped perfectly clean and free from accumulations of gasket cement or carbon which may be upon it. Do not use any abrasive paper for cleaning but rather a flat bladed scraper. Make sure that no odd particles of gasket or carbon fall into the orifices in the casting. If they should, get them blown out.
8. Examine all the valve springs to make sure that they are of the correct length according to the specifications. It will have been noticed when they were being removed whether any were broken, and if they are then they should be replaced. It is a good idea to replace all the valve springs if one is broken as this may be a sign that all of them are weakening.
9. Inside the valve spring collar there is a small rubber ring which acts as an oil seal on the valve stem. New rings are normally supplied with a cylinder head gasket set and it is wise to renew them also.
10 Before reassembling the valves and springs to the cylinder head make a final check that everything is thoroughly clean and free from grit and then lightly smear all the valve stems with engine oil prior to reassembly.

28. Timing Chain and Sprockets - Examination and Renovation

Examine the teeth of both sprockets for wear. Each tooth on the sprocket is in the shape of an inverted 'V' and if the side of the tooth is concave in shape it is an indication that the tooth is worn badly and the sprocket should, therefore, be replaced. If the sprockets are worn and have to be renewed then the chains should also be renewed. If the sprockets are satisfactory, examine the chain to make sure there is no play between the links and if the chain is held out it should not bend when held horizontal. In view of the relative cheapness of these items it is worthwhile putting on a new chain anyway. Examine the tensioner pivot for signs of excessive wear which could cause rattling and also the tensioner itself. If the chain has gouged a deep groove into the tensioner renew it.

29. Camshaft, Camshaft Bearings and Tappets - Examination and Renovation

1. The camshaft lobes should be examined for signs of flats or scoring or any other form of wear and damage. At the same time the tappets should also be examined, particularly on the faces where they bear against the camshaft, for signs of wear. If the case hardened surfaces of the cam lobes or tappet faces have been penetrated it will be quite obvious as there will be a darker, rougher pitted appearance to the surface in question. In such cases, the tappet or the camshaft will need renewal. Where the camshaft or tappet surface is still bright and clean and showing slight signs of wear it is best left alone. Any attempt to re-face either will only result in the case hardened surface being reduced in thickness with the possibility of extreme and rapid wear later on. The skew gear in the camshaft which drives the oil pump shaft and indirectly the distributor also should be examined for signs of extreme wear on the teeth. Here again if the skew gear teeth are very badly worn and ridged, it will mean renewal of the complete camshaft. Examine also in conjunction with this the teeth on the driven gear. The camshaft bearing journals should be perfectly smooth and show no signs of pitting or scoring as should the camshaft bearing shells. Replacement of the camshaft bearing shells is a specialist task as each of the three bearings have to be positioned correctly and must be perfectly lined up with its counterpart. Fortunately, it is rare for the camshaft journals and bearings to wear out at anything like the same rate as the rest of the engine. Having ascertained that the faces of the tappets are satisfactory, check also that the tappets are not a loose fit in their respective bores. It is not likely that they are loosely fitting, but if so they should be renewed.

2. The camshaft thrust plate which retains the camshaft into the cylinder block should also be examined for any signs of ridging or scoring on its thrust face. If there is any sign it should be renewed.

30. Flywheel - Examination and Renovation

1. There are two areas in which the flywheel may have been worn or damaged. Firstly, is on the driving face where the clutch friction plate bears against it. Should the clutch plate have been permitted to wear down beyond the level of the rivets, it is possible that the flywheel has been scored. If this scoring is severe it may be necessary to have it re-faced or even renewed.

2. The other part to examine is the teeth of the starter ring gear around the periphery of the flywheel. The edge of the teeth towards the clutch side of the flywheel are designed with a bevel on them to start with so do not confuse this bevel with wear. If, however, several of the teeth are broken or missing, or the front edges of all teeth are obviously very badly chewed up, then it would be advisable to fit a new ring gear.

3. The old ring gear can be removed by cutting a slot with a hacksaw down between two of the teeth as far as possible, without cutting into the flywheel itself. Once the cut is made a chisel will split the ring gear which can then be drawn off. To fit a new ring gear requires it to be heated first to a temperature of 220ºC, no more. This is best done in a bath of oil or an oven, but not, preferably, with a naked flame. It is much more difficult to spread the heat evenly and control it to the required temperature with a naked flame. Once the ring gear has attained the correct temperature it can be placed onto the flywheel making sure that it beds down properly onto the register. Make sure the bevel edge of the teeth are facing towards the clutch face side of the flywheel. It should then be allowed to cool down naturally. If by mischance, the ring gear is overheated, it should not be used. The temper will have been lost, therefore softening it, and it will wear out in a very short space of time.

5. Although it is not actually fitted into the flywheel itself, there is a bush in the centre of the crankshaft flange onto which the flywheel fits. Although this bush is more correctly associated with the gearbox

or clutch it is mentioned here as well as it would be a pity to ignore it whilst carrying out work on the flywheel. If it shows signs of wear it should be renewed. If suitable extractors are not available to get it out another method is to fill the recess with grease and then drive in a piece of close fitting steel bar. This should force the bush out. A new bush may be pressed in.

31. Oil Pump - Examination and Renovation

1. With the oil pump removed from the engine, it should be inverted and the hexagon headed screws securing the base plate to the pump body removed. The outer rotor ring may then be lifted out and this should be done carefully as if dropped it could easily crack and therefore become unserviceable.

2. The interior of the pump body may then be thoroughly cleaned with petrol or paraffin to remove all traces of oil.

3. The efficiency of any oil pump depends on the clearances between the inner rotor tips and outer rotor and the outer rotor fit in the pump body. These are set to very fine tolerances on manufacture and if any excessive wear occurs then the oil which is normally forced round by the increasing and decreasing size of the apertures between the inner and outer rotors will escape in the increased clearances between them and thus the pumping efficiency and pressure will be reduced at the output side of the pump.

4. The main feature of checking the pump, therefore, is to measure the clearances. The first clearances to measure is that between the ends of the rotors and the face of the body of the pump. This can be done by putting a steel straight edge across the pump body and measuring the gap between it and the faces of both rotors with a feeler blade. The gap should be between .001 and .003 inch (.025mm and .075mm). The next clearance to be measured is that between the tip of the inner rotor and the high point of the convex section of the outer rotor, also with a feeler blade. The gap here should be between .001 and .006 inch (.025 mm and .15 mm).

6. The third clearance to be measured is that between the outside of the outer rotor and the pump body. This measurement should be between .005 inch and .008 inch (.125 to .20 mm).

7. If any of the clearances exceed the limits specified, or if the centre rotor spindle should be slack in its bush then a replacement oil pump should be fitted.

8. It is possible to rectify an excessive gap between the end faces of both rotors and the pump body (the first check made) by filing down the face of the body. This calls for a degree of fitting skill in the use of a file and should only be attempted by somebody who has the ability to file dead square and dead flat and to measurements of a thousandth of an inch. If not done properly this could make the pump far worse than it was originally, and if replaced in this state could cause irreparable damage to the engine in due course.

9. Whilst the pump is dismantled the opportunity should be taken to examine and clean the inlet filter gauze screen. If the engine has been properly looked after this screen should be perfectly clean. If it is not, however, clean it thoroughly in petrol or paraffin and blow it dry. Do not dry it off on any material or cloth which could leave particles remaining hooked up in the gauze.

32. Exhaust and Inlet Manifolds - Inspection

Exhaust and inlet manifolds should be examined for signs of cracks or other breakages, particularly on the mounting lugs. The mating faces of both manifolds where they join the cylinder head should be examined to make sure that they are completely flat and free from pitting or burrs of any sort. Use a straight edge to check the faces of the manifold for distortion. If there is any distortion or signs of severe pitting or burning the manifold should be renewed. Examine also the exhaust manifold to exhaust pipe flange mounting studs. In time these tend to corrode away and are consequently weakened and it is a simple task to extract them and fit new ones. This is well worth doing. Provided the manifolds are sound,

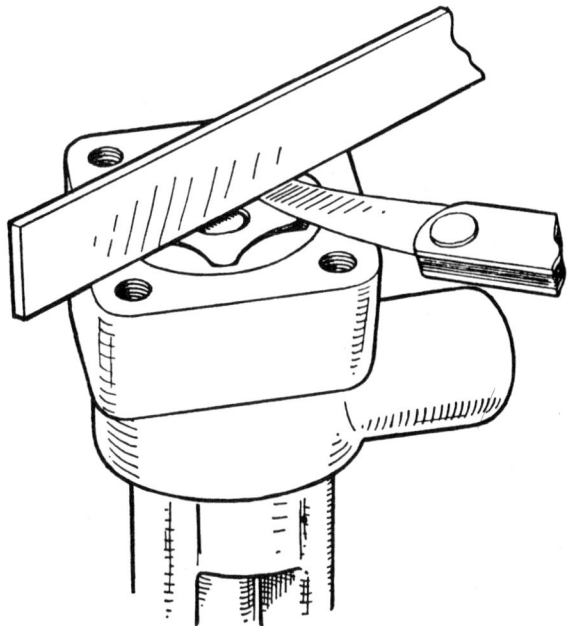

Fig. 1.11. Using straight edge and feeler blade to check oil pump rotor end clearance

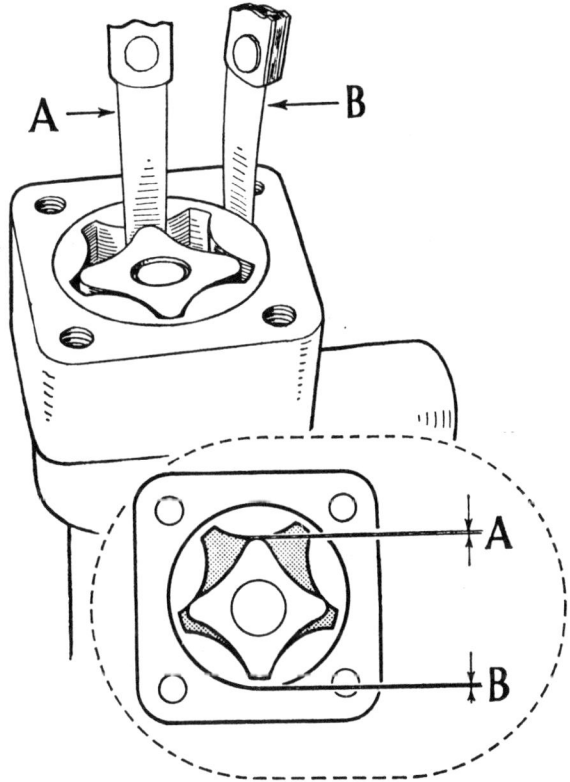

Fig. 1.12. Using feeler gauge to check oil pump.
(A) Rotor top clearance
(B) Outer rotor clearance

accumulations of carbon within the ports may be removed with a wire brush or scraper.

33. Decarbonisation

1. Modern engines, together with modern fuels and lubricants, have virtually nullified the need for the engine to have a 'de-coke' which was common enough only a few years ago. Carbon deposits are formed mostly on the modern engine only when it has to do a great deal of slow speed, stop/start running, for example, in busy traffic and city traffic conditions. If carbon deposit symptoms are apparent, such as pinking or pre-ignition and running on after the engine has been switched off, then a good high speed run on a motorway or straight stretch of road is usually sufficient to clear these deposits out. It is beneficial to any motor car to give it a good high speed run from time to time.

2. There will always be some carbon deposits, of course, so if the occasion demands the removal of the cylinder head for some reason or another, it is a good idea to remove the carbon deposits when the opportunity presents itself. Carbon deposits in the combustion chambers of the cylinder head can be dealt with as described under the section heading 'Cylinder Head - Inspection and Renovation'. The other carbon deposits which have to be dealt with are those on the crowns of the pistons. This work can easily be carried out with the engine in the car, but great care must be taken to ensure that no particles of dislodged carbon fall either into the cylinder bores and down past the piston rings or into the water jacket orifices in the cylinder block.

3. Bring the first piston to be attended to to the top of its stroke and then using a sheet of strong paper and some self adhesive tape, mask off the other three cylinders and surrounding block to prevent any particles falling into the open orifices in the block. To prevent small particles of dislodged carbon from finding their way down the side of the piston which is actually being decarbonised, press grease into the gap between the piston and the cylinder wall. Carbon deposits should then be scraped away carefully with a flat blade from the top of the crown of the piston and the surrounding top edge of the cylinder. Great care must be taken to ensure that the scraper does not gouge away into the soft aluminium surface of the piston crown.

4. A wire brush, either operated by hand or a power drill should not be used if decarbonising is being done with the engine still in the car. It is virtually impossible to prevent carbon particles being distributed over a large area and the time saved by this method is very little.

5. In addition to the removal of carbon deposits on the pistons, it is a good time also to make sure that traces of gasket or any sealing compound are removed from the mating face of the cylinder block top face.

6. After each piston has been attended to, clean out the grease and carbon particles from the gap where it has been pressed in. As the engine is revolved to bring the next piston to the top of its stroke for attention, check the bore of the cylinder which has just been decarbonised and make sure that no traces of carbon or grease are adhering to the inside of the bore.

34. Engine Reassembly - General

It is during the process of engine reassembly that the job is either made a success or a failure. From the very word go there are three basic rules which it is folly to ignore, namely:

1. Absolute cleanliness. The working area, the components of the engine and the hands of those working on the engine must be completely free of grime and grit. One small piece of carborundum dust or swarf can ruin a big end in no time, and nullify all the time and effort you have spent.

2. 'Don't spoil the ship for a ha'porth of tar'. Yes, an old fashioned proverb, but if you have spent many hours and several pounds on new parts it is ridiculous to jeopardise the job for the sake of a seal or a gasket which costs a few pence. One is tempted to say 'Oh it'll be all right'. If you can really convince yourself, well and good, but it will be far better for your peace of mind to get the appropriate new piece even though it may mean a little delay.

3. Don't rush it. The most skilled and experienced mechanic can easily make a mistake if he is rushed. It is no use boasting to your friends that you did the whole job on Saturday and Sunday if it is a smoking wreck on Monday.

Check that all nuts and bolts are clean and in good condition and renew as necessary, all spring washers, lock washer and tab washers, which may have become damaged or unserviceable during dismantling. A supply of clean engine oil and clean cloths (to wipe excessive clean oil off your hands only!) and a torque spanner are the only things which should be required in addition to all the tools used in dismantling the engine.

35. Crankshaft and Main Bearing - Reassembly

1. Stand the cylinder block inverted on the bench and gather together the bearing caps, new bearing shells and have the crankshaft alongside lined up in the way in which it will eventually be placed into the cylinder block. Make sure that the oilways in the crankshaft are all quite clear.

2. Make sure that the bearing housings in the cylinder block are perfectly clean and smooth in preparation for the fitting of the top halves of the main bearing shells. The centre and two end bearing shells have a central groove running through them, whilst the other two are plain. Each bearing shell has an oil hole in it and this must line up with the corresponding hole in the cylinder block. Each shell is notched, and this notch also must line up with the corresponding notch in the cylinder block. Carefully fit each shell into position taking care not to bend, distort or scratch it in any way. When they are in position lubricate the shells with a liberal quantity of clean engine oil.

3. Making sure that the crankshaft is the right way round, next pick it up and very carefully lower it square and straight into position on the shell bearings in the crankcase.

4. The centre and end bearing shell lower halves are also grooved and the other two plain. Again, make sure that the bearing caps are perfectly clean and fit the shells so that the notches in their ends line up and fit snugly into the grooves in the bearing caps. There are no oilways in the bearing caps so that the holes in the bearing shells will not line up with anything.

5. The crankshaft end float is controlled by two semi-circular thrust washers which fit at the sides of the centre main bearing journal. Place these in position and slide them round into the gap between the bearing housing and the flange of the crankshaft, making sure that the grooves in the thrust washers face outwards away from the centre. Once these are in position the end float can be checked by pushing the crankshaft as far as it will go in one direction and measuring the gap between the face of the thrust washer and the machined surface of the flange with a feeler blade. Next arrange all the bearing caps complete with their shells so that you know precisely where each one should go. The front and rear ones are easily identifiable by their particular shape as is the centre one. The others, two and four, are numbered and should be arranged accordingly. As there is the possibility of a seepage of oil through the end main bearing cap mating faces it is permissible to put a very thin smear of non-setting jointing compound onto the outside edge of the vertical face where the bearing cap locates into the crankcase. The precise position is indicated in fig. 1.13, location A. Lubricate the main journals of the crankshaft liberally with clean engine oil and place all the bearing caps in position and fit the bolts. The front main bearing cap has a machined front face and this must line up with the front surface of the cylinder block. Make sure that this is done with a straight edge before finally tightening down the bolts. When all the caps are settled correctly in position, tighten the bolts down evenly, using a torque spanner, to the correct torque as given under the specifications. When this has been done revolve the crankshaft to make sure that

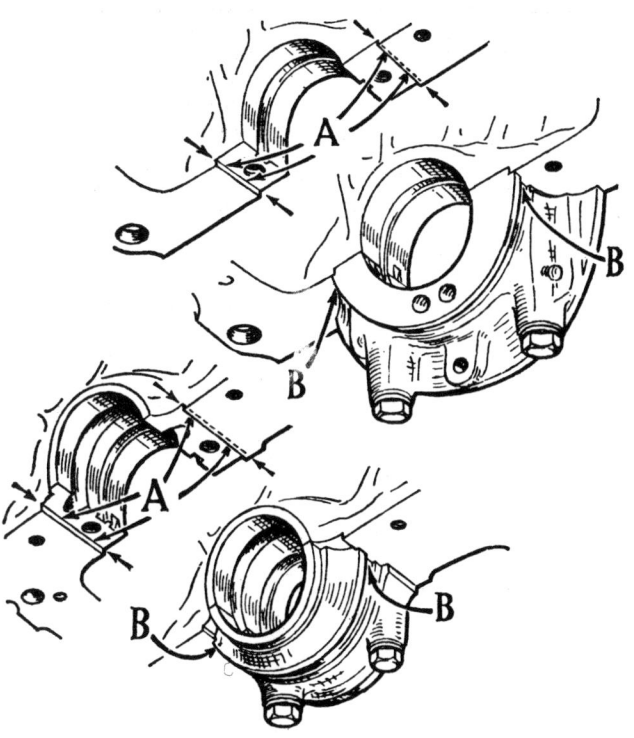

Fig. 1.13. Main Bearing Cap
'A' Use Wellseal here to prevent oil seepage.
'B' Use quick setting jointing compound here at ends of the bearing cap to sump cork gaskets

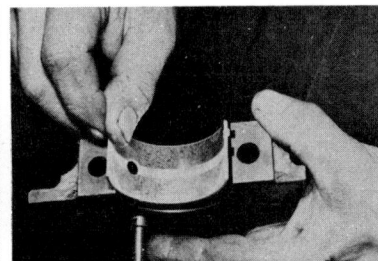

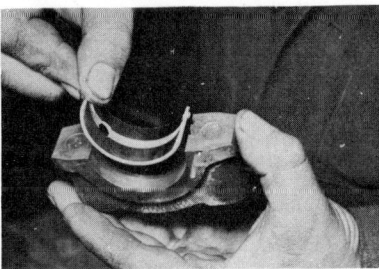

CRANKSHAFT & MAIN BEARING REASSEMBLY – SECTION
35. Fitting main bearing shells and crankshaft replacement.

there are no intermittent tight spots. Any signs that something is binding whilst the crankshaft is being revolved indicates that something is wrong and there may be a high spot on one of the bearings or on the crankshaft itself. This must be investigated or a damaged bearing could result.

36. Pistons, Gudgeon Pins and Connecting Rods - Reassembly

If new pistons are being fitted to the existing connecting rods, it is assumed that the fit of the new gudgeon pins which will be supplied with the pistons is correct in the small end bush of the connecting rod. There is an oil squirt hole on one side of each connecting rod and this faces the right hand side of the cylinder bores. Each piston also has an indication on its top surface showing which is the front so therefore, the piston and connecting rod can be assembled properly to ensure that the offset in the piston is in the correct direction. Make sure the piston is sufficiently warm to enable the gudgeon pin to slide easily through the bosses and then place the gudgeon pin half way into the piston, insert the connecting rod the correct way round, and push the gudgeon pin completely home into position. Fit the circlips into the grooves on each end of the piston to locate the gudgeon pin in position.

37. Piston Rings - Replacement on Pistons

1. Before fitting new piston rings to the old pistons, make sure the ring grooves in the piston are completely clean and free of carbon deposits. A piece of old, broken piston ring is a useful tool for doing this, but make sure that the sharp edge is not permitted to gouge out any pieces of metal. Check also that the specified gap between the edge of the new piston ring and the groove is correct.
2. All rings must be fitted from the top of the piston (a possible exception to this is the bottom oil control ring which is fitted into the skirt of some pistons which are supplied). To get the new rings into position involves spreading them sufficiently to clear the diameter of the piston itself and then moving them down over the existing grooves into their appropriate positions. Care must be taken to avoid straining them to a point where they could break. A piece of thin shim steel or an old feeler gauge blade is a very useful means of guiding the ends of the rings over the grooves to prevent them inadvertently dropping in, rather than passing over each groove. Before fitting the rings to the piston it is important to check that the end gap matches the cylinder bore into which they will eventually be fitted. Push the rings down the bores using the piston until they are about 2½ inches below the top surface of the cylinder head. Then measure the gap. If the gap is too large you have either got the wrong piston rings or the cylinder bores are worn more than you had anticipated. If the gap is too small then it will be necessary to remove a piece of material from the end of the ring. The gap may be increased to the correct specification by clamping the end of the ring in a vice so that a very small portion of the end projects above the top of the vice. Then use a fine file to take off the material in very small quantities at a time. Do not clamp the ring so that the end being filed projects too far above the vice jaws or it may easily be snapped off while the filing is being done. When every ring has been checked and the gaps made correct the rings should be assembled to the piston to prevent them being mixed up with other rings which will be fitted to other bores. Fit the bottom scraper ring first by placing it over the top of the piston and spreading the ends. Move it down the piston a little at a time, taking care to prevent it from snagging in the grooves over which it will pass. The next ring to be fitted is the lower compression ring and this only goes on one way up. The top edge of the ring will be marked 'top' and this, of course, should go uppermost. Don't be misled into thinking that this means that the ring is the top one on the piston. The top compression ring, which is the last one to go on can be fitted either way up on the piston. When all the rings are in position in their grooves, try and arrange the gaps to be equally spaced around the piston. Obviously,

if the gaps of all the rings are in a straight line there will be a much greater tendency for compression loss at that point.

38. Pistons and Connecting Rods and Big End Bearings - Reassembly to Cylinder Block and Crankshaft

1. If new piston rings, on either new pistons or the old pistons, are going into the original cylinder bores it is important that the piston ring gaps should be checked before fitting the piston assemblies. This will mean removing the rings from a new piston in order to check them. In order to assist the bedding in of the new piston rings to the original cylinder bore, it is a good idea to remove the oil glaze which builds up on a bore as an engine becomes more used. This can be done with fine emery cloth, wrapped round a wooden plug of suitable diameter. If the crankshaft is already fitted to the cylinder block, greatest care must be taken during this operation to keep any carborundum particles away from the bearing surfaces. This will involve masking off the bottom end of each cylinder and taking every precaution to prevent contamination. Careful and thorough cleaning out afterwards will also be necessary, so unless you are perfectly sure that you can do this job safely, it is best not to do it at all.
2. To assist in fitting the piston and rings into the bore it is also useful if the top edge of each cylinder bore is chamfered. This gives a lead for the piston rings to run into the bore when they are compressed. The bottom oil control ring is very fragile and is easily broken if restricted.
3. Tap the piston and connecting rod assembly into the top of the block making sure that the front of the piston is towards the front of the engine block and fit a suitable clamp around all the piston rings to compress them into the grooves of the piston. It is possible to improvise a ring compressor out of a suitably sized hose clip, but great care should be exercised if this is done as it is not possible to get it to lie dead flat due to the adjusting screw housing projecting beyond the edge of the clip. This can permit the edge of a piston ring to escape its control and then be trapped against the cylinder block face and consequently break. If a strip of sheet metal is cut from an old tin and used in conjunction with a hose clip this is less likely to happen. With the rings suitably clamped, the piston may then be gently tapped into the bore. Fit a new shell bearing into the connecting rod half of the big end, making sure that the oil hole and notch in the end of the shell line up with the corresponding hole and notch in the connecting rod. Lubricate the big end journal on the crankshaft with clean engine oil and push the connecting rod down onto the journal. Fit a new shell bearing into the cap, lining up the notch accordingly (there is no oil hole in the cap) and replace it onto the big end studs. The big end bearing caps will have been marked on removal as noted in the appropriate section so there should be no difficulty in making sure that the same cap goes onto the same connecting rod the right way round. Refit the self locking nuts which one should check to make sure are of the correct size, and are new, and tighten them down to the correct torque. If you have had the crankshaft reground and the firm which reground it is not actually assembling the pistons and connecting rods to it, it is a good idea to check the fit of each big end bearing onto the crankshaft before actually inserting the pistons into the cylinder block. Then if any high spots are apparent when the bearing is turned on the crankshaft, suitable action can be taken. Defects of this nature are rare but can be caused by poor quality workmanship on the regrinding of the crankshaft or damage to the mating faces of the big end bearing caps where some previous owner has misguidedly filed them down in an attempt to take up any bearing slackness.

39. Camshaft and Tappets - Replacement in Cylinder Block

1. If the tappets have been removed from the cylinder block, then they should not be replaced until the camshaft has been refitted. If the tappets are still in position in the cylinder block and the engine is

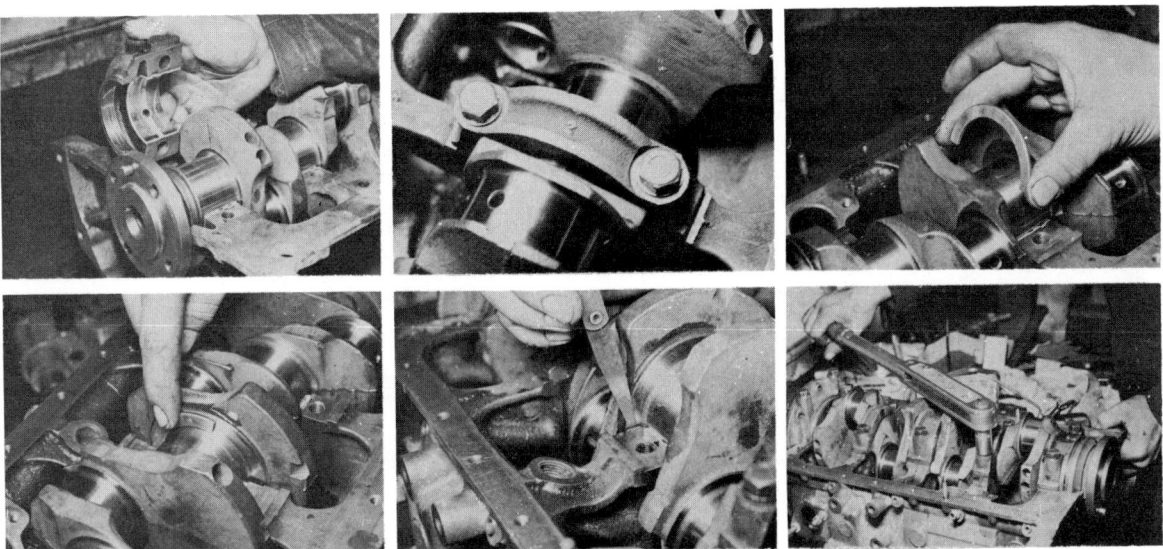

CRANKSHAFT & MAIN BEARING REASSEMBLY — SECTION 35. Fitting thrust washers, checking end float and tightening main bearing caps.

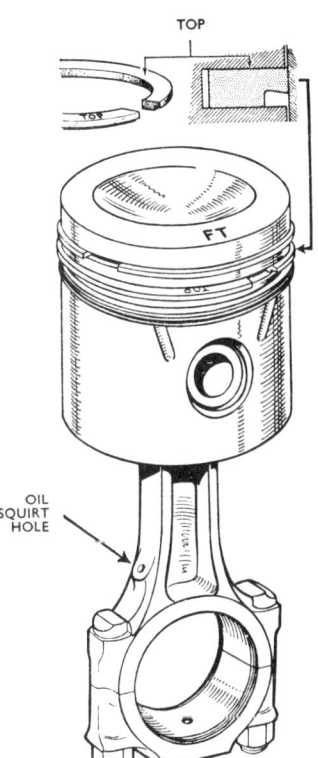

Fig. 1.14. Piston and connecting rod assembly showing relationship of oil squirt hole to F.T. (front mark) on piston crown and correct fitting of lower compression ring.

PISTON & CONNECTING ROD — REASSEMBLY TO CYLINDER BLOCK — SECTION 38. Replacing piston/con-rod assemblies. Fitting big ends.

CAMSHAFT & TAPPETS — REPLACEMENT IN CYLINDER BLOCK — SECTION 39. (Top three photos). Refitting the camshaft and thrust plate. (Lower two photos). Replacing tappets and tappet chest cover after head and rocker gear are replaced.

PISTON, GUDGEON PIN & CONNECTING ROD — REASSEMBLY — SECTION 36. Fitting piston to connecting rod.

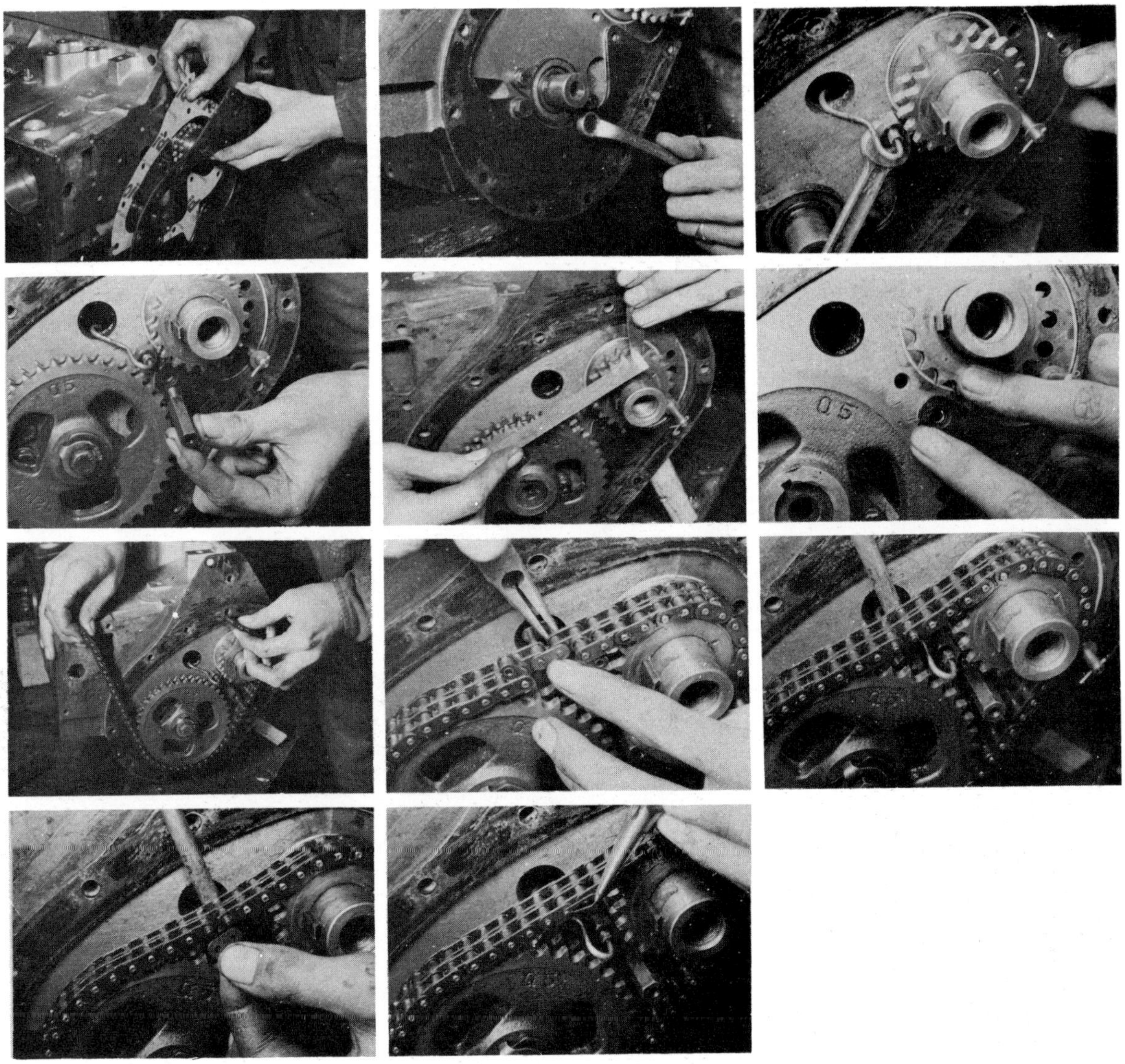

TIMING CHAIN, SPROCKETS, TENSIONER & COVER — REPLACEMENT — SECTION 40. Aligning the timing marks and fitting the chain link.

out of the car it is best to lie it on its side, pushing the tappets up in their bores so that they will not foul the lobes of the camshaft as it is being inserted into position. It should also be noted that if the engine has been completely dismantled the camshaft should always be refitted before the oil pump.

2. Make sure that all the camshaft bearings are in good condition and perfectly clean. Lubricate them with clean engine oil and then carefully replace the camshaft into the cylinder block. The main requirement in doing this is to make sure that the hardened steel lobes of the camshaft do not damage the soft metal bearing surfaces through which they have to pass. When the camshaft is fully home the thrust plate should be replaced and secured by the two bolts. If for any reason the front engine plate has been detached from the block it should be replaced now using a new gasket.

3. To avoid the possibility of the tappets falling out of their locations due to gravity with the engine inverted, it is best to wait until the oil pump and sump have been replaced on the engine and it is, once again, upright. The tappets should be thoroughly cleaned and lubricated with clean oil before replacing them in their appropriate bores.

40. Timing Chain, Tensioner, Sprockets and Cover - Replacement

1. Before fitting the timing chain or sprockets, make sure that the front plate has been put back onto the cylinder block if it was removed. If the timing chain is one which is fitted with a detachable connecting link, then the two sprockets may be replaced on their respective shafts independently of the chain. But it is in fact better to assemble the chain to the sprockets before replacing them. It can be a fiddle to get the connecting link fitted otherwise. Also, if the chain is being replaced with the engine in the car there is the possibility of dropping a piece of the link into the aperture where the oil feed pipe comes out. If this happens the front plate has to come off. When fitting the connecting link note that the two keep plates are different thicknesses - the thicker one goes in the centre. Also the open end of the spring clip should be at the trailing end of the link. The chain revolves in a clockwise direction as viewed from the front. So place the two sprockets inside the chain so that a straight line through the centre of each also passes through the two dimple marks on the edge of the sprockets. These dimple marks should face each ohter. The keys on the crankshaft and camshaft should be positioned so that they line up with the sprockets' keyways when assembled to the chain. The sprockets and chain together should then be placed on the ends of the shafts and pushed forward together until the keyways locate on the keys. Under no circumstances must the camshaft sprocket be driven on by striking. The camshaft could move back and displace the sealing plug at the other end of the block. Draw the sprocket on with a bolt. The crankshaft sprocket may be tapped on.

2. Do not forget to replace the cover mounting stud between the two sprockets if it should have been removed. When the sprockets and chain are satisfactorily assembled check that the timing marks are still correctly lined up. Refit the two lockwashers onto the camshaft sprocket mounting bolt and bend the top lockwasher into a flat on the bolt head.

3. Replace the tensioner arm onto the spindle and refit a washer and new split pin to retain it in position.

4. Replace the oil slinger disc over the crankshaft with the concave side facing outwards. The cover may now be refitted using a new gasket. The tensioner device should be tucked inside the cover and then the cover put on holding the tensioner in position against the chain. Replace all the securing bolts but do not tighten them up at this juncture.

41. Crankshaft Pulley Wheel - Replacement

The crankshaft pulley wheel is a straight fit onto the end of the crankshaft, the key in the crankshaft engaging in the keyway of the pulley wheel. There is no oil seal built into the timing cover round the crankshaft pulley wheel, the latter having a scroll groove machined into the boss to return any oil which may try to seep through. If the timing cover has been removed, it should be loosened before the crankshaft pulley wheel is refitted to the crankshaft. This enables the boss of the flywheel pulley to centralise in the aperture of the cover. However, there is a bolt alongside the aperture which must be tightened before the flywheel pulley is finally driven right on, so in the first instance it is best not to push the pulley wheel right home but to centralise the cover, draw the pulley wheel off and tighten up the particular bolt referred to. If one or two other bolts are also nipped up at the same time the remainder can be tightened down whether the crankshaft pulley wheel may be on or off. If the pulley wheel is a tight fit it may be necessary to drive it on using a block of wood. The bolt which secures the crankshaft pulley wheel into position may be replaced but it is easier if it is left until the engine is reconnected to the gearbox in the car before it is fully tightened. It is easier to lock the engine so that the necessary torque can be applied.

42. Oil Pump - Replacement

1. The oil pump should not be replaced until the camshaft, crankshaft, pistons, connecting rods and timing chain (but not the cover) have all been reassembled into the block.

2. It is important that the teeth of the oil pump driving spindle are properly meshed with the skew gear on the camshaft to enable the distributor drive which comes from the oil pump driveshaft also, to be correctly timed. The upper end of the oil pump drive spindle has an offset slot in it which engages into the bottom of the distributor drive spindle, and it is this slot which must be put in the right position when refitting the oil pump.

3. First of all, it is necessary to put No. 1 piston at the top dead centre. This must also be on the compression stroke and not on the exhaust stroke. If you have just finished assembling the camshaft timing chain and sprockets the crankshaft will be in the correct position provided it has not been turned since that assembly was done. The key in the crankshaft to which the flywheel pulley fits is always uppermost at top dead centre on No. 1 piston. With the timing marks on the sprockets still lined up, this will mean that No. 1 is correctly on the compression stroke T.D.C.

4. Once the crankshaft is positioned correctly with No. 1 piston at top dead centre on compression stroke, the oil pump may be refitted. As the pump is put into position, the spindle will turn due to the curved nature of the gears which mesh together. Initially, therefore, the slot in spindle must be set so that when it turns it will finish up in the position as shown in Fig. 1.16

5. It will be necessary for the mating faces of the pump, and the crankcase where it fits, to be perfectly clean and free from any scratches or burrs. The oil suction pipe, complete with unions, should also be lightly assembled to the oil pump body, as it will not be possible to fit this after the oil pump has been bolted down.

6. It is best for the engine to be lying on its side when refitting the oil pump as in this way it will be easy to look at the position of the driving slot in the top of the spindle. Tighten the pump mounting bolts and the oil suction pipe unions.

7. After the oil pump has been satisfactorily replaced but before fitting the sump it is a good idea to check that the distributor, in fact will be in the correct position when refitted. To do this, replace the distributor temporarily so that its drive spindle engages in the slot in the oil pump spindle and see that the rotor arm of the distributor lines up with the No. 1 plug lead contact when the cap is in position If, however, the precautions as recommended were taken when the distributor was removed, the position of the driving slot will be known for sure when reassembling the engine. The reason for taking these precautions is that it is possible for the driving dog on the end of a distributor shaft to be in a different location in relation to the rotor arm, and unless this is known a lot of time can be wasted when eventually setting up the ignition timing.

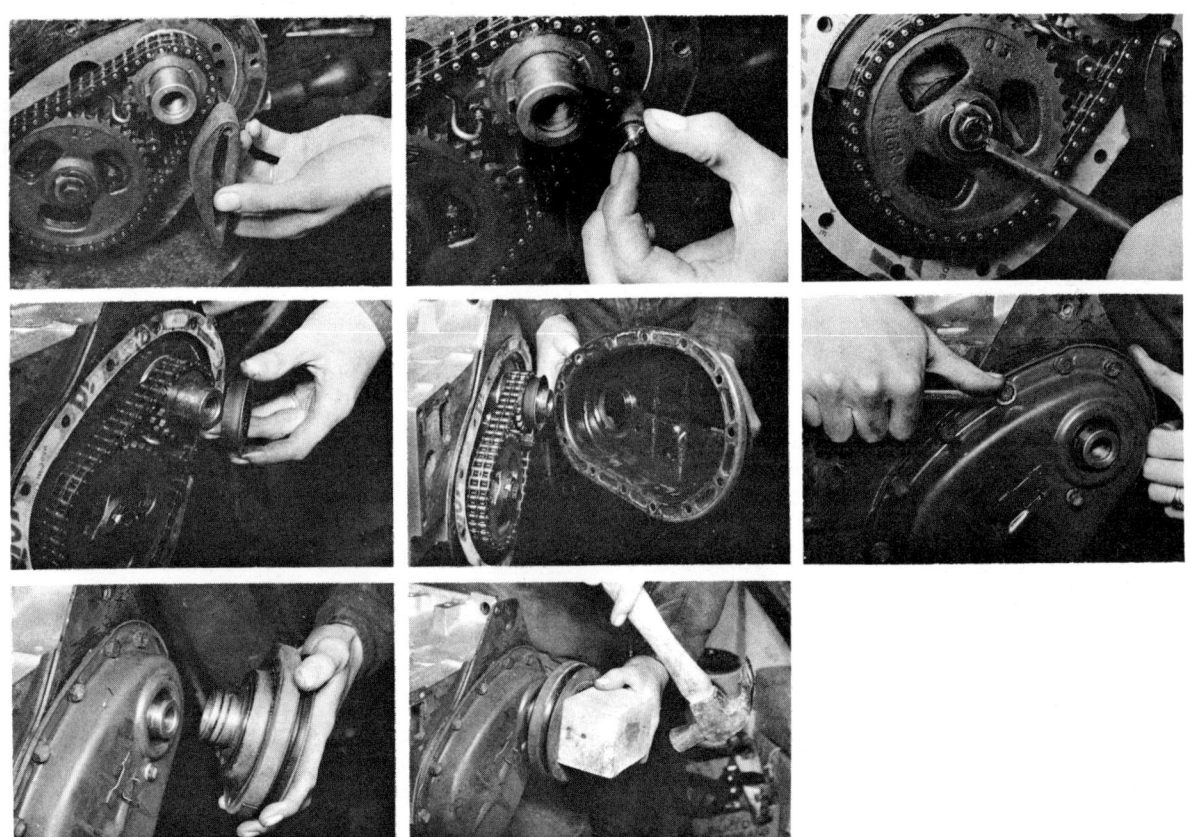

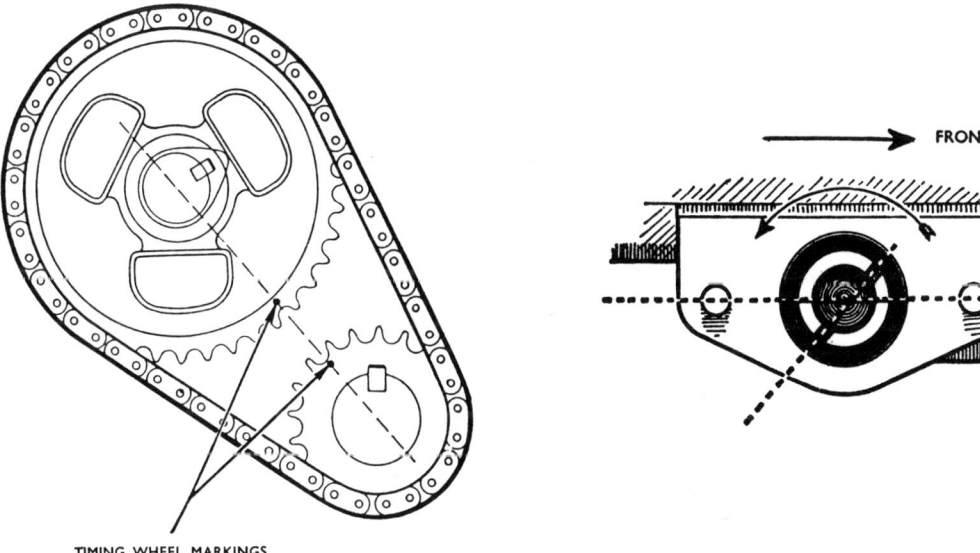

TIMING CHAIN, SPROCKETS, TENSIONER & COVER — REPLACEMENT — SECTION 40. Final assembly and replacement of the timing chain cover and crankshaft pulley.

TIMING WHEEL MARKINGS

Fig. 1.15. Timing chain sprocket line up marks and shaft keyways, No. 1 piston at T.D.C. on compression

FRONT

Fig. 1.16. Position of offset slot in distributor drive at No. 1 T.D.C. firing position. Refer to text for possible variations which may occur.

43. Sump - Replacement

1. Before replacing the sump make quite sure that all big end bearing cap nuts are tight, all main bearing cap bolts are tight, and that the oil pump has been replaced and securely tightened down. Fit a new sump gasket to the mating face on the base of the cylinder block, having first made sure that the face has been thoroughly cleaned of all remnants of old gasket and jointing compound.

2. Clean off all similar traces of gasket and jointing compound from the mating face of the sump itself. The sump gasket comes in four pieces; two semi-circular cork seals which engage in the grooves of the bearing caps at each end of the crankshaft, and two side gaskets which fit the flanges of the sump pan. Fit the side gaskets first to the crankcase. It is not essential to use a jointing compound although many people prefer to do so as a precaution. However, when fitting the cork seals into the grooves of the bearing caps the ends of the seals should be treated with a quick setting jointing compound where they bear onto the ends of the side gaskets. Carefully place the sump in position over the gaskets and locate all the sump holding bolts into position before tightening them up.

4. On engines fitted with aluminium sumps make sure that if the baffle plate has been removed for cleaning that it is replaced before the sump is put back.

44. Flywheel - Replacement

1. Before replacing the flywheel to the crankshaft flange, the mating faces must be examined carefully for any signs of dents or burrs and be cleaned up as necessary. All traces of oil and grit must also be removed, and the locating dowel peg should be in position on the crankshaft flange. Offer up the flywheel to the flange squarely and locate it carefully into position without damaging the edges of the mating faces.

2. Once the flywheel is securely mounted the set bolts should be fitted with new tab washers and progressively tightened up to the specified torque. If possible, it is a good idea to check the flywheel run-out at the outer edge of the clutch facing. If this exceeds a total of .003 inch then it means that the flywheel is not fitted square with the crankshaft and serious vibration problems could result when the engine is running. A micrometer clock gauge will be needed to check this run-out.

45. Valves and Springs - Reassembly to Cylinder Head

1. There are slight differences between the aluminium and cast iron heads in details of assembly but these are minor and will be immediately apparent. The photographs used show an aluminium headed engine which was removed from the car and a cast iron headed version where the head was removed with the engine still in the car.

2. With the head perfectly clean and having carried out all necessary renewals and renovations as required, lightly lubricate the valve stem for the first valve to be replaced and fit it in the guide. If the same valves are being used again they should have been kept in order so that they may go back in the same place.

3. Note that the arrangement of exhaust and inlet valves differs between aluminium and cast iron heads.

4. On aluminium heads place the spring seating washer over the valve lip upwards, followed by the spring and collar. On cast iron heads the lower spring seating washer is not fitted. Note that the collars are fitted with sealing rings in their internal bores and these should be renewed if necessary. The seals are included in the head gasket set.

5. The valve spring compressing tool should then be used to compress the spring sufficiently to enable the split collars to be refitted into the groove of the valve stem. A little grease may be used to assist holding them in position.

6. Release the spring compressor slowly, watching that the collars do not move out of the groove, and then, when the compressor is removed, hit the top of the valve stem to 'bounce' the spring and verify the assembly is secure.

7. Repeat the procedure for each valve in turn, taking care that each valve is replaced in its correct guide.

46. Inlet and Exhaust Manifolds - Replacement

1. If the engine is removed from the car the manifolds may be replaced on the cylinder head whether the head is fitted or not. With the engine in the car and the head removed, it is more convenient to fit them to the head before replacing the head to the engine.

2. A common gasket is used for both inlet and exhaust manifolds although the porting arrangements are different between the iron and aluminium heads. It should be noted also that the two outer inlet ports are fitted with steel ring locating inserts. These should be clean and free from carbon or any sign of damage due to heat. Fit them before the gasket.

3. Put the gasket in position and then assemble the two manifolds to each other before mounting them on the studs.

4. Replace all the six washers and nuts and three bolts and tighten them down evenly. These should be retightened later when the engine is warm. It is considered safer not to replace the carburettor until later although, of course, there is no hard and fast rule about this.

5. Reconnect the exhaust pipe to the exhaust manifold flange after the head has been fitted to the engine and the engine is in the car.

47. Cylinder Head - Refitting to the Cylinder Block

1. Make sure that the new cylinder head gasket is the correct one for the type of head as they are quite different for iron or aluminium.

2. Make sure that the mating surfaces of the head and cylinder block are perfectly clean and flat. Place the gasket in position on the cylinder head. Do not use any sealing compound or grease when fitting it. Make sure it is put in position the right way up. It is marked 'top' on the upper side.

3. If the tappet chest cover plate has been removed from the block it should now be replaced with a new gasket fitted and the bolts done up finger tight into the cylinder block. Make sure the tappets are in position too!

4. Hold the cylinder head over the block and making sure that the oil feed pipe goes through the centre hole (in line with the push rod holes) lower the head gently into place over the two studs.

5. Replace the remaining bolts which hold the tappet chest cover and then tighten all of them evenly. This will ensure that the mating faces of the cover and both the head and block are properly lined up before the head is unmovably tightened down. If a new gasket is not being fitted to the tappet chest cover it may help to guard against possible leaks if the top edge of the gasket is smeared with jointing compound before the head is replaced. This would normally apply only where the engine has not been removed from the car.

6. Replace all the cylinder head bolts and washers and the nuts onto the two studs.

7. All the bolts and nuts should be lightly tightened down equally, and then progressively tightened by about 10 lb/ft. at a time in the correct sequence as shown in Fig.1.17 until the correct total torque has been applied.

8. The length of the two projecting studs will prevent most sockets from reaching the single nut so the second nut should be locked to it when both may be turned together. The top one may be slackened off by holding the bottom one with an open ended spanner after the full tightening has been completed.

OIL PUMP – REPLACEMENT – SECTION 42. Oil pump and delivery pipe ready for tightening down.

SUMP – REPLACEMENT – SECTION 43. Securing baffle and aluminium sump to crankcase.

FLYWHEEL -- REPLACEMENT – SECTION 44. Replacing flywheel and tightening securing bolts to the correct torque.

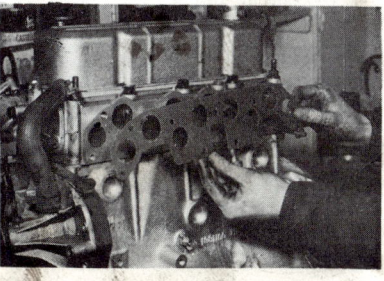

(LEFT) INLET & EXHAUST MANIFOLDS– REPLACEMENT

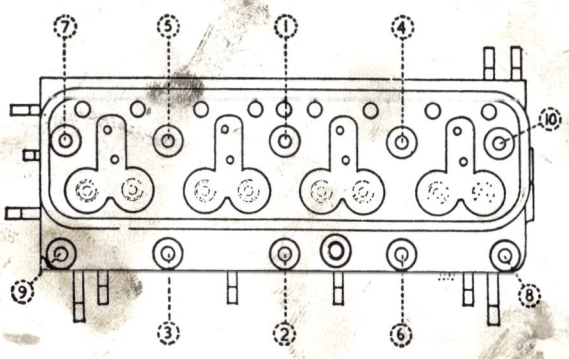

Fig. 1.17. Sequence of tightening of cylinder head bolts/nuts. Slacken in reverse order

48. Valve Rocker Gear - Reassembly and Refitting to the Cylinder Head

1. The rocker should be fitted to the head after the head has been fitted to the block. Otherwise some of the head bolts are not accessible for tightening with a conventional socket spanner. Also a lot of unnecessary slackening of the rocker adjusters will be necessary in order to refit the push rods.
2. Replace the push rods into their appropriate holes and make sure that the lower convex ends engage in the tappets.
3. If the rocker gear has been dismantled reassemble each of the two halves correctly, noting the position of the springs and the standards (see Figs. 1.5 and 1.6).
4. When both halves are assembled check that the two centres of the shafts are open ended. These receive the lubricating oil from the centre T-piece which must be next positioned between the two assemblies with the inlet section pointing downwards.
5. Place the union connector over the oil pipe. It will stay put, as the pipe has a small belled out section to prevent it falling through the head.
6. The whole assembly should then be picked up as a unit and placed in position so that the oil pipe enters the T-piece and each of the push rod ends locates into its respective rocker arm adjuster stud. This will probably take a bit of fiddling. Remember also that the assembly will not sit down in position properly as some valves should be in the open position and the push rods for these will be on the high points of the cams.
7. On aluminium headed engines the standards of the rocker assembly fit over studs whereas on iron heads bolts are used.
8. Replace all washers and nuts or bolts as appropriate and proceed to tighten them down a small and equal amount each in sequence so as to prevent any distortion caused by the resistance of the springs on the open valves. Check once more that the push rods are correctly located.
9. When the standards are all seated flat on the head the nuts or bolts should be tightened to the correct torque of 11 lb/ft.
10 Tighten the oil pipe union.

49. Valve Rocker Clearances - Checking and Adjustment

1. The valve rocker clearances are important as they control the amount a valve opens and when it opens and thus can affect the efficiency of the engine.
2. The clearances should be measured and set by using a feeler blade between the rocker arm and end of each valve stem. This is done when the valve is closed and the tappet is resting on the lowest point of the cam.
3. To enable each valve to be in the correct position for checking with the minimum amount of engine turning the procedure and order of checking should follow the sequence given in the following tables. Note that the order is quite different, depending on whichever type of cylinder head (aluminium or cast iron) is fitted. In both the tables below the valves are numbered 1 to 8, starting from the front of the cylinder head. A valve is fully open when the rocker arm has pushed the valve down to its lowest point.

Cast Iron Head

Open valve	Adjust clearance (hot)
No. 8 (ex)	No. 1 (ex)
No. 6 (in)	No. 3 (in)
No. 4 (ex)	No. 5 (ex)
No. 7 (in)	No. 2 (in)
No. 1 (ex)	No. 8 (ex)
No. 3 (in)	No. 6 (in)
No. 5 (ex)	No. 4 (ex)
No. 2 (in)	No. 7 (in)

Aluminium head

Open valve	Adjust clearance (hot)	
No. 8 (ex)	No. 1 (ex)	
No. 5 (in)	No. 4 (in)	nm)
No. 3 (ex)	No. 6 (ex)	m)
No. 7 (ex)	No. 2 (in)	nm)
No. 1 (ex)	No. 8 (ex)	am)
No. 4 (in)	No. 5 (in)	mm)
No. 6 (ex)	No. 3 (ex)	am)
No. 2 (in)	No. 7 (in)	mm)
		mm)

Refer to Specifications for correct valve clearance

4. Using a screwdriver and spanner first slacken the locknut on the adjusting stud and then put the feeler blade, of thickness appropriate, to the valve being adjusted between the rocker arm and valve stem. Slacken the stud adjuster if the gap is too small to accept the blade.
5. Turn the adjusting screw until the feeler blade can be felt to drag lightly when it is drawn out of the gap.
6. Hold the adjuster with a screwdriver and tighten the locknut. Check the gap once more to make sure it has not altered as a result of locking the stud.
7. If the engine is being assembled on the bench or after the head has been taken off the gaps should be set .002 inch more than specification in the first instance.

50. Engine Reassembly - Final Stages

1. Before replacing an engine into the car, all those ancillary parts which were removed before the engine was stripped should be replaced. These items were listed in Section 7 One possible exception is the carburettor which projects in a somewhat vulnerable way and could be damaged expensively if any mishap occurred on replacing the engine.
2. Refit the rocker gear cover, even though it has to be taken off again, as this will protect the rocker gear from damage and dust. Leave the new gasket to be fitted later.

51. Engine - Replacement in the Car

Generally speaking the replacement of the engine is a reversal of the removal procedure but the following points should be borne in mind.
1. If the engine and gearbox have been removed together, they should be reassembled and replaced together. This takes care of the possible difficulties one may encounter fitting the gearbox input shaft into the clutch. It will mean that the propeller shaft may also remain connected. However, it must not be forgotten that the propeller shaft will need to be introduced into the gearbox rear cover before the unit is in its final position, otherwise the propeller shaft will need to be disconnected at the rear axle pinion flange.
2. When lowering the engine into the car make sure first that it is suspended at the correct attitude. It is difficult and possibly dangerous to have to alter the angle of tilt whilst it is suspended.
3. Always lower the engine very slowly and watch it all round all the way. It is easy to wrench out wire and pipes due to being in too much of a hurry and not noticing these things when they flip back in the way - as they always seem to do.
4. If the engine will not go where it should, look and find out why. Do not try and force anything.
5. Always fit new oil filter and air filter elements.
6. The following check list should ensure that the engine starts safely and with little or no delay:-

a) Fuel pipes to fuel pump and carburettor - connected and tight.
b) Water hoses to radiator and heater - connected and clipped tight.
c) Radiator and cylinder block water drain taps shut.
d) Cooling system filled up.

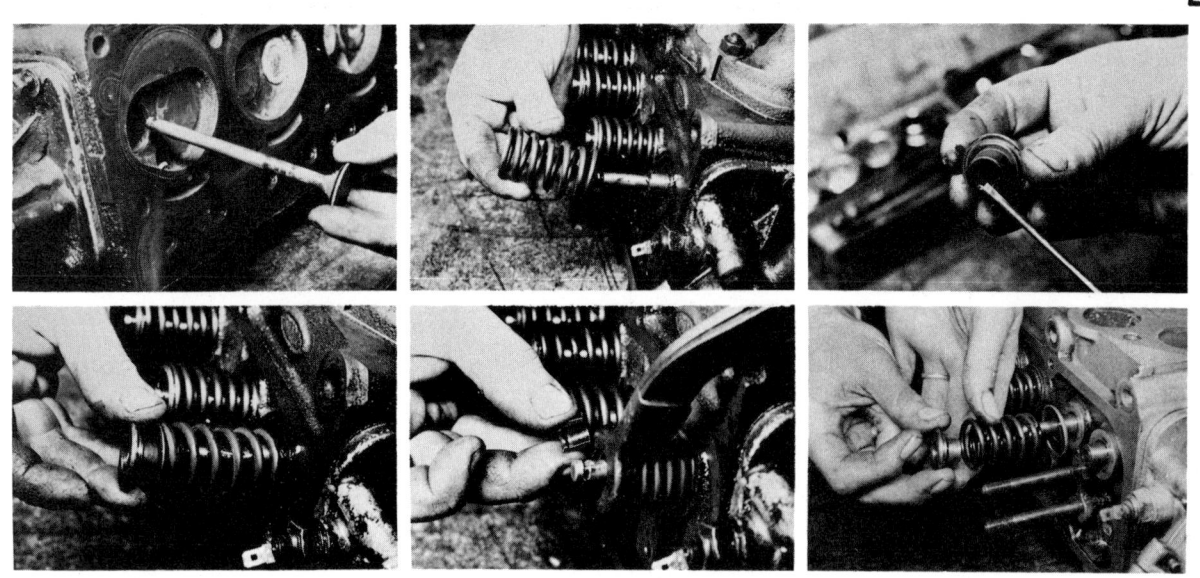

VALVES & VALVE SPRINGS — REASSEMBLY TO HEAD — SECTION 45. Assembly of valves to cylinder head. (Last photo shows aluminium head).

VALVE ROCKER GEAR — REASSEMBLY & FITTING TO CYLINDER HEAD — SECTION 48. (Top five photos). Assembly to cast iron head. (Bottom three photos) Aluminium head.

e) Sump drain plug screwed in tight.

f) Oil filter element screwed on tight.

g) Oil in sump.

h) Oil in gearbox and level plug tight.

i) L.T. wires connected to distributor and coil.

j) Sparking plugs clean and tight.

k) Valve clearances set.

l) H.T. leads from coil, distributor and spark plugs all connected correctly, and securely.

m) Distributor rotor arm fitted.

n) Choke and throttle cables connected and controls operating correctly over full range.

o) Braided earthing cables from engine to body frame secure.

p) Starter motor lead securely connected at both ends.

q) Fan belt fitted and tensioned.

r) Generator leads connected.

s) Oil pressure pipe or sender wire connected.

t) Temperature gauge wire connected.

u) Battery charged and in good condition and leads securely connected to clean terminals.

v) All loose tools removed from engine compartment.

w) All jacks and blocks removed.

7. As soon as the engine starts, run it steadily at a fast tick-over for several minutes and look all round for signs of leaks and loose or unclipped pipes and wires. Watch the instruments and warning lights and stop the engine at the first indications of anything nasty!

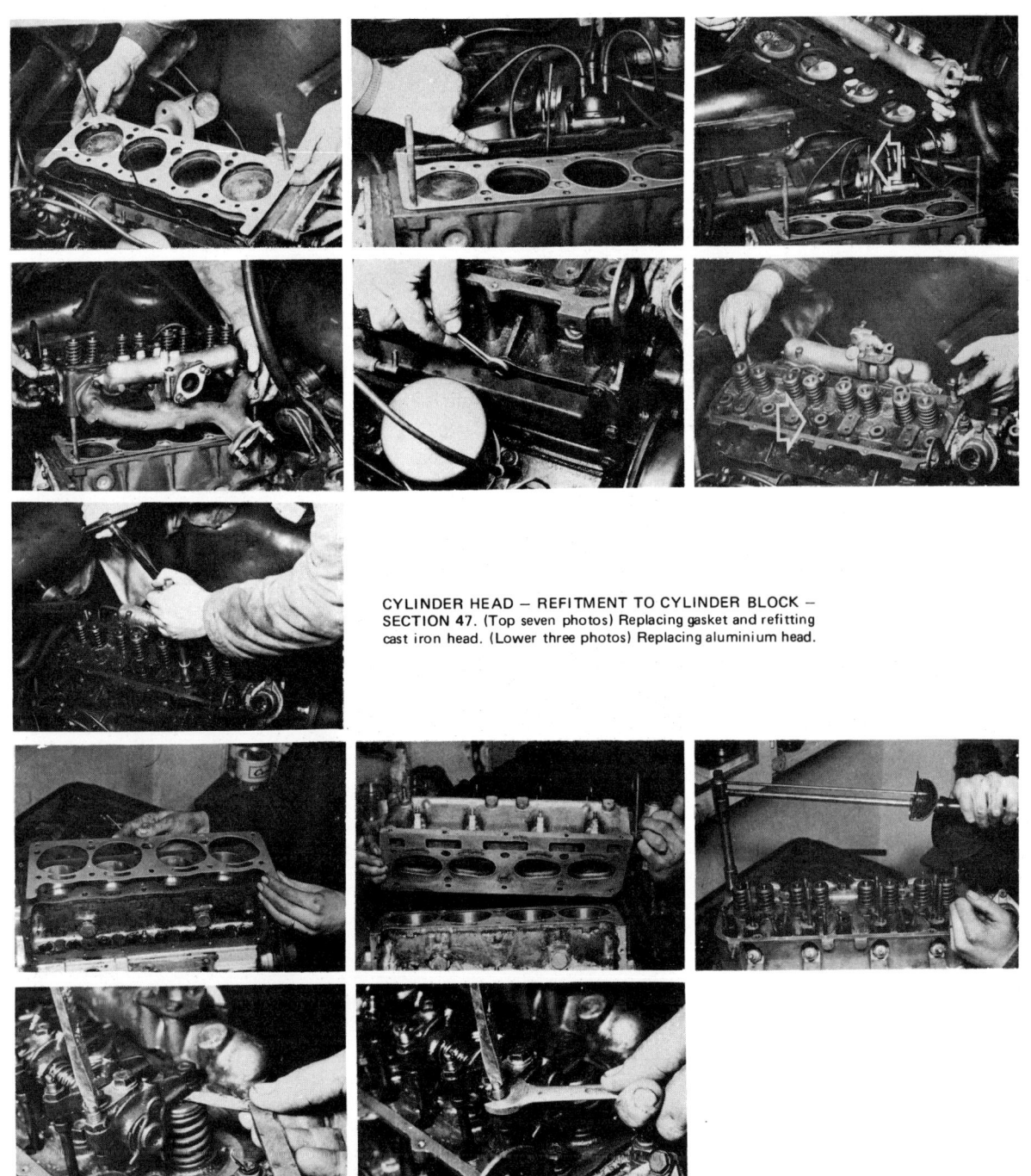

CYLINDER HEAD — REFITMENT TO CYLINDER BLOCK — SECTION 47. (Top seven photos) Replacing gasket and refitting cast iron head. (Lower three photos) Replacing aluminium head.

VALVE ROCKER CLEARANCES — SECTION 49. Checking and adjustment.

Fault Finding Chart -- Engine

Symptom	Reason/s	Remedy
Engine will not turn over when starter switch is operated.	Flat battery. Bad battery connections. Bad connections at solenoid switch and/or starter motor.	Check that battery is fully charged and that all connections are clean and tight.
	Starter motor jammed.	Turn the square headed end of the starter motor shaft with a spanner to free it. Where a pre-engaged starter is fitted rock the car back and forth with a gear engaged. If this does not free pinion remove starter.
	Defective solenoid.	Bridge the main terminals of the solenoid switch with a piece of heavy duty cable in order to operate the starter.
	Starter motor defective;	Remove and overhaul starter motor.
Engine turns over normally but fails to fire and run.	No spark at plugs.	Check ignition system according to procedures given in Chapter 4.
	No fuel reaching engine.	Check fuel system according to procedures given in Chapter 3.
	Too much fuel reaching the engine (flooding).	Check the fuel system as above.
Engine starts but runs unevenly and misfires.	Ignition and/or fuel system faults.	Check the ignition and fuel systems as though the engine had failed to start.
	Incorrect valve clearances.	Check and reset clearances.
	Burnt out valves. Blown cylinder head gasket.	Remove cylinder head and examine and overhaul as necessary.
	Worn out piston rings. Worn cylinder bores.	Remove cylinder head and examine pistons and cylinder bores. Overhaul as necessary.
Lack of power	Ignition and/or fuel system faults.	Check the ignition and fuel systems for correct ignition timing and carburetter settings.
	Incorrect valve clearances.	Check and reset the clearances.
	Burnt out valves. Blown cylinder head gasket.	Remove cylinder head and examine and overhaul as necessary.
	Worn out piston rings. Worn cylinder bores.	Remove cylinder head and examine pistons and cylinder bores. Overhaul as necessary.
Excessive oil consumption.	Oil leaks from crankshaft rear oil seal, timing cover gasket and oil seal, rocker cover gasket, oil filter gasket, sump gasket, sump plug washer.	Identify source of leak and renew seal as appropriate.
	Worn piston rings or cylinder bores resulting in oil being burnt by engine. Smoky exhaust is an indication.	Fit new rings or rebore cylinders and fit new pistons, depending on degree of wear.
	Worn valve guides and/or defective valve stem seals.	Remove cylinder heads and recondition valve stem bores and valves and seals as necessary.
Excessive mechanical noise from engine.	Wrong valve to rocker clearances. Worn crankshaft bearings. Worn cylinders (piston slap).	Adjust valve clearances. Inspect and overhaul where necessary.
	Slack or worn timing chain and sprockets.	Adjust chain and/or inspect all timing mechanism.

NOTE: When investigating starting and uneven running faults do not be tempted into snap diagnosis. Start from the beginning of the check procedure and follow it through. It will take less time in the long run. Poor performance from an engine in terms of power and economy is not normally diagnosed quickly. In any event the ignition and fuel systems must be checked first before assuming any further investigation needs to be made.

Castrol GRADES

Castrol Engine Oils

Castrol GTX

An ultra high performance SAE 20W/50 motor oil which exceeds the latest API MS requirements and manufacturers' specifications. Castrol GTX with liquid tungsten† generously protects engines at the extreme limits of performance, and combines both good cold starting with oil consumption control. Approved by leading car makers.

Castrol XL 20/50

Contains liquid tungsten†; well suited to the majority of conditions giving good oil consumption control in both new and old cars.

Castrolite (Multi-grade)

This is the lightest multi-grade oil of the Castrol motor oil family containing liquid tungsten†. It is best suited to ensure easy winter starting and for those car models whose manufacturers specify lighter weight oils.

Castrol Grand Prix

An SAE 50 engine oil for use where a heavy, full-bodied lubricant is required.

Castrol Two-Stroke-Four

A premium SAE 30 motor oil possessing good detergency characteristics and corrosion inhibitors, coupled with low ash forming tendency and excellent anti-scuff properties. It is suitable for all two-stroke motor-cycles, and for two-stroke and small four-stroke horticultural machines.

Castrol CR (Multi-grade)

A high quality engine oil of the SAE-20W/30 multi-grade type, suited to mixed fleet operations.

Castrol CRI 10, 20, 30

Primarily for diesel engines, a range of heavily fortified, fully detergent oils, covering the requirements of DEF 2101-D and Supplement 1 specifications.

Castrol CRB 20, 30

Primarily for diesel engines, heavily fortified, fully detergent oils, covering the requirements of MIL-L-2104B.

Castrol R 40

Primarily designed and developed for highly stressed racing engines. Castrol 'R' should not be mixed with any other oil nor with any grade of Castrol.

†*Liquid Tungsten is an oil soluble long chain tertiary alkyl primary amine tungstate covered by British Patent No. 882,295.*

Castrol Gear Oils

Castrol Hypoy (90 EP)

A light-bodied powerful extreme pressure gear oil for use in hypoid rear axles and in some gearboxes.

Castrol Gear Oils (continued)

Castrol Hypoy Light (80 EP)

A very light-bodied powerful extreme pressure gear oil for use in hypoid rear axles in cold climates and in some gearboxes.

Castrol Hypoy B (90 EP)

A light-bodied powerful extreme pressure gear oil that complies with the requirements of the MIL-L-2105B specification, for use in certain gearboxes and rear axles.

Castrol Hi-Press (140 EP)

A heavy-bodied extreme pressure gear oil for use in spiral bevel rear axles and some gearboxes.

Castrol ST (90)

A light-bodied gear oil with fortifying additives

Castrol D (140)

A heavy full-bodied gear oil with fortifying additives.

Castrol Thio-Hypoy FD (90 EP)

A light-bodied powerful extreme pressure gear oil. This is a special oil for running-in certain hypoid gears.

Automatic Transmission Fluids

Castrol TQF

(Automatic Transmission Fluid)

Approved for use in all Borg-Warner Automatic Transmission Units. Castrol TQF also meets Ford specification M2C 33F.

Castrol TQ Dexron®

(Automatic Transmission Fluid)

Complies with the requirements of Dexron® Automatic Transmission Fluids as laid down by General Motors Corporation.

Castrol Greases

Castrol LM

A multi-purpose high melting point lithium based grease approved for most automotive applications including chassis and wheel bearing lubrication.

Castrol MS3

A high melting point lithium based grease containing molybdenum disulphide.

Castrol BNS

A high melting point grease for use where recommended by certain manufacturers in front wheel bearings when disc brakes are fitted.

Castrol Greases (continued)

Castrol CL

A semi-fluid calcium based grease, which is both waterproof and adhesive, intended for chassis lubrication.

Castrol Medium

A medium consistency calcium based grease.

Castrol Heavy

A heavy consistency calcium based grease.

Castrol PH

A white grease for plunger housings and other moving parts on brake mechanisms. *It must NOT be allowed to come into contact with brake fluid when applied to the moving parts of hydraulic brakes.*

Castrol Graphited Grease

A graphited grease for the lubrication of transmission chains.

Castrol Under-Water Grease

A grease for the under-water gears of outboard motors.

Anti-Freeze

Castrol Anti-Freeze

Contains anti-corrosion additives with ethyiene glycol. Recommended for the cooling systems of all petrol and diesel engines.

Speciality Products

Castrol Girling Damper Oil Thin

The oil for Girling piston type hydraulic dampers.

Castrol Shockol

A light viscosity oil for use in some piston type shock absorbers and in some hydraulic systems employing synthetic rubber seals. It must not be used in braking systems.

Castrol Penetrating Oil

A leaf spring lubricant possessing a high degree of penetration and providing protection against rust.

Castrol Solvent Flushing Oil

A light-bodied solvent oil, designed for flushing engines, rear axles, gearboxes and gearcasings.

Castrollo

An upper cylinder lubricant for use in the proportion of 1 fluid ounce to two gallons of fuel.

Everyman Oil

A light-bodied machine oil containing anti-corrosion additives for both general use and cycle lubrication.

Chapter 2 Cooling system

Contents

Specifications

Type									Pressurized with centrifugal pump and fan; sealed system with expansion bottle on certain models. Also fitted to certain models is a viscous coupling fan
Radiator ...	...	...	...	...	...	...	...	...;	Two or three row, gilled tube
Radiator cap valve relief pressure			...	...	...	...	...	9 lb/in^2 (0.63 kg/cm^2)

Thermostat:

Opening temperature	...	...	...	...	...	...	...	$82^{\circ}C$ $(180^{\circ}F)$, Later models $79/83^{\circ}C$ $(178/184^{\circ}F)$
By-pass port closed at	...	...	...	...	...	...	...	$95^{\circ}C$ $(203^{\circ}F)$

Coolant capacity (with heater):

Sceptre, Hillman GT and Hunter GT ...	...	...	...	...	13.75 pints (16.5 US pints, 7.8 litres)
All other models	...	...	...	...	...	12.6 pints (15.1 US pints, 7.2 litres)

For torque wrench settings consult page 208.

1. General Description

The engine cooling liquid is circulated round the system on the thermo siphon principle, assisted by a belt driven impeller type pump.

The system is pressurised so that boiling and evaporation will only occur at abnormally high temperatures. The radiator cap valve will lift at a pressure of 9 lbs/in.^{2}. The pressure will then drop, as vapour boils off and passes down the overflow pipe, until the valve re-seats. It is therefore important that the radiator cap is one designed for the system and in good condition. Testing equipment is available at most garages.

The circuit also incorporates a thermostatically controlled valve which restricts the amount of water passing through the radiator until the correct engine operating temperature is reached. This assists rapid warming up and keeps the engine at a constant running temperature regardless of ambient conditions.

The principle of operation is as follows. The water heated by the engine rises out of the cylinder head towards the thermostat which, if cold, is closed. It then diverts via the heater (or heater by-pass pipe if the heater valve is shut) straight to the pump and thence back to the engine.

When the engine warms up a proportion of the warm water will pass via the thermostat valve to the top of the radiator down through which it will pass and cool. The pump will then draw the cold water from the bottom of the radiator and pass it back to the engine (the pump has two inlets). If the engine temperature should rise excessively the thermostat valve will close off the by-pass outlet thus directing all water through the radiator.

Water which may boil off down the radiator overflow pipe passes into a reservoir which maintains a level of liquid covering the end of the overflow pipe. Consequently, any liquid exhausted down the overflow is drawn back by the vacuum conditions created when the system cools down. This greatly reduces the need for regular topping up.

2. Routine Maintenance

1. The coolant level should be checked at least weekly - more often if indications warrant it - by removing the radiator cap. The level should be just below the bottom of the filler neck. If topping up is required use a soft water (rainwater) if possible. This helps to keep deposits to a minimum.

2. Check the fan belt for wear and correct tension and adjust or renew it if needed (See Section   10).

3. The water pump is sealed and need not be touched unless signs of leaking or shaft bearing failure are apparent.

4. In hard water areas removal of deposits using a proprietary chemical de-scaler may be needed from time to time - but not more than annually. A good time to do this is at the change of the seasons when anti-freeze may be used.

3. Cooling System - Draining

1. Stand the car level and remove the radiator cap - slowly and with caution if the engine is very hot (and thus likely to boil when pressure is released).

2. Unscrew the drain tap at the bottom of the radiator, and if the coolant is to be re-used because of anti-freeze, collect it in a clean

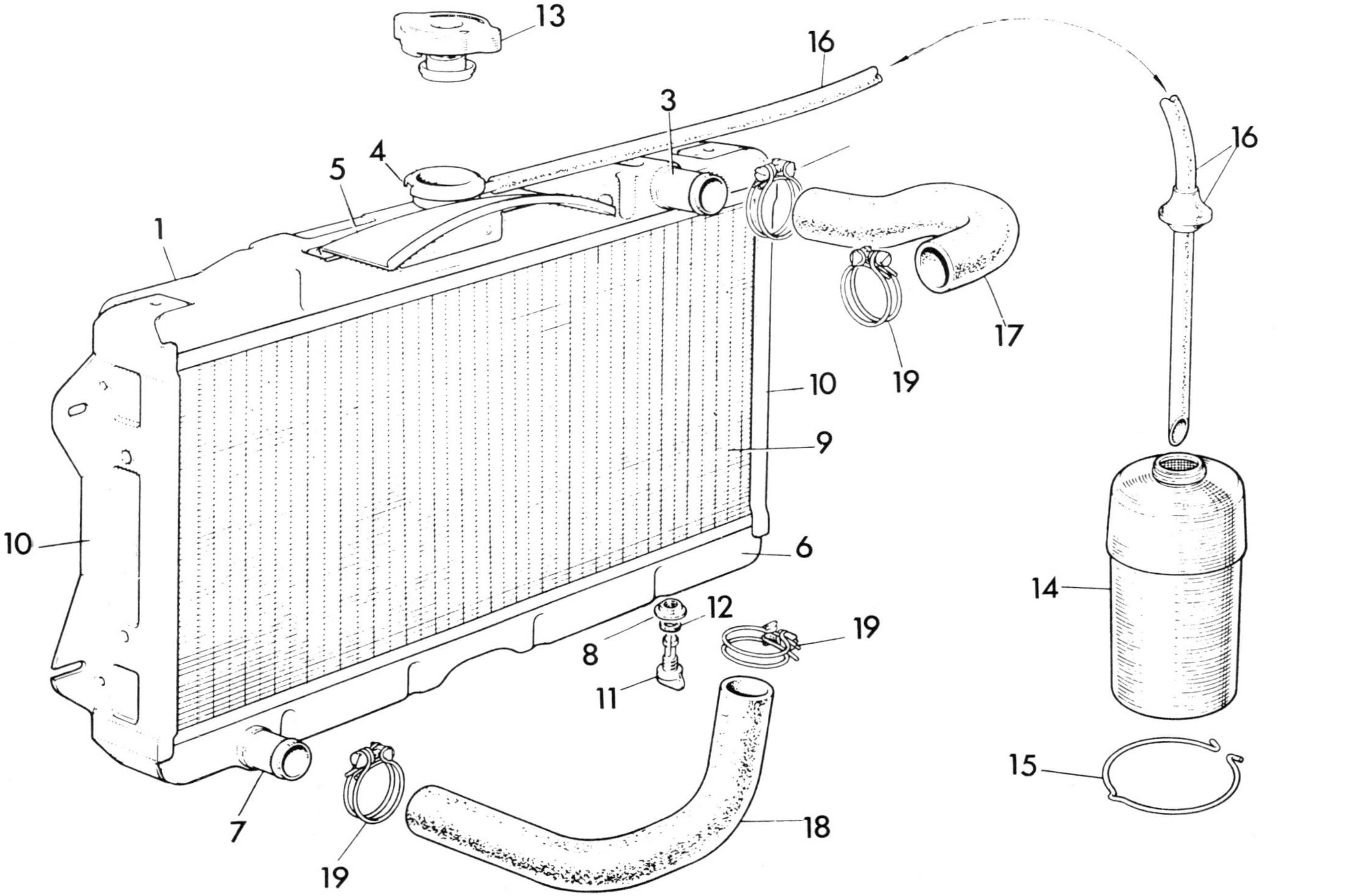

Fig. 2.1. RADIATOR AND HOSES

1 Top tank	5 Fan guard	8 Drain tap boss
3 Top inlet pipe	6 Bottom tank	9 Core
4 Filler neck	7 Bottom outlet pipe	10 Side strap

11 Drain tap	14 Expansion bottle	17 Top hose
12 Washer	15 Clip	18 Bottom hose
13 Filler cap	16 Expansion pipe and cap	19 Hose clip

53

container. If the water is to be completely drained from the cylinder block also, the tap on the left side in the centre of the block should be opened.

3. When the water has ceased flowing poke the drain tap outlets with a piece of wire to check that no loose sediment is blocking them.

4. Cooling System - Flushing

1. Every so often - particularly in hard water areas - it is a good practice to flush out the system to remove any loose sediment, and scale which may have accumulated. The time to do this is when the coolant is being drained or anti-freeze added. With the expansion bottle system, however, the need for topping up is very infrequent so that the deposits of lime and so on, from regular additions of new water, are reduced. The need for flushing, therefore, is usually only caused by some other factor - such as a leak which allow air to enter the system and cause oxidisation or the use of an anti-freeze of a type which may cause corrosion.

2. To check the need for flushing open the radiator drain tap and if the liquid coming out is obviously very dirty and full of solid particles let it run out. If it clears as more runs out and the outflow is in no way restricted then there is no great problem. If, however, constant poking with a piece of wire is needed and the liquid continues very dirty then obviously a flush is needed.

3. To flush out, simply leave the radiator and block drain taps open and after removing the radiator cap, run a hose through the system for about 15 minutes. If the taps show signs of blockage keep poking them out. If the blocking is persistant remove the tap completely so that a larger orifice may permit the obstruction to clear itself. In some bad cases a reverse flush may help and this is easily done by removing the radiator and running the hose into the bottom tank so that it flows out of the filler neck.

4. If the radiator flow is restricted by something other than loose sediment then no amount of flushing will shift it and it is then that a proprietary chemical cleaner is needed. Use this according to the directions and make sure that the residue is fully flushed out afterwards. If leaks develop after using a chemical cleaner, a proprietary radiator sealer may cure them but the signs are that the radiator has suffered considerable chemical corrosion and that the metal is obviously getting very thin in places.

5. Cooling System - Filling

1. Always flush out before refilling.

2. Close both drain taps and fill up slowly. Mix anti-freeze, if being used, with the water before putting it in, making up a total quantity about 2 pints less than the capacity of the system. Then top up with water.

3. Run the engine up to normal temperature and then check the level again. If the level was right up to the neck on filling it will have dropped at least ¼ inch and this level should be retained.

4. Check that the heater works. If it does not there may be an air lock in the system. If it does not work efficiently the thermostat may be stuck open.

6. Radiator - Removal, Inspection, Cleaning and Replacement

1. Drain the cooling system as described earlier in Section 3.

2. Slacken the clip and remove the top radiator hose where it connects to the thermostat housing outlet or to the radiator. Slacken also the clip securing the bottom hose to the radiator and pull off the hose.

3. The radiator is held by four hexagon headed speed screws. When these are removed the radiator may be lifted out.

4. Thoroughly clean the exterior of the radiator. It has presumably been removed in order to repair a leak or for further examination of a suspected blockage (except of course as part of a procedure to get

access to something else).

5. As the radiator tanks and connections are made of brass they can be repaired with solder where exterior leaks are accessible. The technique of soldering is not discussed here but suffice it to say that the surfaces to be joined must be thoroughly cleaned, then tinned and the solder able to 'run' in the repair. It is fruitless merely depositing blobs of solder about the place. It would be better to use a resin filler paste which in fact can be used for such repairs in limited applications. Care must also be taken when soldering to localise any heat used. Otherwise the radiator may start to disintegrate where you least want it to. A leak in the internal parts of the honeycomb, if not severe, can be cured with one of the specialist sealers added to the cooling liquid. If severe, professional attention will be needed. Another way for emergencies only, is to block the whole of the honeycomb in the suspect area with resin filler paste. Old fashioned remedies such as mustard, egg whites and porridge oats added to the water, are not recommended as they have been known to have sinister effects on water pumps and thermostats. There is much less liquid in modern systems and these foodstuffs cannot be digested so readily!

7. Thermostat - Removal, Testing and Replacement

1. If the engine gets too hot or stays too cool; or the heater is inefficient, then the thermostat is probably to blame.

2. Drain out sufficient coolant to lower the level about 4 inches (say a quart) so that no more will be lost when the top radiator hose is next detached from the thermostat housing.

3. Remove the two bolts securing the hose flange to the housing and remove the flange. The thermostat may then be taken out. If it is stuck round the edges carefully clean around the lip with a pointed tool to free it.

4. To test the thermostat, suspend it on a piece of cotton in a pan of water and see how it behaves at the necessary opening temperatures. The valve should start to open within 3°C of the normal operating temperature. Then after another 2 to 3 minutes it should open 3/8 inch (9.5 mm) to the 'by-pass port closed' position. After being once more placed in cooler water it should close within 15 to 20 seconds. On later type thermostats the by-pass valve has been deleted.

5. If a thermostat does not operate correctly it should be renewed. If one is not immediately available leave the old one out to avoid damage by possible overheating of the engine.

6. Refit the thermostat to its housing carefully and make sure it seats snugly. When refitting the housing flange cover, use a new gasket and sealing compound on both sides. If the mating surfaces are badly pitted it may be necessary to clean them up with a file, but make sure the surfaces remain flat.

7. Do not overtighten the securing bolts as the threads in the housing are easily stripped. This is why preparation of the mating surfaces is important to stop leaks.

8. Water Pump - Removal, Dismantling and Replacement

1. If the water pump leaks or the bearing is obviously worn it will need to be removed for renewal or repair.

2. Drain the cooling system and then undo the hoses which are connected to the pump.

3. Slacken the generator mounting bolts and belt tension adjuster bolt so that the fan belt may be removed.

4. Remove the four bolts that hold the fan and pulley to the pulley centre and take the fan and pulley off.

5. When removing a plastic type fan, undo the four screws and remove, together with the spring washers, the metal retaining plate and fan. When refitting the fan, ensure that the retaining plate locates correctly on the locating peg of the fan before securing with the four screws and spring washers.

6. The pump is held to the block by four larger bolts (do not confuse them with the pump assembly bolts) which should be

55

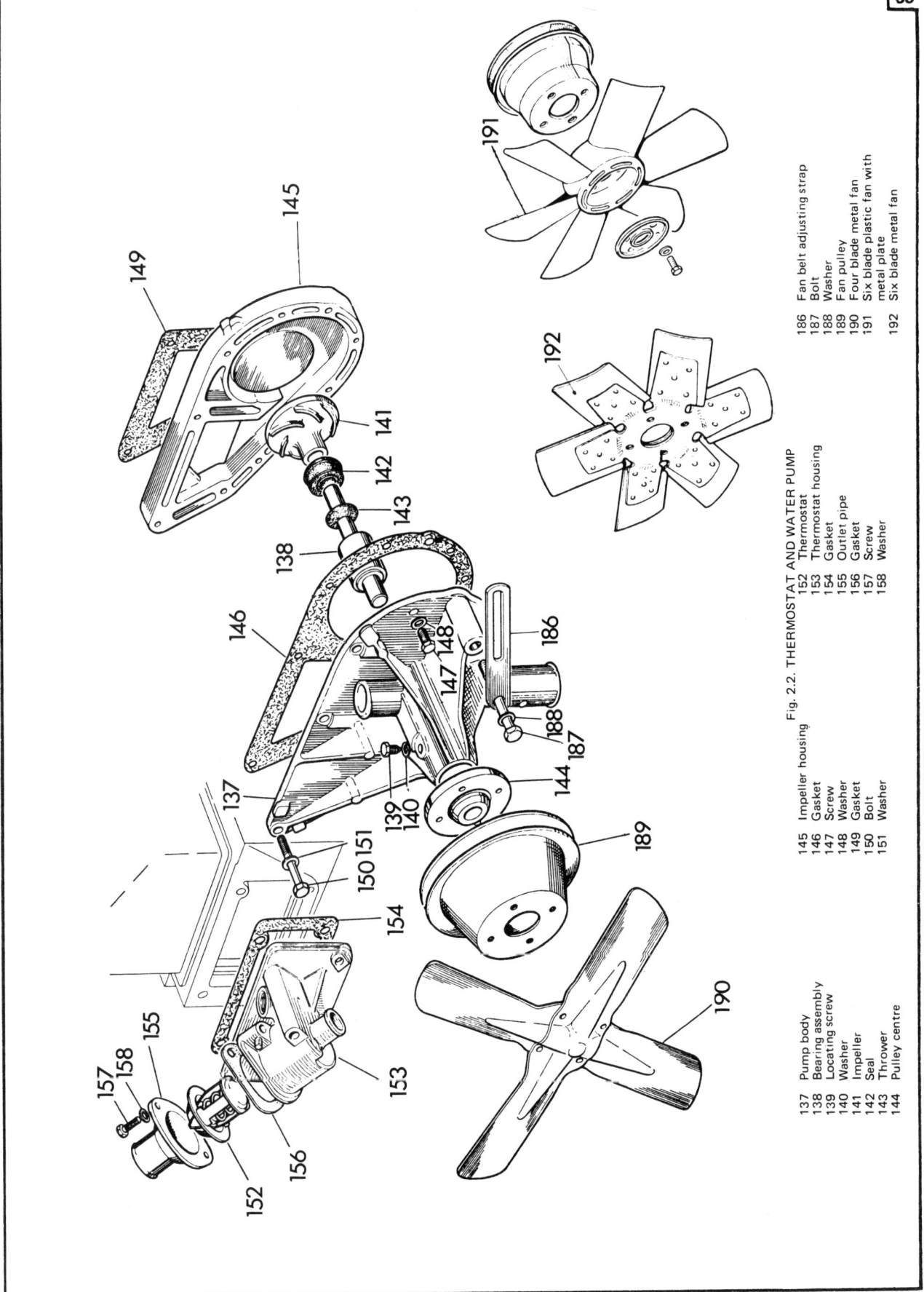

Fig. 2.2. THERMOSTAT AND WATER PUMP

137 Pump body
138 Bearing assembly
139 Locating screw
140 Washer
141 Impeller
142 Seal
143 Thrower
144 Pulley centre

145 Impeller housing
146 Gasket
147 Screw
148 Washer
149 Gasket
150 Bolt
151 Washer

152 Thermostat
153 Thermostat housing
154 Gasket
155 Outlet pipe
156 Gasket
157 Screw
158 Washer

186 Fan belt adjusting strap
187 Bolt
188 Washer
189 Fan pulley
190 Four blade metal fan
191 Six blade plastic fan with metal plate
192 Six blade metal fan

removed and the pump lifted off.

7   Before attempting repairs to the pump find out the relative cost of a new bearing assembly, seal and gasket and weigh this against the cost of a complete unit, new or secondhand, and the time factor involved.

8.   Begin dismantling by removing the screws securing the impeller housing to the body and separating the two. To remove the bearing and spindle assembly first remove the locating screw and then draw the pulley centre off the spindle with a suitable claw extractor.

9.   Warm the pump body in hot water (90°C) in order that the spindle, together with the bearing and impeller, may be pressed out. When this has been done the impeller may be pressed off the spindle. The seal may be removed and replaced when the bearing assembly has been pressed out of the body. The face of the seal is carbon, and both it and the mating face on the body must be perfectly smooth and unscored.

10   Unless one has the use of a proper press, reassembly is tricky. The impeller and pulley centre have to be positioned correctly on the spindle. If pushed on too far or too little the operation of the pump is affected. For this reason repair of the pump should not be undertaken lightly without the proper equipment to hand.

11   When fitting a new seal unit into the pump body it should be smeared with a sealing compound to prevent water seepage. Make sure no traces of sealer get onto the carbon face however.

12   Reassembly is otherwise a reversal of the dismantling procedure. Heat the body once more when pressing the bearing into position and locate it with the screw whilst it is still warm and movable.

13   Before replacing housing and the block the mating faces of both the impeller housing and the block must be perfectly clean and free of traces of old gaskets. Fit a new gasket, using jointing compound, on both sides and tighten the bolts evenly to ensure a watertight joint.

14   Refit the fan and pulley, replace the fan belt and adjust the tension and connect the water hoses. Refill the system with coolant. Examine for leaks when cold and also at normal running temperature.

9. Anti-Freeze

1.   Anti-freeze liquid added to the coolant is now the accepted protection against cold which can freeze the coolant and crack the block. Even though a heater may be available whilst the car is garaged at night, daytime temperatures when the car is parked outside can be low enough to freeze! At very low temperatures a car without anti-freeze can freeze up, whilst running, at the bottom of the radiator. Also a small quantity of water will always remain in the block after draining which could freeze and cause damage.

2.   Anti-freeze has very searching properties and if there are any leaks or wear leaks in the system, it will accentuate them and you may soon notice growths of bluish deposits at the offending places. Make sure, therefore, that the cooling system is in good condition before adding anti-freeze.

3.   Use only anti-freeze liquid to B.S. 3151/3152 which will be an inhibited ethylene glycol mixture. Inhibited to protect attacks on aluminium alloy components.

4.   Mix the required quantity of anti-freeze liquid with half the quantity of clean water required to fill the system. Pour this into the flushed out radiator and top up with clean water. Run the engine straight away to thoroughly disperse the anti-freeze throughout.

5.   The percentages of anti-freeze to use (in relation to the total cooling liquid capacity) are given in the table below.

Solution strength	Frost protection	Safe pump circulation
25%	-15°F (-26°C)	10°F (-12°C)
30%	-28°F (-33°C)	3°F (-16°C)
35%	-38°F (-39°C)	-4°F (-20°C)
40%	-42°F (-41°C)	-10°F (-23°C)
50%	-53°F (-47°C)	-32°F (-36°C)

10. Fan Belt - Removal, Replacement and Adjustment

1.   If the fan belt is obviously badly worn, or stretched so far that it is still too slack at maximum adjustment, it should be renewed. In case of breakage it is wise to carry a spare at all times.

2.   Whether the belt has broken and dropped off, or is being taken off, first slacken the two nuts and bolts on which the generator pivots and then the bolts underneath which lock the long slotted adjusting brace. Do not slacken any of the bolts more than is necessary to just move the generator with a little force.

3.   Leave the generator so that the fan belt may be removed.

4.   Fit a new fan belt over the pulleys and move the generator out until it is tight. Then tighten the bolts. This will be easier to do if the bolts are tight enough to allow the generator to move only when levered. Check the fan belt tension by depressing it between the generator and water pump pulleys. It should not deflect more than ½ inch under 9 lbs. pressure. Do not overtighten the belt or excessive strain will be put on the generator and pump bearings.

5.   After a new belt has run for a few hundred miles check the tension again as the initial stretch may require re-adjustment.

6.   There are no definite rules as regards frequency of checking but it only takes a second every time the oil and water levels are checked.

11. Water Temperature Gauge - Fault Diagnosis and Rectification

1.   If no reading is recorded on the gauge when the engine is hot, the fault is in either the gauge, sender unit or wiring. Do NOT remove the wire from the sender unit and short it to earth to check whether a reading can be obtained. This will burn out the windings of the gauge.

2.   If the fuel gauge is also not functioning the cause may be that the instrument voltage stabiliser unit is faulty.

3.   Otherwise, disconnect the terminal from the transmitter unit and insulate the end of the wire so that it will not short accidentally and damage the gauge.

4.   Then measure the resistance in ohms. between the transmitter terminal and earth when the engine is cold and again when hot. If there is no difference then it is faulty and should be unscrewed and a new one fitted. If there is a variation in resistance measured then the gauge is probably faulty and will need renewal. Make sure first however that the wire from sender to gauge is in order. Details of instrument removal will be found in Chapter 10.

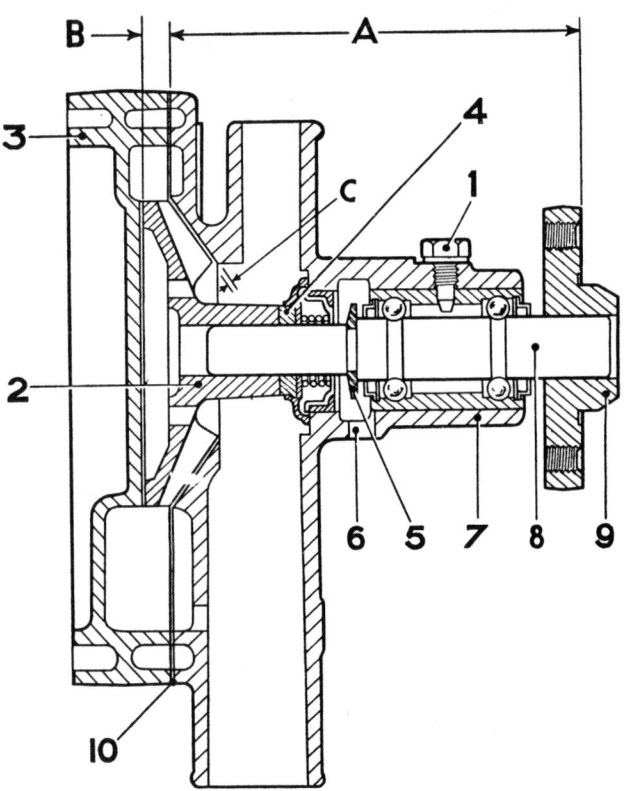

Fig. 2.3. WATER PUMP – SECTION SHOWING CLEARANCES

1	Bearing locating screw	6	Drain hole	Dimensions
2	Impeller	7	Pump body	A 4.088 in. (103.8 mm)
3	Impeller housing	8	Bearing assembly	B .280 in. (7.1 mm)
4	Seal	9	Fan pulley centre	C .010 in. (.25 mm)
5	Water thrower	10	Gasket	

SECTION 3. Cylinder block drain tap beneath exhaust manifold.

SECTION 11. Detaching temperature gauge sender unit lead.

Fault Finding Chart - Cooling System

Symptom	Reason	Remedy
Loss of coolant but no overheating provided coolant level is kept topped up	Reservoir bottle empty. Small leaks in system	Hall fill reservoir bottle. Examine all hoses and connections for signs of cracks and leaks when engine is both cold and hot, stationary and running. If no signs, use proprietary sealer in coolant to stop any invisible leaks.
Coolant level drops in radiator and expansion bottle fills up.	Radiator cap opening pressure too low.	Check and fit new radiator cap of correct type.
Temperature gauge indicates constant overheating but no loss of coolant.	Radiator cap opening pressure too high.	Check and fit new radiator cap of correct type and then diagnose reason for overheating.
Overheating and loss of coolant only when overheated.	Faulty thermostat. Fan belt slipping Engine out of tune due to ignition and/or fuel system settings being incorrect. Blockage or restriction in circulation of cooling water. Radiator cooling fins clogged up. Blown cylinder head gasket or cracked cylinder head. Sheared water pump impeller shaft. Cracked cylinder block. New engine still tight.	Check and renew if faulty. Check and adjust. Check ignition and fuel systems and adjust as required. Check that no hoses have collapsed. Drain, flush out and refill cooling system. Use chemical flushing compound if necessary. Remove radiator and clean exterior as needed Remove cylinder head for examination. Remove pump and check. Remove engine and examine and repair (if possible). Adjust engine speeds to suit until run in.
Engine runs too cool and heater inefficient.	Thermostat missing or stuck open.	Remove housing cover and inspect.

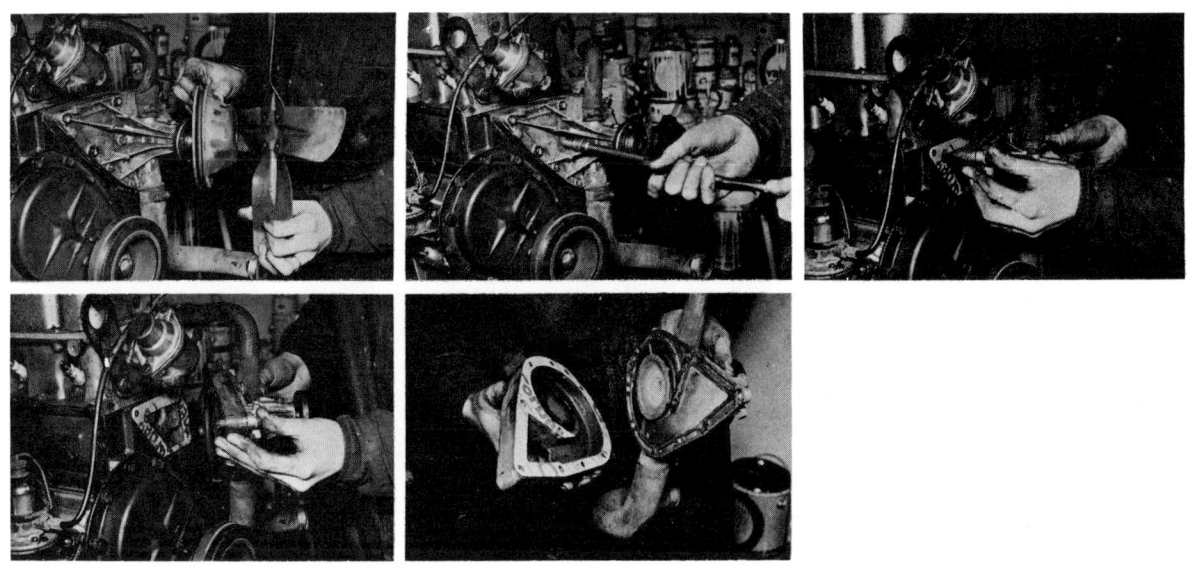

SECTION 8. Removal and separation of water pump components.

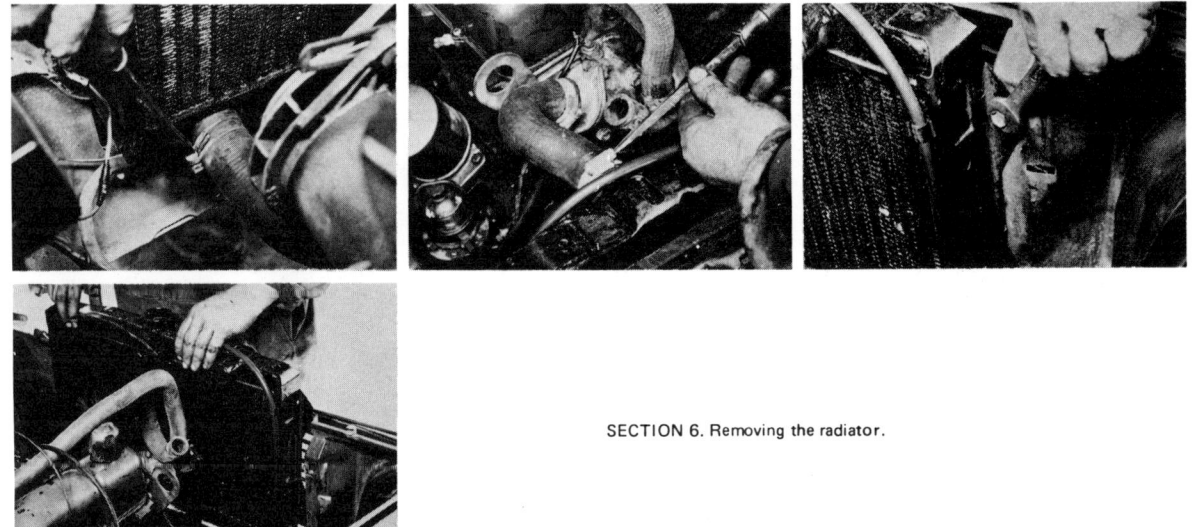

SECTION 6. Removing the radiator.

Chapter 3 Fuel system and carburation

Contents

Specifications

Fuel pump

Type	AC mechanical
Delivery pressure	2¾ - 4¼ lb/in^2 (0.19 - 0.29 kg/cm^2)

Air cleaner ... ... AC Delco (single) or Fram (twin) - dry elements

Carburettor

Type ... ... Stromberg 150 CDS

	Single	*Twin*
Slow running speed	700 - 800 rpm	800 - 900 rpm
Needle:		
Sea level to 5,000 ft (1,500 m)	6P (alum. head)	6R
5,000 to 10,000 ft (1,500 to 3,000 m)	5R	5AC
Over 10,000 ft (3, 000 m)	5T	5AD
Spring	Red (all engines)	Blue
Fast idle adjustment (between screw head and cam)	0.065 in (1.65 mm) for 12 coil spring on cam travel stop. 0.045 in (1.14 mm) for 6 coil spring on cam travel stop,	0.050 in (1.27 mm)
Choke control	Manual	Manual

Fuel tank
Capacity:

All models	10 gallons (12 US gallons, 45.5 litres)

For details of other carburettors, see Chapter 13, page 206.

1 General description

A 10 gallon fuel tank is mounted under the rear of the car and from this fuel is drawn by an AC mechanical pump and delivered to the carburettor.

The pump is operated by an arm actuated by a cam on the camshaft and is located low down forward on the right-hand side of the engine block. The pump incorporates a filter screen. Fuel is delivered to a variety of carburettors according to which model car and the type of engine fitted. The output of the pump exceeds all normal requirements of the single or twin carburettors and fuel level within all carburettors is regulated by a float operated needle valve. When the valve is closed, shutting off the flow, the pump freewheels. The diaphragm is held up by the

pressure in the line until such time as the carburettor needle valve opens allowing the spring action of the pump to resume oscillating the diaphragm and deliver more fuel.

The air taken in through the carburettor is filtered by a renewable paper element.

2 Routine maintenance

1 Every 5,000 miles, or more frequently in very dusty circumstances, remove the air filter element and tap it smartly on a flat surface to dislodge any excess accumulations of dust on the outside. Wipe out the filter housing.

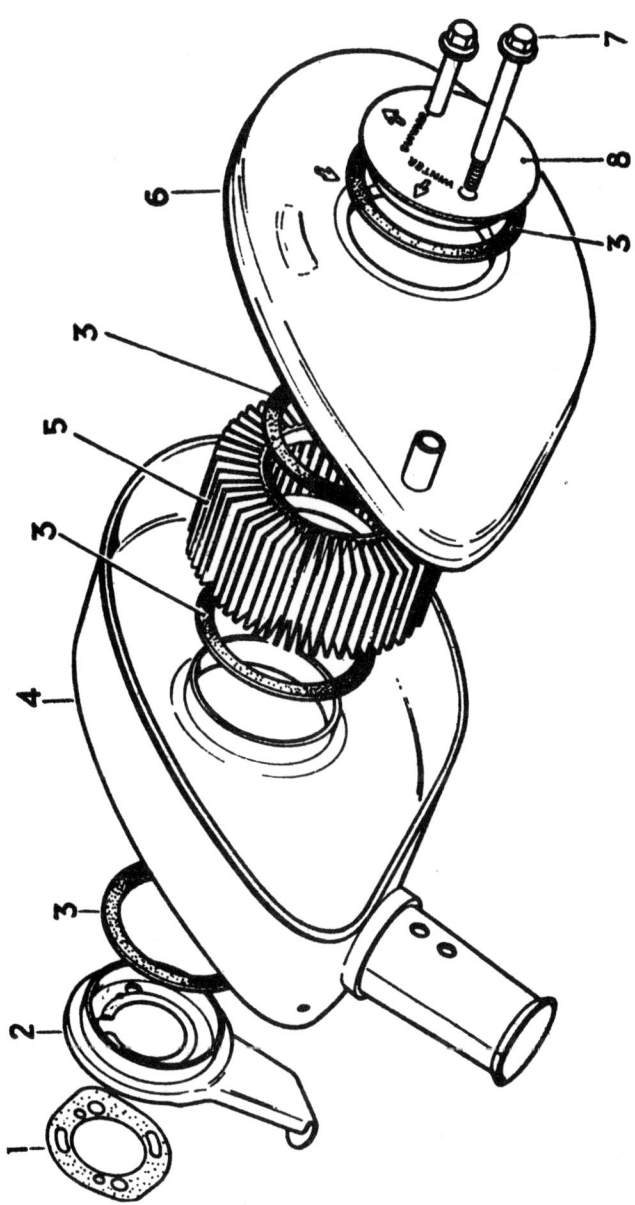

Fig. 3.1. AIR CLEANER

1 Gasket - cleaner to carburettor
2 Throttle return spring plate

3 Sealing ring
4 Main body

5 Paper element
6 Cover

7 Fixing bolts
8 Fixing plate

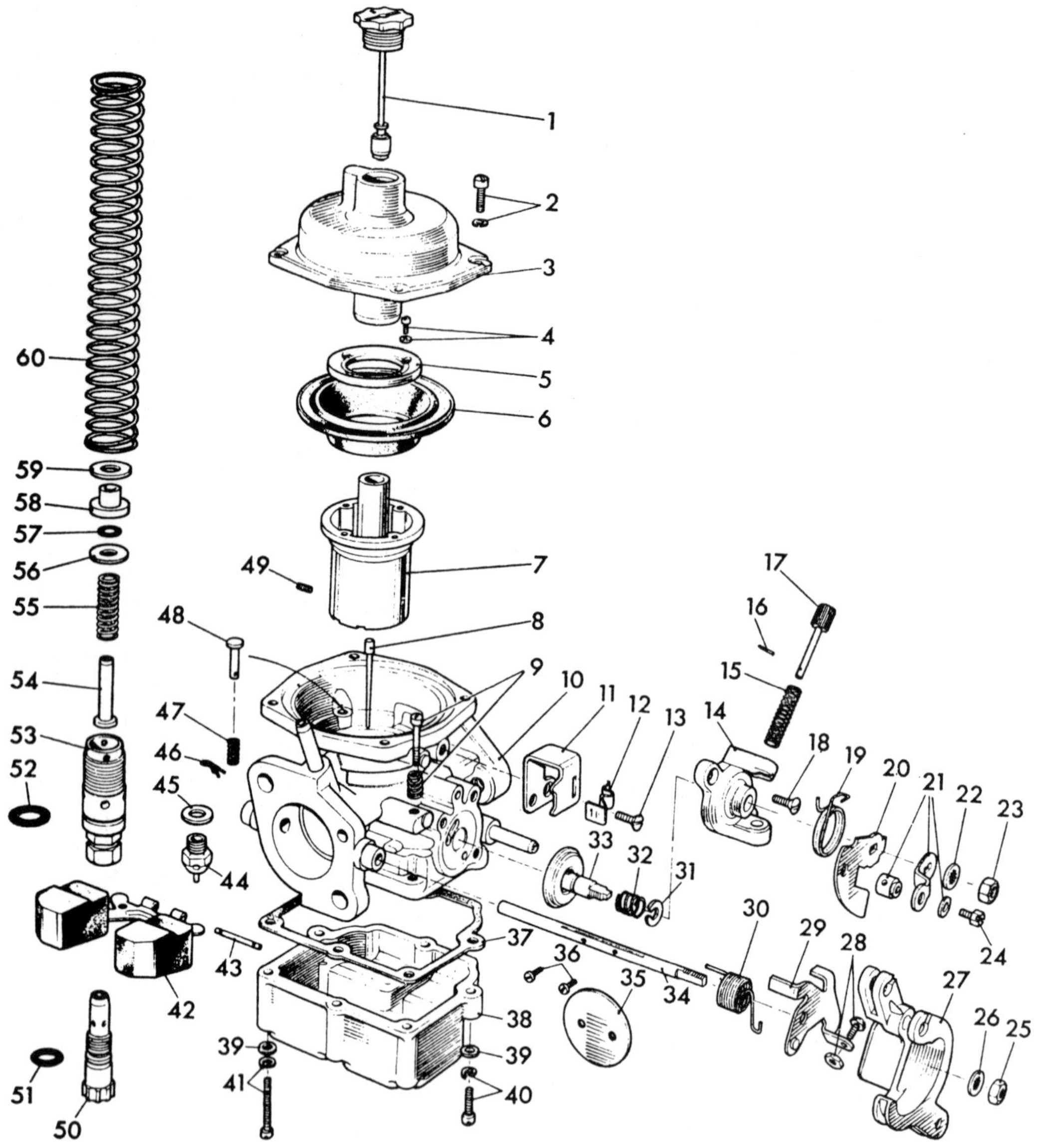

Fig. 3.2. STROMBERG 150 CDS CARBURETTOR (EXPLODED VIEW)

1 Air valve piston damper	17 Travel stop	34 Throttle spindle	50 Jet adjustment
2 Screw and spring washer (4)	18 Fixing screw (2)	35 Throttle valve	51 'O' ring jet adjustment
3 Suction cover chamber	19 Fast idle cam return spring	36 Throttle valve fixing screws	52 'O' ring jet bushing retaining screw
4 Screw and spring washer (4)	20 Fast idle cam	37 Gasket	
5 Diaphragm retaining spring	21 Lever	38 Float chamber	53 Jet bushing retaining screw
6 Diaphragm	22 Washer	39 Washer	54 Jet
7 Air valve piston	23 Nut	40 Screw (short) (2)	55 Jet spring
8 Metering needle	24 Screw	41 Screw (long) (2)	56 Washer
9 Slow running adjustment screw	25 Nut	42 Float assembly	57 'O' ring jet
10 Carburettor body	26 Washer	43 Float pivot pin	58 Jet and centralising bush
11 Choke cable bracket	27 Guide plate	44 Float valve assembly	59 Washer
12 Choke cable clip	28 Adjusting screw	45 Valve seat washer	60 Air valve piston return spring
13 Screw	29 Stop lever	46 Retainer	
14 Starter cover	30 Return spring	47 Spring	
15 Travel stop spring	31 Spring retainer	48 Air valve piston lifting pin	
16 Pin	32 Disc valve spring	49 Locking screw	
	33 Starter assembly disc valve		

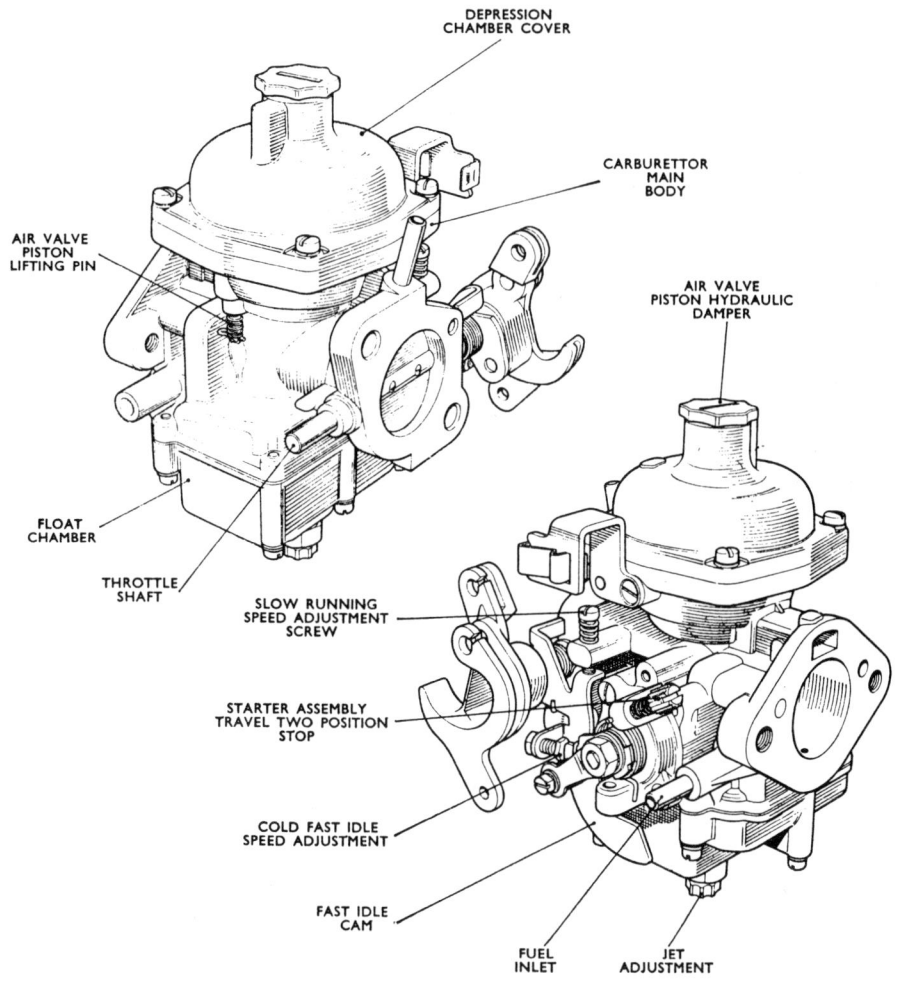

Fig. 3.3. Stromberg 150 CDS Carburettor (External Views)

2. Lubricate all moving pivots on the carburettor controls with one or two drops of engine oil from time to time. There is no hard and fast rule about frequency but when you check the engine oil dipstick a drop off the end can be used for this purpose.

3. Every 1,000 miles check the level of oil in the hydraulic damper piston in the carburettor. See Section 6 for details.

4. Every 5,000 miles remove the fuel pump filter cover and examine the filter gauze after lifting it out. Blow through it to clear any particles. Do not use a cloth as strands of cotton or lint must not get into the system.

5. Every 10,000 miles renew the air filter element.

6. Every 15,000 miles it is beneficial to remove and thoroughly clean the carburettor and float chamber. For procedures refer to the relevant sections in this Chapter.

3. Air Filter Element - Removal and Replacement

1. Unhook the throttle return spring where it hooks into an eye on the back of the air filter housing.

2. Unscrew the two bolts which hold the whole air cleaner assembly to the carburettor. Once these are clear the whole unit may be lifted off and separated to give access to the filter element. Clean out the interior of the filter housing. If the same element is to be refitted tap it on a flat surface to remove any loose accumulations of dust. Do NOT try and wash it, brush it - or blow it with compressed air.

3. When reassembling the unit make sure that the sealing rings are intact and in place. When fitting the element, it should seat snugly over the locating ridges in the housing.

4. The air intake pipe may be positioned for 'Summer' or 'Winter' conditions by revolving the casing, before the bolts are tightened, so that the appropriate indication arrows line up. In the winter position the pipe draws air from a heated shroud round the exhaust pipe.

4. Stromberg 150 CDS Carburettor - Description and Principle of Operation

The Stromberg carburettor is a variable choke design with a single fuel delivery jet. This means that the cross-sectional area of the air intake passage through the carburettor varies according to demands made by the engine. The fuel, which is drawn into the air passage through a jet orifice, is metered by a tapered needle which moves in and out of the jet, thus varying the effective size of the orifice. This needle is attached to, and moves with, the air valve piston which controls the variable choke opening.

At rest, the air valve piston is right down, choking off the air supply and the tapered needle is fully home with the jet virtually cutting off the fuel outlet from the jet. For starting, the cold start lever is first pulled and this sets the cold start device so that fuel may be drawn into the main air passage via an independent passage which is opened up. It also opens the throttle flap a small amount. (On earlier types of Stromberg carburettors the cold start device consisted of lifting the air valve a little mechanically thus drawing the needle out of the jet to provide the richer mixture necessary).

As soon as the engine fires the suction from the engine, or manifold depression, is partially diverted to the upper side of the chamber in which the diaphragm attached to the air valve piston is positioned. This causes the valve to rise and provides sufficient air flow to enable the engine to run. As the throttle is opened further, manifold depression is reduced and now it is the speed of air through the venturi which causes the depression in the upper chamber, thus causing the piston to rise further. If the throttle is opened suddenly, the natural tendency of the air valve piston to rise - causing a weak mixture when it is least required (i.e. during acceleration) - is prevented by a hydraulic damper which delays the piston in its upward travel. The air intake is thus restricted and a proportionately

larger quantity of fuel to air is drawn though.

Under constant speed running conditions the air valve position is balanced by air speed through the venturi, throttle opening and the light pressure of the diaphragm return spring.

5. Stromberg 150 CDS Carburettor - Removal and Replacement

1. The carburettor may be removed prior to engine removal or in order to dismantle and overhaul it.

2. Undo the fuel pipe union from the carburettor.

3. Unhook the throttle return spring from the back of the air cleaner and then undo the two bolts securing the air cleaner to the carburettor and lift it away.

4. Detach the vacuum pipe from the connection to the mounting flange.

5. Slacken the screw securing the cold start inner cable to the operating lever, undo the clip over the cable outer and lift the cable away.

6. Detach the throttle cable from the mounting bracket by undoing the locknut nearest the open end only (otherwise the positioning will be upset). Alternatively, the bracket and cable may be detached together by undoing the bolt holding the bracket to the inlet manifold.

7. Unloop the cable from the throttle lever and take the nipple out of the recess.

8. Undo the two mounting stud nuts holding the carburettor in position. One of these can only be removed completely whilst the carburettor is being drawn back off the studs.

9. Lift away the carburettor.

10 Replacement is a reversal of the removal procedure but take care on the following points.

11 When refitting the cold start cable to the carburettor do not clip the outer in position until the arm has been checked in the fully open position. If the outer is clipped in position, with the end too far down, the limit of travel of the operating arm will be restricted and result in cold start difficulties.

12 Make sure that the throttle and cold start cables are properly clipped to keep their position. If this is not done variations can result in the amount of movement at the operating levers on the carburettor.

6. Stromberg 150 CDS Carburettor - Setting and Adjustments

1. Before making any adjustments to the carburettor settings make sure that your reasons for the adjustment are sound and that you only do one at a time. Check the result of each adjustment after it is made. The Stromberg carburettor is a finely balanced and relatively delicate instrument and can easily be put off tune.

2. Control settings are important. Make sure that the operation of the cold start cable moves the lever easily throughout its full range of movement and returns to its closed position when the control knob is pushed home. Adjustment can be made by repositioning the inner cable relative to the operating arm at the clamping screw. The outer cable can be repositioned as necessary where it clips to the bracket on the carburettor.

3. The throttle cable should also be checked for movement throughout its range. Make particularly sure that when the throttle flap is in the fully open position the position of the accelerator pedal is as far down as it could possibly be, even with the cable disconnected. Otherwise pressure on the pedal will impart severe strain on the cable and more important, on the throttle spindle and bearings. Adjustment should be made at the point where the end of the cable outer is located into the bracket near the carburettor. Slacken the two locknuts and move the outer cable so that when the accelerator pedal is fully depressed the throttle is just fully open.

5. Slow running adjustment is controlled by the throttle stop screw which in turn regulates the position of the throttle flap when the accelerator cable is at rest. The single jet controls fuel mixture throughout the full operational range. If satisfactory slow-running

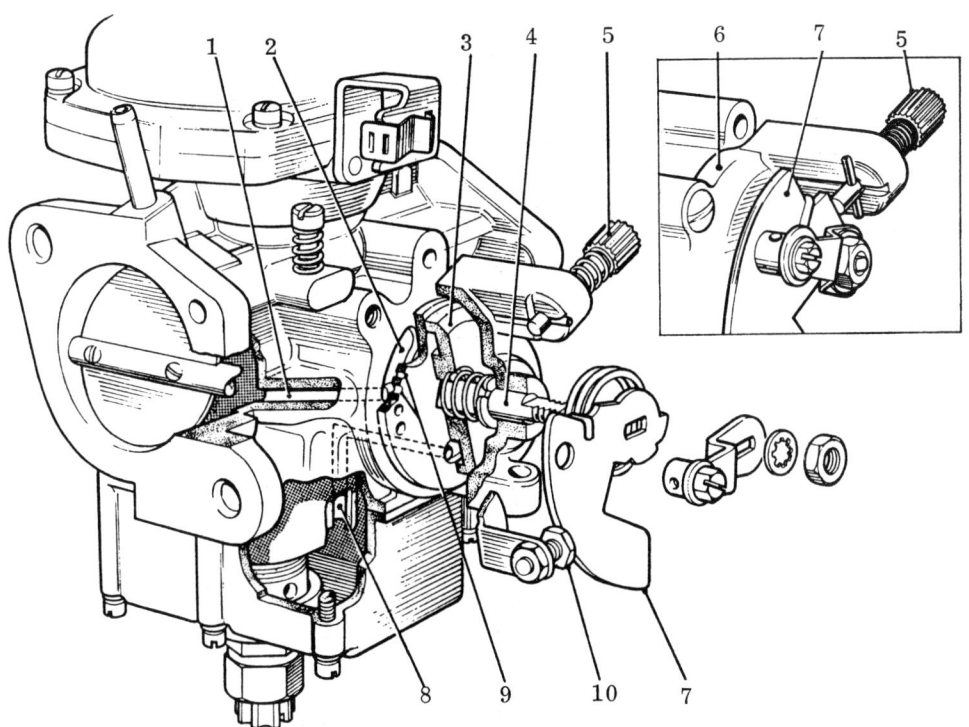

Fig. 3.4. STROMBERG 150 CDS, COLD START DEVICE

1 Drilling for fuel from disc valve
2 Port to fuel feed drilling from disc valve
3 Disc valve
4 Disc valve spindle
5 Two position stop for cold start opening limit
6 Starter device outer housing
7 Fast idle cam
8 Drilling for fuel from float chamber to disc valve
9 Orifices for fuel in disc valve
10 Fast idle adjustment screw

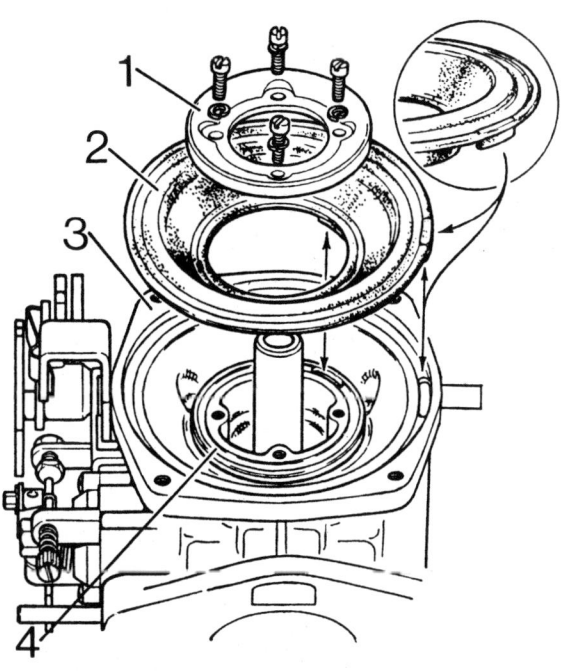

Fig. 3.5. STROMBERG 150 CDS. LOCATION AND SECURING OF DIAPHRAGM TO THE AIR VALVE AND BODY

1 Clamping ring   2 Diaphragm   3 Main body   4 Air valve

cannot be achieved with the throttle stop screw adjustment, then it will be necessary to proceed to the following check which affects the carburettor performance at all speeds.

6. If slow running indicates that further adjustment, other than on the throttle stop screw, is required, first remove the air valve piston damper from the top of the carburettor. Insert a thin rod or screwdriver into the top and use this to hold the piston down. At the same time turn the jet adjustment screw (N.B. NOT the jet bush retainer) upwards so that the jet itself eventually touches the air valve piston. This will be felt when the adjusting screw meets resistance. Release the downward pressure on the valve piston and then check that the piston moves freely. This can be done by lifting the pin and letting it fall. An audible 'click' should be heard as the piston hits the jet bridge. (If this does not occur then the jet will need centralising as described later). Back off the jet adjusting screw two complete turns. Refill the piston damper bore to within 6 mm of its upper edge with clean engine oil (do not use very low viscosity oils). Refit the damper piston. Run the engine until normal temperature is reached and adjust the throttle stop screw to obtain an idling speed of 700/800 r.p.m. It is permissible to move the jet adjuster screw not more than ½ turn in either direction in order to achieve the desired smooth running. If no success is achieved it will be necessary to check the needle position in the piston. This involves partial dismantling and is covered in the next Section.

7. The jet will need to be centralised if movement of the piston valve is binding the needle against the side of the jet orifice. The jet is located in a bush which permits it to move up and down when the jet adjusting screw is turned. The bush is locked into position by the jet bush retaining screw and when this is slackened the jet bushing, together with the jet, is free to move laterally. To centralise the jet, first slacken the jet bushing retainer by ½ turn. Then turn the jet adjusting screw so that the jet is level with the bridge face (as described in the previous adjustment). Then tap the jet bushing retainer to assist the jet to find its position round the needle. The jet bushing retainer screw should then be tightened and the piston lifted with the pin and allowed to drop. An audible click indicates that it is falling to the bottom of its stroke without hindrance. Then re-adjust the jet as described for the last adjustment in paragraph 6.

8. In certain cases of excessive fuel consumption or flooding it may be that the floats or needle valve positions need resetting. For this, dismantling is necessary and the adjustment procedure is incorporated in the next Section.

9. The carburettor is so designed that when the cold start device is used the throttle is automatically opened a specified amount. This ensures that the engine speed is kept up; otherwise the rich mixture would stall the engine at low revolutions. The throttle opening is set by the fast idle adjustment screw. The head of this screw bears against the fast idle cam mounted on the cold start device boss. The screw may be adjusted to give the correct gap between head and cam, with the cold start device closed, after slackening the locknut. The clearances are given under the 'Specifications'.

7. Stromberg 150 CDS Carburettor - Dismantling, Inspection and Reassembly

1. Do not dismantle the carburettor unless it is absolutely necessary. This should be only for cleaning at intervals of 15,000 miles or when systematic diagnosis indicates that there is a fault with it. The internal mechanism is delicate and finely balanced and unnecessary tinkering will probably do more harm than good.

2. Although certain parts may be removed with the carburettor still attached to the engine, nevertheless, it is considered safer to remove it and work over a bench.

3. Having removed the carburettor, take out the piston damper by unscrewing the top cap.

4. Undo the four screws holding the depression chamber cover in position. Mark the edge of the cover and carburettor body so that it may be replaced in the same position. Then carefully lift it off,

watching that the diaphragm return spring does not get stretched in the process. The return spring should be carefully detached from its upper and lower seatings and laid to one side. If this spring is kinked, stretched or treated in any way that may affect its pressure when installed, the balance of the carburettor will be upset. Renew it (with one of the correct colour code) if in doubt.

5. Lift out the air valve piston and diaphragm together. If the diaphragm shows signs of perforation, cracking or other damage it must be renewed. Remove the four screws and washers by which the retaining ring secures it to the piston. Note also that the diaphragm has tabs on its inner and outer edges that locate into slots in the piston and body of the carburettor. When refitting a diaphragm it is most important that the centre section seats properly on the piston. It is easily dislodged when fitting the retaining ring. With the piston removed it is possible to check that the needle is correctly fitted. The shoulder of the needle should be flush with the face of the piston. If not, it may be re-set after slackening the needle locking screw in the side of the piston.

6. The float chamber may be removed next. First unscrew and remove the jet adjusting screw. See that the 'O' ring around it is in good condition. Undo the six screws which hold the float chamber to the carburettor body. The chamber may then be carefully pulled down over the jet bushing retainer. It is not essential to remove the jet and associated parts unless it is being renewed. The resistance to pulling off the float chamber will be the 'O' ring seal which is fitted around the jet bushing retainer. This must be examined for condition.

7. With the float chamber removed the carburettor may be cleaned with petrol or paraffin (nothing else). Use an air jet where possible to blow out the orifices in the body to the cold start device and the main jet area.

8. When the float chamber is removed the floats may be checked for correct setting. With the carburettor in the inverted position and the needle valve in the closed position the highest point of the float should be 15.5 - 16.5 mm above the joint face of the body. Both parts of the float should be equal and if necessary the arm that contacts the needle valve may be bent to adjust the float position. If the floats are apparently set correctly and excessive fuel consumption or flooding has been experienced, it is quite possible that the needle valve is worn so a new one should be fitted. If the needle valve is one which can be separated from its seat, a ridge in the valve face indicates wear.

9. If there is any sign of play between the throttle spindle and the bushes in the body it may be necessary to consider removing the spindle. This can be done after removing the nut holding the throttle operating lever, removing the two screws securing the throttle plate and drawing the spindle out.

10 Reassembly is a reversal of the dismantling procedure. The float chamber gasket need not necessarily be renewed but it is a good idea to fit three new 'O' rings on the jet, jet bushing and jet bushing retainer. When the diaphragm and piston assembly is replaced make sure the tabs fit the grooves.

11 The jet centralisation and adjustment and fast idle cam clearances may be set before replacing the carburettor on the engine.

8. Fuel Pump - Removal and Replacement

1. The fuel pump will need removing if it is to be dismantled for overhaul. Disconnect the fuel lines on the inlet and outlet sides by undoing the union on the inlet side and pulling off the connector pipe on the outlet side.

2. Undo the two nuts holding the pump flange to the crankcase and take the pump off. Keep the spacer and gaskets together and do not discard them. If necessary blank off the fuel line from the tank to prevent loss of fuel.

3. Replacement is a reversal of the removal procedure. Make sure that the total thickness of gaskets and spacer is the same as came off. Check that the fuel line connections are not leaking after starting the engine.

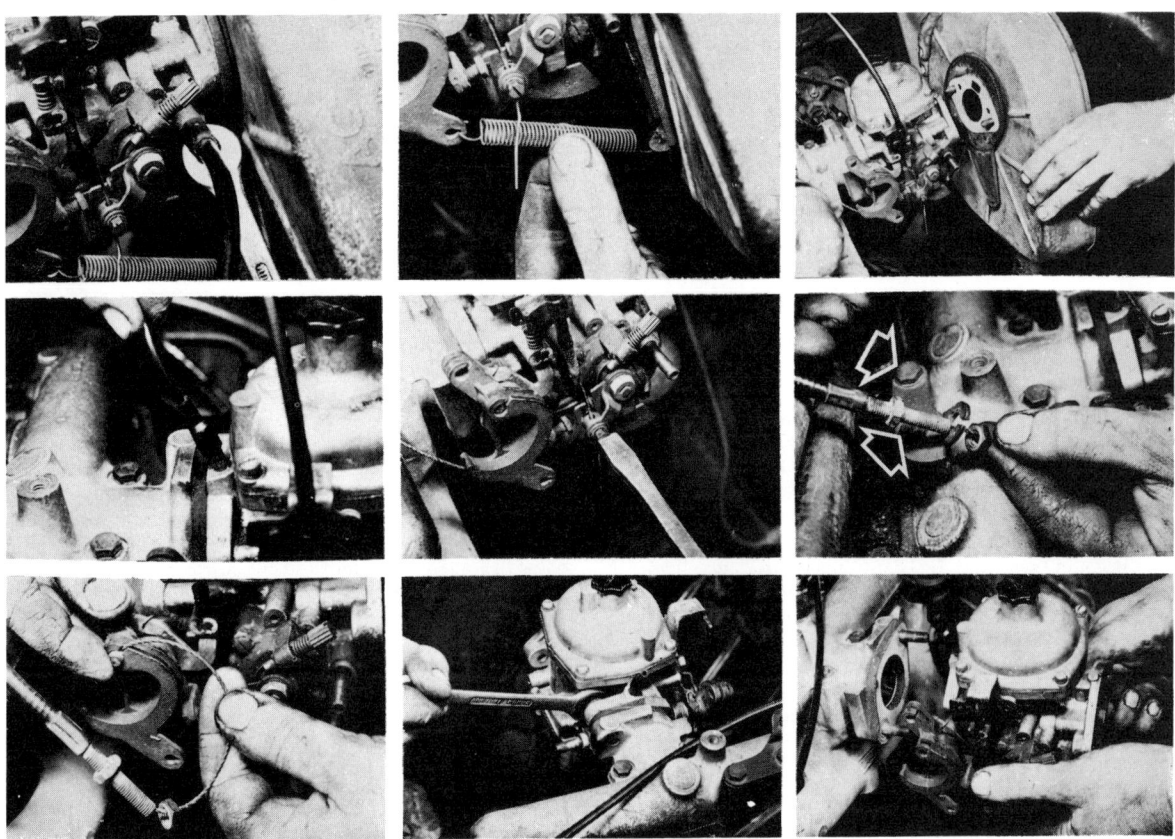

SECTION 5. Single carburettor removal sequence

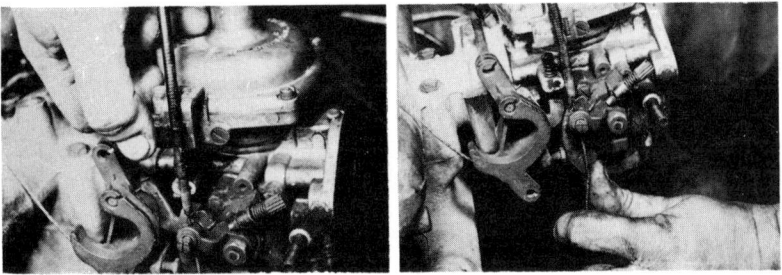

SECTION 5. Ensure the cold start outer cable clears the fully open actuating arm.

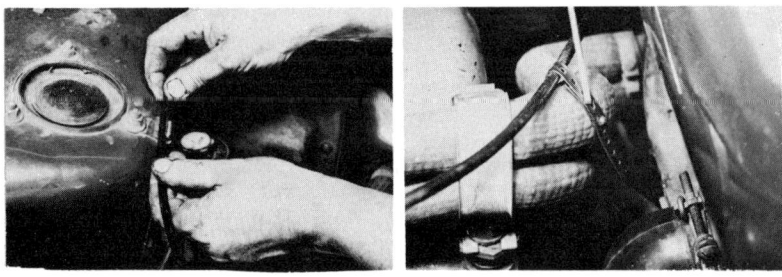

SECTION 5. Clip carburetter cables. Properly in place.

9. Fuel Pump - Inspection, Dismantling and Reassembly

1. First clean the pump exterior thoroughly and mark the edges of the two halves of the body.

2. Undo the cover retaining clip and lift off the cover. The gasket and gauze filter may then be removed.

3. Remove the six screws and washers holding the two halves of the pump together and the top half may then be lifted off.

4. The diaphragm and pull rod should then be pushed down a little against the pressure of the return spring and turned clockwise ¼ of a turn. This will disengage the pull rod from the operating link and the diaphragm may be lifted out.

5. If there are signs of wear in the rocker arm pivot pin, and rocker arm and link bushes then they should be renewed. They can be taken from the pump body by first clamping the rocker arm in a vice and then tapping the body away with a soft faced hammer.

6. The valve assemblies should only be removed from the upper body if renewal is necessary. They are staked into the body and are destroyed when levered out.

7. Examine the diaphragm for signs of cracking or perforation and renew if necessary.

8. The oil seal and retainer in the base of the pump (round the pull rod) should be renewed as a matter of course if the diaphragm is also being renewed. They can be levered out with a screwdriver. The new ones should be pressed in carefully, keeping them square.

9. When fitting new valve assemblies to the body, first fit the seating washers and then place the valves, making sure that they are the correct way up according to inlet and outlet. The body will have to be restaked at six (different) places round the edge so that the assemblies are firmly held in their positions. If this is not done properly and leakage occurs between the valve assembly and the seating ring the pump will not operate efficiently.

10 The rocker arm assembly is refitted to the body by first assembling the link, rocker arm, pivot pin and washers and placing them in position in the pump body. Then locate the spring over the pip on the rocker arm and in the pump body recess. Then tap the pin retainers into the slots in the body so that they are hard up to the pin. The slots should then be staked with a suitable punch so that the retainers are tightly held in position.

11 Place the diaphragm return spring in position in the lower half of the pump. To replace the diaphragm first fit the stem carefully through the oil seals then position the diaphragm so that the tab is in the position shown in Fig. 3.7 . Then press the centre of the diaphragm down which will pass the stem end through the operating link slot. Then, by turning it 90º anti-clockwise, the stem will hook into position correctly.

12 Fit the upper half of the pump body and line up the mating marks. In order to assemble the two halves and the diaphragm properly push the rocker arm upwards so that the diaphragm is drawn level. Then place the six screws in position lightly. It is best if the base of the pump is held in a vice whilst the rocker arm is pushed right up to bring the diaphragm to the bottom of its stroke. A short piece of tube over the rocker arm will provide easy leverage. In this position the six screws should be tightened evenly and alternatively.

13 Fit a new filter bowl gasket carefully in the groove of the upper body, making sure that it does not twist or buckle in the process. Replace the cover and the retaining clip and screw it tight.

14 When the pump is reassembled the suction and delivery pressure can be felt at the inlet and outlet ports when the rocker arm is operated. Be careful not to block the inlet port completely when testing suction. If the rocker arm were to be operated strongly and the inlet side was blocked the diaphragm could be damaged.

10. Fuel Gauge - Tank Sender Unit

1. The fuel gauge sender unit is mounted on the side of the tank where the fuel outlet pipe connection is also made. If the gauge becomes faulty, first check that the sender unit, which is a variable resistance, is giving different resistance readings with both a full and empty tank. If not it should be renewed. Otherwise the gauge is faulty.

2. To remove the sender unit, first disconnect the fuel pipe union. Then engage the locking plate lugs with a suitable tool and turn it anti-clockwise. The unit can then be lifted out. Take care when replacing that the washer is correctly installed and that both joining surfaces are clean and undistorted.

11. Exhaust System

1. When any one section of the exhaust system needs renewal it often follows that the whole lot is best replaced.

2. On new cars the front pipe and silencer is fitted as a single piece. In view of the fact that the front pipe is that which deteriorates less quickly than the rest, replacements are supplied in two parts. Thus it is possible to cut the original pipe and fit the silencer section only. Fig. 3.8 shows the position at which the cut should be made.

3. It is most important when fitting exhausts that the twists and contours are carefully followed and that each connecting joint overlaps the correct distance. Any stresses or strain imparted, in order to force the system to fit the hangar clips, will result in early fractures and failures.

4. When fitting a new part or a complete system it is well worth removing ALL the system from the car and cleaning up all the joints so that they fit together easily. The time spent struggling with obstinate joints whilst flat on your back under the car is eliminated and the likelihood of distorting or even breaking a section is greatly reduced. Do not waste a lot of time trying to undo rusted and corroded clamps and bolts. Cut them off. New ones will be required anyway if they are that bad.

12. Exhaust and Crankcase Emission Control Systems

Although no legislation yet exists in the United Kingdom, models in the Sunbeam Arrow range which are exported to North America, need to conform to the exhaust emission control regulations for new cars which are in force there.

The purpose of the system is to reduce the amount of hydrocarbons in the form of unburnt fuel and carbon monoxide which are vented to atmosphere by the engine and which contribute to pollution of the atmosphere. This section intends to give readers an idea of the Rootes system fitted to single carburettor engines in this range. Different methods are used for different engines. It must also be realised that development of the system is still in its early stages and experience will doubtless evolve modified systems for the future.

Basically the present system needs a modified variable choke carburettor - such as the Stromberg 150 CDS - and a modified distributor. Most of the polluting gases reach atmosphere via the exhaust on overrun conditions when the throttle is shut. Normally the exhaust gases excessively dilute the slow running mixture reaching the engine in these conditions and so prevent proper combustion. The modified system uses the manifold depression, which is at maximum on overrun, to operate this. A control valve which in turn operates a throttle by-pass valve permits a proper mixture to reach the cylinders. This, in turn, increases the engine power and so cuts out the overrun engine braking effect. To counteract this an automatic vacuum retard device is fitted to the distributor which retards the ignition 12 crankshaft degrees. The throttle by-pass valve is incorporated as part of the Stromberg C.D.S.E. carburettor.

Other refinements on the carburettor are a temperature controlled valve which weakens the mixture under light load and idling conditions when the engine is hot. Furthermore, the main jet is fixed and the needle is spring loaded to run off-centre in the jet to improve atomisation. The manifold depression has to reach 21 in. Hg. before the system comes into operation and cuts out when it drops to 18 Hg. (allowing air through the bleed to return the valves to closed

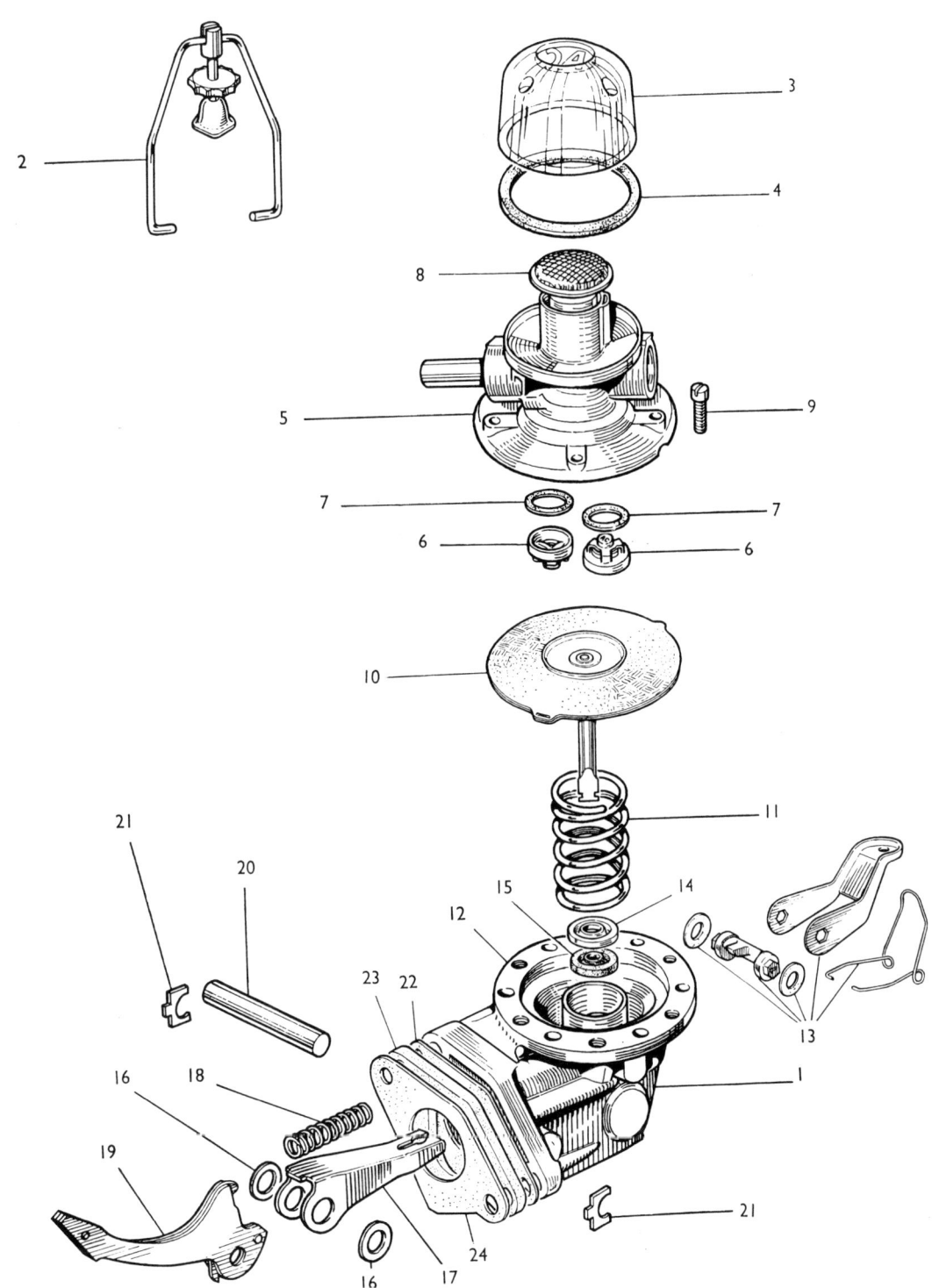

Fig. 3.6. A.C. FUEL PUMP — EXPLODED VIEW

1 Pump assembly
2 Filter bowl clip
3 Filter bowl
4 Sealing ring
5 Upper body
6 Valves

7 Valve seats
8 Filter gauze
9 Screw
10 Diaphragm
11 Diaphragm spring
12 Lower body

13 Hand primer
14 Seal washer
15 Seal
16 Pivot washers
17 Operating link
18 Rocker arm spring

19 Rocker arm
20 Pivot pin
21 Pivot pin retainer
22 Pump gasket
23 Spacer insulator
24 Cylinder block gasket

SECTION 8. Refitting fuel pump and connecting fuel feed pipe.

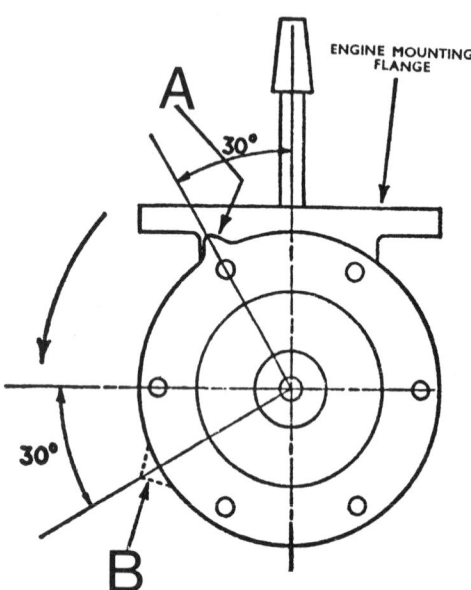

Fig. 3.7. Diagram of fuel pump diaphragm to show position of tabs when inserting the stem (A) and after locking on to the operating link (B)

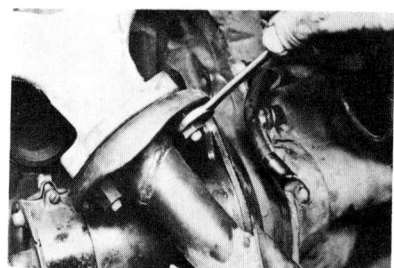

SECTION 11. Detaching nuts holding exhaust pipes to manifold studs.

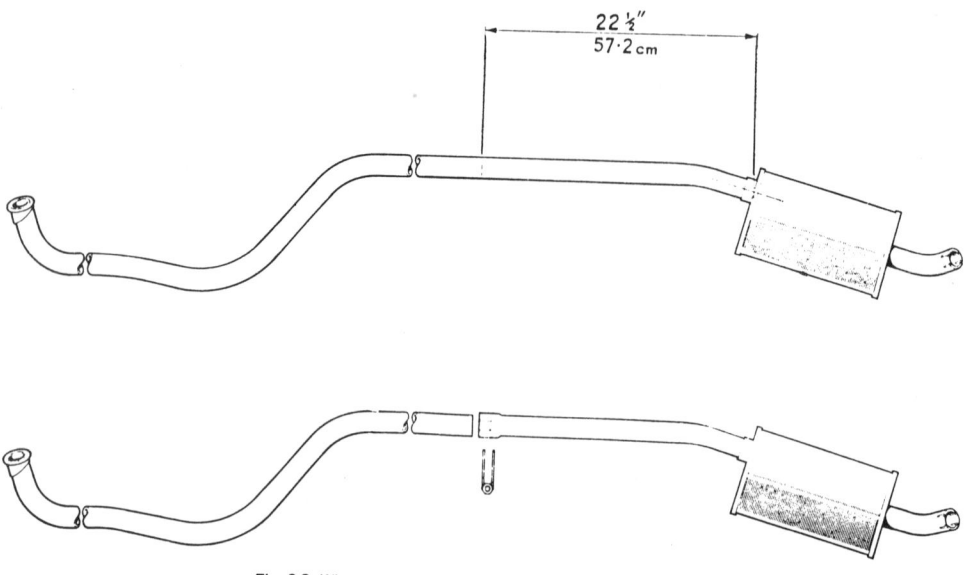

Fig. 3.8. Where to cut the old exhaust pipe when fitting a new silencer

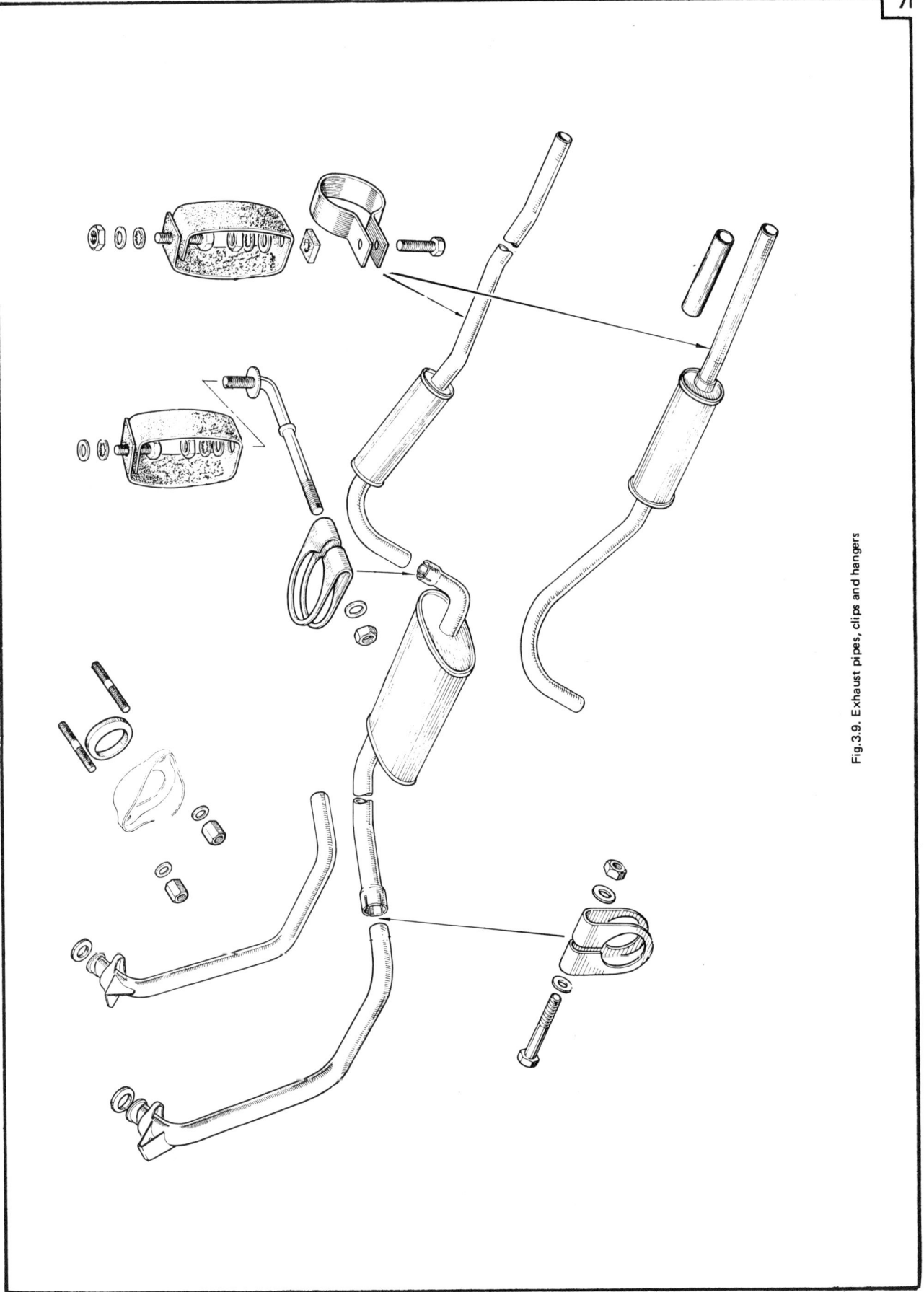

Fig.3.9. Exhaust pipes, clips and hangers

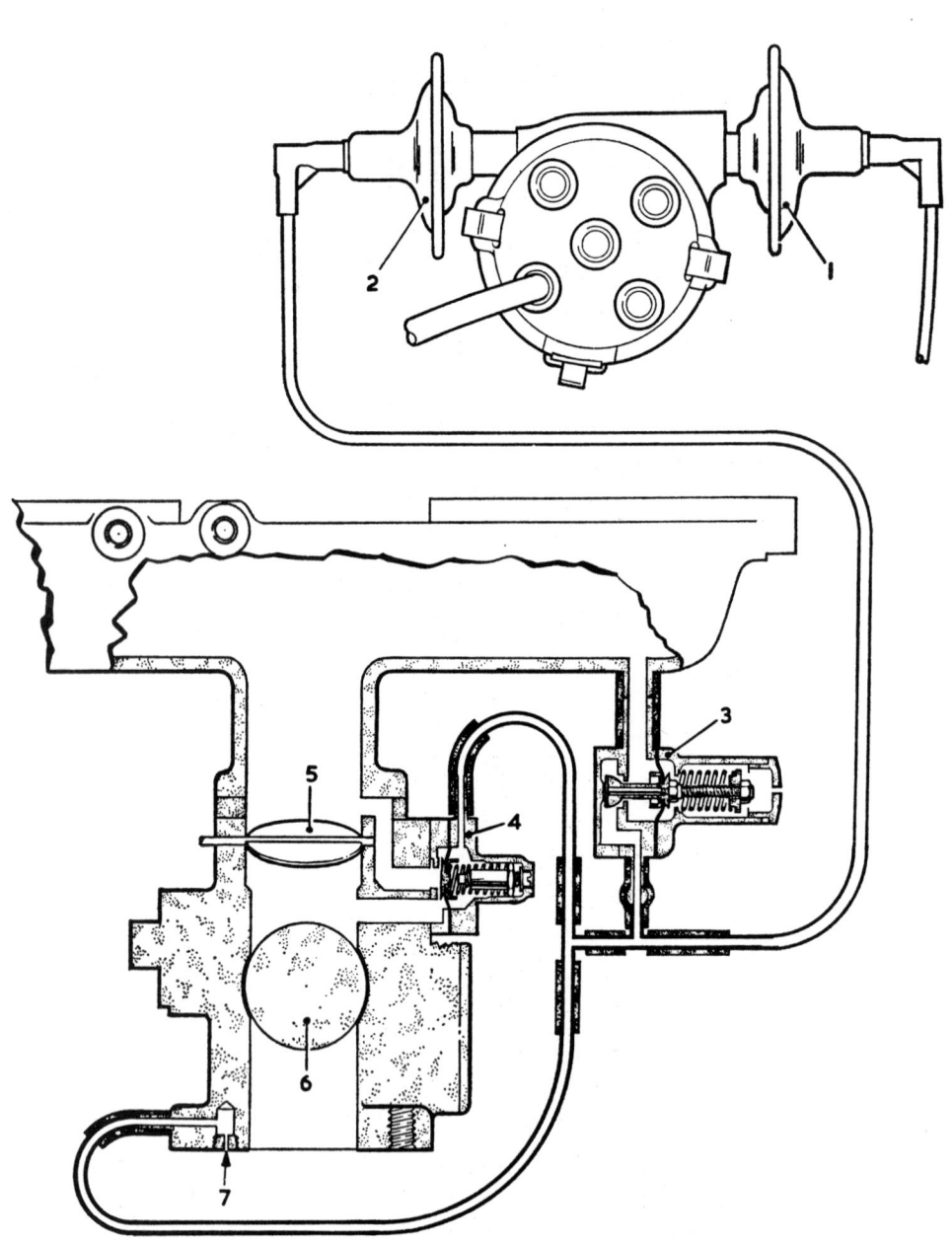

Fig. 3.11. EXHAUST EMISSION CONTROL. SCHEMATIC LAYOUT OF
SINGLE CARBURETTOR SYSTEM. (N.B. TEMPERATURE
CONTROLLED MIXTURE VALVE NOT SHOWN)

1 Distributor vacuum advance
  diaphragm
2 Distributor vacuum retard

  diaphragm
3 Manifold depression control
  valve

4 Throttle by-pass valve
5 Throttle flap
6 Carburettor air-valve piston

7 Calibrated air bleed (closing
  valves when manifold depression goes below 18 in Hg)

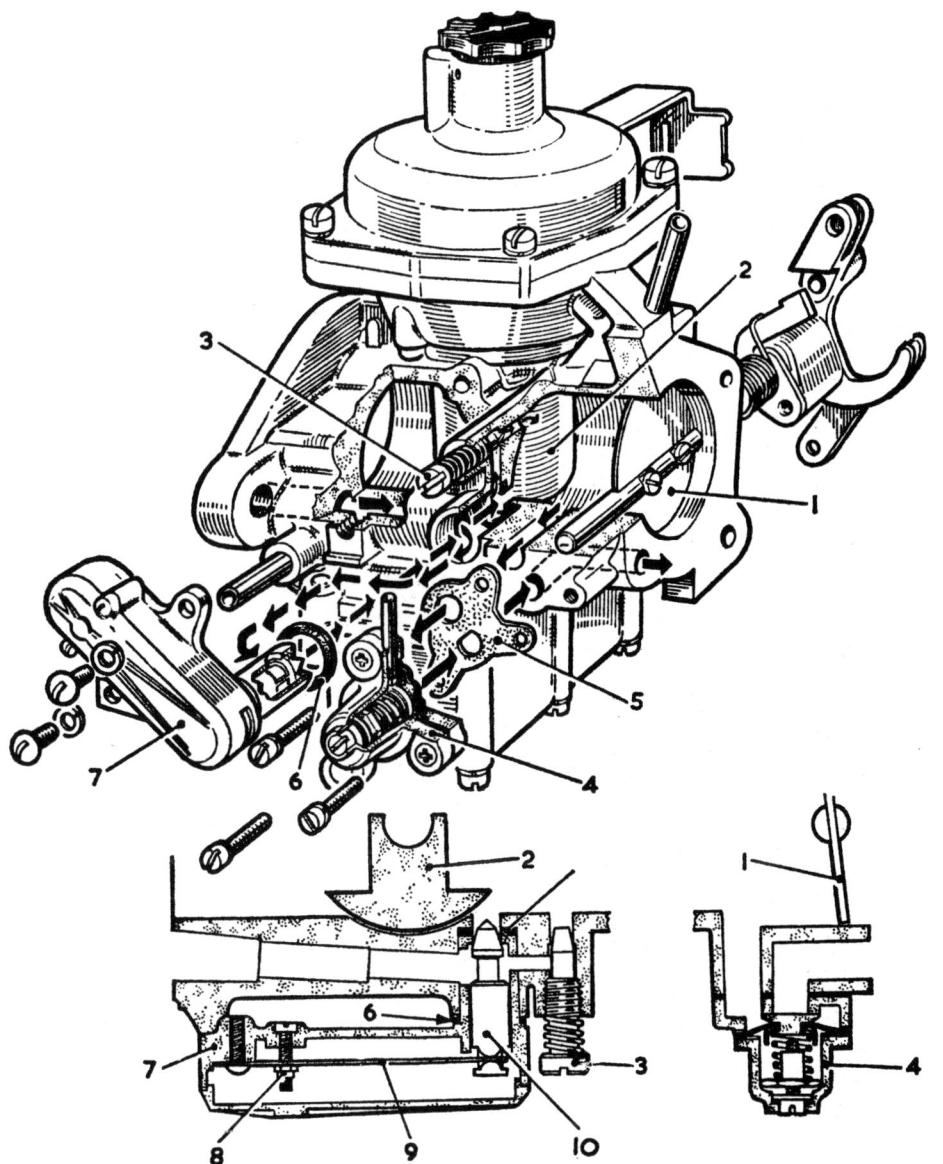

Fig. 3.10. STROMBERG CDSE CARBURETTOR — CUT-AWAY VIEW WITH
DETAIL OF THROTTLE BY-PASS VALVE AND TEMPERATURE
CONTROLLED MIXTURE VALVE

1 Throttle flap	4 Throttle by-pass valve	7 Temperature controlled valve	9 Bi-metal spring
2 Air valve piston	5 Gasket - valve to body	body	10 Valve plunger
3 Slow running air bleed screw	6 Joint ring	8 Adjustment screw	

positions).

It must be appreciated, of course, that all other aspects of engine condition and settings must be as near perfect as possible to achieve the sought after reduction in emission fumes. Valve clearances, plug gaps, points gap, centrifugal and vacuum automatic advance curves and static timing are all equally important.

The overall requirement is, therefore, an engine in a very good state of tune at all times. The extra expense of maintaining this is offset by improved performance and fuel consumption and the knowledge that one is not feeding unwanted elements into the air we breath.

This manual does not intend to go into any detail on the servicing operations necessary as the full implications are not yet known of what the owner may or may not be able to do in the tuning and setting up of such a system on his own car.

It is hoped, however, that this brief summary will give readers an idea of what the whole problem is about and allay any fears, due to lack of knowledge, that the system will be so complex as to be totally beyond their comprehension. This is not so. What is being done in effect, is to develop the existing carburation and ignition systems to ensure that fuel is more carefully metered in and more thoroughly burnt. Future developments will also incorporate filter systems for even more selective containment of the polluting elements of internal combustion emissions.

Fault Finding Chart — Fuel System & Carburation

Unsatisfactory engine performance and excessive fuel consumption are not necessarily the fault of the fuel system or carburetter. In fact they more commonly occur as a result of ignition and timing faults. Before acting on the following it is necessary to check the ignition system first. Even though a fault may lie in the fuel system it will be difficult to trace unless the ignition is correct. The faults below, therefore, assume that this has been attended to first (where appropriate). It also assumes that the engine is not worn out.

Symptom	Reason/s	Remedy
Smell of petrol when engine is stopped	Leaking fuel lines or unions.	Examine all lines and unions for signs of looseness or fractures. Fit new lines or unions as necessary.
	Leaking fuel tank.	Fill fuel tank to capacity and examine carefully at seams, unions and filler pipe connections. Repair as necessary.
Smell of petrol when engine is idling.	Leaking fuel line unions between pump and carburetter.	Check line and unions and tighten or repair.
	Overflow of fuel from float chamber due to wrong level setting or ineffective needle valve or punctured float.	Check fuel level setting and condition of float and needle valve and renew if necessary.
Excessive fuel consumption for reasons not covered by leaks or float chamber faults.	Over-rich jet setting.	Adjust jet.
Difficult starting, uneven running, lack of power, cutting out.	Jet. Blocked or restricted.	Dismantle and clean out float chamber and jet.
	Fuel pump not delivering sufficient fuel.	Check pump delivery and clean or repair as required.
	Air valve piston not operating correctly	Dismantle and examine. Clean and repair as required.

Chapter 4 Ignition system

Contents

Specifications

Type	Coil and distributor
Firing order	1, 3, 4, 2
Coil	Lucas 11.C.12 (HA.12 on some export models)
	AC Delco Remy 100329
	AC Delco Remy 7992170 (5 series)

Spark plugs

All models	Champion N9Y or AC 42XLS
Gap	0.025 in (0.635 mm)

Distributor

	Lucas 25D4	Lucas 4SD4	Ducellier
Type	Lucas 25D4	Same	
Drive	Skew gear on camshaft	Same	Same
Rotation (viewed from above)	Anti-clockwise	Same	Same
Contact breaker gap	0.015 in (0.38 mm)	0.015 in (0.38 mm)	0.016 in (0.4 mm) (initial setting only)
Contact lever spring tension	18/24 oz (0.51/0.68 kg)	18/24 oz (0.51/0.68 kg)	23 oz (0.65 kg)
Cam dwell angle	$60^\circ \pm 3^\circ$	$51^\circ \pm 5^\circ$	$56^\circ \pm 1^\circ$

Ignition timing (nominal) static   ... ... $7 - 9^\circ$ BTDC (1500LC $2 - 6^\circ$ BTDC)

Ignition timing (Dynamic, at 3,000 rpm with vacuum advance pipe disconnected) ... ...

Engine	Head	Carbs	Timing
1500 HC	Iron	Single	$39 - 41^\circ$ BTDC
1725 HC	Iron	Single	$29 - 31^\circ$ BTDC
1725 LC	Iron	Single	$30 - 32^\circ$ BTDC
1725	Alum.	Single	$31 - 33^\circ$ BTDC
1725	Alum.	Twin	$33 - 35^\circ$ BTDC

Distributor/Engine identification table

Engine type	Lucas	Ducellier	Vacuum advance unit marking
1725 Alum. head, single carb	41151, 41183, 41291 or 41462 or 41555	4515	4 - 8 - 5
1725 Alum. head, twin carbs	41077 or 41461 or 41554	4514	4 - 8 - 5
1500 Iron head, HC and LC 1	41170 or 41460 or 41553	4513	4 - 7 - 8
1725 Iron head, HC	41043 or 41458 or 41551	4511	5 - 11 - 7
1725 Iron head, LC	41177 or 41459 or 41552	4512	4 - 8 - 5

Distributor centrifugal advance - decelerating (crank degrees)

Distributor Service No

Crank rpm	41077 or 41461	41151	41183	41291 or 41462	41043 or 41458	41177 or 41459	41170 or 41460	41553 (Lucas) 4513 (Ducellier)	41551 (Lucas) 4511 (Ducellier)	41555 (Lucas) 4515 (Ducellier)	41554 (Lucas) 4514 (Ducellier)
500	–	—	—	—	—	—	—	—	—	—	—
600	--	—	—	—	—	—	—	—	0 - 2	—	—
750	—	0 -1	0 -1	0 -1	0 - 6	—	—	—	—	—	—
800	—	—	—	—	—	0 - 2	0 - 2	0 - 2	—	—	0 - 4
1000	2 - 6	2 - 6	2 - 6	1 - 4	6 - 12	—	—	—	6 - 12	0 - 4	—
1200	—	—	—	—	—	3 - 7	—	—	—	—	—
1500	8 - 12	12 - 16	12 - 16	7 - 11	—	—	8 - 12	—	—	—	—
1600	—	—	—	—	—	—	17 - 21	17 - 21	—	—	—
2000	15 - 19	16 - 20	16 - 20	13 - 17	14 - 18	13 - 17	20 - 24	—	—	—	10 - 14

2100	—	—	—	—	—	—	—	—	—	—	—
2400	—	—	—	—	—	—	—	—	—	18 - 22	20 - 24
2700	—	—	—	—	—	—	—	—	18 - 22	—	24 - 28
3000	24 - 28	22 - 26	22 - 26	22 - 26	21 - 25	20 - 24	28 - 32	28 - 32	—	22 - 26	—
3200	—	—	—	—	—	—	—	—	—	—	—
3500	24 - 28	25 - 29	25 - 29	25 - 29	24 - 28	23 - 27	32 - 36	—	—	—	—
3600	—	—	—	—	—	—	—	—	—	26 - 30	—
4000	—	—	—	—	—	—	—	36 - 40	—	—	—
4200	—	—	—	—	—	—	—	—	—	—	—
4800	—	—	—	—	—	—	—	—	32 - 36	—	—

Note: The static advance angle must be added to these figures when testing the distributor on the engine, with the vacuum pipe disconnected

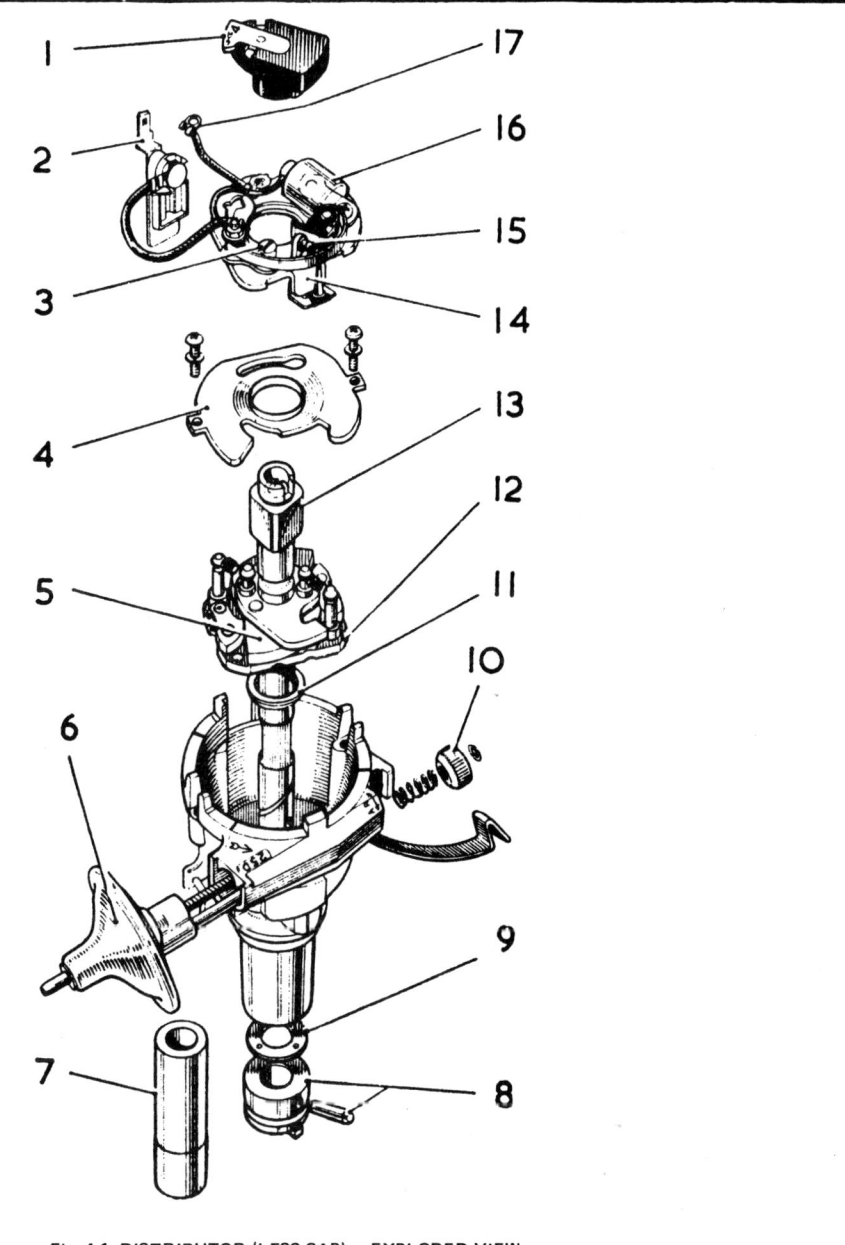

Fig. 4.1. DISTRIBUTOR (LESS CAP) — EXPLODED VIEW

1 Rotor arm	5 Centrifugal advance control	9 Thrust washer	14 Contact breaker moving plate
2 LT terminal	weights	10 Vernier adjustment nut	15 Contacts
3 Fixed contact plate securing	6 Vacuum advance control unit	11 Distance collar	16 Condenser
screw	7 Bearing bush	12 Action plate	17 CB earth connector
4 Contact breaker base plate	8 Dog and pin	13 Cam	

Distributor vacuum advance (crank degrees)

Distributor service no.

Hg in	41077 0 / 41461	41151	41183	41291 or 41462	41043 or 41458	41177 or 41459	41170 or 41460	41553 (Lucas) 4513 (Ducellier)	41551 (Lucas) 4511 (Ducellier)	41555 (Lucas) 4515 (Ducellier)	41554 (Lucas) 4514 (Ducellier)
2½	0 - 1	0 - 1	0 - 1	0 - 1	—	0 - 1	—	—	—	0 - 1	0 - 1
3	——	—	—	—	—	—	0 - 1	0 - 1	—	—	—
4	—	—	—	—	0 - 1	—	0 - 5	—	0 - 1	—	—
5	1 - 7	1 - 6	1 - 6	1 - 6	—	1 - 7	—	—	—	1 - 6	1 - 6
6	—	—	—	—	0 - 4	—	5 - 14	5 - 14	—	—	—
7	6 - 10	6 - 10	6 - 10	6 - 10	—	6 - 10	—	—	—	6 - 10	6 - 10
7½	—	—	—	—	—	—	—	—	—	—	—
8	—	—	—	—	4½ - 8½	—	12 - 18	12 - 18	4½ - 8½	—	—
8½	—	—	—	—	—	—	—	—	—	—	—
10	—	—	—	—	9 - 13	—	—	—	9 - 13	—	—
11	8 - 12	8 - 12	8 - 12	8 - 12	—	8 - 12	—	—	—	8 - 12	8 - 12
15	—	—	—	—	12 - 16	—	14 - 18	14 - 18	12 - 16	—	—

1. General Description

In order that the internal combustion engine with spark ignition can operate properly, it is essential that the spark is delivered at the sparking plug electrodes at the precise moment it is required. This moment varies - in relation to the position of the pistons and crankshaft - depending on the speed and loading of the engine. This control of the spark timing is automatic (on early cars the control was manual). When it is realised that at 50 m.p.h. approximately 100 sparks per second are being produced then the importance of the need for precise setting is realised. The majority of minor faults and cases of poor performance and economy can be traced to the ignition system.

The principles are as follows:- Battery voltage (12 volts) is fed through a circuit which passes through a coil developing high voltage.

Without going into electrical principles it is sufficient to say that when the 12 volt circuit is 'made', current is fed into a capacitor (condenser). When the circuit is broken the condenser discharges its current into the low voltage line and a high voltage current is boosted from the core of the coil and along the H.T. lead. This current is delivered to the centre contact of the distributor cap and from there, via the rotor arm, to each of the other four contacts in turn. Each of these is linked by a 'high tension' lead to each sparking plug.

Obviously the timing of the break in the circuit decides the moment at which the spark is made. The contact points (or breaker points!) are in effect a switch. Not only do they open and close four times for every 2 revolutions of the crankshaft - delivering a spark to the four plugs in turn - they also open earlier or later in relation to the position of the crankshaft/pistons. Ignition advance and retard are the terms used to express this condition and it is measured in degrees - being degrees of angle of any crank on the shaft. Zero degrees is top dead centre, being the highest point of the arc made by a crank. Timing setting is therefore expressed as so many degrees B.T.D.C. (before top dead centre).

In order to vary the ignition timing the contact points mounting plate can rotate a limited amount relative to the centre spindle. This is controlled by the vacuum advance device which works from the suction (depression) in the engine inlet manifold. Secondly, the contact opening cam is able to revolve a certain amount round the centre spindle. This is controlled by spring loaded weights which move out under centrifugal force. When they move out the spindle to cam position is altered.

Timing varies with different engines but normally ranges from the static (at rest) advance of approximately 8° B.T.D.C. to 36° B.T.D.C. The vacuum advance device is concerned only with smooth running and economy at the lower engine speeds and part throttle openings. When accelerating and under open throttle conditions the centrifugal control is the only one in operation. The static timing is important of course as the two automatic timing advance devices start from this point and consequently if it is incorrect the whole range is affected. The vernier adjustment on the vacuum advance unit alters the static ignition setting entirely - not just for the vacuum advance part.

2. Routine Maintenance

a) Sparking plugs (5,000 miles)

Remove the plugs and thoroughly clean away all traces of carbon. Examine the porcelain insulation round the central electrode inside the plug and if damaged discard the plug. Reset the gap between the electrodes. Do not use a set of plugs for more than 10,000 miles. It is false economy.

b) Distributor

Every 5,000 miles remove the cap and rotor arm and put one or two drops of engine oil into the centre of the cam recess. Smear the surfaces of the cam itself with petroleum jelly. Do not over lubricate as any excess could get onto the contact point surfaces and cause ignition difficulties.

Every 5,000 miles examine the contact point surfaces. If there is a build up of deposits on one face and a pit in the other it will be impossible to set the gap correctly and they should be refaced or renewed. Set the gap when the contact surfaces are in order.

c) General

Examine all leads and terminals for signs of broken or cracked insulation. Also check all terminal connections for slackness or signs of fracturing of some strands of wire. Partly broken wire should be renewed.

The H.T. leads are particularly important as any insulation faults will cause the high voltage to 'jump' to the nearest earth and this will prevent a spark at the plug. Check that no H.T. leads are loose or in a position where the insulation could wear due to rubbing against part of the engine.

3. Distributor - Contact Points - Adjustment

1. Remove the distributor cap by unclipping the two leaf springs, one each side of the distributor.
2. Pull off the rotor arm from the cam spindle.
3. First examine the points by carefully levering them apart with a small screwdriver or something similar. If the faces of the circular contacts are pitted or rough then they cannot be properly set and should be removed for renewal or cleaning up.
4. If the faces are clean then turn the engine so that the moving arm of the breaker rests with the follower on one of the four high points on the cam. The engine can be turned by engaging a gear and moving the car.
5. Select a feeler blade (.015 in. (0.4 mm)) and place it between the points. If the gap is too great, slacken the fixed point locking screw and move the plate to alter the gap. If the gap is too small the feeler

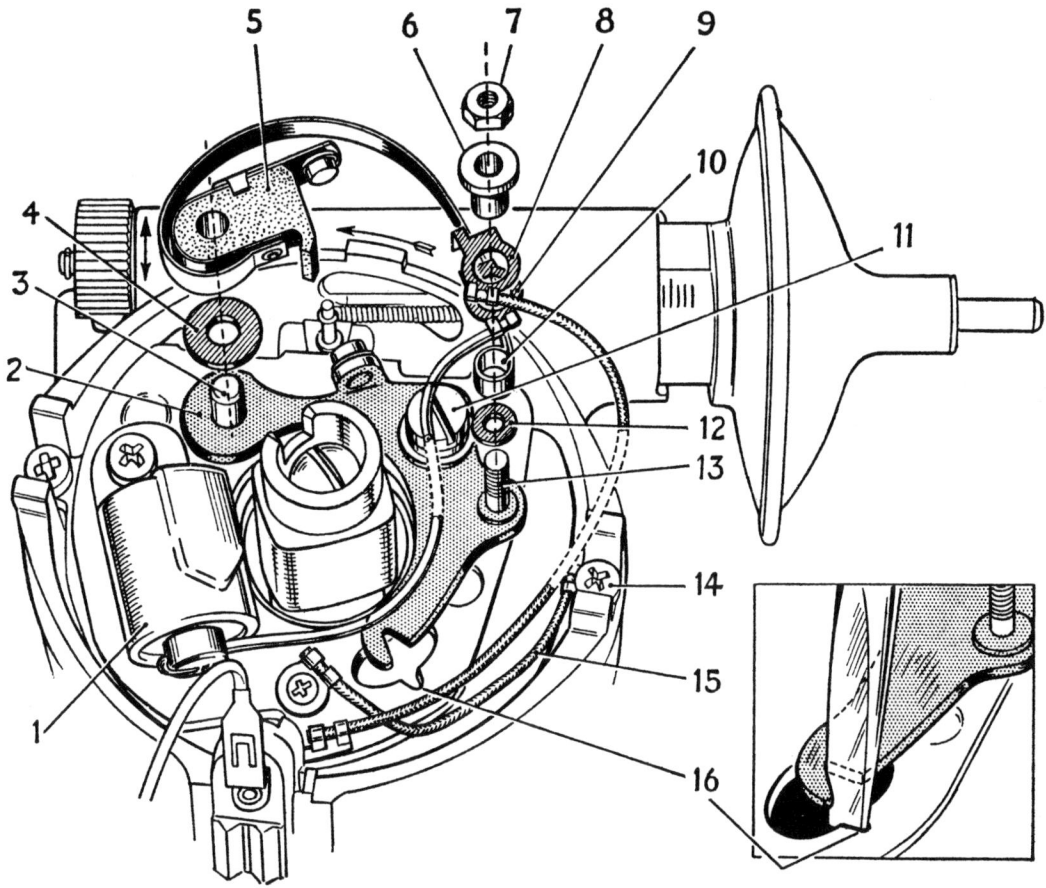

Fig. 4.2. CONTACT BREAKER POINTS — EXPLODED VIEW

1 Condenser
2 Fixed contact plate
3 Moving contact pivot post
4 Fibre insulating washer
5 Moving contact

6 Nylon insulating sleeve
7 Terminal nut
8 Lead from coil
9 Lead to condenser
10 Moving contact spring eye

11 Fixed contact plate securing screw
12 Fibre insulating washer
13 Terminal post
14 Contact base plate

securing screw (and earth wire connection)
15 Earth wire
16 Screwdriver notch for adjustment

blade may still fit between the points as the spring loaded arm can simply move back. When setting them, therefore, the feeler gauge blade should only be a very light touch on each contact face.

6. Lock the fixed plate screw and recheck the gap. Replace the rotor arm making sure that the lug in the rotor recess is fully engaged in the slot on the cam spindle.

7. Check the inside of the distributor cap before replacing it and verify that the four contacts are clean and the centre carbon brush is intact and moves freely.

4. Distributor - Contact Points - Removal and Replacement

1. The contact points will need removal if the surfaces are bad enough to require renewal or re-facing. Generally it is best to renew the contacts completely as re-facing never produces a surface as good as the original (unless done professionally which would cost more than the new ones!) and they will deteriorate again much more rapidly.

2. Remove the distributor cap and rotor arm as described in the previous Section and remove the fixed plate locking screw.

3. Undo the small nut on the terminal post which also secures the end of the spring and lift off the washer and nylon insulating sleeve. The two circular tags from the coil and condenser leads may then be taken off and the spring contact lifted off at the pivot post. The fixed contact can also now be lifted out.

4. Replacement is a reversal of the removal procedure. Modern contact sets are sometimes supplied as a complete assembly which can be fitted and connected as a single unit. If the new points are in separate pieces the assembly on the terminal post is very important. If you did not notice the order in which the pieces came off, the correct order of replacement is - Fixed contact onto the base plate, insulating washer over the terminal post (NOT the pivot post), spring contact, lead connectors onto terminal post, nylon sleeve on terminal post, plain washer and nut. This assembly insulates the spring side of the contacts from earth except when the points are closed.

5. Distributor - Condenser - Testing, Removal and Replacement

1. A faulty condenser causes interruptions in the ignition circuit or total failure. Elaborate testing methods are pointless as the item is cheap to renew.

2. If the contact points become pitted after a relatively small mileage (under 1,000) and if starting is difficult then it is a good idea to replace the condenser with the points. Another way to check is to remove the distributor cap and turn the engine so that the points are closed. Then switch on the ignition and open the points using an insulated screwdriver. There should be a small blue spark visible but if the condenser is faulty there will be a fat blue spark.

3. To remove the condenser disconnect the lead from the contacts terminal post and remove the crosshead screw securing the condenser mounting bracket to the plate. Fit a new one in the reverse order.

6. Distributor - Removal and Replacement

1. The distributor will need removal if there are indications that the drive spindle is a sloppy fit in the bushes (causing contact gap setting difficulties) or if it is to be dismantled and thoroughly cleaned and checked. It should also be removed before the oil pump is taken out.

2. Before removing the distributor it is helpful to prevent future confusion if the engine is positioned with No. 1 piston at T.D.C. on the firing stroke. This can be done by noting the position of the No. 1 plug lead in the cap and then turning the engine to T.D.C. so that the rotor is adjacent to the No. 1 plug position in the cap. (The cap, of course, will be removed to do this.) For details see Section 8 - 'Ignition Timing'.

3. Detach the plug leads from the spark plugs and the coil H.T. lead

from the distributor cap or coil. Remove the cap by unclipping the leaf spring clip at each side.

4. Pull off the L.T. wire connector at the distributor and remove the suction pipe from the vacuum advance unit.

5. Undo the two bolts securing the flange of the distributor body to the block. Do not undo the upper clamp bolts or clamp unless the distributor is being renewed. It will keep the timing at least in the right area.

6. Lift the distributor out. Before proceeding any further, note the position of the eccentric slot in the end of the drive shaft inside the distributor mounting recess in the block. This will give a firm timing reference if the oil pump is to be removed.

7. Replacement is a reversal of the removal procedure. Check that the rubber sealing ring between the flange and block is in good condition. Line up the eccentric tongue on the distributor shaft with the slot in the drive shaft and when the sleeve of the body is being pushed down be prepared to rotate the shaft either way a little so as to engage the drive.

7. Distributor - Dismantling, Inspection and Reassembly

1. If the distributor is causing trouble with the ignition system it is often a good idea to fit a completely new unit. Without the proper test equipment it is difficult to diagnose whether or not the centrifugal and vacuum automatic advance mechanisms are performing as they should. However, play in the shaft bushes can be detected by removing the rotor arm and gripping the end and trying to move it sideways. If there is any movement then it means that the cam cannot accurately control the contact points gap. This must receive attention.

2. With the distributor removed take off the rotor, condenser and contact points as described in Section 4.

3. Unhook the vacuum advance link from the edge of the contact breaker moving plate and then take out the two screws at the edge of the base plate which secure it to the body of the distributor.

4. Pull the nylon L.T. lead terminal from the groove in the side of the distributor and the two plates may then be lifted out.

5. If the shaft is being removed to renew the bushes do NOT dismantle the centrifugal advance mechanism as it is not necessary. Remove the small circlip from the end of the threaded shank of the vacuum advance vernier adjustment. This will enable the knurled screw to be taken right off. Note the position of the vernier scale on the advance unit. The vacuum unit can then be also withdrawn.

6. Remove the pin securing the offset driving dog with a flat nosed punch and the shaft complete with cam and centrifugal advance mechanism may be taken out. Note the relative position of the dog offset to the cam rotor slot.

7. To renew the bush first press or drive out the old one from inside the distributor body.

8. The bush is stepped at its lower end for ¾ inch (19 mm). Before fitting a new bush it should be soaked in engine oil for at least 24 hours - or hot oil for 2 hours - before fitting. It is made of sintered copper/iron and retains its lubricant due to porosity. The new bush should be pushed in from the lower end, the small diameter part first. When the shoulder part reaches the body the bush should be pressed in with a shouldered mandrel in a press or vice. Any attempt to drive it in - even using blocks of wood - will almost certainly cause it to break up. The bottom of the bush should be flush with the distributor body and it should protrude very slightly at the top inside.

9. When fitted the bush should be drilled through in line with the shaft oil drain hole in the body. Make sure there are no burrs or loose metal particles anywhere in the bush.

10 Refit the shaft, lubricate with engine oil. If it is tight it will need 'running in' by hand until there are no traces of binding. The bush must not be reamed as this will impair its self lubricating properties. Do not forget the distance collar on the shaft under the action plate.

11 If the centrifugal advance device is to be dismantled first remove the two springs very carefully so as not to kink, distort or stretch

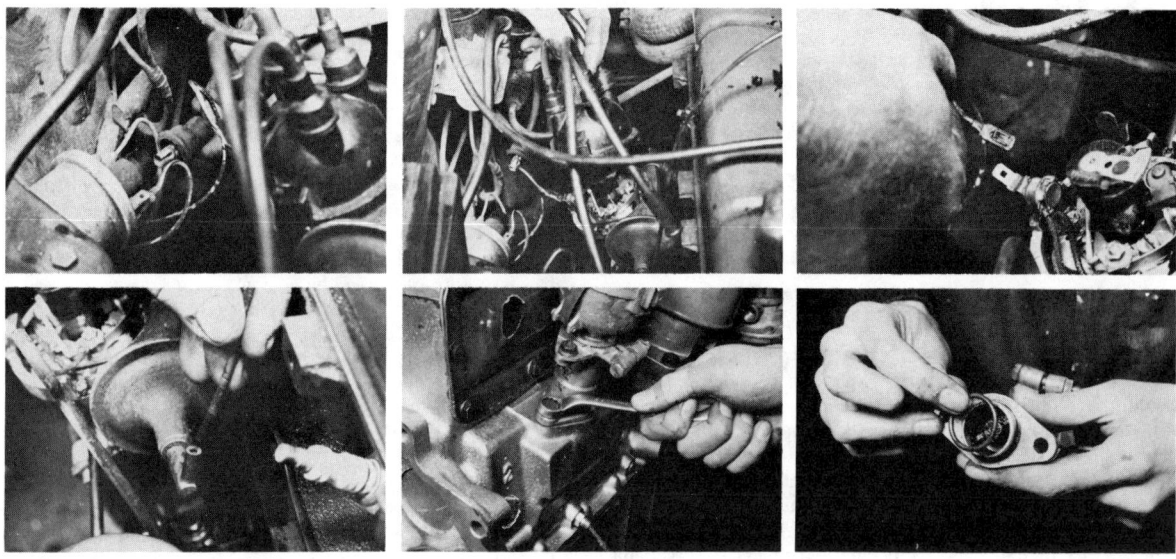

SECTION 6. Sequence of operations for removing distributor and checking the condition of the 'O' ring.

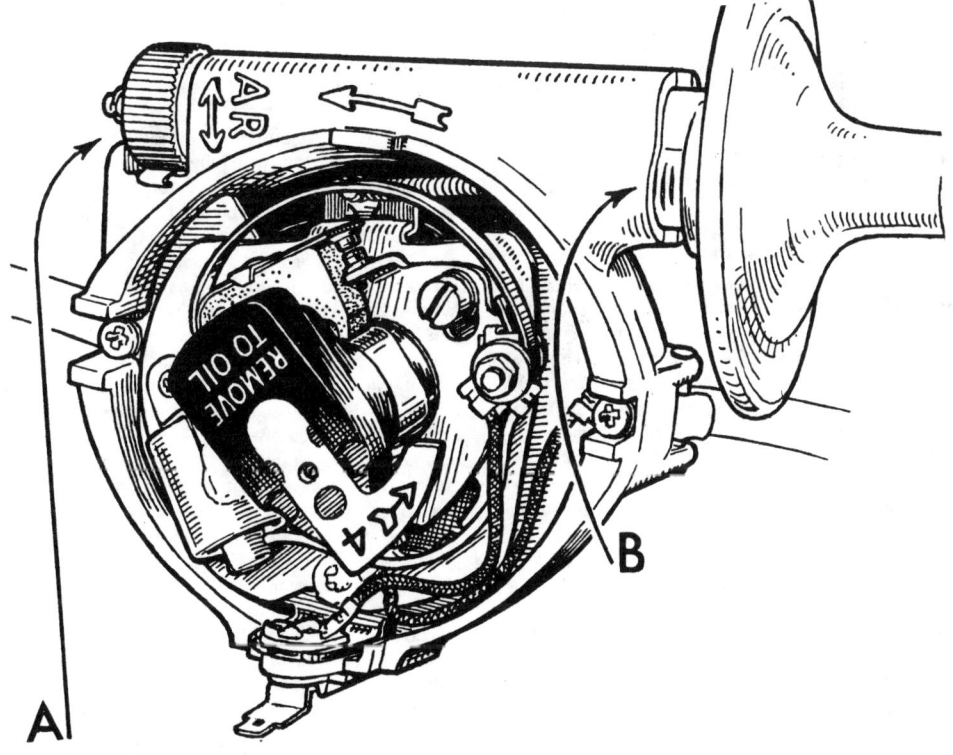

Fig. 4.3. Distributor - Vacuum advance control. Static advance may be adjusted by vernier adjustment screw (A) and indicated on scale (B). Scale is shown in central position (2 divisions)

them. Then note the position of the cam rotor arm slot relative to the offset drive dog on the bottom of the shaft and unscrew the screw in the top of the cam securing it to the shaft. The cam may then be lifted off followed by the counter weights.

12 Reassembly of the distributor is a reversal of the dismantling process. Take care to see that the cam rotor arm slot is in the same relative position with the driving dog as before and do not stretch the centrifugal springs. Smear the contact breaker base plate with a thin film of oil or grease between it and the moving plate. Make sure the drive dog retaining pin is peened over sufficiently to prevent it working loose.

8. Ignition Timing

1. It is necessary to time the ignition when it has been upset due to overhauling or dismantling which may have altered the relationship between the position of the pistons and the moment at which the distributor delivers the spark. Also, if maladjustments have affected the engine performance it is very desirable, although not always essential, to reset the timing starting from scratch. In the following procedures it is assumed that the intention is to obtain standard performance from the standard engine which is in reasonable condition. It is also assumed that the recommended fuel octane rating is used. It is possible today to have an engine checked on special equipment designed to indicate where different faults may be. These instruments are excellent for indicating what may be wrong with your engine in a variety of areas. They do not, however, compute the full combination of settings needed to get the best possible performance from your particular engine as it is. The final check for ignition timing depends solely on the performance of the car on the road in all the variety of conditions that it meets.

2. The static or datum timing is getting the spark to arrive at a particular position of the crankshaft. (See Section 1). Most manufacturers stick to the convention of using No. 1 cylinder for this adjustment and the Hillman is no exception. From the specifications we know that the static timing is say, 8° Before Top Dead Centre. The range of 6° - 10° given is intentional. No two engines are identical. Neither are the combined operations of their components. So we start in the middle of the possible range.

3. The crankshaft pulley wheel, keyed to the front of the crankshaft, is marked with a series of notches (or lines on those models with damper pulley wheels). A pointer is fitted to the front of the timing gear cover. If the engine is revolved clockwise T.D.C. on No. 1 piston will be achieved when the LAST notch (or line) comes up to the pointer. Do this and then look at the distributor cap and see at which position the H.T. lead from No. 1 sparking plug connects. Then remove the cap and see whether the top of the rotor arm is facing the No. 1 plug contact. If it is, good! If not then the engine must be turned another complete revolution to the T.D.C. mark again. The rotor arm should then be in the correct position. Should the rotor arm still be way out, check whether the distributor body can be rotated enough to compensate by slackening the clamp and trying it. It may be possible, with alterations to plug lead lengths. Such a state of affairs usually indicates that the oil pump drive spindle is out of position. With luck it will not have to be repositioned. (See Chapter 1 - 'Oil Pump Replacement'.).

4. Now the engine should be set at the correct static advance position. Each notch, or line, represents 5° so for 8° advance turn the engine back 1½ notches/lines from the T.D.C. mark.

5. As discussed in the opening Section the spark is produced when the contact points in the L.T. circuit open. It is now necessary to slacken the distributor clamping screw so that the body of the distributor may be turned (whilst the rotor spindle stays still). Also the vernier control on the vacuum advance should be set in the centre of the range to give scope for equal fine adjustment either way later. This central position is with two divisions of the scale showing. The distributor should now be turned slightly, one way or the other,

so that the contact points are fully open on the cam. The contact gap MUST be set correctly. As it is difficult to see exactly when the points are just closed a means of doing this electrically is necessary. Use a continuity tester or a 12 volt bulb and a jumper lead. If the latter is used, put one lead to the terminal where the coil L.T. lead joins the distributor and the other to a good earth on the engine block. With the ignition switched on the bulb will now light. Turn the body of the distributor anti-clockwise until the light just goes out. Then, lightly holding the rotor arm with clockwise pressure, turn the body clockwise again until the light just comes on again. Then tighten the clamping screw. If desired the correctness of the setting can be checked with a stroboscopic timing light but such a device is not essential for accurate setting of the static timing.

6. The performance of the engine should now be checked by road testing. Make any adjustments by turning the vernier adjustment wheel a measured number of 'clicks' - start by increasing the advance - and road test after each adjustment. One complete revolution of the vernier adjuster is equivalent to a 3° crankshaft movement and 1 division on the scale represents 4°.

7. Should the owner wish, he may check the vacuum and centrifugal advance characterisations of the distributor. For this he will need to employ an accurate tachometer and a stroboscopic timing light. Using the table for the degrees of advance at various engine revolutions he may calculate whether the distributor is doing its job properly. It must be remembered that these are ranges of degrees rather than precise figures. If the distributor was seriously wrong then the performance of the car would be noticeably affected. Should the distributor be suspected of malfunction in this respect it would be best to get it tested on the specialised equipment available at some garages or simply fit a new one. Often the cost of thorough checking (which involves removing the distributor if it is to be done very precisely) is not far short of the cost of a new unit.

9. Sparking Plugs and H.T. Leads

1. With the development of modern technology and materials, sparking plugs are generally very reliable and require minimal attention. When they are due for checking and cleaning it is good practise to have them thoroughly sand blasted, gapped and checked under pressure on the machine that most garages have installed. They can also be used as good indications of engine condition, particularly as regards the fuel mixture being used and the state of the pistons and cylinder bores. Check each plug as it is possible that one cylinder condition is different from the rest. Plugs come in different types to suit the particular type of engine. A 'hot' plug is for engines which run at lower temperatures than normal and a 'cold' plug is for the hotter running engines. If plugs of the wrong rating are fitted they can either damage the engine or fail to operate properly. Under normal running conditions a correctly rated plug in a properly tuned engine will have a light deposit of a brownish colour on the electrodes. A dry black sooty deposit indicates an over-rich fuel mixture. An oily blackish deposit indicates worn bores or valve guides. A dry hard whitish deposit indicates too weak a fuel mixture. If plugs of the wrong heat range are fitted they will have similar symptoms to a weak mixture together with burnt electrodes (plug too hot) or to an over-rich mixture caked somewhat thicker (plug too cold). Do not try and economise by using plugs beyond 10,000 miles. Unless the engine remains in exceptionally good tune, reductions in performance and fuel economy will outweigh the cost of a new set.

2. The H.T. leads and their connections at both ends should always be clean and dry and, as far as possible, neatly arranged away from each other and nearby metallic parts which could cause premature shorting in weak insulation. The metal connections at the ends should be a firm and secure fit and free from any signs of corrosive deposits. If any lead shows signs of cracking or chafing of the insulation it should be renewed. Remember that radio interference suppression is required when renewing any leads.

Measuring plug gap. A feeler gauge of the correct size (see ignition system specifications) should have a slight 'drag' when slid between the electrodes. Adjust gap if necessary

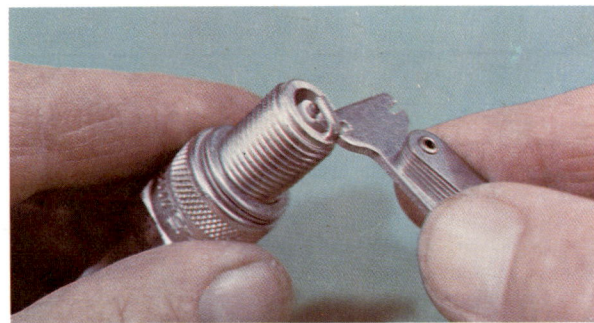

Adjusting plug gap. The plug gap is adjusted by bending the earth electrode inwards, or outwards, as necessary until the correct clearance is obtained. Note the use of the correct tool

Normal. Grey-brown deposits lightly coated core nose. Gap increasing by around 0.001 in (0.025 mm) per 1000 miles (1600 km). Plugs ideally suited to engine and engine in good condition

Carbon fouling. Dry, black, sooty deposits. Will cause weak spark and eventually misfire. Fault: over-rich fuel mixture. Check: carburettor mixture settings, float level and jet sizes; choke operation and cleanliness of air filter. Plugs can be re-used after cleaning

Oil fouling. Wet, oily deposits. Will cause weak spark and eventually misfire. Fault: worn bores/piston rings or valve guides; sometimes occurs (temporarily) during running-in period. Plugs can be re-used after thorough cleaning

Overheating. Electrodes have glazed appearance, core nose very white - few deposits. Fault: plug overheating. Check: plug value, ignition timing, fuel octane rating (too low) and fuel mixture (too weak). Discard plugs and cure fault immediately

Electrode damage. Electrodes burned away; core nose has burned, glazed appearance. Fault: initial pre-ignition. Check: as for 'Overheating' but may be more severe. Discard plugs and remedy fault before piston or valve damage occurs

Split core nose (may appear initially as a crack). Damage is self-evident, but cracks will only show after cleaning. Fault: pre-ignition or wrong gap-setting technique. Check: ignition timing, cooling system, fuel octane rating (too low) and fuel mixture (too weak). Discard plugs, rectify fault immediately

10. Ignition Faults - Symptoms, Reasons and Remedies

Engine troubles normally associated with, and usually caused by, faults in the ignition system are:-

a) Failure to start when the engine is timed.
b) Uneven running due to misfiring or mistiming.
c) Smooth running at low engine revolutions but misfiring when under load or accelerating or at high constant revolutions.
d) Smooth running at higher revolutions and misfiring or cutting-out at low speeds.

a) First check that all wires are properly connected and dry. If the engine fails to catch when the starter is operated do not continue for more than 5 or 6 short burst attempts or the battery will start to get tired and the problem made worse. Remove the spark plug lead from a plug and turn the engine again holding the lead (by the insulation!) about ¼ inch from the side of the engine block. A spark should jump the gap audibly and visibly. If it does then the plugs are at fault or the static timing is very seriously adrift. If both are good, however, then there must be a fuel supply fault, so go on to that.

If no spark is obtained at the end of a plug lead detach the coil H.T. lead from the centre of the distributor cap and hold that near the block to try and find a spark. If you now get one, then there is something wrong between the centre terminal of the distributor cap and the end of the plug lead. Check the cap itself for damage or damp, the 4 terminal lugs for signs of corrosion, the centre carbon brush in the top (is it jammed?) and the rotor arm.

If no spark comes from the coil H.T. lead check next that the contact breaker points are clean and that the gap is correct. A quick check can be made by turning the engine so that the points are closed. Then switch on the ignition and open the points with an insulated screwdriver. There should be a small visible spark and, once again, if the coil H.T. lead is held near the block at the same time a proper H.T. spark should occur. If there is a big fat spark at the points but none at the H.T. lead then the condenser is done for and should be renewed.

If neither of these things happen then the next step in this tale of woe is to see if there is any current (12 volts) reaching the coil (+ terminal). (One could check this at the distributor, but by going back to the input side of the coil a longer length of possible fault line is bracketed and could save time).

With a 12v bulb and piece of wire suitably connected (or of course a voltmeter if you have one handy) connect between the + or 'SW' terminal of the coil and earth and switch on the ignition. No light means no volts so the fault is between the battery and the coil via the ignition switch. This is moving out of the realms of just ignition problems - the electrical system is becoming involved in general. So to get home to bed get a piece of wire and connect the + terminal of the coil to the + terminal on the battery and see if sparks occur at the H.T. leads once more.

If there is current reaching the coil then the coil itself or the wire from its '—' terminal to the distributor is at fault. Check the '—' or CB terminal with a bulb with the ignition switched on. If it fails to light then the coil is faulty in its L.T. windings and needs renewal.

b) Uneven running and misfiring should first be checked by seeing that all leads, particularly H.T., are dry and connected properly. See that they are not shorting to earth through broken or cracked insulation. If they are, you should be able to see and hear it. If not, then check the plugs, contact points and condenser just as you would in a case of total failure to start.

c) If misfiring occurs at high speed check the points gap, which may be too small, and the plugs in that order. Check also that the spring tension on the points is not too light thus causing them to bounce. This requires a special pull balance so if in doubt it will be cheaper to buy a new set of contacts rather than go to a garage and get them to check it. If the trouble is still not cured then the fault lies in the carburation or engine itself.

d) If misfiring or stalling occurs only at low speeds the points gap is possibly too big. If not, then the slow running adjustment on the carburettor needs attention.

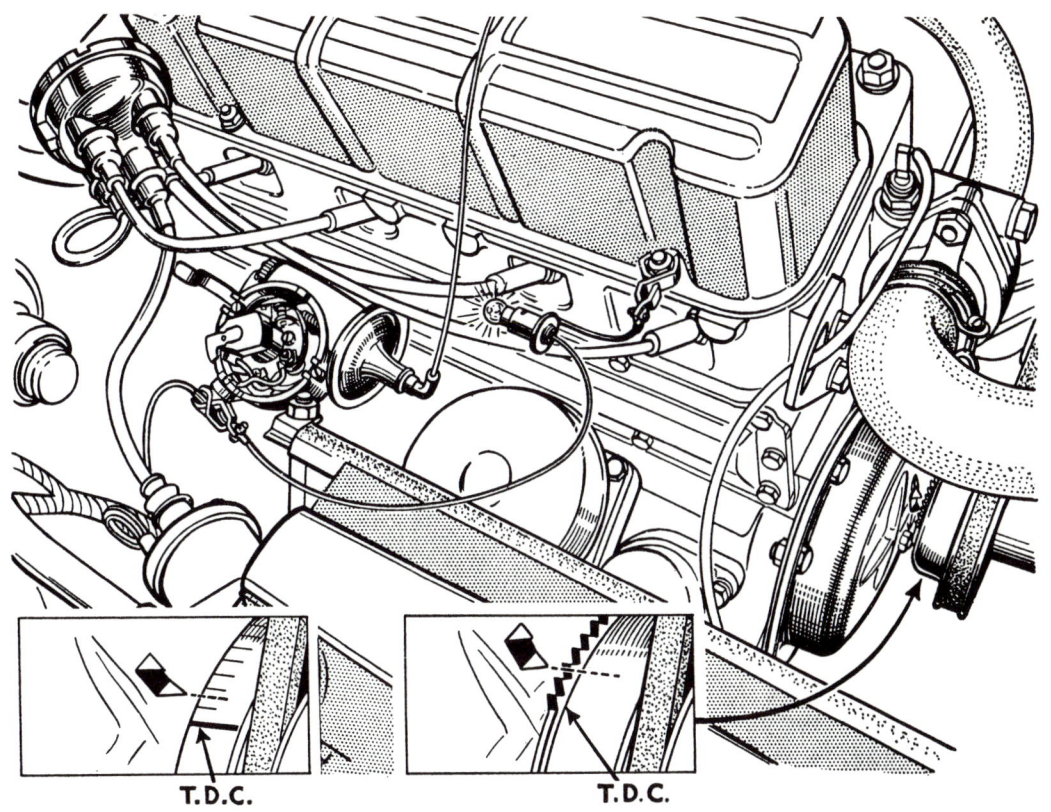

Fig. 4.5. Static Ignition Timing - Drawing showing inset the position of pointer and notches/lines. 8° advance is indicated in the drawing.

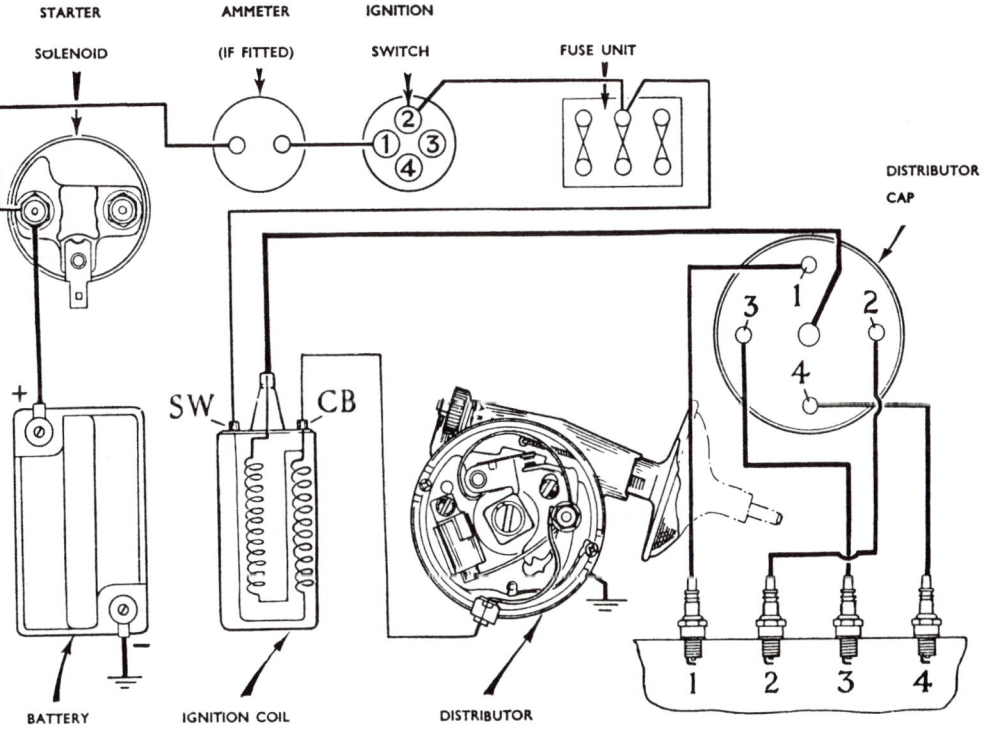

Fig. 4.6. Ignition system - showing L.T. 12 volt primary circuit and H.T. circuit in heavy lines.

Chapter 5 Clutch and actuating mechanism

Contents

Specifications

Type	Borg and Beck or Laycock diaphragm spring, hydraulically operated

Driven plate

Diameter	7½ in (19 cm) Hunter GLS 8½ (21.6 cm)
Number of springs	Four
Colour of springs:	
Single carb models	Light grey
Twin carb models	Two orange/violet and two white/light green

Clutch assembly

Adjustment	On pedal only
Thrust bearing	Carbon ring
Master cylinder bore	5/8 in (15.875 mm)
Slave cylinder bore	1 1/8 in (28.575 mm)

1 General description

All models have a diaphragm spring single plate hydraulically operated clutch. The cover assembly which incorporates the diaphragm spring and pressure plate bolts to the flywheel, sandwiching the friction disc between them. The friction disc has a splined hub which engages with the splined input shaft of the gearbox. The friction material on both sides of the plate is gripped by the cover and flywheel surfaces in much the same way as brake shoes grip the drums and when the clutch pedal is depressed the pressure plate is pulled off by the diaphragm spring.

The centre section of the friction plate is spring cushioned against the outer part to take up any shock and help ensure a smooth drive take up.

The diaphragm spring is mounted on shouldered studs between two fulcrum rings and is attached to both pressure plate and cover by tangentially positioned straps. When pressure is applied to the centre of the diaphragm the outer edge moves in the opposite direction, drawing the pressure plate with it.

The friction disc between the pressure plate and flywheel is free floating along the input shaft splines and as it gets thinner with wear so the pressure plate automatically moves forward to take it up under the pressure of the diaphragm spring.

In turn, the travel of the operating lever is compensated by the hydraulic clutch piston moving fractionally further along the cylinder in the rest position. The pressure is applied to the centre of the diaphragm by a carbon faced thrust ring pivot mounted at the end of the operating lever. No adjustments are necessary.

2 Routine maintenance

Every 5,000 miles or 3 months (minimum) have a look at the level of the fluid in the reservoir (look at the brake fluid reservoir too!). If the level is a little bit down top it up. If the level is a lot down there must be a reason - probably a leak. Trace the pipe to both ends and if signs of fluid leaking are apparent take the necessary action. Keep the reservoir cap clean and the air vent hole clear. Lubricate the pedal cross shaft bushes with a few drops of engine oil.

3 Hydraulic system (clutch) - bleeding

1 The need for bleeding the cylinders and fluid line arises when air gets into it. Air gets in whenever a joint or seal leaks or part has to be dismantled. Bleeding is simply the process of venting the air out again.
2 Make sure the reservoir is filled and obtain a piece of 3/16 inch bore diameter rubber tube about 2 to 3 feet long and clean jam jar. A small quantity of fresh, clean hydraulic fluid is also necessary. necessary.
3 Detach the cap (if fitted) on the bleed nipple at the clutch. cylinder and clean up the nipple and surrounding area. Unscrew the nipple ¾ turn and fit the tube over it. Put about ½ inch of fluid in the jar and put the other end of the pipe in it. The jar can be placed on the ground under the car.
4 The clutch pedal should then be depressed quickly and released slowly until no more air bubbles come from the pipe. Quick pedal

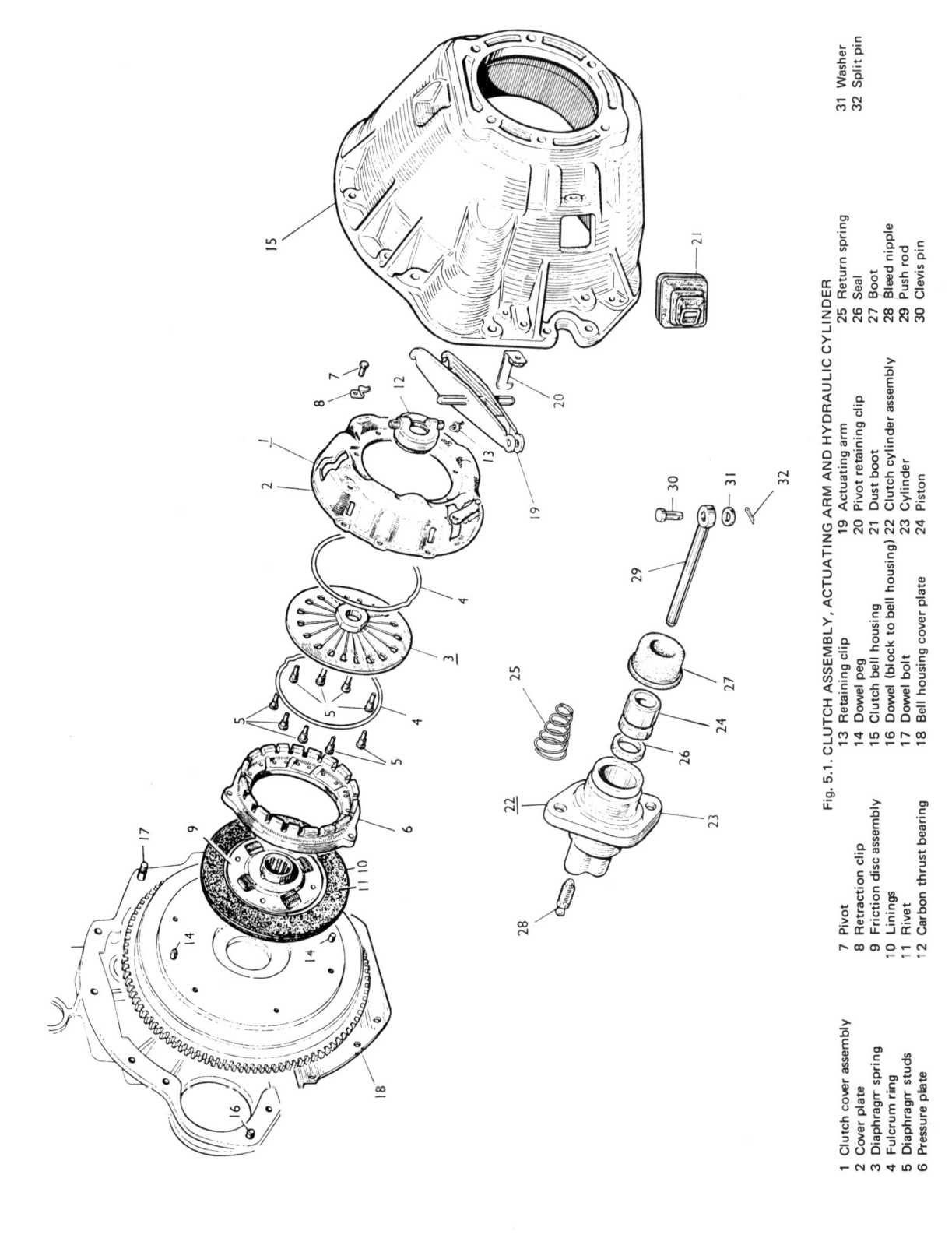

Fig. 5.1. CLUTCH ASSEMBLY, ACTUATING ARM AND HYDRAULIC CYLINDER

1 Clutch cover assembly
2 Cover plate
3 Diaphragm spring
4 Fulcrum ring
5 Diaphragm studs
6 Pressure plate

7 Pivot
8 Retraction clip
9 Friction disc assembly
10 Linings
11 Rivet
12 Carbon thrust bearing

13 Retaining clip
14 Dowel peg
15 Clutch bell housing
16 Dowel (block to bell housing)
17 Dowel bolt
18 Bell housing cover plate

19 Actuating arm
20 Pivot retaining clip
21 Dust boot
22 Clutch cylinder assembly
23 Cylinder
24 Piston

25 Return spring
26 Seal
27 Boot
28 Bleed nipple
29 Push rod
30 Clevis pin

31 Washer
32 Split pin

action carries the air along rather than leave it behind. Keep the reservoir topped up.

5. When the air bubbles stop tighten the nipple at the end of a down stroke.

6. Check that the operation of the clutch is satisfactory. Even though there may be no exterior leaks it is possible that the movement of the pushrod from the clutch cylinder is inadequate because fluid is leaking internally past the seals in the master cylinder. If this is the case, it is best to replace all seals in both cylinders.

4. Clutch Operating Cylinder - Removal, Dismantling, Assembly and Replacement

1. The clutch cylinder is fixed to the rear left hand side of the clutch bellhousing flange by two bolts. If it is to be removed for overhaul, first seal the cap of the fluid reservoir with a piece of plastic film (to minimise fluid loss)' and undo the pipe where it joins the cylinder. Then remove the two mounting bolts, disengage the pushrod from the piston inside the rubber boot, and lift the unit out. (If the cylinder is merely being moved out of the way for gearbox renewal the pipe need not be detached).

2. Remove the rubber boot. If a little air pressure is applied to the fluid inlet it will force the piston out of the cylinder - or it may be possible to shake it out. If the piston is seized, removal may be difficult. Soak the assembly in methylated spirits and if this does not release it buy a new unit. The cylinder bore will almost certainly be damaged anyway.

3. The seal may be removed from the piston by levering it off out of the groove. Note that the feathered side of the seal faces into the cylinder so that a new seal must be fitted the same way onto the piston. Pistons vary. Some have a flat end into the cylinder, others have two concave ends and the inner end is the one to which the seal groove is nearest. Thoroughly clean the cylinder and piston with methylated spirit or clean hydraulic fluid and fit a new seal by stretching it over the piston into the groove. The lip faces INTO the cylinder.

4. Replace the piston into the cylinder using a little fluid to lubricate the walls and make sure the lip of the seal does not get turned back. Replace the rubber boot so that it locks into the outer groove. It is quite a good idea to smear a little rubber grease (not ordinary grease) around the end of the piston under the boot.

5. Replacement is a reversal of the removal procedure. Make sure the unit is fitted on the rear side of the bellhousing flange - it is possible to put it on the front!

6. Bleed the system as described in the previous section.

5. Clutch Master Cylinder - Removal, Dismantling, Assembly and Replacement

1. The master cylinder and fluid reservoir are a single unit and indications of something wrong with it are if the pedal travels down without operating the clutch efficiently (assuming, of course, that the system has been bled and there are no leaks).

2. To remove the unit from the car first seal the cap with a piece of film to reduce fluid wastage whilst dismantling the pipes. Alternatively, the fluid may be pumped out from the clutch cylinder bleed nipple by opening the nipple and depressing the pedal several times.

3. From inside the car remove the split pin and clevis pin which attaches the pushrod assembly to the clutch pedal. It will be necessary to remove the parcel tray for this which is held by a screw at each end and plastic buttons to the side panels. When the pushrod is free remove the spring retainer collar and return spring.

4. From the engine compartment undo the hydraulic union of the pipe outlet from the cylinder and pull the pipe out and to one side. Undo the two bolts holding the whole unit to the vertical face of the bulkhead and take it out.

5. To dismantle the assembly first remove the rubber boot and then

with a pair of contracting circlip pliers remove the circlip from the internal bore of the cylinder. The piston assembly may then be drawn out. The trap valve can be ejected by blowing through the cylinder outlet orifice.

6. Thoroughly clean all the component parts and the cylinder and orifices with methylated spirit or clean hydraulic fluid.

7. Reassembly is a reversal of the dismantling process, using a new trap valve and seal cups as necessary. A complete repair kit will include everything required. Before fitting new seals, however, examine the cylinder bore for any signs of pitting, ridging or scoring. Any such signs mean that the cylinder is unserviceable and should be renewed. This normally means replacement of the whole assembly.

8. It is most important that the seals and washers are assembled into the cylinder in the correct order and the right way round. This order can be seen from the exploded drawing (Fig. 5.3). The main cup seal should have its lip facing the interior of the cylinder and the dome washer between it and the piston should have the convex surface against the head of the piston. The secondary cup seal should be carefully fitted into the groove at the outer end of the piston, also with its lip facing forward into the cylinder.

9. Ensure that the circlip is finally fitted securely into the groove and replace the rubber boot.

10 Refit the unit to the car in the opposite order to removal and refill the reservoir with fresh fluid of the correct specification. It is false economy to re-use the old fluid. Bleed the system as described in Section 3 and then check that the clutch movement is satisfactory and no leaks are apparent.

6. Clutch Pedal - Removal and Replacement

1. It may be necessary to remove the pedal if the bush and cross shaft are worn so much that operation is affected.

2. To detach either of the two control pedals it is necessary first to withdraw the whole assembly.

3. First remove both brake and clutch master cylinders from the car. Then remove the four nuts inside the car, which hold the mounting plate to the bulkhead and disconnect the bracing bracket from the steering column. The whole lot can then be lifted out from the engine compartment. Take out the split pin from the cross shaft and the pedals may be removed. Renew the shaft or pedal as necessary. When refitting the pedals and cross shaft make sure the wave washer is correctly placed between the clutch pedal boss and the mounting plate on the cross shaft.

4. The assembly is replaced in reverse order of removal.

7. Clutch - Removal

1. If it is necessary to renew the friction plate or examine the clutch in any way it will be first of all necessary to remove the gearbox (see Chapter 6) in order to get at it. If the engine has been removed then the clutch is, of course, accessible. Once the gearbox is removed or the engine taken out the succeeding operations are the same, although work is easier with the engine out when no pit or ramp is available. If the engine and gearbox have been removed from the car together they will have to be separated of course.

2. Before removing the clutch cover bolts mark the position of the cover in relation to the flywheel so that it may be put back the same way.

3. Slacken off the cover retaining bolts ½ a turn at a time in a diagonal fashion evenly so as to relieve the diaphragm spring pressure without distorting it.

4. When the bolts are removed the friction plate inside will be released and the cover can be pulled off the locating dowel pegs.

8. Clutch - Inspection and Renovation

1. Unfortunately it is not possible to inspect the clutch without

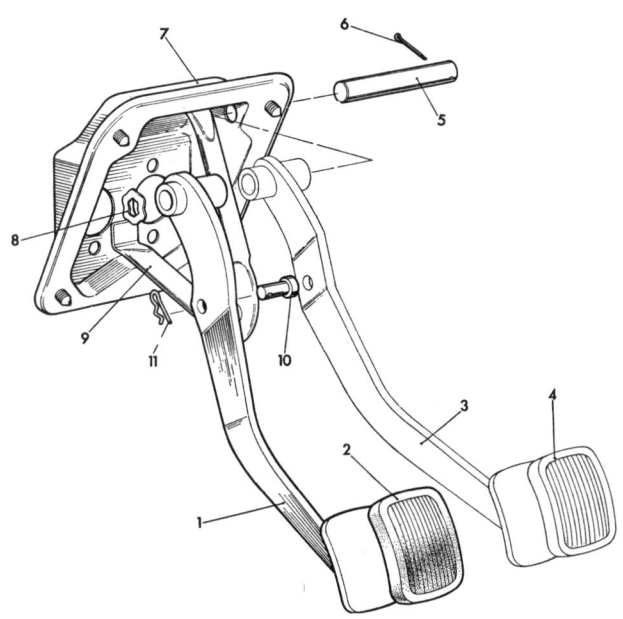

Fig. 5.2. CLUTCH PEDAL AND MOUNTING ASSEMBLY

1 Clutch pedal	4 Pedal pad	7 Mounting plate	10 Clevis pin
2 Pedal pad	5 Pedal cross-shaft	8 Wave washer	11 Split pin
3 Brake pedal	6 Cotter pin	9 Steering steady bracket	

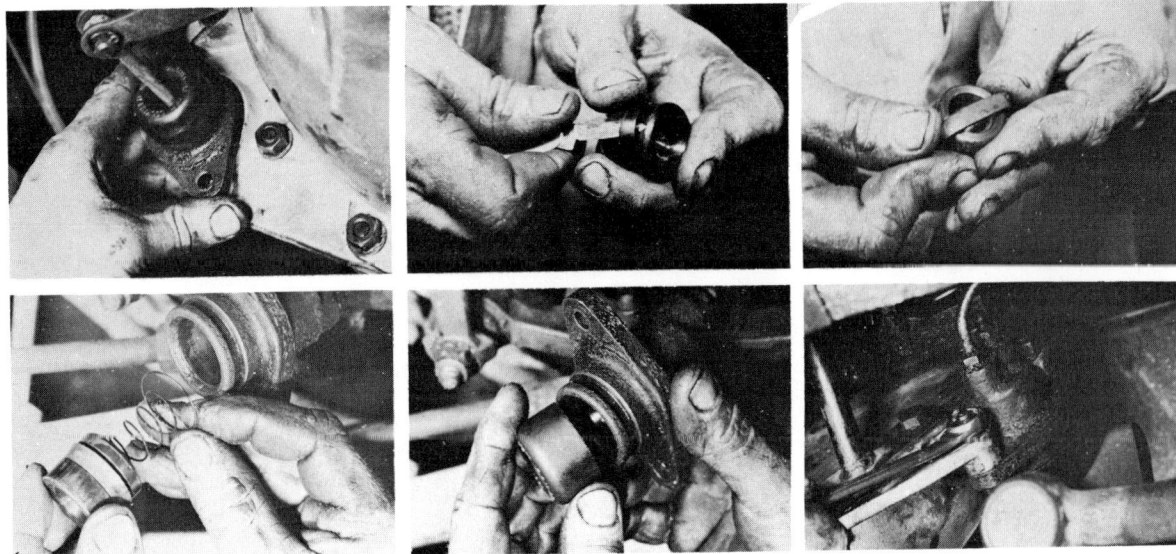

SECTION 4. Removal of clutch hydraulic cylinder, renewal of piston seal, reassembling and replacment.

going to the considerably trouble of removing the assembly. Consequently, one waits for trouble to develop or makes a decision to check and overhaul it any way at a specific mileage. Wear of the clutch friction plate depends a great deal on how the car has been driven. Habitual clutch slipping will obviously cause rapid wear. If it is assumed that the friction disc will need replacement at 35,000 miles and will be worth replacing at 25,000 miles there will be no significant waste of time and money if the work is done. Of course, a history of the car is very valuable for this decision. If, on the other hand, trouble is awaited, action must be taken immediately it occurs; otherwise further more costly wear could occur. Trouble usually comes in the form of slipping, when the engine speeds up and the car does not; or squealing, denoting that the friction material is worn to the rivets; or juddering denoting all sorts of things (see 'Faults' Diagnosis). Wear on the carbon thrust release ring which presses onto the centre of the diaphragm every time the clutch is operated could also cause squealing if the wear was extreme. If the clutch is not examined when wear is apparent the faces of the flywheel and pressure plate may be severely scored and call for costly replacement.

2. Having decided to dismantle the clutch, first examine the faces of the flywheel and the pressure plate. If these are smooth and shiny you may smile. If they are slightly ridged or scored frown a bit but stay happy in the knowledge that a new friction disc will be enough to regain satisfactory performance. If there is severe scoring, curse mildly and be prepared to buy a new pressure plate assembly and/or flywheel. It is possible to skim the face of the flywheel but engineering advice should be sought. If a new flywheel is obtained it will have to be matched to balance the same as the original. If you hurriedly put the badly scored surfaces back together with a new friction plate you will achieve short-lived results only. After a few thousand miles the same old trouble will recur and judder will always be present in some form or another.

3. The friction plate lining surfaces should be at least $1/32$ in. (.8 mm) above the heads of the rivets, otherwise the disc is not really worth putting back. If the friction lining material shows signs of chipping or breaking up or has black areas caused by oil contamination it should also be renewed. Oil contamination will be confirmed by signs of oil which may be visible on the flywheel or in the bellhousing (on the gearbox). Consideration must be given to curing any such leaks before refitting the clutch assembly. Linings can be obtained for fitting the existing clutch discs but it is hardly worth it. With a new assembly you know that the splines and the disc itself are in good condition.

9. Clutch - Replacement

1. If the original cover is being re-used line up the marks made before removal, and support the friction plate on one finger between cover and flywheel so that the larger boss faces the flywheel. Friction discs are normally marked 'This side to flywheel'.

2. Locate the cover on the dowel pegs in the flywheel and then place all the cover bolts in position and screw them up lightly by hand.

3. It is necessary to line up the centre of the friction disc with the exact centre of the flywheel. This is easily done if a piece of shouldered bar can be placed in the counter bore at the flywheel centre with the larger diameter supporting the friction disc. If you do not have such a thing, the disc may be lined up by eye if the engine is out of the car. For the man flat on his back on a cold concrete floor with his eyes full of grime it is certainly worthwhile making up some sort of centralising tool from a piece of broom handle or tube to get reasonably accurate positioning. If this is not done great difficulty (and possible damage to the gearbox input shaft) may be experienced when the time comes to refit the gearbox to the engine.

4. With the friction plate centralised the cover bolts should be tightened diagonally, evenly and progressively so that the diaphragm spring will not be distorted. Remove the centralising tool. Before refitting the gearbox to the engine do not forget to check the clutch thrust release bearing and operating mechanism.

5. Refit the gearbox (Chapter 6) and bleed the hydraulic system if it has been disturbed.

10. Clutch Operating Lever and Thrust Release Bearing - Dismantling, Inspection and Reassembly

1. When the clutch pedal is depressed the hydraulic clutch cylinder piston actuates the lever which pivots in the bellhousing and forces a carbon faced thrust ring or bearing against the steel boss at the centre of the diaphragm spring. In time the carbon ring will wear away and if this condition is allied to a well worn friction plate difficulty may be experienced in disengaging the clutch due to the limit of piston travel being reached before the diaphragm has been depressed sufficiently. A new carbon thrust ring face projects ¼ inch approximately from the housing and should be renewed if it is significantly less than this.

2. To renew the release bearing the clutch bellhousing and gearbox must be separated from the engine. The bearing is held to the actuating arm by two spring steel clips which, when released, allow it to be drawn off over the gearbox input shaft. Replacement is a reversal of the removal procedure. Should the release arm require removal the pivot pin clip holding it in position may be released by undoing the nut on the outside of the bellhousing. Once again, do **not** undo this without supporting the engine and gearbox. You will not be able to get it back.

11. Clutch Faults - Diagnosis and Remedy

1. Provided the clutch is not intentionally slipped excessively, or the pedal used as a footrest, which may wear out the carbon thrust ring more quickly than normal, the only malfunction of the clutch one would expect would be routine wear of the friction plate. This normal wear will become obvious as the clutch starts to slip; that is the engine turns normally but the car fails to accelerate properly or slows down on hills. In such cases the clutch must be examined and repaired immediately if necessary. Delay could be more costly. The gearbox will have to be taken off for this job.

2. Squealing noises from the clutch (and make sure they **are** from the clutch and not the fan belt or water pump) are most likely to come from a worn out clutch release bearing. The actual efficiency of the clutch may not be immediately affected but damage could be caused to the thrust boss on the diaphragm if no action is taken. Another reason for squealing could be a worn out or oil contaminated friction plate. In such instances the next symptom one could expect would be clutch slip. Do not wait for that however as the friction plate rivets could be scoring up the flywheel or pressure plate surfaces. Once again inspection and repair involves gearbox removal.

3. Failure to disengage the clutch (sometimes referred to as 'clutch spin') when the pedal is fully depressed, can be caused by one or more of several factors. Symptoms are the total inability or considerable difficulty in engaging any gear at rest - and when a gear is engaged it will be accompanied by a nasty crunch and the car bucking forwards (or backwards!). First check that the hydraulic system is moving the actuating lever when the pedal is depressed. An empty fluid reservoir or visible leaks will indicate that the system is malfunctioning. If the hydraulics are all right then the fault may be due to the friction plate sticking to the pressure plate or flywheel due to rusted splines which prevent it from floating fore and aft on the gearbox input shaft. This is not unusual if the car has been standing unused for a long time. Try engaging a gear, with the engine stopped and handbrake on; then depress the clutch and try starting the engine. If the clutch is seized solid the engine will not turn over but if you are lucky and the engine starts and the clutch can be slipped it should be possible to get it back to normal operation after using it a few times. Rust on the friction faces as well as on the splines will have the same effect and can be cured by the same treatment. If the clutch spin does not eventually disappear completely then some

SECTION 10 — Removal of thrust bearing and actuating arm.

SECTION 9 — Replacing and securing clutch assembly with centralising mandrel in position.

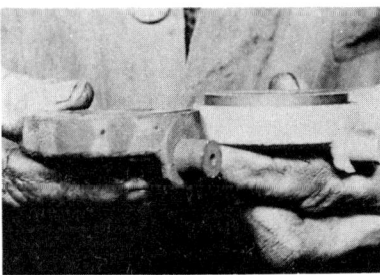

SECTION 10 — Comparison of worn and new carbons in clutch thrust bearings.

other defect such as distortion on the pressure faces may be the cause and this will involve dismantling. Thirdly, the cause could be a worn out thrust bearing allied to a well worn clutch plate. Squealing noises, each time the clutch is operated, will be an indication of this and dismantling will be necessary.

4. Another fault is judder - particularly to be noticed when the clutch is taking up the drive. Although the symptom is noticed when the clutch is operated, the clutch is not necessarily the culprit. Check the condition of the engine mountings - two forward and one under the gearbox. If the engine vibrates and rocks excessively when started up it would indicate that they are spongy or broken. Then check that the universal joints on the propeller shaft are not worn and that the back axle and suspension are secure and free from excessive backlash. Defective rear dampers can also cause drive judder. If diagnosis finally indicates that the fault lies in the clutch it will be caused by wear, contamination, distortion in one or other of the components and dismantling will be needed to ascertain for sure what is causing it.

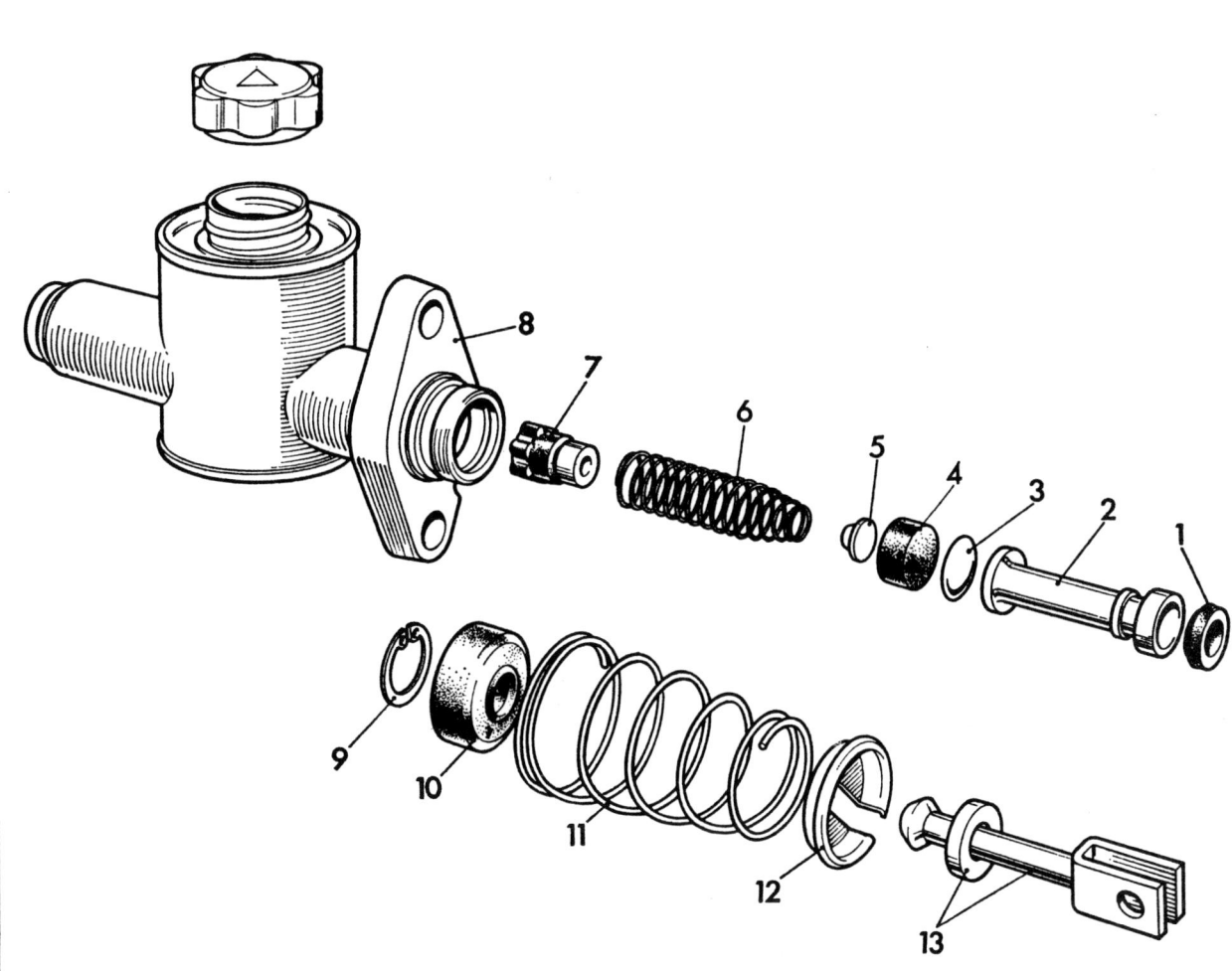

Fig. 5.3. CLUTCH MASTER CYLINDER

1 Secondary cup	5 Spring retainer	9 Circlip	13 Push rod assembly
2 Piston	6 Spring	10 Rubber boot	
3 Piston washer	7 Trap valve assembly	11 Pedal return spring	
4 Cup	8 Cylinder	12 Spring retainer	

Chapter 6 Gearbox

Contents

Specifications

Type	Four forward speeds, all synchromesh and reverse. Forward gears are helical cut and reverse is a straight cut spur gear
Bearings	
Mainshaft	Front spigot, needle rollers; rear, ball
Layshaft	Needle rollers
Primary shaft	Ball
Primary shaft spigot bearing	Oilite or wax-impregnated bush (later models have a needle roller bearing)
Reverse gear	Phosphor bronze bush
Adjustment	
Mainshaft	None
Layshaft	Selective assembly
Layshaft (endfloat)	0.006 - 0.008 in (0.15 - 0.20 mm)
1st speed wheel endfloat	0.004 - 0.009 in (0.10 - 0.23 mm)

Ratios

	Standard	Close ratio
Top	1.000 : 1	1.000 : 1
Third	1.392 : 1	1.296 : 1
Second	2.140 : 1	1.993 : 1
First	3.353 : 1	3.122 : 1
Reverse	3.569 : 1	3.323 : 1

Overdrive (where fitted)

	'D' type	'J' type
Ratio	0.803 : 1	0.797 : 1
Operating pressure:	lb/in^2 (kg/cm^2)	lb/in^2 (kg/cm^2)
GLS	510 - 530 (35.8 - 37.3)	340 - 370 (23.9 - 26.0)
All other models	480 - 500 (33.7 - 35.2)	340 - 370 (23.9 - 26.0)
Residual pressure	—	12 - 25 (0.8 - 1.8)

Speedometer drive gears

	4.22 Standard	3.89 Overdrive	3.89 Standard & automatic	3.70 Sceptre Automatic	3.70 Standard & auto, except Sceptre
Driving gear	4	4	4	4	4
Pinion	15	15	14	14	13

Capacities

Standard	3½ pints (4.2 US pints, 1.9 litres)
With 'D' type overdrive	4½ pints (5.4 US pints, 2.5 litres)
With 'J' type overdrive	5 pints (6 US pints, 2.8 litres)

For full details of the overdrive units and automatic gearbox, refer to Chapter 13, page 206.

1. General Description

The gearbox is a constant mesh four forward and one reverse speed unit with synchromesh fitted on all four forward speeds.

The input shaft and mainshaft are mounted in the casing on ball bearings and locate into each other on needle rollers.

The laygear cluster revolves on needle roller bearings on the fixed layshaft; end float is controlled by a thrust washer at each end fitted between the casing and the laygear. With the exception of reverse, all gears are helically cut.

Gear selection is by three forks running on three separate rails and the forks are held in their neutral and selection positions by spring loaded detent balls housed in each fork, which engage in grooves in the rails.

The selector lever operates the forks through a remote control which permits a short, positive action lever to be used. Reverse gear selection position is achieved by overcoming a spring loaded plunger which bears on the base of the gear shift lever at the end of the remote control housing.

2. Routine Maintenance

1. Apart from checking the oil level in the gearbox every 5,000 miles the manufacturers state that draining and refilling with fresh

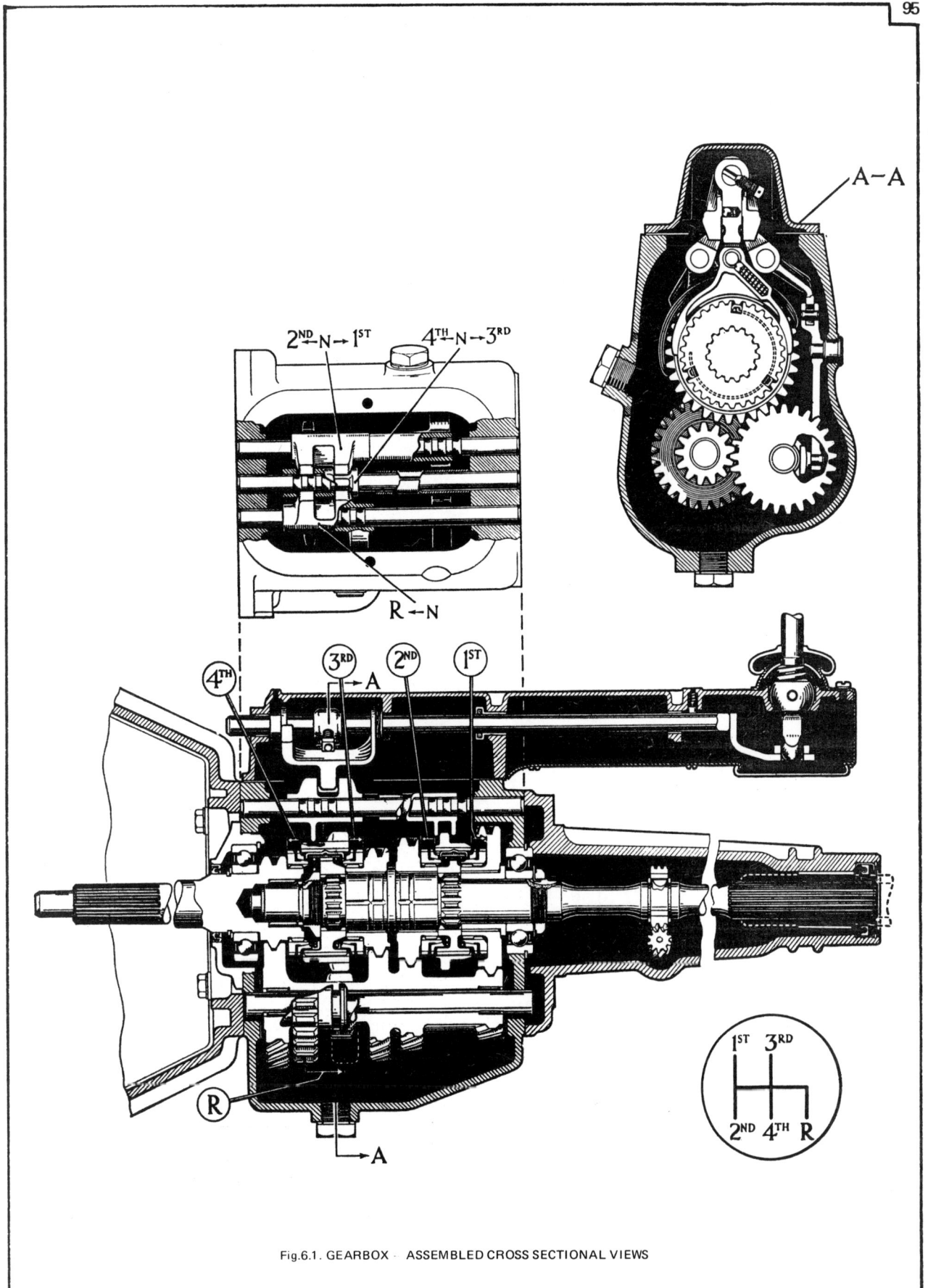

Fig.6.1. GEARBOX · ASSEMBLED CROSS SECTIONAL VIEWS

Fig. 6.2. GEARBOX – EXPLODED VIEW

1 Casing
2 Filler level plug
3 Washer
4 Drain plug
5 Washer
6 Front cover
7 Oil seal
8 Gasket
9 Rear extension cover
10 Bush
11 Oil seal
12 Circlip
13 Gasket
14 Input shaft
15 Needle rollers
16 Spacer
17 Bearing
18 Oil shield
19 Spacer ring
20 Circlip

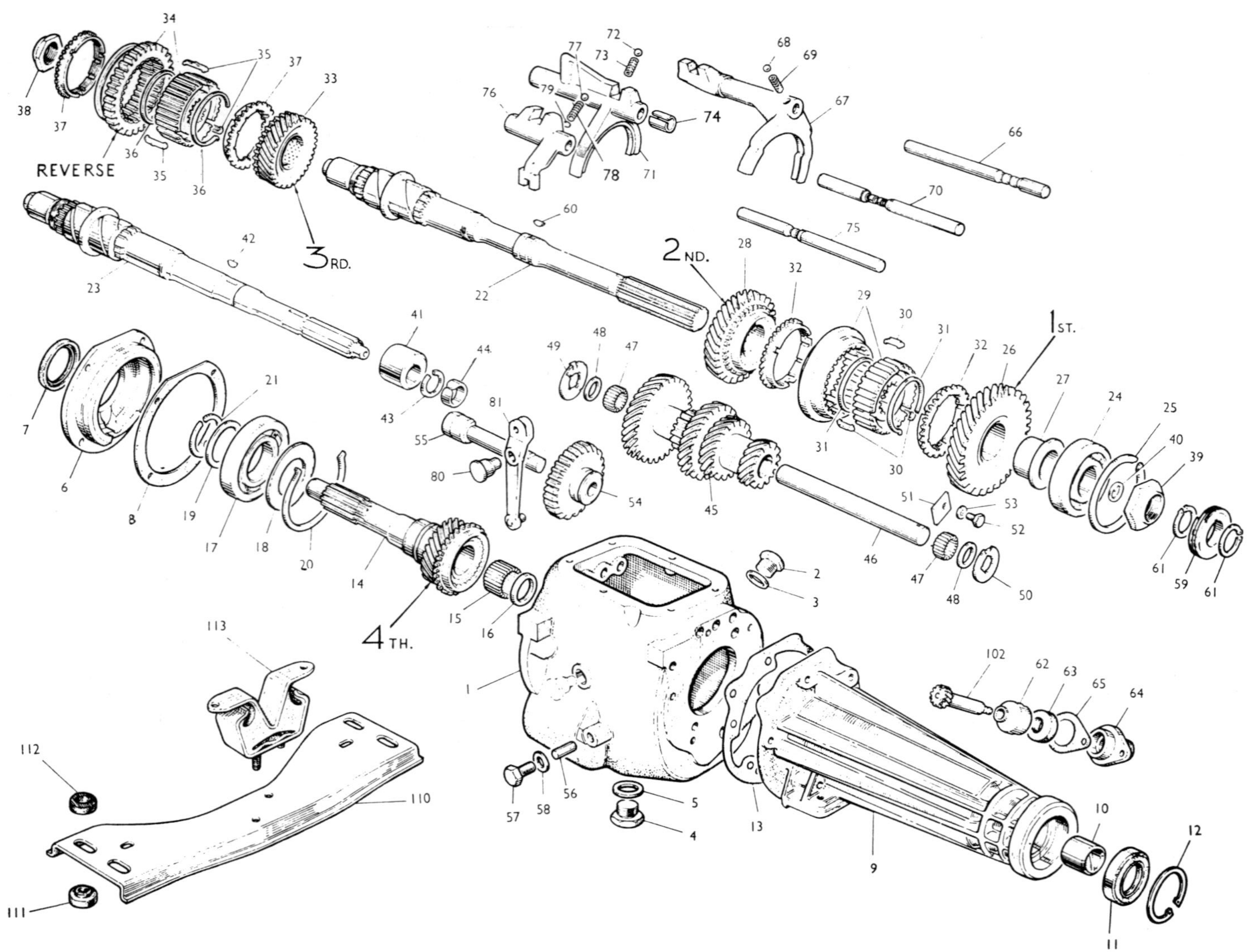

21 Circlip
22 Mainshaft
23 Overdrive mainshaft
24 Bearing (mainshaft)
25 Circlip
26 1st gear
27 Boss
28 2nd gear
29 Synchro-hub assembly 1st/2nd gear
30 Blocker bar
31 Retaining clip
32 Baulk ring
33 3rd gear
34 Synchro-hub assembly 3rd/4th gear
35 Blocker bar
36 Retaining clip
37 Baulk ring
38 Nut mainshaft front
39 Nut mainshaft rear
40 Lock washer
41 Cam, overdrive oil pump
42 Woodruff key
43 Circlip
44 Retaining ring
45 Lay gear
46 Lay shaft
47 Needle rollers
48 Retaining ring
49 Thrust washer - front
50 Thrust washer - rear
51 Locking plate
52 Bolt
53 Washer
54 Reverse idler gear
55 Reverse idler gear shaft
56 Locking pin
57 Screw
58 Washer
59 Speedometer - drive wheel
60 Woodruff key
61 Circlip
62 Speedometer - pinion bearing
63 Seal
64 Cable adaptor
65 Gasket

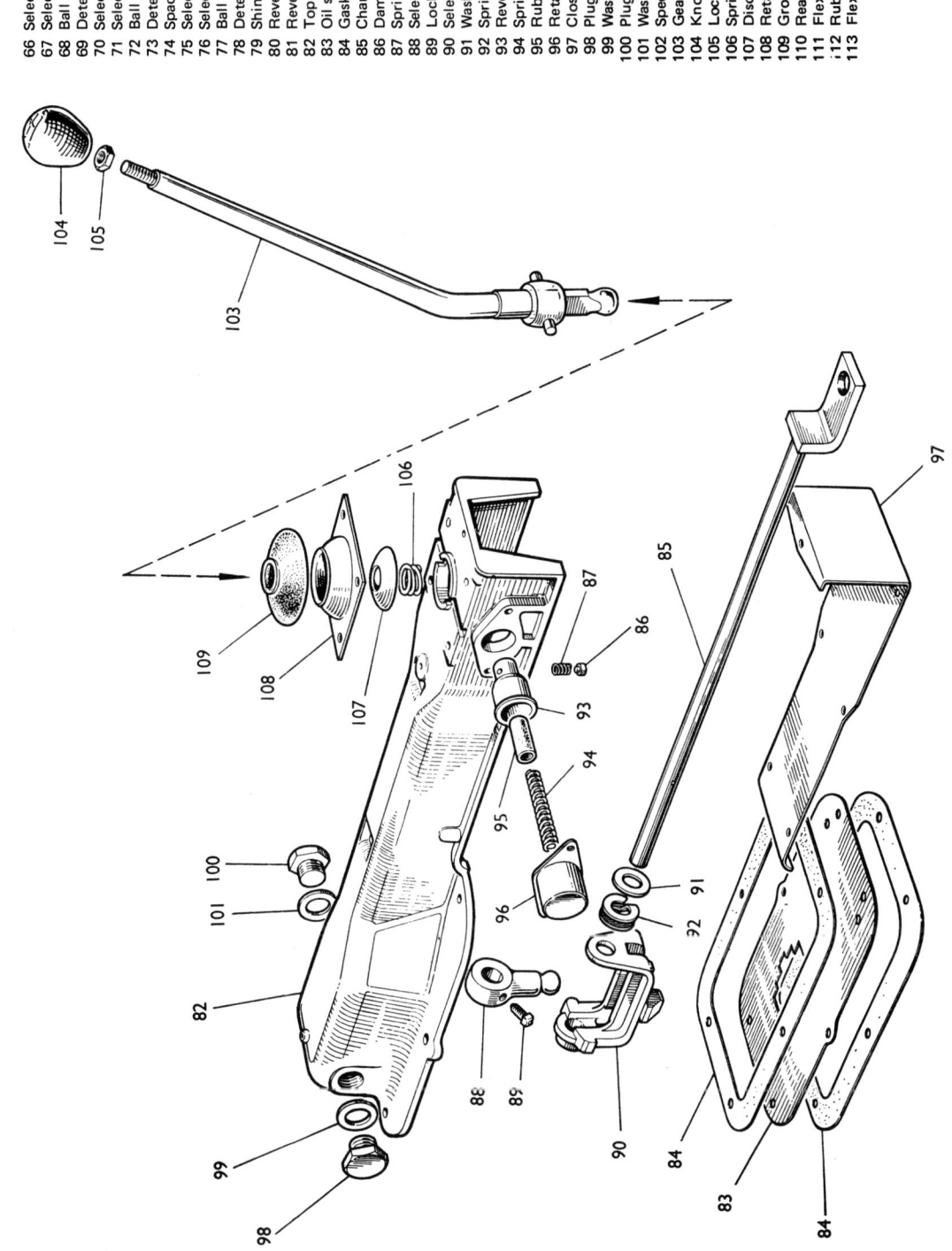

66 Selector rail 1st/2nd gear
67 Selector fork 1st/2nd gear
68 Ball
69 Detent spring
70 Selector rail 3rd/4th gear
71 Selector fork 3rd/4th gear
72 Ball
73 Detent spring
74 Spacer sleeve
75 Selector rail reverse
76 Selector fork reverse
77 Ball
78 Detent spring
79 Shim
80 Reverse lever pivot pin
81 Reverse lever
82 Top cover
83 Oil shield
84 Gasket
85 Change shaft
86 Damper pad
87 Spring
88 Selector lever
89 Locking screw
90 Selector safety catch
91 Washer
92 Spring washer
93 Reverse stop plunger
94 Spring
95 Rubber sleeve
96 Retainer
97 Closing plate
98 Plug - reverse light switch hole
99 Washer
100 Plug - overdrive switch hole
101 Washer
102 Speedometer driving pinion
103 Gear change lever
104 Knob
105 Locknut
106 Spring
107 Disc
108 Retaining cap
109 Grommet
110 Rear mounting cross member
111 Flexible insulator
112 Rubber collar
113 Flexible mounting

Fig. 6.3. GEARBOX TOP COVER AND GEARSHIFT (EXPLODED VIEW)

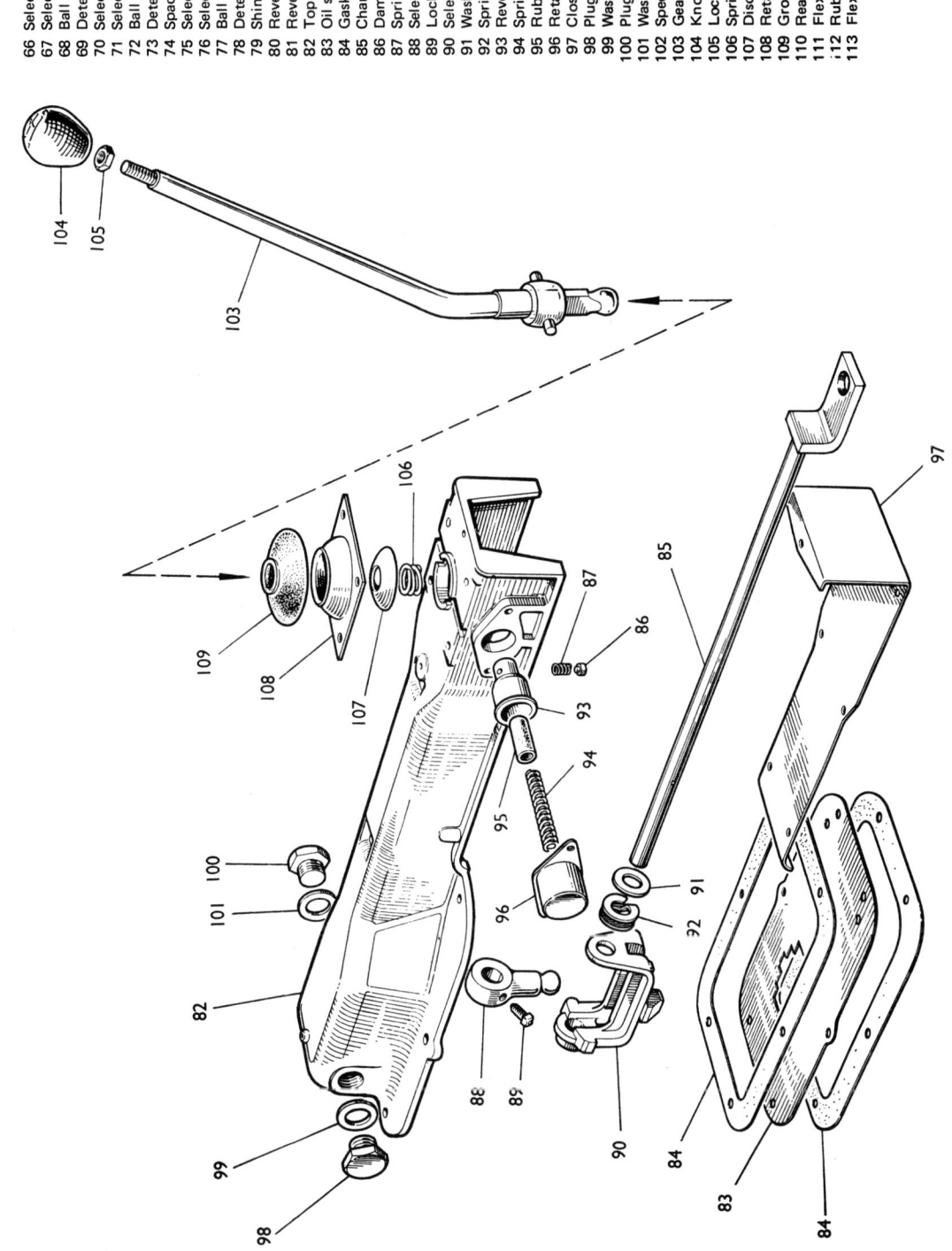

oil is only necessary at intervals of 30,000 miles.

2. To check the oil level in the gearbox the car should be stood on level ground and the filler and level plug, which is mounted on the right hand side of the gearbox casing, removed. A quantity of the correct specification oil should be added until it overflows from the filler hole. In cold weather it may be necessary to wait a little time for this to be seen. Do not overfill the box in such instances otherwise additional internal pressure will be built up when running which may burst oil seals or at least force oil past them.

3. To drain and replenish the gearbox oil first run the car for sufficient time to enable the warmth of the engine to transmit to the gearbox and allow the oil to thin down a little. Then stand the car on level ground and remove both the filler and drain plugs. Allow at least fifteen minutes to drain and then replace the drain plug, preferably with a new washer, and refill with the correct oil to the level plug hole.

3. Gearbox - Removal and Replacement

1. The gearbox may be removed together with the engine in which case the instructions to do this are given in Chapter 1.

2. If the gearbox is being removed on its own, time spent on initial preparation work in raising and supporting the car will be amply repaid later. Ideally, of course, the car would be raised on a hoist or ramp or put over a pit but as most owners will not have this facility, they must certainly acquire a set of four chassis stands to support the car as high as possible safely. The maximum possible clearance between the car and the ground should be obtained to provide the easiest possible access and manoeuvring space for two people when the gearbox is eventually lowered to the ground.

3. Disconnect the battery leads, drain the cooling system and drain the oil from the gearbox. Disconnect the top radiator hose from the engine so that when the engine is tilted it will not be strained.

4. Remove the four bolts securing the rear of the propeller shaft to the pinion flange. Lower it and withdraw it from the gearbox rear extension cover.

5. Unscrew the knob from the gear lever and take out the screws securing the front of the console panel. Pull out the ashtray and remove the two screws inside holding the rear of the console. Lift off the console and disconnect any switch wires, noting their connections and colours.

6. Slide the rubber boot from the base up the lever and take it off.

7. Four setscrews holding the spring retaining cap onto the top of the remote change casing will now be visible and should be removed. This will release the gear lever assembly which can be lifted straight up out of the box.

8. If a reversing light or overdrive is fitted the connecting wire should be detached.

9. It is necessary to detach the centre track rod of the steering gear from the drop arm and slave arm connections. This is so that the bellhousing is not obstructed when the gearbox is drawn back. The centre track rod will still be connected to the outer track rods but it will be possible to drop it the necessary 3 to 4 inches. For details of disconnecting the ball joint pins refer to Chapter 11.

10 On models fitted with steel sumps remove the two brace rods which bolt to the bellhousing and sump flange.

11 Remove the clutch hydraulic cylinder mounting bolts and move the cylinder to one side. The hydraulic system need not be disturbed.

12 For steel sump models, remove the bottom bolts in the bellhousing (which secure the cover plate) and take off the cover plate. On aluminium sump models the bolts hold the sump casting itself to the bellhousing.

13 Remove the starter motor bolts and draw it forward clear of the housing. It may rest alongside the engine if tied with a piece of string to hold it in place.

14 Detach the speedometer drive cable from the rear extension cover by unscrewing the knurled union nut.

15 So that the gearbox may be drawn off the engine the engine has to

be tilted backwards and this is achieved when the rear supporting crossmember is removed. Before removing this however the engine must be supported on a jack which will keep the degree of tilt under control. The head of the jack should be placed under the rear edge of the crankcase on the sump mounting flange (steel sumps) if possible, or otherwise as near the rear of the sump as possible. Put a piece of wood between the jack and sump to spread the load. This latter method applies anyway to engines with aluminium sumps. The crossmember may then be removed by undoing the four rubber bushed mounting bolts - two at each end.

16 Carefully lower the jack so that the engine tilts sufficiently to enable the gearbox to come off when the remainder of the bell-housing bolts are removed. Watch the front of the engine to see that the sump does not foul the anti-roll bar; although when sufficiently tilted the engine may be chocked with wood against the roll bar.

17 The remainder of the bolts holding the bellhousing to the engine may now be removed and the gearbox should be free to move.

18 Two people at least are needed to support the weight of the gearbox. If they are lying underneath the car it is a wise precaution to place some soft padding such as sacks underneath the gearbox. Then, if the weight is suddenly too much it will not be damaged if it falls a bit quick! Whatever else may happen do **not** tilt the gearbox or heave it from side to side whilst it is still mated to the clutch assembly. This could cause strain and damage to the gearbox input shaft or clutch cover.

19 Replacement of the gearbox is a reversal of the removal procedure but the following points have to be borne in mind.

a) The clutch friction disc must be properly centred if the clutch assembly has been disturbed (Chapter 5 refers).

b) The propeller shaft should be replaced so that the mating flanges line up in the same position.

c) Do not forget to replace the oil.

4. Gearbox - Dismantling

1. Before any dismantling begins thoroughly clean off the gearbox exterior with paraffin or a proprietary solvent. This will keep the working area clean and minimise the possibility of dirt and grit being transferred from the exterior to the interior.

2. Next remove the top cover (which incorporates the remote change mechanism) by undoing the six bolts which hold it to the top of the gearbox casing. The oil shield plate underneath should then be lifted off.

3. The clutch thrust release bearing and arm should now be detached as described in Chapter 5. The bellhousing may next be separated from the gearbox casing by undoing the six bolts and washers inside the bellhousing.

4. The mainshaft extension cover is next removed and to do this, first remove the two setscrews holding the speedometer drive gear mechanism to the side of the cover. With these removed the whole assembly may be drawn out. Then undo the bolts holding the extension cover to the rear of the gear casing and draw it off. If wished, the mounting crossmember may be separated from it but it is not essential.

5. The selector rails and forks are next to be dismantled and the first thing to note is that the rails must be driven out from the front towards the rear. Also one should have available dummy selector rails made from $1/16$ inch rod (11 mm). These are used to retain the detent balls and springs in the selector forks when the rail proper is driven out. Otherwise the ball could fly out and get lost. Three shafts are needed, 2 x 2.9 inch (73.6 mm) long and one 4.95 inch (125.7 mm) long. On some models the 3rd/4th selector fork (the one on the centre rail has a long integral boss instead of a spacer tube and for these two long and one short dummy rail are required. Using the dummy shafts drive out the selector rails from the front of the casing starting with the reverse selector rail (the left one). Leave the dummies in position after the rails have been driven out and then lift out the selector forks.

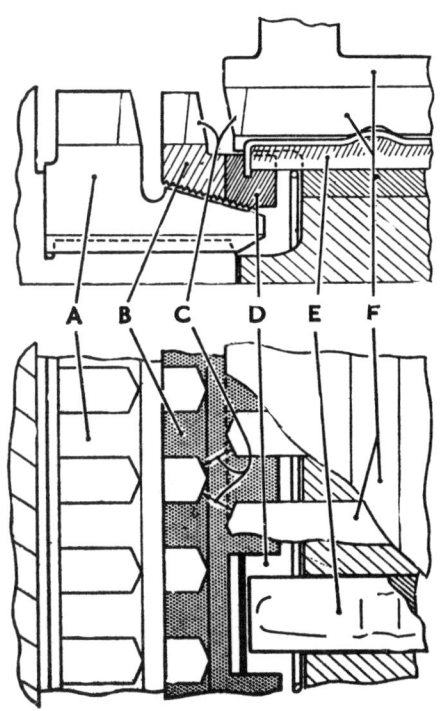

Fig. 6.4. SYNCHRO HUB, CROSS SECTION OF BLOCKER
BARS AND BAULK RINGS TO SHOW OPERATION

A Gear wheel dogs
B Baulk ring
C Sliding sleeve and baulk ring dog teeth faces
D Baulk ring cut-outs
E Blocker bars
F Sliding sleeve

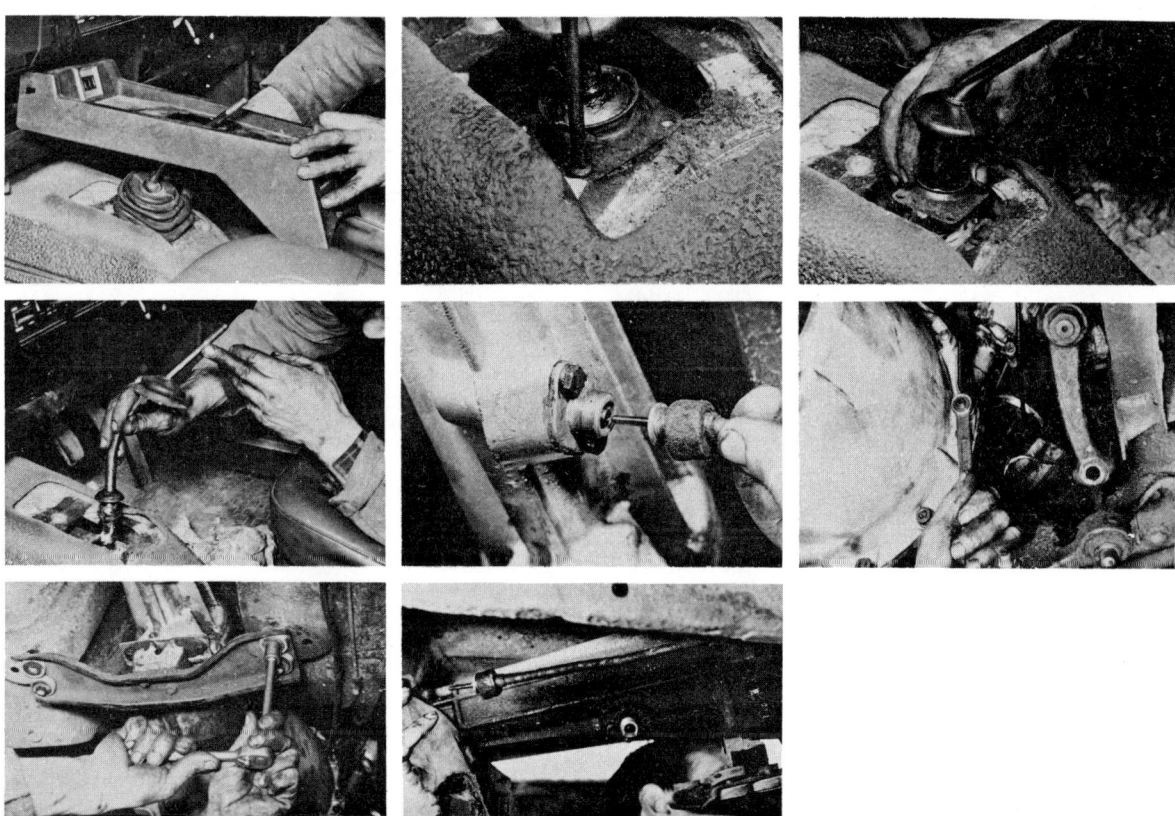

SECTION 3. Removal of console, lever, speedo cable, bellhousing bolts and rear mounting crossmember.

6. The next step is to remove the layshaft so that the laygear cluster may be lowered to the bottom of the box. A dummy shaft will certainly be needed for reassembly so it is best to use it also for dismantling. It should be made from ¾ inch (18 mm) diameter bar or tube and be 6½ inches (165 mm) long. A piece of electrical conduit pipe was used on the occasion when the photographs were taken. First remove the bolt and washer holding the locking plate into the groove at the rear of the casing. Using the dummy layshaft drive the layshaft out from the front of the box. Provided the dummy shaft has not been made too long it will fit flush with the ends of the laygear and permit it to drop the inch or so to the bottom of the casing.

7. If the four nuts (or setscrews) holding the front cover to the casing are now taken out the input shaft, bearing and front cover can all be withdrawn from the casing. The counter bore end of the input shaft houses 23 needle rollers and a spacer ring and these should be taken out now and kept in a suitable container where they will not be lost. The baulk ring on the 3rd/4th synchro hub for 4th gear will now be free to lift off the end of the mainshaft assembly. Ideally, its position should be noted so that the cut-outs will relate to the same hub blocker bars on replacement.

8. The mainshaft assembly is removed through the front of the casing. First remove the two circlips which hold the nylon worm gear for the speedometer in position. Then use the jaw of a large open-ended spanner and a hammer to drive the gear off the shoulder of the shaft rearwards. Remove and retain safely the Woodruff key. To undo the mainshaft nut the shaft will have to be held firm. It can be locked in the box by engaging two gears at once, i.e. sliding the forward hub back on to 3rd gear and the rear hub on to either 1st or 2nd. Alternatively, the shaft can be gripped in the soft metal covered jaws of a vice but help will be needed to support the weight of the casing if this is done. If a lockwasher is fitted bend back the tab and with a suitably large spanner undo the nut and take it and the washer off the shaft. The front end of the mainshaft should now be supported with one hand and the shaft driven forward with a mallet through the rear bearing which will remain where it is. As soon as the shaft is free it can be fed through the front of the casing but 1st gear and its centre bush will have to be slid off the back of the shaft as they are too large to go through the hole. Do not drop them!

9. With the mainshaft assembly removed lift up the laygear from the bottom of the box keeping it horizontal so that the needle rollers in the ends do not fall out unintentionally. Take out also the two thrust washers located one at each end of the laygear between it and the casing.

10 The mainshaft bearing can now be driven out of the casing from the inside using a suitable drift.

11 The reverse idler gear and operating lever do not normally need removal as they rarely cause trouble being comparatively little used. However, if it is necessary a spacer will have to be made. Remove the operating lever and the screw and spindle locking pin from the side of the casing. Then make up a 'U' shaped spacer from some 3/16 flat strip. It should be 5/8 inch (16 mm) long and radiused to fit round the smaller diameter of the idler shaft. The gear can then butt the spacer up to the larger diameter shoulder at the front end of the shaft. Use a brass drift through the rear of the casing placed near the centre of the gear and drive the shaft forward out of the casing. The gearbox is now completely stripped into main assemblies.

5. Gearbox - Examination of Main Assemblies

1 The gearbox has presumably been dismantled because of one of the faults listed under Fault Finding in Section 9. To rectify faulty synchromesh, gear jumping and other operative faults is usually straightforward enough although if total quietness is also demanded it is virtually impossible to guarantee it without renewing everything. Worn gears will still work but not quietly. Examine the input shaft bearing for signs of sloppiness or roughness - it is usually the first component to wear. In any case it is worthwhile fitting a new one

while the box is stripped. Examine the mainshaft bearing similarly.

2 There are four baulk rings, one each side of the two synchroniser hub assemblies but only one of these (for 4th gear) can be renewed without dismantling the mainshaft. The critical wear occurs in the three cut-outs where the blocker bars engage and is difficult to measure unless in comparison with a new one. As a general guide it is worthwhile replacing all four baulk rings anyway and certainly if the synchromesh is at fault.

3 The hubs themselves should be gripped (by hand) and twisted to see if the outer sliding sleeve moves rotationally in relation to the hub. If it does the splines between the hub and sleeve are worn and the whole hub assembly needs renewal.

4 All gears should be examined for signs of chipped teeth and extraordinary wear. They should also be a smooth sliding fit on the shaft and not rock at all.

5 The nose of the mainshaft, which engages in the needle rollers in the counter bore of the input shaft, should be examined for signs of pitting or ridging. If such signs are apparent the only cure is a new mainshaft. Examine the needle rollers also for signs of wear or pitting and renew them all if one looks bad.

6 The layshaft gears should be examined for chipping or extreme wear. The shaft itself may show signs of wear at the ends where the gear runs on the needle roller bearings. If there is severe pitting or ridging then the layshaft should be renewed and new needle roller bearings fitted. The thrust washers at the ends of the laygear should be renewed as a matter of course. The selector mechanism should also come in for some careful examination. Examine the forks to see that they are not worn where they guide the hub sleeve. The 3rd/4th selector runs in a groove in the hub and there should be no play between the hub groove and fork. The 1st/2nd selector fork is grooved to engage and land on the hub and here again there should be no play between the two. An impositive 'feel' in gear changing or jumping out of gear could be caused by insufficient pressure being exerted by the detent springs on the balls when engaged in the selector rail grooves. This can be tested by gripping the selector fork in a soft jawed vice and temporarily replacing the appropriate rail. A suitable clamp and hook should be fitted to the end of the rail so that a pull scale can be attached. The force necessary to pull the rail groove across the ball should be between 25-35 lbs. for forward gears and 40-45 lbs. for reverse. The spring loading can be varied by adding or removing shims underneath the detent spring in the fork. This effectively tensions or relaxes the spring as necessary. If there are signs of wear on the rails or balls they should be renewed; as should any broken springs, of course.

7 Examine the gear casing for any signs of damage or cracks.

8 To summarize, if the gearbox is being dismantled it is worthwhile renewing the following items as a matter of course. (The gaskets are essential.)

Input and mainshaft bearings (2).
Baulk rings (4).
Laygear thrust washers (2).
Gaskets including cover oil seals (set).
Circlips and mainshaft nuts.

9 If there are many other components in an obviously tired condition one must weigh up the advantages of replacing many parts (and ending up with a less than perfect gearbox) against obtaining a fully reconditioned unit on exchange.

6. Gearbox - Input Shaft Bearing - Removal & Replacement

1 The bearing is held into the front cover by a large internal circlip, the ends of which fit in a cut-out in the cover. Remove the circlip. If the edge of the cover is carefully supported between vice jaws, gear facing downwards, the shaft can be driven down with a mallet and the bearing and shaft together will come out of the cover. Next remove the external circlips round the shaft in front of the bearing and the abutment washer behind it. Then support the

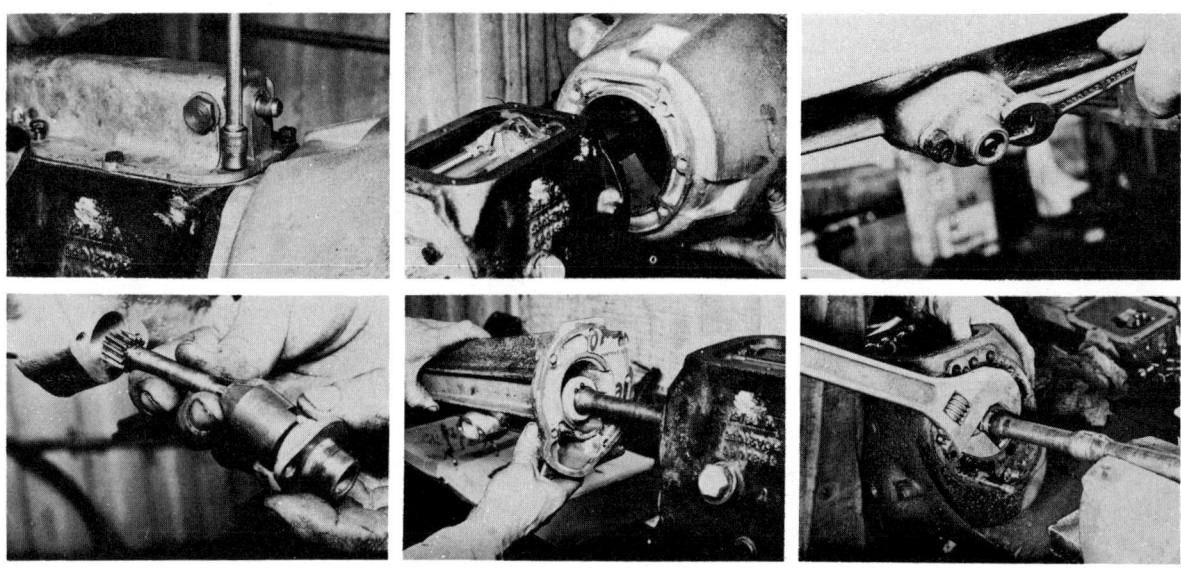

SECTION 4. Removal of top cover, bellhousing, speedo drive, rear cover and main shaft unit.

SECTION 7. Levering the synchro hub assemblies off the main shaft and (right) mainshaft held in vice ready for reassembly.

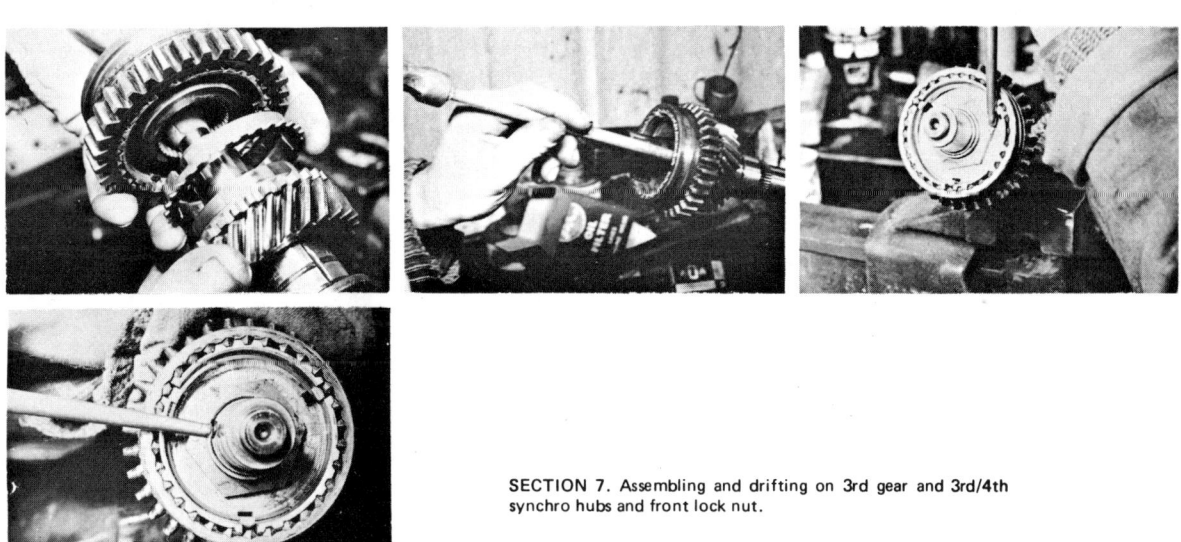

SECTION 7. Assembling and drifting on 3rd gear and 3rd/4th synchro hubs and front lock nut.

bearing on the vice jaws, making sure that the gear teeth are not fouling them and drive the shaft out downwards from the bearing. Remove the shield plate from behind the bearing. Refitting the bearing to the input shaft is a reversal of the removal method. Place the shield over the shaft first and then place the shaft into the bearing. Support the bearing on the **inner** race across the soft clad vice jaws and drive the shaft into it with a mallet. Do not close the vice jaws too far or they will catch the shoulder on the shaft. Make sure the bearing is driven on right up to the limit of the shoulder.

2   The abutment washer comes in one of two thicknesses, .054-.056 inch or .058-.060 inch and the larger of the two should be fitted, if it will go between the bearing and circlip. A new circlip should also be used.

3   It is wise to renew the front cover oil seal also before refitting the bearing and shaft. Drive out the old one from the inside using a suitable punch. Fit the new one in square so that the flexible lip faces the bearing. The shaft and bearing may now be driven into the cover. One note of caution here. There are occasions when the lip of the oil seal stubbornly refuses to go onto the seal land on the shaft but sticks on the shoulder before reaching it, thus forcing the inner part of the seal back. This is no good as the seal will soon wear out and leak. To guide the lip of the seal onto the land a tube made up of flexible shim steel will be needed to put round inside the seal and over the shaft land. This can then be withdrawn after the bearing is fully home inside the front cover.

Refit the large circlip locking the bearing and shaft into the cover.

7. Gearbox Mainshaft - Dismantling and Reassembly

1. The difficult parts to shift on the mainshaft are the two synchro hub assemblies which are the only items now left to remove. They are a splined press fit onto the shaft. They have to be moved by pressure as opposed to striking. If no press equipment is handy two long levers with lipped ends (tyre levers) are essential. It is best also to try and avoid dismantling them unless it is absolutely necessary. If they do happen to fly apart, it will be impossible to know where each blocker bar came from and how the splines were mated. It will not mean that the hub is useless but wear will be accelerated when unmatched surfaces come together on reassembly. For those who wish to inspect the hubs in detail, information is given at the end of this Section.

2. Grip the plain section of the tail end of the shaft in the padded jaws of a vice so that the two hub assemblies are tilted upwards. To remove the front nut requires a large socket or tubular spanner. If none is available cut a nick near one of the corners of the nut and undo it with a steel drift and hammer. The locking ring is peened into the groove but this will automatically come away when the nut turns. If this locking ring is seriously chewed up when the nut is removed a new one should be obtained to ensure safe locking up when reassembled.

3. With the nut removed the two levers should be placed between the 2nd and 3rd gear wheels which is where the dividing shoulder on the shaft is located. Leverage will force the 3rd gear and hub one way and/or the 2nd gear and hub the other. Further leverage can be then obtained between the shoulder and the gear. Each hub assembly, followed by the gear wheel, can then be taken off. The main shaft is then completely stripped.

4. If a hub assembly is suspected of being worn and is to be dismantled, first mark with a coloured wax crayon or a small dab of paint, the relative positions of the hub and outer sleeve and each blocker bar to its groove in the hub. Then slide the outer sleeve off the hub and the blocker bars and spring circlips will fall free. Then replace the sleeve on the hub. It should slide freely but with no other movement possible. The internal teeth on the sliding sleeve should have flat faces and be free from grooves or ridges. The blocker bars should be identical in length and top profile. The blocker bar circlips should not show signs of wear where they rest on the edges of the bars and the turned over end should not touch the inner face of the bar (see Fig. 6.5). If it does, carefully grind a little off. When

reassembling the hub fit the circlips so that when viewed from their own side the hooked end is at the anti-clockwise tail of the clip. Do not put both hooked ends into the same blocker bar. If a hub is badly worn the whole assembly should be renewed, bearing in mind, of course, the overall condition of the gearbox.

5. Reassemble the mainshaft by first clamping it in a vice by the plain section of the rear end, using soft jaws in the vice. Third gear should then be placed over the nose of the shaft. (3rd gear is the smallest of the three gears on the mainshaft - top gear is on the input shaft.) The helical tooth part of the gear abuts the shoulder on the shaft. Then place a baulk ring over the gear cone, making sure that it is the right type. (The two rings on the 3rd/4th hub are different from those on the 1st/2nd hub.) The hub assembly is next put on with the selector fork groove of the outer sleeve towards the nose of the shaft. This will be a drive fit onto the splines and two things have to be carefully watched. You do not want the thing to fly apart when putting it on so when driving it on with a drift hit the centre of the boss only. At the same time keep an eye on the baulk ring to make sure the three cut-outs line up on the blocker bars of the hub when it is driven fully home. The large front nut should next be fitted. Strictly speaking, a new one should be used because the old self locking ring will almost certainly line up with the used part once more against the groove. However, it is known for them to be re-used provided the locking ring is not severely disturbed on removal. The nut should be tightened to a torque of 80 lbs/ft. and the locking ring staked into the groove. If you have to tighten up using a hammer and drift, use a 2 lbs. hammer and take it as far as it will go.

6. Remove the mainshaft from the vice and support it vertically in the jaws, tail end upwards clamping the nose between soft jaw plates. 2nd gear is fitted next (the middle size of the three), placed with the helical teeth abutting the shoulder. Place a baulk ring over the cone of the gear wheel. Just like the 3rd/4th hub this one has to be driven on to the splines and thus should be done with the drift against the centre hub only. Note also that the selector fork land of the outer sleeve is next to the 2nd gear wheel.

8. Rear Cover - Removal and Refitting of Oil Seal

The rear cover oil seal should be renewed if the gearbox is dismantled and of course **must** be if it is obviously leaking. It is possible to do this job with the gearbox still in the car after removing the propeller shaft. First take out the circlip which retains it (if fitted). There are three ways of getting the old seal out. If you can borrow a proper extractor tool it can be drawn out quite easily with the gearbox on or off the car. If not, then it can be driven out with a long drift against the inside of the seal provided, of course, that the rear cover is removed from the gearbox. This may also be done with the gearbox still in the car but will involve removal of the propeller shaft, speedometer drive gear and the rear support crossmember first. The third method is to cut the old seal away from the outside with a cold chisel. This method will require great care to avoid damaging the bore of the case where the seal fits. The new seal should be driven in firmly and square, open side inwards, with a suitably sized drift, such as an old piston (as was used in the photographs).

9. Gearbox - Assembly

1. Before assembly begins, make sure that every part is perfectly clean, including the interior of the casing and that a supply of clean oil, grease and the necessary new parts and gaskets are available. A proprietary jointing compound should also be handy as all gaskets should be coated with it on fitting.

2. Check first that the endfloat of the lay gear is correct. Place the two thrust washers in position so that the pips fit the cut-outs in the casing. Put the laygear in position (without the shaft) between them and measure the gap between the end of the gear and the face of a

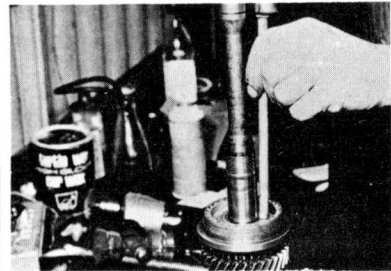

SECTION 7. Assembling and drifting on 2nd gear and 1st/2nd synchro hub assembly.

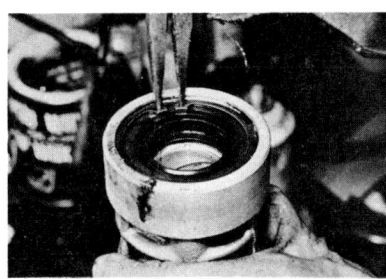

SECTION 8. Removal and refitting of oil seal in rear cover.

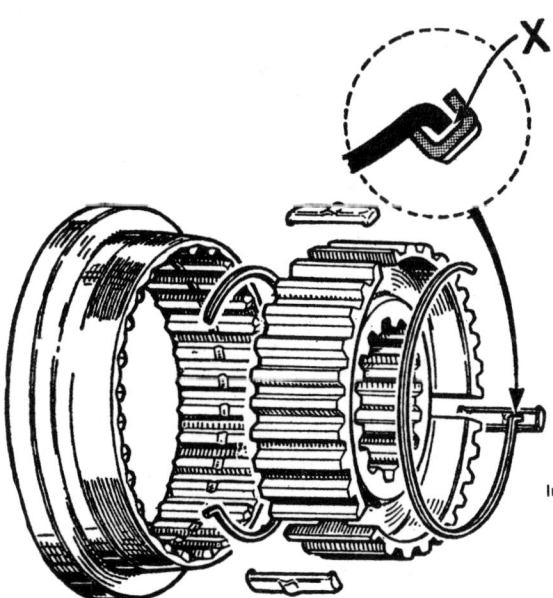

X

Fig.6.5. SYNCHRO HUB — EXPLODED VIEW
Inset Gap 'X' which should exist between the end of the retaining
clip and recess in the blocker bar.

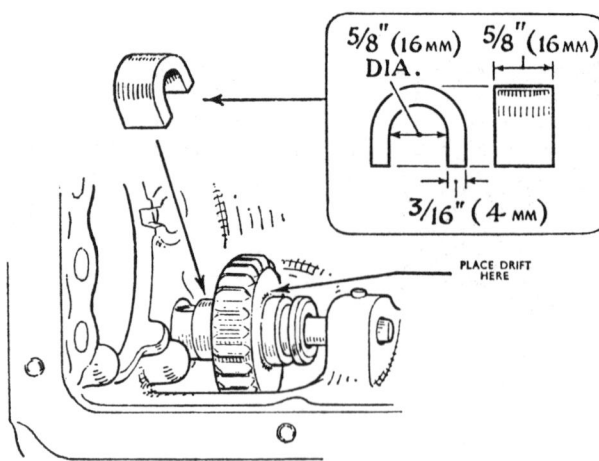

5/8" (16 MM) 5/8" (16 MM)
DIA.

3/16" (4 MM)

PLACE DRIFT HERE

Fig. 6.6. REVERSE IDLER GEAR
Drawing showing dimensions of spacer required to drift out the shaft.

SECTION 9. Fitting mainshaft bearing into casing.

SECTION 9. Reverse idler gear and selector in position.

SECTION 9. Fitting needle rollers, spacers, dummy layshaft, into laygear and then into gearbox casing.

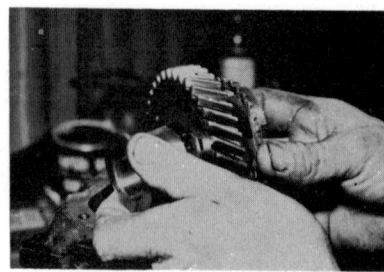
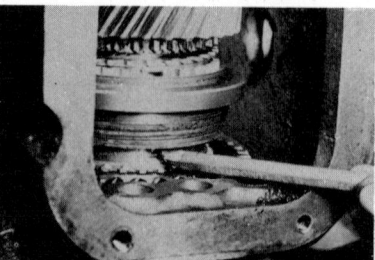

SECTION 9. Preparing 1st gear boss and baulk ring followed by assembly of main shaft into box ensuring that the baulk ring cut-outs are lined up with the synchro hubs.

SECTION 9. Fitting needle rollers into the input shaft. Spacer and baulk ring onto the main shaft.

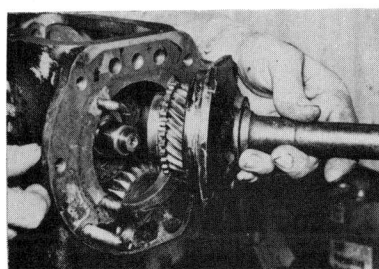

SECTION 9. Replacing and securing input shaft to gearbox.

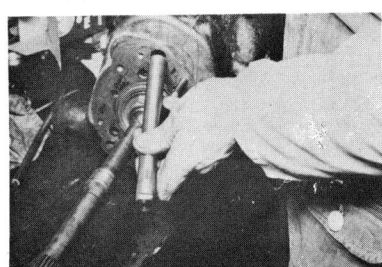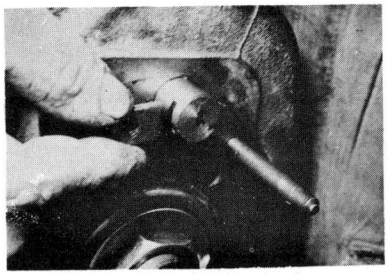

SECTION 9. Fitting and securing the layshaft.

SECTION 9. Placing in order, selector forks 1st/2nd, 3rd/4th, and reverse.

thrust washer with a feeler gauge. It should be between .006 - .008 inch (.15 - .20 mm) and if necessary a front thrust washer of a different thickness may be obtained from a Rootes/Chrysler parts store.

3. Fit the mainshaft bearing into the casing before anything else. First the circlip should be fitted into the outer race and the bearing tapped square into the casing. The **wider** part of the race (the circlip is off centre) goes into the casing.

4. Begin assembling by fitting the reverse idler gear assembly so that the flat on the smaller end of the shaft will engage with the pin in the interior supporting lug in the casing. Replace the operating lever with the pin in the groove of the gearwheel.

5. The laygear should now be prepared by fitting the 27 needle rollers into each end, holding them in position with thick grease. Then put the spacer ring on top of the rollers and put the dummy shaft into position in the gear. Put the cluster into the gearbox with the larger gear towards the front and let it rest on the bottom. At the same time position the thrust washers at each end so that they line up as near as possible with the layshaft holes in the casing. They should be fitted so that the pips locate in the cut-outs in the casing and if smeared with grease they will not move around. In subsequent operations care should be taken not to disturb them. If they move out of line from the shaft holes too far it may be impossible to position them again when the time arrives to fit the layshaft. And that is one of the last things to be done.

6. The mainshaft can now be put into the casing from the front, tail end first. Get first gear with its centre boss and baulk ring ready and when the end of the mainshaft is inside the box put the baulk ring on first, cut-out side towards the hub, followed by the gear wheel and boss. The gear wheel cone side goes towards the baulk ring and the flange of the boss is towards the tail end of the shaft. The mainshaft can then be put through the bearing in the casing.

7. The whole gearbox should now be carefully positioned over the vice jaws so that the mainshaft bearing is supported by the jaws and the rear of the mainshaft points downwards. The shaft is then driven downwards with a mallet and at the same time an eye must be kept on the 1st/2nd synchro hub and 1st gear baulk ring. As the gap between the gear and rear bearing diminishes the baulk ring must be positioned so that the three cut-outs line up with the blocker bars in the hub. If the fit of the shaft into the bearing is not too tight the final positioning may be done more easily with the gearbox horizontal once again on the bench. (Watch that the bearing is not inadvertently driven back out of the casing!)

8. The mainshaft locking unit can now be fitted. First fit the lock-washer and then run the nut up to it. Check once again that the first gear baulk ring is properly located and that the bearing circlip is fully up to the casing. Do not tighten the nut fully at this stage.

9. The gearbox is now ready to receive the input shaft assembly. First place the spacer ring over the nose of the mainshaft with the chamfered edge inwards, followed by the last of the four baulk rings which goes on to the front of the 3rd/4th hub. The three cut-outs should engage with the blocker bars. A little dab of grease will help to hold it in position until the input shaft is fitted.

10 The counter bore of the input shaft should be smeared with thick grease and the 23 needle rollers put into position. Then place a new gasket in position on the cover having smeared on both sides with jointing compound to ensure an oil tight seal. The assembly should then be located on the nose of the mainshaft engaging the front cover over the four studs in the casing. The flat on the front cover should be horizontal at the upper edge so that the oil drain hole in the casing is at the lower edge. Replace the nuts and tighten them up fully.

11 Now is the time to fit the layshaft. First make sure that the thrust washers are in position and then carefully turn the box upside down so that the lay gear drops into mesh with the mainshaft gears and input shaft. Make final adjustments to the position of the thrust washers and then insert the layshaft from the rear of the gear casing, plain end leading. Carefully tap it through the lay gear, driving the dummy shaft ahead. Do **not** pull the dummy shaft out

ahead of the layshaft. If a single needle roller were to move out of position it could be a considerable fiddle getting it back into position again. As soon as the layshaft is home line up the locking slot so that the locking plate and bolt can be fitted and tightened.

12 The mainshaft nut can now be tightened to 80 lbs/ft. of torque. If a suitable torque spanner is not available full force on a 129 shifter will be adequate. The mainshaft can be locked, whilst tightening the nut, by locking both synchro hubs on to two gears at the same time. Otherwise the mainshaft should be manoeuvred so that it can be clamped in the vice whilst the weight of the gearbox is still supported properly. Move the hubs to neutral when finished. Punch the lockwasher onto a flat of the nut when fully tightened. Give the mainshaft a spin to ensure that everything is revolving freely and smoothly.

13 Next refit the speedometer drive gear inner circlip and Woodruff key. Drive on the gear with an open ended spanner jaw and fit the second circlip.

14 The selectors are fitted next. Provided dummy rails have been used no difficulty need be experienced. First fit the 3rd/4th selector fork in position (this is the one with the groove in the fork) then the 1st/2nd fork and finally the reverse selector, fitting the small forked arm over the pin on the reverse operating lever.

15 The rails are fitted next starting with the 1st/2nd gear selector rail. This is the one with the three detents nearest the end of the rail and should be tapped in from the rear of the casing with the long plain section leading. The dummy rail will be driven ahead.

16 The 3rd/4th gear selector rail goes next in the centre. This rail has three detents nearer the centre than the 1st/2nd rail and should be pushed in with the shorter plain section first. As soon as it is through the casing fit the sleeve over the end (if there is one) and then continue driving it through the fork. Once again the dummy rail will be driven ahead of it.

17 Finally insert the reverse selector rail, being the one with only two detents. The shorter plain section goes in first from the rear of the casing.

18 When all rails are fitted the ends should be flush with the casing. With the gears in neutral the cut-outs in the tops of the forks should line up with each other.

19 For those who have decided not to use dummy rails the appropriate shims and springs should be placed in the hole in the fork. The ball can then be held to the end of a suitable rod with a blob of grease and put into position and pressed down whilst the rail proper is moved forward to trap it. A steady hand and some patience are needed here and it must also be remembered that if a ball, with a blob of grease attached, is dropped into the box it might just stick in an awkward place and be very difficult to shake out. If this should happen remove the springs and shims from the forks before inverting the box and if necessary use a quantity of paraffin to flush it out.

20 Next fit a new gasket onto the mating face of the rear cover, having treated it with jointing compound on both sides, and offer up the cover to the casing. Replace the bolts and tighten them up.

21 There are two gaskets for the top cover, one above and one below the splash shield. Treat both with jointing compound before fitting them and the splash shield into position and replacing the top cover. Refit the top cover bolts and tighten them down evenly.

22 It is a good idea at this stage to refit the gear lever into the top cover remote control extension so that the selection of gears can be checked. Check that the reverse stop plunger and spring are well greased and tight, and that the selector lever and screw are absolutely tight on the gearshift shaft.

23 Replace the clutch bellhousing and clutch operating lever and thrust bearing.

10. Gearbox - Fault Finding

Faults in the gearbox can range from small buzzing noises and minor snags in engaging gears to serious faults such as loud howling whines, vibrations or great difficulty in remaining in or getting into

SECTION 9. Tightening rear mainshaft nut and lock washer and fitting speedo wheel drive.

SECTION 9. Placing in order, selector forks rail 1st/2nd, 3rd/4th, and reverse.

SECTION 9. Positioning detent balls when dummy rails are not used.

gears in general. For serious faults the only thing to do is remove the gearbox and have a look, or just renew it unseen with a new or secondhand unit. For minor faults, other than those which can be positively identified as coming from the base of the gear lever which can be easily got at, it is more a matter of how long the fault or irritating noise can be tolerated before doing something about it. Once something starts to wear to a noticable degree other things may also start to deteriorate rapidly.

Unfortunately, the amount of trouble to rectify a minor fault will be the same as for a major one - removal and dismantling of the gearbox. One may save something on the cost of spares required but even this is open to doubt as accurate diagnosis can only be made when the gearbox is stripped. Some faults can go on for thousands of miles without getting noticeably worse or affecting anything else - a worn baulk ring for example, failure of a bearing on the other hand could wreck the whole assembly in a few hundred miles. The list of faults and causes below are intended to give the owner some help and guidance in deciding **when** to take action in the light of the degree of seriousness. All the faults require removal and dismantling of the gearbox except where stated.

Fault Finding Chart - Gearbox

Fault	Cause	Major or Minor
Sloppy gear lever and rattles	Worn ball joint and pins or loose reverse stop plunger.	Minor - can be repaired with gearbox in position.
	Loose selector lever in top cover over gearbox.	Serious - loose locking screw could drop in gearbox.
Ineffective synchromesh on one or more gears.	Worn baulk rings. Worn blocker bars.	Minor - can go on for many miles.
Jumps out of one or more gears.	Weak detent springs. Worn selector forks. Worn engagement dogs. Worn synchro hubs.	Depends on how many gears involved and whether driving safety is affected.
Whining, roughness, vibration allied to other faults.	Bearing failure and/or overall wear.	Major - could break up and lock transmission which is dangerous.
Noisy and difficult gear engagement.	Clutch not operating correctly.	—
Sloppy and impositive gear selection	Overall wear throughout the selector mechanism.	Major - could be dangerous in that driver is unable to control car properly.

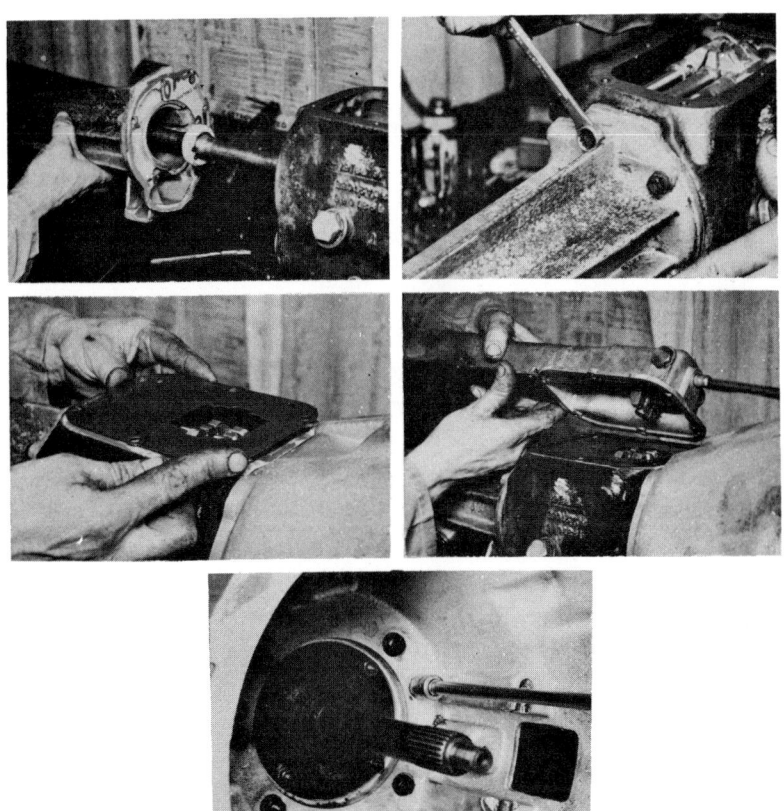

SECTION 9. Refitting rear extension, cover splash, top cover and bellhousing.

Chapter 7 Propeller shaft and universal joints

Contents

Specifications

Type	...	...	...	...	...	...	...	...	...	Tubular, single piece or divided with rubber-mounted centre bearing

Universal joints	...	...	...	...	...	...	...	...	Sealed needle roller bearings

For details of the two-piece propshaft, refer to Chapter 13.

1 General description

Engine power is transferred from the engine to the rear axle and wheels through the gearbox and a rotating propeller shaft.

Due to the up and down motion of the rear axle, the flexibility of the engine/gearbox mountings and the variations in distance between the gearbox and the pinion flange on the rear axle final drive unit, the propeller shaft has a universal joint at each end and a splined sleeve at the forward end. The two universal joints permit the drive to be transmitted with the shaft out of alignment. The splined sleeve slides on the splined end of the gearbox mainshaft thus compensating as required for the variations in effective length of the propeller shaft. The splies are lubricated from the gearbox and the universal joints are pre-packed with grease on assembly and should need no further attention.

2 Routine Maintenance

No specific maintenance is necessary. Examine the universal joints from time to time for signs of wear.

3 Propeller shaft - removal and replacement

1   Jack up the rear of the car or position it over a pit or ramp. If jacked up support the body side members with proper stands.
2   If the rear wheels are off the ground it will be necessary to apply the handbrake or engage a gear whilst undoing the pinion flange bolts. Otherwise the propeller shaft will turn.
3   Mark the relationship of the two flanges to each other with a file notch or punch mark and then undo the four nuts and bolts. Before removing the last one, make sure the propeller shaft will not drop on your head and also place a container under the rear end of the gearbox extension cover to catch any oil drips.
4   Move the shaft forward a little to disengage the flange register, then lower it and draw the front end from the gearbox. Do not let the sleeve or its internal splines get damaged or contaminated with grit in any way.
5   Replacement is a reversal of the removal procedure. Make sure that the sleeve end is a good fit on the splines with no backlash (if there is any it may mean renewal of both the sleeve and gearbox mainshaft). The oil seal in the gearbox rear cover should be in good condition also (see Chapter 6). The mating marks of the flanges should be lined up to their previous positions.

4 Universal joints and splines - inspection and repair

1   Wear in the needle roller bearings is indicated by vibration or 'clunks' in the transmission, particularly when the drive is being taken up or when going to over-run. (Backlash in the rear axle has the same effect so check that too if symptoms occur).
2   It is easy to check the needle roller bearings whilst the propeller shaft is still in position. Try to turn the shaft with one hand and grip the flange or sleeve on the other side of the joint with the other hand. There should be no movement between the two. If there is any, the bearings will need renewal.
3   The splines of the sliding sleeve should be a smooth sliding fit on the gearbox mainshaft and no trace of rotational backlash should be apparent. If there is any serious backlash the repair could be costly as both the gearbox mainshaft and the sleeve may need renewal (although a new sleeve only may suffice). Any significant signs of ridging on the outer surface of the sleeve may be the cause of oil leaks from the rear of the gearbox and a new seal may not be sufficient to rectify the trouble. Much depends on the degree of wear apparent and the owner will have to decide whether a new sleeve is worthwhile.

5 Universal Joints - dismantling and fitting new bearings

1   Clean away all traces of dirt from the whole assembly and then remove the circlips which hold each set of needle roller bearings in position. If the circlip is tight tap the face of the bearing cup inside it which may be jamming it in its groove.
2   The bearing should come out if the edges of the yoke ears are tapped with a mallet. If, however, they are very tight it should be possible to shift them, pressing them between the jaws of a vice using two distance pieces. Two different size socket spanners are ideal and it will be possible to force one out sufficiently far to enable it to be gripped by another suitable tool (pliers or vice again) and drawn out. Take care not to damage the yokes. If the

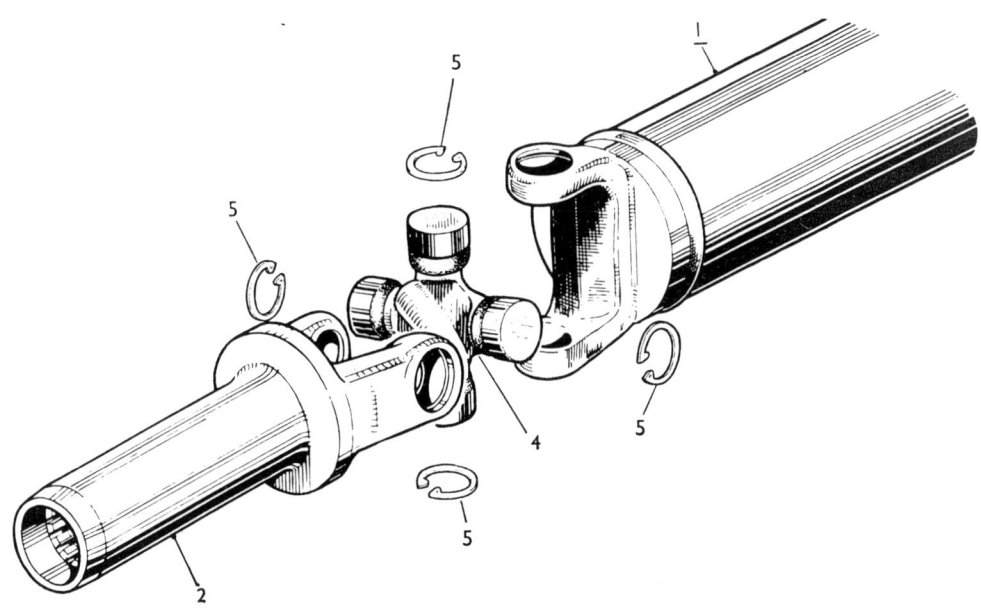

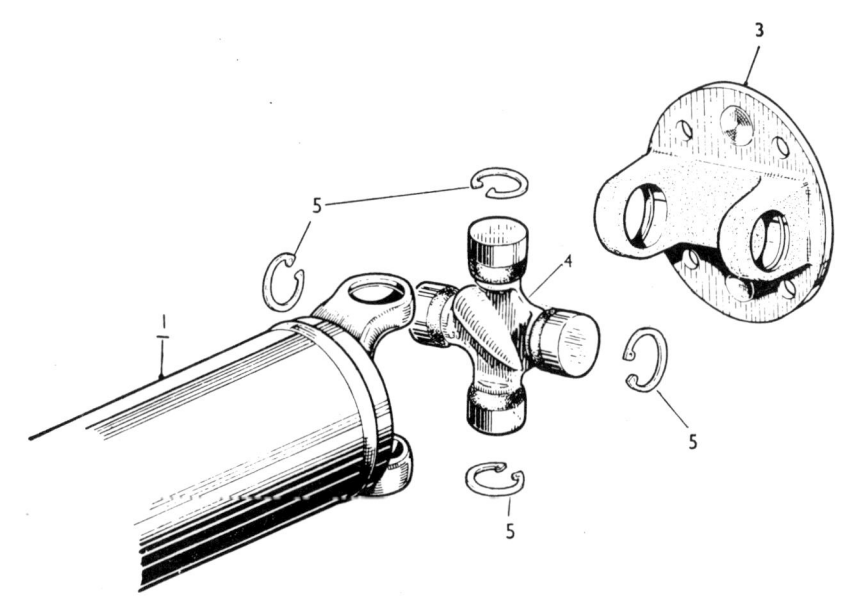

Fig. 7.1. PROPELLER SHAFT AND
UNIVERSAL JOINTS
(EXPLODED VIEW)

1 Propeller shaft
2 Splined sliding sleeve
3 Pinion flange coupling
4 Journal spider with needle
   roller bearings
5 Circlips

seized up or worn so badly that the holes in the yokes are oval then a new yoke will be needed - and if this is on the propeller shaft then that will have to be acquired too as the whole assembly is balanced and parts are not supplied separately.

3. New bearings will be supplied with new seals and circlips. Make sure the needles are correctly in position and the cup 1/3 full of grease. Put the gaskets and retainers on the four journals of the spider. Each cup may then be tapped through the yoke onto the spider journal. Fit all four on one joint before putting the circlips in position and make sure everything moves freely.

SECTION 3. Removing flange coupling bolts and withdrawing the sliding splined sleeve.

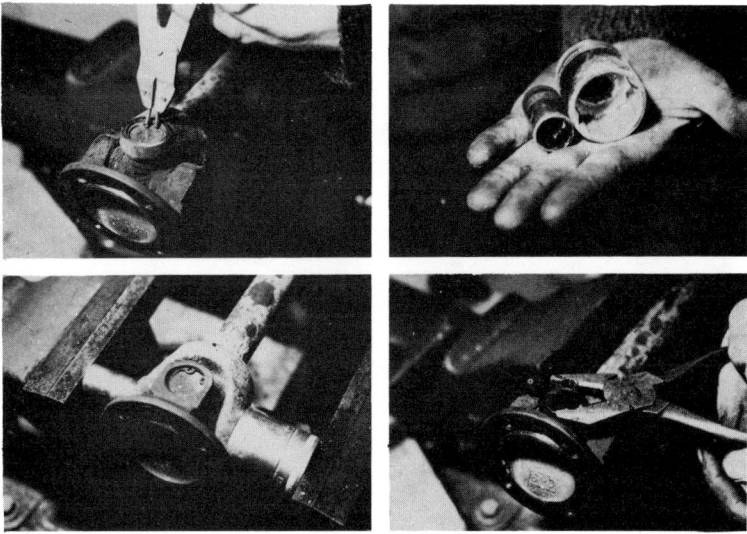

SECTION 5. Removing needle roller bearings using sockets as drifts between the vice jaws.

Chapter 8 Rear axle

Contents

Specifications

Type ... ...   Semi-floating, hypoid bevel gears

Bearings
Pinion ... ...   Taper roller
Differential and crownwheel assembly ... ...   Taper roller
Hub ... ...   Ball

Adjustment
Hypoid bevel pinion ... ...   Shims
Differential assembly ... ...   Shims
Crown wheel to pinion (backlash) ... ...   0.005 - 0.009 in (0.127 - 0.229 mm)

Number of teeth

Crownwheel	38) 4.22	35) 3.89	37) 3.70
Pinion	9)	9)	10)

Final drive ratios ... ...   4.22 : 1   3.89 : 1   3.70 : 1

Overall ratios

	Standard gearbox	Close ratio gearbox	Standard gearbox	Close ratio gearbox	Standard gearbox	Close ratio gearbox
Top (overdrive)	—	3.39	3.12	3.12	—	—
Top	4.22	4.22	3.89	3.89	3.70	3.70
Third (overdrive)	—	4.39	4.35	4.05	—	—
Third	5.87	5.47	5.41	5.04	5.15	4.80
Second	9.04	8.42	8.32	7.75	7.92	7.37
First	14.16	13.18	13.04	12.14	12.41	11.55
Reverse	15.07	14.03	13.88	12.92	13.20	12.30

Capacity ... ...   1¾ pints (2.1 US pints, 1 litre)

1 General description

The rear axle is of the semi-floating type incorporating a hypoid crownwheel and pinion with a two pinion differential. The crownwheel and pinion and differential are mounted as an assembly in the differential carrier and this is bolted to the front of the banjo type axle housing. This means that the axle does not have to be disturbed in order to remove and examine the differential and final drive.

2 Routine maintenance

1 Every 5,000 miles remove the level plug located in the right-hand horizontal web of the differential casing. The oil should be level with the bottom of the threads in the hole and in order to see this the use of a hand mirror will help. Top up with the recommended oil as required.
2 Every 30,000 miles remove the level/filler plug and drain plug after a run, when the axle should be a little warmer than

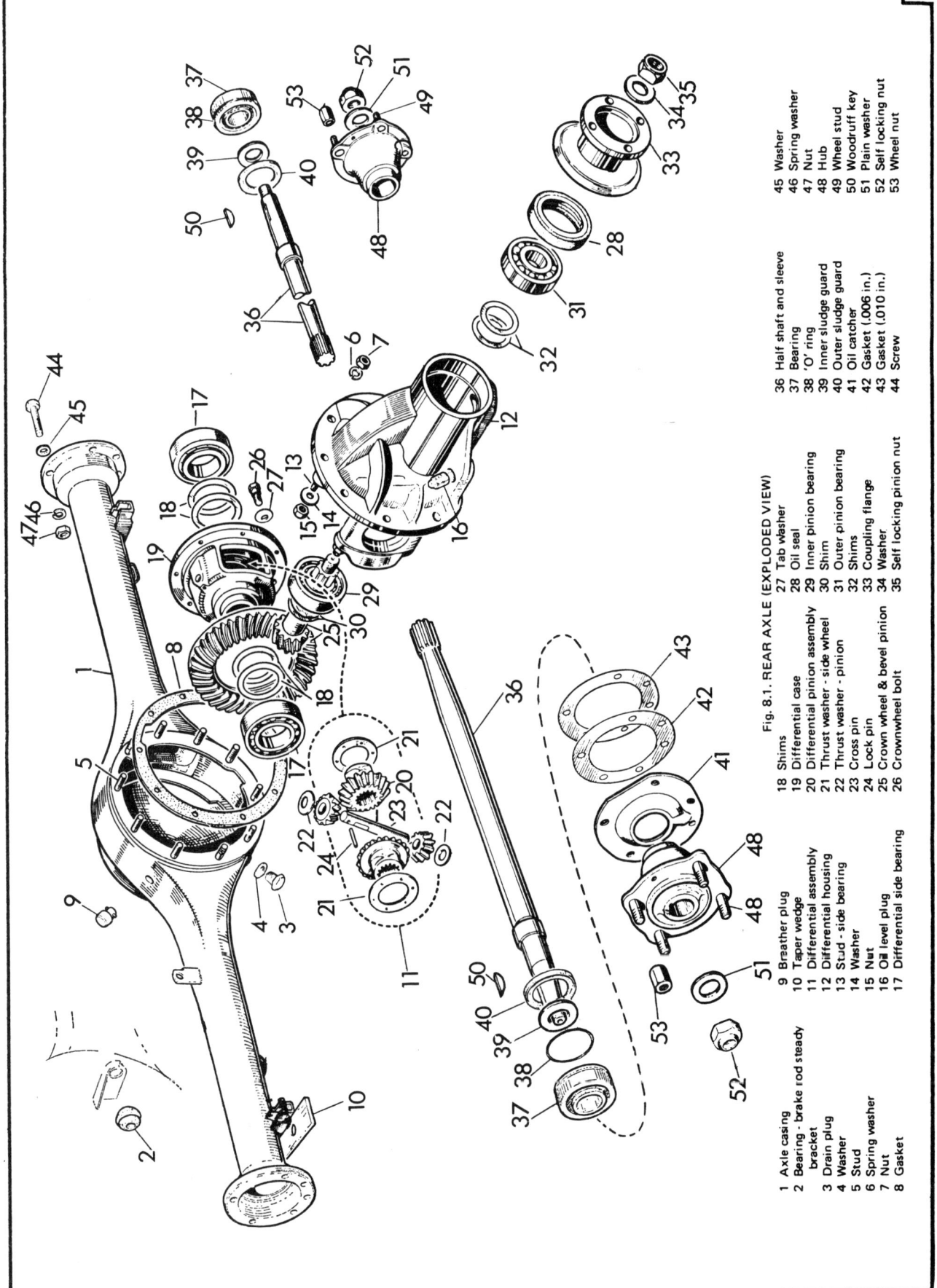

Fig. 8.1. REAR AXLE (EXPLODED VIEW)

1 Axle casing
2 Bearing - brake rod steady bracket
3 Drain plug
4 Washer
5 Stud
6 Spring washer
7 Nut
8 Gasket
9 Breather plug
10 Taper wedge
11 Differential assembly
12 Differential housing
13 Stud - side bearing
14 Washer
15 Nut
16 Oil level plug
17 Differential side bearing
18 Shims
19 Differential case
20 Differential pinion assembly
21 Thrust washer - side wheel
22 Thrust washer - pinion
23 Cross pin
24 Lock pin
25 Crown wheel & bevel pinion
26 Crownwheel bolt
27 Tab washer
28 Oil seal
29 Inner pinion bearing
30 Shim
31 Outer pinion bearing
32 Shims
33 Coupling flange
34 Washer
35 Self locking pinion nut
36 Half shaft and sleeve
37 Bearing
38 'O' ring
39 Inner sludge guard
40 Outer sludge guard
41 Oil catcher
42 Gasket (.006 in.)
43 Gasket (.010 in.)
44 Screw
45 Washer
46 Spring washer
47 Nut
48 Hub
49 Wheel stud
50 Woodruff key
51 Plain washer
52 Self locking nut
53 Wheel nut

normal and drain the oil out. Refill with 3½ pints of the recommended oil. If wished, the recommended amount of a proprietary grade of molybdenum disulphide may be added as an aid to wear reduction and reducing friction.

3. Check that the breather plug is clear when checking the oil level.

3. Half Shafts, Bearings and Oil Seals - Removal and Replacement

1. The half shafts may be withdrawn without disturbing the differential gear. They are removed in order to renew the bearings or oil seals or if the differential is to be removed. Read the whole of this Section before starting work.

2. Jack up the car at the rear and support it firmly on proper stands. Remove the rear wheels, free the handbrake and remove the brake drums. (Details in Chapter 9).

3. Remove the clevis pin from the handbrake linkage and disconnect the hydraulic brake pipe from the wheel cylinder. (Details in Chapter 9).

4. Remove the nuts and bolts securing the oil catcher plate and brake backplate to the axle casing flange. The half shaft hub, bearing and backplate are now held in position as an assembly by the fit of the outer race of the bearing into the axle casing. Ideally the use of a proper impact hammer removal tool is needed to draw the assembly out. This consists of a flange which bolts to the wheel studs and to which is fitted a long shaft extension with a sliding weight on it. The sliding weight is hit against a flange at the extremity of the shaft and this draws the axle out. Whatever you do, this principle - of attaching a suitable bracket and striking point to the wheel studs - must be followed. No part of the axle assembly itself must be struck. A sustained pull is also quite ineffective and will probably only result in heaving the car off the stands. So get something suitable organised in advance or you will be wasting your time. One possibility is to use an old wheel rim bolted to the studs and then strike it from the inside with something suitably heavy. The success or otherwise of this method depends on access and the ability to get a good swing at it. Whatever method is used the car should be firmly supported.

6. It is essential that proper facilities are also available if the bearing/oil seal is to be renewed. The bearing has to be drawn off the outer end of the shaft. First, therefore, the hub has to be removed. It is held by a nut on to a keyed taper at the end of the shaft. A proper puller to get this off is essential otherwise the end of the shaft may be damaged. The bearing may then be pulled off, also using a suitable tool which can bear on the end of the shaft and pull against the inner race of the bearing. A keen owner may be able to make up a suitable puller but the time and effort involved should be weighed against the advantage of handing the shaft to someone with the necessary equipment for fitting a new bearing.

7. Behind the bearing is a very tight fitting sleeve round the shaft. This serves to grip the bearing inner race against the hub. When the bearing is removed, therefore, the sleeve has to be moved about 1/32 inch (1 mm) towards the outer end of the shaft so that when a new bearing is pressed on, the hub will finally be drawn up against the bearing and the bearing will force the sleeve back. The force needed will be sufficient to grip the inner race of the bearing. It will be seen, therefore, that to attempt this work with nothing more than a hammer, chisel and hope will be almost certainly doomed to failure.

8. When fitting the new bearing (having first moved the sleeve into position on the shaft) make sure that the inner sludge guard is fitted to the shaft first and that the oil seal which is incorporated in the bearing, faces inwards. The bearing should be pressed on until the sludge plate is just held between the inner race and sleeve on the shaft - no further. Then put the back plate and dust cover in position followed by the hub. When the hub is drawn on with the nut the bearing will be finally moved into position as required. The nut needs tightening to 180 lbs/ft.

9. When replacing the half shaft the splines at the inner end should first pick up the splines in the differential side gears. Then enter the bearing into the axle casing recess until the outer edge of the race is nearly flush with the casing. Then bolt up the back plate evenly, which

will draw the bearing completely into position.

10 Reconnect the hydraulic pipe and handbrake linkage, refit the brake drum and bleed the brakes.

4. Differential Carrier - Removal and Replacement

1. Jack up the car and support it on stands as for half shaft removal. Drain the oil from the back axle by removing the drain plug. The half shaft should then be removed sufficiently far for the inner ends to disengage from the differential side pinions. The propeller shaft should then be dismantled from the rear axle pinion flange. It is not necessary to draw it out from the gearbox provided it can be conveniently rested out of the way on one side.

2. Undo the ten nuts and washers holding the differential carrier to the casing. The whole unit can then be drawn forward off the studs and taken out.

3. When replacing the assembly ensure that the mating faces are perfectly clean and free from burrs. A new gasket coated with sealing compound should also be used. Otherwise refitting is a reversal of the removal operation.

5. Differential, Crownwheel and Pinion - Overhaul

1. At some point in the life of a rear axle an owner is faced with the need to cure either a severe back lash or an unacceptable whine or noise level. Such symptoms usually indicate worn bearings coupled with worn gears to a varying degree. Due to the fact that rebuilding and setting up a differential assembly is a specialised job, calling for training and experience, any owner contemplating such work should first seriously consider the relative economics of obtaining parts and rebuilding (with the possibility of an unsuccessful result) compared with obtaining a complete assembly either new or secondhand from a breaker. This manual does not, therefore, detail the step by step procedures of assembly. Dismantling is no problem at all. The specifications and exploded drawing should enable someone with experience to get on with it. If the pinion oil seal is leaking a new one may be fitted after first removing the pinion nut and flange. The old seal may be dug out with a pointed tool, taking care not to damage the casing. A new one should be sealed on installation with compound on the outside and pressed on the inner lip. These oil seals rarely fail and if one does then it is likely that the pinion bearings have also failed. In such cases the fitting of a new seal would be a waste of time.

6. Rear Axle - Removal and Replacement

1. Removal of the rear axle should be a rare occurence and the most likely reason is if the differential unit has gone and a replacement assembly obtained from a breaker is being fitted complete, rather than just the differential assembly.

2. Jack up the rear of the car and support the body under the side frame allowing the axle and springs to hang free. Remove the wheels.

3. Disconnect the propeller shaft (Chapter 7) and the dampers at their lower mountings only (Chapter 11).

4. Disconnect the handbrake linkage at both hubs and from the bracket on the axle casing. Also disconnect the hydraulic flexible brake hose coupling at the union with the rigid pipe (not at the three way connector) (see Chapter 9). Protect the ends of the fluid lines from dirt.

5. Remove all the 'U' bolts clamping the axle to the springs and then withdraw the axle from one side between the springs and the body.

6. When refitting the axle make sure it is correctly located with the correct spring seats and clamps in position (see Chapter 11) and tighten the 'U' bolt nuts to the correct torque of 35 lbs/ft. Reconnect the handbrake linkage and hydraulic lines and bleed the hydraulic system.

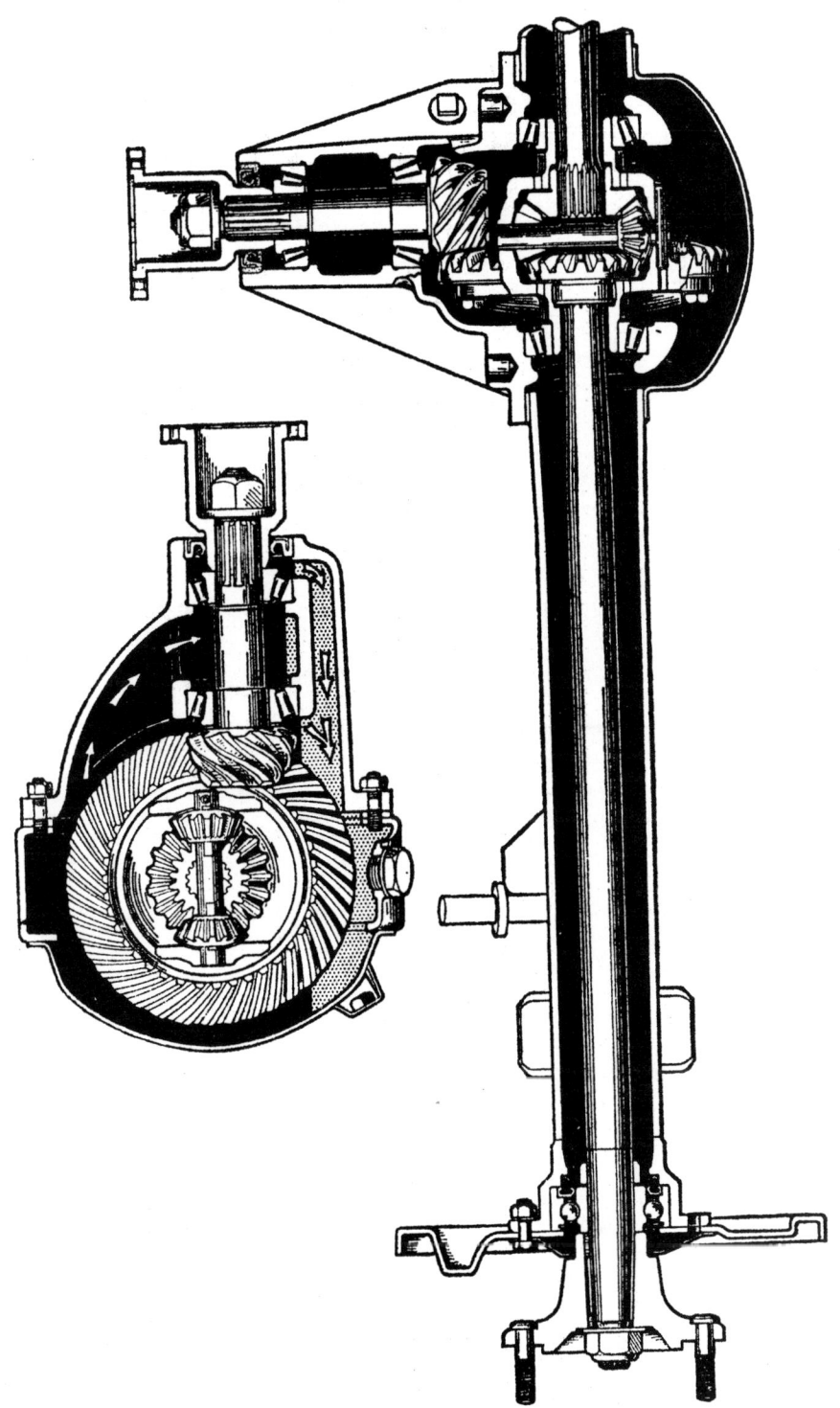

Fig. 8.2. REAR AXLE (vertical and horizontal cross section)

Chapter 9 Braking system

Contents

Specifications

Type		Lockheed hydraulic
Brake diameters		
Front disc		9.6 in (24.4 cm)
Rear drum		9 in (22.9 cm)
Lining width		1.75 in (4.5 cm)

	Non-servo cars and cars fitted with accessory servo kit	Servo-assisted cars
Front brakes		
Lining material	Mintex 78 or M108	Don 22* or Ferodo 2430F
Colour code**	RGRGR	RRYY* or BWWWB
Total area	16 in^2 (103.2 cm^2)	20 in^2 (129.0 cm^2)
Rear brakes		
Lining material	Don 202	Don 24
Colour code	RRR	—R—RRR
Total area	59.4 in^2 (383.2 cm^2)	59.4 in^2 (383.2 cm^2)

Master cylinder bore		¾ in (19.05 mm)
Caliper cylinder bore		2 1/8 in (53.975 mm)
Rear cylinder bore		¾ in (19.05 mm)
Maximum disc run-out		0.004 in (0.10 mm)
Servo (if fitted)		Lockheed type 6

* Early Sceptre cars were fitted with this lining, but latest material must be used in sets for replacement
** Colour identification. R = Red, B = Blue, Y = Yellow, G = Green, W = White, —R— = a long strip

1 General description

All models are fitted with Lockheed disc brakes at the front and drum brakes and shoes at the rear. All are hydraulically operated by the foot pedal and the independent handbrake operates the rear drum brakes only by an independent mechanical linkage.

No adjustment to the brakes is necessary as the pistons for the disc pads move forward automatically (without retracting) as the pads wear. The hydraulic fluid in the system is automatically increases from the reservoir as the capacity increases when the pistons move forward. The rear brake shoes are automatically adjusted by a mechanical ratchet which restricts retraction as the linings wear.

The retraction of the pistons which force the pads against the discs is a frictional distance and is governed only by the minute distortion of the fluid seal in the bore of the cylinder. The rear shoes however are spring retracted and the override ratchet device holds them closer to the drums as the linings wear. The ratchet is

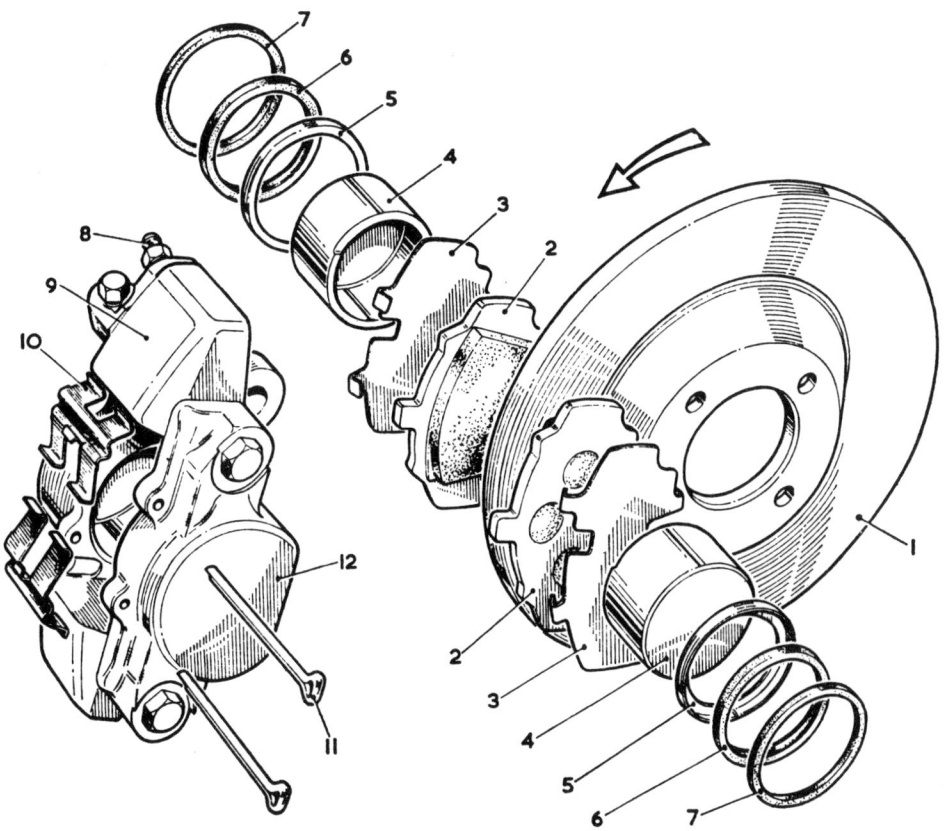

Fig. 9.1. DISC BRAKE — EXPLODED VIEW OF PADS, DISC & PISTON
COMPONENTS (Early model with Shims)

1 Disc	4 Pistons	7 Fluid seals	10 Steady springs
2 Brake pads	5 Dust seal retainer	8 Bleed nipple	11 Split pins
3 Anti-squeal shims	6 Dust seals	9 Inner half of caliper	12 Outer half of caliper

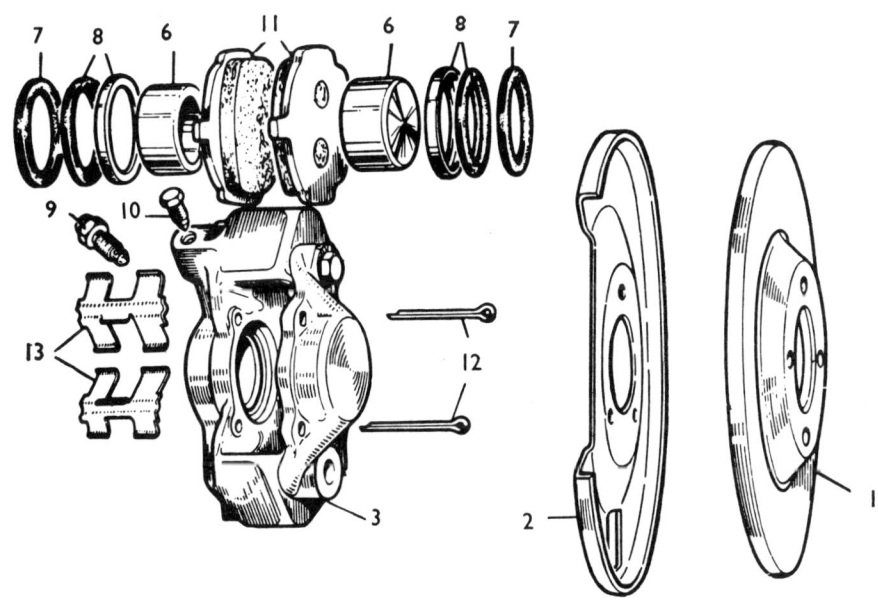

Fig. 9.2. DISC BRAKE — EXPLODED VIEW OF PADS, DISC AND PISTON
COMPONENTS (Later type - no shims)

1 Disc	6 Piston	9 Bleed nipple	12 Split pin
2 Splash shield	7 Fluid seal	10 Plug	13 Steady springs
3 Caliper body	8 Dust seal and retainer	11 Pads	

operated and takes up as needed each time the brakes are applied.

2. Routine Maintenance

1. Every week remove the hydraulic fluid reservoir cap, having made sure that it is clean and check the level of the fluid which should be just below the bottom of the filler neck. Check also that the vent hole in the cap is clear. Any need for regular topping up, regardless of quantity, should be viewed with suspicion and the whole hydraulic system carefully checked for signs of leakage.

2. Every 5,000 miles the brake pads and shoes should be examined to check the thickness of friction lining material remaining. Rear shoe linings should be renewed when the material has almost reached the level of the rivet heads. If the rivets ever rub on the drums they will cause scoring and reduced braking efficiency. The disc pads should be renewed when minimum thickness is $1/8$ inch (3 mm). If one pad shows signs of wearing more than another they may be changed over to the other side of the disc (on some earlier models only). At the same time as friction material is examined the hydraulic pipes and unions should be examined for any signs of damage or corrosion. Brake lining wear varies according to driving style but no set of disc pads should be expected to last more than 15,000 miles. The rear brake shoe linings will probably last half as long again. Make sure the handbrake functions properly at all times.

3. Every 10,000 miles remove the air filter from the servo unit (if fitted) and clean or renew it.

4. Every 25,000 miles it is good policy to renew all hydraulic cylinder seals as a matter of routine, together with the fluid and flexible hoses. Any repair work in the interior should also, of course, be taken into account.

5. If you have just acquired a secondhand car it is strongly recommended that all brake drums, pads, shoes and discs are thoroughly examined for condition and wear immediately. Even though braking efficiency may be excellent the friction materials could be nearing the end of their useful life and it is as well to know this without delay. Similarly, the hydraulic cylinders, pipes and connections should be carefully examined for leaks or chafing. Faults should be rectified immediately. It should be remembered that three year old cars will be subject to safety tests and that apart from safety, which is paramount, defects in the system even though they may not yet affect stopping power, will possibly cause the vehicle to fail the test.

3. Disc Pads - Removal, Inspection and Replacement

1. If the brake pads have worn down to a friction material thickness of $1/8$ inch (3 mm) they should be renewed as soon as possible. If one pad is worn on one side of the disc more than the other (this often happens - the inner pad wears faster) it was in order in some early models to change them over; provided, of course, neither has reached the minimum permissible thickness. However, later models and replacement pads are handed. (The pads are identified by a rectangular cut away portion in the trailing edge of the plate). These pads cannot be moved to the other side of the same disc although they can be moved to the same position on the other disc. In order to check pad thickness, jack up the car and remove the wheel. The edge of the pad will then be visible in the caliper which is mounted on the forward side of the disc.

2. To remove the pads depress the steady springs to relieve the pressure on the split pins and draw out the split pins. If the pads are then rotated upwards a little they can be eased out of the calliper.

3. When fitting new pads it will be necessary to ease the pistons back into their bores to accommodate the thicker material. First examine the fluid reservoir because when the pistons move back the level will rise and it should not be allowed to overflow. Then move the pistons back by exerting steady pressure with a flat blade between piston head and disc. At the same time check that the anti-squeal cut-out portion of the piston crown is across the line of disc rotation on the

lead inside, i.e., upwards in this instance. If it is not rotate the piston carefully until it is. Where the later type pads are fitted, without shims, the cut-out of the piston should be approximately angled at 25° from a line across the direction of disc travel.

4. When the gap is wide enough for the pads to go in lead in the top edge first and then hold the front lug and rotate the pad downwards so that it fits snugly in position. The shim plates (if used) should be slipped in between the pads and the pistons. (Note that later models and new pads have no shims.) Place the steady springs in position with the longer legs facing each other and refit the split pins, spreading the ends a little to keep them in position.

5. Operate the brake pedal until firm pressure is felt. Then rotate the wheel to ensure that no binding is taking place (although the pads may noticeably just touch the disc). Always fit new pads of the correct specification and if a different type must be used make sure it applies to both front wheels.

4. Discs - Inspection, Removal and Replacement

1. Brake discs rarely give trouble but very severe use in unusually wet or dirty conditions may cause distortion or scoring. If it does not run true the performance of the brakes can be seriously affected. The amount of 'out-of-true' or run-out should not exceed .004 inch (.1 mm).

2. To check the discs jack up the car and first make sure that the hub bearing is in good condition. It may be necessary to tighten the bearing nut to eliminate any play which could exist due to the castellations of the nut and split pin position.

3. If a dial gauge micrometer is mounted against the surface of the disc while turning it, the amount of run-out can be measured. After checking re-adjust the hub bearing (Chapter 11). If the disc is heavily scored or damaged it should be renewed.

4. A damaged disc should only be reground as a last resort if no replacement is available. It will cost about the same if done properly. A maximum of .010 inch (.25 mm) may be removed from each side, each side must be ground off equally and the maximum run-out between mounting and rubbing faces is .002 inch (.05 mm). Rubbing faces must be parallel to .001 inch (.025 mm).

5. To remove a disc, first take off the calliper assembly (it is not necessary to disturb the hydraulics) as described in Section 9. Then remove the hub (and disc with it) as described in Chapter 11 for renewal of front wheel bearings.

6. The disc may then be removed from the hub by undoing the four bolts and washers.

7. Fitting a disc is the reverse procedure, being careful to ensure that the mating faces of the disc and hub are perfectly clean and free from burrs or high spots. Wash off the protective coating off a new disc also. Tighten the bolts evenly to the specified torque of 32 lb/ft.

8. Replace the hub, adjust the bearing and refit the calliper. If the previous pads are being used allow time for bedding in before full braking efficiency is achieved.

5. Brake Drums and Shoes - Removal, Inspection and Replacement

1. Jack up the car and remove the roadwheel. Block the front wheels and release the handbrake.

2. The drum is located over the four wheel studs and is positioned by a single countersunk screw into the hub which should be removed. The drum may then be pulled straight off the studs. If it seems stuck fast it will be due to binding at the roots of the wheel studs. A little easing fluid and a tap with a mallet on the edge should shift it. Do not hit the drum with a hammer as it is brittle and could easily fracture. It sometimes happens that very badly scored and worn drums can 'mesh' their grooves into the surfaces of the brake linings to such an extent that the drum cannot be pulled off; the automatic adjuster being inaccessible for release. On later models the mechanism can be reached and released by drilling a $5/16$ inch hole at a radius of 2.55 inch - opposite the locating screw. This is really rather a

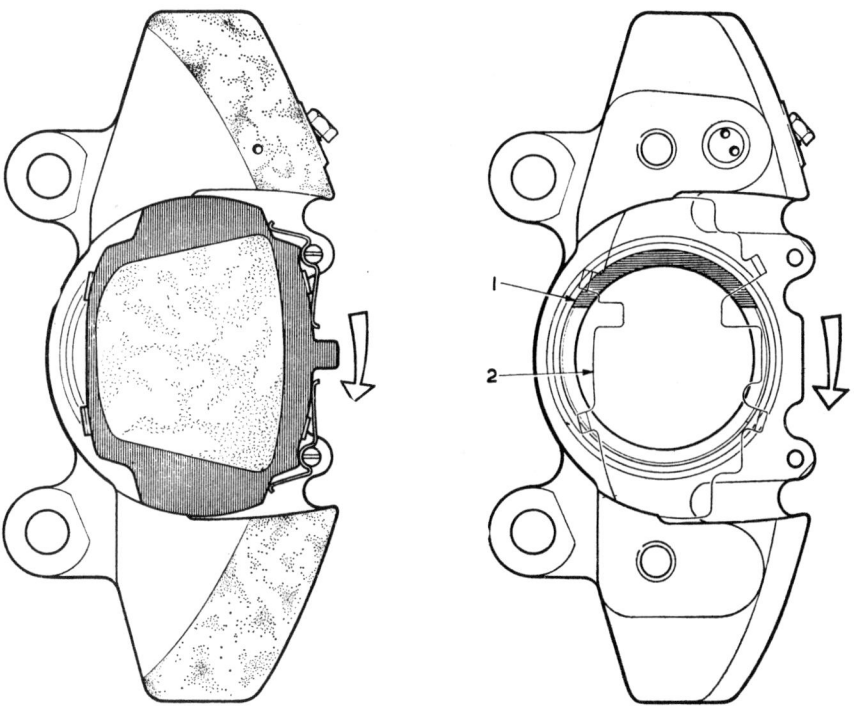

Fig. 9.3. Section through caliper showing locations of pad, shim and piston cut-out (early models)
1 Cut-out   2 Shim

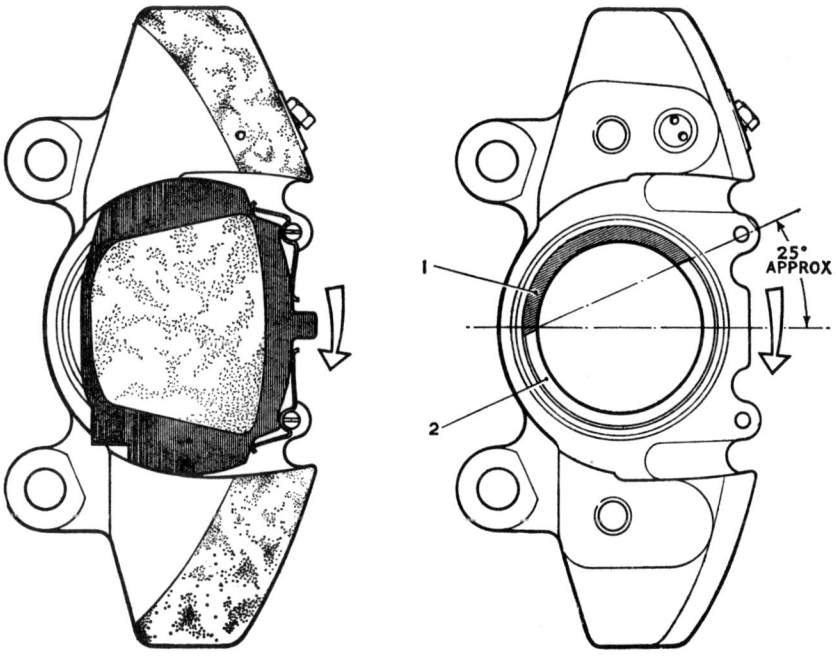

Fig. 9.4. Section through caliper showing locations of pad and piston cut-out when new type pads are fitted to early model calipers
1   Piston cut-out   2   Contact of piston to pad

waste of time if the drum is to be renewed anyway. If you cannot actually break the drum to pieces with a hammer without risk of damaging the hub then cut it off - or cut nicks in it and try splitting it with a cold chisel. If you cut into the shoes inside as well it does not matter as they are going to need renewal too.

3. With the drum removed brush out any dust and examine the rubbing surface for any signs of pitting or deep scoring. The surface should be smooth and bright but minor hairline scores are of no consequence and could have been caused by grit or brake shoes with linings just worn to the rivets. A drum that is obviously badly worn should be renewed. A perfectly satisfactory replacement can often be obtained from a breakers yard. It is no economy having drums tuned up on a lathe (unless you can have it done for nothing!). Also, as the radius is altered if the rubbing surfaces are machined out, standard shoes will not match properly until a lot of bedding in has taken place and re-radiused the linings.

4. The brake shoes should be examined next. There should be no signs of contamination by oil and the linings should be above the heads of the rivets. If the level is close (less than $1/32$ inch) it is worth changing them. If there are signs of oil contamination they should be renewed also and the source of oil leakage found before it ruins the new ones as well.

5. To remove the shoes (having, of course, removed the drum) first detach the steady posts from the centre of each shoe. This can be done by holding the head with one pair of pliers and rotating the dished, slotted washer 90° so that it unlocks from the post and comes off with the spring behind it.

6. Next note which holes the pull-off springs fit into in the shoes. Then lift the head of each brake shoe (the end not on the hydraulic piston) against spring tension out of its slot on the backplate. This will relieve some of the tension and the other ends of the shoes can be similarly lifted out at the cylinder end.

7. Before fitting new shoes check that the wheel cylinder is free to move in the backplate slot (early models) and that the backplate is not distorted and is securely bolted on. (If it has to be taken off first, take out the halfshaft as described in Chapter 8). Also see that the hydraulic piston moves freely and that there are no fluid leaks. Be careful not to let the piston come right out of the cylinder or it will be necessary to bleed the brakes after it is put back.

8. To refit the shoes first arrange them as shown in the drawing with the retractor springs hooked into the correct holes. The double coil spring goes next to the cylinder with the hook ends outwards in the two outer holes in the shoes. The other spring fits with the hook ends outwards also but using the next to last hole in the trailing end of the leading shoe. (A leading shoe is one where the leading end in relation to the drum rotation is where the piston force is applied.) The tappet should be screwed fully into the adjuster wheel to ease assembly. When the shoes are in position the adjuster wheel can be rotated to expand the shoes just far enough to allow the drum to be refitted. Replace the steady pins, springs and lock washers. Centralise the shoes so that the drum will go on easily.

9. When the drum has been replaced operate the brakes to check that they do not bind. It is possible for light binding to occur initially, in which case they should be checked again after a few miles motoring.

6. Handbrake - Adjustment and Cable Renewal

1. There is rarely any need to touch the handbrake as the automatic adjustment of the rear brake shoes also adjusts the handbrake operation. The only need for adjustment is when the cable stretches unduly or after fitting a new one. The principle of operation is simple. The inner cable runs to one wheel and the reaction of the outer cable when tension is applied is transferred to the other wheel by a rod. The mounting is on the differential cover of the rear axle. The end of the inner cable is connected to the brake wheel lever by a clevis on an adjuster screw. By slackening the locknut the adjuster can be screwed into the clevis, thus shortening the cable and taking up any excessive handbrake lever travel.

2. Due to the rear brake shoes being self adjusting, care must be taken to avoid over tensioning of the handbrake cable otherwise the brakes may bind on. When adjustments are being carried out, therefore, the following procedure ensures that this cannot happen. First jack up the rear wheels so they are both off the ground together. Make sure the front wheels are securely chocked. Set the handbrake lever off and then lift it one notch on the ratchet. Slacken the cable adjuster and pump the foot brake to make sure the automatic adjustment is fully taken up. Make sure also that the wheel cylinders are sliding freely in the backplate (early models) and return to rest normally after pulling on the operating lever. Then disconnect the clevis from the lever by removing the clevis pin and alter the screwed adjuster until it can be refitted without moving the lever or without pulling on the cable to give any tension. Refit the clevis. After operating the hand lever a few times to settle the linkage the lever should travel six to eight notches before the brakes are fully on.

3. To fit a new cable it is first necessary to remove the handbrake lever. This is attached to the door sill by two bolts. Remove these, taking care to keep the distance pieces safely as they are essential to correct positioning. The end of the cable is then accessible and can be detached by removing the clevis pin. The other end is detached similarly and the outer cable is released from the brake rod by compressing the spring and releasing the spring retainers from round the cable. Replacement is a reversal of this process and the handbrake should be adjusted as previously described.

7. Hydraulic Fluid Pipes - Inspection, Removal and Replacement

1. Periodically and certainly well in advance of the M.O.T. test if due, all brake pipes, connections and unions should be completely and carefully examined. Fig. 9.5 shows the composition of all such pipes and unions in the system.

2. Examine first all the unions for signs of leaks. Then look at the flexible hoses for signs of fraying and chafing (as well as for leaks). This is only a preliminary inspection of the flexible hoses as exterior condition does not necessarily indicate interior condition which will be considered later.

3. The steel pipes must be examined equally carefully. They must be thoroughly cleaned and examined for signs of dents or other percussive damage, rust and corrosion. Rust and corrosion should be scraped off and, if the depth of pitting in the pipes is significant, they will need replacement. This is most likely in those areas underneath the car body and along the rear axle where the pipes are exposed to the full force of road and weather conditions.

4. If any section of pipe is to be removed, first of all take off the fluid reservoir cap, line it with a piece of polythene film to make it airtight and screw it back on. This will minimise the amount of fluid dripping out of the system when the pipes are removed.

5. Rigid pipe removal is usually quite straightforward. The unions at each end are undone and the pipe drawn out of the connection. The clips which may hold it to the car body are bent back and it is then removed. Underneath the car exposed unions can be particularly stubborn, defying the efforts of an open ended spanner. As few people will have the special split ring spanner required, a self-grip wrench (Mole) is the only answer. If the pipe is being renewed new unions will be provided. If not then one will have to put up with the possibility of burring over the flats on the union and use a self-grip wrench for replacement also.

6. Flexible hoses are always fitted to a rigid support bracket where they join a rigid pipe, the bracket being fixed to the body frame and/or suspension unit. The rigid pipe unions must first be removed from the flexible union. Then the locknut securing the flexible pipe to the bracket must be unscrewed, releasing the end of the pipe from the bracket. As these connections are usually exposed they are more often than not rusted up and a penetrating fluid is virtually essential to aid removal (try 'Plus-Gas'). When undoing them, both halves must be supported as the bracket is not strong enough to support the torque required to undo the nut and can easily be snapped off.

7. Once the flexible hose is removed examine the internal bore. If

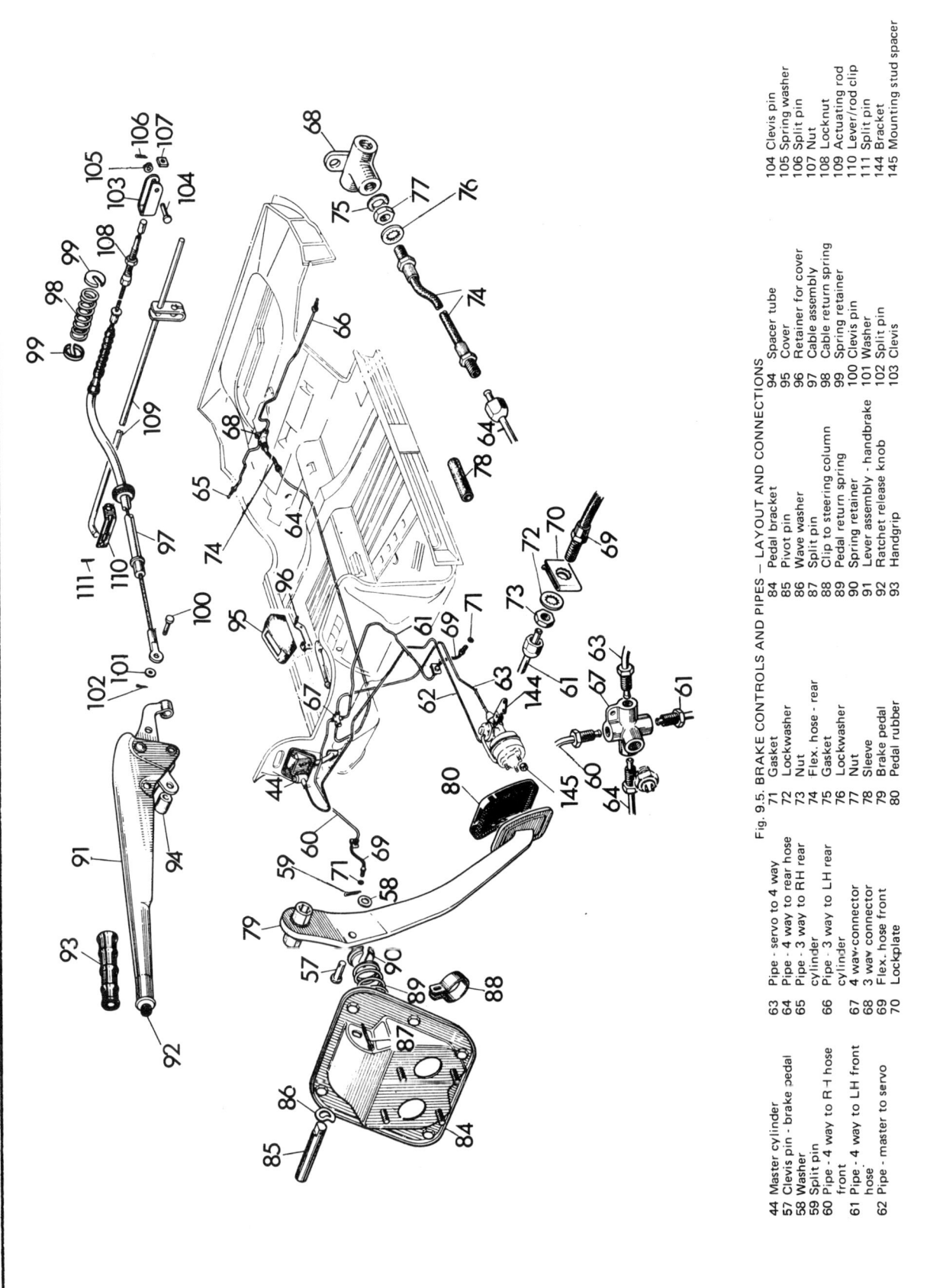

Fig. 9.5. BRAKE CONTROLS AND PIPES — LAYOUT AND CONNECTIONS

44 Master cylinder
57 Clevis pin - brake pedal
58 Washer
59 Split pin
60 Pipe - 4 way to R-I hose front
61 Pipe - 4 way to LH front hose
62 Pipe - master to servo
63 Pipe - servo to 4 way
64 Pipe - 4 way to rear hose
65 Pipe - 3 way to RH rear cylinder
66 Pipe - 3 way to LH rear cylinder
67 4 way-connector
68 3 way connector
69 Flex. hose front
70 Lockplate

71 Gasket
72 Lockwasher
73 Nut
74 Flex. hose - rear
75 Gasket
76 Lockwasher
77 Nut
78 Sleeve
79 Brake pedal
80 Pedal rubber

84 Pedal bracket
85 Pivot pin
86 Wave washer
87 Split pin
88 Clip to steering column
89 Pedal return spring
90 Spring retainer
91 Lever assembly - handbrake
92 Ratchet release knob
93 Handgrip

94 Spacer tube
95 Cover
96 Retainer for cover
97 Cable assembly
98 Cable return spring
99 Spring retainer
100 Clevis pin
101 Washer
102 Split pin
103 Clevis

104 Clevis pin
105 Spring washer
106 Split pin
107 Nut
108 Locknut
109 Actuating rod
110 Lever/rod clip
111 Split pin
144 Bracket
145 Mounting stud spacer

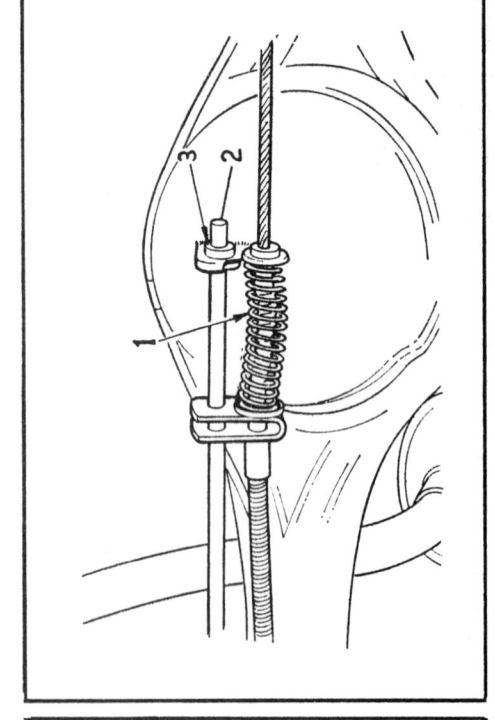
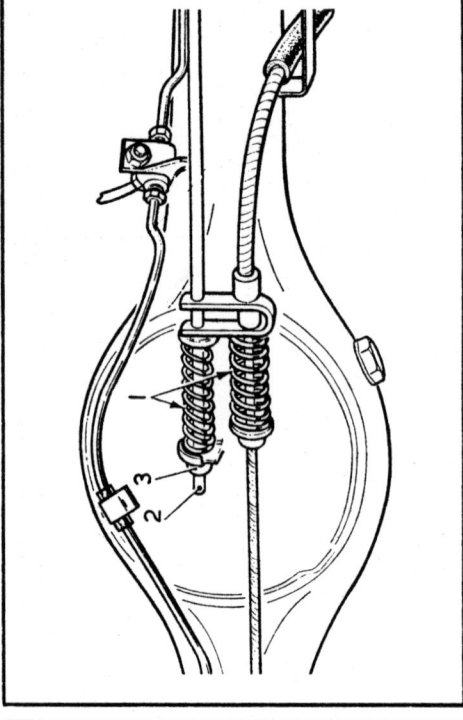
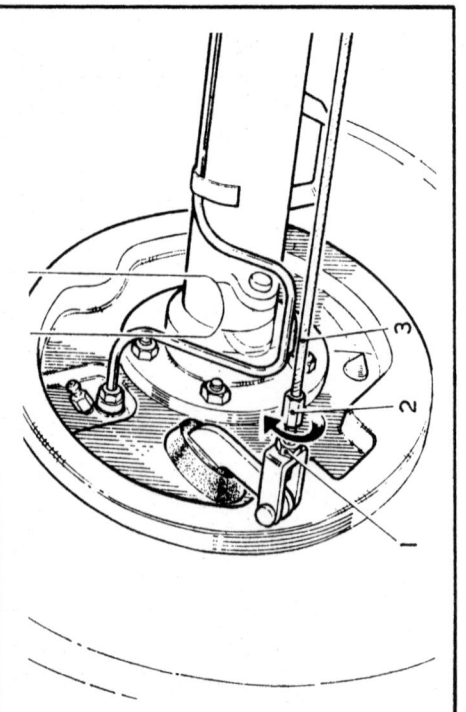

LATER MODELS

EARLY MODELS

Adjusters

Compensators

Fig. 9.6. REAR BRAKES, HANDBRAKE LINKAGES & ADJUSTERS

1 Locknut   2 Adjuster unit   3 Cable, inner

1 Return spring   2 Operating rod   3 Rod bearing

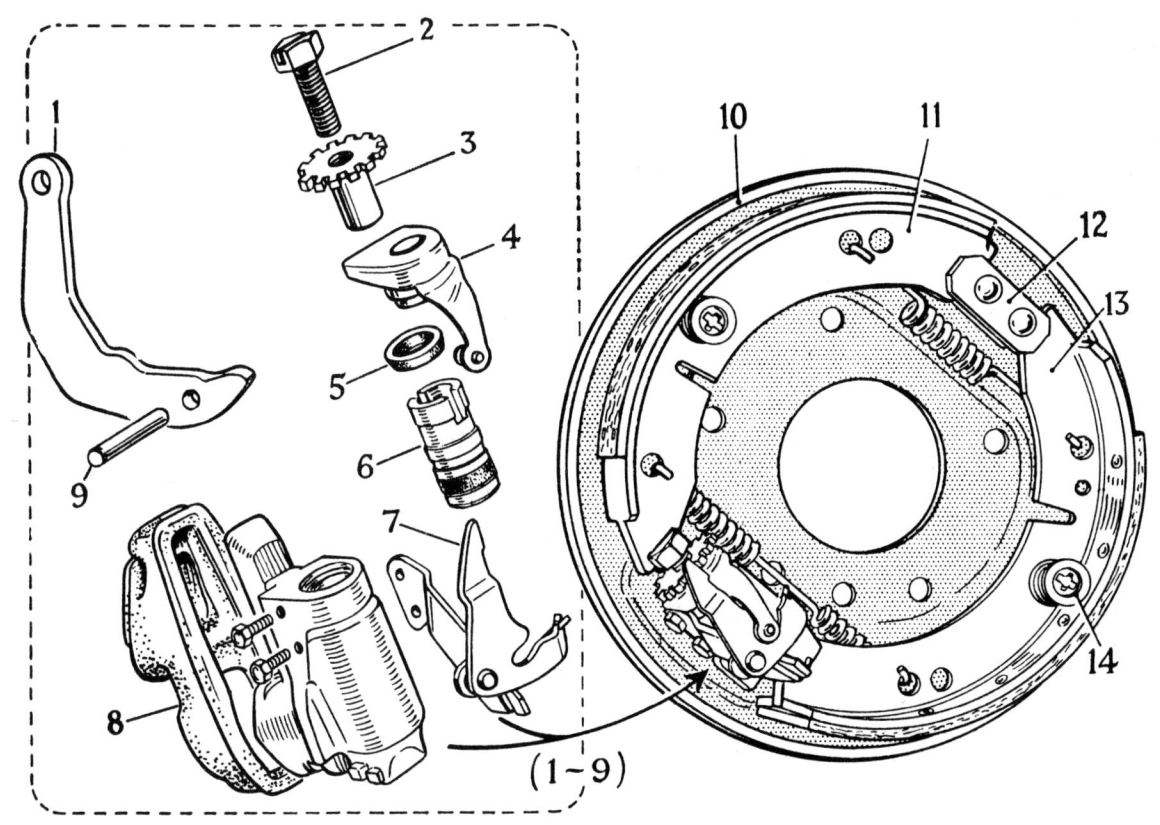

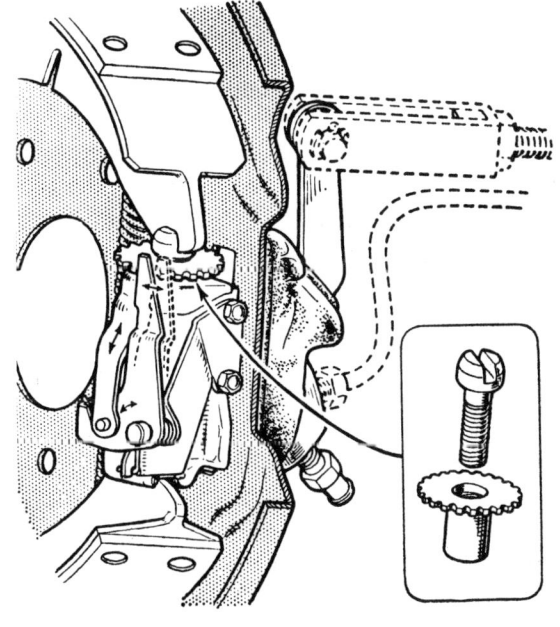

Fig. 9.7. EXPLODED & ASSEMBLED VIEWS OF
EARLY SLIDING CYLINDER TYPE
SELF ADJUSTING MECHANISMS
FOR REAR BRAKES

1 Wheel cylinder lever
2 Tappet
3 Adjuster wheel
4 Outer piston & pressing
5 Seal
6 Seal and inner piston
7 Adjuster pawl
8 Rubber dust cover
9 Pivot pin
10 Backplate
11 Leading brake shoe
12 Fixed abutment
13 Trailing brake shoe
14 Steady post

(1~9)

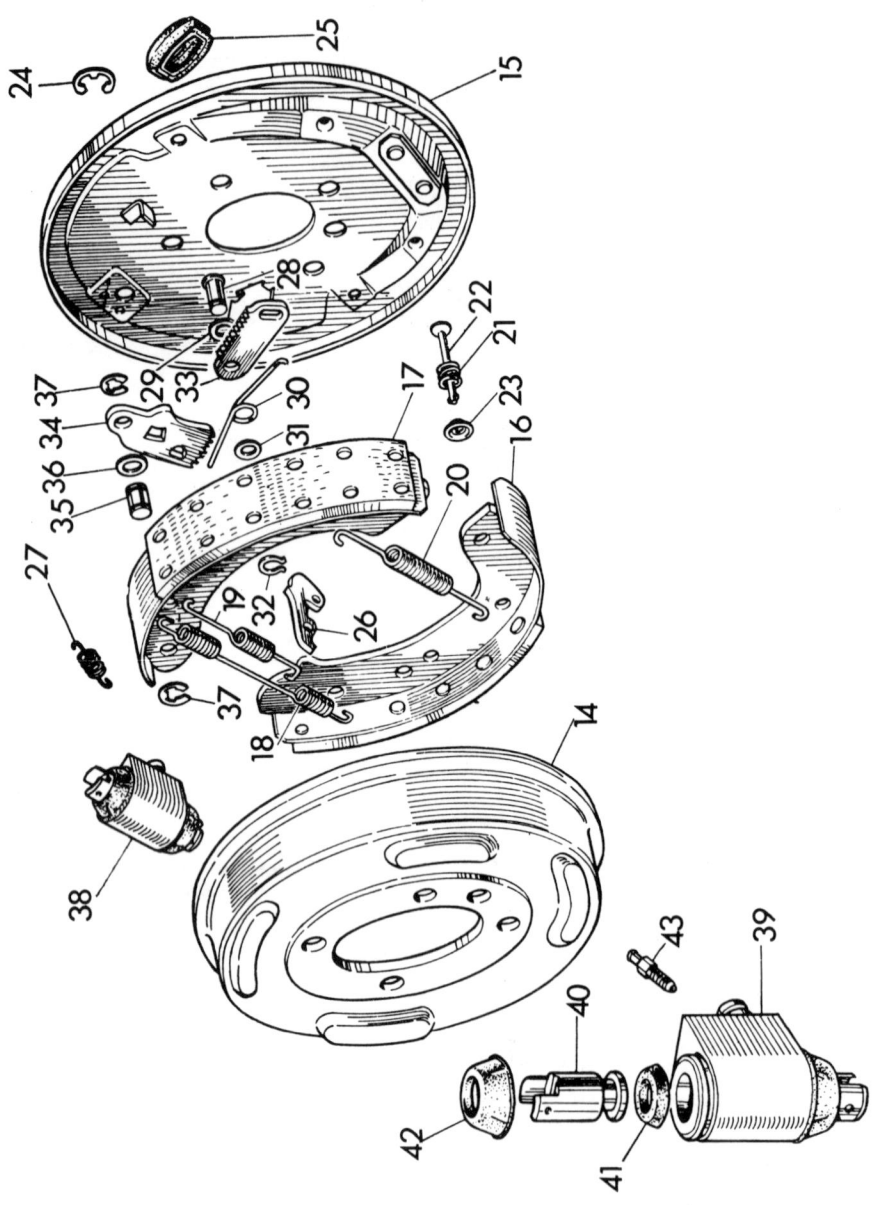

Fig. 9.8. REAR BRAKE ASSEMBLY & SELF ADJUSTING MECHANISM
(LATER TYPE) WITH DOUBLE PISTON SLAVE CYLINDER

14 Drum
15 Backplate
16 Shoe
17 Lining
18 Retractor spring

19 Retractor spring-handbrake lever
20 Retractor spring
21 Tensioning spring
22 Steady pin
23 Retainer cup

24 Circlip - cylinder retaining
25 Rubber boot
26 Handbrake lever
27 Shoe to piston link spring
28 Clevis pin - lever pivot

29 Washer
30 Ratchet lever spring
31 Washer
32 Circlip
33 Lower ratchet lever

34 Upper ratchet lever
35 Pivot pin - upper lever
36 Washer
37 Circlip
38 Wheel cylinder assembly

39 Wheel cylinder
40 Piston
41 Seal
42 Boot
43 Bleed nipple

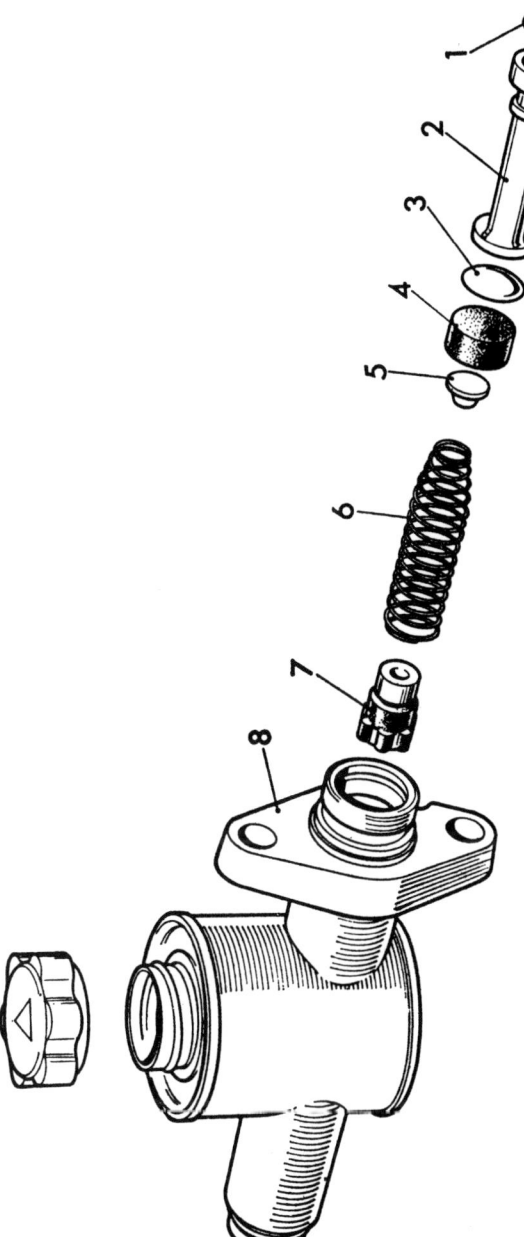

Fig. 9.9. MASTER CYLINDER (EXPLODED VIEW)

1 Secondary cup seal
2 Piston
3 Piston washer

4 Primary cup seal
5 Spring retainer
6 Return spring

7 Trap valve
8 Cylinder body

clear of fluid it should be possible to see through it. Any specks of rubber which come out, or signs of restriction in the bore, mean that the inner lining is breaking up and the pipe must be replaced.

8. Rigid pipes which need replacement can usually be purchased at any local garage where they have the pipe, unions and special tools to make them up. All that they need to know is the pipe length required and the type of flare used at the ends of the pipe. These may be different at each end of the same pipe.

9. Replacement of pipes is a straightforward reversal of the removal procedure. It is best to get all the sets (bends) in the pipe made preparatory to installation. Also any acute bends should be put in by the garage on a bending machine otherwise there is the possibility of kinking them and restricting the bore area and fluid flow.

10 With the pipes replaced, remove the polythene from the reservoir cap and bleed the system as described in Section 13

8. Hydraulic Wheel Cylinders (Rear) - Inspection and Repair

1. If it is suspected that one or more of the wheel cylinders is malfunctioning, jack up the suspect wheel and remove the brake drum as described in Section 5.

2. Inspect for signs of fluid leakage around the wheel cylinder and if there are any, proceed as described in paragraph 5.

3. Next get someone to press the brake pedal very gently a small amount. Watch the wheel cylinder and see that the piston moves out a little. On no account let it come right out or it will need reassembly and bleeding. On releasing the pedal pressure make sure that the retraction springs on the shoes move the piston back into position without delay. If the piston moves satisfactorily make sure also that the cylinder body is free to slide endways in the slot in the backplate. If it should be seized it will mean that only one brake shoe is being applied.

4. If there is a leak, or the piston does not move (or only moves very slowly under excessive pressure) then the rubber piston seals will need renewal at least.

5. Seal the reservoir cap and remove the brake shoes as described in Section 5.

6. Disconnect the brake fluid pipes where they enter the cylinder and plug the ends of the lines to minimise loss of fluid.

7. Remove the split pin and clevis pin from the handbrake operating link and the rubber dust cover.

8. The cylinder is retained by two U shaped clips and these can be drawn out by inserting a pointed instrument in the base of the U. On later models the cylinder is fixed and has a double piston, each operating one end of both shoes.

9. Then pull out the piston, complete with seal and the spring. Examine the piston and cylinder for signs of wear or scoring and if there are any the whole assembly must be renewed. If they are in good condition only the seal needs renewal. Pull the old one off the piston and thoroughly clean the whole assembly using clean hydraulic fluid or methylated spirit.

10 Fit the new seal to the piston so that the lip faces away from the centre of the piston.

11 Lubricate the components in hydraulic fluid before reassembly which is carried out in the reverse order. Make sure the lip of the seal on the piston enters the cylinder first.

12 When refitting the cylinder to the backplate the handbrake link must be positioned correctly.

13 Reconnect the handbrake cable and hydraulic pipes and replace the brake shoes and drum as described in Section 5. Bleed the hydraulic system as described in Section 13

9. Disc Callipers - Inspection, Removal and Repair

1. Any indications of fluid leaks or piston seizures in the front brake callipers will mean that they have to be removed for repair.

2. Jack up the car and remove the wheel and brake pads as described in Section 3.

3. To facilitate piston removal depress the brake pedal now to force them out as far as they can go up to the disc.

4. Seal the fluid reservoir cap with polythene sheet and disconnect the hydraulic pipe union from the body of the calliper.

5. The calliper is held to the stub axle by two bolts. Do not under any circumstances loosen the other bolts as these hold the two halves of the calliper together. The calliper can then be lifted away.

6. Provided the pistons are not seized they can be drawn out by hand but in any case if some air pressure can be applied to the fluid inlet it will make things easier. If one piston is very tight try using methylated spirits to ease it. If drastic measures are necessary try and confine any damage to the piston rather than the calliper body.

7. Remove the dust seals and retaining rings from the annular grooves in the cylinder bores and then pull out the piston fluid seals from their grooves.

8. Examine the pistons and bores for signs of wear and scores. If there are signs of wear the whole assembly will probably need replacement.

9. The cylinders and pistons should be thoroughly cleaned in fluid or methylated spirits and care taken to avoid contamination by dirt or mineral oils.

10 Before reassembly lubricate the parts with hydraulic fluid and begin by placing the piston seal in the cylinder in its groove and inserting next the bellows so that its outer lip engages in the top cylinder groove. Then fit the dust seal and retaining ring making sure that they fit flush and square. The piston should be inserted carefully after lubricating with fluid or special disc brake lubricant. On pistons with anti-squeal cut-outs make sure these are correctly positioned as mentioned in Section 3.

11 The calliper may now be refitted to the stub axle. Tighten the bolts to a torque of 60 lbs/ft.

12 Replace the pads and shims as described in Section 3, reconnect the hydraulic pipe and bleed the system as described in Section 13. Replace the wheel and road test the car.

10. Master Cylinder - Removal and Replacement

1. If the disc calliper pistons and rear wheel hydraulic cylinders are in order and there are no leaks elsewhere, yet the brake pedal still does not hold under sustained pressure then the master cylinder seals may be presumed to be ineffective. To renew them the master cylinder must be removed.

2. Disconnect the master cylinder pushrod from the brake pedal by removing the clevis pin.

3. Unscrew the hydraulic pipe union and push the pipe to one side.

4. Remove the two nuts and washers holding the master cylinder to the bulkhead and lift the unit away. Empty the contents of the reservoir into a clean container.

5. Replacement is a reversal of the removal procedure, after which the braking system must be completely bled.

11. Master Cylinder - Dismantling, Overhaul and Reassembly

1. Unless there are obvious signs of leakage any defects in the master cylinder are usually the last to be detected in the hydraulic system.

2. Before assuming that a fault in the system is in the master cylinder the pipes and wheel cylinders should all be checked and examined as described in Sections 7 and 8.

3. Remove the master cylinder from the car as described in the previous Section.

4. Dismantle and reassemble the unit as described for the clutch master cylinder in Chapter 5.

12. Servo Unit - Removal, Overhaul and Reassembly

1. The servo unit, fitted to some cars, is an additional source of power boost to the hydraulic system for brake application. It uses

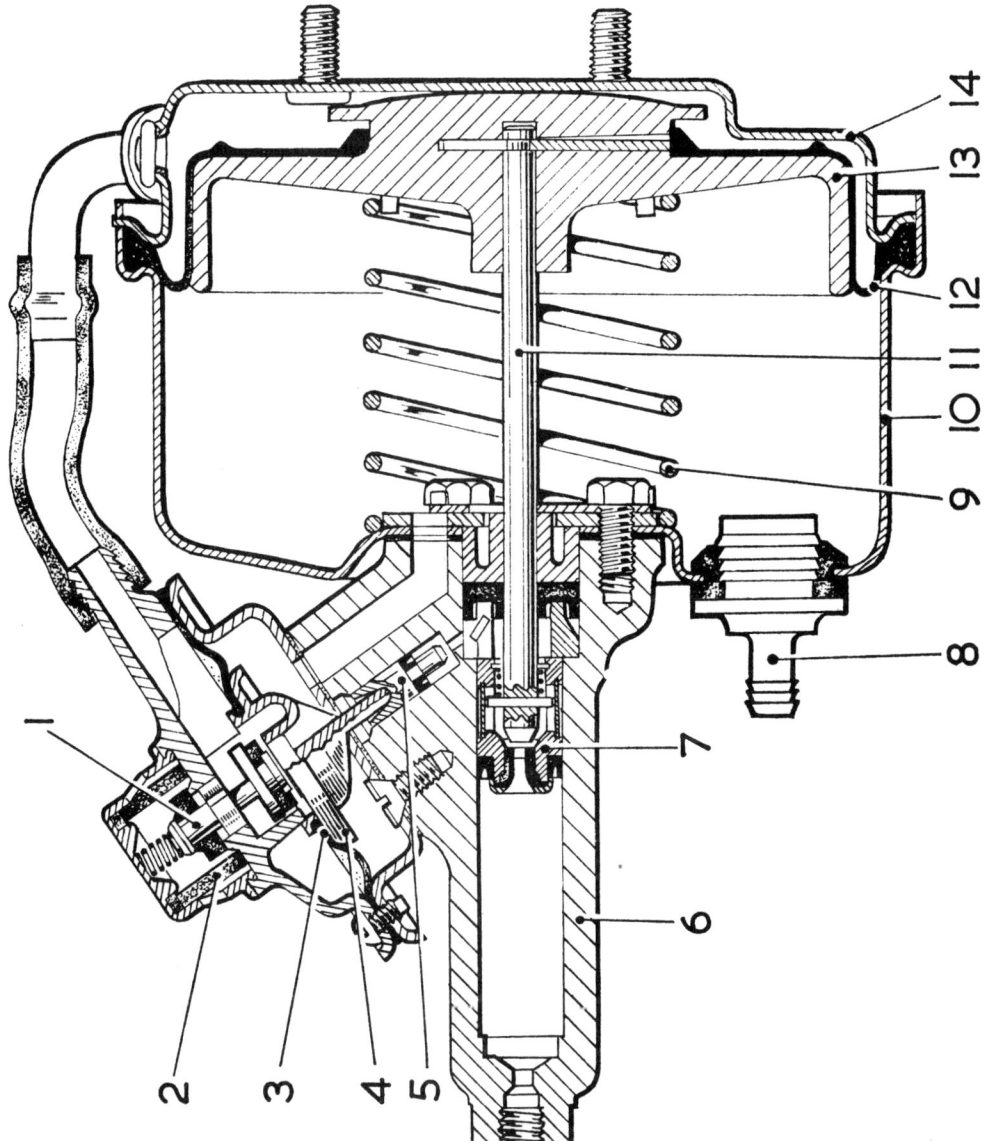

Fig. 9.10. CROSS SECTION OF ASSEMBLED SERVO UNIT (LOCKHEED TYPE 6)

1 Air valve and air valve
  return spring
2 Air filter
3 Air valve diaphragm
4 Air valve diaphragm support

5 Air valve piston
6 Slave cylinder
7 Slave cylinder piston
8 Vacuum connection and
  non-return valve

9 Servo return spring
10 Servo shell
11 Push rod
12 Servo rubber
13 Piston

14 Servo end cover

the vacuum from the inlet manifold on a larger diameter diaphragm. This drives a piston in an intermediate hydraulic slave cylinder, thus supplementing the pressure applied on the foot pedal. If the servo unit should fail, the hydraulic system will still be open to permit pressure from the master cylinder to reach the wheel cylinders. If the servo unit needs removal for any reason, it must be remembered that no braking will be available, other than from the handbrake, unless a direct hydraulic line is made between the master cylinder and the four way connector.

2. The servo is mounted low down on the left hand wing valance panel. To remove it first disconnect the battery and remove the carburettor air cleaner. Loosen the clamping bolt on the bracket clip at the slave cylinder end and disconnect the vacuum pipe from either the inlet manifold or the servo. Seal the master cylinder reservoir cap with polythene sheet to minimise fluid loss and then disconnect both the hydraulic pipes at the servo slave cylinder. Try and cap the pipe ends with something to keep out dirt and keep in the fluid. Undo the nuts holding the shell and mounting bracket to the bodywork and lift the unit out.

3. Before dismantling the unit make sure the exterior is perfectly clean and prepare an equally clean work bench on which to work. A complete repair kit which includes diaphragms and seals for the air valve, vacuum piston and hydraulic piston, should be obtained in advance.

4. Grip the servo unit in a well padded vice by the slave cylinder body with the air valve uppermost.

5. Remove the rubber pipe from the end cover connection.

6. Undo the screws securing the plastic air valve cover and lift off the cover assembly complete, which comprises the filter and valve. If the air valve is suspect a new assembly which is part of the complete repair kit will have to be obtained. (i.e. these individual parts cannot be obtained separately).

7. The dome containing these items is a snap fit into the air valve cover.

8. Remove the rubber diaphragm and its plastic support, and the three valve housing securing screws will then be revealed. Undo these and take off the housing and joint washer.

9. To get the air control valve piston out of its cylinder will require a low pressure inside the slave cylinder. This can be done by blocking one of the two hydraulic fluid unions on the slave cylinder with a finger and applying air pressure from a foot pump to the other. When it is out remove the rubber cup from the piston (for replacement).

10 The non return valve which is mounted in a rubber grommet can be pushed out by thumb pressure. Remove the grommet also.

11 It is now necessary to remove the end cover from the main servo shell. This is a twist fit bayonet type of connection and to remove it calls for an anti-clockwise twist as far as the stops in the cover will permit; when it will come off. Although there is a special tool for this (C2030) one can achieve the same result by drilling three holes in a plate to which the vacuum shell can be bolted and then clamp the plate in the vice and twist the cover off.

12 Put the unit back into the vice as before. To remove the diaphragm it is not necessary to free the retaining key from the pushrod. Turn the diaphragm support so that the retaining key points downwards. Then supply light fluctuating pressure to the backplate against the main return spring and the retaining key will drop out.

13 Hold on to the diaphragm support and take it and the diaphragm and the return spring from the servo shell.

14 The bolts holding the servo shell to the slave cylinder are now exposed. Bend back the locking plate tabs from the bolt heads and remove the bolts, locking plate and abutment plate.

15 The shell can now be taken from the slave cylinder. Retrieve the washer between the two.

16 The pushrod can now be drawn from the slave cylinder together with piston assembly.

17 Slide the bearing cup and spacer off the pushrod noting the order and position in which they came off.

18 Prise the rubber seal off the slave piston.

19 If the rod is to be detached from the piston the following action will be required but a new retaining clip will be needed. It should not normally be necessary to separate them. Open up the retaining clip by twisting a small screwdriver in the join and this will expose the connecting pin which can be pushed out. This disconnects the slave piston from the connecting rod. This unit is now completely dismantled.

20 Examine all rubber cups and seals for wear and replace as necessary. If the air valve unit is in good condition and it is only necessary to clean the filter, blow it through with a tyre foot pump. Do not use any cleaning fluids or lubricants on the filter.

21 Wash all slave cylinder components in clean hydraulic fluid, and remove any deposits from the slave cylinder walls in the same way. If the slave cylinder is scored then it must be replaced.

22 Reassembly must be done in very clean conditions as a single speck of grit in the wrong place can cause total malfunction. It is best to wash your hands, get new clean cloths and lay out all the components on a sheet of clean white paper. Five minutes' extra attention now could save you another complete dismantling operation later.

23 Use clean hydraulic fluid as a lubricant when reassembling the hydraulic components.

24 If the piston and pushrod were separated push the rod into the rear of the piston against the spring until the connecting pin hole is open. Fit the pin followed by the retaining clip. It is important to ensure that the clip fits snugly in its groove. Any protrusions will score the cylinder wall.

25 Refit the rubber seal to the slave piston using only the fingers, ensuring that the lips of the seal face away from the pushrod.

26 Lubricate (with hydraulic fluid only) the cylinder bore and insert the piston. Then replace in correct order, over the pushrod the spacer cup and bearing into the mouth of the slave cylinder. Ensure that each item placed into the cylinder has its sealing lips neither bent nor turned back and that each is bedded individually in turn.

27 The servo shell is now already in the reverse order as given in paragraph 10. If the locking plate has been used more than once before (i.e. if the servo has already been twice dismantled) a new one should be fitted. Tighten the bolts evenly to a torque figure of 17 lb/ft. and tap up the locking plate tabs.

28 To replace the diaphragm, support and spring pull out the pushrod as far as possible. Fit the spring and diaphragm support ensuring that the spring ends are correctly located over the abutment plate and the diaphragm support boss.

29 Press the diaphragm support over the pushrod with the key slot facing upwards and when the groove in the pushrod and the slot in the diaphragm are lined up insert the key.

30 Ensuring that the support and diaphragm are quite clean and dry fit the diaphragm to the support, gently stretching the inner edge to ensure that it seats properly in the groove of the support.

31 Smear the outer edge of the diaphragm with disc brake lubricant (not grease or hydraulic oil). This prevents it from binding when the lid cover is refitted to the servo shell.

32 If no service tool is available fix the end cover onto the vehicle mounting bracket (if you did not leave it there when taking it off) using the normal mounting units. Offer up the servo unit to the end cover so that when twisted clockwise the pipe will line up with the elbow on the end cover when the turn is completely up to the stops.

33 With the unit back on the bench replace the non return valve and its mounting grommet.

34 To replace the air valve assembly first fit the rubber piston cup to the spigot of the piston ensuring that the lips face away from the spigot shoulder. Lubricate the cup with a little hydraulic fluid and insert it into the slave cylinder, taking care that the lips do not get bent back.

35 Fit the joint washer and valve housing to the slave cylinder using the three securing screws.

36 Fit the diaphragm support into the diaphragm and make sure that the inner ring fits snugly into the groove in the support. Then place the spigot of the support into the hole in the air valve piston. Use no lubricants.

37 Line up the screw holes in the diaphragm and the valve housing.

38 If the air filter and dome have been removed now is the time to

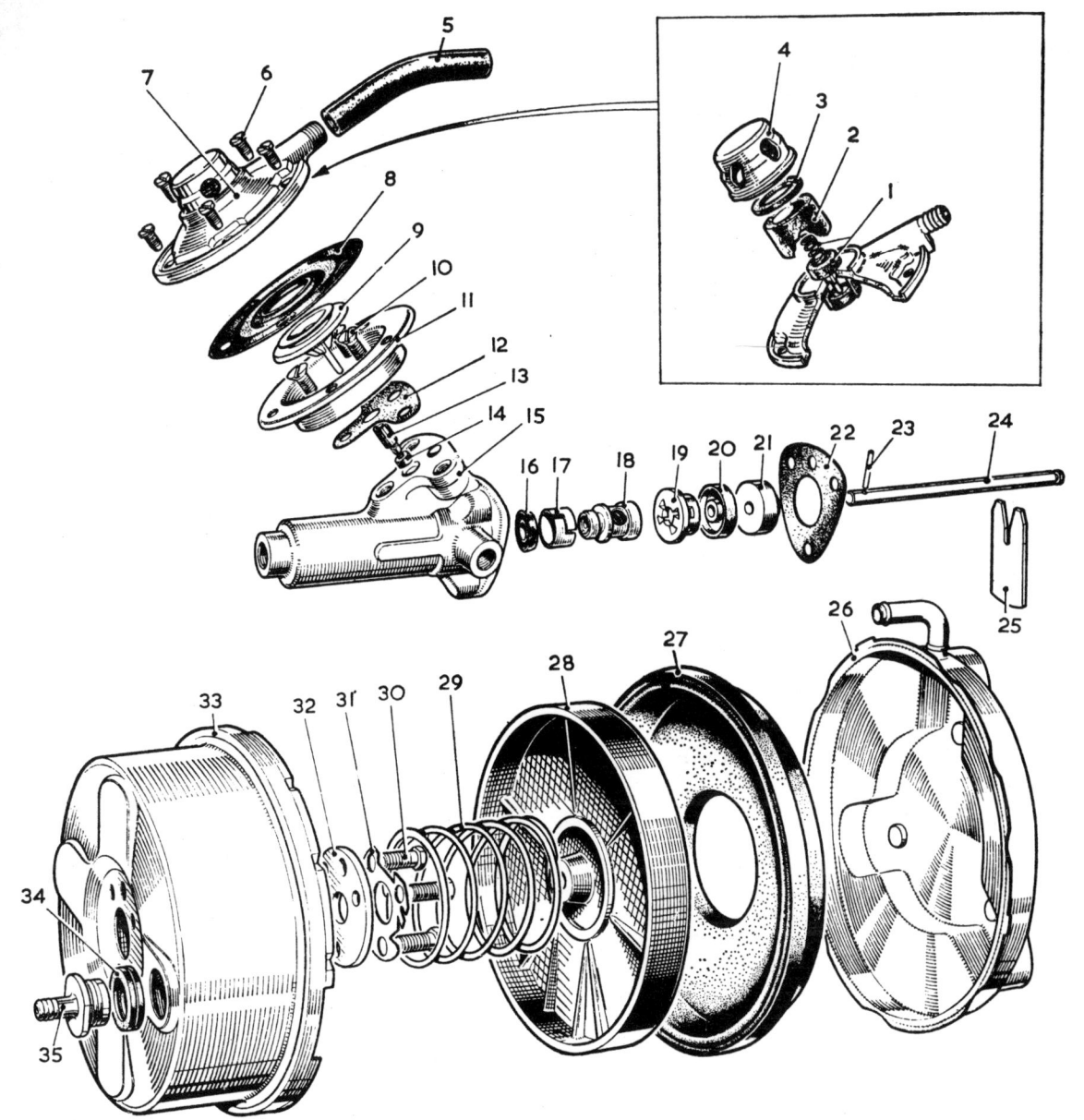

Fig. 9.11. LOCKHEED TYPE 6 SERVO UNIT (EXPLODED VIEW)

1 Air valve and air valve return spring	11 Air valve unit lower housing	21 Plastic bearing
2 Air filter	12 Joint - air valve unit to slave cylinder	22 Joint - slave cylinder to servo shell
3 Sorbo washer	13 Air valve piston	23 Retainer pin - piston (19) to push rod (24)
4 Air valve cover dome	14 Air valve piston rubber cup	24 Push rod
5 Connecting hose	15 Slave cylinder	25 Retaining key - push rod (24) to diaphragm support (28)
6 Air valve cover fixing screws	16 Slave piston rubber seal	26 End cover
7 Air valve unit cover	17 Retainer for connecting pin (23)	27 Servo rubber diaphragm
8 Air valve diaphragm	18 Slave cylinder piston	28 Diaphragm support
9 Air valve diaphragm support	19 Plastic spacer	29 Servo return spring
10 Air valve fixing unit securing screws	20 Rubber cup	

30 Bolts - slave cylinder to servo shell	
31 Locking plate	
32 Abutment plate	
33 Servo shell	
34 Rubber seal mounting - vacuum non-return valve	
35 Vacuum connection and non-return valve - plastic	

snap the complete assembly back into the air valve cover.

39 Place the valve cover over the diaphragm so that the projections in the cover engage the slots in the diaphragm. Replace all five securing screws finger tight. Tighten them down firmly, but not overtight, in a progressive pattern roughly North, South, East, West. This tightening sequence is important as the air valve must seat evenly and precisely. Any leak renders the whole servo inoperative.

40 Refit the rubber pipe from the valve cover port to the end cover elbow.

41 Replacement of the unit on the car is a reversal of the removal procedure. Keep all pipes well clear of the exhaust. Bleed the hydraulic system in the normal manner when reconnected and test without delay.

13. Hydraulic System - Bleeding

1. The system should need bleeding only when some part of the system has been dismantled which would allow air into the fluid circuit; or if the reservoir level has been allowed to drop so far that air has entered the master cylinder.

2. Ensure that a supply of clean non-aerated fluid of the correct specification is to hand in order to replenish the reservoir during the bleeding process. It is advisable, if not essential, to have someone available to help, as one person has to pump the brake pedal while the other attends to each wheel. The reservoir level has also to be continuously watched and replenished. Fluid bled out should not be re-used. A clean glass jar and a 9-12 inch length of $1/8$ inch internal diameter rubber tube that will fit tightly over the bleed nipples is also required.

3. Bleed the front brakes first as these hold the largest quantity of fluid in the system.

4. Make sure the bleed nipple is clean and put a small quantity of fluid in the bottom of the jar. Fit the tube onto the nipple and place the other end in the jar under the surface of the liquid. Keep it under the surface throughout the bleeding operation.

5. Unscrew the bleed screw ½ turn and get the assistant to depress and release the brake pedal in short sharp bursts when you direct him. Short sharp jabs are better than long slow ones because they will force any air bubbles along the line ahead of the fluid rather than pump the fluid past them. It is not essential to remove all the air the first time. If the whole system is being bled, attend to each wheel for three or four complete pedal strokes and then repeat the process. On the second time around operate the pedal sharply in the same way until no more bubbles are apparent. The bleed screw should be tightened and closed with the brake pedal fully depressed which ensures that no aerated fluid can get back into the system. Do not forget to keep the reservoir topped up throughout.

6. When all four wheels have been satisfactorily bled depress the foot pedal which should offer a firmer resistance with no trace of 'sponginess'. The pedal should not continue to go down under sustained pressure. If it does there is a leak or the master cylinder seals are worn out. For dual braking systems read Section 17 for different procedures.

14. Brake Pedal - Removal and Replacement

Should the brake pedal pivot shaft become excessively sloppy due to wear in the pivot shaft there could be a lot of lost motion between the initial movement of the pedal and application of the brakes. This is not a satisfactory state of affairs. To remove the pedal and shaft assembly follow the procedures as laid down for the clutch pedal in Chapter 5, Section 6

15. Stop Light Switch

The stop light switch is a pressure operated contact mounted in the hydraulic system on the face of the fourway connector. If the brake lights do not work when the pedal is depressed check first that the bulbs are all right. Then remove both leads from the terminals on the switch and touch them together. With the ignition switched on the brake lights should now work. If they do, the switch is faulty and should be unscrewed and a new one fitted. Bleed the hydraulic system afterwards.

16. Dual Braking System - Description

Models for the North American market have to be fitted with dual braking systems to meet the safety laws. It is possible that the law or the manufacturers may decide that the same feature is necessary for the domestic market also. The dual braking system consists of two separate hydraulic circuits which are operated from a tandem master cylinder. Should there be a break in one circuit with consequent loss of pressure it means that there is still the other remaining to halt the car. Obviously the two circuits are each for the front and rear brakes. All dual brake system models are fitted with servo assistance to the front wheel circuit only. In addition, a pressure failure switch is incorporated into the hydraulic circuit so that immediate indication is given of the failure of one circuit. It consists of a double ended piston held in central balance in a cylinder, between the opposing pressure of each hydraulic circuit. Should one pressure differ from the other the piston will move and operate a switch which lights an indicator on the instrument panel. The same light is operated by a switch on the handbrake also - which helps to indicate that the electrics are working properly.

17. Tandem Master Cylinder and Pressure Failure Switch - Removal, Overhaul and Replacement

1. The cylinder is disconnected by undoing the hydraulic pipe unions and unscrewing the two mounting bolts in the same way as for a conventional cylinder. Before attempting to dismantle the unit it is essential to have a complete repair kit available. Special circlip pliers are also needed. The conventional variety will not reach the circlips in the bore of the cylinder.

2. Remove the rubber boot and pushrod and place the cylinder in a soft-jawed vice with the bore mouth upwards. Push down the spring retainer and this will reveal a 'Spirolox' locking ring in a groove in the cylinder wall. Carefully hook this out using a small screwdriver, pushing the end in an anti-clockwise direction. Then remove the retainer and spring.

3. Remove the first circlip and then pull off the nylon bearing and cup seal from the primary piston. This will involve moving the piston up and down in the bore. Then remove the plain washer.

4. The second circlip is now accessible and should be removed. The piston assembly and stop washer can now be drawn out of the cylinder.

5. To fit new seals the pistons will have to be separated. This can be done by compressing the spring between them and punching out the pin from the end of the primary piston which hooks into the loop from the secondary piston.

6. Apart from the cup already taken out, there are three main cups and two piston washers fitted to the pistons. Note carefully how these are fitted and where, before pulling them off. The odd one out is in fact that on the rear end (the connecting link end) of the secondary piston. The internal bore is larger and there are no dimples in the lip.

7. Maintaining scrupulous cleanliness fit the new cups and washers in position and reassemble the pistons. Examine carefully the bore of the cylinder which should show no signs of scoring or damage. The cups on the secondary piston should have their lips pointing towards the end of the piston and the washer behind the head cup should have the concave side against the seal cup. The same applies to the washer behind the cup of the primary piston.

8. When reassembling the pistons to the cylinder make sure the lips

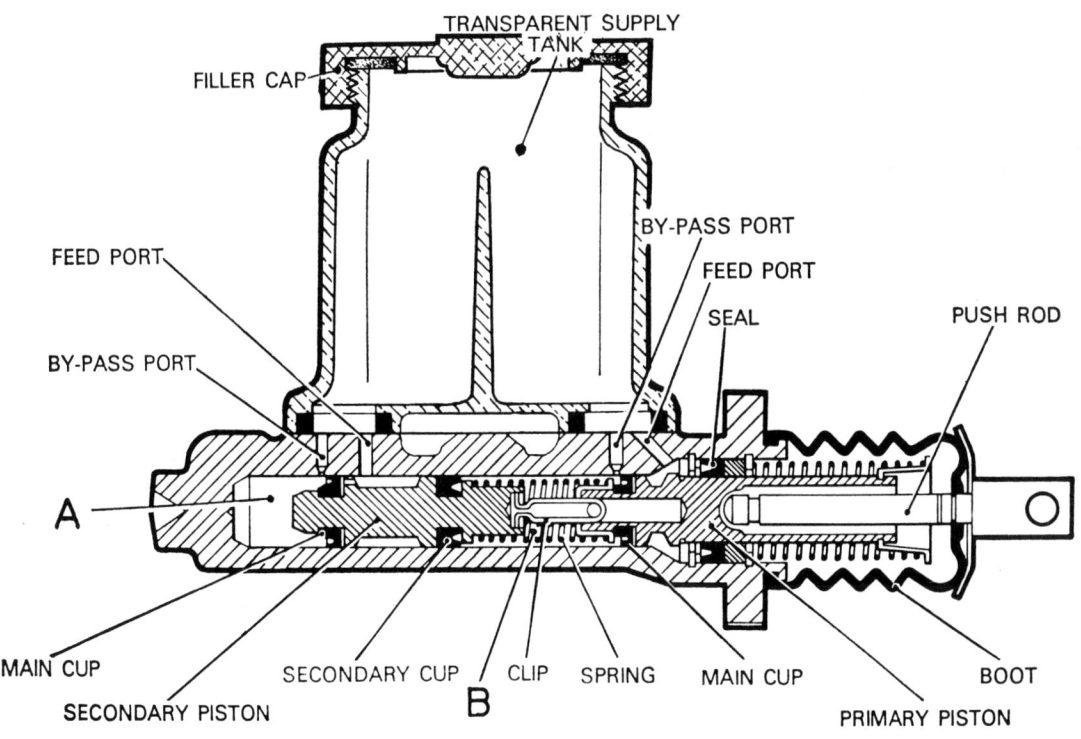

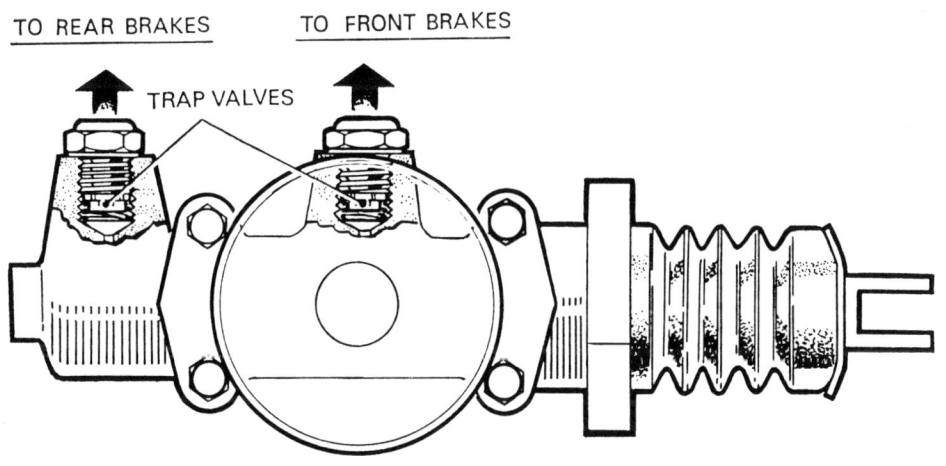

Fig. 9.12. TANDEM MASTER CYLINDER (CROSS SECTIONS)
A Rear brake fluid chamber
B Front brake fluid chamber

of the cups are not turned back. The stop washer should be put over the end of the primary piston (when it is in the bore) and the piston assembly pressed down until the circlip groove is revealed. Make sure the circlip fits securely. After assembly coat the inside and beaded edges of the rubber boot with special rubber grease and insert the pushrod into the boot and the rear of the piston. Then fit the boot over the cylinder with the small hole facing away from the supply tank.

9. If the trap valves are to be taken out of the two outlet pipe unions in the cylinder first carefully remove the adaptor fittings and discard the copper gaskets which must be renewed each time they are taken out.

10 The seals of the pressure equalizing switch may need renewal and this is simply done by first unscrewing the switch and withdrawing it. Then undo the end cap and pull out the piston. The seals may then be removed.

11 To bleed the hydraulic system on a dual braking system requires a slightly different approach from normal because the pressure equalising switch has to be balanced in a central position. Ensure first there is no residual vacuum in the servo by operating the brake pedal several times. Do not restart the engine. Begin bleeding with the **rear** brakes and if the rear brake system only has been opened then a bleed valve on the front system will also have to be opened at the same time to permit fluid to be released. After finishing the rear brakes, bleed the front. If the pressure warning light should remain on (hand brake off!) after completing the bleeding, open a rear bleed nipple and apply light pressure to the brake pedal. Immediately the light goes out close the bleed valve and then release the pedal. If the light should stay on, even after one complete down stroke of the pedal, close the bleed valve at the end of the pedal stroke and then do the same thing at one of the front brakes. If the warning light flashes on and off intermittently when the brakes are applied then there must be a pressure variation between the two systems which must be fully investigated.

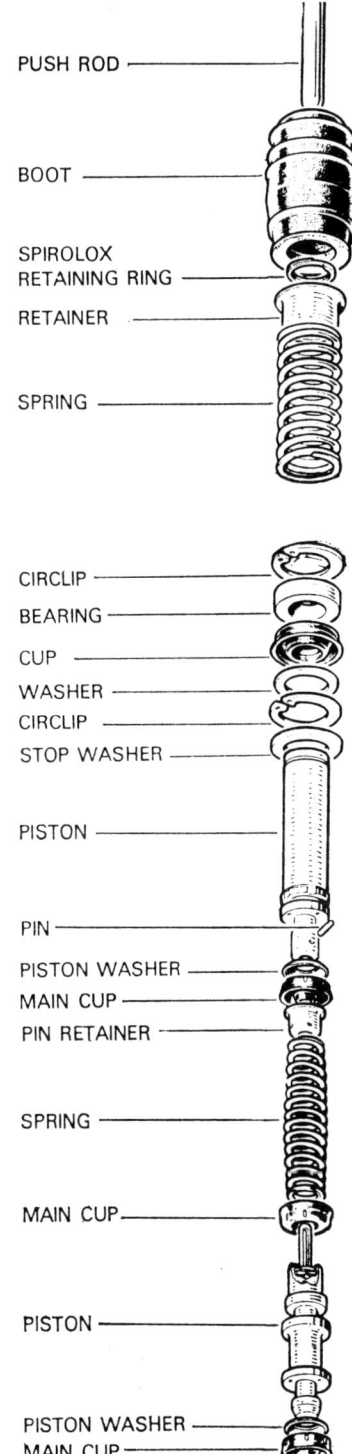

PUSH ROD

BOOT

SPIROLOX
RETAINING RING

RETAINER

SPRING

CIRCLIP
BEARING
CUP
WASHER
CIRCLIP
STOP WASHER

PISTON

PIN

PISTON WASHER
MAIN CUP
PIN RETAINER

SPRING

MAIN CUP

PISTON

PISTON WASHER
MAIN CUP

Fig. 9.13. TANDEM MASTER CYLINDER
Exploded view of piston assembly.

Fault Finding Chart — Braking System

Before diagnosing faults from the following chart, check that any braking irregularities are not caused by:—

1. Uneven or incorrect tyre pressures
2. Incorrect 'mix' of radial and cross-ply tyres
3. Wear in the steering mechanism
4. Defects in the suspension and dampers
5. Misalignment of the body frame

Symptom	Reason	Remedy
Pedal travels a long way before the brakes operate	Automatic adjuster on rear shoes not functioning	Check and repair rear brake automatic adjusters.
	Disc pads or linings excessively worn.	Inspect and renew as necessary.
Stopping ability poor, even though pedal pressure is firm	Linings, pads, discs or drums badly worn or scored.	Dismantle, inspect, and renew as required.
	One or more calliper pistons or rear wheel cylinders seized, resulting in some pads/shoes not pressing against discs/drums.	Dismantle and inspect cylinders and repair or renew as necessary.
	Brake pads or linings contaminated with oil.	Renew pads or linings and repair source of oil contamination.
	Wrong type of pads or linings fitted (too hard).	Verify type of material which is correct for the car and fit it.
	Brake pads or shoes incorrectly assembled.	Check for correct assembly.
	Servo unit (where fitted) not functioning.	Check and repair as necessary.
Car veers to one side when brakes are applied.	Brake pads on one side are contaminated with oil.	Renew pads and repair source of oil contamination.
	Hydraulic pistons in callipers are partially or wholly seized on one side.	Inspect calliper pistons for correct movement and repair as necessary.
	A mixture of pad materials used between sides.	Standardize on types of pads fitted.
	Unequal wear between sides caused by partially seized hydraulic pistons in brake callipers.	Check pistons and renew pads and discs as required.
Pedal feels spongy when the brakes are applied.	Air is present in the hydraulic system.	Bleed the hydraulic system and check for any signs of leakage.
Pedal feels springy when the brakes are applied.	Rear brake linings not bedded into the drums (after fitting new ones).	Allow time for new linings to bed in.
	Master cylinder, brake calliper or drum backplate mounting bolts loose.	Tighten mounting bolts as necessary.
	Severe wear in rear drums causing distortion when brakes are applied.	Renew drums and linings.
Pedal travels right down with little or no resistance and brakes are virtually non-operative.	Leak in hydraulic system resulting in lack of pressure for operation of wheel cylinders.	Examine the whole of the hydraulic system and locate and repair the source of the leak(s). Test after repairing each and every leak source.
	If no signs of leakage are apparent the master cylinder internal seals are failing to sustain pressure.	Overhaul the master cylinder. If indications are that seals have failed for reasons other than wear, all the wheel cylinder seals should be checked also and the system completely replenished with the correct fluid.
Binding, juddering, overheating.	One, or a combination of causes given in the foregoing sections.	Complete and systematic inspection of the whole braking system.

137

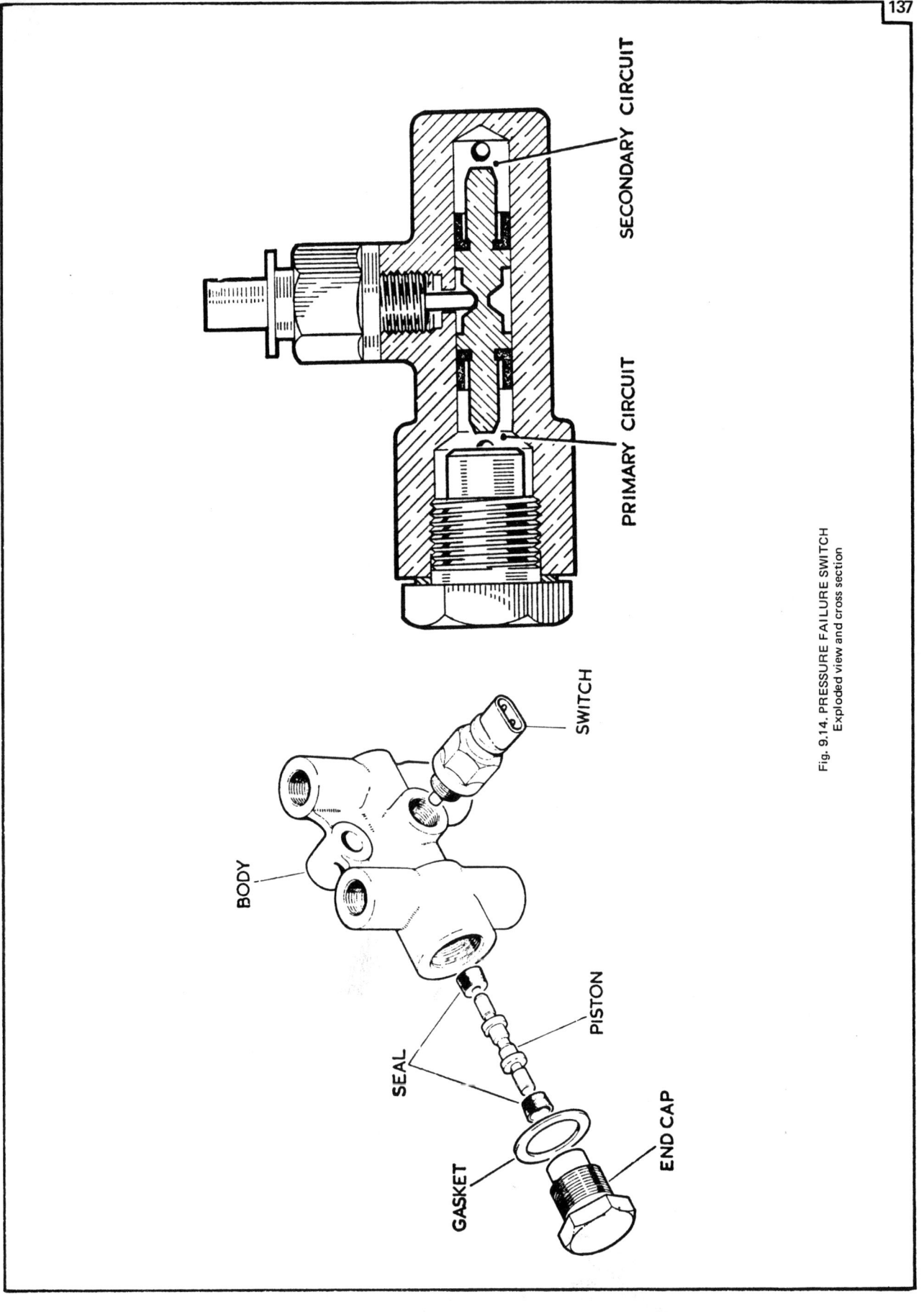

SECONDARY CIRCUIT

PRIMARY CIRCUIT

SWITCH

BODY

SEAL

PISTON

GASKET

END CAP

Fig. 9.14. PRESSURE FAILURE SWITCH
Exploded view and cross section

Chapter 10 Electrical system

Contents

Specifications

Battery

Number of plates	...	...	...	...	...	...	9	11
Capacity of 20 hr rating (amp. hr)	...	...	...	...	...	39 - 40	50 - 55
Voltage and polarity	...	...	...	...	...	...	12 volt negative earth	

DC generator

Type	...	...	...	...	...	...	...	Lucas C40-1 or C40L, shunt wound, two-pole, two brush
Maximum output (cold)	...	...	...	...	...	...	C40-1	C40L
Amps ...	...	...	...	...	...	...	22	25
at rpm	...	...	...	...	...	...	2275	2275
at volts	...	...	...	...	...	...	13.5	13.5
Load (ohms) ...	...	...	...	...	...	...	0.49	0.54
Cutting-in speed (cold) ...	...	...	...	...	...	1350 rpm (max) at 13 volts	
Field resistance ...	...	...	...	...	...	...	5.9 ohms	
Minimum length of brushes	...	...	...	...	...	¼ in (6.4 mm)	
Brush spring tension:								
New brushes ...	...	...	...	...	...	...	30 oz (0.85 kg)	
Brushes worn to ¼ in (6.4 mm)	...	...	...	...	...	15 oz (0.42 kg)	
Control box type	...	...	...	...	...	...	RB340, current/Voltage regulator	

Alternator

					10AC	16AC	15ACR	16ACR	DN460
Type	...	...	...	...	10AC	16AC	15ACR	16ACR	DN460
Regulated voltage	...	...	...	13.9 - 14.3	13.6 - 14.4	13.6 - 14.4	13.6 - 14.4	13.6 - 14.4
DC output (amps)	...	...	...	35	34	28	34	25
Rotor resistance (ohms)	...	...	3.47	4.3	4.3	4.3	2.6 - 2.9
Minimum brush length in (mm)	...	5/32 (4)	0.2 (5)	0.2 (5)	0.2 (5)	0.2 (5)
Brush spring tension (oz)	...	7½ - 8½ at 13/32 in	7 - 10	9	9	8 at ¾ in
Brush spring tension (g)	...	...	210 - 240 at 10 mm	198 - 283	255 - 368	255 - 368	227 at 19 mm
						Brush face flush with brush box			
Warning lamp control	...	...	...	3AW	—	—	—	—
Field isolating relay	...	...	...	6RA	—	—	—	—
Control box type	...	...	...	4TR	8TR	8TR	8TR or 14TR	Motorola
Rectifier pack model	...	...	...	—	4DS5	4DS5	4DS5	—
Warning lamp bulb (watts)	...	...	2.2	3	3	3	3

Starter

	M35G - 1	M35G	M35J, M35J PE
Type	M35G - 1	M35G	M35J, M35J PE
Lock torque	8.2 lb/ft (1.13 kg/m)	8.6 lb/ft (1.19 kg/m)	7 lb/ft (0.97 kg/m)
at amps	370	280	350 - 370
Light running current	45 amps	60 amps	65 amps
at rpm	9,500/11,000	5,500/6,000	8,000/10,000
Minimum brush length	5/16 in (7.9 mm)	5/16 in (7.9 mm)	3/8 in (9.5 mm)
Brush spring tension:			
New brushes	30 - 34 oz (850 - 910 gm)	30 - 34 oz (850 - 910 gm)	28 oz (800 gm) with new
Minimum with worn brushes ...	25 oz (711 gm)	25 oz (711 gm)	brush protruding 1/16 in (1.5 mm) horn brush box

Lamp bulbs

	Lucas reference	Rating
Headlamp (single circular)	Lucas Mk 10 sealed beam	60/45W
Headlamp (rectangular):		
with bulb, early models	451	80/60W
later models	410	45/40W
Headlamp (rectangular)	Sealed beam	75/60W
Headlamp (twin):		
Outer	No. 2A	50/37½W
Inner	No. 1A	50W
Sidelamp, glove box lamp, wing flasher	989	5W
Front and rear indicators, reversing lamp	382	21W
Stop and tail	380	21/5W
Rear number plate, boot lamp	501 or 989	5W capless or 5W
Interior (roof) lamp	254	6W
Panel (instrument) lamps	987	2.4W
Warning lamps, clock	501 or 989	5W capless or 5W

Wiper motor

Type	Lucas D L3A	Lucas 15W
Normal light running current	3.3 amps	1.5 amps
Normal final gear speed	44 - 48 rpm	46 - 52 rpm
High speed running current (light)	2.5 amps	2 amps
High speed final gear speed (light)	60 -70 rpm	60 - 70 rpm

Fuses

Early models have 3 fuses rated at 35 amp. Later cars (Series 4, 5 and 6 have an eight fuse unit. See Chapter 13).

1 General description

The electrical system is 12 volt and apart from the ignition which is dealt with in Chapter 4, the main items are:-

a) Battery - lead/acid, 12 volt, negative earth.
b) Dynamo driven by the fan belt, coupled with a voltage and current regulator or:
c) Alternator driven by the fan belt, coupled with a voltage and current regulator.
d) Electro-mechanical starter motor. One of three types is fitted. One throws a pinion into engagement with the flywheel ring gear as soon as the motor shafts starts to revolve. The other two engage the pinion with the flywheel ring gear by means of a solenoid and then power is switched to the motor itself.

The battery provides starting power and a reserve, should the loading of the equipment exceed the output of the dynamo. (Where an alternator is fitted this rarely happens). When the dynamo or alternator is not fully loaded the extra current available is used to charge the battery. When the battery is fully charged and the load demand is light the output of the dynamo or alternator is regulated so that overcharging does not damage the battery.

2 Battery - Removal and Replacement

1 The battery is situated at the front right hand side of the engine compartment.
2 Disconnect the earth lead (negative) from the terminal by unscrewing the centre screw and twisting the terminal cover off. Do not use any striking force or damage could be caused to the battery. Then remove the positive lead in the same way.
3 Slacken off the nuts holding the battery clamp stays until the assembly can be disengaged sufficiently to lift the battery out.
4 Lift the battery out, keeping it the right way up to prevent spillage of the electrolyte.
5 Replacement is a reversal of this procedure. Replace the positive lead first and smear the terminal posts and connections beforehand with petroleum jelly (not grease) in order to prevent corrosion.

3. Battery - Maintenance and Inspection

1. Check the battery electrolyte level weekly by lifting off the cover or removing the individual cell plugs. The tops of the plates should be just covered with the liquid and if not, add distilled water so that they are just covered. Do **not** add extra water with the idea of reducing the intervals of topping up. This will merely dilute the electrolyte and reduce charging and current retention efficiency. On batteries fitted with patent covers, troughs, glass balls and so on, follow the instructions in the handbook or marked on the cover of the battery to ensure correct addition of water.

2. Keep the battery clean and dry all over by wiping it with a dry cloth. A damp top surface could cause tracking between the two terminal posts with consequent draining of power.

3. Every three months remove the battery and check the support tray clamp and battery terminal connections for signs of corrosion - usually indicated by a whitish green crystalline deposit. Wash this off with clean water to which a little ammonia or washing soda has been added. Then treat the terminals with petroleum jelly and the battery mounting with suitable protective paint to prevent the metal being eaten away. Clean the battery thoroughly and repair any cracks with a proprietary sealer. If there has been any excessive leakage the appropriate cell may need an addition of electrolyte rather than just distilled water.

4. If the electrolyte level needs an excessive amount of replenishment and no leaks are apparent it could be due to overcharging as a result of the battery having been run down and then left to recharge from the vehicle rather than an outside source. If the battery has been heavily discharged for one reason or another it is best to have it continuously charged at a low amperage for a period of many hours. If it is charged from the car's system under such conditions the charging will be intermittent and greatly varied in intensity. This does not do the battery any good at all. If the battery needs topping up frequently, even when it is known to be in good condition and not too old, then the voltage regulator should be checked to ensure that the charging output is being correctly controlled. An elderly battery however may need topping up more than a new one because it needs to take in more charging current. Do not worry about this provided it gives satisfactory service.

5. When checking a battery's condition a hydrometer should be used. On some batteries where the terminals of each of the six cells are exposed a discharge tester can be used to check the condition of any one cell also. On modern batteries the use of a discharge tester is no longer regarded as useful as the replacement or repair of cells is not an economic proposition. The tables below give the hydrometer readings for various states of charge. A further check can be made when the battery is undergoing a charge. If, towards the end of the charge, when the cells are meant to be 'gassing' (bubbling), one cell appears not to be, then it indicates that the cell or cells in question are probably breaking down and the life of the battery is limited.

4. Battery - Charging and Electrolyte Replenishment

1. It is possible that in winter time when the load on the battery cannot be recuperated during normal driving time (from a dynamo) external charging is desirable. This is best done overnight at a 'trickle' rate of 1—1.5 amps. Alternatively a 3—4 amp. rate can be used over a period of four hours or so. Check the specific gravity in the latter case and stop the charge when the reading is correct. Most modern charging sets reduce the rate automatically when the fully charged state is neared. Rapid boost charges of 30—60 amps, or more may get you out of trouble or can be used on a battery that has seen better days anyhow. They are not advisable for a good battery that may have run flat for some reason.

2. Electrolyte replenishment should not normally be necessary unless an accident or some other cause such as contamination arises. If it is necessary then it is best to first discharge the battery completely and then tip out all the remaining liquid from all cells.

Then acquire a quantity of mixed electrolyte from a battery shop or garage according to the specifications in the table below. The quantity required will depend on the type of battery but 3—4 pints should be more than enough for most. When the electrolyte has been put into the battery a slow charge - not exceeding one amp - should be given for as long as is necessary to fully charge the battery. This could be up to 36 hours.

Specific gravities for hydrometer readings - (check each cell)

Electrolyte temperature 60°F (15.6°C)

	Climate below 80°F (26.7°C)	Climate above 80°F (26.7°C)
Fully charged	1.270-1.290	1.210-1.230
Half charged	1.190-1.210	1.130-1.150
Discharged completely	1.110-1.130	1.050-1.070

Note:- If the electrolyte temperature is significantly different from 60°F (15.6°C) then the specific gravity reading will be affected. For every 5°F (2.8°C) it will increase or decrease with the temperature by .002.

5. Dynamo - Maintenance and Testing

1. The fan belt tension should be checked every 5,000 miles at least. In fact it is easy enough to do when the bonnet is raised for any other purpose. The belt is correctly adjusted when a total of 5/8 inch deflection can be obtained in the centre of the longest free run of belt. To adjust the tension slacken the three generator mounting bolts and swing it in the required direction. Tighten the bolt in the slotted bracket first and check the tension again before finally tightening the other two. If in doubt as to the final adjustment setting always err on the side of the belt being a little slack rather than too tight. If too tight, excessive strain will be imposed on the dynamo and water pump bearings. If too slack it will slip and squeal and you will soon find out.

2. The dynamo shaft bush at the commutator end should also receive two or three drops of engine oil through the hole in the end cover every 5,000 miles.

3. If the dynamo is suspected of being faulty it may be checked quite easily without taking it from the car. Make sure first that the fan belt is adjusted correctly, the two lead terminals are clean and securely connected and that the battery terminals are clean and tight. Also verify that the terminal connections on the control box 'D' and 'F' are those that come from the 'D' and 'F' terminals on the dynamo and that the leads are intact and unbroken. This can be done with a continuity test on each wire.

4. Next pull off the leads from the terminal on the dynamo and then join the terminals with a short length of non-insulated wire. Using crocodile clips, attach a voltmeter with the positive lead to the centre of the bridge wire on the dynamo terminals and the negative to a good earth nearby. Switch off all ancillary equipment. Start the engine and increase the revolutions smoothly to a maximum of 1,000 r.p.m. The voltmeter should rise immediately with no fluctuations, to give a reading of 15 volts. Do not increase engine speed in an attempt to increase the voltage if it is low. If the voltage is sub-normal the dynamo should be removed for further examination. If a radio suppressor is fitted between the 'D' terminal and earth check again with this removed before deciding the dynamo is faulty. The suppressor may be faulty.

6. Dynamo - Removal and Replacement

1. Slacken the two dynamo retaining bolts and the nut on the sliding link, and move the dynamo in towards the engine so that the fan belt can be removed.

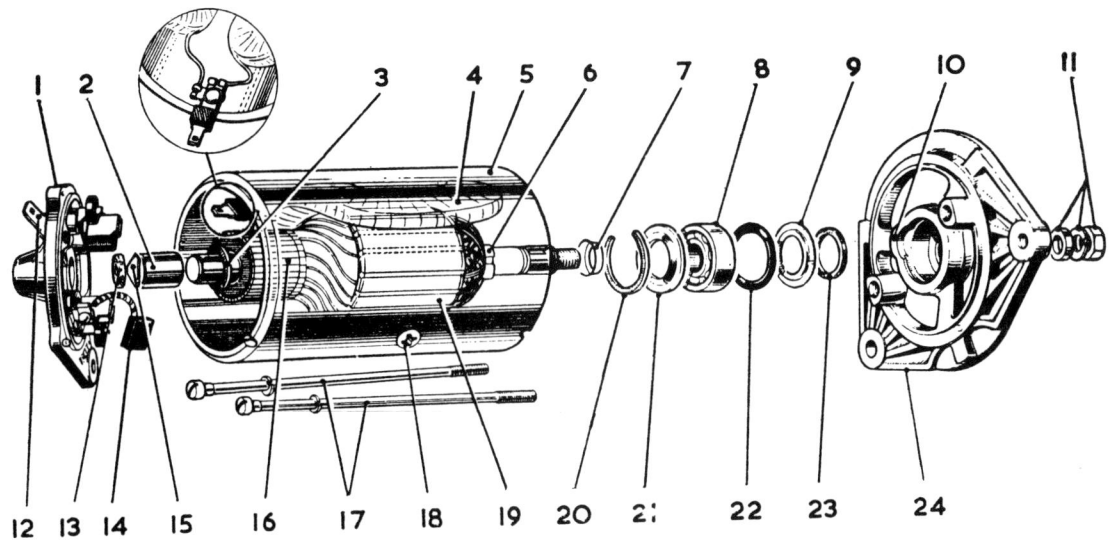

Fig. 10.1. DYNAMO C40L – EXPLODED VIEW

1 Commutator end bracket	7 Retaining cup	13 Felt ring
2 Bronze bush	8 Drive end bearing	14 Carbon brush
3 Fibre washer	9 Pressure ring plate	15 Felt ring retainer
4 Field winding	10 Extractor notch	16 Commutator
5 Yoke	11 Nut and washers	17 Through bolts
6 Armature shaft	12 Terminal 'D'	18 Pole-shoe screw

19 Armature
20 Circlip
21 Bearing retaining plate
22 Pressure ring
23 Felt ring
24 Drive end bracket

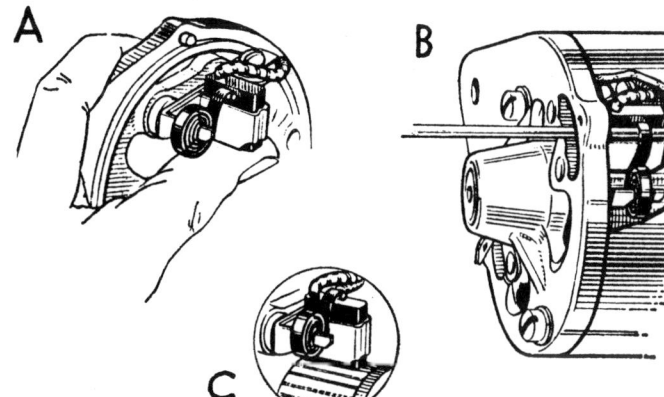

Fig. 10.2. DYNAMO BRUSH GEAR
A   Fitting the spring to hold the brush up in the holder
B   Hooking up the spring through the endplate to replace
it on the brush.
C   Correctly fitted brush.

SECTION 2. Lifting out the battery.

2. Disconnect the two leads from the dynamo terminals.

3. Remove the nut from the sliding link bolt, and remove the two upper bolts. The dynamo is then free to be lifted away from the engine.

4. Replacement is a reversal of the above procedure. Do not finally tighten the retaining bolts and the nut on the sliding link until the fan belt has been tensioned correctly.

7. Dynamo - Dismantling, Repair and Reassembly

1. Clamp the dynamo in a vice and remove the two through bolts which hold the assembly together.

2. Remove the commutator end bracket by pulling it straight off the end of the armature shaft.

3. Remove the generator from the vice and draw the drive end bracket complete with armature from the yoke or casing.

4. Do not dismantle further at this stage. Examine the carbon brushes in the holders of the commutator end bracket. They may be lifted out of their holders after the pressure springs are hooked out. The length of the brushes should be no less than ¼ inch (6.4 mm). If required fit new ones which are supplied with new leads. Note that the C40 and C40L have a different type of brush fitted.

5. Examine next the commutator end of the armature. This should not be burnt or scored in any way. First clean it off with a little petrol on a rag. Any traces of pitting, scoring or burring, if slight, can be cleaned off with fine glass paper. Do not use emery paper. Make sure that there are no flat spots, by tearing the glass paper into strips and use it by drawing it round the commutator evenly. Do not try and clean off too much by this method as the commutator must remain circular in section.

6. To test the armature is not difficult but a voltmeter or bulb and 12 volt battery are required. The two tests determine whether there may be a break in any circuit winding or if any wiring insulation is broken down. Figs. 10.3 and 10.4 show how the battery, voltmeter and probe connectors are used to test whether (a) any wire in the windings is broken or (b) whether there is an insulation breakdown. In the first test the probes are placed on adjacent segments of a clean commutator. All voltmeter readings should be similar. If a bulb is used instead it will glow very dimly or not at all if there is a fault. For the second test any reading or bulb lighting indicates a fault. Test each segment in turn with one probe and keep the other on the shaft. Should either test indicate a faulty armature the wisest action in the long run is to obtain a replacement dynamo altogether. The field coils may be tested if an ohmmeter or ammeter can be obtained. With an ohmmeter the resistance (measured between the terminal and the yoke) should be 6 ohms. With an ammeter, connect it in series with a 12 volt battery again from the field terminal to the yoke. A reading of 2 amps. is normal. Zero amps or infinity ohms indicate an open circuit. More than 2 amps or less than 6 ohms indicates a breakdown of the insulation. Unless you can get the field coils readily repaired it is better to obtain a replacement unit.

7. The drive end bearing should have no play but in the event that it also needs renewal (very rare except where the fan belt has been persistently over-tight) first remove the pulley nut and washers and draw off the pulley. Then tap the Woodruff key out of the shaft using a screwdriver under one end. Be careful to guard against it flying off and getting lost. Remove the circlip from the bearing housing which will release the bearing retaining plate. If the end cover is now supported across the jaws of a vice, with the armature hanging down the end of the shaft may be tapped with a soft faced mallet to drive it out of the bearing housing with the bearing. The bearing itself can next be taken off the shaft by the same method. When fitting a new bearing make sure it is thoroughly packed with grease and fit it into the end cover first making sure that the pressure ring and retaining plate are all assembled correctly. Refit the circlip. Then place the retaining cup over the armature shaft so that the open end faces the armature. Then the end cover may be supported over the vice jaws and the armature carefully tapped through the bearing with a mallet. Refit the spacer, then the Woodruff key, followed by the pulley, washer and nut.

8. Finally, if new brushes have been fitted, make sure that they are a free sliding fit in their holders. If there are any signs of sticking they may be relieved by careful rubbing with a fine file. The bearing face of each brush should be concave to match the commutator.

9. Replace the armature/drive end cover assembly into the main yoke and then prepare to fit the commutator end cover by hooking back the brush springs on to the sides of the brushes which should be drawn back. The brushes will then be held and can be released and the springs brought to bear after the end cover has been assembled (see Fig. 10.2)

10 Note that both end covers have locating pips which register in corresponding cut-outs in the yoke. When fitting the commutator end cover, see that the blade terminal of the field coil connection fits in the proper slot and that the insulating sleeve round it is intact. Replace the through bolts and before tightening them right up, check that the end plates are fully and correctly in position. Spin the armature to ensure it is not binding or touching the field coils and then unhook the brush springs and lower the brushes onto the commutator with the springs on top. Finally, place a few drops of engine oil in the oil hole of the commutator bearing bush.

8. Alternator - Description and Maintenance

1. The alternator is a generator capable of producing alternating current which is rectified into direct current so that it may be used in the car electrical system to charge the battery. Its main advantage is that it is lighter, more robust and has a much higher output at low engine revolutions. Incorporated in the charging circuit there are also:-

a) A relay to switch the energising current to the field winding when the ignition switch is turned on.

b) A sealed control unit.

c) Warning lamp control unit.

Of these the sealed control unit (only) is capable of being adjusted but it is considered that the average keen owner is best advised to leave it alone.

2. Maintenance is minimal. Both bearings, one ball and one needle roller, are sealed and the only items subject to any wear are the slip ring carbon brushes but this is minimal. Otherwise the only regular attention needed is to make sure that the ventilation holes in the slip ring end cover are kept clear and that like the dynamo, the fan belt tension is maintained correctly.

9. Alternator - Precautions and Testing

1. If the charging system of the car develops a fault one cannot set about finding out where it may be, in the same way as one could do for a dynamo. Trial and error procedures and connections are out. Due to the relatively sophisticated electronic circuity, the polarity of the system (positive and negative) is very important and wrong connections can cause damage, even if the motor is not running.

2. Before carrying out any tests to find out what trouble may exist in the circuit the following precautions **must** be observed:-

a) Never disconnect the battery with the alternator running.

b) Observe the polarity of the system throughout.

c) Make sure the battery polarity is suitable. A mistaken reverse connection will damage the diode rectifiers.

d) Do not earth the brown/yellow cable if disconnected at 'AL' on the warning lamp control.

e) Do not earth the brown/green cable if disconnected from the alternator.

f) Always disconnect the battery earth before disconnecting the alternator ouput cable.

g) Disconnect battery terminals before connecting an external

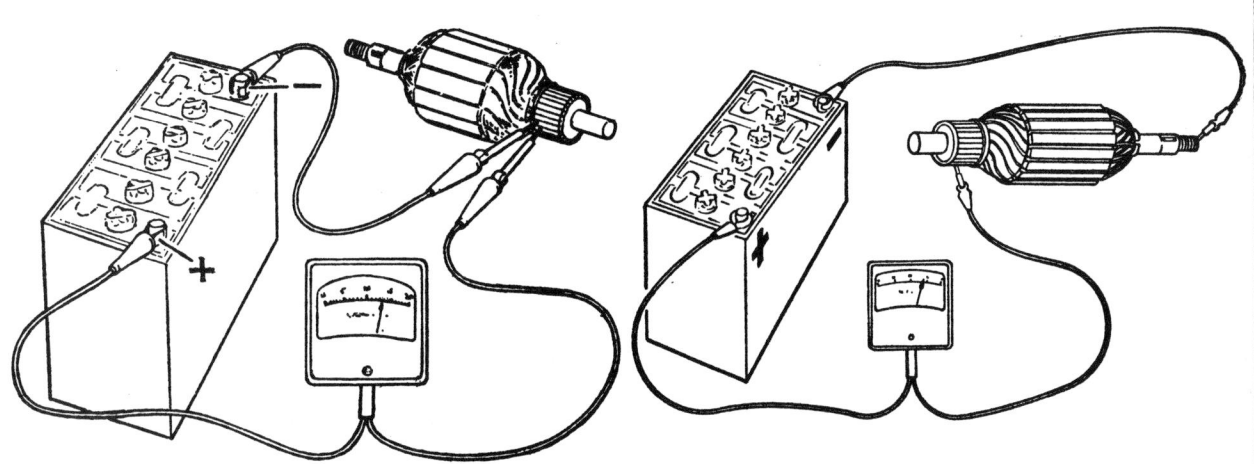

Fig. 10.3. Dynamo armature - Testing for open circuit

Fig. 10. 4. Dynamo armature - Testing for insulation of windings

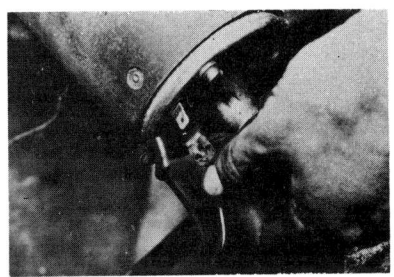

SECTION 6. Terminal connections on dynamo.

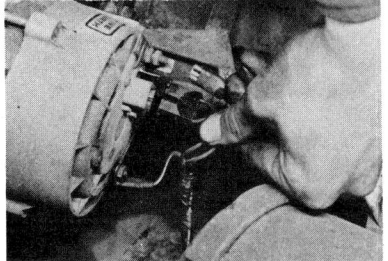

SECTION 10. Terminal connections on alternator.

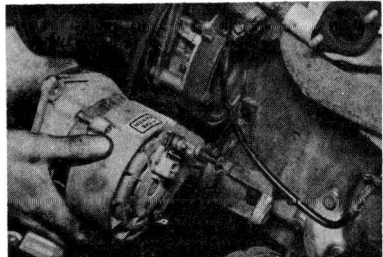

SECTION 10. Removing the alternator.

charging source.

h) A booster battery connection must always be made in parallel - i.e. negative to negative - positive to positive.

j) Always disconnect the battery and alternator if electric welding is to be done in the bodywork.

2. With the foregoing precautions firmly in mind, the owner should be able to carry out the following basic tests which will be able to point out which component may be faulty.

a) Check the fan belt for wear and tension.

b) Disconnect the battery earth cable.

c) If no ammeter is fitted, disconnect the main output lead from the alternator and wire in an ammeter (of 75 amps capacity) between the lead and the terminal.

d) Disconnect the 'F' and '—' leads from the voltage regulator and join them together.

e) Reconnect the battery earth lead, switch on and run the engine speed up to 2,100 r.p.m. A 25 amp reading should be obtained. If a low reading is obtained the circuit connections are badly made (especially earth) or the alternator is faulty. If there is no reading at all, check that there is voltage across the two field terminals by applying a voltmeter. If there is no voltage then the 6RA isolating relay is faulty. (Conversely there should be no voltage across these two terminals when the ignition switch is off.)

f) If the 6RA relay appears faulty continue the test by disconnecting the lead from terminal C2 and connect it temporarily to C1. If the alternator output is now correct a new relay unit is indicated.

g) If the alternator output is still incorrect then the control unit may be faulty. The way to test this is to fit another control unit which is known to be in order.

h) If the alternator output is wrong yet again then the alternator must be faulty.

10. Alternator - Removal and Replacement

Disconnect the battery leads. The alternator is then removed in the same manner as the dynamo. Note that the two main mounting bolts are underneath.

11. Alternator - Dismantling and Reassembly

1. The keen owner should only dismantle the alternator if he has verified that it is in fact faulty. Even then he should only dismantle it with the limited intention of examining the slip ring brushes which can be easily renewed.

2. Remove the shaft nut, spring washer, pulley and fan and then mark the drive end bracket, starter laminations and slip ring end cover so that they can be reassembled the same way. Then undo the three through bolts and take out the end bracket and rotor.

3. At the other end remove the terminal nuts and washers, insulators, brush box screws and 2BA bolt.

4. The stator and heat sink assembly may then be taken out.

5. The brushes are held in by tongues at the root of each field terminal blade and can be removed by closing up the tongues. Check the brushes are at least the specified minimum length of 5/32 inch (4 mm). Renew them if necessary, checking that they slide freely in their holders. Clean the faces of the slip rings with a petrol moistened cloth while the opportunity presents itself.

6. Reassemble the alternator in the reverse order and if the brushes have been renewed test the output. If the alternator is still not serviceable it should be exchanged for another unit.

12. Starter Motor - General Description

1. The starter motor is mounted on the clutch bellhousing on the left hand side of the engine. It is secured by two bolts. It has four field coils and four commutator brushes, two of which are earthed. When the motor spins the drive pinion is thrown forward on a spiral spline to engage with the flywheel ring gear which is then turned. When the engine fires the overrun of the flywheel throws the pinion back out of mesh.

2. A starter motor is not normally looked at until it goes wrong. However, it is worthwhile giving a periodic check - say, every 5,000 miles. This can be done by sliding back the band in order to expose the commutator and brush gear. If an air jet can be used to blow out the dust so much the better. Any signs of dust should be cleaned off with petrol on a cloth and the commutator can be wiped dry with a non fluffy cloth. Make sure that the connections are perfectly clean and tight. It will also be possible to see if any of the brushes are very badly worn.

13. Starter Motor Cicruit - Testing

If the starter motor fails to turn the engine when the switch is operated there are four possible reasons why:-

a) The battery is no good.

b) The electrical connections between switch, solenoid, battery and starter motor are somewhere failing to pass the necessary current from the battery through the starter to earth.

c) The solenoid switch is no good.

d) The starter motor is either jammed or electrically defective.

To check the battery, switch on the headlights. If they go dim after a few seconds the battery is definitely unwell. If the lamps glow brightly, next operate the starter switch and see what happens to the lights. If they go dim then you know that power is reaching the starter motor but failing to turn it. Therefore, check that it is not jammed by fitting a suitable spanner over the squared end of the shaft and making sure it turns easily. If it is not jammed the starter will have to come out for examination. If the starter should turn very slowly go on to the next check.

If, when the starter switch is operated, the lights stay bright, then the power is not reaching the starter. Check all connections from battery to solenoid switch to starter for perfect cleanliness and tightness. With a good battery installed this is the most usual cause of starter motor problems. Check that the earth link cable between the engine and frame is also intact and cleanly connected. This can sometimes be overlooked when the engine is taken out.

If no results have yet been achieved turn off the headlights, otherwise the battery will go flat. You will possibly have heard a clicking noise each time the switch was operated. This is the solenoid switch operating but it does not necessarily follow that the main contact is closing properly. (N.B. if no clicking has been heard from the solenoid it is certainly defective). The solenoid contact can be checked by putting a voltmeter or bulb across the main cable connection on the starter side of the solenoid and earth. When the switch is operated, there should be a reading or lighted bulb. If not, the solenoid switch is no good. (Do not put a bulb across the two solenoid terminals. If the motor is not faulty the bulb will blow.) If, finally, it is established that the solenoid is not faulty and 12 volts are getting to the starter then the starter motor must be the culprit.

14. Starter Motor - Removal and Replacement

1. Disconnect the battery to prevent accidental short circuits.

2. Remove the main cable from the terminal post on the starter motor.

3. Undo the two bolts - one above and one below, holding the motor to the bellhousing. It may then be drawn out. In the photographs the exhaust pipe is disconnected from the manifold but this is not necessary to remove the starter.

4. Replacement is a reversal of the removal procedure. Make sure that the main terminal is away from the engine, i.e., do not fit the

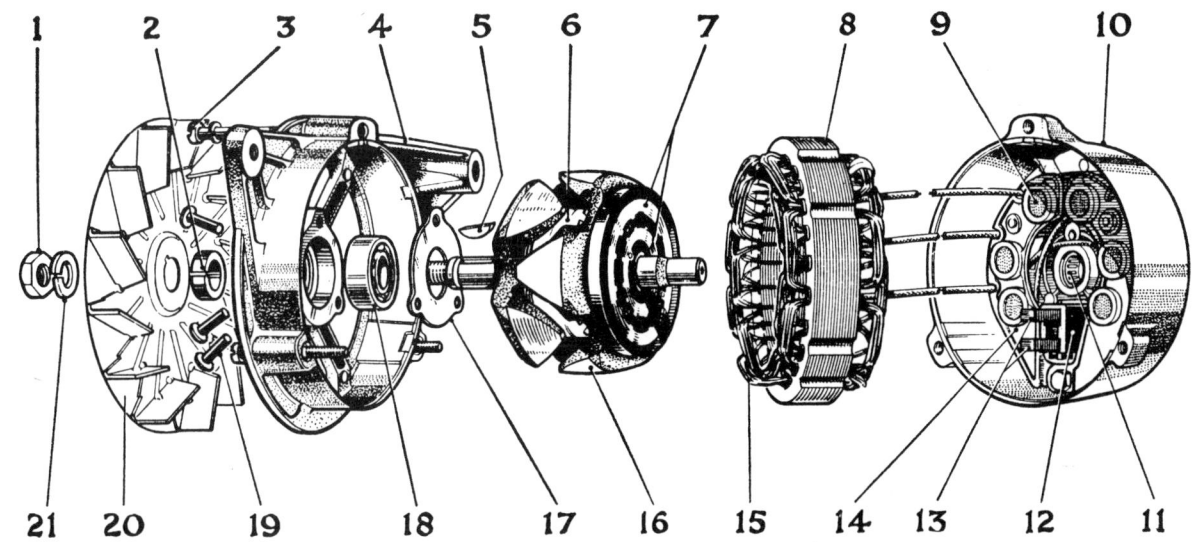

Fig. 10.5. ALTERNATOR — EXPLODED VIEW

1 Shaft nut	7 Slip-rings	13 Brushes	19 Bearing retaining-plate rivets
2 Bearing collar	8 Stator laminations	14 Diode heat sink	20 Cooling fan
3 'Through' fixing bolts (3)	9 Silicon diodes	15 Stator windings	21 Spring washer
4 Drive-end bracket	10 Slip-ring end-cover	16 Rotor	
5 Woodruff key	11 Needle-roller bearing	17 Bearing retaining-plate	
6 Rotor (field) winding	12 Brush box moulding	18 Ball bearing	

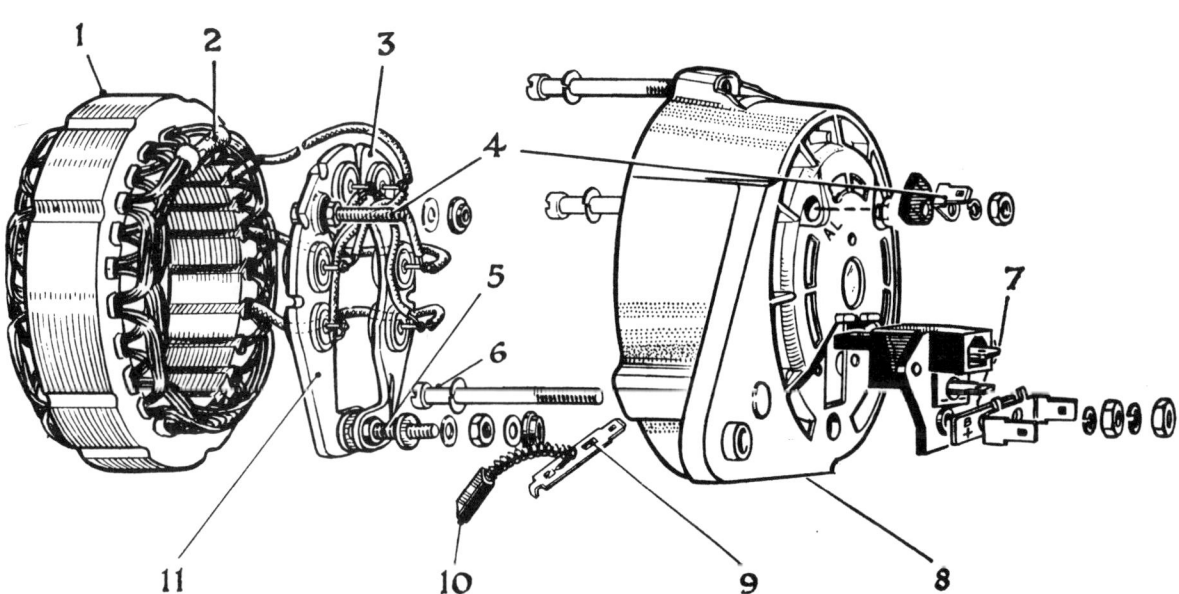

Fig. 10.6. ALTERNATOR — DETAILED EXPLODED VIEW OF BRUSH GEAR AND RECTIFIER DIODES IN END COVER

1 Stator	4 Warning light terminal 'AL'	8 Slip-ring end-cover	11 Positive heat sink and cathode base diode (red)
2 Star point	5 Output terminal (+)	9 Terminal blade retaining tongue	
3 Negative heat sink and anode base diodes (black)	6 'Through' fixing bolts (3)	10 Rotor slip-ring brush	
	7 Field terminal (2)		

starter the wrong way up.

15. Starter Motor - Dismantling, Repair and Reassembly

1. Grip the motor in a vice if possible and remove the band cover over the brush gear.

2. Using a piece of stiff hooked wire pull back each of the four carbon brush springs and lift each brush from its holder.

3. Unscrew the two through bolts and the commutator end bracket may then be taken off. The pinion end bracket complete with armature and drive assembly may then be removed from the yoke.

4. Before proceeding further, it is advisable to check that both the armature and field coils are in order. There is no point in renewing bearings and brushes if the guts of the motor are useless. To test the armature proceed in exactly the same way as for the dynamo armature described in Section 7 To test the field coils for continuity is also straightforward. A 12 volt bulb and battery connected in series can be applied with prods to the connections of the field coil brushes. The bulb should light. This, however, only indicates continuity - the insulation could be in a poor state even so and to test this with surety requires a voltage of more than 12 - 110 volts to be exact - and this calls for a transformer. If you have been able to rig up 110 volts (A.C. will do) wire a 110 volt bulb (a 220 volt will do) into the circuit and prod between the field coil terminal and the yoke of the motor. If the lamp lights (or glows dimly with a 220 volts bulb) then the insulation is broken down and the field coils need renewal.

5. If either the armature or field coils are in need of renewal it is recommended that a complete exchange unit be obtained.

6. If both armature and field coils are in order then check that the bearing bushes are not worn. If they are they may be renewed in the same fashion as described for the commutator end bush of the dynamo in Section 7. To renew the bush in the driving end plate will require the starter pinion assembly to be removed first, in order to withdraw the shaft. This is explained in Section 16. If the carbon brushes are below minimum length of $5/16$ inch (7.9 mm) they should also be renewed.

7. The two brushes attached to the end cover (not insulated) can be unsoldered and new ones clipped in and re-soldered to the terminal eyelets. The other two brushes connected to the field coils need a little care and attention. Originally they have been resistance brazed to aluminium end tags of the coils. Aluminium cannot be soldered so the old leads must be cut, leaving sufficient copper (at least $1/8$ inch/3 mm) to solder the new leads onto. The insulation must also be in perfect condition because no part of the connecting wire must touch the yoke. When soldering the flexible lead make sure that no solder runs along the braid. This would reduce its flexibility and possibly cause it to fracture.

8. Reassembly of the starter motor is a reversal of the dismantling process. The brushes are replaced in the holders after the end cover has been replaced but before this is done each brush should be checked in its holder to ensure it slides smoothly and freely. Wipe the surfaces with a petrol dampened cloth if sticking occurs and if more than this is needed the sides may be smoothed with a very fine file. Before putting the end cover in place make sure that the brushes are so arranged that they can be easily hooked into position and that their leads are not trapped. Remember also that the springs should all be conveniently ready. The brushes should not be able to fit into the wrong brush boxes but it is worth noting that the two fixed to the end plate only go into holders to which they are attached at the base. (The other two holders are insulated from the end plate.)

16. Starter Motor Drive Pinion - Dismantling, Repair and Reassembly

1. Persistent jamming or reluctance to disengage indicates that the starter pinion assembly needs attention. The starter motor should first of all be removed.

2. With the starter motor removed, thoroughly clean with petrol the drive pinion, taking care to keep any liquid from running into the motor. If there is a lot of dirt to clean off, this could be the sole trouble. The pinion should move freely in a spiral movement along the shaft against the light spring and return easily on being released. To do this the spiral splines must be completely clean and free of oil. (Oil merely collects dust and gums up the splines.) Both springs should be intact. The larger one acts as a shock absorber when the moving pinion engages the stationary flywheel ring gear.

3. Should either spring be broken, or the spiral splines be badly worn, preventing the pinion from moving smoothly, it will be necessary to remove the starter and drive from the shaft. This requires the heavy spring to be compressed so that the jump ring which locates in a groove round the shaft inside the shaft collar can be removed. This calls for either a special tool or a device to be made up which will enable the spring to be compressed between the jaws of a vice. Such a device has to be very robust to overcome the strength of the spring so unless you have some suitable metal available it would be advisable to borrow one.

4. With the jump ring removed the components of the drive assembly can be removed from the shaft. Renew any parts as necessary, noting that if the pinion is renewed the spiral splined sleeves should also be renewed. Reassembly is a reversal of the dismantling procedure, once again requiring the services of the device to compress the buffer spring.

17. Pre-Engaged Starters - Description, Maintenance and Testing

1. The motor part of the pre-engaged starter is no different from the inertia type. The difference is in the method of engaging the driving pinion with the flywheel ring gear. The starter solenoid switch, in addition to making the electrical connection, now also operates a lever which moves the pinion into mesh with the ring gear just before the power is switched to the motor. This results in quieter operation and reduces much of the shock loading on the starter motor. To prevent the engine driving the starter, should the pinion stick, the drive is through a one-way roller type clutch. Also, the pinion is spring loaded, so that in the event of an exact abutment of gear teeth preventing engagement the solenoid will still continue and make power contact and the pinion will move into engagement automatically as soon as the shaft moves. The operating lever, which connects the solenoid plunger to the pinion, pivots on an eccentric pin so that the pinion engagement may be set correctly in relation to the switch contacts.

2. Maintenance and testing procedures are the same as for the other type of starter but, of course, in this case the solenoid switch is mounted on the starter motor casing itself.

18. Pre-Engaged Starters - Removal and Replacement

Removal and replacement is the same as for the inertia type with the additional requirement that the two feed wires to the solenoid need pulling off the Lucar connections.

19. Pre-Engaged Starters - Dismantling and Reassembly

1. Having removed the starter motor from the car the solenoid unit may be removed after disconnecting the link cable to the motor from the main terminal.

2. The solenoid plunger can be then disengaged from the lever in the drive end bracket.

3. Take off the brush gear band cover and lift out the two insulated brushes from their holders. Then remove the two through bolts which hold both end covers to the yoke.

4. Take the end bracket off the commutator and then slacken the locknut on the eccentric pivot bolt and unscrew the pivot bolt from the drive end bracket.

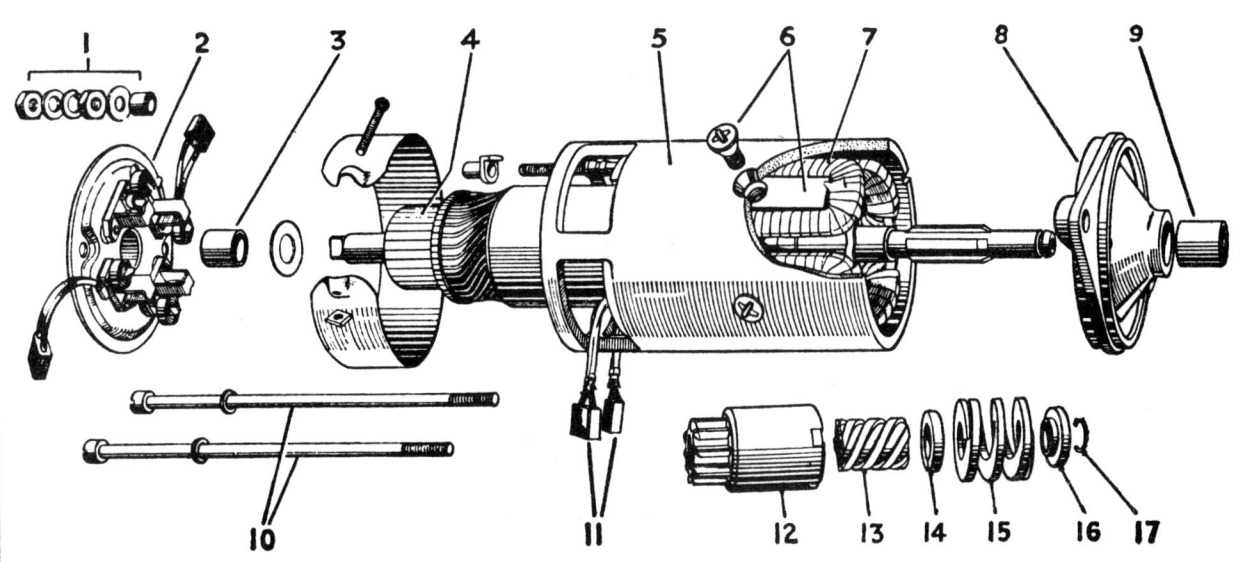

Fig. 10.7. STARTER MOTOR — INERTIA TYPE — EXPLODED VIEW

1 Terminal nuts and washer	6 Pole shoes and screws	11 Insulated brushes	16 Shaft collar
2 Commutator end bracket	7 Field coils	12 Pinion and barrel assembly	17 Jump ring
3 Bearing bush	8 Drive-end bracket	13 Screwed sleeve	
4 Commutator	9 Bearing bush	14 Buffer washer	
5 Yoke	10 Through bolts	15 Main spring	

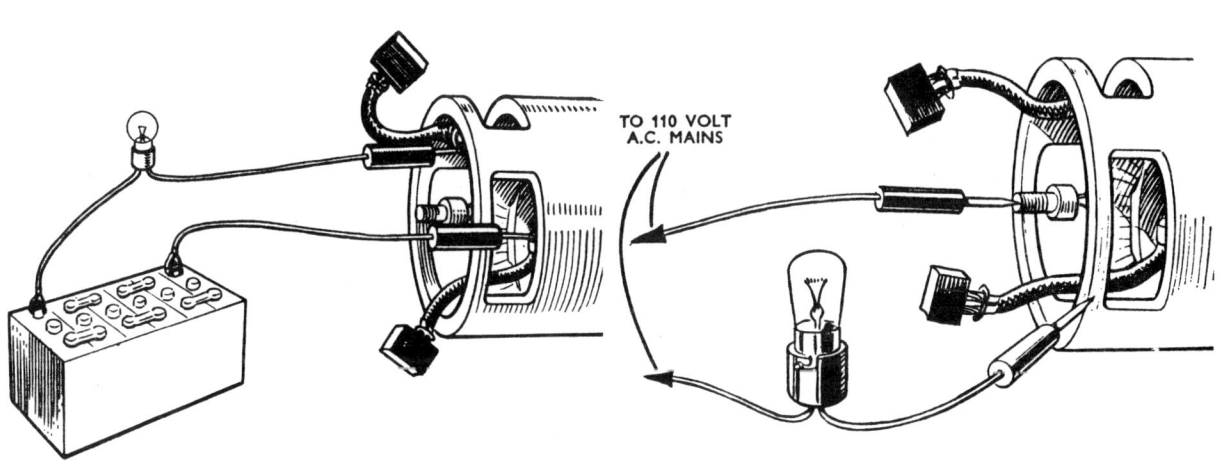

Fig. 10.8. Connection for starter motor field coil continuity test.

Fig. 10.9. Connection for starter motor field coil insulation test.

 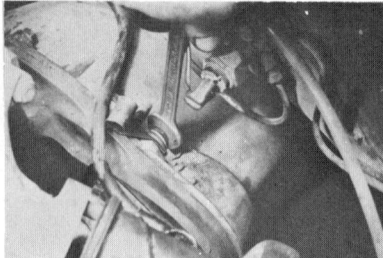 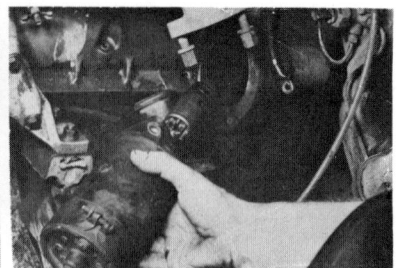

SECTION 14. Disconnecting and removing the starter motor.

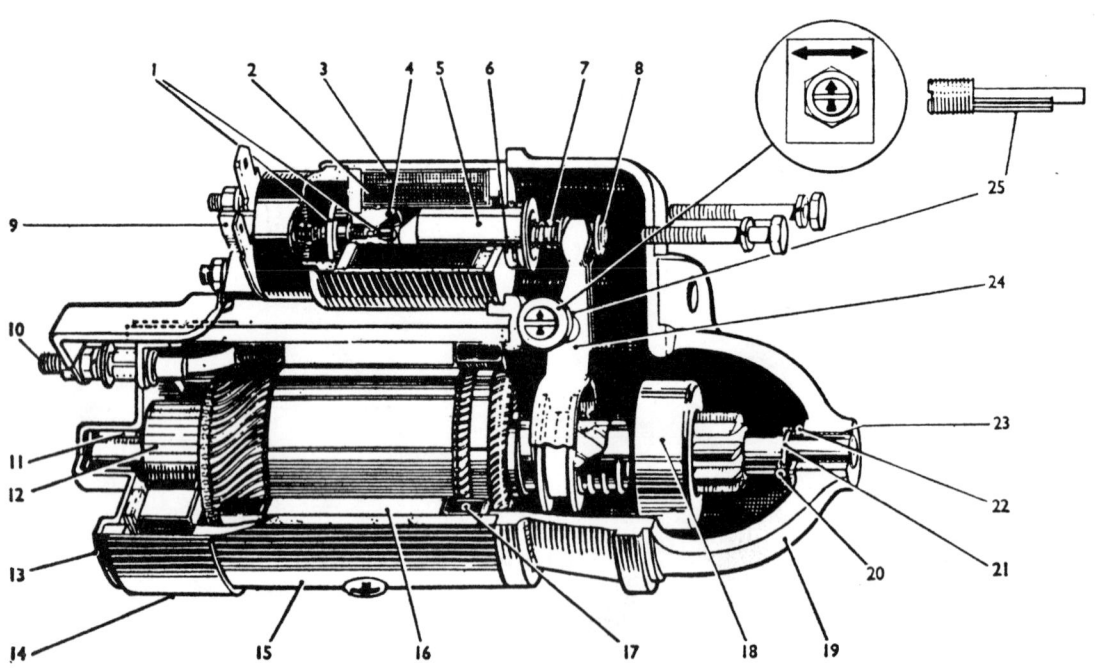

Fig. 10.10. STARTER MOTOR — PRE-ENGAGED TYPE — CROSS SECTION

1 Spindle and moving contact assembly	7 Lost motion spring	14 Band cover	21 Jump ring
2 Series winding	8 Sliding collar	15 Yoke	22 Thrust washer
3 Shunt winding	9 Solenoid unit	16 Pole shoes	23 Bronze bush
4 Core	10 Main terminal	17 Field coils	24 Engaging lever
5 Plunger	11 Bronze bush	18 Roller clutch	25 Eccentric pivot pin
6 Pinion retraction spring	12 Commutator	19 Drive end bracket	
	13 Commutator end bracket	20 Thrust collar	

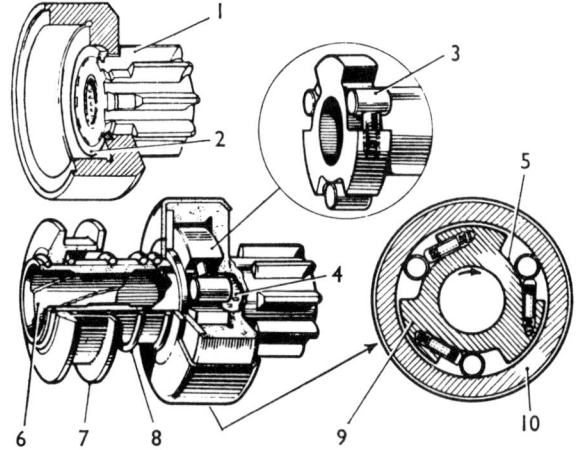

Fig. 10.11. DETAILS OF PRE-ENGAGED STARTER
PINION AND ROLLER CLUTCH

1 Alternative construction   5 Cam tracts
  (pinion pressed and   6 Driving sleeve
  cleat-ringed into   7 Operating bush
  driven member)   8 Engagement spring
2 Soft metal cleating ring   9 Driving member
3 Spring loaded rollers   10 Driven member (with
4 Bush   pinion)

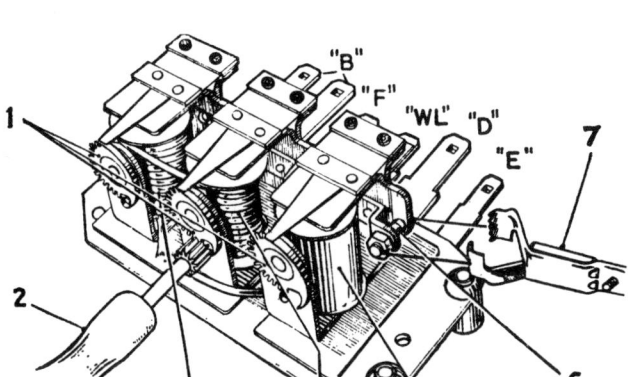

Fig. 10.12. CONTROL BOX (LUCAS RB340)
DYNAMO ONLY

1 Adjustment cams   5 Voltage regulator
2 Lucas setting tool   6 Voltage regulator contacts
3 Cut-out relay   7 Clip
4 Current regulator

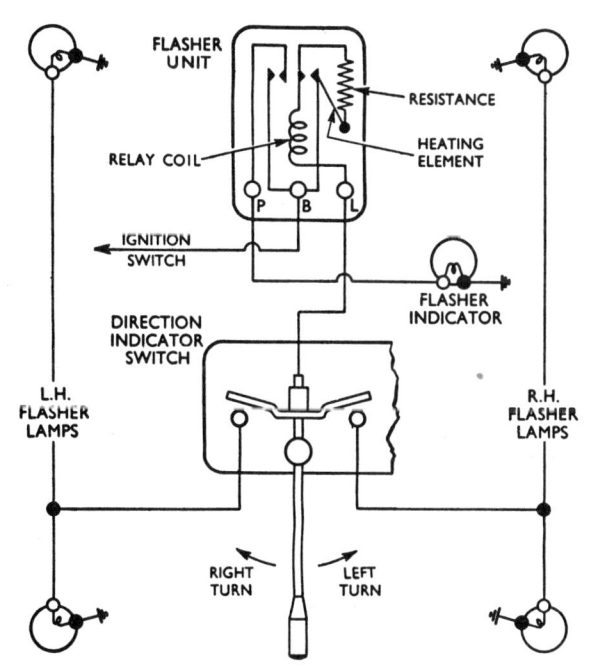

Fig. 10.13. Flasher circuit - Schematic diagram

5. The armature can now be removed from the drive end bracket and the engaging lever after that. Note which way round the lever goes.

6. If the thrust collar on the armature shaft is depressed a small jump ring is revealed. Remove this and the collar and the drive unit can be drawn off. The driving pinion and clutch are a single assembly but can be separated from the grooved operating bush by pushing back the bush to reveal another jump ring. This can be removed, thus releasing the bush from the spindle.

7. Checking of the armature field coils and subsequently bearing bushes and brushgear should be carried out as described in Section 15.

8. Reassembly is a reversal of the removal procedure. All the components of the drive pin and bearings should be liberally greased on assembly. Adjustment of the eccentric pin may be necessary. The best way is to connect a 6 volt supply between the small terminal of the solenoid and the solenoid casing. This will draw in the plunger as far as the springs which the low power will not permit it to overcome. If the pinion is held back lightly (towards the armature) to take up any lost motion the gap between the end of the pinion and the thrust collar should be .010 inch (.28 mm). The eccentric pin should be moved to achieve this. The arrow head on the pivot bolt should point only towards the arrowed arc marked in the bracket as the adjustment range is through 180º only.

20. Control Box (Dynamo Only) - Regulators and Cut-Outs - General Description

1. The control box comprises three units; two separate vibrating armature-type single contact regulators and a cut-out relay. One of the regulators is sensitive to changes in current and the other to changes in voltage.

2. Adjustment can only be made with a special tool which resembles a screwdriver with a multi-toothed blade. This can be obtained through Lucas agents.

3. The regulators control the output from the dynamo depending on the state of the battery and the demands of the electrical equipment, and ensure that the battery is not overcharged. The cut-out is really an automatic switch and connects the dynamo to the battery when the dynamo is turning fast enough to produce a charge. Similarly it disconnects the battery from the dynamo when the engine is idling or stationary so that the battery does not discharge through the dynamo.

21. Cut-Out and Regulator Contacts - Maintenance

1. Every 10,000 miles check the cut-out and regulator contacts. If they are dirty or rough or burnt place a piece of fine glass paper **(do not use emery paper or carborundum paper)** between the cut-out contacts, close them manually and draw the glass paper through several times.

2. Clean the regulator contacts in exactly the same way, but use emery or carborundum paper and not glass paper. Carefully clean both sets of contacts from all traces of dust with a rag moistened in methylated spirits.

22. Voltage Regulator Adjustment

1. The regulator requires very little attention during its service life, and should there be any reason to suspect its correct functioning tests of all circuits should be made to ensure that they are not the reason for the trouble.

2. These checks include the tension of the fan belt, to make sure that it is not slipping and so providing only a very low charge rate. The battery should be carefully checked for possible low charge rate due to a faulty cell, or corroded battery connections.

3. The leads from the generator may have been crossed during replacement, and if this is the case then the regulator points will have

stuck together as soon as the generator starts to charge. Check for loose or broken leads from the generator to the regulator.

4. If after a thorough check it is considered advisable to test the regulator, this should only be carried out by an electrician who is well acquainted with the correct method, using test bench equipment.

5. Pull off the Lucar connections from the two adjacent control box terminals 'B'. To start the engine it will now be necessary to join together the ignition and battery leads with a suitable wire.

6. Connect a 0-30 volt voltmeter between terminal 'D' on the control box and terminal 'WL'. Start the engine and run it at 2,000 r.p.m. The reading on the voltmeter should be steady and lie between the limits detailed in the specifications.

7. If the reading is unsteady this may be due to dirty contacts. If the reading is outside the specified limits stop the engine and adjust the voltage regulator in the following manner.

8. Take off the control box cover and start and run the engine at 2,000 r.p.m. Using the correct tool turn the voltage adjustment cam anti-clockwise to raise the setting and clockwise to lower it. To check that the setting is correct, stop the engine, and then start it and run it at 2,000 r.p.m. noting the reading. Refit the cover and the connections to the 'WL' and 'D' terminals.

23. Current Regulator Adjustment

1. The output from the current regulator should equal the maximum output from the dynamo which is 22 amps. To test this it is necessary to bypass the cut-out by holding the contacts together.

2. Remove the cover from the control box and with a bulldog clip hold the cut-out contacts together.

3. Pull off the wires from the adjacent terminals 'B' and connect a 0-40 moving coil ammeter to one of the terminals and to the leads.

4. All the other load connections including the ignition must be made to the battery.

5. Turn on all the lights and other electrical accessories and run the engine at 2,000 r.p.m. The ammeter should give a steady reading between 19 and 22 amps. If the needle flickers it is likely that the points are dirty. If the reading is too low turn the special Lucas tool clockwise to raise the setting and anti-clockwise to lower it.

24. Cut-Out Adjustment

1. Check the voltage required to operate the cut-out by connecting a voltmeter between the control box terminals 'D' and 'WL'. Remove the control box cover, start the engine and gradually increase its speed until the cut-outs close. This should occur when the reading is between 12.6 and 13.4 volts.

2. If the reading is outside these limits turn the cut-out adjusting cam (1 in the illustration) by means of the adjusting tool, a fraction at a time clockwise to raise the voltage and anti-clockwise to lower it.

3. To adjust the drop off voltage bend the fixed contact blade carefully. The adjustment to the cut-out should be completed within 30 seconds of starting the engine as otherwise heat build-up from the shunt coil will affect the readings.

4. If the cut-out fails to work, clean the contacts, and, if there is still no response, renew the cut-out and regulator unit.

25. Fuses

A fuse unit is mounted on the bulkhead and contains three circuit fuses and two spares. The connections are made to the back of the fuse panel by Lucar connectors and reference to the wiring diagram shows the relevant circuit connections.

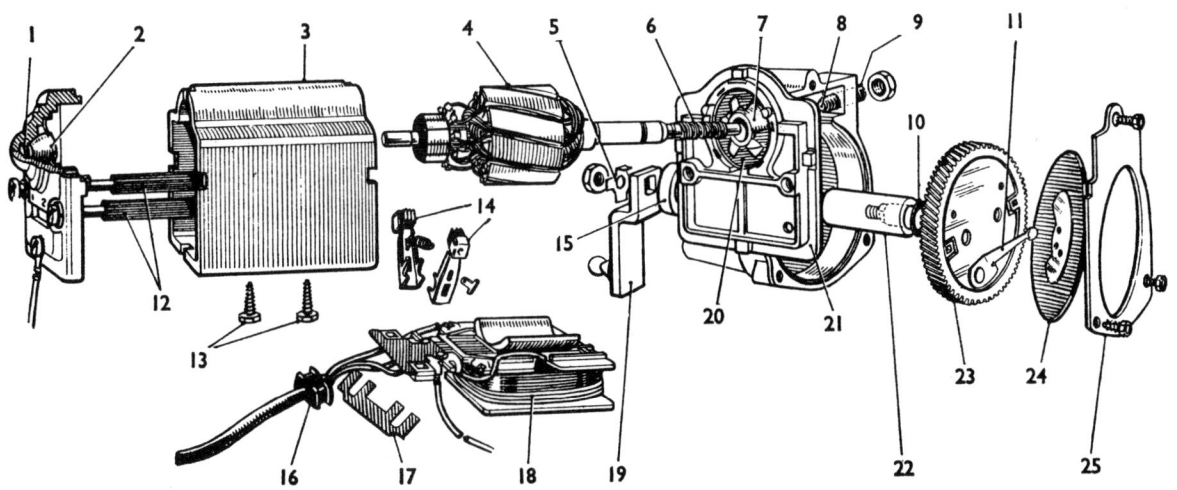

Fig. 10.14. WINDSCREEN WIPER MOTOR DL3A TWO-SPEED
EXPLODED VIEW

1	Thrust pad	8	Thrust pad	15	Bush
2	Self-aligning bearing	9	End-play adjuster	16	Grommet
3	Yoke	10	Washer	17	Brush lever retainer
4	Armature	11	Moving contact	18	Field coil
5	Tab washer	12	Through bolts	19	Rotating output crank
6	Worm gear	13	Pole-piece screws	20	Bearing retaining ring
7	Self-aligning bearing	14	Brushgear	21	Drive end bracket

22 Porous bronze bush
23 Final gear
24 Limit switch fixed contact plate
25 Gearbox cover

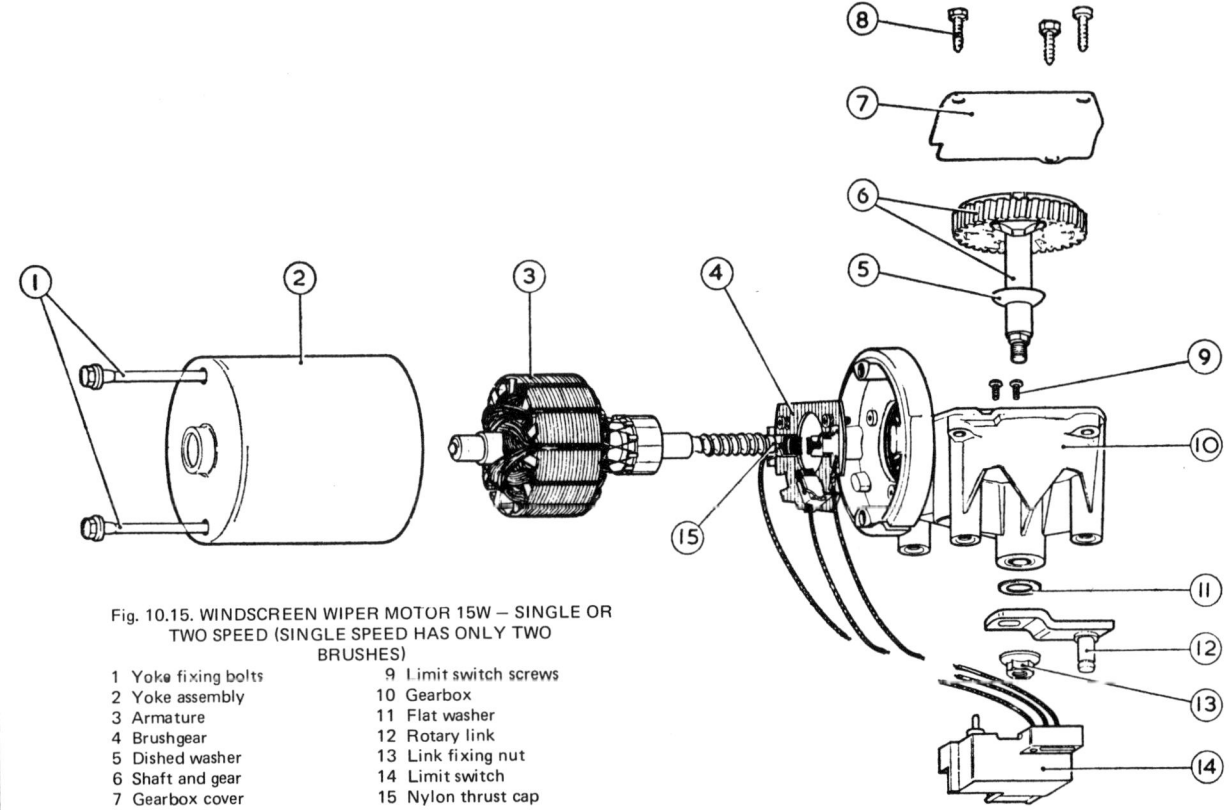

Fig. 10.15. WINDSCREEN WIPER MOTOR 15W — SINGLE OR
TWO SPEED (SINGLE SPEED HAS ONLY TWO
BRUSHES)

1	Yoke fixing bolts	9	Limit switch screws
2	Yoke assembly	10	Gearbox
3	Armature	11	Flat washer
4	Brushgear	12	Rotary link
5	Dished washer	13	Link fixing nut
6	Shaft and gear	14	Limit switch
7	Gearbox cover	15	Nylon thrust cap
8	Cover fixing screws		

26. Direction Indicator Flasher Circuit - Fault Tracing and Rectification

1. The unit which causes the lights to flash intermittently is contained in a three inch long cylinder clipped under the dashboard. If has three terminals at one end.
2. If the flashers fail to work properly first check that all the bulbs are serviceable and of the correct wattage. Then check that the nuts which hold the lamp bodies to the car are tight and free from corrosion. These are the means by which the circuit is completed and any resistance here could affect the proper working of the coils in the flasher unit.
3. If there is still no success, bridge the 'B' and 'L' terminals on the flasher unit. When the switch is operated the lights should go on (on the appropriate side) and stay on. If they do the flasher unit is faulty. If they do not go on first make quite sure that with the ignition switched on current is reaching the 'B' terminal at the flasher circuit. If it is then the indicator switch is faulty. If it is not, then the connection from the ignition switch to the flasher unit is faulty (via the fuse).

27. Windscreen Wipers and Drive Motor - Fault Diagnosis

1. If the wipers fail to operate first check that current is reaching the motor. This can be done by switching on and using a voltmeter or 12 volt bulb and two wires between the '+' terminal on the motor and earth. On two speed motors there are three leads from the motor and there should be a reading from two of them.
2. If no current is reaching the motor check whether there is any at the switch. If there is then a break has occurred in the wiring between switch and motor.
3. If there is no current at the switch go back to the ignition switch and so isolate the area of the fault.
4. If current is reaching the motor but the wipers do not operate, switch on and give the wiper arms a push - they or the motor could be jammed. Switch off immediately if nothing happens otherwise further damage to the motor may occur. If the wipers now run the reason for them jamming must be found. It will almost certainly be due to wear in either the linkage of the wiper mechanism or the mechanism in the motor gearbox.
5. If the wipers run too slowly it will be due to something restricting the free operation of the linkage or a fault in the motor. In such cases it is well to check the current being used by connecting an ammeter in the circuit. If it exceeds three amps something is restricting free movement. If less, then the commutator and brush gear in the motor are suspect.
6. If wear is obviously causing malfunction or there is a fault in the motor it is best to remove the motor or wiper mechanism for further examination and repairs.

28. Windscreen Wiper Motor and Mechanism - Removal and Replacement

1. Disconnect the battery and then remove the air intake grille in front of the windscreen. It is held in position by three screws. Detach the water pipe from it at the same time.
2. Remove the wiper blades and arm assemblies by pulling them off the splined spindles. Be careful not to bend the arms - the boss should be levered a little if it is tight.
3. Remove the nut, washers and rubber bushes holding the spindles to the bulkhead.
4. From inside the car, remove the screws and studs securing the parcel shelf and also the R.H. demister air tube which is held onto the heater box by two nuts.
5. Remove the glove box lid by undoing the five screws and unhooking the check strap. Then remove the two screws holding the box itself in position and lift that out.

6. The cables leading to the motor are next disconnected and the large self-tapping screw which holds the motor and mechanism to the bulkhead bracket is then removed. The whole assembly can then be lifted out.
7. When refitting the assembly make sure that the earthing cable is refitted to the securing screw and that the rubber bushes are fitted exactly as they came off.

29. Windscreen Wiper Mechanism and Motor - Dismantling and Reassembly

1. The DL3A motor fitted to earlier models was superseded by the 15W type. The DL3A was a two-speed unit, whereas the 15W is two-speed only on those cars fitted with alternators.
2. The exploded drawings indicate the layout of both motors and by removing the through bolts it is easy enough to examine the commutator and brush gear. Normally, however, if a wiper motor fails it is usually for reasons of excessive loading due to wear or jamming of the wiper arm link mechanism and consequently the renewal of the complete motor is the best answer. Brush gear can be obtained separately if it is conclusive that this is the only fault. Similarly, the large gear wheel and spindle can be obtained. Any serious wear in the armature spindle bushes however, is not a matter of simply renewing the bushes as these are part of the end covers.
3. If a new motor is fitted (or the old one successfully repaired) it is important to make sure that the wiper arm mechanism operates smoothly and freely, otherwise the motor could be ruined yet again. The nylon crankpin bushes should be renewed if worn and the wiper spindles should be a good fit in the sleeves. If in doubt renew the whole assembly.

30. Windscreen Washer - Fault Finding

1. The washer is a simple pump which draws water from a reservoir and pumps it along a pipe which goes to the jets. It is operated by the combined wiper/washer switch.
2. If nothing comes out of the jets when the pump is operated, disconnect the pipe from the jets. This will soon tell you if the jets are blocked or not. If no water comes down the pipe trace all the pipes and connections to be sure that there are no breaks or hardened kinks or flattened sections. Blow through the pipes to make sure they are clear.
3. As a last resort, remove the pump from the back of the instrument panel (Section 36 or 37) and check its operation with a piece of pipe in a bowl of water. If it does not pump you will have to buy a new one.

31. Horns - Fault Finding and Remedy

1. Should either or both horns fail to work the first thing to do is make sure that current is reaching the horn terminals. This can be done by connecting a 12 volt test lamp to the feed wire and pressing the horn button with the ignition switch on. If the bulb lights then the fault must lie in the horn or the horn mounting. The tightness and cleanliness of the horn mounting is important as the circuit is made to earth through the fixing bolt. The connections should, of course, be a clean tight fit on the horn terminals.
2. If no current is reaching the horn check the fuse (No. 1) and wiring connections as indicated in the wiring diagram.
3. Having established that the fault is in the horn the adjusting screw can be used. Do not touch the centre screw which is pre-set and is not to be adjusted. The adjusting screw is near the terminals and can be tuned in either direction. Anti-clockwise tuning reduces and eventually cuts out any sound and the correct setting is at a point where sound becomes correct just after cut in when tuning clockwise. When doing adjustments the fuse is likely to blow so fit a piece of heavy wire across the fuse bridge temporarily.
4. If a satisfactory note cannot be obtained then the horn must be

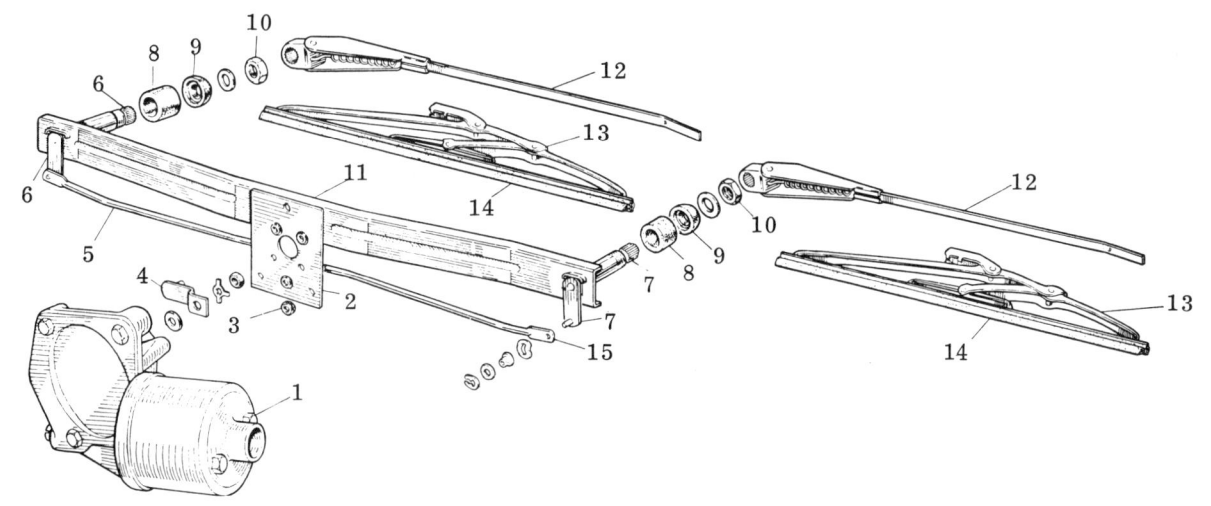

Fig. 10.16. WINDSCREEN WIPER MECHANISM – EXPLODED VIEW

1 Motor unit	5 Primary link L.H.	9 Bush - front	13 Blade assembly
2 Mounting bracket	6 Spindle L.H.	10 Locknut	14 Squeegee
3 Nut	7 Spindle R.H.	11 Link set	15 Primary link R.H.
4 Rotary link	8 Bush - rear	12 Wiper arm	

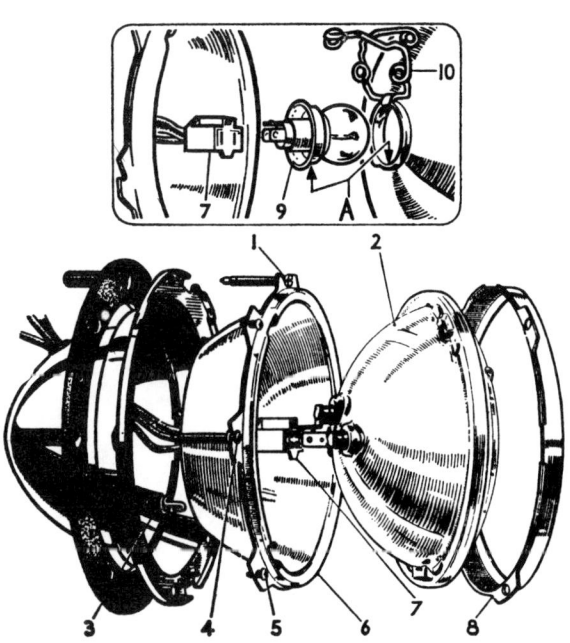

Fig. 10.17. HEADLAMP – F700 Mk.10 – ROUND – EXPLODED VIEW

1 Vertical adjustment screw	4 Horizontal adjustment screw	6 Seating rim	9 Bulb) European
2 Sealed beam light unit	5 Rim retaining screw	7 Adaptor	10 Bulb retainer) type
3 Tensioning spring		8 Unit rim	A. Bulb locations

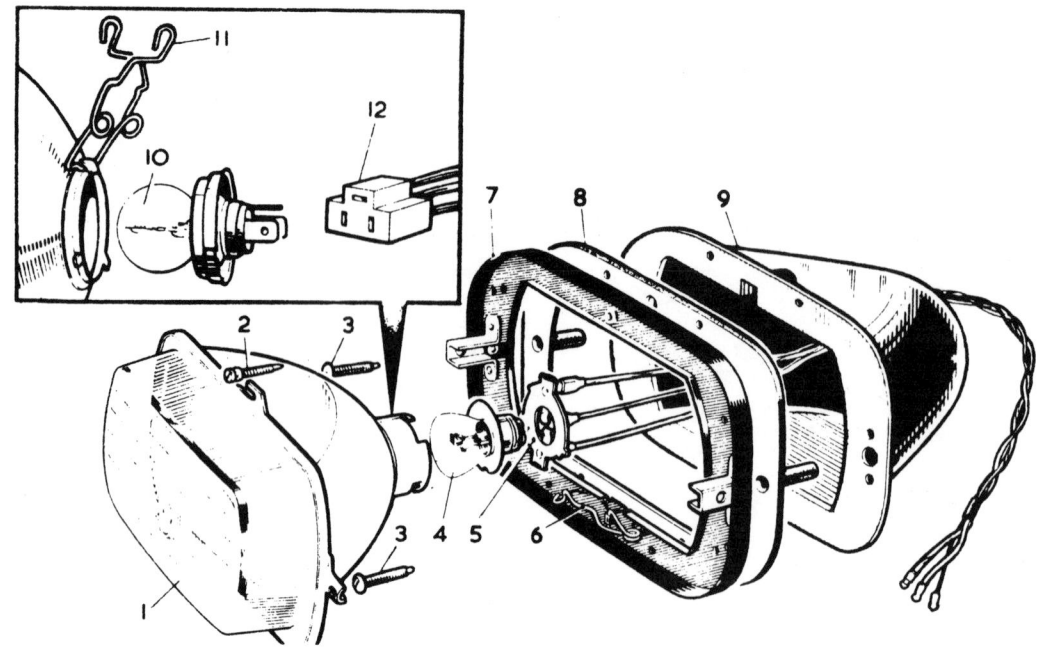

FIG. 10.18. 2FR RECTANGULAR HEADLAMP — EXPLODED VIEW.
INSET SHOWS LATER TYPE LAMP.

1 Light unit	5 Contact plate	9 Lamp cover
2 Vertical adjustment screw	6 Spring clip	10 Bulb
3 Horizontal adjustment screw	7 Seating rim	11 Spring clip for bulb
4 Bulb	8 Rubber gasket	12 Cable connector

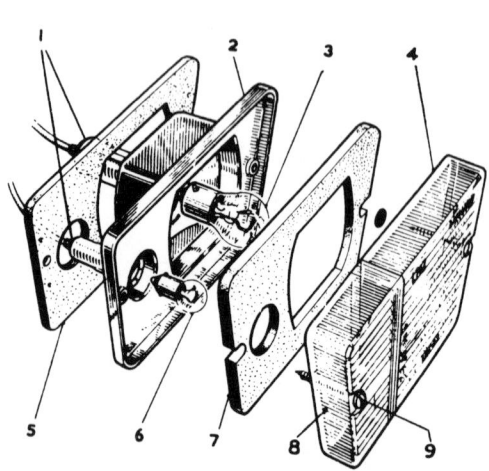

Fig. 10.19. FRONT SIDE LAMP AND FLASHER
ASSEMBLY — EXPLODED VIEW

1 Bulb holders	6 Side light bulb
2 Lamp body	7 Rubber lens gasket
3 Flasher bulb	8 Side light lens
4 Flasher lens	9 Fixing screw
5 Rubber mounting gasket	

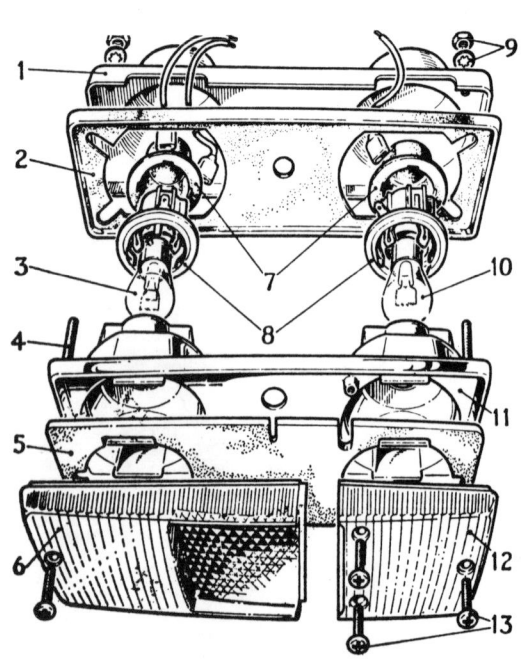

Fig. 10.20. REAR SIDE LAMP, STOP AND
FLASHER ASSEMBLY — EXPLODED VIEW

1 Rear plastic cover	7 Rubber sealing caps
2 Rubber mounting gasket	8 Bulb holders
3 Stop-tail light bulb	9 Lamp fixing nuts
4 Lamp body fixing stud	10 Flasher-light bulb
5 Lens sealing rubber	11 Lamp body
6 Stop-tail light lens and reflector	12 Flasher-light lens
	13 Fixing screws

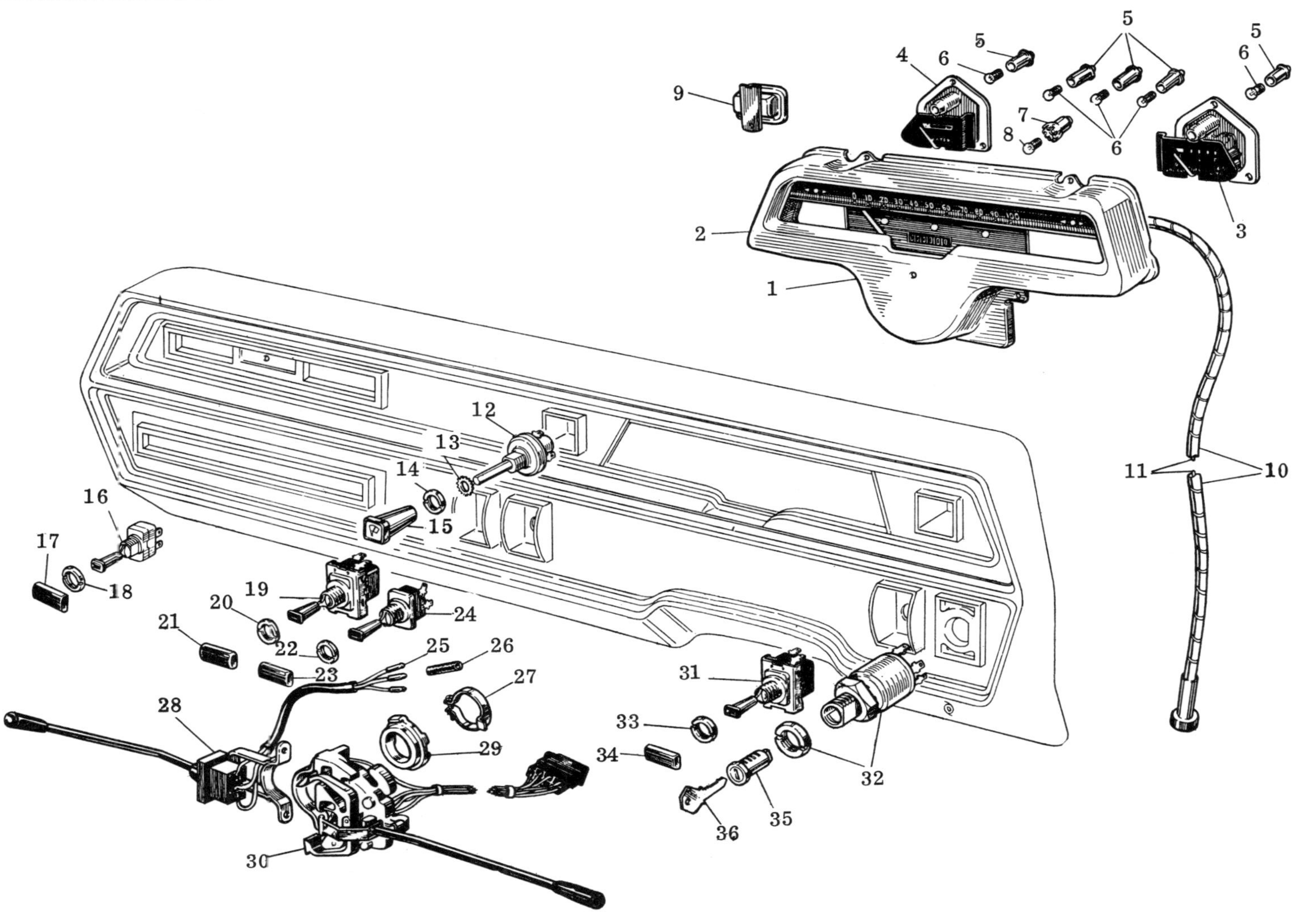

Fig. 10.21. INSTRUMENT LAYOUT MINX — HUNTER (Early models)

1	Instrument housing	8	Bulb	14	Locking ring	21	Knob	27	Cancelling striker	31	Lighting switch
2	Speedo head unit	9	Voltage regulator (instruments)	15	Knob	22	Locking ring	28	Direction indicator switch	32	Ignition switch
3	Fuel gauge	10	Speedo cable outer	16	Glove box switch	23	Knob	29	Cancelling striker bush	33	Locking ring
4	Temperature gauge	11	Speedo cable inner	17	Switch knob	24	Panel light switch	30	Horn, dip, flasher switch	34	Knob
5	Lamp holders	12	Wiper/washer switch	18	Locking ring	25	Direction indicator connections			35	Lock barrel
6	Lamp bulbs	13	Lock washer	19	Blower switch	26	Insulating sleeve			36	Key
7	Lamp holder			20	Locking ring						

renewed.

32. Headlamps - Adjustment, Removal and Replacement

1. The F700 Mk. 10 circular or 2FR rectangular headlamp may be fitted. The circular one is normally a sealed beam unit with a replaceable bulb version for some European versions. The rectangular type is fitted with a replaceable bulb. There is a difference between the early and later type bulbs fitted to the rectangular headlamps. See Fig. 10.18.
2. To renew the lamp unit either for renewal or bulb replacement, first of all remove the grille which is held in position by crosshead screws.
3. For circular lamps next remove the screws holding the unit rim. Do not confuse these with the two adjusting screws which should not be disturbed. Then draw the unit forward. For rectangular lamps remove the wire securing clip underneath the unit. Then draw the unit forward until it can be rotated clockwise a little in order to disengage from the vertical adjustment screw.
4. With the lamp unit clear the wires may be detached or in the case of replaceable bulbs the holder may be unclipped and drawn from the reflector. The bulb may then be taken out.
5. When replacing the circular unit make sure that the three projections on the rear are correctly positioned. The top one is so marked.
6. Beam setting should normally be done with the proper optical equipment but a good guide can be obtained by using the alignment diagram as given. This shows how the lights should aim in the main beam condition with two people in the front of the car. The car should face squarely a vertical surface at a distance of 25 feet (7.6 metres). Each lamp should be masked whilst the other is adjusted by means of the vertical and horizontal adjustment screws provided.

33. Front Side Lamp and Flasher Assembly

1. The units are not interchangeable from one side of the car to the other.
2. To renew bulbs first remove the two screws which hold the two-colour lens in position. Do not disturb the rubber lens seal unless it has deteriorated and needs renewal.
3. The bulbs may then be removed by pressing and twisting anti-clockwise.
4. Both bulbs are single filament and the bayonet caps will fit either way round.
5. When replacing the lens do not overtighten the screws or the rubber seal will be over-compressed and made less effective.
6. It is important for correct completion of the circuit that the bulb holder sleeves and the unit fixing screws are all quite free of any signs of corrosion or rust. Also they must be tight. Intermittent operation or lamp dimness is usually caused by these faults.

34. Rear Side, Stop and Flasher Lamp Assemblies

1. The units are not interchangeable from one side of the car to the other.
2. Each lens is separate, so depending on which bulb needs renewal, remove the appropriate lens. The stop/tail light lens is held by one screw and clips under the other lens so care should be exercised when removing it.
3. Bulbs are removed by pressing and turning anti-clockwise. If they are very tight it may be necessary to remove the bulb holders from the rear of the clamp.
4. The stop/tail lamp bulb is a double filament type with an offset bayonet pin so it will only fit the holder one way round.
5. When replacing the lenses do not overtighten the screws.

6. In cases of malfunction make sure that the lamp fixing nuts and the earth wire connection to one of the fixing studs are all corrosion-free and tight before checking the wiring circuit.

35. Dip, Flasher, Main Beam and Horn Switch

1. The switch is mounted on the steering column and if any or all of its parts go wrong, it has to be renewed as a complete unit.
2. To test the switch, the cowl round the steering column should be removed and the wires disconnected at the nearby snap connectors. By bridging the appropriate wires according to the colour coding in the wiring diagram, each part of the switch's function can be verified.
3. The switch is held to the steering column by two screws securing a clip and can be removed by simply unscrewing them.
4. When refitting a switch it should be positioned so that the flasher self cancelling cam is set centrally when the wheels are in a straight ahead position.

36. Instrument Panel and Instruments (Minx and Hunter) - Checking, Removal and Replacement

1. The temperature gauge, fuel gauge, instrument voltage regulator and speedometer are all housed in a rectangular shaped unit fitted to the back of the main panel. To remove any of these items it is easiest in the long run to remove the whole unit first.
2. Disconnect the battery and detach the cables from the gauges and voltage stabiliser on the back of the unit. The speedometer cable should be disconnected from the instrument together with the trip setting cable.
3. Pull the six panel and warning lights out of their sockets.
4. Remove the four screws securing the housing to the back of the panel and lift it out.
5. The gauges and voltage stabiliser may be detached by undoing their fixing screws and renewed if necessary. Do not renew either the temperature gauge or fuel gauge until it is quite certain that their respective sender units are working (see Chapters 2 and 3 for details). Should both gauges have failed at the same time it is quite likely that the voltage stabiliser is faulty so check this before fitting new gauges. A continuity test across the two terminals 'B' and 'I' will indicate whether total failure has occurred or not.
6. The individual switches on the lower half of the main panel may be detached by unscrewing the slotted chrome ring, pulling off the finger bar and then withdrawing the switch from the back of the panel. It is best to leave the wires connected until after the switch is out so that correctness of reconnecting is assured.
7. The combined windscreen wiper/washer pump switch can be removed in the same manner. The knob is held on by a spring loaded plunger which must first be released in order to pull it off. The pump and switch can be renewed separately if needed.

37. Instrument Panel and Instruments (Vogue and Gazelle) - Checking, Removal and Replacement

1. The instrument panel is of polished wood veneer and the instruments are detachable individually from the front.
2. The temperature gauge, ammeter and oil pressure gauge (Vogue) are contained in a circular instrument cluster whilst the speedometer and fuel gauge are individually mounted. First disconnect the battery. Then detach all connecting wires, speedo cable, oil pressure pipe and panel lights as necessary from the instrument or cluster, depending on which is to be removed. Then release the stirrup which holds each instrument (or cluster) to the panel by undoing the knurled nuts. These should only need undoing with the fingers. The instrument may then be drawn out from the front of the panel.

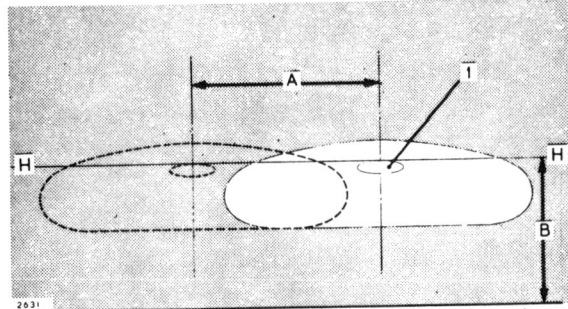

A. DISTANCE BETWEEN HEADLAMP CENTRES
B. HEIGHT OF HEADLAMP CENTRES MINUS 2 in. (5 mm)
H. HORIZONTAL LINE 2 in. (5 mm) BELOW HEADLAMP CENTRES
I. CONCENTRATED AREA OF LIGHT
Tolerance: 6 in. (152 mm) left to 6 in. right at 25 ft (7.5 m) (1 = 5 in.
(127 mm) at 25 ft (7.5 m).

Fig. 10.22a. Main beam pattern for 7 in. round headlamps and early
type 2FR headlamps with bulb No. 451. Also No. 1 (inner) lamps of
four headlamp system

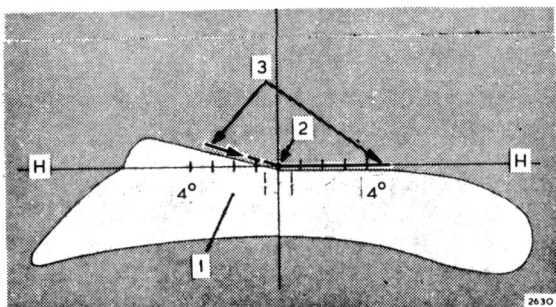

1. CONCENTRATED AREA OF LIGHT
2. BEAM 'KINK' AIMING POINT
3. BEAM 'CUT-OFF', ie LIGHT/DARK BOUNDARY
H. HORIZONTAL LINE 4 in. (102 mm) BELOW HEADLAMP CENTRES
Tolerance of kink aim point: from vertical line on screen to 6 in.
(152 mm) left ONLY at 25 ft (7.5 m). Tolerance to right not permitted.
1º = 5 in. (127 mm) at 25 ft (7.5 m).

Fig. 10.22b. Dipped (meeting) beam pattern for later type 2FR
headlamps with bulb No. 410 or 411. Also 4FR headlamps

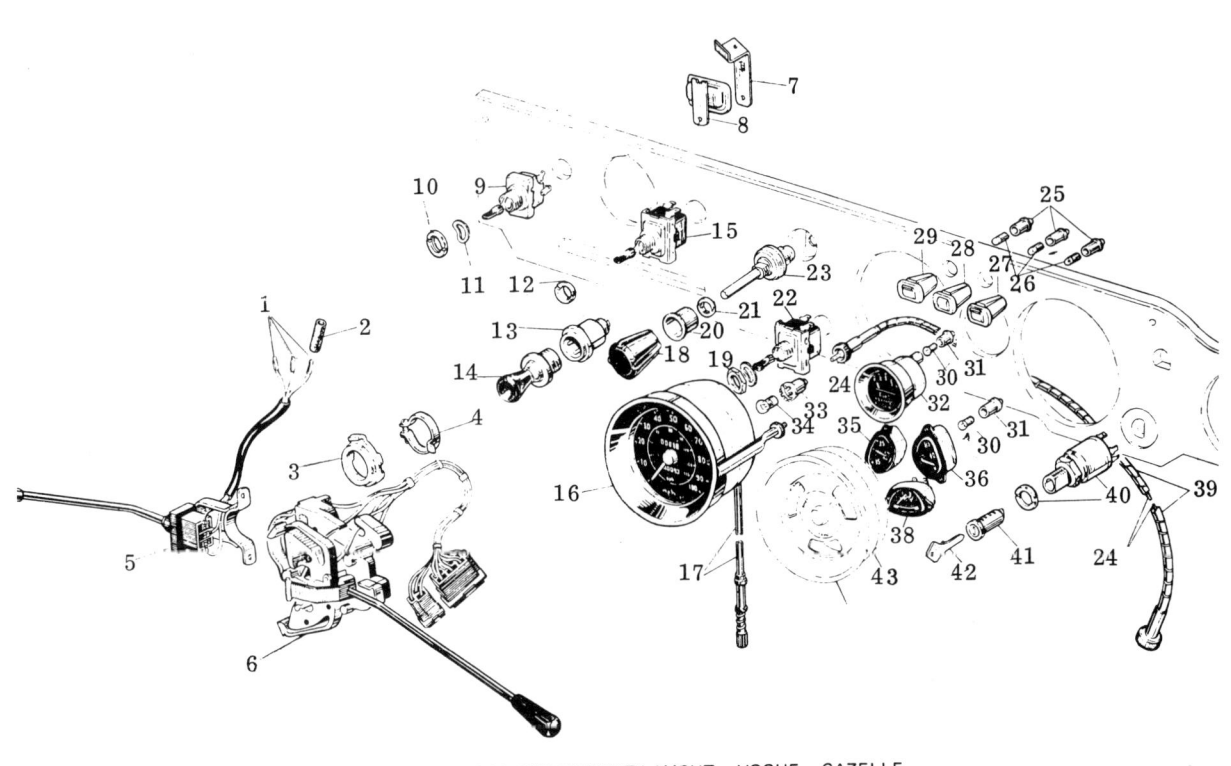

Fig. 10.23. INSTRUMENT LAYOUT — VOGUE — GAZELLE

1 Direction indicator connect-ions	12 Locking ring	24 Speedometer inner cable	36 Oil pressure gauge
2 Insulating sleeve	13 Cigarette lighter socket	25 Warning lamp holders	38 Temperature gauge
3 Cancelling striker bush	14 Cigarette lighter element	26 Wiper switch	39 Speedometer cable
4 Striker	15 Blower switch	27 Warning lamp lens	40 Ignition switch
5 Indicator switch	16 Speedometer head	28 Warning lamp lens	41 Lock barrel
6 Horn, dip & flasher switch	17 Trip setting cable	29 Warning lamp lens	42 Key
7 Mounting bracket	18 Light switch knob	30 Instrument bulb	43 Instrument bezel
8 Instrument voltage regulator	19 Locking ring	31 Bulb holder	
9 Panel light switch	20 Bezel	32 Fuel gauge	
10 Locking ring	21 Locking ring	33 Bulb holder	
11 Wave washer	22 Wiper switch	34 Instrument bulb	
	23 Light switch	35 Ammeter	

3. Before renewing any gauges the precautions as mentioned in the previous section should be taken and in the case of the oil pressure gauge giving no reading make sure you have some oil in the engine sump first!

4. The instrument voltage stabiliser is mounted on the steering column support bracket behind the panel.

5. Individual knobs and switches are removed from the panel in the same way as for the Minx/Hunter models.

Fault Finding Chart - Electrical System

The following chart does not include fault finding in connection with starting failure or engine running which is covered in Chapters 1 (Engine) and 4 (Ignition). **It also assumes that a good battery is fitted and that the earth link strap is properly connected from engine to body frame.**

Before anything else **always** check that the battery terminal connections are **clean** and tight.

Symptom	Cause	Remedy
When the ignition is switched on the oil and generator warning lights do not light.	Blown bulbs Broken circuit wire or loose connection Defective oil pressure sender	If engine starts anyway the bulb(s) will be defective (generator). Check oil sender by touching wire to earth. Check fuse box and control box connections.
When engine speeds up generator light stays lit	Loose or broken fan belt Defective generator Defective control box	Check fan belt tension. Test generator in car. Test control box in car.
When engine is running the oil pressure warning light stays lit. (Check causes in order)	No oil Severe leak in lubricating system Oil pressure switch defective Oil pump defective	Stop engine. Check lubricant level and system for leaks. Check lead is fitted to sender switch tightly. Change sender switch. Check oil pump by slackening oil filter and running engine to see if oil is pumped out.
Battery goes flat after a few days yet generator warning light goes out normally	Loose fan belt resulting in dynamo/alternator not timing fast enough. Dynamo/alternator output inadequate Control box malfunctioning	Check fan belt. Test dynamo/alternator output in car and overhaul as necessary. Test control box in car.
No road lights at all when switched on	Broken feed wire. (The headlamps are not fused)	Trace wiring circuit to headlamp switch.
No side lights	Blown fuse or broken connection	Check fuse. Trace which bulb causes failure if fuse keeps blowing and then check circuit.
Some bulbs fail to operate	Blown bulb Bad or dirty bulb holder connection	Remove bulb and test and clean up bulb holder. Check earth connections of units which complete the circuit to earth through the body of the unit.
Stop lights do not work	Broken feed wire to circuit in question Blown bulb(s) Defective switch Broken wire	Check circuit. Check bulb and connection. Short out terminals of switch and see if lights come on when ignition is switched on. If they do switch is U/S. Trace wiring circuit.
Fuel gauge registers incorrectly	Faulty voltage regulator sender unit or gauge	Check as described in this Chapter.
Water temperature gauge registers incorrectly	Faulty voltage regulator sender unit or gauge	Check as described in this Chapter.
Horn faulty	Switch defective, bad earth connection or broken circuit Faulty horn	By pass switch to check if horn is all right. Then check feed to horn. See details in this Chapter.
Windscreen wipers not working properly	Mechanism jammed Mechanism worn out Defective switch Defective motor	Give wipers a push to see if they will start. Then check out as described in detail in this Chapter.

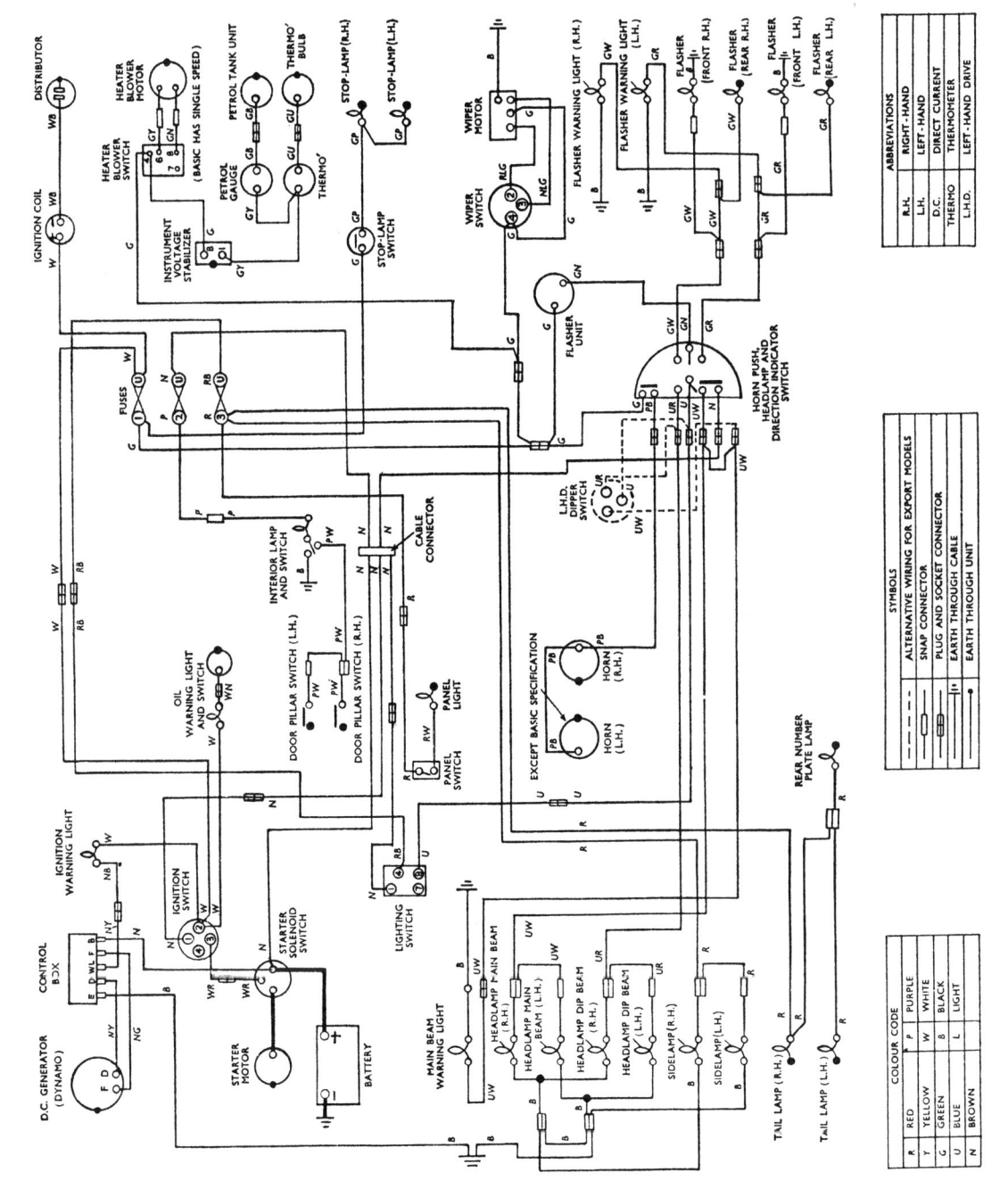

Fig. 10.24. Minx Saloon and Estate with dynamo

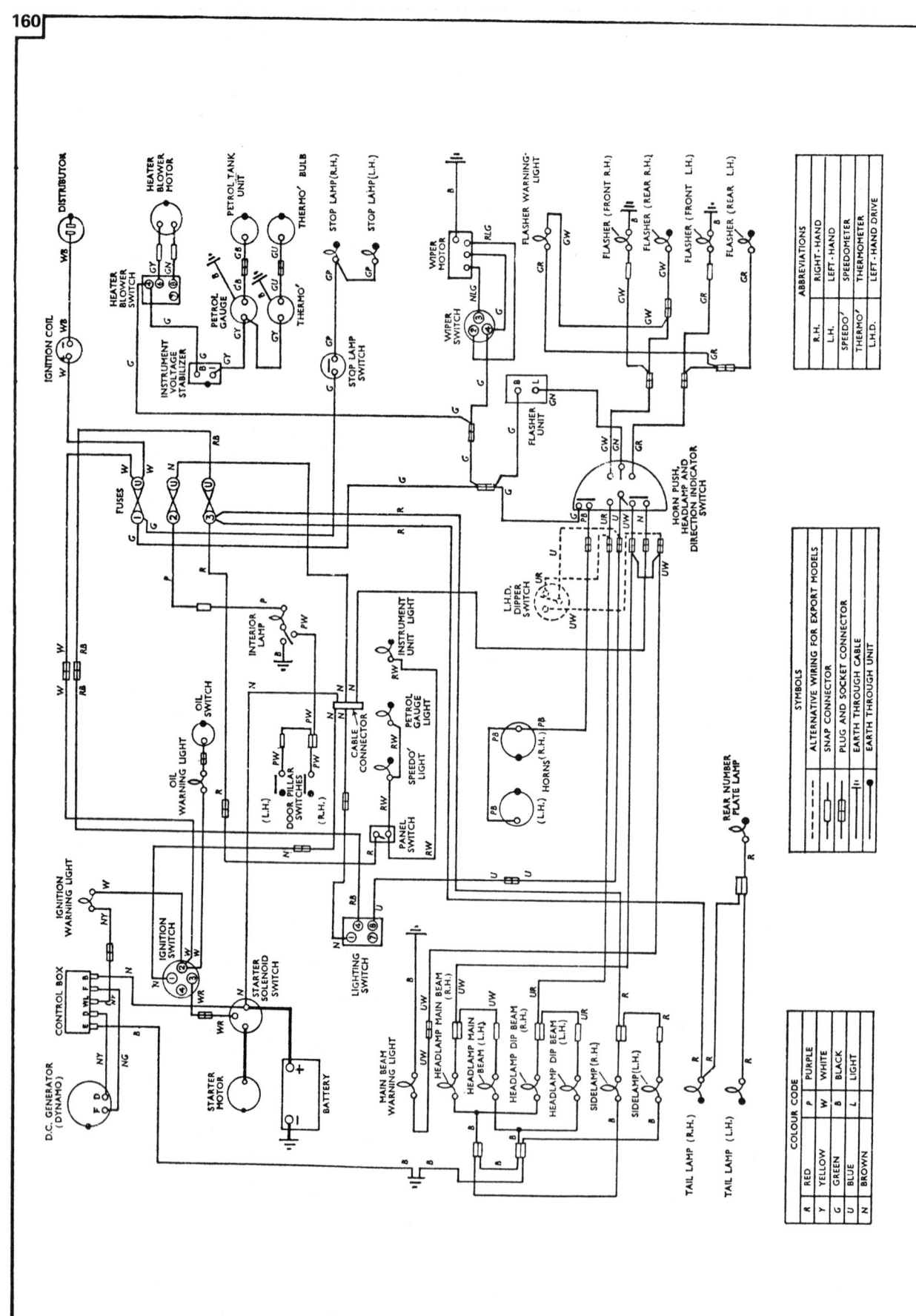

Fig. 10.25. Gazelle and early Hunter fitted with dynamo

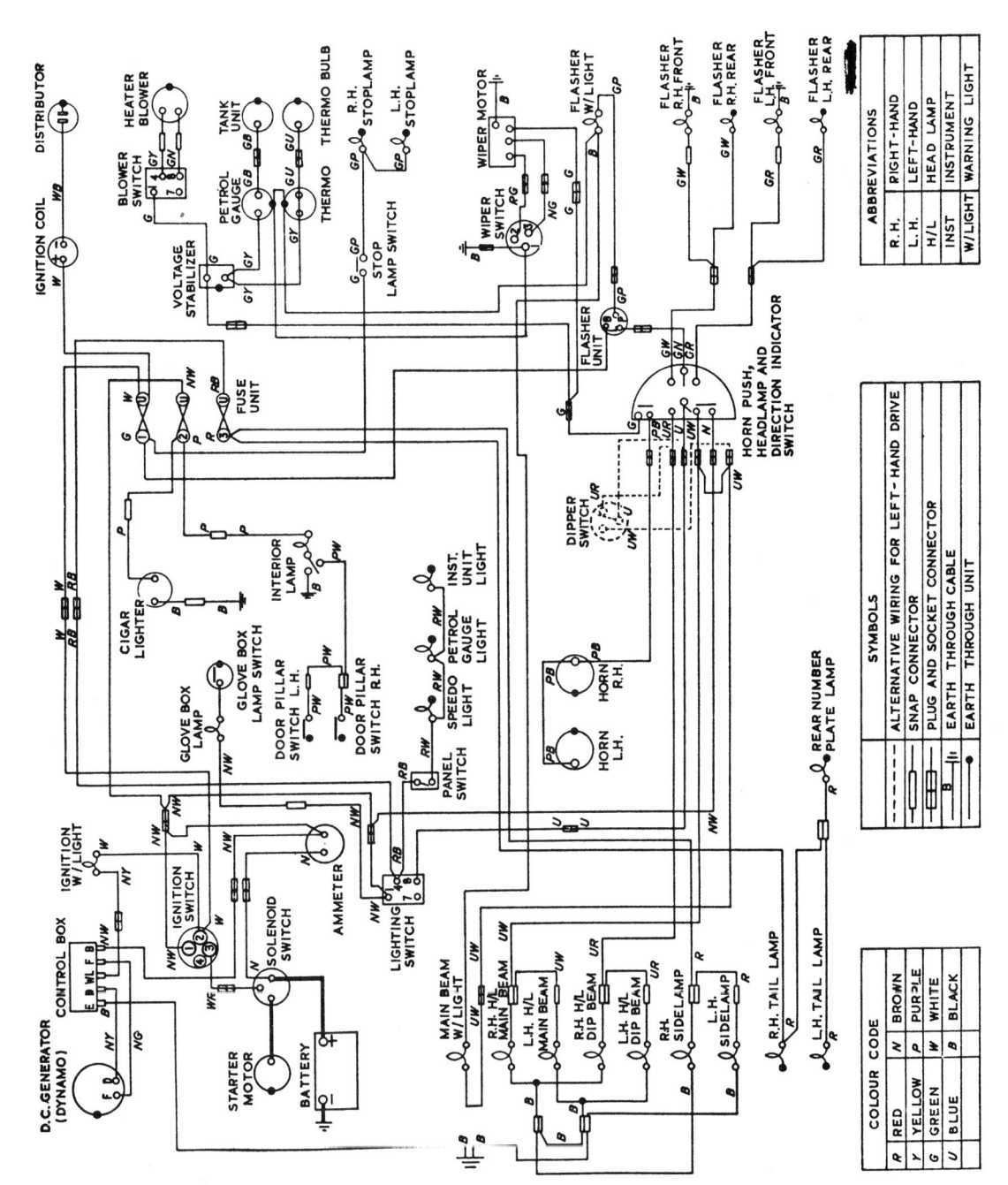

Fig. 10.26. Vogue Estate fitted with D.C. generator (dynamo)

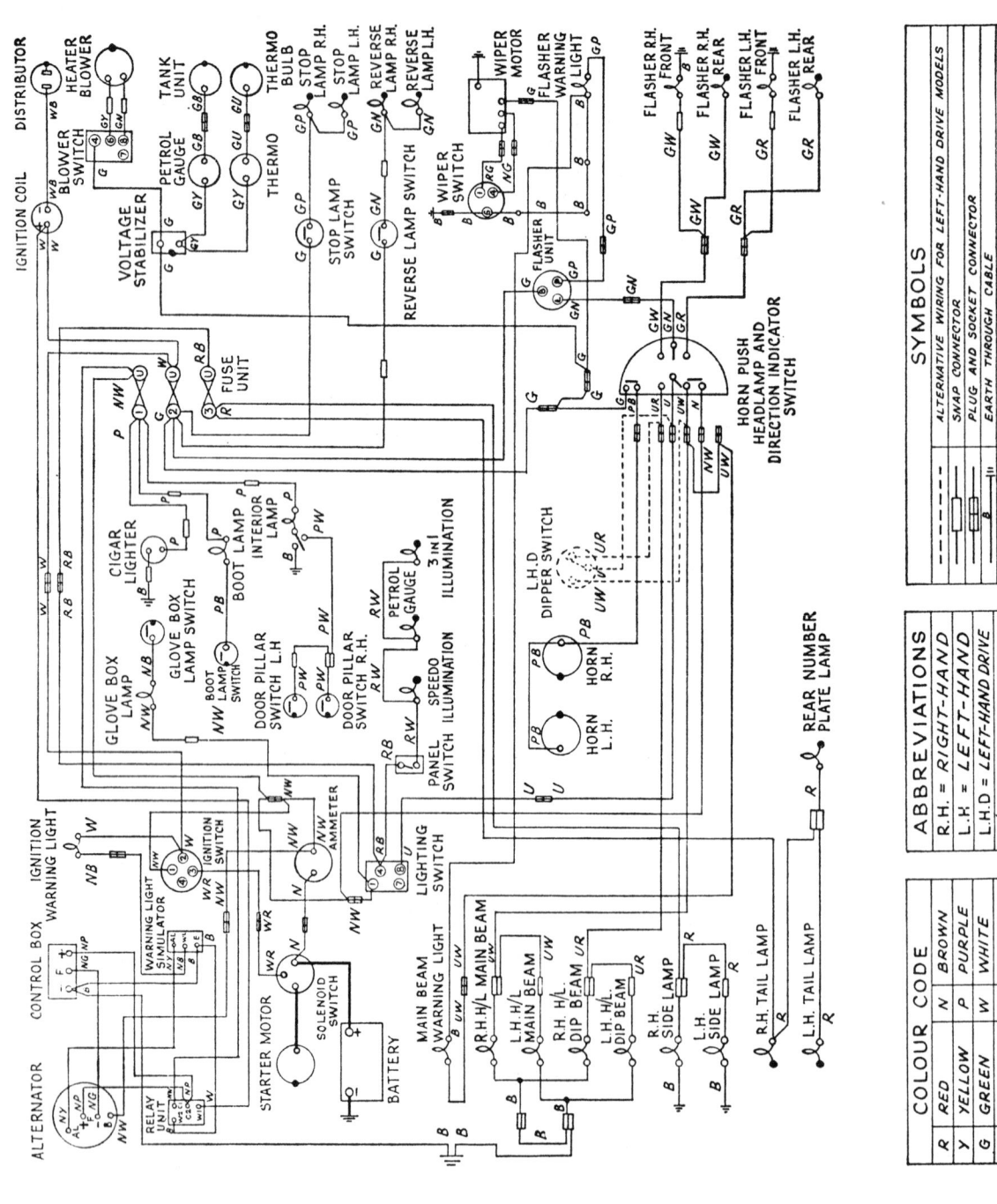

Fig. 10.27. Vogue Saloon and Estate fitted with alternator (10AC)

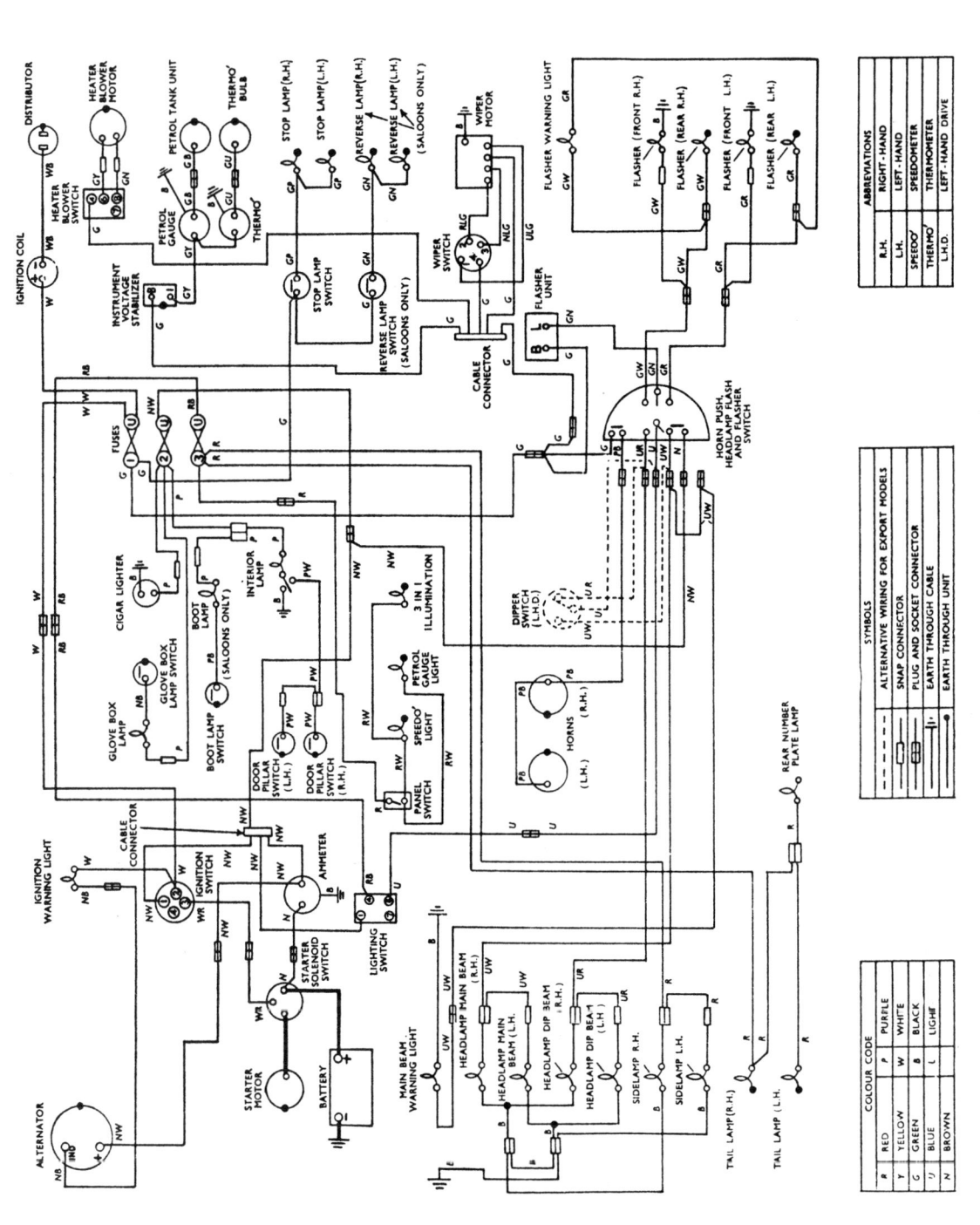

Fig. 10.28. Vogue Saloon and Estate fitted with 16ACR alternator

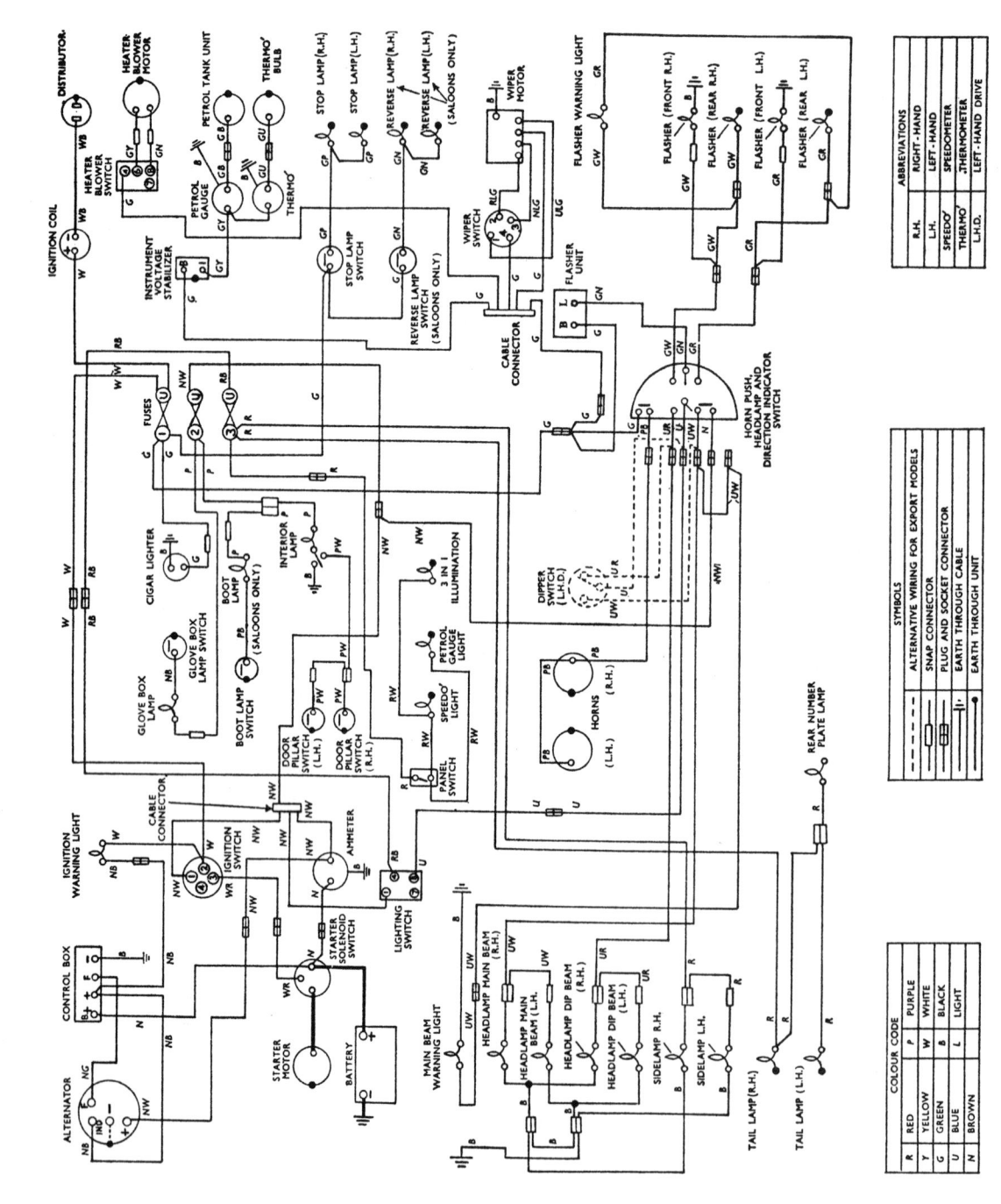

Fig. 10.29. Vogue Saloon and Estate fitted with alternator

Chapter 11 Suspension, dampers and steering

Contents

Specifications

Front suspension

Type ... ... Independent MacPherson type strut with anti-roll bar

Damper ... ... Armstrong telescopic, integral with strut

Spring

	Standard	*Heavy duty*
Inside diameter:		
Early models	4.5 in (11.4 cm)	4.5 in (11.4 cm)
Later models	4.3 in (11 cm)	4.3 in (11 cm)
Free length	14.15 in (35.9 cm)	12.9 in (32.8 cm)
Laden length:		
Early models	7.2 in (18.3 cm)	7.7 in (19.6 cm)
Later models	6.7 in (17 cm)	7.3 in (18.5 cm)
Laden load	625 lb (283.5 kg)	625 lb (283.5 kg)

Front hub endfloat ... ... 0.0015 - 0.004 in (0.040 - 0.10 mm)

Toe-in (track) ... ... 1/8 in $\pm$ 1/16 in (3 mm $\pm$ 1.5 mm) (30' $\pm$ 15')

Camber ... ... Zero $\pm$ ¾°

Castor ... ... ¼° negative $\pm$ ½°

Steering axis inclination ... ... 11¾° $\pm$ ¾°

Toe-out on turns ... ... Nil, wheels parallel at 20° turn

Wheel angles at full lock ... ... Inner 35°, outer 33°

Rear suspension

Type ... ... Asymmetric semi-elliptic springs

Dampers ... ... Telescopic direct acting, Girling Monitube, or Woodhead Monroe

Springs (general data)	*No. of leaves*	*Unladen camber (on car)*
Standard saloon	3 or 4	1.5 in (38.1 mm) positive
DL, Super and GL saloons	3	—
HD saloon	4	2.5 in (63.5 mm) positive
DL and GL Estate cars	4	2 in (50.8 mm) positive
HD Estate car	5 + 1 helper	2.25 in (57.2 mm) positive
Sceptre	3 or 4	1.5 in (38.1 mm) positive
Sceptre (later models)	3	—
Sceptre Estate car	4	—
GLS	4	1.5 in (38.1 mm) positive
GT	3	—

Steering

Type ,.. ... ... Burman F-type recirculating ball

Ratio ... ... 16.4 : 1

Turns, lock to lock 3 1/3

Turning circle:

Early models	33 ft 6 in (10.2 m)
Later models	34 ft 2 in (10.4 m)

Rocker shaft endfloat ... ...   Zero - 0.004 in (Zero - 0.10 mm)

Inner shaft bearing pre-load ... ...   0.002 - 0.004 in (0.05 - 0.1 mm)

Worm helix head ... ...   5/8 in (15.8 mm)

Capacity (steering unit) ... ...   0.56 pint (0.67 US pint, 0.32 litre)

Wheels

Wheel type ... ...   Ventilated pressed steel disc

Rim size ... ...   4½J x 13 safety ledge; 5J x 13 hump (safety ledge - later models)

Tyre sizes and pressures lb/in² (kg/cm²)

		5.60 x13 Early Saloons	6.00 x 13 Early Saloons	Early Estate Cars	Super DL and GL	155SR x 13 GT	Sceptre	165SR x 13 GT	DL Estate GL Estate Sceptre Estate
Front	... ...	24 (1.7)	25 (1.8)	24 (1.7)	24 (1.7)	26 (1.8)	26 (1.8)	24 (1.7)	24 (1.7)
Rear	... ...	24 (1.7)	25 (1.8)	24 (1.7)	24 (1.7)	26 (1.8)	26 (1.8)	24 (1.7)	24 (1.7)
Front	... ...	28 (2)	30 (2.1)	26 (1.8)	24 (1.7)	26 (1.8)	26 (1.8)	24 (1.7)	24 (1.7)
Rear	... ...	28 (2)	30 (2.1)	36 (2.5)	24 (1.7)	26 (1.8)	26 (1.8)	24 (1.7)	24 (1.7)
Front	... ...	28 (2)	30 (2.1)	26 (1.8)	26 (1.8)	26 (1.8)	26 (1.8)	24 (1.7)	24 (1.7)
Rear	... ...	28 (2)	30 (2.1)	36 (2.5)	30 (2.1)	30 (2.1)	30 (2.1)	26 (1.8)	32 (2.2)

1   Up to four occupants
2   Continuous high speed
3   Four occupants plus luggage

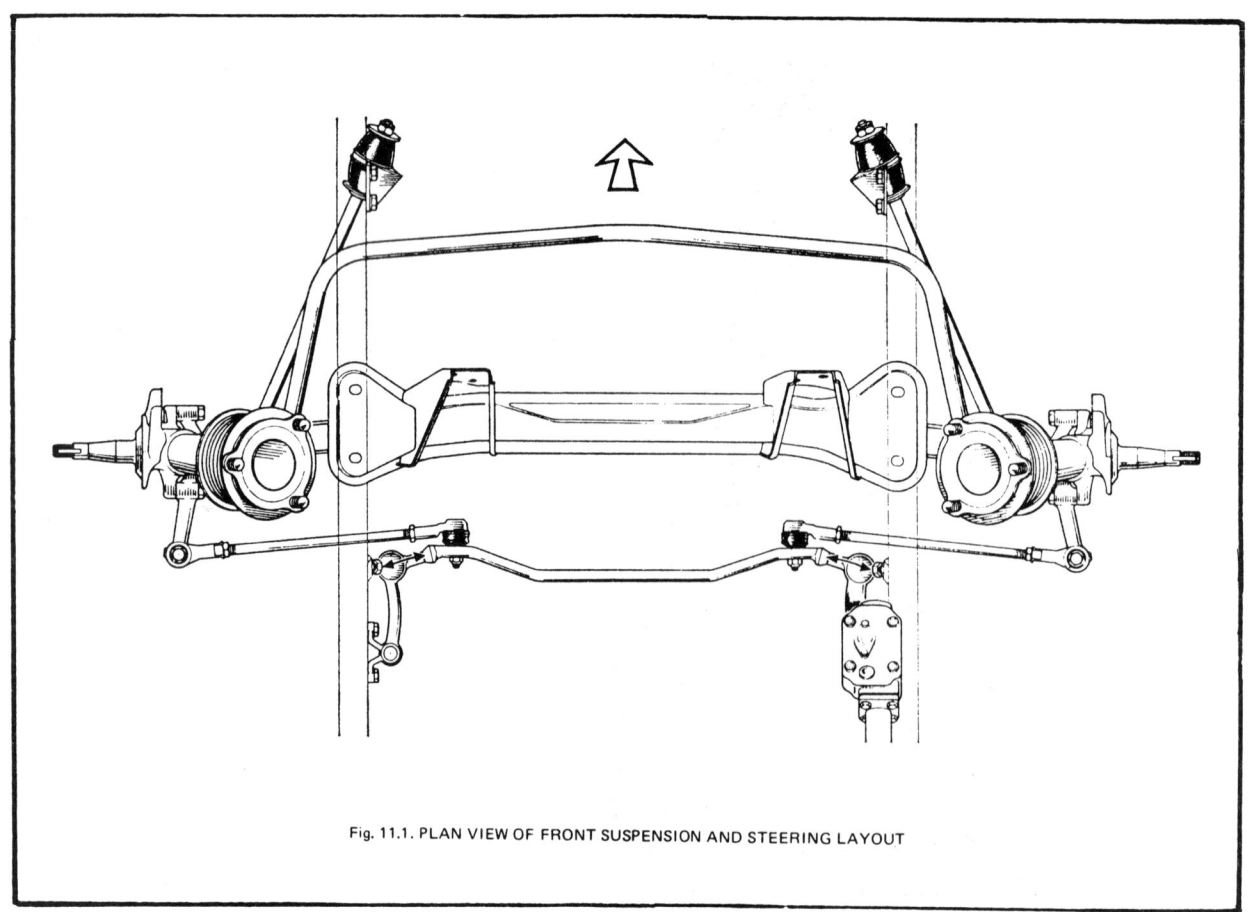

Fig. 11.1. PLAN VIEW OF FRONT SUSPENSION AND STEERING LAYOUT

1. General Description

The independent front suspension consists of the well tried MacPherson strut system, having been used by another large car producer for many years, and more recently adopted for a legendary European car.

It comprises a single telescopic damper unit, the foot so designed to carry the wheel hub and brake assembly. A coil spring surrounds the damper. The top of the unit fits into a rubber mounted thrust bush in a reinforced section of the wing.

The lower end of the unit is linked to the front crossmember at each side by a radius arm and fore and aft stabilisation is from a rod mounted forward to the side frame members. An anti-roll bar is also fitted across the car between the suspension units.

Rear suspension is by conventional semi-elliptic leaf springs, the springs being mounted on rubber bushed shackle pins. Telescopic hydraulic dampers are used.

The steering gear is a recirculating ball worm and nut unit which connects to the wheels via a drop arm, a centre track rod, a relay lever and two outer track rods connected to the steering arms on each wheel.

2. Routine Maintenance

As practically the whole of the suspension and steering connects via either bonded rubber bushes or pre-packed and sealed ball joints the bulk of any routine maintenance would be better described as routine inspection. The only two items requiring addition or replacement of lubricant from time to time are the steering box and the front wheel bearings.

Every 5,000 miles the filler plug of the steering box and the surrounding area should be cleaned, removed and the oil level checked. The level should be up to the bottom of the filler hole. Top up with 90 EP oil if necessary (Castrol Hypoy).

Every 15,000 miles the front hubs should be removed and the bearings flushed out and repacked with grease (Castrol L.M.).

Inspection of the steering linkage ball joints, suspension bushes and damper mountings should be undertaken at every 5,000 miles service and components renewed as necessary. For the owner who does his own maintenance this inspection is the area which is most often neglected. The fact that no grease can be pumped in or no adjustment made anyway tends to deter the owner from going to the trouble of jacking the suspension off the ground and examining the whole system properly. Any fault means expense; the components cannot be repaired - only renewed. This manual wishes to stress the importance of this less interesting aspect of owner car care. The fact that there is nothing to show for ones efforts, except the possibility of further expense and work is the necessary part of the whole which justifies an owner in regarding himself as competent to maintain his own car completely. It should be a matter of pride that no one else should be able to point first to defects in the steering and suspension.

3. Springs and Dampers - Inspection

1. The safety of a car depends more on the steering and suspension than anything else and this is the reason why the compulsory tests made for vehicles over three years old pay attention to the condition of all the steering and suspension components.

2. The rear suspension should be examined for broken spring leaves. This will usually be obvious as the car will be down on the side

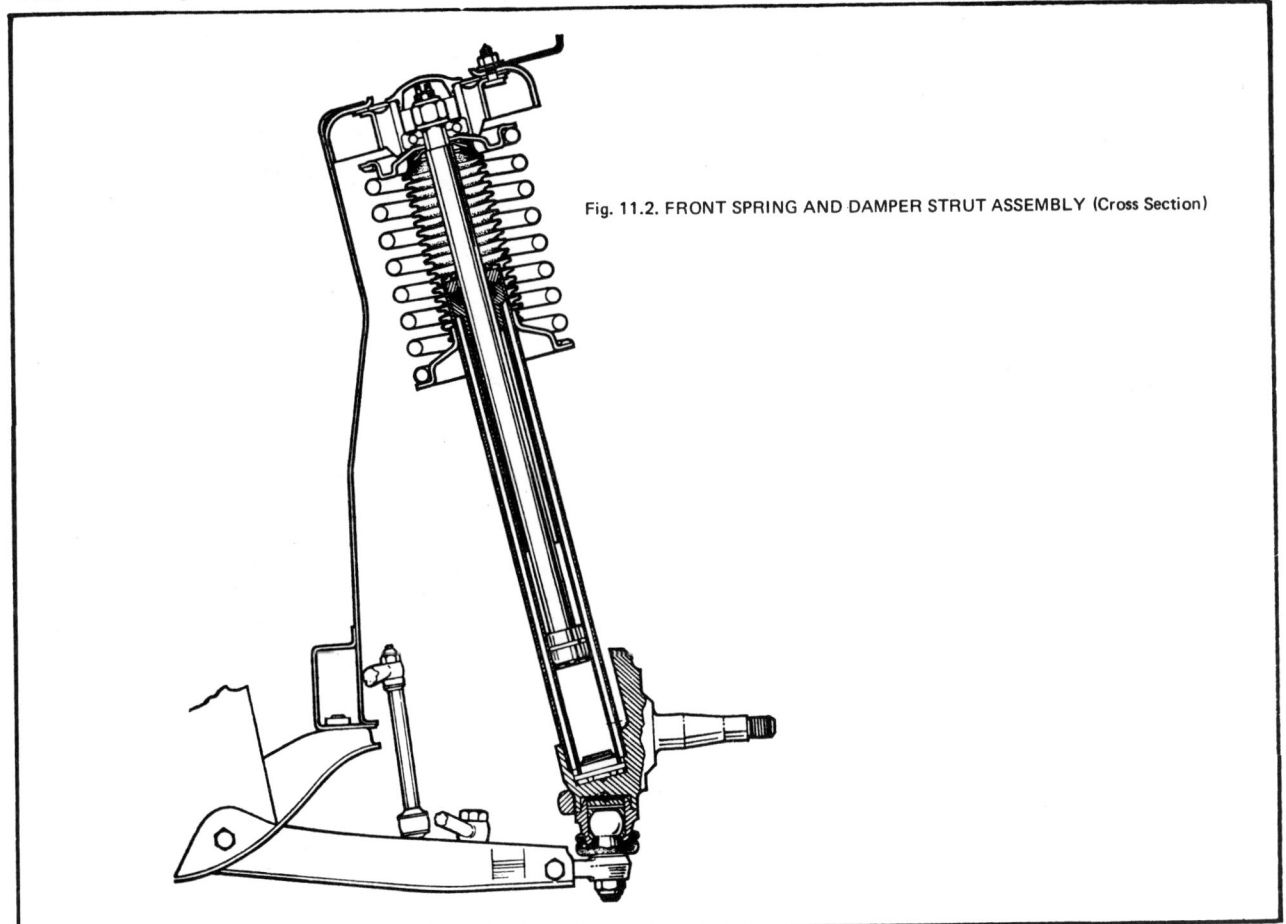

Fig. 11.2. FRONT SPRING AND DAMPER STRUT ASSEMBLY (Cross Section)

affected. Such broken leaves must be renewed.

3. The spring hangar and shackle pin bushes may be checked by jacking up the body and at the same time watching to see if there is any movement between the shackle pins and the frame when the weight is gradually shifted. As mud normally collects round these mounting points a badly worn bush is usually immediately apparent because the movement prevents the mud from caking.

4. Check for any signs of movement also in the 'U' bolts clamping the springs to the axle tube. If any one is loose check first that the axle is correctly located in the spring seat before tightening the 'U' bolt.

5. The top and bottom anchorage points of the hydraulic damper should be firm. If there are signs of oil on the outside of the lower cylinder section it indicates that the seals have gone and the damper must be renewed. The damper may also have failed internally and this is more difficult to detect. It is usually indicated by excessive bounce at the rear end and axle patter or 'tramp' on uneven surfaces. When this occurs remove the shock absorber in order to check its damping power in both directions. The best test of any suspension system is on the road. Static tests of dampers are not entirely conclusive and further indications of failure, either front or rear, are noticeable pitching (bonnet goes up and down!) when the car is braked and stopped sharply, excessive rolling on fast bends, and a definite feeling of insecurity on corners, particularly if the road surface is uneven. If in doubt it is a good idea to drive over a roughish road and have someone follow to watch how the wheels behave. Excessive up and down 'patter' of any wheel is quite obvious and denotes a defective damper.

6. The front suspension should be checked by first jacking the car up so that the wheel is clear of the ground. Then place another jack under the track control arm near the outer end. When the arm is raised by the jack any movement in the suspension strut ball stud will be apparent. So also will any wear in the inner track control arm bush. There should be no vertical or horizontal play whatsoever in either the ball joints or bushes at each end of the track control arms.

4. Stabiliser Bar - Removal and Replacement

1. The stabiliser bar could become ineffective if bent or if its mounting bushes became loose.

2. Leave the weight of the car on the front wheels and remove the nuts and washers securing the ends of the bar to the top ends of the link pins from the track control arms.

3. Then remove the two bolts securing the 'U' clamps and bushes to the side frame members. (These clamps are the ones which need detaching when it is necessary to lower the stabiliser bar for engine removal.)

4. The stabiliser bar can then be removed.

5. Renew any rubber bushes showing signs of deterioration. When refitting, particularly if new bushes have been used on the side frame clamps, it will help if the brackets are compressed by a 'G' cramp to ease refitting of the securing bolts. Tighten the nuts to the specified torque.

5. Track Control Arm Ball Joint - Removal and Replacement

1. Inspection will indicate whether there is any free play in the outer ball joint and if there is the joint will need replacement.

2. The joint is flanged and bolted to the base of the suspension strut and secured to the lower arm by a taper pin and nut into the eye of the carrier on the end of the arm.

3. Jack up the car, support it with a stand under the side member and remove the road wheel.

4. It improves accessibility if the disc calliper hub and dust plate are also taken off but this is not essential - especially if you have a pit or elevator. Next undo the two bolts holding the ball joint to the foot of the strut. It should then be possible to move the lower arm away from the bottom of the strut. If any difficulty is encountered, another jack can be placed under the hub or hub spindle to raise the

strut a little.

5. The ball joint nut should now be removed from the bottom of the ball joint pin. The tapered pin is often a stubborn item to get out of the carrier. If you do not have a proper claw clamp or slotted tapered steel wedges available to apply the necessary pressure, success can often be achieved by placing one hammer head on one side of the carrier and hitting the opposite side with another. This, in effect, squeezes the taper out of its seating.

6. When fitting a new ball joint make sure that the mating flange faces are clean and free from scores or burrs so that they fit perfectly flush. Fit it to the strut first and tighten the bolts to the specified torque. Then clean the taper pin and the bore in the carrier and fit them together. Tighten the nut to the specified torque.

6. Track Control Arm and Bushes - Removal and Replacement

1. If the inner pivot bushes on the track control arm are worn out the arm will have to be removed in order to renew them.

2. With the weight of the car still on the front suspension first remove the bottom nut of the link pin which connects the stabiliser bar to the arm.

3. Jack up the front of the car and support it on stands placed under the side members. Remove the road wheel from the side being dealt with.

4. Remove the large vertical bolt which holds the eye of the radius rod to the suspension arm (this also goes through the inner end of the carrier arm). Then remove the horizontal bolt that holds the carrier arm to the end of the suspension arm.

5. If the pivot bolt at the inner end of the arm is now removed the arm may be taken out.

6. New bushes should be fitted to the inner end and in addition all the self locking nuts used should be renewed. Otherwise reassembly is a simple reversal of the removal procedure. Tighten all nuts and bolts to the specified torque. It is advisable to get the steering alignment checked after assembly.

7. Front Suspension Strut Assembly - Removal and Replacement

1. If the damping part of the suspension unit is not working properly, or the spring is broken and needs renewing, it will be necessary to remove the whole unit from the car first. Carefully prise out the dust cap from the thrust bearing in the wing valance and unscrew the nut by **one turn only** using tool number P5025 or a similar device (see Section 8, paragraph 5).

2. Jack up the front of the car and support it on stands underneath the side members. Detach the brake calliper from the hub as described in Chapter 9.

3. Undo the two bolts which hold the steering arm to the foot of the strut but leave the arm connected to the track rod.

4. Remove the two bolts securing the steering arm to the foot of the strut, allowing the steering arm to remain connected to the outer track rod. Undo and remove the two bolts that secure the lower balljoint to the strut. Release the joint and leave the balljoint attached to the carrier.

5. Support the lower end of the strut on a block or jack before the next step of detaching it at the upper end.

6. The upper end is held to the wing valance by three studs from which the nuts should now be removed. The centre nut should not be touched. The whole unit may now be lifted away from the car.

7. When replacing the assembly renew all self locking nuts and tighten them to the correct torque settings. It is important that rubber mountings should not be over-tightened. It is advisable to have the steering alignment checked after fitting.

8. Front Suspension Strut Assembly - Overhaul

1. Unless you are able to borrow the correct special tools needed

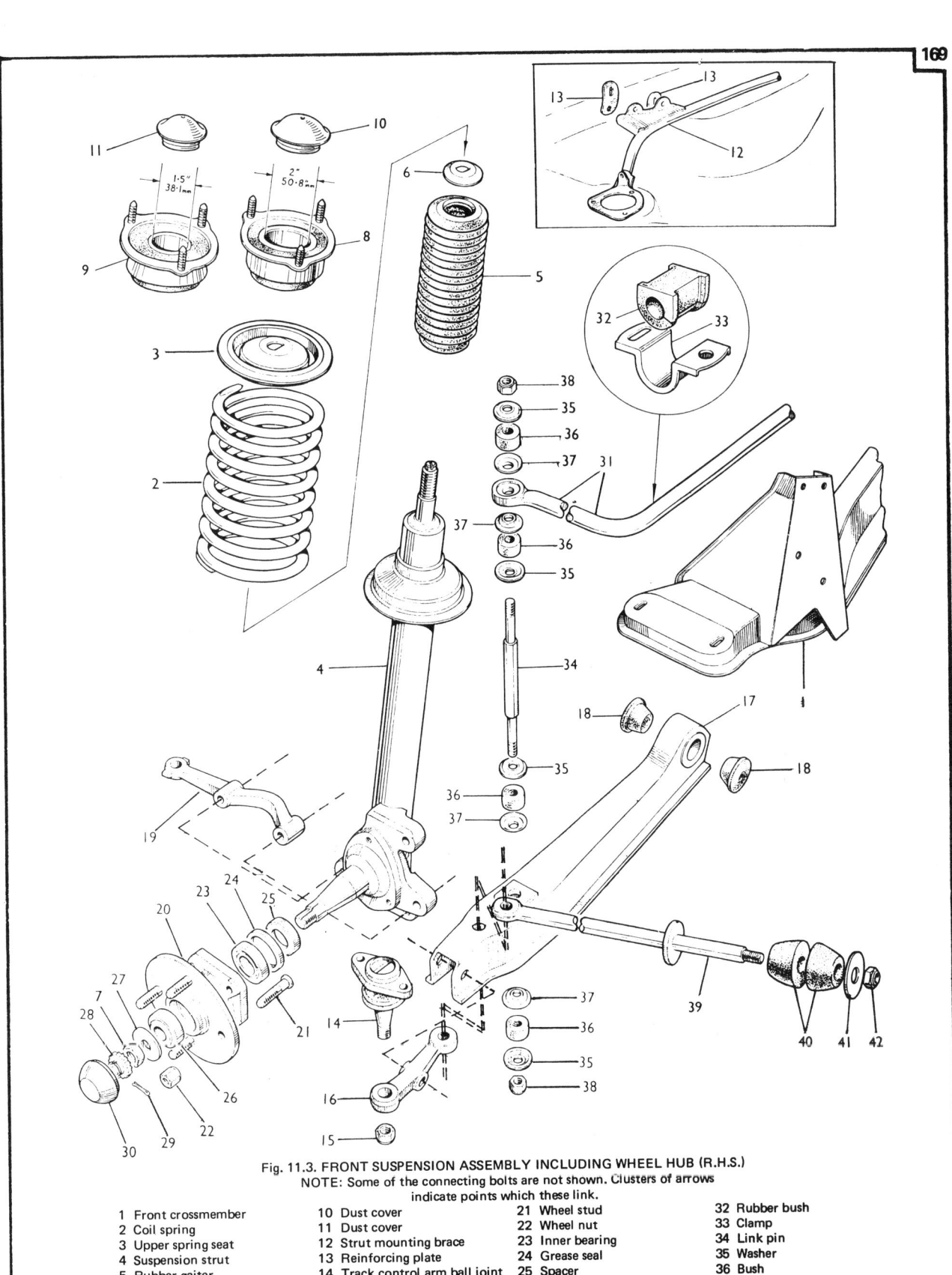

Fig. 11.3. FRONT SUSPENSION ASSEMBLY INCLUDING WHEEL HUB (R.H.S.)
NOTE: Some of the connecting bolts are not shown. Clusters of arrows
indicate points which these link.

1 Front crossmember	10 Dust cover	21 Wheel stud	32 Rubber bush
2 Coil spring	11 Dust cover	22 Wheel nut	33 Clamp
3 Upper spring seat	12 Strut mounting brace	23 Inner bearing	34 Link pin
4 Suspension strut	13 Reinforcing plate	24 Grease seal	35 Washer
5 Rubber gaiter	14 Track control arm ball joint	25 Spacer	36 Bush
6 Thrust bearing washer	15 Self-locking nut	26 Outer bearing	37 Washer
7 Hub bearing nut	16 Ball joint carrier	27 Washer	38 Nut - self locking
8 Thrust bearing unit	17 Track control arm	28 Lock cap	39 Radius rod
(machined type)	18 Bushes	29 Split pin	40 Rubber bushes
9 Thrust bearing unit	19 Steering arm	30 Dust cap	41 Washer
(pressed type)	20 Hub	31 Stabiliser bar	42 Nut - self-locking

to dismantle the strut assembly you could cause damage to both the damper and strut. So unless you are quite sure, we recommend that you get specialist help.

2. To dismantle the unit it is convenient to refit it to a road wheel, place the road wheel on a bench and steady the strut by putting a wooden wedge between it and the tyre wall.

3. To remove the thrust bearing unit the pressure of the spring has to be relieved with a compressor tool (RG521) . If a tool other than that specially designed is used it must be remembered that although the amount of compressing required is minimal it must be able to relieve the spring to its free length; so must have sufficient travel.

4. Fit the tool securely and squarely on the spring, bolt heads upwards, and compress it evenly until the pressure is taken off the thrust bearing unit.

5. Remove the dust cap and using tool P5025 the thrust bearing nut can be undone. The tool is in two parts. One part is a screwdriver engaging in the slot in the top of the damper piston rod to prevent it turning and the other is a socket wrench to undo the nut. A suitable tool can be improvised with a long tubular spanner and T-handled screwdriver but you will certainly need two pairs of hands to deal with it.

6. The washer and bearing unit may then be taken off. The spring compressor should then be released evenly until the spring tension is completely relieved. Remove the spring together with its upper seat.

7. If it is desired to remove the damper unit from the strut, remove the rubber gaiter and push the piston rod right into the strut. Then knock back the staking which locks the sealing nut into the strut tube.

8. The gland nut is one with four dog slots in it to accept once again a special tool (RG525). Do not attempt to undo this nut with a hammer and pin punch because one slip which may ruin the very fine threads, will be the virtual end of the whole unit.

9. With the gland nut removed take out the rubber 'O' ring and from inside the top edge of the strut the damper rod should be pulled out, dislodging the guide bush and seal assembly from the top of the strut at the same time.

10 Drain out the oil which is not re-usable.

11 Reassembly is simply a repeat of the dismantling process in reverse but before commencing operations the following paragraphs should be read and pondered over. Remember that the safety of the car depends much on this unit.

a) The whole unit must be scrupulously clean, inside and out, before reassembly begins. Use petrol to clean out and let it dry off afterwards.

b) 350 c.c. of fresh oil (Armstrong Fluid 788) is required for each damper unit and should be initially divided between the damper unit and the strut. It will be necessary to lift the damper guide bush out of the stop tube to get this oil in. The damper should then be primed with one or two long steady strokes of the piston until resistance is equal in both directions.

c) Fit a new seal and 'O' ring and also a new gland nut.

d) Make sure that everything is properly lined up when fitting the gland nut and keep the damper piston rod pulled out at all stages of reassembly.

e) The threads of the gland nut are very easily crossed unless extreme care is taken. Also make sure that the threads on the end of the piston rod are not damaged during reassembly. Stake the gland nut as before.

f) Always fit a new gaiter to protect the damper piston.

g) Do not refit a spring that does not correspond closely to the free length dimensions given in the specifications. When compressing the spring, to refit the upper bearing bush, care is needed to engage the piston rod in the thrust bearing plate and to prevent the piston being pushed back too far into the strut.

h) Observe all the torque wrench loadings on the various nuts with accuracy. If the thrust bearing nut is overtight the steering will be stiff and the thrust bearing overloaded, causing early failure.

i) The special tools required for dismantling will all be required for the same uses in reassembly.

9. Rear Springs and Dampers - Removal and Replacement

1. To renew the rear dampers jack up the car under the axle and remove the wheel for ease of access. Then remove the lower anchor bolt, nut and lockwasher and pull the bottom of the damper from its location.

2. From inside the boot remove the locknut from the top mounting spindle and then grip the flats on the spindle with a suitable spanner so that the second nut can be undone and removed.

3. The damper may then be taken out from underneath. When refitting make sure first that all the rubber mountings and steel bushes are in good condition. Renew them if necessary. New bushes may come with the damper.

4. The rear springs must be detached either to renew a broken leaf or to renew the mounting bushes at the front or rear. Jack up the car and support it on stands at the rear and then support the axle on a jack at a point away from the spring mountings. Remove the road wheel.

5. Detach the lower end of the damper from the mounting.

6. Thoroughly clean off all the dirt from the 'U' bolts and shackle pins and soak the nuts and threads with a suitable easing fluid such as 'Plus-Gas'.

7. Remove the 'U' bolt nuts and jack up the axle a little way to separate it from the springs.

8. Remove the nut and washer from the front hanger bolt. This may prove very stubborn and if it needs driving out replace the nut to try and protect the threads. In any case one should be prepared to renew the bolt.

9. When removing the shackle plates at the rear end of the spring both nuts must first be removed as the two halves each comprise one shackle pin and plate and need separating. Here again the pins may be very difficult to shift and it is not unknown to have to have to cut them off.

10 A broken spring can be replaced as a complete unit or the individual leaf can be renewed. If the leaf only is being replaced new spring clips, rivets and inserts will be required to reassemble the leaves. A replacement unit can usually be found at a breaker's and this is the simplest and cheapest way to go about it.

11 When reassembling the rubber bushes for the shackles use some soapy water to lubricate them. The front spring hanger bush is a press fit unit into the spring. It will have to be driven out and a new one pressed in if it needs renewal. Note that there were different types of bush fitted to the front hanger over a period of time. The very early versions were fitted with an eccentric bolt hole which was positioned at 12 o'clock. These bushes are no longer used and the new replacements, still having an eccentric bolt hole, require that the hole be positioned at 10.30, i.e., 45° up from the horizontal at the front. Other bushes have central bolt holes and others again have a triangular section. The latter require that one lobe of the triangle is positioned at 10.30 in the spring eye like the eccentric version. The point about this variety of bushes is that they must be the same on both rear springs. Otherwise some funny things can happen to the rear axle position under certain load and acceleration conditions. So if a new type of bush is fitted in one spring the same should also be fitted in the other. Another feature which occurs in earlier models is the fitting of a steel wedge between the top leaf and the axle pad. Where these are fitted make sure that the thick end faces forwards. Some early Hunters and Vogues had no wedges and none should be fitted except in serious cases of vibration.

12 When refitting the spring to the hangars it is usually easier to fit the front end first. Then replace the shackle pins and bushes. Replace the nuts but do not tighten them yet. Then lower the axle and position it so that it locates correctly onto the spring (and wedge if fitted) and put the 'U' bolts and clamp plate in position. Tighten up the 'U' bolt nuts only moderately.

13 The damper should next be fitted to the lower mounting.

14 The car should then be lowered to the ground, bounced a few times to settle the bushes and then all the nuts tightened to the specified torque.

15 The specifications give the spring cambers for the various models -

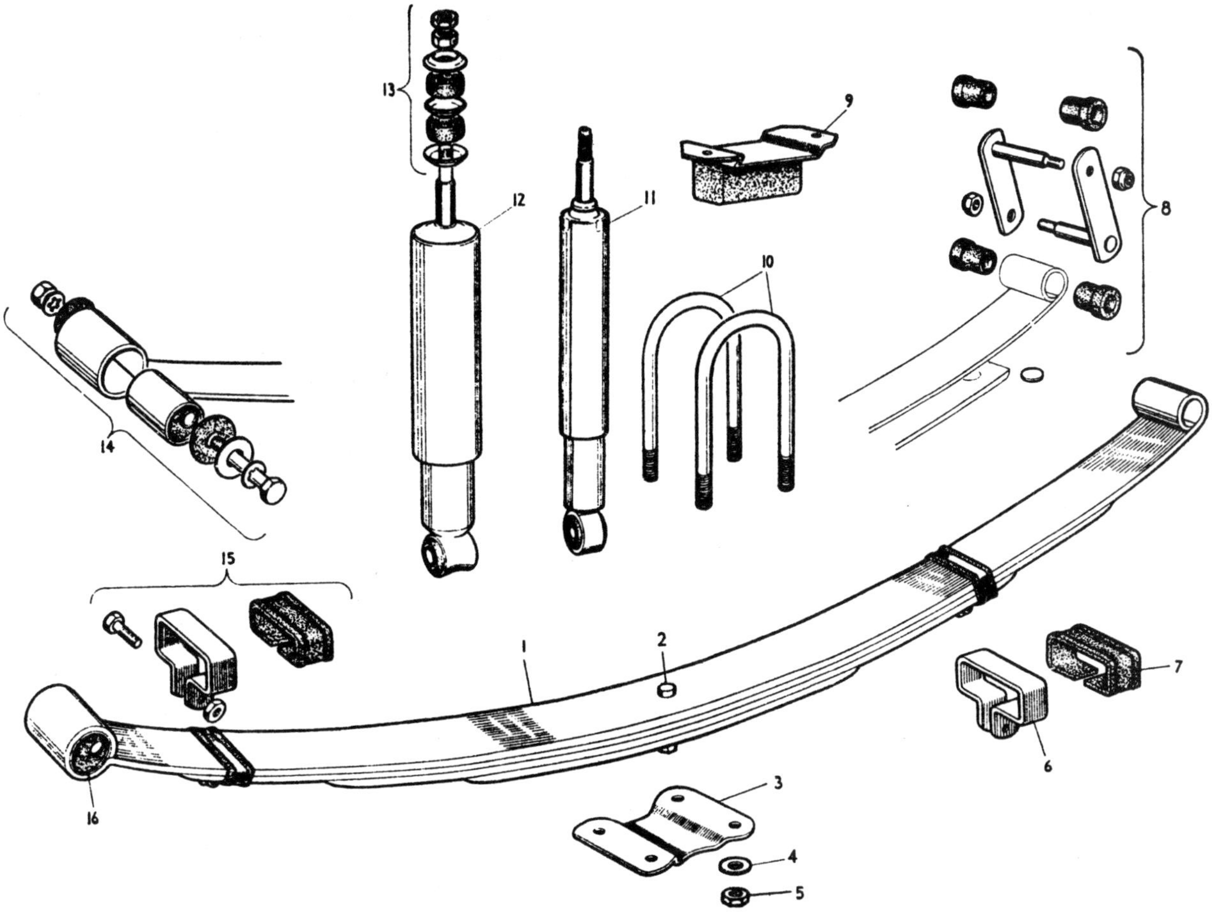

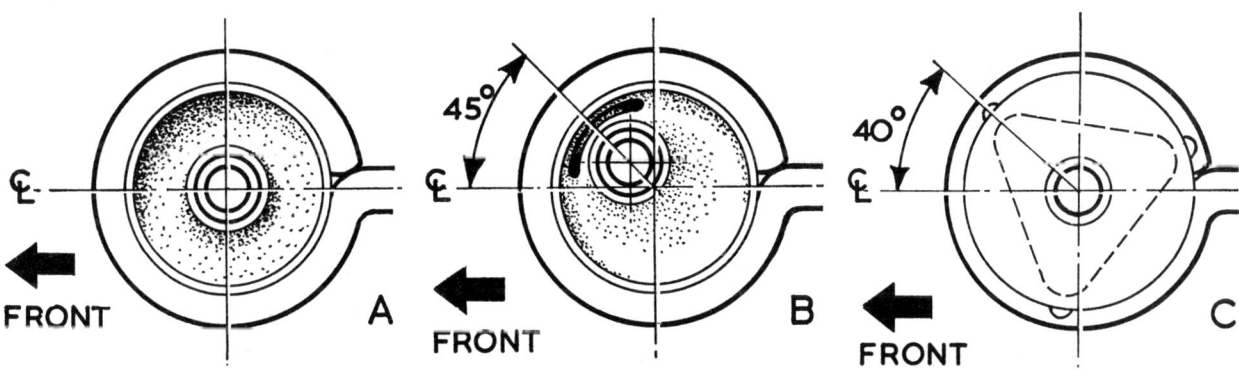

Fig. 11.4. REAR SUSPENSION & DAMPER

1 Main leaf	6 Spring clip	11 Damper - Girling monitube	15 Clip and rubber assembly
2 Dowel bolt	7 Spring clip rubber	12 Damper - Woodhead-Monroe	16 Eccentric bush - front eye
3 Spring retainer	8 Rear shackle assembly	13 Damper - top mounting	
4 'U' bolt washer	9 Bump/torque reaction rubber	assembly	
5 'U' bolt nut	10 'U' bolts	14 Front eye assembly	

Fig. 11.5. DIFFERENT TYPES OF REAR SPRING FRONT EYE BUSHES
A Steel jacketed centre pin   B Steel jacketed eccentric pin
C Flanged triangular section

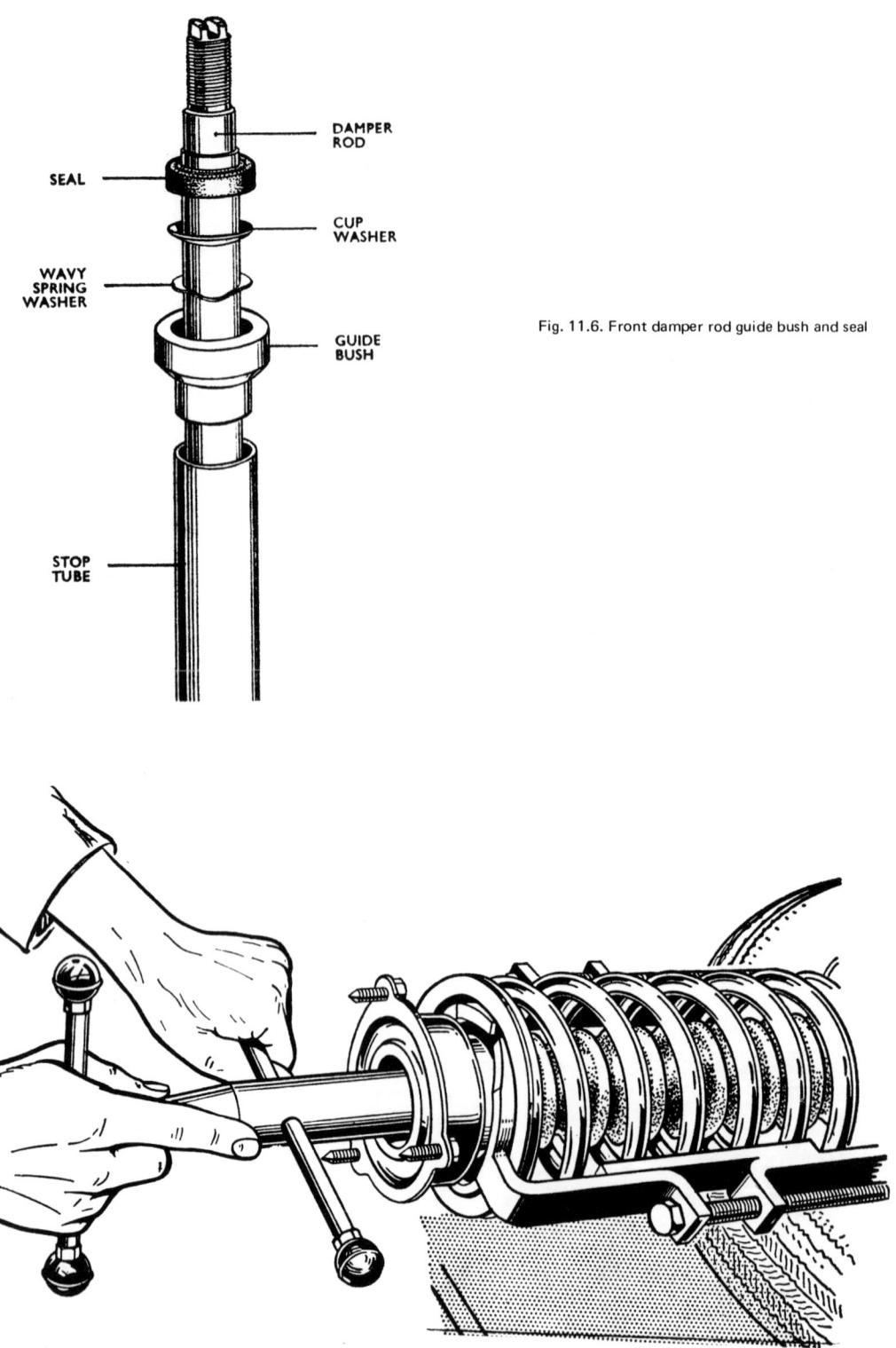

DAMPER ROD

SEAL

CUP WASHER

WAVY SPRING WASHER

GUIDE BUSH

STOP TUBE

Fig. 11.6. Front damper rod guide bush and seal

Fig. 11.7. Dismantling front strut showing spring compressor and special tool P5025 for undoing thrust bearing nut in position.

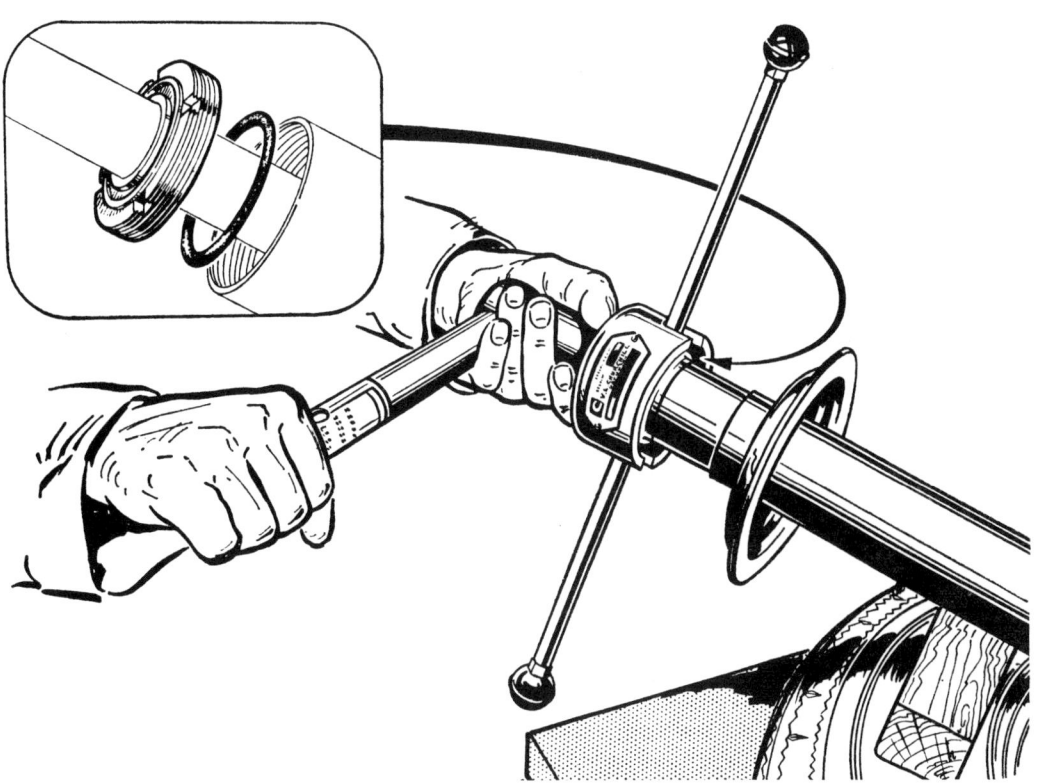

Fig. 11.8. Special tool RG525 with torque wrench incorporated for fitting the gland nut to the strut. Inset shows details of gland nut and 'O' ring.

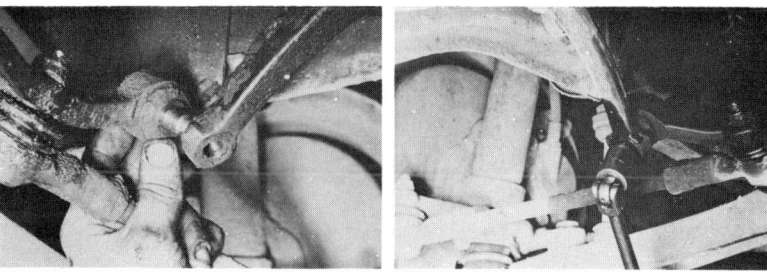

SECTION 11. Replacing the centre track rod to the idler arm and drop arm (R.H. drive).

the camber being the amount of 'bow' in the spring - which is measured as the distance between the centre of the top leaf and a straight line drawn through the centre line of the front hanger bolt and lower rear shackle pin. The easiest way to check this is to measure the vertical height of the centre line of the two bolts and the underside of the axle tube from the ground. Put the car on a smooth level surface in order to do this properly. With the known length of the spring between the hangar bolts the dimensions can be scaled on paper and the camber distance calculated.

10. Steering Gear and Linkage - Inspection

1. Wear in the steering gear and linkage is indicated when there is considerable movement in the steering wheel without corresponding movement at the road wheels. Wear is also indicated when the car tends to 'wander' off the line one is trying to steer. There are three main steering 'groups' to examine in such circumstances. These are the wheel bearings, the linkage joints and bushes and the steering box itself.
2. First jack up the front of the car and support it on stands under the side frame members so that both front wheels are clear of the ground.
3. Grip the top and bottom of the wheel and try to rock it. It will not take any great effort to be able to feel any play in the wheel bearing. If this play is very noticeable it would be as well to adjust it straight away as it could confuse further examinations. It is also possible that during this check play may be discovered also in the lower suspension track control arm ball joint (at the foot of the suspension strut). If this happens the ball joint will need renewal as described in Section 5.
4. Next grip each side of the wheel and try rocking it laterally. Steady pressure will, of course, turn the steering but an alternated back and forth pressure will reveal any loose joint. If some play is felt it would be easier to get assistance from someone so that while one person rocks the wheel from side to side, the other can look at the joints and bushes on the track rods and connections. Excluding the steering box itself there are seven places where the play may occur. The two outer ball joints on the two outer track rods are the most likely, followed by the two inner joints on the same rods where they join the centre track rod. Any play in these means renewal of the ball joint. Next are the two swivel bushes, one at each end of the centre track rod. If play is detected in these then the whole track rod will need to be renewed as the bushes are not obtainable separately. The last point to check is the pivot of the relay or idler arm which supports the centre track rod on the side opposite the steering box. This unit is bolted to the side frame member and any play calls for renewal of the unit.
5. Finally, the steering box itself is checked. First make sure that the bolts holding the steering box to the side frame member are tight. Then get another person to help examine the mechanism. One should look at, or get hold of, the drop arm at the bottom of the steering box while the other turns the steering wheel a little way from side to side. The amount of lost motion between the steering wheel and the drop arm indicates the degree of wear somewhere in the steering box mechanism. This check should be carried out with the wheels first of all in the straight ahead position and then at nearly full lock on each side. If the play only occurs noticeably in the straight ahead position then the wear is most probably in the worm and/or nut. If it occurs at all positions of the steering then the wear is probably in the rocker shaft bush. An oil leak at this point is another indication of such wear. In either case the steering box will need removal for closer examination and repair.
6. Many owners consider removing shims at one of the two places they are fitted, thinking thereby to compensate for wear. This can be done but the beneficial results, if any, will be very short lived. The wear which has taken place and which will be taken up by removal of the shims will not be properly compensated. The top cover shims, which control rocker shaft endfloat, will not rectify wear in the bush. Their removal will merely keep the shaft running out of alignment -

albeit with less play initially. But stiffness will probably result and wear will continue at an accelerated rate until the situation will soon be worse than it was originally. The other shims, between the column flange and the box, pre-load the two ball races (which are not adjustable) on the shaft inside the box. If there is noticeable end float on the shaft due to worn bearings, the removal of shims will take up the float but the already worn bearings will wear much faster as a result. To sum up it must be understood that the shims are used to set up unworn components as they should be set up. The shims are not designed as a means of subsequent adjustment in order to compensate for wear. If they are used in this manner, play will be removed initially (but with the likelihood of stiffness and steering irregularity) but wear will accelerate and result in an equal or increased amount of play.

11. Steering Linkage - Removal and Replacement

1. The ball joints on the two outer track rods and the swivel bushes on the centre track rod are all fitted into their respective locations by means of a taper pin into a tapered hole and secured by a self-locking nut. In the case of the four ball joints (two on each of the outer track rods) they are also screwed onto the rod and held by a locknut. The two other ball joints have left-hand threads.
2. To remove the taper pin first remove the self locking nut. On rare and happy occasions the taper pins have been known to simply pull out. More often they are well and truly wedged in position and a clamp or slotted steel wedges may be driven between the ball unit and the arm to which it is attached. Another method is to place the head of a hammer (or other solid metal article) on one side of the hole in the arm into which the pin is fitted. Then hit it smartly with a hammer on the opposite side. This has the effect of squeezing the taper out and usually works, provided one can get a good swing at it.
3. When the taper pin is free, grip the shank of the joint and back off the locknut. Move this locknut just sufficiently to unlock the shank as its position is a guide to fitting the new joint. Then screw the ball joint off the rod.
4. It is most important when fitting new ball joints to first ensure that they are screwed on to the rod the same amount and then, before tightening the locknut, that they are correctly angled. So, after connecting everything up and before tightening the locknuts set the steering in the straight ahead position and see that the socket of the ball joint is square with the axis of the ball taper pin. If this is not done the whole joint could be under extreme strain when the steering is on only partial lock.
5. If the centre track rod bushes require that the track rod be renewed then it will be necessary first to detach the inner ball joints of the outer track rods from it. The two swivel joints can then be removed from the drop arm and idler arm respectively and the unit removed.
6. As has been mentioned already any play in the idler arm bush means that the centre track rod should be detached from it and the whole unit unbolted from the side frame and renewed.
7. When any part of the steering linkage is renewed it is advisable to have the alignment of the steering checked at a garage equipped with the proper equipment. Although a new joint properly replaced may be satisfactory without further attention there are exceptions, particularly if the recent history of the car is not known. Some misguided individual could have altered the outer track rod settings thinking to cure a steering fault that was caused by wear.

12. Steering Gear - Removal and Replacement

1. The steering gear or steering box as it is often called, is integral with the steering column and shaft and its removal and replacement is not a quick job. Do not therefore start dismantling it without having first decided what is needed to put it right. Remember that if the bush is worn out the new one could well need reaming out and

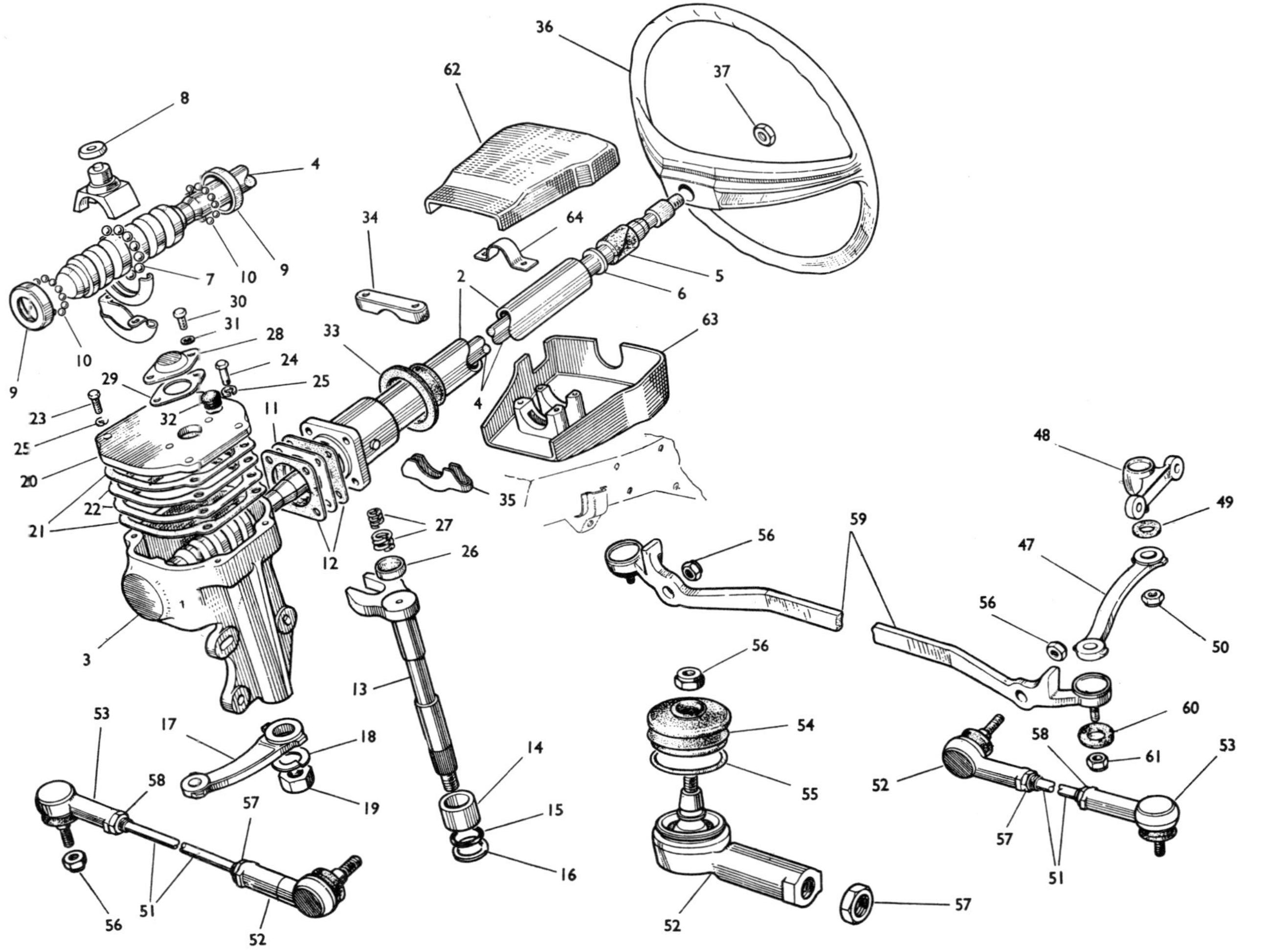

Fig. 11.9. STEERING BOX, COLUMN AND LINKAGE

2 Outer column tube
3 Steering box
4 Inner column shaft and worm gear
5 Felt bush
6 Retaining washer
7 Recirculating balls
8 Nut guide roller
9 Bearing race
10 Bearing balls

11 Shim
12 Gaskets
13 Rocker shaft
14 Bush
15 Seal
16 Seal retainer
17 Drop arm
18 Lock washer
19 Nut
20 Top cover

21 Gaskets
22 Shims
23 Screw
24 Dowel screw
25 Spring washer
26 Thrust button
27 Thrust springs
28 Retaining cap
29 Joint
30 Cap screw

31 Star washer
32 Filler plug
33 Grommet
34 Clamping bracket - upper half
35 Clamping bracket - lower half
36 Steering wheel
37 Nut
47 Idler (relay) arm

48 Idler pivot
49 Dust cover
50 Self-locking nut
51 Outer track rod
52 Ball joint R.H. thread
53 Ball joint L.H. thread
54 Rubber boot
55 Retainer ring
56 Self-locking nut
57 Rod lock nut R.H. thread

58 Rod locknut L.H. thread
59 Centre track rod
60 Dust cover
61 Self-locking nut
62 Cowl - upper half
63 Cowl - lower half
64 Cowl clamp

this involves specialist tools. If the unit is badly worn it is almost certain that the quickest and cheapest repair is going to be the fitting of another one. It is unusual for only one part to be worn and the cost of the component parts together would be little less than that for the assembly.

2. On right-hand drive cars it is necessary to lower the front cross-member to provide sufficient clearance to get the whole unit out from under the car. It is also necessary to have at least two feet ground clearance in order to get the column out.

3. First disconnect the battery and then remove the upper and lower halves of the cowl around the upper end of the steering column by taking out the screws from underneath. Then detach the direction indicator switch and overdrive switch if fitted.

4. Next remove the steering wheel. This can be done by first prizing out the motif in the centre. Then mark the position of the wheel in relation to the shaft - which will simplify replacement if the same shaft is being put back. Undo the nut and the wheel can be pulled off.

5. Move the front seat right back and pull the carpet back from the scuttle. Then remove the screws and clips holding the parcel shelf in position and then undo the two clamps holding the column in position.

6. To lower the front crossmember means detaching the engine from its forward mounting so the weight will have to be supported by other means. In view of the fact that the car has to be raised much higher than usual at the front it is not really practicable or safe to think in terms of supporting the engine from underneath. It is better to support it from above by means of lifting tackle suspended from a beam or some suitably padded strut across the top of the engine compartment, from which a hook or sling may be attached to the slinging eye at the front of the engine.

7. With the car raised on stands and the weight of the engine supported, the engine mounting bolts should be removed. Then the two bolts on each side which hold the crossmember to the side frame should be taken out and the crossmember allowed to come down as far as it can.

8. Detach the end of the centre track rod from the drop arm.

9. The three bolts holding the steering box to the side frame should now be slackened and, before removal, the position of any shims between the box and the wheel arch noted. The shims must be carefully guarded as they should go back as before even if a new box is fitted.

10 The steering box and column can now be manoeuvred out from under the car.

11 On left-hand drive models the removal of the crossmember is unnecessary. If the air cleaner and clutch slave cylinder are taken off, the whole column can be swung horizontal. The upper end should be protected against oil coming out. The box end can then be lifted upwards inside the engine compartment and the whole assembly drawn out from above.

12 Replacement is a reversal of the removal procedure with the following points borne in mind. Assemble all the mounting bolts and column clamping brackets loosely before tightening anything. The shims between the box and wing panel should be in position and the rubber grommet round the column where it passes through the scuttle. The alignment of the column with the upper and lower clamps is important as when everything is tight there should be no twist or stresses built up. This is why it may be necessary to increase or reduce the shims at the steering box mounting. Do not forget to fill the box with oil on completion and it is advisable to check the front wheel alignment also.

13. Front Wheel Bearings - Adjustment

1. Jack up the front wheels, together or in turn, and remove the hub caps. Then check the bearings as described in Section 10, to verify that they do in fact need adjusting. Then prise off the bearing dust cap. This can usually be dislodged by a few sideways taps with a hammer.

2. When the bearing nut is exposed withdraw the split pin and the castellated lock cap that goes over the nut.

3. If it is possible to use a torque wrench tighten the bearing nut, spinning the wheel all the while, to a torque of 15-20 lb/ft. Then back off one flat and refit the lock cap and fit a new split pin. If no torque wrench is available tighten the nut with a tubular spanner as much as you can without using a tommy bar and then continue as described.

4. If, during the adjustment and afterwards, the bearing feels rough or the wheel tends to bind in any position it is possible that one or both of the hub bearing races is worn out in which case they should be renewed.

5. Replace the dust cover which should not be filled with grease.

14. Front Hubs and Bearings - Removal and Replacement

1. When the 15,000 mile service calls for repacking the hubs with grease the hubs must be taken off the spindles. To renew the bearings is a procedure following on from this.

2. Jack up the car, support it on stands and remove the front wheels.

3. Detach the brake callipers from the discs as detailed in Chapter 9.

4. Remove the bearing dust covers and then take out the split pin and remove the castellated lock cap followed by the nut and washer.

5. The hub and disc assembly may now be drawn off and the roller bearing may be taken out from each side of the hub.

6. If flushing and repacking is all that is being done, the inside of the hub should now be thoroughly cleaned out with paraffin to remove all old grease. The roller bearings should be cleaned similarly. Dry them off thoroughly and then work new grease into the roller bearings. The hub should be packed with grease only as much as is indicated in the cross-section drawing. Clean off the spindle and make sure the grease seal is in good condition. Remove the seal and distance piece if the bearings are being renewed.

7. If the bearings are being renewed the inner races of each one will have to be driven out of the hub. This can be done with a suitable drift through the bore of the hub. Be careful to drive the races out straight and square and do not damage the bore of the hub where they fit. Then fit the inner races of the new bearings into the hub, making sure that the larger internal diameter of each race faces outwards.

8. Next pack the rollers and hub with grease as previously described and place the rollers of the inner bearing in position.

9. The bearing seal should next be pressed into the hub with the lip towards the bearing. Then the special distance piece should be pushed into the centre of the seal with the bevelled side facing outwards.

10 The hub can then be replaced on the axle spindle and the rollers of the outer bearing fitted, followed by the washer and nut.

11 Adjust the bearings as described in the previous Section and replace the dust cap.

12 Refit the brake calliper and road wheel.

15. Steering Alignment

1. To obtain true and accurate steering the correct alignment of the front wheels is essential. Misalignment can be positively dangerous and, incidentally, wears the tyres out at a great rate.

2. Before assuming that your steering is misaligned and therefore in need of adjustment (only) the following factors must first of all be checked:-

a) Tyre pressures.
b) Wheels - trueness and balance.
c) Wheel bearings - adjustment or wear.
d) Steering linkage - ball joints and swivels.
e) Steering box - wear.

3. If all the foregoing are in order then the wheel alignment may be checked knowing that any fault is beyond the scope of visual inspection without special equipment.

4. Steering alignment comprises more than just setting the toe-in of

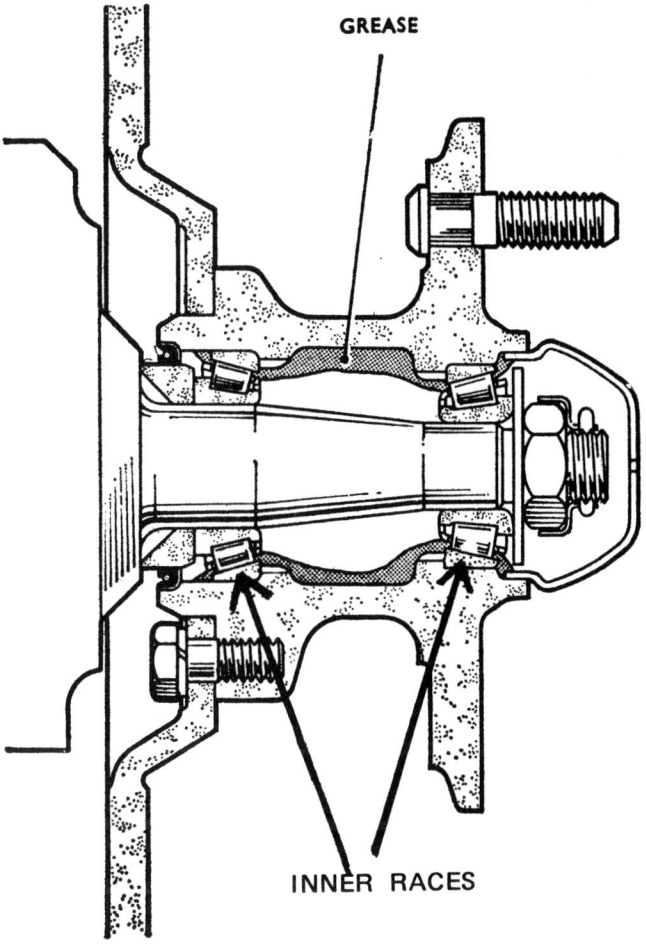

GREASE

INNER RACES

Fig. 11.10. FRONT WHEEL HUB ASSEMBLY SHOWING GREASE PACKING AND INNER BEARING RACES

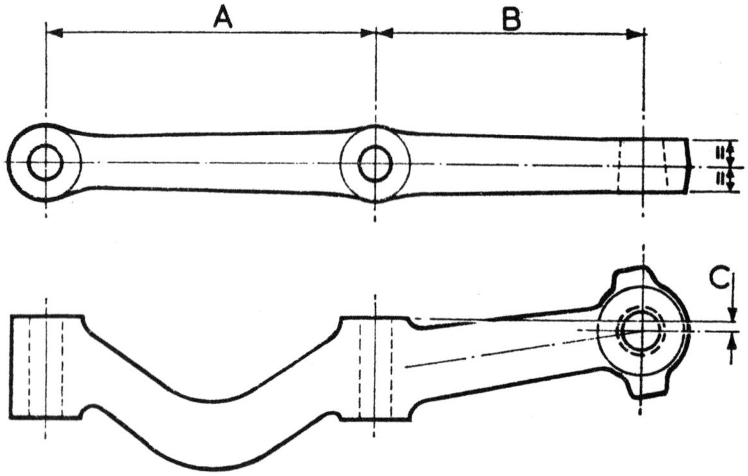

STEERING ARM
A   3.8 in. (96.52 mm)
B   3.02 in. (76.71 mm)
C   .14 in. (3.56 mm)

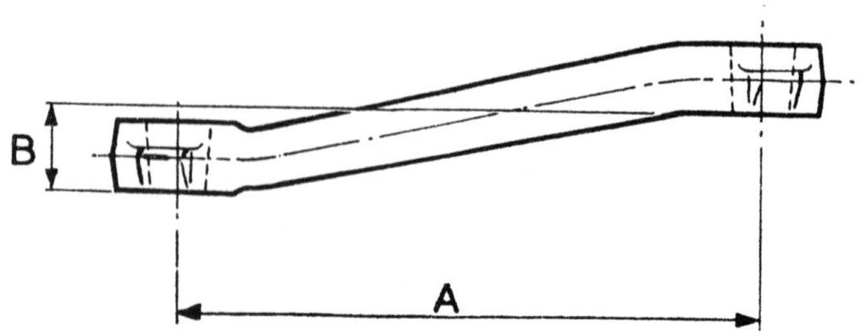

IDLER ARM
A   5.0 in. (127 mm) hole centre lines parallel
B   .7 in. (17.78 mm)

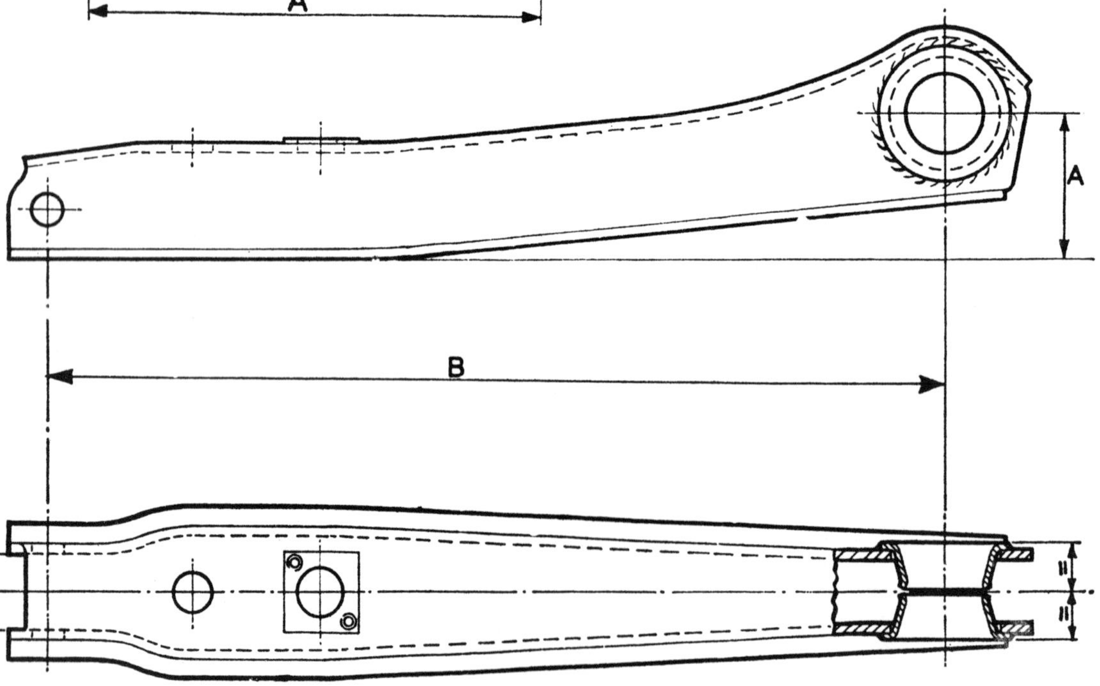

TRACK CONTROL (LOWER SUSPENSION ARM)
A   1.88 in. (47.75 mm)
B   12.1 in. (307.34 mm)

Fig. 11.11. DIMENSION DETAILS OF COMPONENTS ON WHICH STEERING ALIGNMENT DEPENDS (PAGE 1)

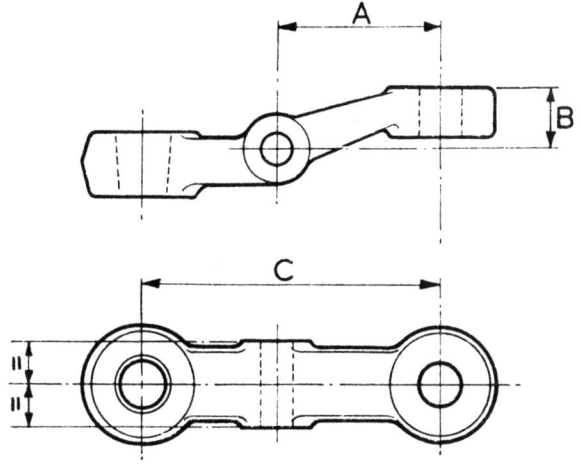

TRACK CONTROL ARM BALL JOINT CARRIER
A 1.96 in. (49.78 mm)
B   .72 in. (18.29 mm)
C 3.58 in. (90.93 mm)

STUB AXLE
A Faces parallel at right angles to spindle centre line
B 2.45 in. (62.23 mm)
C Concentric bearing surfaces

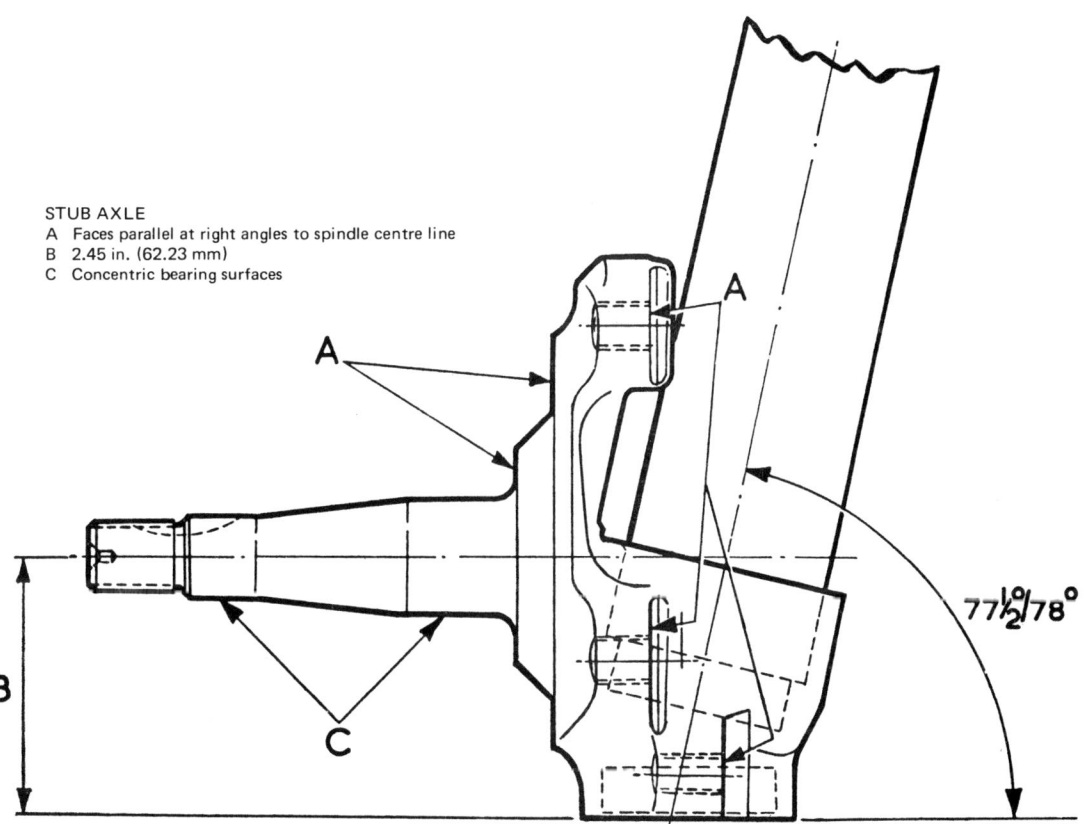

$77\tfrac{1}{2}/78^{\circ}$

Fig. 11.11. DIMENSION DETAILS OF COMPONENTS ON WHICH STEERING ALIGNMENT DEPENDS (PAGE 2)

the wheels. Camber angle, castor angle, steering axis inclination and wheel angle on turns are also part of the alignment checking process. Of this total of five alignment features only one can be adjusted - namely, toe-in. Toe-in is adjusted by the outer track rods. All other angles are controlled by the angles and dimensions of the component parts of the steering and the bushes and ball joints which link them together.

5. It is not possible to check the steering alignment without proper gauge equipment. It is imperative that any checking is done on the correct equipment and you would be well advised to go to a Chrysler/Rootes agent for this service. This is because in addition to the alignment measuring gear, the suspension at front and rear has

to be pre-set to a fixed datum before checking begins. (This is done by loading the body and fitting special dimension blocks at certain points - details are not given here). The steering geometry alters under different loads and attitudes and the specifications are at datum position. If the agents should advise that after setting the toe-in correctly some other aspect of the steering geometry is incorrect then it means that one or more components have been distorted out of shape (provided of course that all the joints and bushes are in order). In such circumstances the components which affect the alignment will have to be removed and their dimensions individually checked. Details of the components and their dimensions are given in Fig. 11.11

Fault Finding Chart - Suspension - Dampers - Steering

Before beginning to diagnose faults from the list below first make quite sure that any irregularities are not caused by:-

1. Incorrect tyre pressures.
2. Incorrect mix of radial and cross-ply tyres.
3. Misalignment of bodyframe or rear axle.
4. Binding brakes.

Symptom	Reason	Remedy
Steering wheel can be rotated more than an inch or so before road wheels move.	Wear in the linkage or steering box. Steering box mounting bolts loose.	Inspect linkage and renew parts as necessary.
Car difficult to keep in a consistent straight line - steering 'wanders'.	As above. Front wheel hub bearings loose or worn. Worn track control arm ball joint. Steering alignment incorrect (tyre wear will indicate this).	As above. Adjust or renew. Inspect and renew if necessary. Check.
Steering stiff and heavy.	Excessive wear or seizure in the steering linkage joints and control arm ball joint. Steering alignment incorrect.	Check all steering linkage and the steering box and renew as necessary. Check.
Wheel wobble and vibration.	Wheels out of balance. Wheels buckled. General wear. Broken spring(s).	Get professional balancing done. Renew wheel. Inspect and overhaul steering. Renew.
Excessive pitching and rolling - particularly on corners and when braking.	Defective dampers or springs.	Inspect and renew as required.

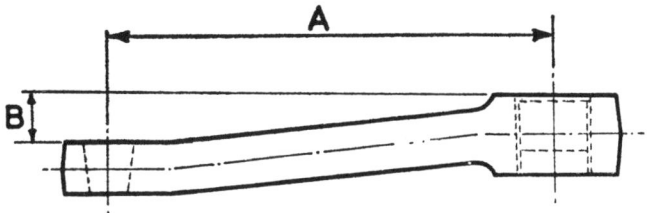

DROP ARM
A 5.0 in. (127 mm) hole centre - lines parallel
B   .5 in. (12.7 mm)

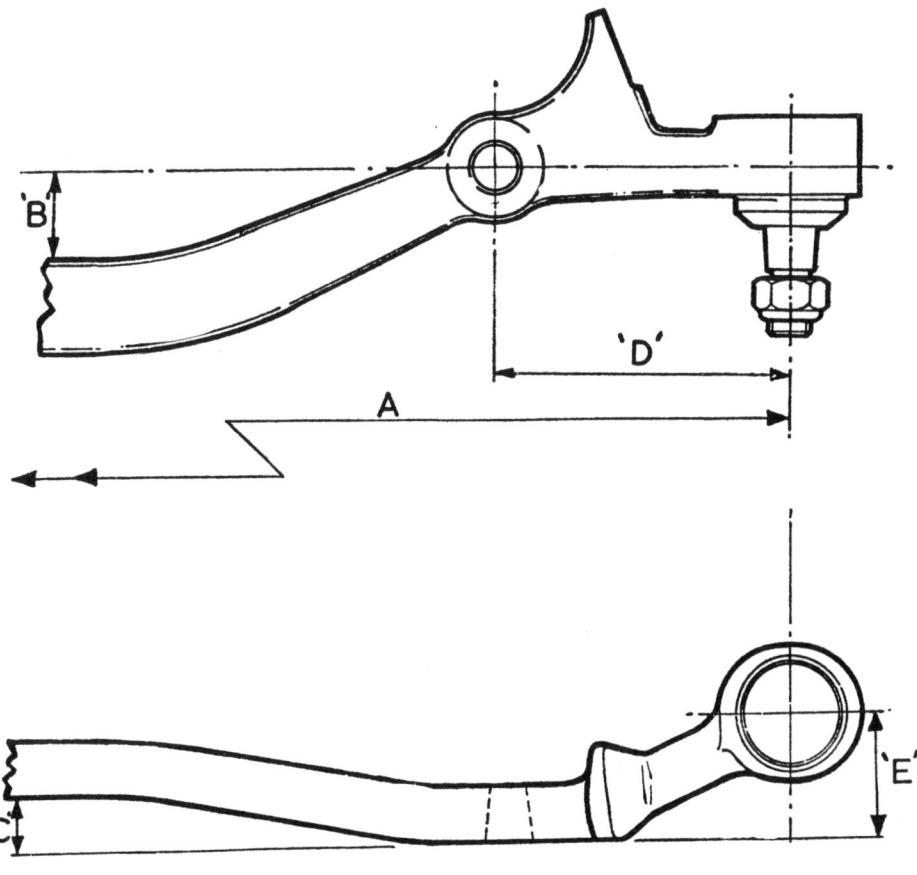

CENTRE TRACK ROD
A 23.75 in. (603.25 mm) between ball pin centres
B   .94 in. (23.88 mm)
C   .54 in. (13.72 mm)
D 3.21 in. (81.53 mm)
E 1.28 in. (32.51 mm)

Fig. 11.11. DIMENSION DETAILS OF COMPONENTS ON WHICH STEERING ALIGMENT DEPENDS (PAGE 3)

Chapter 12 Bodywork and underframe

Contents

1. General Description

The combined body shell and underframe is an all welded unitary structure of sheet steel pressings. Openings in the shell provide for the engine compartment, luggage boot, doors and windows. The rear suspension is bolted directly to the side frame members of the unit at each end of the leaf springs. A detachable crossmember is bolted to the side members at the bottom of the engine compartment and this braces the structure, supports the forward end of the engine/gearbox unit and provides the lower attachment points for the front suspension struts. A shorter tranverse member is bolted across the transmission tunnel section just to the rear of the engine compartment and this is the third support point for the engine/gearbox unit, the gearbox rear extension being flexibly mounted on it. All models have four doors and there are estate versions of the Vogue, Minx and Hunter having an additional rear door hinged at the top.

The wing aprons are reinforced where the upper bearing thrust units of the suspension strut assemblies are bolted to the bodywork.

2. Maintenance - Body Exterior

1. The general condition of a car's bodywork is the one thing that significantly affects its value. Maintenance is easy but needs to be regular and particular. Neglect - particularly after minor damage - can quickly lead to further deterioration and costly repair bills. It is important also to keep watch on those parts of the bodywork not immediately visible, for example the underside, inside all the wheel arches and the lower part of the engine compartment.
2. The basic maintenance routine for the bodywork is washing - preferably with a lot of water from a hose. This will remove all the loose solids which may have stuck to the car. It is important to flush these off in such a way as to prevent grit from scratching the finish. The wheel arches and underbody need washing in the same way, to remove any accumulated mud which will retain moisture and tend to encourage rust. Paradoxically enough, the best time to clean the underbody and wheel arches is in wet weather when the mud is thoroughly wet and soft. In very wet weather the underbody is usually cleaned of large accumulations automatically and this is a good time for inspection.
3. Periodically, it is a good idea to have the whole of the underside of the car steam cleaned, engine compartment included, so that a thorough inspection can be carried out to see what minor repairs and renovations are necessary. Steam cleaning is available at many garages and is necessary for removal of accumulation of oily grime which sometimes collects thickly in areas near the engine, gearbox and back axle. If steam facilities are not available there are one or two excellent grease solvents available which can be brush applied. The dirt can then be simply hosed off. Any signs of rust on the underside panels and bracing members must be attended to immediately. Thorough wire brushing followed by treatment with an anti-rust compound, primer and underbody sealer will prevent continued deterioration. If not dealt with the car could eventually become structurally unsound and therefore unsafe.
4. After washing the paintwork wipe it off with a chamois leather to give a clear unspotted finish. A coat of clear wax polish will give added protection against chemical pollutants in the air and will survive several subsequent washings. If the paintwork sheen has dulled or oxidised use a cleaner/polisher combination to restore the brilliance of the shine. This requires a little more effort but is usually because regular washing has been neglected! Always check that door and ventilator drain holes and pipes are completely clear so that water can drain out. Brightwork should be treated the same way as paintwork. Windscreens and windows can be kept clear of the smeary film which often appears if a little ammonia is added to the water. If glasswork is scratched a good rub with a proprietary metal polish will often clean them. Never use any form of wax or other paint/chromium polish on glass.

3. Maintenance - Body Interior

Mats and carpets should be brushed or vacuum cleaned regularly to keep them free of grit. If they are badly stained, remove them from the car for scrubbing or sponging and make quite sure that they are dry before replacement. Seat and interior trim panels can be kept clean with a wipe over with a damp cloth. If they do become stained (which can be more apparent on light coloured upholstery) use a little liquid detergent and a soft nailbrush to scour the grime out of the grain of the material. Do not forget to keep the headlining clean in the same way as the upholstery. When using liquid cleaners inside the car do not over-wet the surfaces being cleaned. Excessive damp could get into the upholstery seams and padded interior, causing stains, offensive odours or even rot. If the inside of the car gets wet accidentally it is worthwhile taking some trouble to dry it out

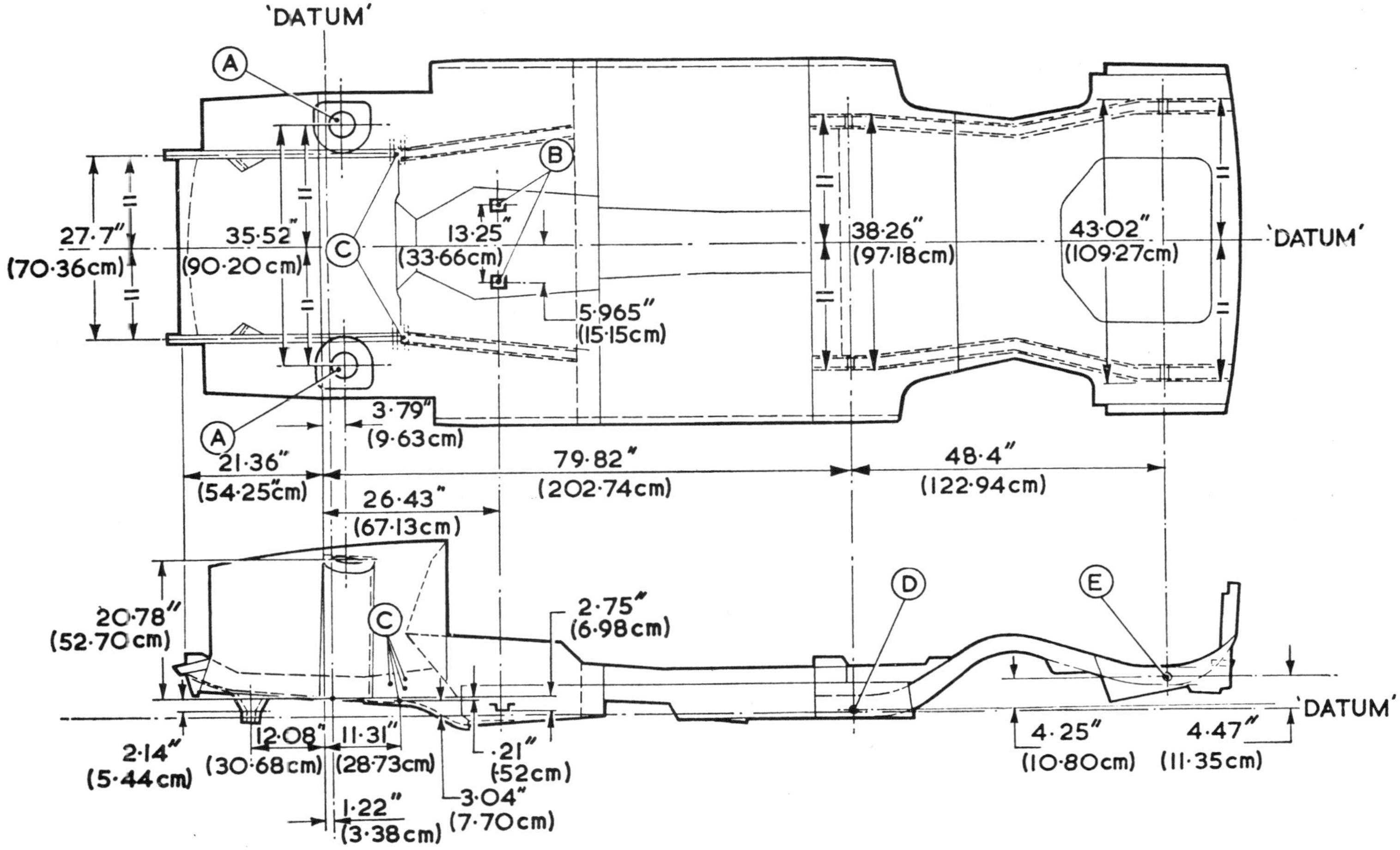
'DATUM'
A
B
C
27·7"
(70·36cm)
35·52"
(90·20 cm)
13·25"
(33·66cm)
5·965"
(15·15cm)
38·26"
(97·18cm)
43·02"
(109·27cm)
'DATUM'
3·79"
(9·63cm)
A
21·36"
(54·25cm)
79·82"
(202·74cm)
48·4"
(122·94cm)
26·43"
(67·13cm)
20·78"
(52·70cm)
C
2·75"
(6·98cm)
D
E
2·14"
(5·44cm)
12·08"
(30·68cm)
11·31"
(28·73cm)
·21"
(·52cm)
3·04"
(7·70cm)
1·22"
(3·38cm)
'DATUM'
4·25"
(10·80cm)
4·47"
(11·35cm)

Fig. 12.1. DIAGRAM OF UNDERFRAME DIMENSIONS

A Frcnt suspension upper mounting
B Engine rear mounting
C Steering gear mounting
D Rear spring front eye bolt
E Rear spring shackle pin

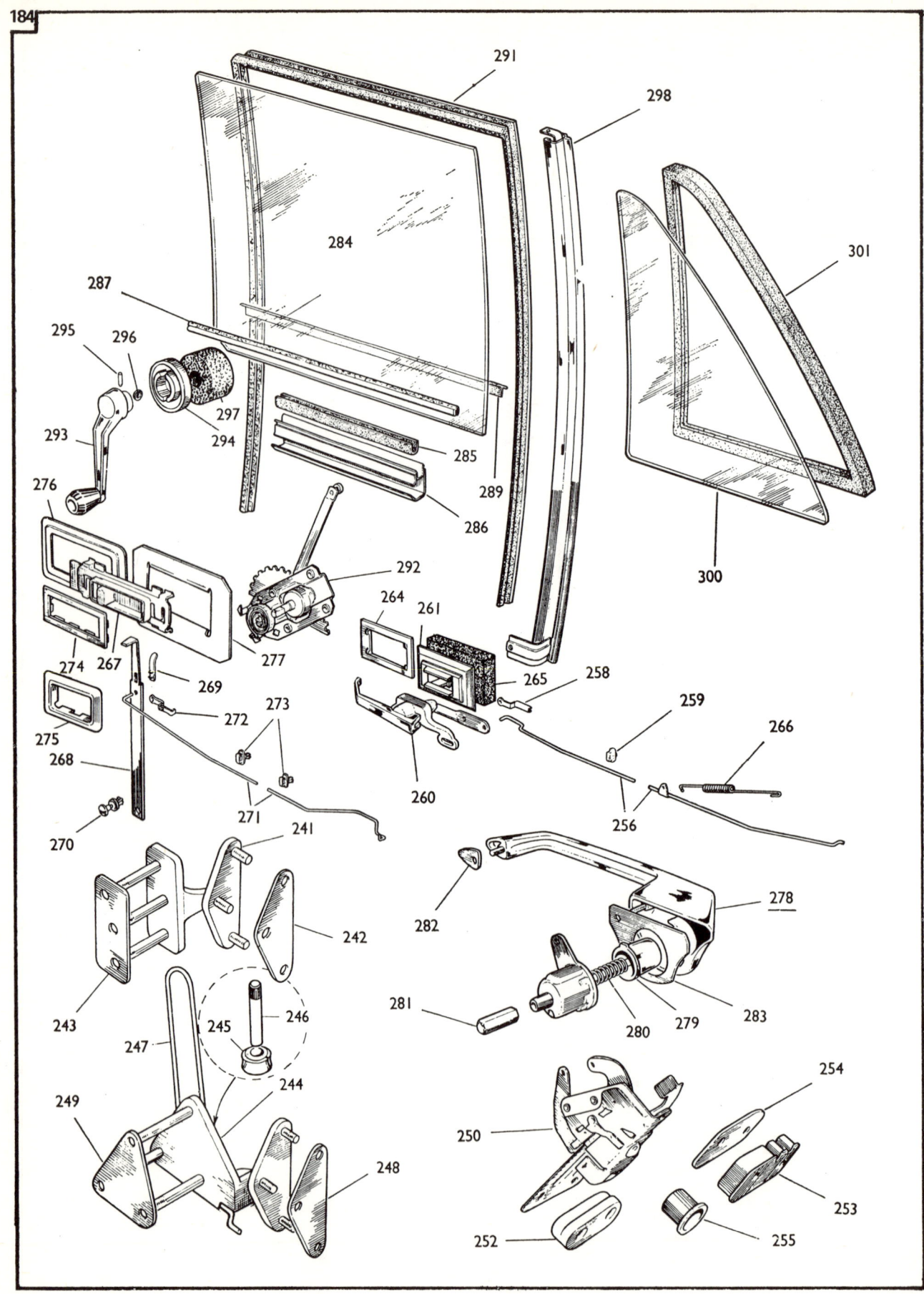

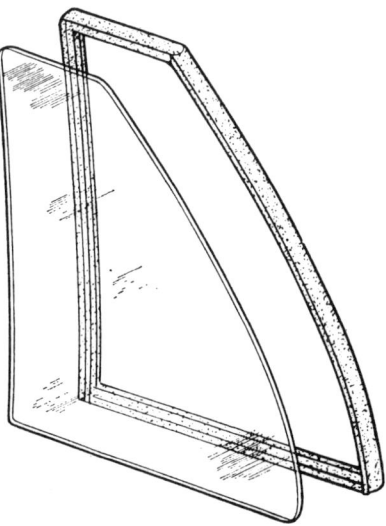

Fig. 12.2a. ESTATE REAR LIGHT

Fig. 12.2. (opposite page) REAR DOOR FITTINGS

241 Upper hinge	256 Remote control rod	273 Anti-rattle clip	287 Inner sill seal
242 Spreader plate to door	258 Clip	274 Escutcheon	289 Outer sill seal
243 Spreader plate to body	259 Anti-rattle clip	275 Escutcheon	291 Glass rim channel
244 Lower hinge & check link	260 Inside door handle	276 Retainer	292 Regulator
245 Check link roller	261 Escutcheon	277 Retainer	293 Handle
246 Retainer pin	264 Retainer	278 Outside handle	294 Escutcheon
247 Torsion hinge	265 Seal	279 Push button screw	295 Cross pin
248 Spreader plate to door	266 Return spring	280 Spring	296 Rubber pad
249 Spreader plate to body	267 Locking bolt	281 Contact nut	297 Foam pad
250 Door lock assembly	268 Locking bolt lever	282 Seating washer front	298 Division channel
252 Dovetail	269 Lever pad	283 Seating washer rear	300 Fixed glass (saloon)
253 Striker plate	270 Pivot	284 Main glass	301 Weather strip
254 Anti-burst plate	271 Locking link	285 Glazing rubber	302 Weather strip
255 Dovetail striker	272 Clip - link to lever	286 Lifting channel	303 Fixed glass (estate)

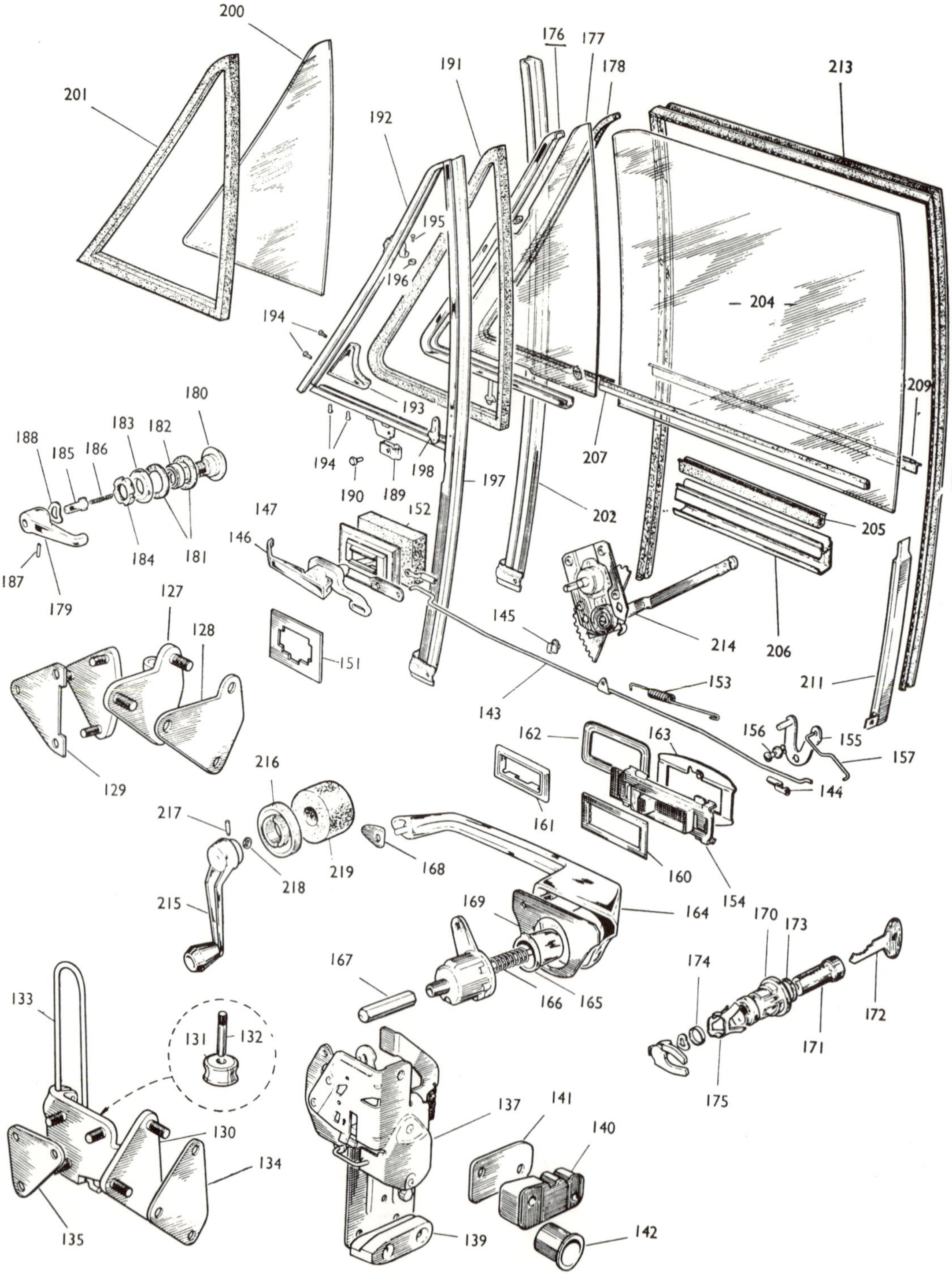
200
201
176
177
178
191
213
192
195
196
204
194
209
180
183
182
188
185
186
193
194
190
189
198
197
207
147
152
202
205
146
184
181
187
179
127
128
145
214
206
151
153
211
143
129
162
163
156
155
157
144
161
216
217
219
218
168
160
154
215
169
164
170
173
167
174
133
131
132
166
165
172
171
175
137
141
140
130
134
135
139
142

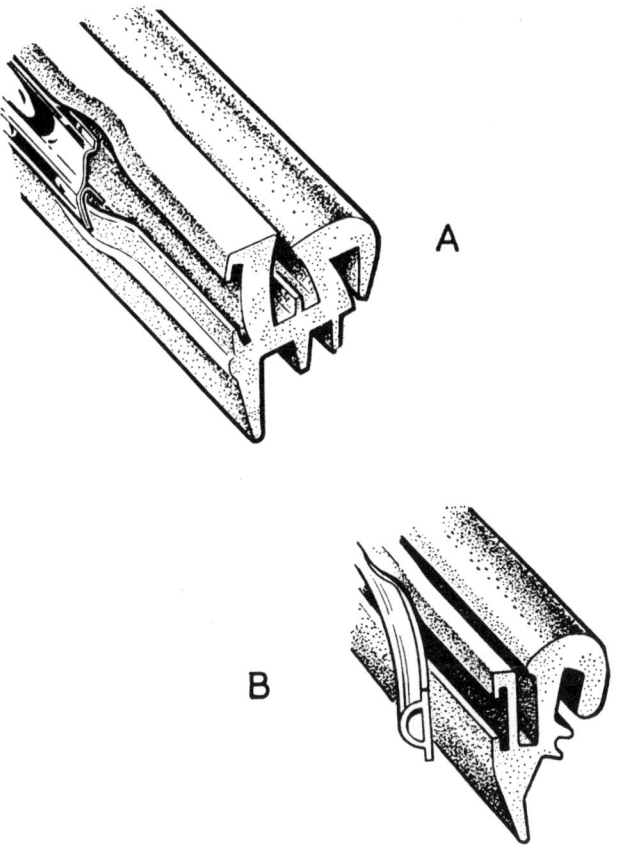

A

B

Fig. 12.4. (left) Cross section of windscreen/window sealing strips
with metal mouldings 'A' and plastic 'B'

Fig. 12.3. (opposite page) FRONT DOOR FITTINGS

127 Upper hinge	153 Handle return spring	176 Frame	196 Spacer
128 Spreader plate to door	154 Locking bolt	177 Quarter light	197 Division channel
129 Spreader plate to body	155 Lever locking bolt	178 Glazing rubber	198 Catch plate
130 Lower hinge	156 Pivot	179 Locking handle - quarterlight	200 Fixed glass
131 Check link roller	157 Locking link	180 Boss and peg	201 Weatherstrip
132 Retainer pin	160 Escutcheon	181 Sealing washer	202 Division channel
133 Torsion spring	161 Escutcheon	182 Cone washer	204 Main glass
134 Spreader plate to door	162 Retainer	183 Special washer	205 Glazing rubber
135 Spreader plate to body	163 Retainer	184 Locking ring	206 Lifting channel
137 Lock assembly	164 Outside handle	185 Push button	207 Inner sill seal
139 Dovetail	165 Push button screw	186 Spring	209 Outer sill seal
140 Striker plate	166 Spring	187 Spring pin	211 Support channel
141 Anti-burst plate	167 Contact nut	188 Wave washer	213 Glass rim channel
142 Dovetail striker	168 Seating washer	189 Clip	214 Regulator
143 Remote control rod	169 Seating washer	190 Screw	215 Handle
144 Clip - rod to lock	170 Lock	191 Weatherstrip	216 Escutcheon
145 Anti-rattle clip	171 Lock cylinder	192 Frame & vertical divider strip	217 Cross pin
146 Inside handle	172 Key	193 Corner block	218 Rubber pad
147 Escutcheon	173 Seating washer	194 Screw	219 Pram pad
151 Escutcheon retainer	174 Pin retainer	195 Pivot pin	
152 Seal	175 4-prong retainer		

properly, particularly where carpets are involved. Do NOT leave oil or electric heaters inside the car for this purpose. If, when removing carpets or mats for cleaning, there are signs of damp underneath, all the interior of the car floor should be uncovered and the point of water entry found. It may only be a missing grommet, but it could be a rusted through floor panel and this demands immediate attention as described in the previous section. More often than not both sides of the panel will require treatment.

4. Minor Repairs to Bodywork

1. A car which does not suffer some minor damage to the bodywork from time to time is the exception rather than the rule. Even presuming the gate post is never scraped or the door opened against a wall or high kerb there is always the likelihood of gravel and grit being thrown up and chipping the surface, particularly at the lower edges of the doors and sills.

2. If the damage is merely a paint scrape which has not reached the metal base, delay is not critical but where bare metal is exposed action must be taken immediately before rust sets in.

3. The average owner will normally keep the following 'first aid' materials available which can give a professional finish for minor jobs:-

a) An anti-rust primer.
b) Cellulose filler (or stopper) for minor scratch filling.
c) Resin filler paste for filling larger areas and depths.
d) Assorted grades of 'wet and dry' abrasive paper.
e) Cellulose primer.
f) Matched finish paint for brush or aerosol application.

4. Where the damage is superficial (i.e. not down to the bare metal and not dented) fill the scratch or chip with sufficient filler to smooth the area, rub down with paper and apply the matching paint.

5. Where the bodywork is scratched down to the metal, but not dented, clean the metal surface thoroughly and apply a suitable metal primer first - such as red lead or zinc chromate. Fill up the scratch as necessary with filler and rub down with wet and dry paper. Apply the matching colour paint.

6. If more than one coat of colour is required rub down each coat with cutting paste before applying the next.

7. If the bodywork is dented, first beat out the dent to conform as near as possible to the original contour. Avoid using steel faced hammers - use hard wood mallets or similar and always support the panel being beaten with a hardwood or metal 'dolly'. In areas where severe creasing and buckling has occurred it will be virtually impossible to reform the metal to the original shape. In such instances a decision should be made whether or not to cut out the damaged piece or attempt to re-contour over it with filler paste. In large areas where the metal panel is seriously damaged or rusted the repair is to be considered major and it is often better to replace a panel or sill section with the appropriate piece supplied as a spare. When using filler paste in largish quantities make sure that the directions are carefully followed. It is false economy to rush the job as the correct hardening time must be allowed between stages and before finishing. With thick applications the filler usually has to be applied in layers - allowing time for each layer to harden. Sometimes the original paint colour will have faded and it will be difficult to obtain an exact colour match. In such instances it is a good scheme to select a complete panel - such as a door or boot lid - and spray the whole panel. Differences will be less apparent where there are obvious divisions between the original and resprayed areas.

5. Major Repairs to Bodywork

Major repairs are required after accident damage or where rust has attacked and eaten away large areas of panelling. Where rust has attacked and weakened structural stress points - such as the front

suspension top mountings and rear spring attachment points - and after accident damage, metal work repairs are essential. Accident damage means that the whole structure must be checked for alignment. Damage to one part may affect the whole, due to the principle of construction. If the bodywork is left misaligned the car will be dangerous due to bad-handling properties - and uneven stresses will be placed on steering and transmission causing abnormal wear or total failure. Rust damaged stress points may be repairable - it depends on the extent and how much has to be cut away before reaching sound metal to which new pieces may be satisfactorily and safely welded. All such metalwork is beyond the scope of most owners and should be left to professionals. Where large patches of wings or door sills or other non stressed panels need patching, it is possible to use resin filler supported on a wire mesh frame. Here again the deciding factor is whether there is sufficient sound metal in the nearby area on which to hang the repair. In any event all the surrounding area must be thoroughly cleaned of rust and treated otherwise any repair will eventually be once more surrounded with rusted metal and liable to fall away. Much also depends on the age and overall condition of the car as to what sort of repair is economically suitable.

6. Hinges, Catches and Locks - Maintenance

The hinges and door latches should be wiped clean of grease and grime and a few drops of light oil applied occasionally. An oil with a graphite additive is particularly good. Do not over-oil as the excess merely runs out and collects more dirt. Wipe over after oiling. Other places which often stiffen up unnoticed and need a drop of oil are the bonnet and boot lid hinges and the bonnet release and safety catches.

7. Doors - Tracing and Silencing Rattles

Having established that a rattle does come from the door(s) check first that it is not loose on its hinges and that the latch is holding it firmly closed. The hinges can be checked by rocking the door up and down when open to detect any play. If the hinges are worn at the pin the whole hinge will need renewal. When the door is closed the panel should be flush with the pillar. If not then the hinges or latch striker plate need adjustment. The door hinges are held to the door and frame by three studs on each hinge plate. Access to the nuts is from behind the door and body and the trim should be removed first as described in the next section. The fitting of new hinges requires assistance if damage to the paintwork is to be avoided. To adjust the setting of the door catch first slacken the screws holding the striker plate to the door pillar just enough so that it can be moved but will hold its position. Then close the door, with the latch button pressed, and then release the latch. This is so that the striker plate position is not drastically disturbed on closing the door. Then set the door position by moving it without touching the catch, so that the panel is flush with the bodywork. This will set the striker plate in the proper place. Then carefully release the catch so as not to disturb the striker plate, open the door and tighten the screws. Rattles within the door will be due to loose fixtures or missing anti-rattle pads and for this the next section explains how to deal with window glass, regulators and so on.

8. Doors - Removal and Replacement of Glass, Quarter Lights, Regulators, Locks and Catches

1. Whatever work is to be done inside the door, the trim panel will have to come off, and this involves first removing the window winder handle. To do this press back the circular escutcheon behind the handle and push out the pin which will be disclosed. The handle may then be pulled off followed by the escutcheon ring. On front doors, slide a flat blade (scraper or putty knife) behind the bottom edge of

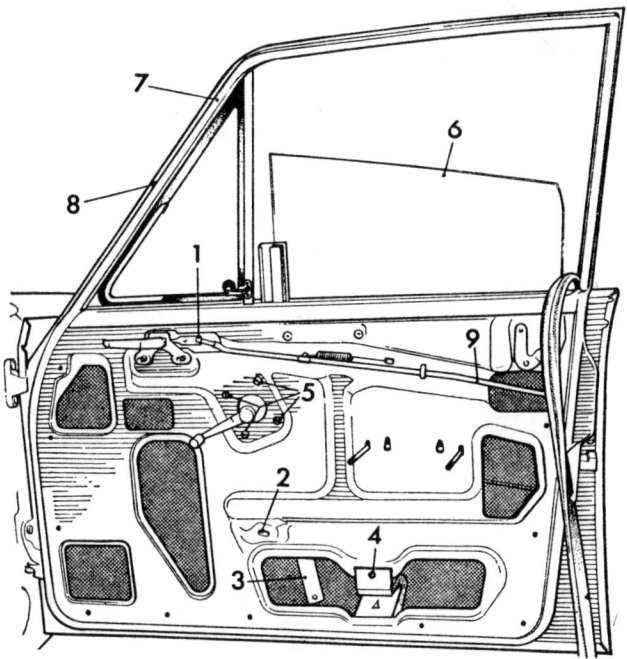

Fig. 12.5. VIEW OF FRONT DOOR SHOWING MAIN ITEMS AFFECTED WHEN
REMOVING WINDOWS AND LOCKS

1 Remote control link coupling
2 Locating screw, dividing
   channel
3 Regulator arm
4 Bottom stop bracket screw
5 Regulator fixing screw
6 Door glass
7 Pop rivet - frame support
8 Quarter light top hinge screw
9 Remote control link

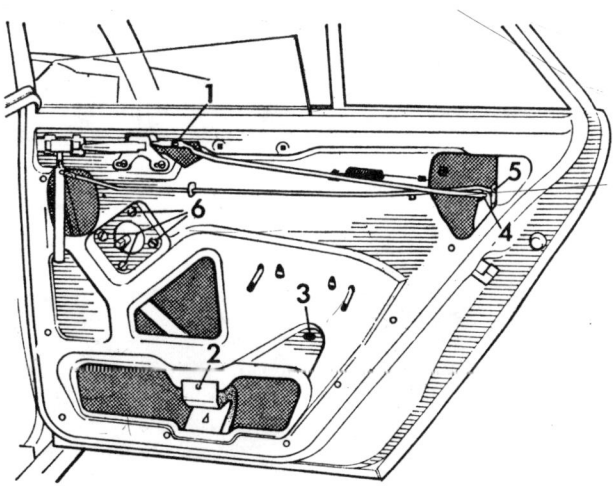

Fig. 12.6. VIEW OF REAR DOOR SHOWING MAIN
ITEMS AFFECTED WHEN REMOVING
WINDOWS AND LOCKS

1 Remote control link coupling
2 Locating screw bottom stop
   bracket
3 Locating screw dividing
   channel
4 Remote control link
5 Remote control lock coupling
6 Regulator fixing screws

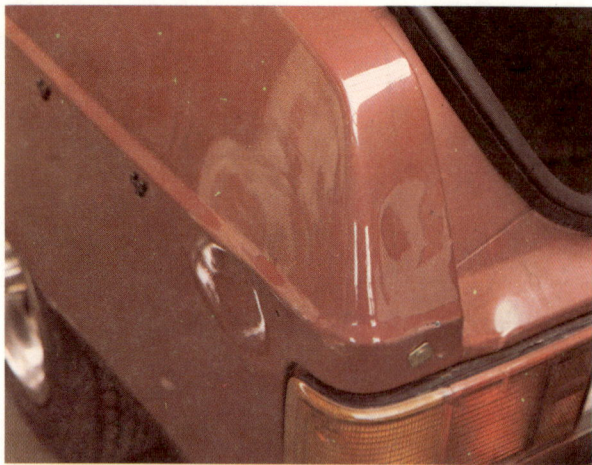

This sequence of photographs deals with the repair of the dent and scratch (above rear lamp) shown in this photo. The procedure will be similar for the repair of a hole. It should be noted that the procedures given here are simplified - more explicit instructions will be found in the text

In the case of a dent the first job - after removing surrounding trim - is to hammer out the dent where access is possible. This will minimise filling. Here, the large dent having been hammered out, the damaged area is being made slightly concave

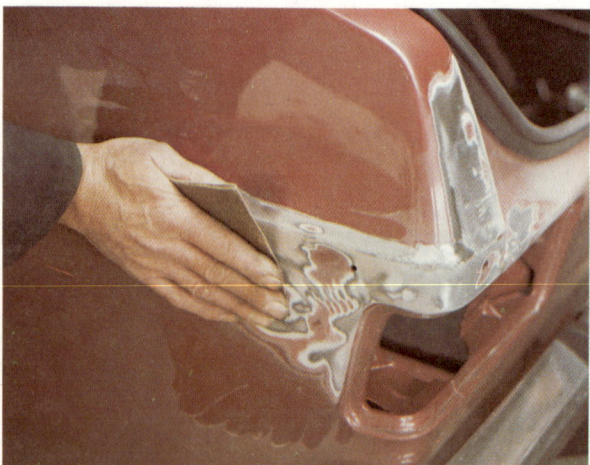

Now all paint must be removed from the damaged area, by rubbing with coarse abrasive paper. Alternatively, a wire brush or abrasive pad can be used in a power drill. Where the repair area meets good paintwork, the edge of the paintwork should be 'feathered', using a finer grade of abrasive paper

In the case of a hole caused by rusting, all damaged sheet-metal should be cut away before proceeding to this stage. Here, the damaged area is being treated with rust remover and inhibitor before being filled

Mix the body filler according to its manufacturer's instructions. In the case of corrosion damage, it will be necessary to block off any large holes before filling - this can be done with zinc gauze or aluminium tape. Make sure the area is absolutely clean before ...

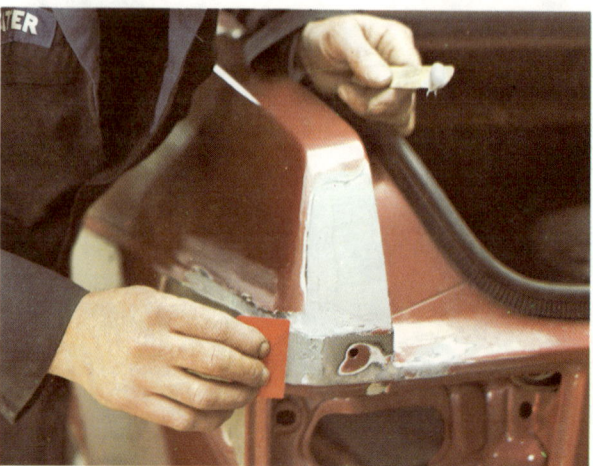

... applying the filler. Filler should be applied with a flexible applicator, as shown, for best results: the wooden spatula being used for confined areas. Apply thin layers of filler at 20-minute intervals, until the surface of the filler is slightly proud of the surrounding bodywork

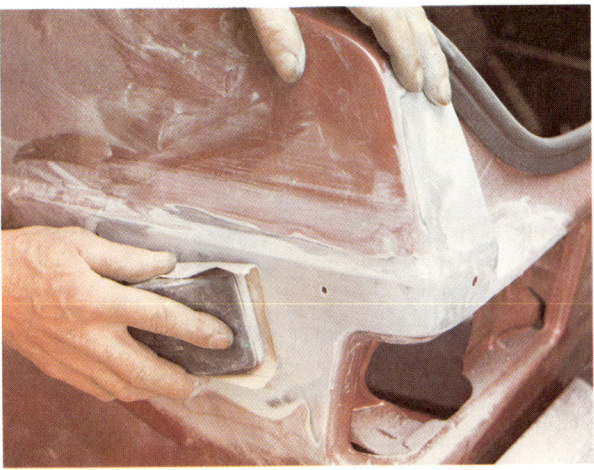

Initial shaping can be done with a Surform plane or Dreadnought file. Then, using progressively finer grades of wet-and-dry paper, wrapped around a sanding block, and copious amounts of clean water, rub-down the filler until really smooth and flat. Again, feather the edges of adjoining paintwork

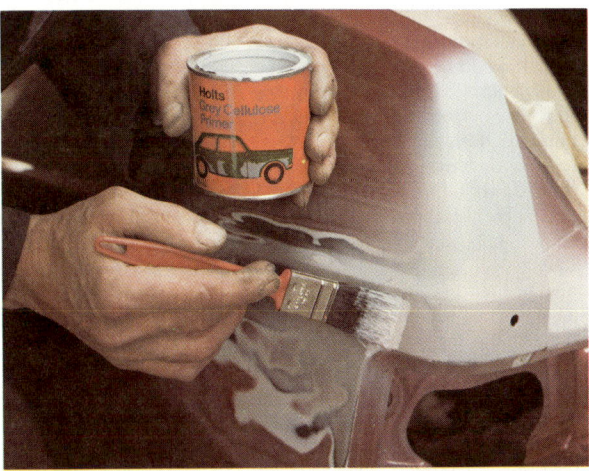

The whole repair area can now be sprayed or brush-painted with primer. If spraying, ensure adjoining areas are protected from over-spray. Note that at least one-inch of the surrounding sound paintwork should be coated with primer. Primer has a 'thick' consistency, so will fill small imperfections

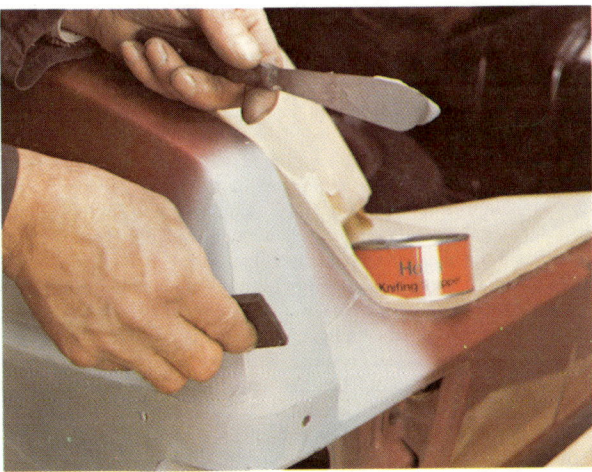

Again, using plenty of water, rub down the primer with a fine grade of wet-and-dry paper (400 grade is probably best) until it is really smooth and well blended into the surrounding paint-work. Any remaining imperfections can now be filled by carefully applied knifing stopper paste

When the stopper has hardened, rub-down the repair area again before applying the final coat of primer. Before rubbing-down this last coat of primer, ensure the repair area is blemish-free - use more stopper if necessary. To ensure that the surface of the primer is really smooth use some finishing compound

The top coat can now be applied. When working out of doors, pick a dry, warm and wind-free day. Ensure surrounding areas are protected from over-spray. Agitate the aerosol thoroughly, then spray the centre of the repair area, working outwards with a circular motion. Apply the paint as several thin coats.

After a period of about two-weeks, which the paint needs to harden fully, the surface of the repaired area can be 'cut' with a mild cutting compound prior to wax polishing. When carrying out bodywork repairs, remember that the quality of the finished job is proportional to the time and effort expended

the trim panel and run it along until it comes up against a clip. Then lever the clip out. Continue like this making sure that the leverage is applied close to the clips, otherwise you might pull them out of the trim panel. When the clips are clear, pull the panel down to free the top edge from the garnish rail. On rear doors the panel is held at the bottom by three self tapping screws so remove these and draw the panel down in the same way.

2. The garnish rail along the top of the door sill is held by retaining screws. Remove these, lift the rail free of the top edge of the door and ease it over the interior door handle. Watch that the locking slide does not fall from the handle.

3. If wished, the remote handle may now be detached by removing the link clip and taking out the handle securing bolts.

4. To remove the window winder mechanism, undo the bottom stop bracket screw and take out the stop bracket. Then replace the winder handle temporarily and lower the window to the bottom of the door. Then undo the screws holding the winder mechanism and slide the operating arm out of the channel at the bottom of the glass. Then lift the glass up to the door and prop it in position there. Lift out the winder mechanism from the bottom of the door.

5. To remove the door exterior handle undo the two nuts securing it inside the door outer panel.

6. To remove the lock mechanism disconnect the remote lever link (as already mentioned) and after undoing the screws take the lock out from inside the door.

7. Whichever window (quarter light or main window) needs to be removed from the front door the quarter light has to come out first and a pop rivet has to be drilled out which will need replacement. First lower the window after removing the bottom stop bracket and then remove the screw which holds the lower end of the vertical dividing strip between the quarter light and main window. Remove the operating arm from the channel at the bottom of the glass. Remove the rubber weatherstrip from the outside of the door sill and the felt strip from the inside edge. Then take the rubber channel from the window frame. At the top of the vertical dividing strip a pop rivet secures it to the door frame. Drill this out and then undo the screw which holds the top quarter light hinge to the door frame. The quarter light complete with strip may then be lifted out of the door. On back doors the quarter light is fixed and does not need to be removed before the main window. However, the vertical dividing strip which is held by a screw and pop rivet, as in the front door, has to be taken out in the same way.

8. To remove the main window of both front and rear doors turn it through 90º so that the bottom edge is towards the door centre and then lift it out.

9. If the rear quarter light glass is to be removed it may now be pulled out of the rubber channel strip. When replacing this one, seal the glass into the channel with a suitable proprietary sealing compound.

10 Replacement of all door components is a straightforward reversal of the removal sequence. When refixing the vertical dividing strip make sure the main window runs up and down easily before tightening the lower fixing screw.

9. Bonnet (Hood) - Removal and Replacement

1. When in position and closed the bonnet should fit centrally in the aperture and line up flush with the surrounding bodywork. The fore and aft and vertical positions at the hinge end can be adjusted by repositioning the vertical slotted bonnet bracket on the horizontally slotted hinge plate. The forward end is adjusted by the position of the catch post in the centre of the bonnet. By undoing the locknut where it is mounted on the bonnet it can be screwed in or out as necessary, altering the height at which it hooks under the release catch.

2. To remove the bonnet it should be propped open and cloth placed under the rear corners to protect the paintwork. Two people are needed to remove the bonnet easily as support is required while the hinge bolts are undone. However, it is possible for one person to

do it by supporting the rear corners on wooden blocks while undoing the hinge bolts. Great care is needed as the whole bonnet tries to pitch to one side off the front prop stay, so be warned! Before slackening the hinge bolts, mark the relative positions of the two brackets so that the need for adjustment is minimised on replacement.

10. Boot (Trunk) Lid - Removal and Replacement

The fitting of the lid into the aperture follows the same principles as for the bonnet and the hinge end is adjusted in the same way. The height of the closing end is adjusted by raising or lowering the catch post which is clamped to the inner edge of the compartment rear panel.

11. Windscreen and Rear Windows (Saloons and Estate Cars) - Removal and Replacement

1. Two people are needed when working on the windscreen, one inside and one outside the car. The screen or window is held solely by the rubber sealing strip but the lip of the seal is treated with sealing compound where it contacts the glass surfaces and the body aperture flange on the outside.

2. First remove the windscreen wiper arms, rear view interior mirror and the sun visors. Then, using a blunt edge, such as the handle end of an ordinary nail file, ease the outer lip of the sealing rubber away from the glass in order to break the sealing compound adhesion.

3. Using a similar blunt instrument next ease the inner lip of the rubber (inside the car) over the body flange at one of the top corners. Once this is started, firm hand pressure applied from inside will force the windscreen out. Make sure someone is ready outside to support the glass when it becomes free.

4. When the screen (or window) is out, remove the weatherstrip and clean away all traces of sealer. In cases of a broken windscreen make sure all broken pieces are removed (if the same strip is being re-used).

5. When fitting a new screen, first make sure that the edges of the new screen are ground bevelled and that no chips or cracks in the edge are apparent. They are potential starters for future cracks across the screen. This must be watched, particularly if you are getting a secondhand screen from a broken car. Next support the screen on a stand, suitably padded against scratching, front side upwards, so that the edges are not obstructed. Then fit the weatherstrip to the screen. Next, the outer face of the strip against the glass should be treated with sealer injected from a flat nozzle that may be inserted under the lip. Such nozzles are usually provided with a good proprietary sealer. Then fit the metal or plastic mouldings into the recess of the strip. This is best done by putting one edge of the moulding or beading under one edge in the beading and then using the same blunt article to ease the other edge in. Do NOT leave the moulding until after the screen is fitted - it will be very much more difficult to fit. With metal mouldings fit the two joining clips afterwards. With plastic beading the join should be in the bottom centre of the glass and the ends cut square to make a neat butt joint.

6. Next find a piece of strong cord which is long enough to fit into the weatherstrip body flange groove with two long ends left over. Do NOT use thin string as this could cut through the rubber. Put this into the groove - a piece of small bore tube through which the string can be fed often helps to get it in position easily. The loose ends should cross at the centre of the top edge. After the string is in position a further application of sealer should be made to the side of the channel which will bear against the outside face of the body flange.

7. The screen should next be placed centrally in the aperture with the ends of the cord hanging inside the car. The inner edge of the strip can then be pulled over the flange with the cord. If difficulty is experienced in keeping the weatherstrip in position on the glass after fitting the string use self adhesive tape over it onto the glass. This will tear away when the cord is finally pulled out.

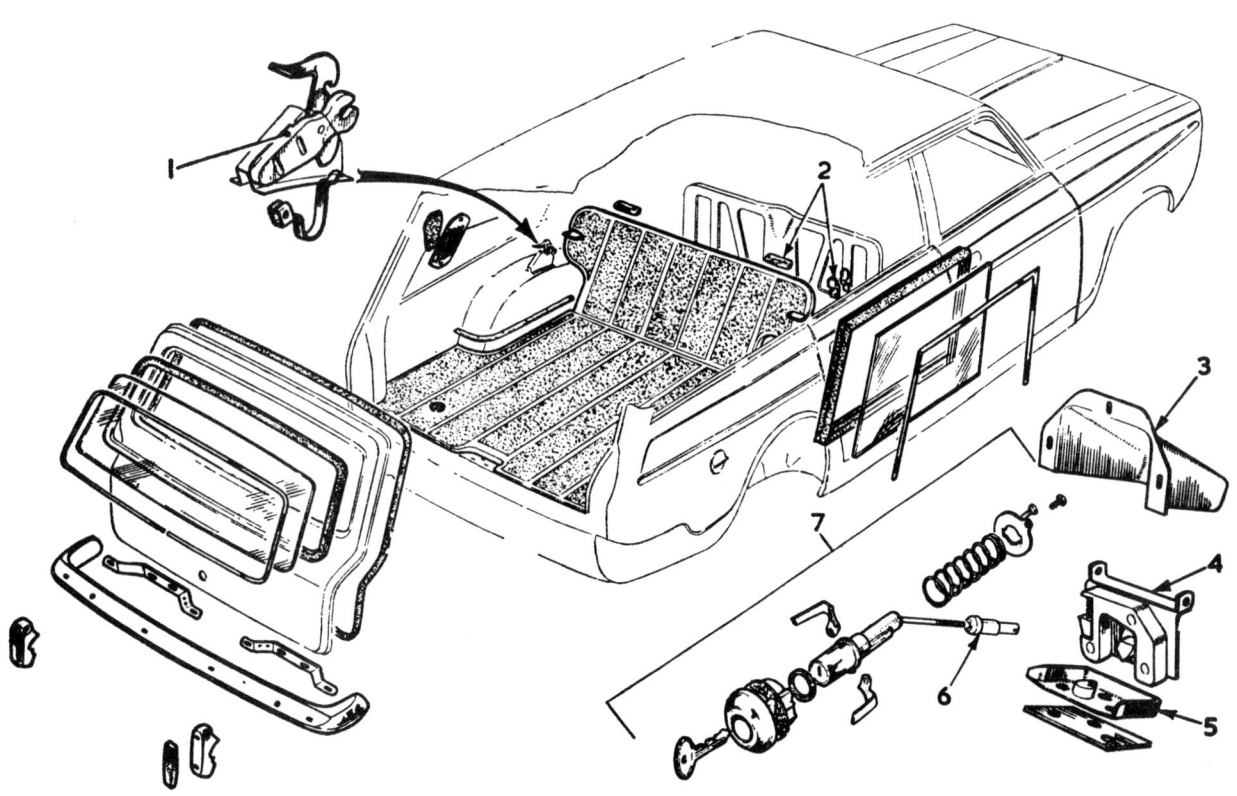

Fig. 12.7. MAIN COMPONENTS OF ESTATE
CAR VERSION

1 Rear seat squab catch   5 Striker plate
2 Rear seat squab support   6 Thimble
3 Lock cover   7 Button and cylinder assembly
4 Lock

SECTION 9. Removal of bonnet hinge bolts. Bonnet propped on wooden blocks.

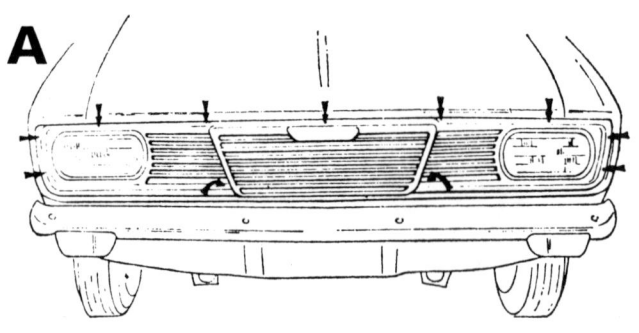

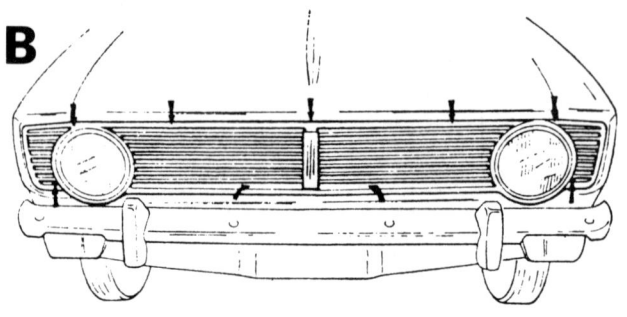

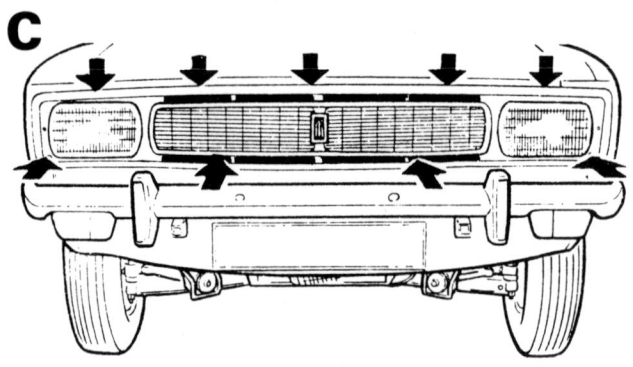

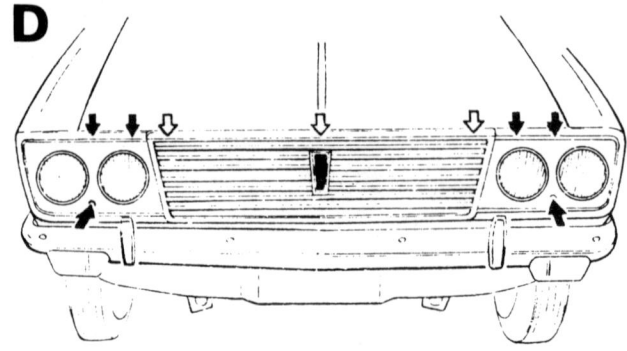

FIG. 12.8. RADIATOR GRILLE FIXING POINTS
A Vogue and Gazelle
B Minx and early Hunter
C Later type Hunter
D Sceptre

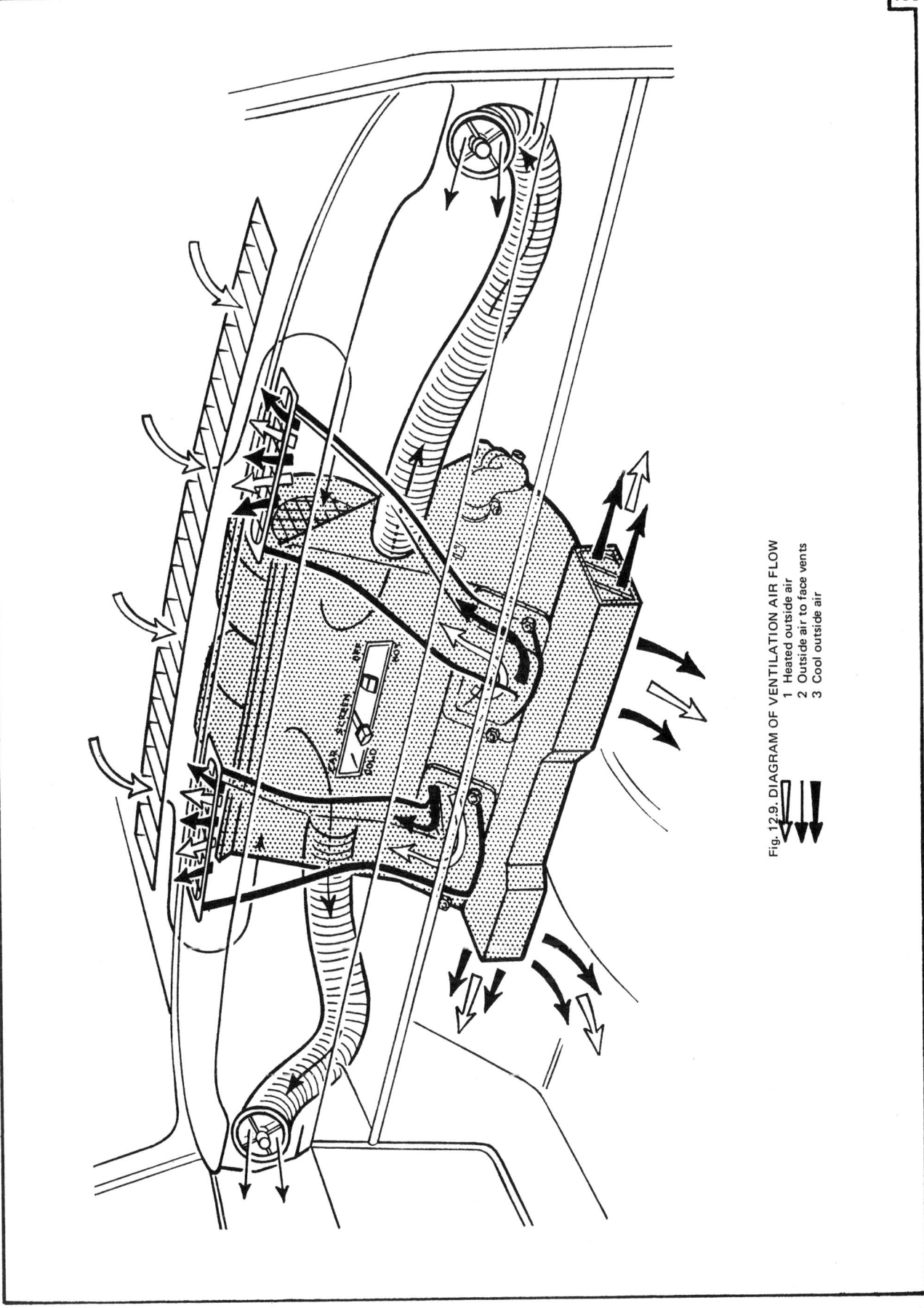

Fig. 12.9. DIAGRAM OF VENTILATION AIR FLOW

1 Heated outside air
2 Outside air to face vents
3 Cool outside air

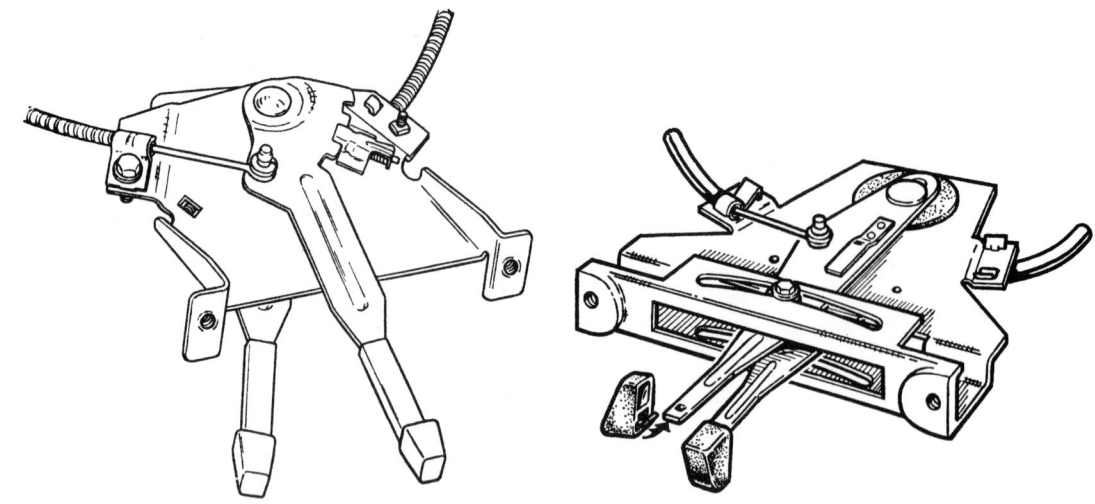

Fig. 12.10. HEATER CONTROL SHOWING TWO TYPES FITTED

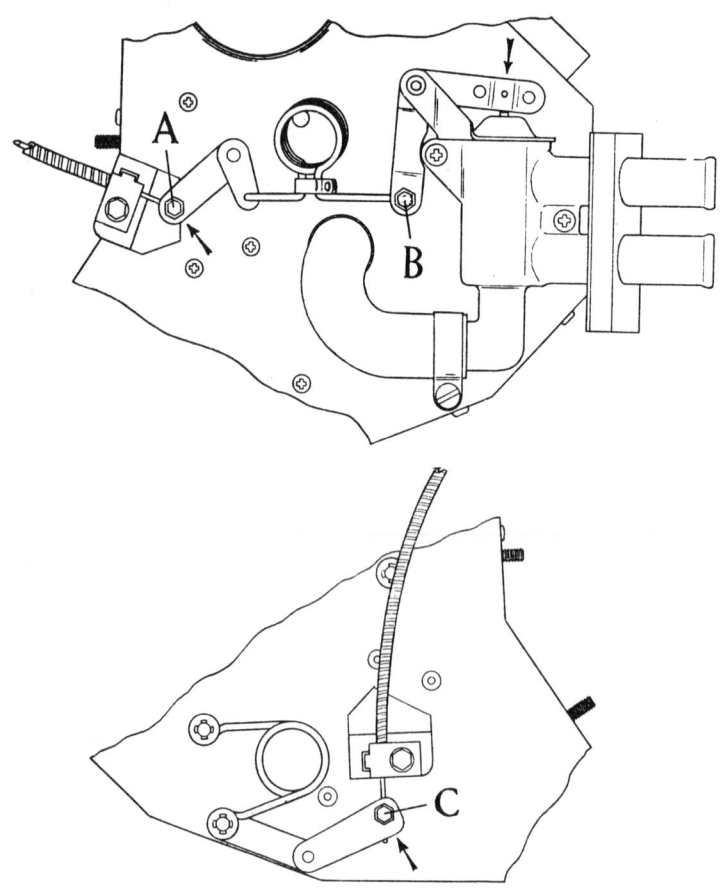

Fig. 12.11. HEATER CABLE ADJUSTMENT POINTS
A MIXING VALVE   B WATER VALVE   C DISTRIBUTOR VALVE

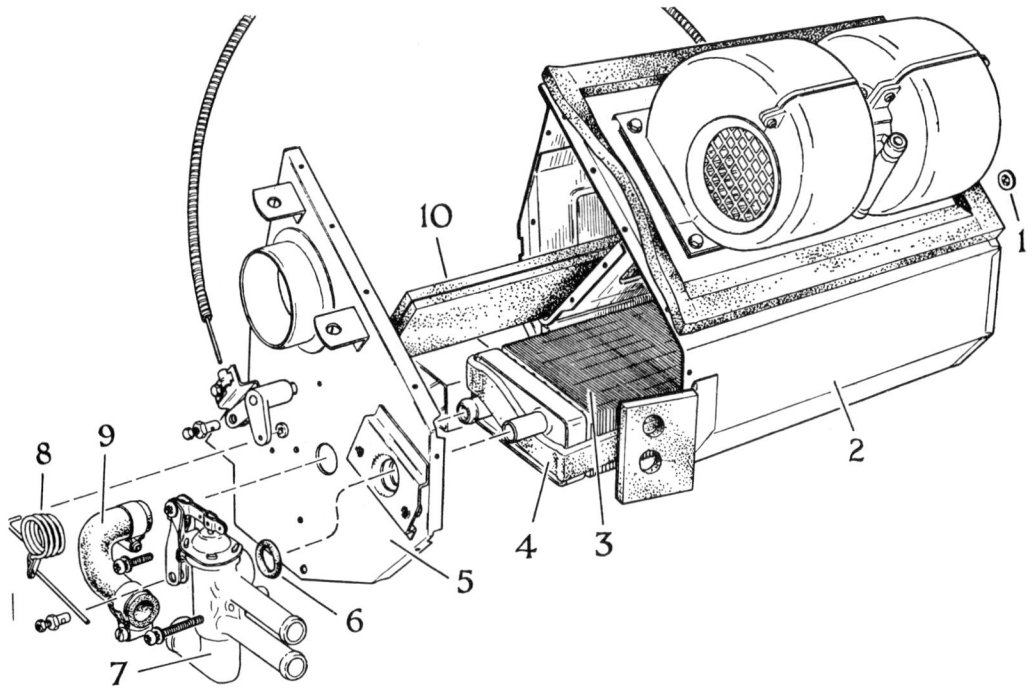

Fig. 12.12. HEATER AND BLOWER UNIT

1 Mixing valve shaft retainer clip	3 Heater matrix	6 'O' ring seal	9 Hose valve to matrix
	4 Seal	7 Water valve	10 Mixing valve flap
2 Heater casing	5 End cover	8 Valve operating link	

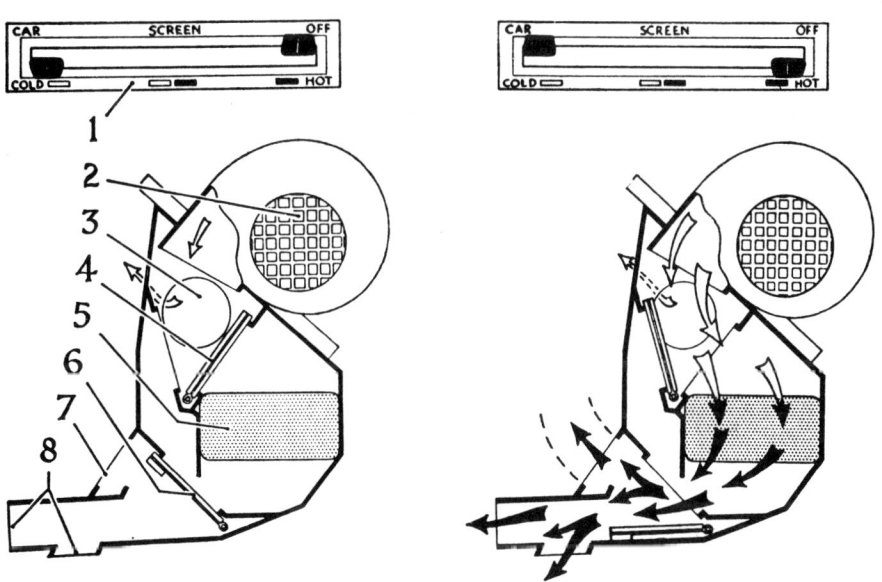

Fig. 12.13. Two cross section views (schematic) of the heater to show
position of flaps and air flow in the 'off' and 'cold' position
and the 'car' and 'hot' position

1 Control panel	3 Outlet to face ducts	5 Heater matrix	7 Screen air outlet
2 Blower	4 Air mixing valve flaps	6 Distributor valve flap	8 Car air outlets

12. Radiator Grilles - Removal and Replacement

All radiator grilles are held in place by self-tapping screws and the illustration shows where these are located. When removed the grille may be lifted off. Replacement is a reversal of this procedure but get all screws started before tightening any.

13. Heating and Ventilating System - Description and Adjustment

1. The system comprises a water heated matrix, linked into the engine radiator circuit but not controlled by the thermostat so that hot water reaches the heater as soon as it is available. Air enters the system through the grille over the scuttle and, depending on the control settings, is either partially or wholly heated and directed to screen, interior or both. The controls operate the mixing valve, distribution valve and water valve. The top lever of the two marked 'off, screen, car' controls the distribution flap. In the 'off' position no air passes to either the car or screen. In the 'screen' position all air is directed to the screen vents for demisting and in the 'car' position most air is directed into the car with some bled off towards the screen. The other lever, marked 'cold - hot' operates both the air 'mixing' flap and the water valve. They both operate simultaneously when the lever is moved away from cold. The water valve lets hot water into the heater matrix and the mixing flap lets a proportion of the inlet air past the heater. In the 'hot' position all air flows past the heater. The water valve is fully open before mixer flap completely cuts off the cold air inlet. The air flow is boosted when necessary by the twin rotor blow fan. A pair of independent fresh air inlet ducts, with outlets one at each end of the dashboard, is also installed. This is not affected by the controls and cannot be heated. The direction and flow of the air is controlled by the air valves at the ends of the ducts.

2. If the heater seems to be malfunctioning, make sure that a thermostat is installed in the cooling system and working properly (see Chapter 2).

3. In order to make sure the air valves are working they can be checked and adjusted at the heater ends of the cables. Release the cable at the lever trunnion ('A' in Fig12.11) and set the mixing flap control to 'cold'. The lever should then be set as far as it will go in a clockwise direction (as arrowed in Fig 12.11 and the cable clamped up. The water valve which is operated by the same cable should be set at the same time by undoing the trunnion clamp ('B' in Fig. 12.11)and pressing the top arm down (as arrowed). Then tighten the clamp once more.

4. The distributor valve cable is set in the same manner but the lever is moved as far as possible clockwise ('C' in Fig.12.11). Check the full range of operation after adjustment to ensure the flap valves are seating correctly at each extremity.

14. Heater Controls and Cables - Removal and Replacement

1. To renew either cable, the control assembly has to be withdrawn from the fascia panel. First disconnect the battery to minimise the possibility of short circuits behind the fascia panel and disconnect both cables at the heater end adjustment trunnions (Section 13).

2. Remove the radio, console and parcel shelf and then the escutcheon, held by two screws, round the control levers. On later models take off the detachable knobs.

3. Two screws, accessible through the aperture, hold the assembly in position and when these are removed it can be drawn forward, bringing the cables with it. Each cable is clamped and can be detached and the inner cable lifted off the lever peg.

4. When fitting a cable make sure the end of the outer does not project beyond the edge of the clamp (or spring clip). Adjust the levers, after replacement, as described in Section 13.

15. Heater Unit, Blowers and Water Valve - Removal and Replacement

1. Disconnect the battery and partially drain the cooling system, keeping the coolant if anti-freeze has been added. Disconnect the inlet and outlet hoses from the water valve.

2. Remove the controls as described in Section 14.

3. Remove the face vent air hoses from the heater end and the demist tubes which run up to the windscreen.

4. Disconnect the two blower cables at the snap connections and release the cable harness where it is clipped to the body of the heater unit.

5. Four screws, two each side, which hold the unit to the mounting, should now be undone. If it is carefully moved to one side it can now be lifted out.

6. To remove the water valve disconnect the short hose between the valve and matrix and release the operating link at the trunnion. The two crosshead securing screws should then be removed and the valve withdrawn. Note the 'O' ring seal which fits between the valve and matrix. This must be renewed when refitting the valve.

7. To remove the heater matrix (having removed the unit from the car and taken off the water valve) take off the air mixing valve shaft retainer clip from the end opposite the lever and then remove all the screws holding the end cover in position. The end cover, together with the mixing valve can be withdrawn and the matrix lifted out.

8. The blower units are serviced as complete assemblies and no spares are supplied by Chrysler for repair. In fact they are assembled and balanced on original assembly and the clearances between rotors and casings are very fine. Dismantling is not, therefore, recommended. To remove the blowers the heater unit should be taken from the car. Attach a draw wire to each of the cables and then remove the six screws holding the blowers to the casing. The draw wires should be left in position on the casing for refitting the leads when replacing the blowers. Note the earth wire attached to one of the centre screws.

9. When reassembling the unit it is important for quietness and proper operation that all sealed joints are made good and that the foam padding is everywhere in good condition and correctly positioned.

Chapter 13 Supplement

Contents

Hillman Hunter GLS Saloon

Introduction

This supplement has been added to cater for the various production changes which have been incorporated in the Hunter range since original publication of the Owner's Workshop Manual. The supplement also includes details of the GT version, Humber Sceptre and the Holbay engined GLS.

Wherever possible, the latest specifications have been included in the existing Chapter and reference must be made there for the required information. If, because of practical reasons, not all of the specifications could be incorporated, reference will be made to the page of the Supplement on which they continue.

References will also be found, at the end of the Specifications of the existing Chapters, to new components which have been added to the Hunter range and a description, together with working procedures where necessary, will be found on the page number stated.

Specifications

The Specifications listed are revised or supplementary to the main Specifications, found at the start of each Chapter.

Engine

Engine performance (DIN Standard 70 020))

Engine details	Compression ratio and pressure*	Fuel Octane requirement	BHP (Imperial at rpm	Maximum torque at rpm*
1725 Twin carb aluminium head				
320 camshaft	9.6 : 1 190/210 lb in^2 (13.4/14.8 kg cm^2)	97	95 at 5000	109 lb ft (15 kg m, 148 Nm at 4300)
298 camshaft	9.2 : 1 160/180 lb in^2 (11.3/12.7 kg cm^2)	97	79 at 5200	91 lb ft (12.6 kg m, 124 Nm at 3800)
295 camshaft **	9.2 : 1 160/180 lb in^2 (11.3/12.7 kg cm^2)	97	79 at 5100 (82 at 5200, models with viscous fan)	93 lb ft (12.9 kg m, 126 Nm at 3300)
1725 Single carb aluminium head				
260 camshaft	9.2 : 1 160/180 lb in^2 (11.3/12.7 kg cm^2)	97	67 at 4800	87 lb ft (12 kg m, 118 Nm at 2800)
295 camshaft **	9.2 : 1 160/180 lb in^2 (11.3/12.7 kg cm^2)	97	72 at 5000 (74 at 5100, models with viscous fan)	90 lb ft (12.5 kg m, 122 Nm at 3000)
1725 Iron head				
HC260 camshaft	8.4 : 1 150/170 lb in^2 (10.6/12 kg cm^2)	97	61 at 4700	85 lb ft (11.8 kg m, 115 Nm at 2600)
LC260 camshaft	7.5 : 1 125/135 lb in^2 (8.8/9.5 kg cm^2)	89	57 at 4500	84 lb ft (11.6 kg m, 114 Nm at 2500)
1500 Iron head				
HC255 camshaft	8.4 : 1 150/170 lb in^2 (10.6/12 kg cm^2)	97	54 at 4600	73 lb ft (10.1 kg m, 99 Nm at 2500)
LC255 camshaft	7.5 : 1 125/135 lb in^2 (8.8/9.5 kg cm^2)	89	49 at 4500	68 lb ft (9.4 kg m, 92 Nm at 2500)

Compression ratio identification:

HC - High compression
LC - Low compression

**Commencing serial numbers:*

GL - LH059 7
GL - Estate LH150 7

M - 1500 Low compression
N - 1500 High compression   (later chassis no. system)
Q - 1725 High compression
P - 1725 Low compression

GT - LH031 7
Alpine - LH100 7
Sceptre - LH090 7
Rapier - LH 190 7

Note: *The camshaft identification numbers listed above represent the camshaft lift in thousandths of an inch. The compression pressures listed are as measured with the carburettor air valve and butterfly held open, spark plugs removed, and the starter turning at normal cranking speed.*

Valve timing (in crank degrees)

		1725				1500	
		Twin carb			Single carb		
Cylinder head	Alum.	Alum.	Alum.	Iron	Alum.	Alum.	Iron
Camshaft lift (in)*	0.298	0.295	0.320	0.260	0.260	0.295	0.255
Inlet opens BTDC**	57°	38°	58°	47°	51°	38°	37°
Inlet closes ABDC**	91°	72°	66°	86°	89°	72°	64°
Exhaust opens BBDC** ...	90°	72°	84°	82°	85°	72°	67°
Exhaust closes	44°	38°	40°	36°	40°	38°	22°
Exhaust valve clearance - and closing position BTDC checking timing chain replacement	0.100 in (2.5 mm)	0.100 in (2.5 mm)	0.100 in (2.5 mm)	0.100 in (2.5 mm)	0.100 in (2.5 mm)	0.100 in (2.5 mm)	0.100 in (2.5 mm)
if suspect	10.5°	7°	30°	20°	18.5°	7°	26.5°

*For application see Engine Performance on page 202.
** At normal valve clearances.

Models fitted with Holbay engine

Engine - general

Compression ratio	9.6 : 1
*Compression pressure	190/210 lb/in^2 (13.3/14.8 kg/cm^2)
Fuel octane requirement	96 - 98

*Taken HOT with the throttles held fully open, all spark plugs removed, at starter cranking speed.

Performance

		Later models
Max. BHP		
Gross	110	
Net	93	95 (DIN)
at rpm	5,200	5,000
Max. torque		
Net	106 lb ft (14.7 kg m)	109 lb ft (15.1 kg m)
at rpm	4,000	4,300
Max. BMEP		
Net	172 lb in^2 (12.1 kg cm^2)	156 lb in^2 (10.9 kg cm^2)
at rpm	4,000	4,300

Cylinder head

Valve clearances (hot)	
Inlet	0.013 in (0.33 mm)
Exhaust	0.013 in (0.33 mm)

Valve timing, with normal running clearance of 0.013 in

Inlet opens	BTDC 58°
Inlet closes	ABDC 66°
Exhaust opens	BBDC 84°
Exhaust closes	ATDC 40°
Valve springs	Dual
Free length	1.584 in (40.2 mm) inner — 1.694 in (43.0 mm) outer
Length fitted	1.280 in (32.5 mm) inner — 1.400 in (35.5 mm) outer
Load fitted	28.3 lb (12.8 kg) inner — 52 lb (23.6 kg) outer

Exhaust valve closing point for checking timing chain replacement, if suspect ... ... — 30° BTDC with valve clearance of 0.100 in (2.5 mm)

Piston

Type	Solid skirt
Material	Aluminium alloy tin-plated
Overall height	2.848 in (72.33 mm)
Rings	
Compression	Two
Scraper	One

Max. permissible weight variation per set ... ...   2 drams (3.55 grms)
Diameter

Grade A	3.2080/3.2076 in (81.48/81.47 mm)
Grade B	3.2084/3.2080 in (81.49/81.48 mm)
Grade C	3.2088/3.2084 in (81.50/81.49 mm)
Grade D	3.2092/3.2088 in (81.51/81.50 mm)
Grade E (for service use only)	3.2096/3.2092 in (81.52/81.51 mm)

Piston skirt clearance measured at right-angle to gudgeon pin hole
at bottom of skirt ... ...   0.0022/0.003 in (0.05/0.07 mm)

Fuel system
Carburettor ... ...   Twin Weber 40 DCOE

		Earlier models	
Slow running speed	1,000 rpm		
Choke size	30 mm	30	30
Auxiliary venturi	35 mm	45	35
Main jet	115	100	115
Pilot (idling) jet	F.18/50	45 F.4	F.18/50
Air correction jet	200	140	200
Pump jet	35	35	35
Starting jet (fuel)	140 F.5	60 F.5	F1/120
Starting air jet	100	100	100
Starting mixture bush	80 mm	60	60
Float level setting	7.5 mm	8.5	7.0

Air cleaner ... ...   Dry element type

Ignition system
Ignition advance control ... ...   Fully automatic centrifugal without vacuum advance (5-Series).
Fully automatic centrifugal with vacuum retard.

Ignition timing

Static	6° - 8° BTDC
Dynamic	26° BTDC @ 3,000 rpm

Ignition timing

Static (5-Series)	13° - 15° BTDC
Dynamic (5-Series)	25° BTDC @ 3,000 rpm

Sparking plugs

Make and type	Champion N9Y
Size	14 mm
Gap	0.025 in (0.635 mm)

Distributor

Make and type	Lucas 23 D4	Lucas 43 D4	Lucas 45 D4
Service number	41239	41454 or 41556	41604
Dwell angle	60° ± 3°	51° ± 5°	51° ± 5°

Centrifugal advance
Decelerating on engine

Crank rpm*	Crank degrees*
3500	18° - 22°
3000	17° - 21°
2000	13° - 17°
1000	6° - 10°
800	2° - 6°

No advance below 500 rpm

Vacuum advance ... ...   Not fitted

Centrifugal advance (5-Series)

Centrifugal advance - decelerating		Vacuum retard	
Crank rpm	Crank degrees*	Mercury ins	Crank degrees
4200	14 - 18	11	8
3200	10 - 14	10	6
2100	6 - 10	8½	3
1200	0 - 2	7½	1

Vacuum retard unit marking 7 - 11 - 4R

Notes:

*The ignition static advance angle must be added to these figures when testing the distributor on the engine with the vacuum diaphragm disconnected.

Clutch

Type	Diaphragm spring
Driven plate - diameter	8½ in (21.6 cm)

Overdrive
Pump pressure

'D' type ... ... 510/530 lb in^2 (35.85/37.26 kg cm^2)

'J' type ... ... 340/370 lb in^2 (23.90/26.00 kg cm^2)

Rear axle

	Rapier H 120	Hunter GLS	
Final drive ratio	3.89 : 1	3.70 : 1	3.89 : 1
Overall ratios			
Overdrive top	3.12 : 1 ('D' type)	—	3.10 : 1
	3.10 : 1 ('J' type)		
Top	3.89 : 1	3.70 : 1	3.89 : 1
Overdrive third	4.05 : 1 ('D' type)	—	4.02 : 1
	4.02 : 1 ('J' type)		
Third	5.04 : 1	4.79 : 1	5.04 : 1
Second	7.75 : 1	7.37 : 1	7.75 : 1
First	12.14 : 1	11.55 : 1	12.14 : 1
Reverse	12.92 : 1	12.29 : 1	12.92 : 1
Road speed per 1,000 engine rpm (direct top)	17.29 mph	18.18 mph	17.29 mph
	(27.8 kph)	(29.3 kph)	(27.8 kph)

Wheels and tyres
Wheel type ... ... Deep pressed steel (no nave plates)

Rim size ... ... 5J x 13 hump rim (safety ledge - later models)

Tyre size ... ... 165 SR x 13 radial ply

Tyre pressures lb/in^2 (kg/cm^2)

	Hunter GLS
Front *	26 (1.8)
Rear	24 (1.7)
Front **	26 (1.8)
Rear	26 (1.8)

*all conditions except fully laden.
**fully laden.

Dimensions

	Hunter GLS
Track (front and rear)	4 ft 4¾ in (134.0 cm)
Overall height	4 ft 7¾ in (141.7 cm)
Ground clearance (laden)	5½ in (14.1 cm)
Turning clearance (between kerbs)	34 ft 2 in (10.4 m)

Kerb weight ... ... 2110 lb (957 kg)

North America Specifications (Arrow sedan)

Valve clearance
Exhaust ... ... 0.014 in

Inlet ... ... 0.012 in

Valve timing
Inlet opens BTDC ... ... 19°

Inlet closes ABDC ... ... 57°

Exhaust opens BBDC ... ... 61°

Exhaust closes ATDC ... ... 15°

Fuel system
Carburettor ... ... Single Stromberg CDSE

Slow running speed

   Manual 850

   Automatic in 'D' 750

Metering needle ... ... B 5A P*

Piston return spring ... ... Red, 0.040 in dia wire

Fast idle adjustment (between adjustment screw head and fast idle cam) ... ... 0.045 - 0.055 in

*VERY IMPORTANT: If a needle is replaced, one with the same identification as the needle removed must be fitted

Ignition system

Sparking plugs	Champion N9Y
Gap	0.025 in
Ignition timing	7º BTDC Static and running at correct idling speed
Coil	11.C.12 or H.A.12

Distributor

Type	Lucas 25 D4
Direction of rotation, viewed from above	Anti-clockwise
Contact breaker gap	0.015 in
Contact lever spring tension (measured at free contact end) ...	18 - 24 oz
Cam dwell angle	60º ± 3º
Service no	41237
Advance curve number	ECM 914
Vacuum advance unit markings	5 - 11 - 7

Distributor centrifugal and vacuum advance (crankshaft degrees)

Centrifugal advance*		Vacuum advance	
Crankshaft rpm	Crankshaft degrees	Inches Hg	Crankshaft degrees
1000	0 - 2	4	0 - 1
1500	11 - 15	—	—
2000	15 - 19	6	0.- 4
2500	18 - 22	—	—
3000	21 - 25	8	4½ - 8½
3500	25 - 29	10	9 - 13
		15	12 - 16

*The static ignition advance angle must be added to these figures when testing the distributor on the engine.

Specifications (continued from Chapter 3)

Stromberg 150 CD-3

	Single carb		Twin carbs
	Aluminium head	Iron head	Aluminium head
Slow running speed	870/930 rpm	770/830 rpm	900/960 rpm
Needle			
Sea level to 5000 ft (1500 m)	B5CL	B5CM	B5CK
5000 ft to 10000 ft (1500 to 3000 m)	B5CQ	B5CS	B5CV
Over 10000 ft (3000 m)	B5CR	B5CT	B5CW
Fast idle speed adjustment (between screwhead and fast idle cam)	0.05 in (1.27 mm)	0.045 in (1.14 mm)	0.040 in (1.01 mm)
Choke control	Manual	Manual	Manual

SU HS4

Slow running speed	770 - 830 rpm (Iron head) 870 - 930 rpm (Aluminium head)
Needle	AAK
Spring	Green
Choke control	Manual

SU HS4C

	Aluminium head	Iron head
Slow running speed	870 - 930 rpm	770 - 830 rpm
Needle	ABZ	ABW
Spring	Yellow	Yellow
Choke	Manual	Manual

Specifications (continued from Chapter 6)

Type D overdrive unit - Specifications

	Dimension		Clearance
Gearbox mainshaft			
Shaft dia. at sunwheel bush	7/8 in − 0.001 in (22.225 − 0.025 mm)		
	− 0.002 in (− 0.050 mm)		
Sunwheel bush i.d	0.877 to 0.878 in (22.276 to 22.301 mm)		
Shaft dia. at rear steady	9/16 in + 0.0000 in (14.288 + 0.0000 mm)		0.005/0.003 in
	− 0.0005 in (− 0.013 mm)		(0.127/0.003 mm)
Piston bores, diameter	7/8 in ± 0.0005 in (22.225 ± 0.013 mm)		
Pump			
Plunger diameter	3/8 in − 0.0004 in (9.525 − 0.010 mm)		
	− 0.0008 in (− 0.020 mm)		
Pump body plunger bore	3/8 in + 0.0008 in (9.525 + 0.020 mm)		0.0016/0.0002 in
	− 0.0002 in (− 0.005 mm)		(0.040/0.005 mm)

Pump spring free length	...	...	...	...	...	...	2 in	(5 cm)	
Valve spring free length	...	...	...	...	...	...	1 in	(2.5 cm)	
Roller pin	...	...	...	...	...	...	¼ in ± 0.00025 in	(6.350 ± 0.006 mm)	
Bush bore for pin	...	...	...	...	...	...	¼ in + 0.002 in	(6.350 + 0.050 mm)	0.00225/0.00075 in
							− 0.001 in	(− 0.025 mm)	(0.056/0.020 mm)
Bush o.d	...	...	...	...	...	...	3/8 in − 0.0014 in	(9.525 − 0.035 mm)	
							− 0.0005 in	(− 0.012 mm)	
Roller i.d	...	...	...	...	...	...	3/8 in + 0.0009 in	(9.525 + 0.023 mm)	
							− 0.0000 in	(− 0.000 mm)	

Miscellaneous

Clutch movement (nominal)	...	...	...	...	...	0.050 in	(1.7 mm)
Clutch spring free length	...	...	...	...	...	1.667 in	(42.34 mm)
Pump plunger spring free length	...	...	...	...	2 in	(51 mm)
Relief valve spring free length	...	...	...	...	1.182 in	(30.02 mm)

Type J overdrive unit - Specifications

							Dimension		Clearance
Cam									
Cam o.d	...	...	...	...	...	...	1.4590/1.4600 in	(37.059/37.084 mm)	0.0010/0.0030 in
Pump strap i.d	...	...	...	...	...	...	1.4610/1.4620 in	(37.109/37.135 mm)	(0.025/0.076 mm)
Mainshaft									
Oil transfer dia.	...	...	...	...	...		0.9640/0.9650 in	(24.486/24.511 mm)	0.0010/0.0030 in
Maincase i.d at oil transfer	...	...	...	...		0.9960/0.9670 in	(24.536/24.562 mm)	(0.025/0.076 mm)
Dia. at sunwheel	...	...	...	...	...		0.9410/0.9430 in	(23.901/23.952 mm)	0.004/0.008 in
Sunwheel bush i.d	...	...	...	...	...		0.9470/0.9490 in	(24.054/24.105 mm)	(0.102/0.203 mm)
Dia. at spigot	...	...	...	...	...		0.5620/0.5625 in	(14.275/14.288 mm)	0.0003/0.0018 in
Spigot bearing i.d	...	...	...	...	...	...	0.5628/0.5638 in	(14.295/14.321 mm)	(0.008/0.046 mm)
Operating pistons									
Piston dia.	...	...	...	...	...	...	1.2492/1.2497 in	(31.731/31.743 mm)	0.0003/0.002 in
Dia. of operating cylinder	...	...	...	...		1.2500/1.2512 in	(31.750/31.781 mm)	(0.008/0.051 mm)
Pump									
Dia. of plunger	...	...	...	...	...	...	0.4996/0.5000 in	(12.690/12.700 mm)	0.0003/0.0013 in
Pump body bore	...	...	...	...	...		0.5003/0.5009 in	(12.708/12.723 mm)	(0.008/0.033 mm)
Relief valve									
Relief valve piston o.d	...	...	...	...		0.2496/0.2498 in	(6.340/6.345 mm)	0.0002/0.0015 in
Relief valve body i.d	...	...	...	...	...		0.2500/0.2505 in	(6.350/6.363 mm)	(0.005/0.038 mm)
Dashpot piston o.d	...	...	...	...	...		0.9370/0.9373 in	(23.780/23.807 mm)	0.0002/0.0015 in
Dashpot sleeve i.d	...	...	...	...	...		0.9375/0.9385 in	(23.812/23.838 mm)	(0.005/0.038 mm)
Miscellaneous									
Sliding member travel	...	...	...	...	...		0.070/0.095 in	(1.79/2.41 mm)	

Automatic transmission

Type	...	...	...					Borg Warner Model 35 (3-speed) or Model 45 (4-speed)
Fluid capacity (from dry)	...	...	...	...	...	...		11¼ pints (6.4 litres) - Model 35
								10½ pints (6 litre) - Model 45
Fluid type	...	...	...	...	...	...	...	Castrol TQF

Transmission gear ratios

									Model 35	Model 45
1st	...	...	...	...	...	...	...	...	2.39 : 1	3.00 : 1
2nd	...	...	...	...	...	...	...	...	1.45 : 1	1.94 : 1
3rd	...	...	...	...	...	...	...	...	1.00 : 1	1.35 : 1
4th	...	...	...	...	...	...	...	...	—	1.00 : 1
Reverse	...	...	...	...	...	...	...	...	2.09 : 1	4.60 : 1

The above ratios are multiplied by the torque converter ratio given below:

2.00 : 1	...	...	...	...	...	...	...	...	(Model 35, L, D, N, R, P selections)
2.00 : 1	...	...	...	...	...	...	...	...	(Model 35, 1, 2, D, N, R, P selections - early models)
2.3 : 1	...	...	...	...	...	...	...	...	(Model 35, 1, 2, D, N, R, P selections - later models)
2.00 : 1	...	...	...	...	...	...	...	...	(Model 45)

Shift speeds

The shift speeds given below are typical for the models in the Hunter range. Where shift speeds are occurring a long way outside than given, a Chrysler dealer should be consulted for further information.

Early models (BW 35)

Throttle position	'D' selected	mph	km/hr
Light	1 - 2	3 - 7	5 - 11
Light	2 - 3	5 - 10	8 - 16
Full	1 - 2	22 - 27	35 - 43
Full	2 - 3	34 - 44	55 - 70
*Forced	1 - 2	33 - 40	53 - 64
*Forced	2 - 3	50 - 60	80 - 96
*Kickdown	3 - 2	47 - 56	76 - 90
*Kickdown	3 - 1	26 - 33	42 - 53

Later models (BW 35)

Throttle position	'D' selected	'I' selected	mph	km/hr
Light throttle	1 - 2	—	7 - 12	11 - 19
Light throttle	2 - 3	—	11 - 16	18 - 25
Forced throttle	1 - 2	—	32 - 41	51 - 66
Forced throttle	2 - 3	—	60 - 68	96 - 109
Kickdown	3 - 2	—	52 - 65	83 - 104
Kickdown	2 - 1	—	21 - 33	34 - 53
Zero throttle	—	2 - 1	7 - 10	11 - 16

BW 45

Throttle position	Gear change	mph	km/hr
Light throttle	1 - 2	6 - 9	9 - 14
Light throttle	2 - 3	8 - 13	13 - 21
Light throttle	3 - 4	13 - 20	21 - 32
Forced throttle	1 - 2	24 - 28	39 - 45
Forced throttle	2 - 3	40 - 47	65 - 76
Forced throttle	3 - 4	58 - 68	94 - 110
Kickdown	4 - 3	65 - 52	105 - 84
Kickdown	3 - 2, 4 - 2	38 - 30	61 - 49
Kickdown	2 - 1, 4 - 1	21 - 17	34 - 27
Zero throttle	3 - 1	3 - 0	5 - 0

Torque wrench settings

Engine

	lb f ft	kg f m
Cylinder head bolts and nuts (iron and aluminium heads, **cold** only)	45	6.22
(Using RG 225A)	39	5.39
Cylinder head studs in cylinder block	11	1.52
Valve rocker standard nuts and bolts	11	1.52
studs	9	1.24
Manifolds to cylinder head 3/8 in nuts and bolts	33	4.56
5/16 in nuts and bolts	16	2.21
Manifold studs in cylinder head 3/8 in	15	2.07
5/16 in	13	1.80
Connecting rod nuts	29	4.01
Main bearing cap bolts	55	7.60
Flywheel to crankshaft bolts	39	5.39
Clutch to flywheel bolts	16	2.21
Crankshaft pulley bolt	50	6.91
Camshaft sprocket bolt	34	4.70
Sump to cylinder block	7	0.97
Sparking plugs	12	1.66

Cooling system

	lb f ft	kg f m
Viscous fan drive - centre fixing bolt	12	1.66
Fan to viscous drive unit fixing bolts	5	0.69

Gearbox

	lb f ft	kg f m
Clutch housing studs in gearbox casing	12	1.66
Front cover studs in gearbox casing	8	1.11
Rear cover studs in gearbox casing	12	1.66
Clutch housing to gearbox casing - nuts	34	4.70
Front cover to gearbox casing - nuts	13	1.80
Rear cover to overdrive adaptor - nuts	13	1.80
Mainshaft rear bearing - nut	80	11.06
Synchro hub	80	11.06
Drain and filler plugs	37	5.12
Reverse gear idler spindle	9	1.24
Top cover to gearbox casing - bolts	4	0.55
Speedometer adaptor to end cover - bolts	4	0.55
Clutch withdrawal lever clip - bolt	4	0.55
Layshaft spindle locking plate - screw	4	0.55
Rear cover to gearbox casing - bolt	13	1.80

Overdrive 'D' Type

	lb f ft	kg f m
Nuts, overdrive to adaptor plate	13	1.80
Plug, pump valve	12 - 15	1.66 - 2.07

	lbf ft	kgf m
Plug, relief valve	12 - 15	1.66 - 2.07
Plug, drain	12 - 15	1.66 - 2.07

Overdrive 'J' type
Nuts, overdrive to adaptor plate	13	1.80
Nuts, rear case to main case	13	1.80
Nuts, bridge piece	7	0.97
Ring nut, ouput shaft	50 - 60	6.91 - 8.29
Plug, pressure take-off	9 - 15	1.24 - 2.07
Plug, dashpot	16	2.21
Plug, pump	16	2.21
Plug, filter	16	2.21
Sump setscrews	7	0.97
Solenoid	30 - 40	4.15 - 5.53

Automatic transmission
Converter to drive disc	32	4.4
Drive disc to crankshaft	40	5.5
Transmission case to coverter		
(BW 35)	9	1.2
(BW 45 - M10)	28	3.9
(BW 45 - M12)	38	5.3
Sump to transmission		
(BW 35)	9	1.2
(BW 45)	5.4	0.75
Inhibitor switch		
(BW 35)	7	0.97
(BW 45)	3.6	0.5
Sump drain plug	12	1.6

Propeller shaft (split)
Coupling to front shaft nut	90	12.44
Propeller shaft front to propeller shaft rear	17	2.35
Centre bearing to brackets	12	1.66

Rear axle
Pinion nut	110	15.21
Axle shaft nut	190	26.27
Crown wheel bolts	47	6.50
Differential bearing cap nuts	52	7.19
Differential housing to casing	11	1.52

Brakes
Disc to hub	32	4.24
Caliper to stub axle carrier	60	8.29
Back plate to axle casing	18	2.49
Bleed screws front	9	1.24
rear	2	0.28
Union nuts (male and female)	8	1.11

Road wheels
Road wheel nuts	47	6.50

Front suspension
Crossmember to body	52	7.19
Lower link to crossmember	28	3.87
Brake reaction rods - front nuts		
Early models	26	3.59
Late models	40	5.53
Brake reaction rods - rear bolts	67	9.26
Anti-roll bar - mounting bolts	28	3.87
link nuts	15	2.07
Lower swivel bearing - main ball pin nut	43	5.94
to strut	17	2.35
to lower link	34	4.70
Top strut bearing - centre nut (maximum)	35	4.84
using adaptor P 5026, set wrench to	29	4.01
housing body	15	2.07
Steering arm to stub carrier	38	5.25
Strut gland nut	27	3.73

Rear suspension							lb f ft	kg f m
Rear spring U-bolts	...	...	...	...	...	...	34	4.70
Rear spring shackle nuts		...	...	...	...	...	25	3.46
Rear spring front eye bolt		...	...	...	...	...	28	3.87
Dampers (upper fixing)		...	...	...	...	...	6	0.83
(lower fixing)	...	...	...	...	...	...	28	3.87
Dampers (Estate car) upper and lower fixing				...	...	...	14	1.94
Steering								
Steering box to underframe		...	...	...	...	...	31	4.29
Relay lever to underframe		...	...	...	...	...	31	4.29
Steering linkage ball pin nuts	...		...	...	...	...	40	5.53
Drop arm (swing lever) to rocker shaft			...	...	...	...	75	10.37
Relay lever to relay shaft		...	...	...	...	...	30	4.15
Rocker shaft cover to steering box		...	...	...	...	...	20	2.76
Outer column to steering box	...		...	...	...	...	20	2.76

Engine

1 Inlet and exhaust manifold, twin carburettor type - removal and refitting

1 Partially drain the cooling system to permit removal of the inlet and outlet hoses from their connections on the inlet manifold.

2 Remove the air cleaner (refer to Chapter 3 if necessary).

3 Disconnect the brake servo vacuum pipe from the inlet manifold.

4 Remove the accelerator cable bracket (two 7/16 in. AF nuts), then disconnect the cable from the carburettor throttle lever.

5 Disconnect both choke cables at the carburettors and the fuel feed pipe at the tee-piece.

6 Remove one 9/16 in AF nut, two ½ in AF bolts and two 9/16 in AF bolts and lift away the inlet manifold complete with the carburettor.

7 Remove four ½ in AF steel nuts and four ½ in AF bolts, and four ½ in AF brass nuts on the exhaust pipe flange and lift away the exhaust manifold.

8 Replacement is a reversal of the removal procedure, following which it will be necessary to ensure that the choke cables are properly adjusted. Do not forget to refill the cooling system.

2 Cylinder head bolts - retightening after 500 miles of running

Note: The following procedure must be carried out with the engine cold after:

A Fitting a new cylinder head gasket.

B Fitting a new or reconditioned engine.

C Purchase of a new car.

1 Remove the rocker gear as detailed in Chapter 1, Section 8. **Note:** This step is not necessary if Churchill tool number RG 255A is used.

2 Recheck the tightness of the bolts in the order shown in Fig. 1.17, by first slackening each bolt by one flat, then retightening to the correct torque. If the special Churchill tool is used, it should be set to an **indicated** torque of 39 lb f ft (5.4 kg fm).

3 On completion, refit the rocker gear (if removed) and rocker cover, referring to Chapter 1 as necessary.

B	1. INDENTATION	FRONT INDICATION AND COMPRESSION IDENTIFICATION MARK
		HIGH COMPRESSION, 1500 cc
		LOW COMPRESSION, 1500 cc
		HIGH COMPRESSION, 1725 cc
		LOW COMPRESSION, 1725 cc
	2. L, M or H	GUDGEON PIN BORE DIAMETER GRADING LETTER L, LOW, M, MEDIUM, H, HIGH
	3. A, B, C, D or E	PISTON DIAMETER GRADING LETTER

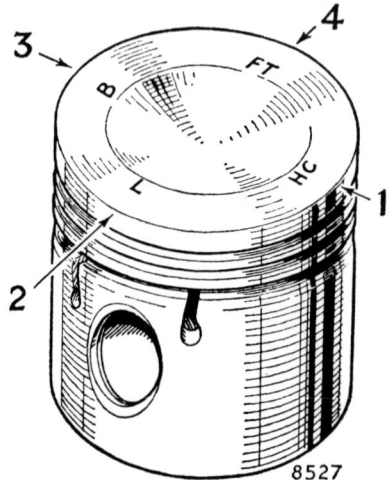

Fig. 13.2. ALTERNATIVE MARKINGS ON THE PISTON CROWN

A	1. HC or LC =	COMPRESSION RATIO INDICATION HC, HIGH COMPRESSION LC, LOW COMPRESSION
	2. L, M or H =	GUDGEON PIN BORE DIAMETER GRADING LETTER L, LOW, M, MEDIUM, H, HIGH
	3. A, B, C, D or E =	PISTON DIAMETER GRADING LETTER
	4. FT =	FRONT — MARK SHOWING FITTING POSITION IN ENGINE

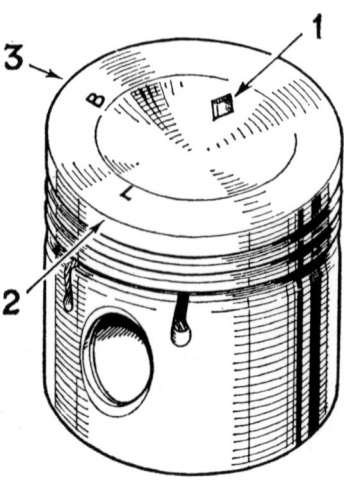

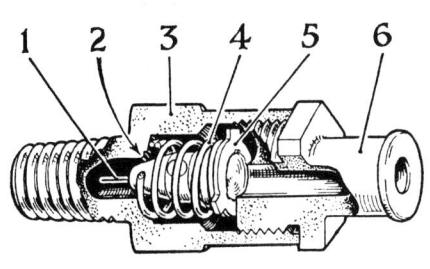

Fig. 13.3. CRANKCASE VENTILATION REGULATION VALVE

1 Bleed
2 Valve seat
3 Valve body
4 Spring
5 Valve poppet
6 Outer end (inlet)

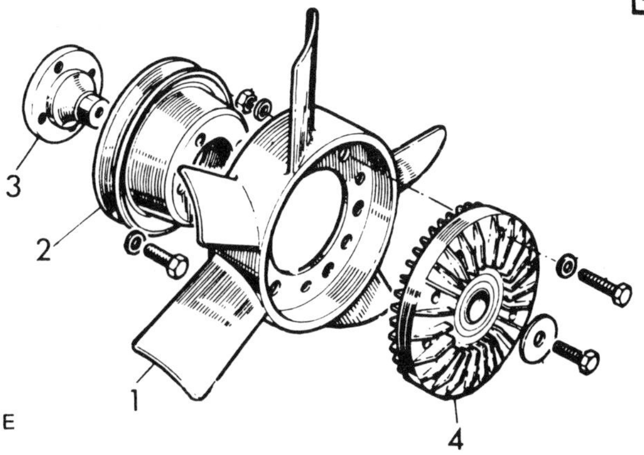

Fig. 13.4. EXPLODED VIEW OF HOLSET VISCOUS FAN
DRIVE UNIT

1 Plastic type fan blades
2 Pulley
3 Hub
4 Drive unit

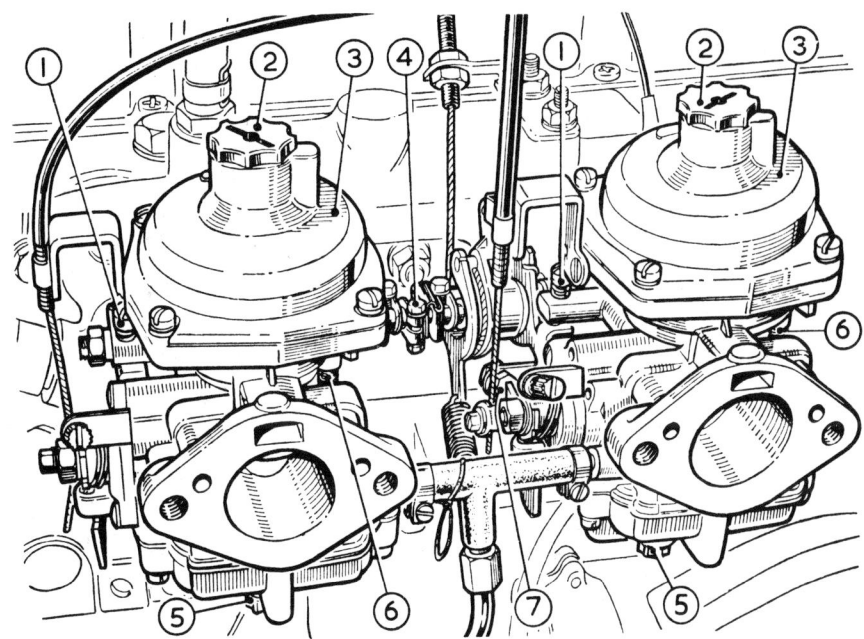

Fig. 13.5. THROTTLE SYNCHRONISATION AND JET ADJUSTMENT OF TWIN
STROMBERG 150 CDS CARBURETTORS

1 Slow running speed
adjustment screw
2 Air valve piston hydraulic
damper
3 Depression chamber cover
4 Coupling clamping bolt
5 Jet adjustment
6 Air valve piston lifting pin
7 Fast idle speed adjustment
screw

Fig. 13.6. EXPLODED VIEW OF TWIN CARBURETTOR AIR
FILTERS

1 Throttle return spring
attachment bracket
2 Air cleaner to carburettor
flange gaskets
3 Air cleaner backplate
4 Air cleaner elements
5 Air cleaner casing
6 Distance pieces - four
7 Air cleaner fixing bolts -
four
8 Air cleaner intake

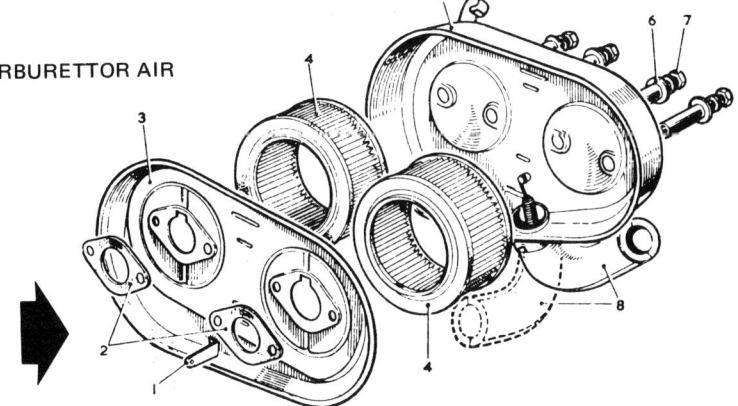

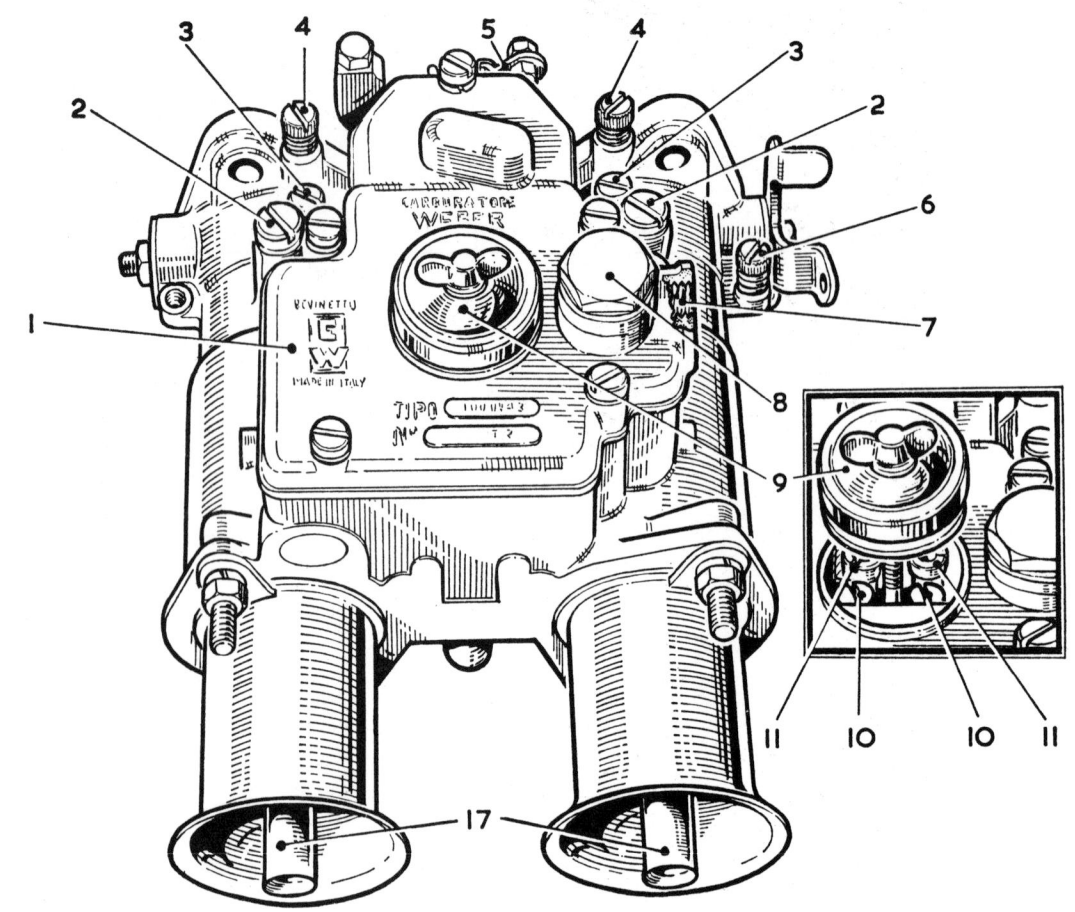

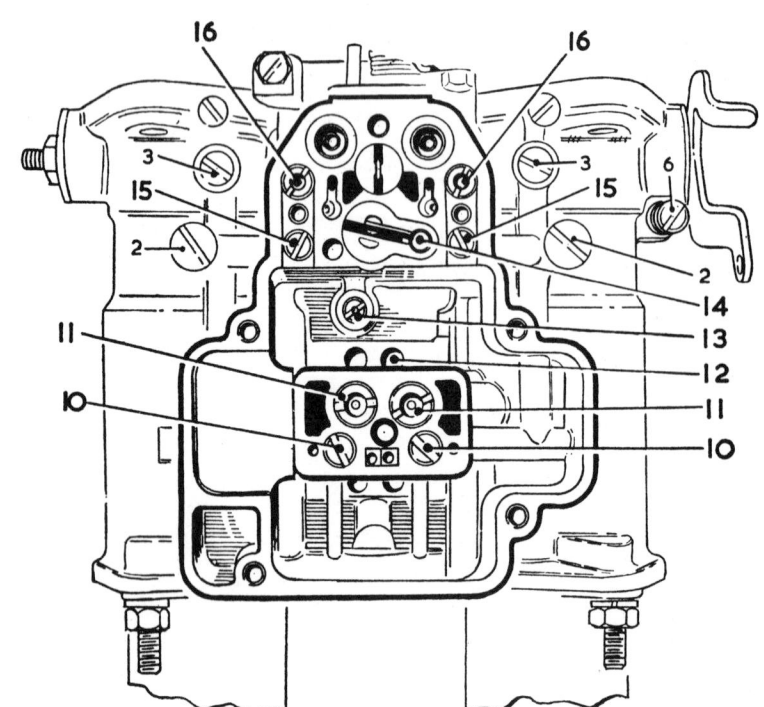

Fig. 13.7. THE WEBER 40 DCOE
CARBURETTOR WITH AND WITHOUT
THE TOP COVER FITTED

1 Float chamber cover
2 Accelerator pump jets
3 Progression hole inspection cover screws
4 Slow running mixture volume control
   screws
5 Cold start device operating lever
6 Slow running speed adjustment screw
7 Fuel inlet
8 Fuel filter cover
9 Removable cover for jet assemblies
10 Slow running jet assemblies
11 Main jet - emulsion tube - air correction
   jet assemblies
12 Feed holes to well below main and slow
   running jets
13 Accelerator pump inlet valve
14 Accelerator pump
15 Accelerator pump outlet valves
16 Starter jets
17 Small venturi extensions

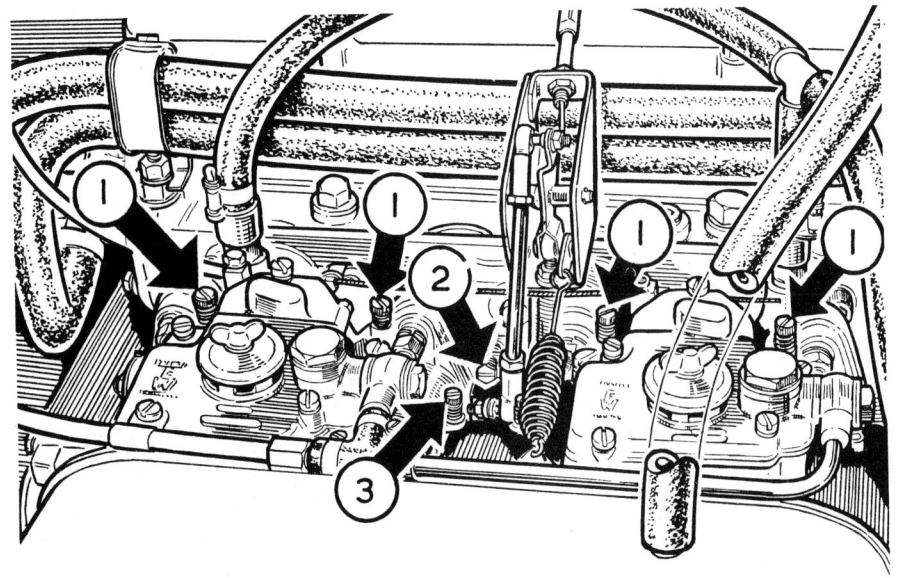

Fig. 13.8. SLOW RUNNING AND SYNCHRONIZING ADJUSTMENTS WITH WEBER DCOE CARBURETTORS

1 Slow running mixture volume control screws

2 Carburettor synchronizing adjustment screw

3 Slow running speed adjustment screw

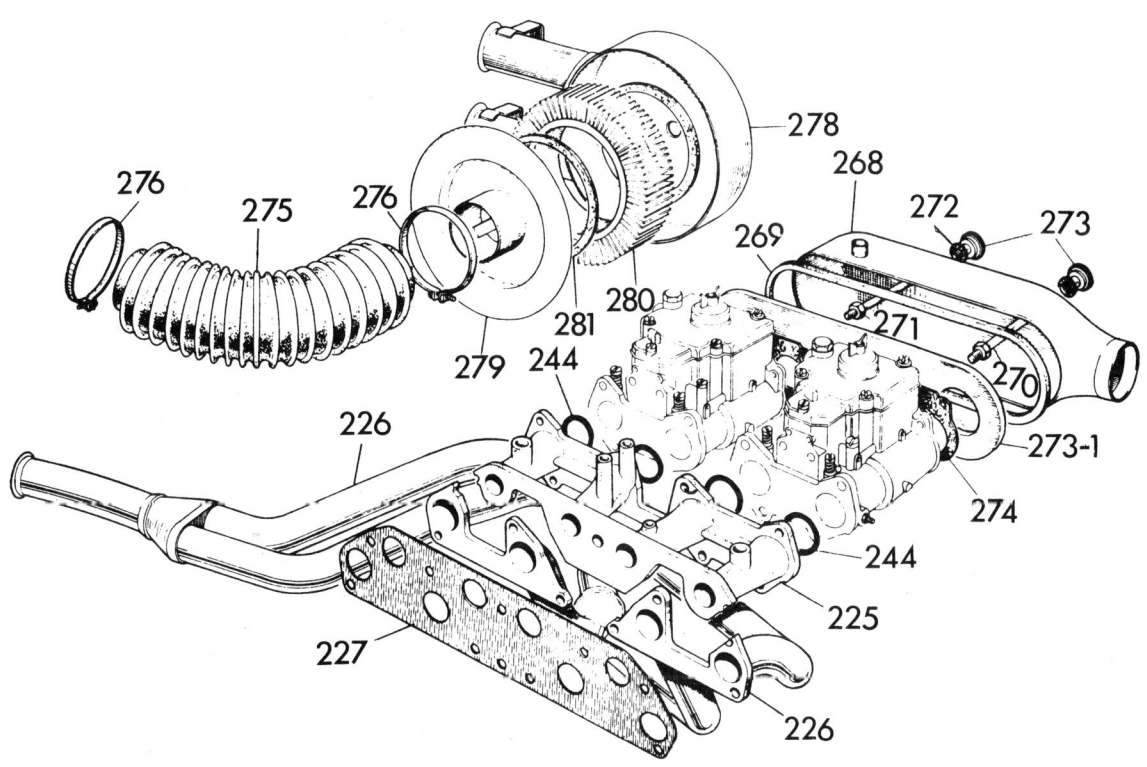

Fig. 13.9. AIR CLEANER, MANIFOLDS & AIR BOX FITTED WITH WEBER DCOE CARBURETTORS

225	Inlet manifold	268	Air box	272	Fibre washer	276	Clip
226	Exhaust manifold	269	Gasket	273	Nut	278	Air filter cover
227	Manifold gasket	270	Stud	273/1	Backplate	279	Filter body
244	Sealing rings	271	Locknut	274	Gasket	280	Filter element
				275	Air hose	281	Sealing ring

3 Crankshaft spigot bearing

Manual gearbox

The crankshaft spigot bearing fitted to later cars is of the needle roller bearing type. Previously, a plain, sintered bush was used and when it becomes necessary to replace either type, the needle roller bearing must be used.

To remove the bush a special tool is available or an alternative method would be to use grease. Fill the recess behind the bush and then insert a close fitting bar. Strike the end of the bar with a hammer and, by hydraulic pressure, the bush will eventually be forced out. A special tool, No. CB 0005 with adaptor CB 0005-2 must be used to insert the needle roller bearing, to ensure that it is correctly positioned.

1 Place the adaptor on the main tool spigot, with the boss away from the handle.
2 Place the new crankshaft bearing over the spigot with the internal oil seal facing toward the adaptor so that, when fitted, the seal is nearest the flywheel end of the crank.
3 Tap the bearing into the crank recess as far as is possible.
4 The bearings are pre-packed with lubricant and no extra lubrication is recommended.

Automatic transmission

The spigot bearing fitted to models with an automatic transmission is made of steel and is also specified when a replacement is necessary. The purpose of this bush is only to centralise the torque converter. The removal and installation procedures follow the same lines as for the manual gearbox.

4 Engine mountings - removal and refitting n

1 To remove a front mounting, initially, remove the lifting eye from the rear left-hand side of the cylinder head and move it to the front left-hand side. Now take the weight of the engine on the lifting eye and remove the front mounting fixing bolts and nuts.
2 To remove a rear (gearbox) mounting, support the gearbox on a jack placed beneath the drain plug, then remove the attachment nuts and bolts.
3 Where an engine mounting damper is fitted, it can be removed by taking out the ½ in AF nut, spring washer and flat washer from the upper mounting, followed by the 9/16 in AF bolt and shakeproof washer from the lower mounting. Lift out the damper by moving its upper end over the threaded end of the upper mounting spindle.
4 Replacement of all items is a straightforward reversal of the removal procedure.

5 Closed crankcase ventilation system - general description

1 The system comprises a regulating valve fitted to the inlet manifold, a flame trap and three connecting hoses. The regulator valve outer end connects to the tappet chamber cover plate, or the oil filler tube on the rocker cover. The flame trap connects via hoses between the carburettor and the rocker cover.
2 When the engine is idling, manifold depression draws the poppet valve onto its seat to restrict the amount of air passing through the unit. When the throttle opens, the decrease in manifold depression permits the spring to lift the poppet valve from its seat and allows fumes and air to pass into the inlet manifold. Clean ventilating air can then pass from the carburettor through the flame trap and into the engine.
3 **Note:** Incorrect operation of the valve will result in unsatisfactory idling.

6 Regulating valve and flame trap - dismantling, cleaning, inspection and reassembly

1 Pull off the hoses to the valve and flame trap. Remove the valve from the manifold.
2 Dismantle the valve and clean all the parts carefully in petrol or paraffin. Do not stretch or fully compress the spring.
3 Check the condition of the spring, valve seat and poppet valve. If unsatisfactory from the point of view of wear, corrosion or damage, the spring must be renewed; poppet valve or valve seat deterioration will entail renewal of the complete valve.
4 Clean the rubber hoses and flame trap by swilling them in petrol or paraffin then shaking dry.
5 Reassemble the valve unit ensuring that the spring and poppet valve are correctly located, then refit the valve to the manifold.
6 Refit the flame trap with the rocker cover connection at its lowest point to allow any surplus oil to drain back into the engine.
7 Refit the hoses.

7 Regulating valve - testing

1 With the valve connected to the manifold, but with the hose connection removed and the engine switched off, use a short rod and check that the poppet valve is free to move and will return under spring action.
2 Run the engine at idling speed and check that it is unaffected by pressing the poppet valve onto its seat.
3 Increase the engine speed to around 3000 rpm, and then release the throttle and check that the engine returns to the idle condition. If this does not occur, a fault in the valve unit is indicated.

8 Holbay engine - differences from standard 1725 cc engine

The following list summarizes the differences between engines fitted to GLS models and standard 1725 cc engines with an aluminium head.

1 *Cylinder head - modified ports and combustion chambers.*
2 *Exhaust valves - new material specification.*
3 *Valve springs - different rating and improved quality.*
4 *Valve spring cups - hardened.*
5 *Pushrods - tubular.*
6 *Valve/rocker clearances - revised.*
7 *Rocker cover - cast aluminium.*
8 *Inlet manifold - four branch type.*
9 *Exhaust manifold - new design.*
10 *Manifold/head gasket - new design.*
11 *Camshaft - new design (also used on some other models - see Specifications).*
12 *Piston - flat top, similar to Minx 1500 cc piston but 0.4 in (10 mm) shorter in overall height. (For clearance and grading see Specifications).*
13 *Flywheel - new design for 8½ in (216 mm) diameter clutch.*
14 *Oil filter base - tapping for temperature gauge transmitter.*
15 *Distributor - new model without vacuum advance. Vacuum retard on later models.*

9 Inlet manifold (Holbay engine) - removal and refitting nt

1 This is basically identical to the twin carburettor version described earlier in this Section, but there are two fixing nuts in the centre, and a 5/16 in Allen key is required to remove the manifold end screws. There is no need to remove the carburettors.
2 Replacement is a reversal of the removal procedure.

10 Exhaust manifold (Holbay engine) - removal and refitting

1 Initially remove the inlet manifold and carburettors as des-

cribed previously, then remove the exhaust manifold by following the procedure described for twin carburettor versions earlier in this Section. **Note:** the clip which secures the manifold to the exhaust pipe after its 'Y' junction.

2 Replacement is a reversal of the removal procedure.

11 Cylinder head (Holbay engine) - removal and refitting

1 The procedure for cylinder head removal is similar to that for standard versions. However, it is necessary to remove the inlet manifold and disconnect the exhaust manifold, before removal of the head.

2 Cooling system

1 Viscous type cooling fan drive unit - description

1 On certain models a Holset viscous fan coupling unit is fitted between the water pump pulley and the fan blades. The unit is similar to a torque converter and acts in a manner similar to a slipping clutch. It has a limited torque output and restricts the fan speed to 3500 rev/min in order to reduce noise and power absorption.

2 Viscous type cooling fan - removal and refitting

Note: In some instances it may be necessary to remove the radiator from the car before the coupling and fan can be removed.

1 Unscrew and remove the centre bolt which secures the drive unit to the water pump pulley flange.

2 Withdraw the fan complete with drive unit.

3 Unscrew and remove the four bolts which secure the fan to the drive unit and separate the two components.

4 Do not attempt to dismantle or repair the drive unit but renew it as an assembly if necessary.

5 Refitting is a reversal of removal, but tighten the centre bolt to a torque of 12 lb f ft (1.7 kg fm) only.

3 Fuel System

1 Stromberg 150CDS twin carburettors - slow running

Adjustments and synchronisation

1 Synchronising twin carburettors should only be carried out after checking spark plugs, points and valve clearances and the engine has reached operating temperature (not overheated under a closed bonnet).

2 Remove the air cleaner and both piston dampers.

3 Temporarily tie the throttle return spring outer end to the fuel pipe tee-piece between the carburettors.

4 Remove both depression chamber covers and lift out the air valve pistons and return springs.

5 Remove both needles from the air valve pistons, check their type with details given in Specifications Section and refit as described for single carburettors in Section 7 of Chapter 3.

6 Refit the air valve pistons, return springs and depression chamber covers ensuring that the diaphragms are correctly located (Fig. 3.5).

7 Hold each air valve piston down (as described for single carburettors) in turn, screw up the jet adjuster (5) (Fig. 13.5) until it makes contact with the air valve piston.

8 Check that each air valve piston falls freely, if not, centralise the jets as described in Section 6 of Chapter 3.

9 Refill the damper bores with engine oil to within ¼ in (6 mm) of the upper edge, and then screw each jet adjuster down exactly 2 turns.

10 Unscrew the fast idle speed adjustment screw (7) until it is well clear of the cam on the front carburettor.

11 Slacken the most accessible clamping bolt (4) on the carburettor throttle couplings.

12 Slacken the slow running screws (1) until they are well clear of the throttle levers, then rotate each screw until a 0.002 inch feeler gauge is just gripped between them and the throttle levers, with the throttle butterflies in the closed position. Now rotate each screw clockwise by two turns.

13 Tighten the clamp bolt (4).

14 Start and run the engine until it regains normal operating temperature. If needed, adjust the jet adjusters not more than half a turn each way from the previously set position and re-adjust each slow running screw by an equal amount to improve the overall idling conditions.

15 Obtain a length of small bore rubber hose and listen to the 'hiss' of incoming air at the carburettor air inlets with the engine running. If the 'hiss' is greater at one than the other, slacken the clamp bolt (4) and adjust the screw (1), on each carburettor if necessary, until synchronized.

16 With the clamp bolt still loose, adjust each carburettor slow running mixture screw (5) until the highest engine speed is obtained without moving the throttle. Always commence with a weak setting (i.e. mixture screw high) and work towards a rich setting (i.e mixture screw down), when adjusting the slow running mixture.

17 Retighten the clamp bolt whilst making sure that the slow running screws rest on their abutment points on the throttle levers.

18 Adjust the fast idle speed screw (7) to obtain the specified adjustment between its domed head and the fast idle cam (ensure that the choke control knob is pushed fully home).

19 On completion, refit the piston damper, air cleaner and throttle return spring.

2 Stromberg 150CDS twin carburettors - removal and refitting

1 Removal of twin carburettors is similar to removal of a single carburettor as detailed in Section 5 of Chapter 1. There are, however, four bolts retaining the air cleaner and only the rear carburettor has a vacuum pipe connection.

2 When withdrawing the carburettors, take care not to bend the coupling, which must be removed if any work is to be undertaken on either carburettor.

3 When replacing carburettors, ensure that they are synchronised correctly. Replacement is otherwise a reversal of the removal procedure.

3 Air cleaner with twin Stromberg carburettors - removal, cleaning and refitting

1 The procedure is identical to that given in Section 3 of Chapter 3, except that four retaining bolts are used.

4 Choke control with twin Stromberg carburettors - renewal and adjustment

1 Disconnect both outer and inner cables at the carburettor ends.

2 Draw the cables through the bulkhead grommets into the inside of the car.

3 Thread a ¾ in (19 mm) AF box spanner over the two cables and remove the nut behind the instrument panel to permit the assembly to be withdrawn.

4 Refit the rear cables in the reverse order to removal.

5 To adjust the cables, set the control knob 1/8 in (3 mm) from the fully home position, then tighten the pinch bolt on the carburettor starter assembly operating lever.

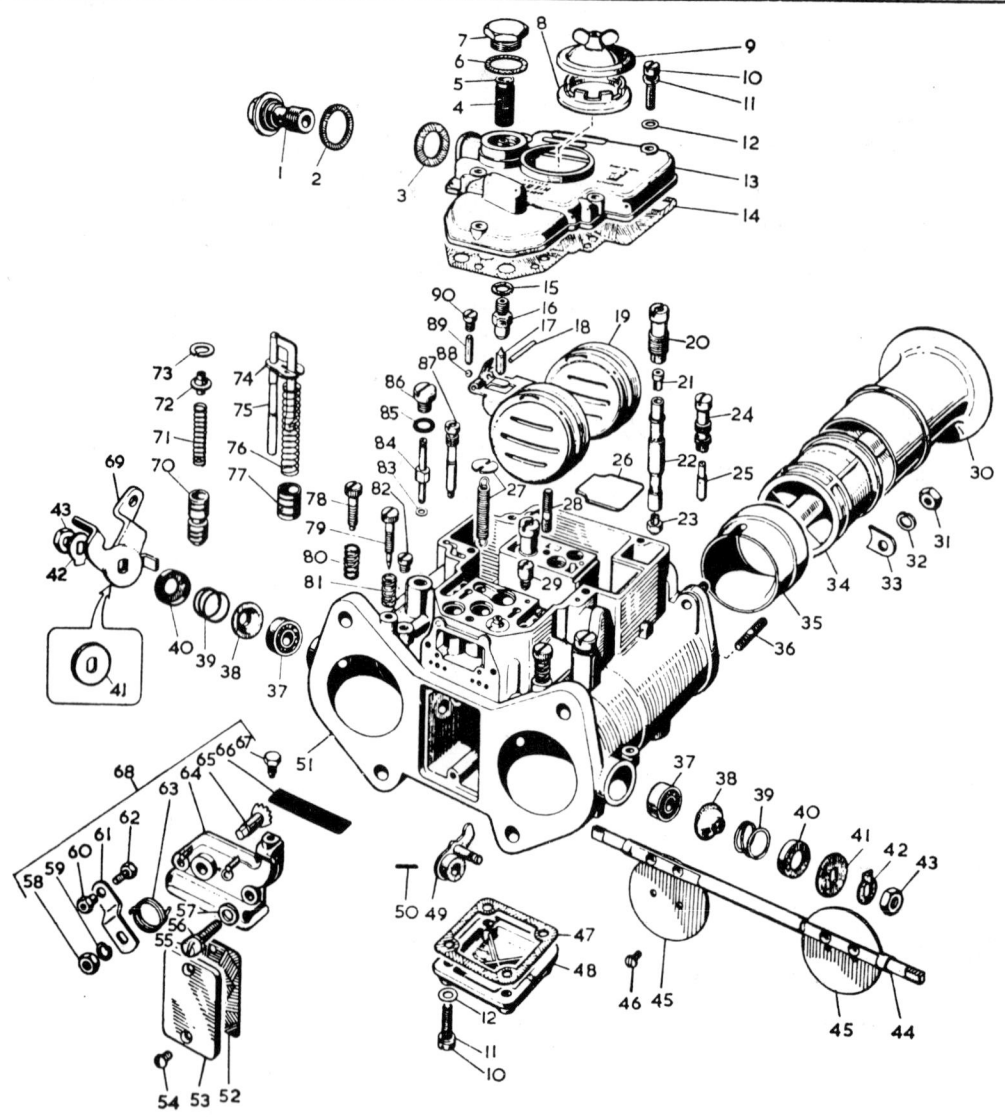

Fig. 13.10. PARTS OF THE WEBER 40 DCOE CARBURETTOR

1 Fuel inlet union	24 Slow running jet holder	46 Screw
2 Washer	25 Slow running jet	47 Gasket
3 Washer	26 Cover plate	48 Cover plate
4 Filter gauze	27 Spring and anchorage	49 Accelerator pump control
5 Bushing	28 Stud	lever
6 Washer	29 Accelerator pump inlet	50 Pin
7 Filter cover plug	valve	51 Carburettor body
8 Float chamber air vent	30 Air inlet	52 Gasket
9 Jet inspection cover	31 Nut	53 Cover plate
10 Screw	32 Spring washer	54 Screw
11 Spring washer	33 Plate	55 Screw
12 Brass washer	34 Auxiliary venturi	56 Spring washer
13 Float chamber cover	35 Large venturi	57 Washer
14 Gasket	36 Stud	58 Nut
15 Washer	37 Bearing	59 Spring washer
16 Needle valve body	38 Dust cover	60 Choke cable attachment
17 Needle valve	39 Spring	61 Starter device operating
18 Pin	40 Cover	lever
19 Twin floats	41 Distance washer	62 Screw
20 Emulsion tube holder	42 Lock washer	63 Return spring
21 Air correction jet	43 Nut	64 Cold start device body
22 Emulsion tube	44 Throttle spindle	65 Starter shaft
23 Main jet	45 Throttle plates	66 Gauze

67 Screw
68 Cold start device assembly
69 Throttle lever
70 Starter valve
71 Return spring
72 Spring guide and retainer
73 Spring ring
74 Retainer plate
75 Accelerator pump control rod
76 Return spring
77 Piston
78 Slow running adjustment screw
79 Volume control screw
80 Spring
81 Spring
82 Progression hole cover screw
83 Gasket washer
84 Accelerator pump jet
85 Sealing ring
86 Screw plug
87 Starting jet
88 Ball valve
89 Weight
90 Screw

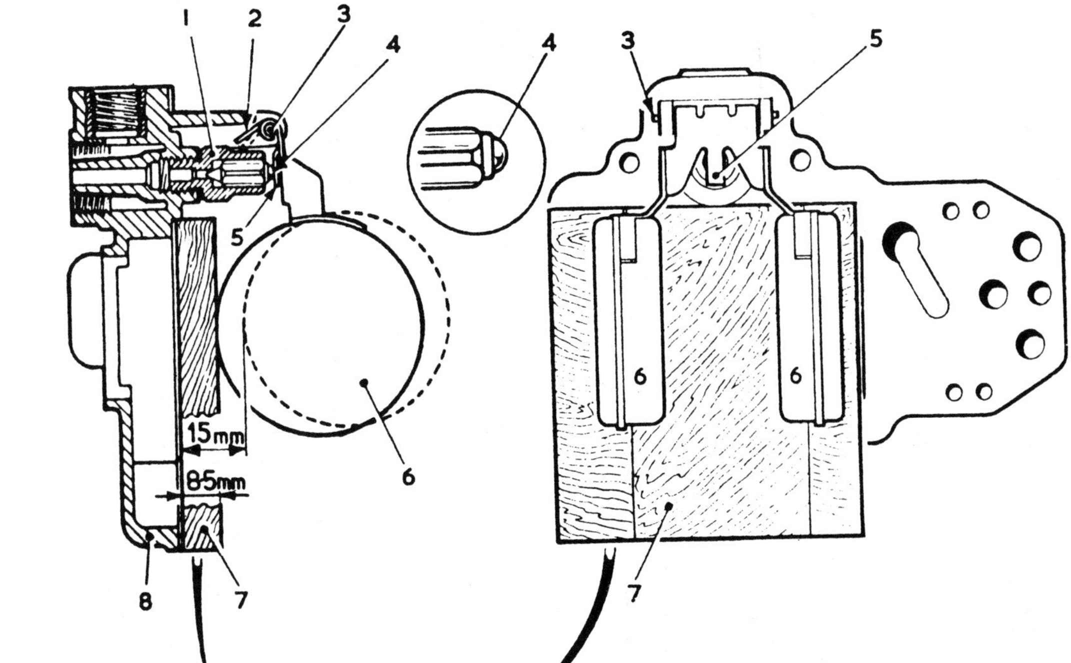

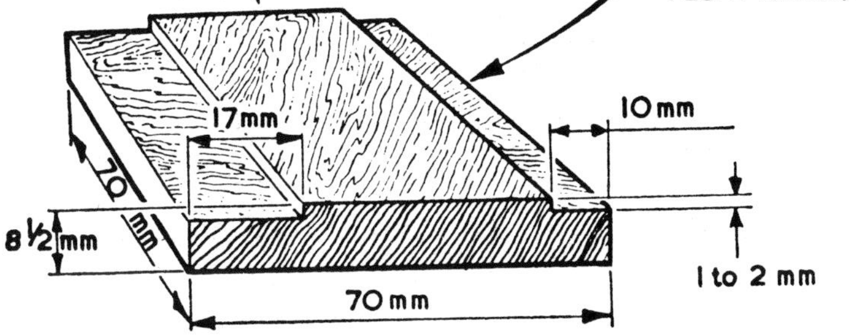

Fig. 13.11. METHOD OF CHECKING WEBER CARBURETTOR
FLOAT LEVEL, AND DETAILS OF GAUGE REQUIRED

1 Needle valve body
2 Float lever travel limit stop
3 Fulcrum pin
4 Needle valve - spring loaded
   damping device end
5 Float lever - tab bent for
   level adjustment
6 Float
7 Hardwood gauge - used for
   float level check
8 Float cover assembly

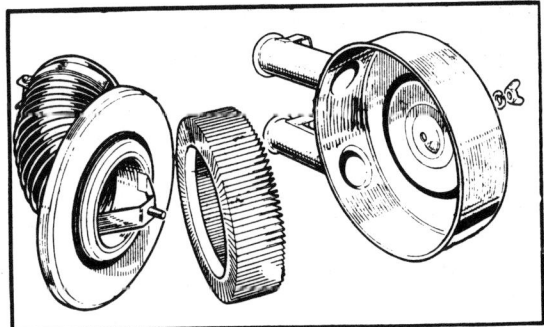

Fig. 13.12. Air cleaner (exploded view) with twin Weber DCOE
carburettors

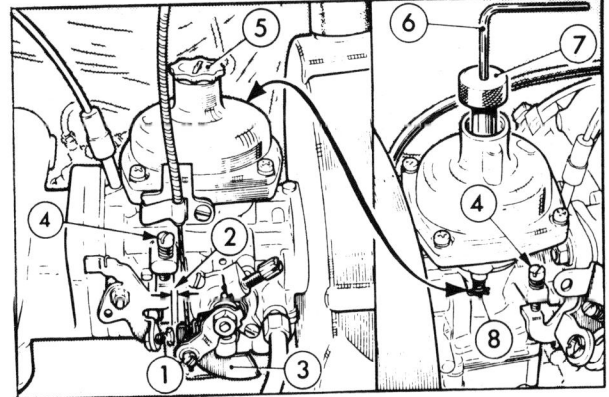

Fig. 13.13. STROMBERG 150 CD3 ADJUSTMENT SCREWS

1 Fast idle
2 Fast idle screw to cam gap
3 Fast idle cam
4 Slow running adjustment
   screw (alternative positions)

5 Air valve piston damper
6 & 7 Adjustment tool for
   metering needle
8 Air valve piston
   lifting pin

Fig. 13.14. SECTIONAL VIEW OF STROMBERG TYPE 150
CD3 CARBURETTOR AND ADJUSTMENT TOOL
1   Air valve piston hydraulic damper
2   Sleeve
3   Cover
4   Depression chamber
5   Flexible diaphragm
6   Air space
7   Diaphragm retaining ring
8   Air passage
9   Air valve piston guide spindle
10 Air valve piston
11 Metering needle adjustment retainer
12 'O' ring seal
13 Metering needle adjustment screw
14 Metering needle holder and bias spring
15 Fixed metering jet
16 Metering needle
17 Fuel inlet needle valve
18 Float pivot
19 Float
20 Float chamber
21 'O' ring seal
22 Plug
23 Throttle valve
24 Depression feed hole
25 Carburettor body
26 Vacuum (distributor) advance connection
27 Inner component of adjustment tool
28 Outer component of adjustment tool
29 Locating peg
30 Air valve piston return spring
31 Metering needle spring loaded locating
    screw

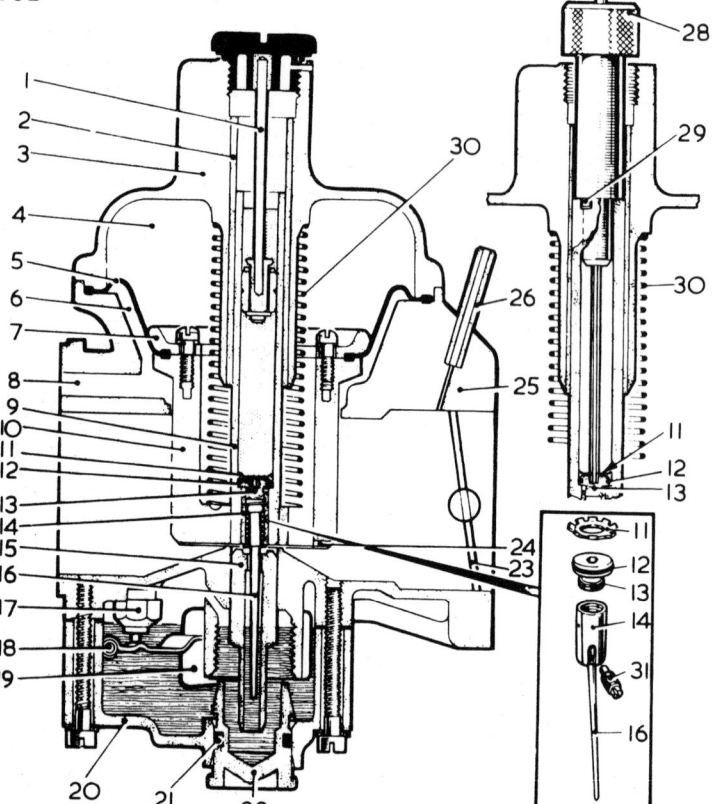

5 Weber 40DCOE carburettor - general description

The Weber DCOE carburettor has two throttle barrels of
equal diameter, each barrel being fitted with similar size venturis,
jets and fuel passageways, which are fed from a single float
chamber between the two barrels. A single accelerator pump
feeds the two accelerator pump jets when the accelerator pedal is
depressed, and a single cold starting device feeds fuel into each
barrel when brought into action by operation of the choke
control.

By using two of these carburettors fitted to a manifold with
four separate ports connecting the four throttle barrels of the
two carburettors to the four inlet ports of the cylinder head, the
advantages of one carburettor for each cylinder are obtained.
The throttle shafts of the two carburettors are linked and
synchronised so that all four throttles operate together.

This arrangement gives increased power and torque because
the carburettors supply each cylinder individually, and are not
restricted by the limitations of a common inlet manifold system.

6 Weber 40DCOE carburettors - adjustments

1   Before carrying out any adjustments to the Weber carburettors read Sections 6.1 and 6.3 inclusive in Chapter 3, with
reference to carburettor controls.
2   Referring to Fig. 13.8, slow running adjustment is controlled
by the screw (3) between the two carburettors. Clockwise
rotation increases the idling speed and anticlockwise rotation
decreases it. If, after obtaining the correct idling speed of 1,000
rpm, the running appears to be uneven, the carburettors will
have to be synchronised.
3   Thoroughly warm up the engine, then remove the carburettor

air box. Check the tightness of all manifold and carburettor
retaining nuts and bolts to ensure there are no air leaks which
could cause the uneven running.
4   Screw in the mixture control screws (1) lightly onto their
seats, then back them off half a turn each. Start up the engine
and adjust the throttle stop screw until the engine runs at
1,000-1,200 rpm.
5   Listen, with a suitable length of pipe, at the same point on
each air intake. A similar hiss should be heard from each one. If
the hiss is different adjust the synchronising screw (2) until a
similar hiss is obtained.
6   Listening to the engine very carefully, or with an assistant in
the car watching the tachometer, adjust each mixture control
screw by no more than 1/12th of a turn at a time until the
highest engine speed is obtained as each screw is adjusted. Clockwise movement of the screws weakens the mixture and anti-
clockwise richens it. If there is no response to these adjustments
it indicates that there is an air leak either at the inlet manifold
gasket or at the joint between the carburettor and the inlet
manifold.
7   Finally, adjust the slow running to 1,000 rpm with the
adjustment screw (3). Short out each spark plug in turn and if
the adjustments have been done correctly there should be the
same falling off of revs as each plug is shorted out.

7 Weber 40DCOE carburettors - removal and refitting

1   The operations for removing the Weber 40DCOE carburettors
are much the same as those for removing the Stromberg 150CDS
units described previously, so only brief instruction will be given
in this Section.

2 Disconnect the air cleaner hose at the carburettor air box end by releasing the clip (Fig. 13.9).
3 Remove the air box from the carburettor by undoing the two long through bolts and nuts.
4 Disconnect the fuel pipe at the T-piece between the carburettors and disconnect the throttle operating rod at its upper end at its ball joint with the cable lever.
5 Disconnect both choke cables at the carburettor ends, then remove all eight nuts, spring and flat washers holding the carburettors to the inlet manifold, and withdraw the carburettors, still connected together. Note the rubber sealing rings between the carburettors and the manifold.
6 To refit the carburettors reverse the above procedure but carefully note the following points:
7 The rubber sealing rings mentioned above are used to make an air-tight joint between the carburettors and the manifold in conjunction with double coil spring washers under the carburettor flange fixing nuts. This setup gives a certain amount of flexibility to the carburettor mounting which minimises the vibration which can cause excessive aeration of the fuel.
8 The rubber sealing rings can be re-used if they are in good condition, but the coil spring washers should always be replaced by new ones once the carburettors have been removed.
9 The carburettor flange fixing nuts must be tightened evenly so that there is a gap of 0.020 - 0.025 in (0.5 to 0.6 mm) between the spring washer coils when the gaps between the carburettor and inlet manifold flanges are parallel.
10 This can be achieved on the lower nuts by tightening them down until the spring washers are just fully compressed and then undoing each nut a quarter of a turn. This must be done after all the easily accessible nuts have been correctly tightened and the coil gaps set correctly.

8 Weber 40DCOE carburettors - dismantling for cleaning

1 Do not dismantle the carburettor unless you are absolutely certain that there is a fault within it, as unnecessary tinkering can well upset the fine balance within the instrument.
2 Referring to Fig. 13.7, remove the circular cover (9) by undoing the wing nut on its top, and remove the slow running jets (10) and the air correction jets (11).
3 Now remove the two accelerator pump jets (2) and undo the progression hole inspection cover screws (3).
4 Remove the float chamber cover (1) by undoing the five retaining screws and take out the starter jets (16).
5 Undo and remove the fuel filter cover plug (8) from the float chamber cover and take off the gauze filter. Wash it in petrol and dry it with low pressure compressed air if available.
6 Allow the floats to hang down as low as possible and with compressed air blow through the fuel feed hole (7) which is normally covered by the filter.
7 Remove all fuel and any dirt or water that may have accumulated from the float chamber and the well below the main jets which is accessible through the small hole (12).
8 Carefully blow through all the jets previously removed with compressed air. DO NOT under any circumstances use wire or any hard object to clean the jets, as this will enlarge or score them and thereby upset the workings of the carburettor.
9 Having cleaned all the jets, replace them in their locations. Before replacing the float chamber cover it is worth checking that the float level is correct.
10 Fig. 13.11 shows the method of checking the float level and gives dimensional details of a small gauge that needs to be made up.
11 Check that the float can move freely on its fulcrum pin (3). Also examine the float lever (5) for signs of pitting where it contacts the needle valve. If wear is present it must be renewed as it can cause faulty operation of the needle valve.
12 Check that the needle valve body (1) is screwed tightly into its housing and that the pin ball end (4) of the spring loaded damping device in the needle valve is not jammed.

13 Hold the float chamber cover (8) in a vertical position so that the weight of the float allows the float lever to just contact the needle valve. It must not move the ball end of the needle damper pin. In this position both floats should just contact the 8.5 mm steps on the gauge when placed between the cover gasket face and the floats at their highest points. The soldered seams on the floats must not make contact with the gauge.
14 If the float level is found to be incorrect carefully bend the lever tab (5) to correct it. Take care when bending the tab to keep its face at right angles to the needle centre line.
15 Having got the float level correct, check that the total float movement from its level position to its lowest point is 6.5 mm (0.256 in). This is in fact 15 mm (0.591 in) from the gasket face on the cover. This movement, if wrong, can be corrected by bending the lug (2).
16 Once all is correct, refit the float chamber cover.

9 Air cleaner with Weber 40DCOE carburettors - removal, cleaning and refitting

1 Initially turn the front wheels on to right lock, then release the clip holding the air intake flexible pipe to the carburettor air box.
2 Pull off the flexible pipe.
3 Remove the two 7/16 in AF screws and one ½ in AF nut that secure the cleaner to the wing valance and lift away the cleaner. Do not lose the washers under the ½ in AF nut.
4 Unscrew the wing nut on the air cleaner and remove the cover.
5 Take out the element, noting that rubber sealing rings are used under each end of the filter element.
6 Clean out the casing and, if the element is to be refitted, tap it on a hard surface to remove surface dust then use a low pressure air line directed sideways onto the filter surface (not directly at it) to remove any remaining dust.
7 If it is required to remove the air box from the carburettor, simply unscrew the retaining nuts. When refitting, use a gasket cement on the gasket fitted between the air box and backplate.
8 Reassembly and refitting is essentially a reversal of the removal procedure, but ensure that the element/cover sealing rings are undamaged and properly located.
9 When refitting the air cleaner to the wing valance, liberally grease the nut and screws to preclude rusting.

10 Stromberg 150CD-3 carburettor - general description

This unit differs from the model CDS by having a fixed metering jet but an adjustable metering needle. This is adjusted internally by means of a special tool (Fig. 13.13) which can be purchased through Chrysler agents.

11 Stromberg 150CD-3 carburettor - setting and adjustment

1 Operation, dismantling, cleaning and reassembly of this type of carburettor is similar to that described for CDS types and reference should be made to Chapter 3.
2 Run the engine to normal operating temperature (on the road) and raise the bonnet immediately on stopping to prevent excessive engine heat build up. Adjust the slow running speed in accordance with that specified by turning the screw (4) Fig. 13.13.
3 If the idling speed is 'lumpy' or erratic, lift the pin (8) with the finger through a distance of about 3/32 in (2.4 mm) and then immediately release it. If the engine speed increases during this operation then the mixture is too rich. If the engine speed stays the same or momentarily decreases but then recovers, then the mixture is correct. If the engine stalls on depressing the lifting pin then the mixture is too weak.

4   Where adjustment of the mixture is required, a special tool must be obtained from a Stromberg/Zenith agent or a Chrysler dealer The tool comprises an inner member similar to an Allen key which engages with the metering needle adjustment screw, and an outer tubular member which incorporates a peg to engage with the air valve piston damper bore slot. During adjustment, the inner member is turned while the outer member is held quite still to prevent the rubber diaphragm twisting or tearing.

5   Before raising or lowering the metering needle, check that the basic setting of the needle is correct. To do this, unscrew and pull out the air valve piston damper (1) Fig. 13.14. Remove the carburettor top cover (3) and then withdraw the air valve piston/rubber diaphragm assembly. Invert the assembly and using a straight edge check that the shoulder of the metering needle or its Delrin washer (if fitted) is flush with the air valve piston lower face. If not, engage the inner member of the adjusting tool and rotate the metering needle until the correct basic setting is obtained.

6   Refit the air valve piston/diaphragm ensuring that the alignment lug on the periphery of the diaphragm locates correctly in the recess in the carburettor body. Refit the carburettor top cover and check that the air valve piston rises and falls freely by depressing the lifting pin. If the piston sticks, loosen the cover screws and gently tap the cover then retighten the screws. If it still sticks, lift the cover and rotate it through 90° at a time and test in each new cover position until the piston rises and falls freely.

7   Insert both components of the adjuster tool into the carburettor damper orifice ensuring that the outer member engages securely with the air valve piston bore slot. If the carburettor is being adjusted without having first checked the basic setting of the metering needle then the damper bore will contain oil. This will make it very difficult to insert the adjuster tool and even pressure will have to be exerted on the outer member until the damper oil is ejected through the channels provided in the tool.

8   To enrich the mixture, rotate the inner member of the tool in a clockwise direction and to weaken it, rotate in an anti-clockwise direction. Do not rotate the inner member of the tool more than one turn in either direction from the basic setting position or the metering needle will become disengaged from its holder. Should this happen, remove the air valve piston/diaphragm assembly and re-engage the metering needle with its holder by supporting the lower face of the needle while exerting pressure on the holder with the adjuster tool and turning it at the same time.

9   The mixture can be adjusted by rotating the tool with the engine running but any downward pressure on the tool will close the air valve piston and stall the engine. It will therefore be more satisfactory if the tool is rotated not more than 1/8th of a turn at a time and removed from the carburettor before starting the engine and checking the effect of the needle adjustment as previously described in paragraph 3. Where adjustment is being carried out with the engine running and it stalls, rev the engine on restarting to clear the inlet manifold before checking the idling quality.

10 Reset the fast idle gap in accordance with that given in the Specifications and refill the damper bore with engine oil to within ¼ in (6 mm) of the upper edge. Refit the piston damper.

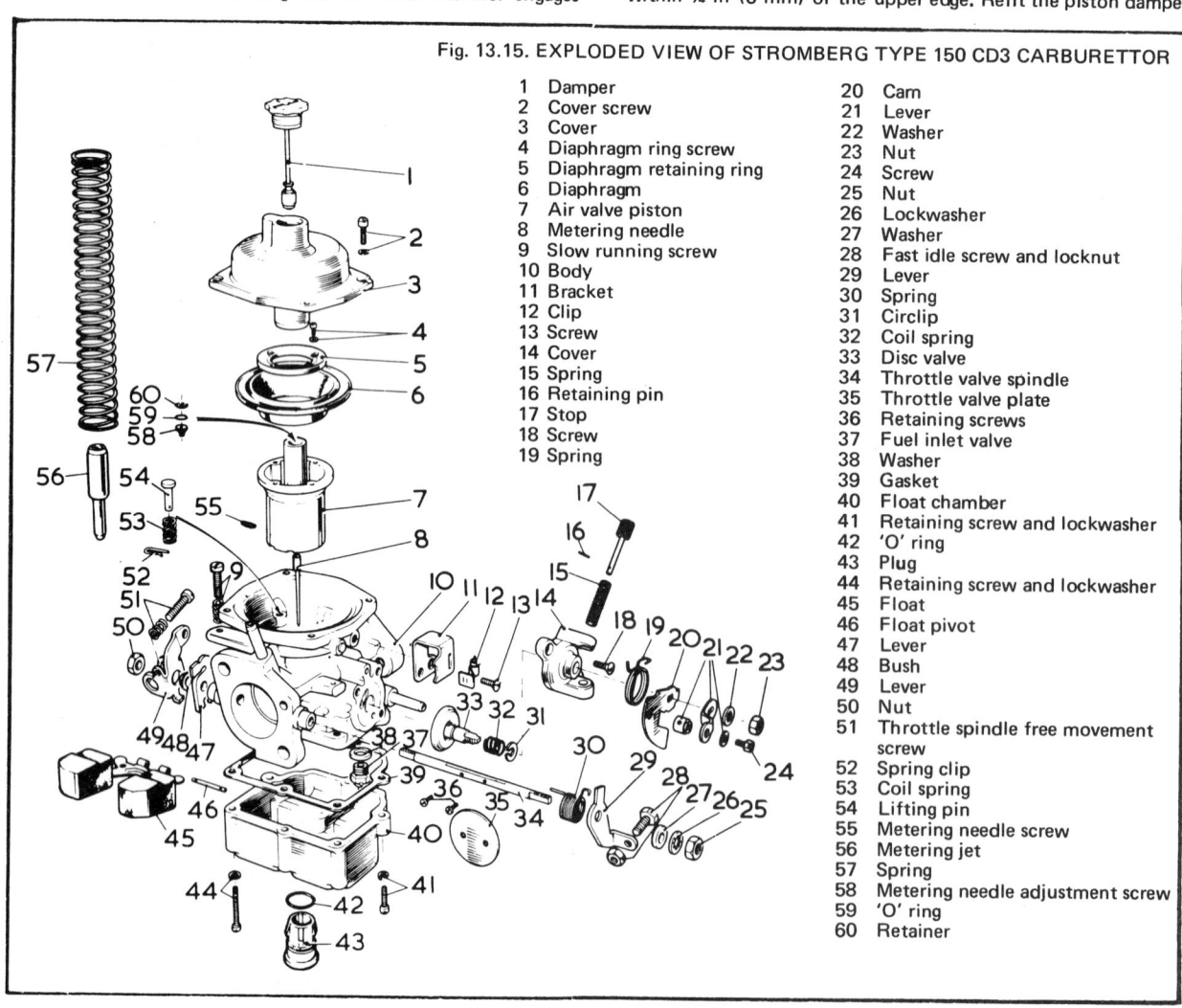

Fig. 13.15. EXPLODED VIEW OF STROMBERG TYPE 150 CD3 CARBURETTOR

1 Damper
2 Cover screw
3 Cover
4 Diaphragm ring screw
5 Diaphragm retaining ring
6 Diaphragm
7 Air valve piston
8 Metering needle
9 Slow running screw
10 Body
11 Bracket
12 Clip
13 Screw
14 Cover
15 Spring
16 Retaining pin
17 Stop
18 Screw
19 Spring
20 Cam
21 Lever
22 Washer
23 Nut
24 Screw
25 Nut
26 Lockwasher
27 Washer
28 Fast idle screw and locknut
29 Lever
30 Spring
31 Circlip
32 Coil spring
33 Disc valve
34 Throttle valve spindle
35 Throttle valve plate
36 Retaining screws
37 Fuel inlet valve
38 Washer
39 Gasket
40 Float chamber
41 Retaining screw and lockwasher
42 'O' ring
43 Plug
44 Retaining screw and lockwasher
45 Float
46 Float pivot
47 Lever
48 Bush
49 Lever
50 Nut
51 Throttle spindle free movement screw
52 Spring clip
53 Coil spring
54 Lifting pin
55 Metering needle screw
56 Metering jet
57 Spring
58 Metering needle adjustment screw
59 'O' ring
60 Retainer

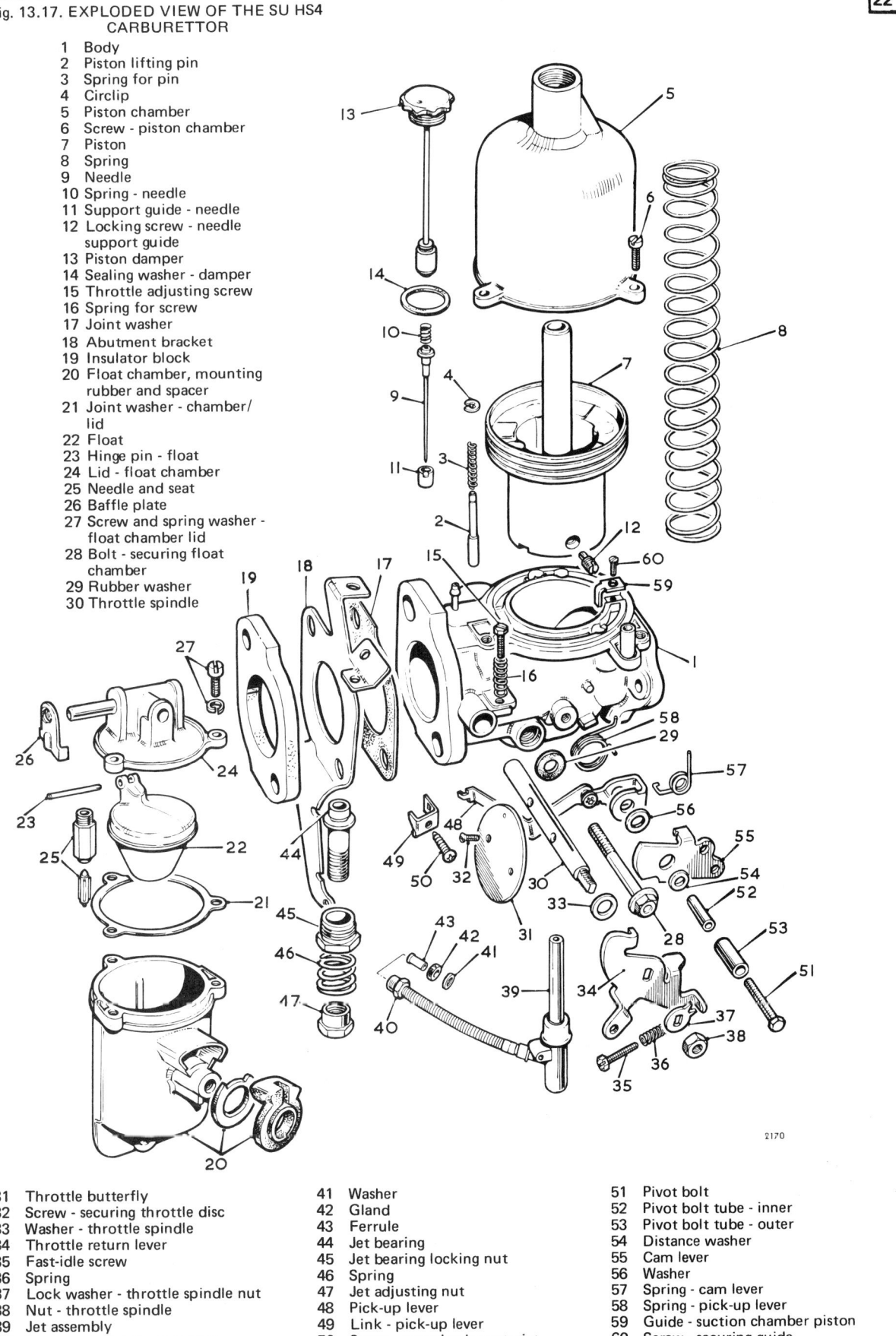

Fig. 13.17. EXPLODED VIEW OF THE SU HS4 CARBURETTOR

1 Body
2 Piston lifting pin
3 Spring for pin
4 Circlip
5 Piston chamber
6 Screw - piston chamber
7 Piston
8 Spring
9 Needle
10 Spring - needle
11 Support guide - needle
12 Locking screw - needle support guide
13 Piston damper
14 Sealing washer - damper
15 Throttle adjusting screw
16 Spring for screw
17 Joint washer
18 Abutment bracket
19 Insulator block
20 Float chamber, mounting rubber and spacer
21 Joint washer - chamber/lid
22 Float
23 Hinge pin - float
24 Lid - float chamber
25 Needle and seat
26 Baffle plate
27 Screw and spring washer - float chamber lid
28 Bolt - securing float chamber
29 Rubber washer
30 Throttle spindle

31 Throttle butterfly
32 Screw - securing throttle disc
33 Washer - throttle spindle
34 Throttle return lever
35 Fast-idle screw
36 Spring
37 Lock washer - throttle spindle nut
38 Nut - throttle spindle
39 Jet assembly
40 Sleeve nut - jet flexible pipe

41 Washer
42 Gland
43 Ferrule
44 Jet bearing
45 Jet bearing locking nut
46 Spring
47 Jet adjusting nut
48 Pick-up lever
49 Link - pick-up lever
50 Screw - securing lever to jet

51 Pivot bolt
52 Pivot bolt tube - inner
53 Pivot bolt tube - outer
54 Distance washer
55 Cam lever
56 Washer
57 Spring - cam lever
58 Spring - pick-up lever
59 Guide - suction chamber piston
60 Screw - securing guide

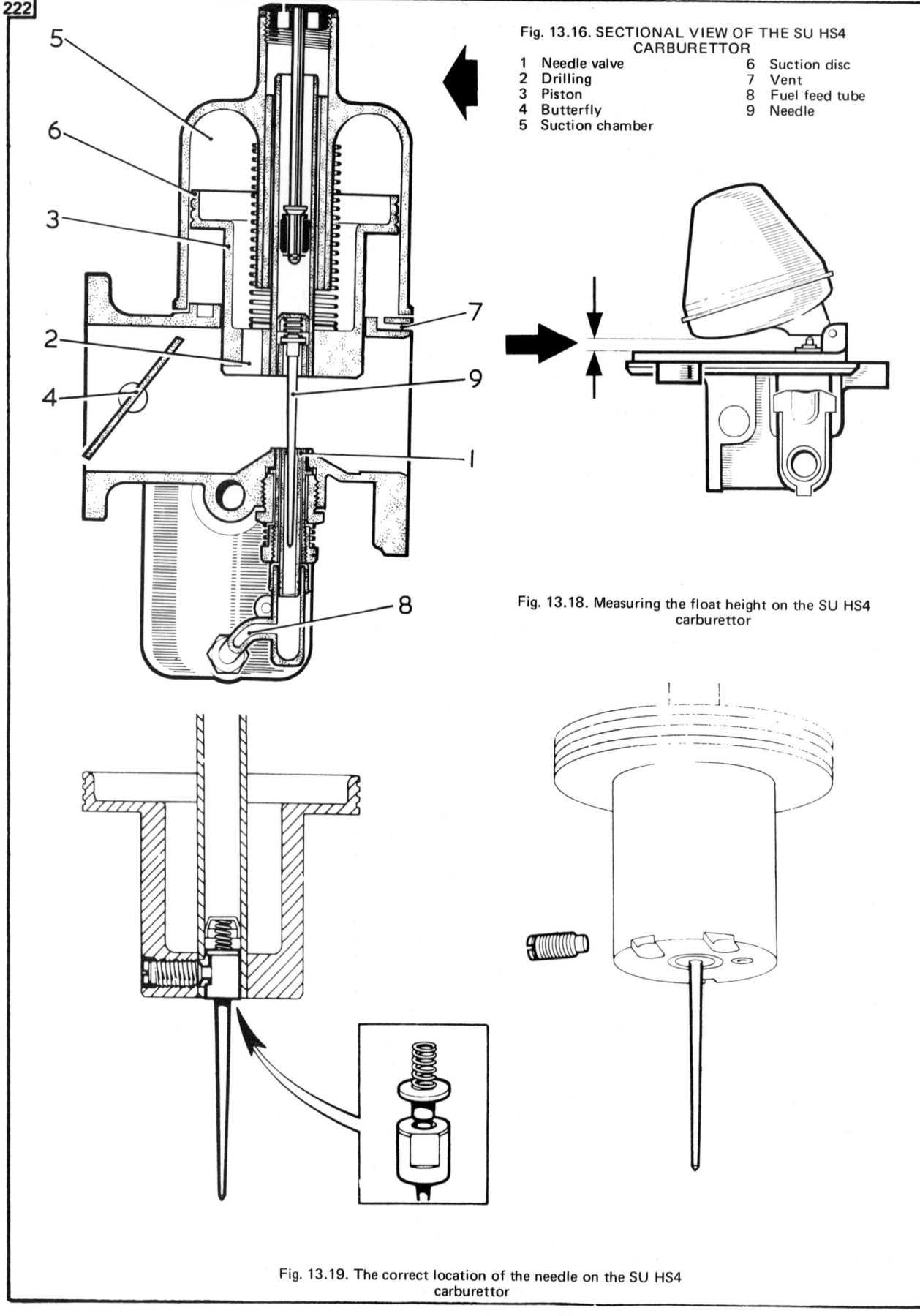

Fig. 13.16. SECTIONAL VIEW OF THE SU HS4
CARBURETTOR

1	Needle valve	6	Suction disc
2	Drilling	7	Vent
3	Piston	8	Fuel feed tube
4	Butterfly	9	Needle
5	Suction chamber		

Fig. 13.18. Measuring the float height on the SU HS4
carburettor

Fig. 13.19. The correct location of the needle on the SU HS4
carburettor

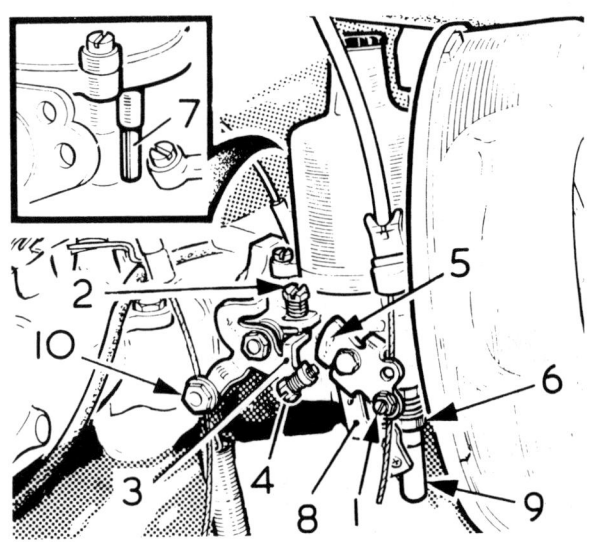

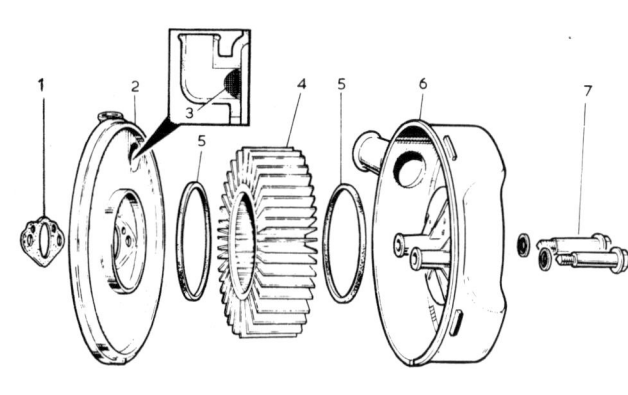

Fig. 13.20. ADJUSTMENT POINTS FOR THE SU HS4 CARBURETTOR

1 Choke control wire	6 Jet adjusting nut
2 Throttle adjusting screw	7 Piston lifting pin
3 Throttle lever arm	8 Jet lever
4 Fast idle screw	9 Jet
5 Mixture control cam lever	10 Throttle control wire attachment

Fig. 13.21. THE SU CARBURETTOR AIR CLEANER

1 Gasket	5 Sealing rings
2 Cover	6 Body
3 Gauze screen	7 Securing bolts
4 Element	

12 Stromberg 150CD-3 twin carburettors - adjustment

1 Where twin carburettors of this type are fitted, check the basic setting of each metering needle as described in the previous Section. Also carry out the procedures of paragraphs 1, 2 and 3 in Section 1.

2 Unscrew the fast idle speed adjustment screw (2) (Fig. 13.13) until it is well clear of the cam on the front carburettor.

3 Slacken the more accessible clamp bolt on the couplings located between the carburettors.

4 Check that the accelerator cable is not holding the throttle open. Slacken off both carburettor slow running speed adjustment screws until their ends are well clear of the throttle levers. From this position rotate each screw exactly two turns in a clockwise direction. Tighten the interconnecting coupling clamp bolt.

5 With the engine at normal operating temperature start the engine and check the mixture as described in the previous Section, adjusting each carburettor, if necessary, with the special tool.

6 Check for synchronisation by referring to the procedure given for 150CD3 carburettors at the beginning of the Fuel System Section (paragraphs 15 and 17).

7 Reset the fast idle gap in accordance with that given in the Specifications and refill the damper bores with engine oil to within ¼ in (6 mm) of the upper edge.

8 On completion, refit the piston damper, air cleaner and throttle return spring.

13 SU HS4 carburettor - general description

1 The variable choke SU carburettor, is a relatively simple instrument. It is similar to the Stromberg carburettor in that it has only one variable jet fitted to deal with all possible conditions.

2 Air passing rapidly through the carburettor draws petrol from the jet so forming the petrol/air mixture. The amount of petrol drawn from the jet depends on the position of the tapered carburettor needle, which moves up and down the jet orifice according to the engine load and throttle opening, thus effectively altering the size of jet so that exactly the right amount of fuel is metered for the prevailing road conditions.

3 The position of the tapered needle in the jet is determined by engine vacuum. The shank of the needle is held, at its top end, in a piston which slides up and down the dashpot in response to the degree of manifold vacuum.

4 With the throttle fully open, the full effect of inlet manifold vacuum is felt by the piston, which has an air bleed into the choke tube on the outside of the throttle. This causes the piston to rise fully, bringing the needle with it. With the accelerator partially closed, only slight inlet manifold vacuum is felt by the piston (although, of course, on the engine side of the throttle the vacuum is greater), and the piston only rises a little, blocking most of the jet orifice with the metering needle.

5 To prevent the piston fluttering and giving a richer mixture when the accelerator pedal is suddenly depressed, an oil damper and light spring are fitted inside the dashpot.

6 The only portion of the piston assembly to come into contact with the piston chamber or dashpot is the actual piston rod. All the other parts of the piston assembly, including the lower choke portion, have sufficient clearance to prevent any direct metal to metal contact which is essential if the carburettor is to function correctly.

7 The correct level of the petrol in the carburettor is determined by the level of the float chamber. When the level is correct the float rises, and, by means of a lever resting on top of it, closes the needle valve in the cover of the float chamber. This closes off the supply of fuel from the pump. When the level in the float chamber drops as fuel is used in the carburettor, the

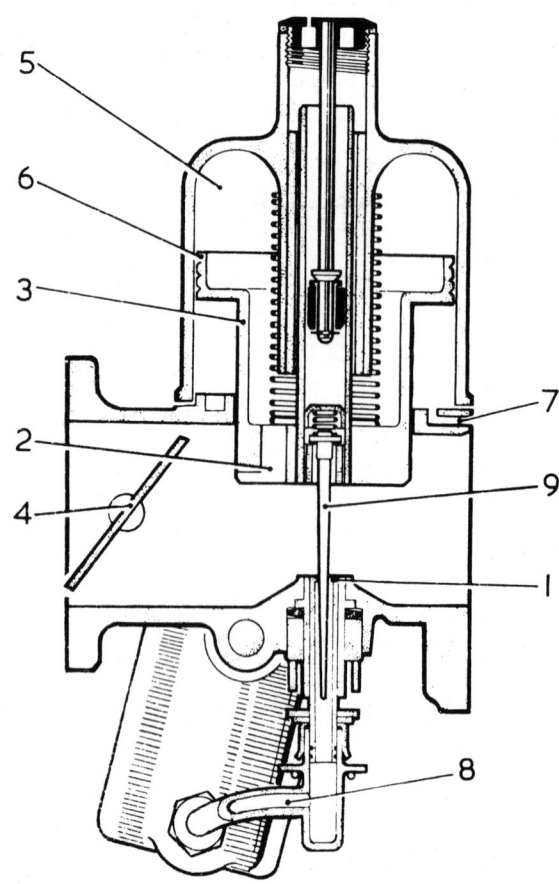

Fig. 13.22. SU HS4C SECTIONAL VIEW

1 Jet	6 Suction disc
2 Drillings	7 Vent
3 Piston	8 Nylon tube
4 Throttle disc	9 Fuel metering needle
5 Chamber	

float drops. As it does, the float needle is unseated so allowing more fuel to enter the float chamber and restore the correct level.

14 SU HS4 carburettor - removal and refitting

1 Disconnect the fuel feed pipe at the inlet to the float chamber.
2 Remove the air cleaner.
3 Disconnect the throttle and choke operating cables at the carburettor.
4 Pull off the vacuum connection.
5 Remove the nuts and spring washers securing the carburettor to the manifold, then pull the carburettor, joint washer, abutment bracket and insulator away.
6 Refitting is a reversal of the removal procedure, following which it will be necessary to top up the piston damper oil level (see next Section) and adjust the choke and throttle cables.

15 SU HS4 carburettor - dismantling and reassembly

1 Unscrew the piston damper and lift away from the chamber and piston assembly. Recover the fibre washer.

2 Using a screwdriver or small file, scratch identification marks on the suction chamber and carburettor body so that they may be fitted together again in their original position. Remove the three suction chamber retaining screws and lift the suction chamber from the carburettor body leaving the suction chamber in situ.
3 Lift the piston spring from the piston, noting which way round it is fitted, and remove the piston. Invert it and allow the oil in the damper bore to drain out. Place the piston in a safe place so that the needle will not be touched or the piston roll onto the floor. It is recommended that the piston be placed on the neck of a narrow jar with the needle inside so acting as a stand.
4 Mark the position of the float chamber lid relative to the body, and unscrew the three screws holding the float chamber lid to the float chamber body. Remove the lid and withdraw the pin thereby releasing the float and float lever. Using a spanner or socket remove the needle valve assembly.
5 Release the pick-up return spring from its retaining lug.
6 Support the plastic moulded base of the jet and remove the screw retaining the jet pick-up link and link bracket.
7 Carefully unscrew the flexible jet tube sleeve nut from the float chamber and lift away the jet assembly from the underside of the carburettor body. Note the gland, washer and ferrule at the end of the jet tube.
8 Undo and remove the jet adjustment nut and spring. Also unscrew the jet locknut and lift away together with the brass washer and jet bearing.
9 Unscrew and remove the lever pivot bolt and spacer. Detach the lever assembly and return the springs noting the pivot bolt tubes, skid washer and the locations of the cam and pick-up lever springs.
10 Close the throttle and lightly mark the relative position of the throttle disc and carburettor flange.
11 Unscrew the disc retaining screws, open the throttle and ease the disc from its slot in the throttle spindle.
12 Bend back the tabs of the lockwasher securing the spindle nut. Undo and remove the nut and detach the lever arm, washer and throttle spindle.
13 Should it be necessary to remove the piston lifting pin, push it upwards and remove the securing clip. Lift away the pin and spring.
14 Reassembly is a straight reversal of the dismantling sequence, following which the piston damper should be topped up with engine oil to within ½ in (13 mm) of the top of the hollow piston rod.

16 SU HS4 carburettor - examination and repair

The SU carburettor is most reliable, but even so, it may develop one of several faults which may not be readily apparent unless a careful inspection is carried out. The common faults the carburettor is prone to are:

1 *Piston sticking*
2 *Float needle sticking*
3 *Float chamber flooding*

In addition, the following parts are susceptible to wear after high mileages and as they vitally affect the economy of the engine they should be checked and renewed where necessary, every 24,000 miles (38,600 km):
a) The carburettor needle: If this has been incorrectly fitted at some time so that it was not centrally located in the jet orifice, then the metering needle will have a tiny ridge worn on it. If a ridge can be seen then the needle must be renewed. SU carburettor needles are made to very fine tolerances and, should a ridge be apparent, no attempt should be made to rub the needle down with fine emery paper.
b) The carburettor jet: If the needle is worn it is likely that the rim of the jet will be damaged where the needle has been striking it. It should be renewed, otherwise fuel consumption will suffer.

The jet can also be badly worn or ridged on the outside from where it has been sliding up and down between the jet bearing every time the choke has been pulled out. Removal and renewal is the only answer.
c) Check the edges of the throttle and choke tube for wear. Renew if worn.
d) The washers fitted to the base of the jet and under the float chamber lid may leak after a time and can cause a great deal of fuel wastage. It is wise to renew them automatically when the carburettor is stripped down.
e) After high mileages the float chamber needle and seat are bound to be ridged. They are not an expensive item to replace and must be renewed as a set. They should never be renewed separately.

17 SU HS4 carburettor - piston sticking

1 The hardened piston rod which slides in the centre guide tube in the middle of the dashpot is the only part of the piston assembly (which comprises the jet needle, suction disc, and piston choke) which should make contact with the dashpot. The piston rim and the choke periphery are machined to very fine tolerances so that they will not touch the dashpot or the choke tube walls.
2 After high mileages wear in the centre guide tube may allow the piston to touch the dashpot wall. This condition is known as sticking.
3 If piston sticking is suspected and it is wished to test for this condition, rotate the piston about the centre guide tube at the same time sliding it up and down inside the dashpot wall, then that portion of the wall must be polished with a metal polish until clearance exists. In extreme cases, fine emery cloth can be used.
    The greatest care should be taken to remove only the minimum amount of metal to provide the clearance, as too large a gap will cause air leakage and upset the function of the carburettor. Clean down the walls of the dashpot and the piston rim and ensure that there is no oil on them. A trace of oil may be judiciously applied to the piston rod.
4 If the piston is sticking, under no circumstances try to clear it by trying to alter the tension of the light return spring.

18 SU HS4 carburettor - float needle sticking

1 If the float needle sticks, the carburettor will soon run dry and the engine will stop, despite there being fuel in the tank.
    The easiest way to check a suspected sticking float needle is to remove the inlet pipe at the carburettor and turn the engine over on the starter motor. In the latter case remove the LT lead on the ignition coil so that the engine does not start. If fuel spurts from the end of the pipe (direct it towards the ground, into a wad of cloth or into a jar) then the fault is almost certain to be a sticking float needle.
2 Remove the float chamber, dismantle the valve and clean the housing and float chamber out thoroughly.

19 SU HS4 carburettor - float chamber flooding

If fuel emerges from the small breather hole in the cover of the float chamber, this is known as flooding. It is caused by the float chamber needle not seating properly in its housing: normally this is because a piece of foreign matter is jammed between the needle and needle housing. Alternatively, the float may have developed a leak or be maladjusted so that it is holding open the float chamber needle valve even though the chamber is full of petrol. Remove the float chamber cover, clean the needle assembly, check the setting of the float as described later in this Chapter and shake the float to verify if any petrol has leaked into it.

20 SU HS4 carburettor - float chamber fuel level adjustment

1 It is essential that the fuel level in the float chamber is always correct as otherwise excessive fuel consumption may occur.
2 Remove the float chamber/lid assembly and invert it.
3 With the needle valve held closed by the weight of the float only, there should be a gap of 1/16 to 3/16 in (1.6 to 4.76 mm) between the float and the rim of the float chamber lid. If the gap is outside these limits, the float must be renewed.

21 SU HS4 carburettor - jet centering

1 This operation is always necessary if the carburettor has been dismantled: but to check if this is necessary on a carburettor in service, first lift the piston by means of the piston lifting pin and then let it fall under its own weight. It should fall onto the bridge making a soft metallic click.
2 Disconnect the jet link from the bottom of the jet, and the nylon flexible tube from the underside of the float chamber. Gently slide the jet and the nylon tube from the underside of the carburettor body. Next unscrew the jet adjusting nut and lift away the nut and the locking spring. Refit the adjusting nut without the locking spring and screw it up as far as possible without forcing. Replace the jet and tube, but there is no need to reconnect the tube.
3 Slacken the jet locking nut so that it may be rotated with the fingers only. Unscrew the piston damper and lift away the damper. Gently press the piston down onto the bridge and tighten the locknut. Lift the piston using the lifting pin and check that it is able to fall freely under its own weight. Now lower the adjusting nut and check once again. If this time there is a difference in the two metallic clicks, repeat the centering procedure until the sound is the same for both tests.
4 Gently remove the jet and unscrew the adjusting nut. Refit the locking spring and jet adjusting nut. Top up the damper with oil, if necessary, and replace the damper. Connect the nylon flexible tube to the underside of the float chamber and finally reconnect the jet link.

22 SU HS4 carburettor - needle replacement

1 Should it be necessary to fit a new needle, first remove the piston and suction chamber assembly, marking the chamber for correct reassembly in its original position.
2 Slacken the needle clamping screw and withdraw the needle, guide and spring from the underside of the piston.
3 To refit the needle assembly fit the spring and guide to the needle and insert the assembly into the piston making sure that the guide is fitted flush with the face of the piston, and the flat on the guide positioned adjacent to the needle guide locking screw. Screw in the guide locking screw.

23 SU HS4 carburettor - adjustments and tuning

1 Top up the piston damper with engine oil until it is ½ in (13 mm) above the top of the hollow piston rod.
2 Run the engine up to normal operating temperature then switch off and disconnect the choke control wire (see Fig. 13.20).
3 Unscrew the throttle adjusting screw until **just** clear of the throttle lever arm when the throttle is closed. Check that the fast idle screw is not touching the mixture control cam lever.
4 Turn the throttle adjusting screw 1½ turns clockwise.
5 Check that the piston falls freely and the jet is centred correctly (see Sections 17 and 21).
6 Turn the jet adjusting nut two turns downwards then restart the engine and adjust the throttle adjusting screw to obtain the

correct idling speed.

7 Turn the jet adjusting nut down to richen or up to weaken the mixture until the fastest idling speed, consistent with even running, is obtained. Readjust the idling speed if necessary.

8 Raise the piston lifting pin about 1/32 in (0.8 mm) after all free movement has been taken up. If the engine speed increases considerably the mixture is too rich; if it decreases immediately, the mixture is too weak. If the mixture is correct a momentary slight increase in idling speed will occur, then the normal idling speed will be resumed. Readjust the mixture if necessary.

9 Reassemble the choke control cable through the pivot pin and clamp the wire so that there is approximately 1/16 in (1.6 mm) free movement at the control knob before the jet lever moves.

10 Run the engine up to normal operating temperature, pull the choke knob out to just take up the free play, then adjust the fast idling to approximately 1000 rpm.

24 Air cleaner with HS4 carburettor - removal, cleaning and refitting

1 The procedure for removal, cleaning and replacement of the air cleaner is similar to that given in Section 3 of Chapter 3, except that the throttle return spring is not clipped to the casing, and there is a gauze screen on the cover at the rocker housing hose connection which should be cleaned with paraffin or petrol, then blown dry with compressed air.

25 SU HS4C carburettor - description

The HS4C carburettor is very similar to the HS4 and most of the procedures apply to both carburettors. The main differences, however, lie in the throttle, choke and jet adjustment linkages. Also, the air filters are of a different design and layout. The differences between the two carburettors are shown in the various illustrations in this Supplement.

26 SU HS4C carburettor - adjustments

When idling, fuel is supplied through the jet to give the correct fuel discharge for idling with the engine at its normal operating temperature. The effective discharge area is determined by the position of the jet, which is set, through a linkage, by a jet adjusting screw.

Idling adjustment

1 Check the throttle for correct operation and signs of sticking.
2 Referring to Fig. 13.24, disconnect the choke cable (1) and remove the air filters (Section 27).
3 Ensuring that the fast idle screw (4) remains clear of the control cam (5), unscrew the throttle screw (2) until it is just clear of the throttle lever with the throttle closed, then turn the screw clockwise 1½ full turns.
4 Lift the piston with the lifting pin (7), and check that if falls freely with a 'click' onto the jet bridge when the pin is released. If the piston shows any tendency to stick, remove the suction chamber and piston as follows:

a) *Clean the exterior of the carburettor.*
b) *Unscrew and remove the piston damper (with washer, if fitted).*
c) *Remove the suction chamber screws and lift the chamber from the body.*
d) *Remove the piston spring, lift out the piston assembly and empty away any oil remaining in the piston rod.*
e) *Thoroughly clean the bore of the suction chamber and the piston using a cloth moistened with petrol or methylated spirit. **Do not use any abrasive compounds for***

cleaning.
f) *Check the needle for damage or if the jet is obstructed by dirt. Check that the needle shank is flush with the underside of the piston.*

5 Refit the piston and suction chamber and, using the lifting pin, check that the piston falls freely onto the bridge.
6 Lift the piston until the jet is visible. Turn the adjusting screw (6) anti-clockwise until the jet is flush with the bridge, or as high as possible without exceeding the bridge height.
7 Turn the jet adjusting screw (6) two turns clockwise.
8 Unscrew the piston damper and remove from the piston. Top up with engine oil until the level is ½ in (13 mm) above the top of the hollow piston rod. Refit the damper and the air cleaner.
9 Start the engine and run it at a fast idle speed until it reaches its normal operating temperature, then allow to run for a further five minutes. Increase the engine speed to 2,500 rpm for 30 seconds, and then allow the engine to idle.
10 Adjust the throttle screw (2) to give the correct idling speed.
11 Turn the jet screw (6) clockwise to enrich, or anti-clockwise to weaken, until the fastest idle speed is obtained. Turn the screw anti-clockwise until the engine speed just begins to drop. Now turn in a clockwise direction the minimum amount necessary to regain the fastest speed.
12 Check the idling speed and adjust if necessary.
13 Check for correct mixture strength by gently raising the lifting pin (7) by about 1/32 in (0.8 mm) whereupon, if the mixture is correct, the engine speed will increase for a moment and then resume its former speed. If the mixture is too rich, the engine speed will increase and if it is too weak, will decrease. Re-adjust if necessary.
14 Re-connect the choke cable and adjust if necessary as described in the following paragraphs.

Choke cable adjustment

Reconnect the choke cable into the pivot pin, ensuring that with the fast idle cam against its stop, a 1/16 in (1.5 mm) movement exists before the cam moves. Pull out the choke knob until the jet is about to move. Adjust the fast idle screw until a speed of 1,750 rpm is reached (engine at its normal operating temperature). Lock the screw with the locknut.

Throttle cable adjustment

Adjust the cable by means of the threaded end of its outer cable at the bracket, so that correct idling is achieved when the pedal is released and full throttle opening just obtained when the pedal is pushed down onto the floor covering.

27 SU HS4C - air filter - removal and refitting

The procedures are similar to that of the air filter fitted to the HS4 carburettor, except that, after removing the two bolts securing the filter to the carburettor, four screws have to be removed to separate the cover and body, to gain access to the filter element. The remainder of the removal sequence and the installation follow the same lines as the HS4.

28 Exhaust emission control

1 Cars supplied for the US market need to comply with regulations governing the control of exhaust emissions and in general, should never be tampered with. Where any adjustment or repair is required it should be carried out by a properly equipped Chrysler agent or carburettor specialist, since in all cases it is necessary to carry out a rigorous step-by-step fault diagnosis procedure.

2 After the first 600 miles (from new) it is necessary for the following service checks to be carried out:

1 *Check valve/rocker clearances.*

2 Check contact points gap.

3 Check idling speed and quality.

4 Check dynamic ignition timing when idling.

5 Check time for engine speed to fall from 2500 rpm to idle - 4 to 6 seconds permitted.

3   At intervals of 4,000 miles it is necessary for the following

service checks to be carried out: Items 3, 4 and 5 in paragraph 2.

4   At intervals of 8,000 miles it is necessary for the following service checks to be carried out:

1 Check the spark plug gap.

2 Check all the items in paragraph 2.

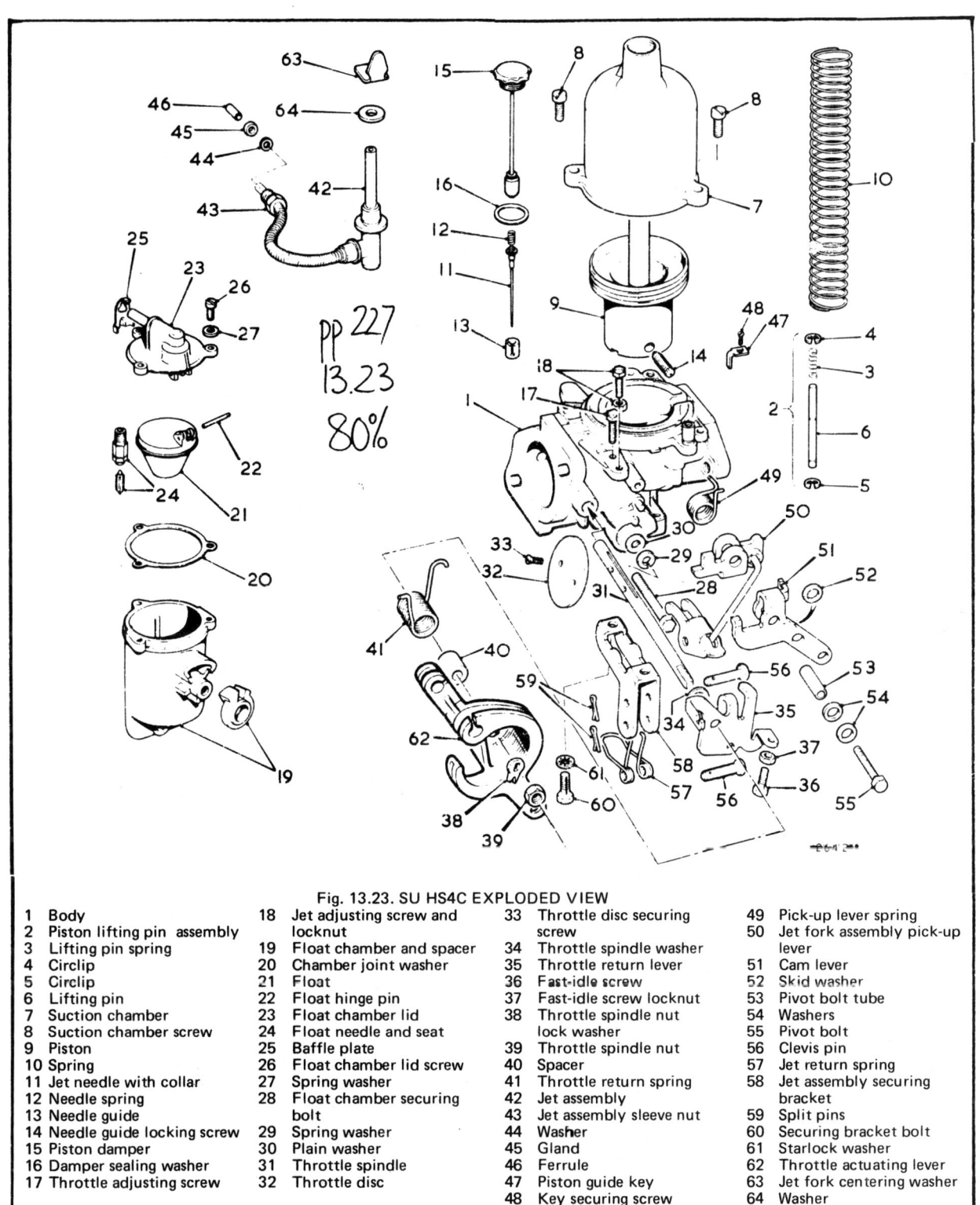

Fig. 13.23. SU HS4C EXPLODED VIEW

1	Body	18	Jet adjusting screw and locknut	33	Throttle disc securing screw	49	Pick-up lever spring
2	Piston lifting pin assembly	19	Float chamber and spacer	34	Throttle spindle washer	50	Jet fork assembly pick-up lever
3	Lifting pin spring	20	Chamber joint washer	35	Throttle return lever	51	Cam lever
4	Circlip	21	Float	36	Fast-idle screw	52	Skid washer
5	Circlip	22	Float hinge pin	37	Fast-idle screw locknut	53	Pivot bolt tube
6	Lifting pin	23	Float chamber lid	38	Throttle spindle nut lock washer	54	Washers
7	Suction chamber	24	Float needle and seat	39	Throttle spindle nut	55	Pivot bolt
8	Suction chamber screw	25	Baffle plate	40	Spacer	56	Clevis pin
9	Piston	26	Float chamber lid screw	41	Throttle return spring	57	Jet return spring
10	Spring	27	Spring washer	42	Jet assembly	58	Jet assembly securing bracket
11	Jet needle with collar	28	Float chamber securing bolt	43	Jet assembly sleeve nut	59	Split pins
12	Needle spring	29	Spring washer	44	Washer	60	Securing bracket bolt
13	Needle guide	30	Plain washer	45	Gland	61	Starlock washer
14	Needle guide locking screw	31	Throttle spindle	46	Ferrule	62	Throttle actuating lever
15	Piston damper	32	Throttle disc	47	Piston guide key	63	Jet fork centering washer
16	Damper sealing washer			48	Key securing screw	64	Washer
17	Throttle adjusting screw						

Fig. 13.24. IDLING, THROTTLE CABLE AND CHOKE CONTROL ADJUSTMENT
1   Mixture control (choke) cable   5   Mixture control cam
2   Throttle adjusting screw   6   Jet adjusting screw
4   Fast idle adjusting screw   7   Piston lifting pin

4   Ignition System

1   Lucas 43D4 and 45D4 distributors - general note

1   These distributors are slightly smaller than the earlier 23D4 and 25D4 distributors which they supersede. No vacuum unit is fitted and on the 43D4 there is no vernier adjuster.

2   Ignition timing where a 43D4 or 45D4 distributor is fitted

1   The procedure for ignition timing is identical to that given in Chapter 4, Section 8, except that in paragraph 5 note that the coil LT lead terminated inside the distributor on a terminal assembly.

3   Lucas 43D4 and 45D4 distributors - maintenance and adjustment

1   Every 5,000 miles (8000 km) release the two spring clips which retain the distributor cap in position, and remove the distributor cap and rotor arm. Apply two or three drops of engine oil to the felt pad which is located in the distributor cam recess.
2   Refer to Fig. 13.26 and remove the movable contact breaker arm by lifting the spring (16) out of the white nylon insulator (17) and the contact point from its hollow pivot (11). Apply a thin smear of high melting point grease to the outside of the hollow pivot.
3   Apply a smear of the same grease to the high points of the distributor cam.
4   Apply one drop of engine oil through the centre plate holes (15) (Fig. 13.27). This operation applies only to the type 45D4 distributor and it should be noted that neither type of distributor requires lubrication of the centrifugal advance mechanism.
5   Prise the contact points apart and check their faces for pitting. Minor 'pips' or 'craters' may be removed from the contact point faces by dressing them squarely on an oilstone or by drawing a strip of fine emery cloth between them. If the points are badly pitted or burned then they must be renewed.

6   To remove the points, push the LT and condenser (capacitor) lead connecting plate (18) from the looped end of the movable contact spring arm (16) (Fig. 13.26).
7   Unscrew and remove the locking screw and washers which secure the fixed contact breaker arm and lift the complete contact breaker set from the distributor baseplate.
8   Separate the two points simply by pulling the movable arm from the hollow pivot.
9   Refitting the points is a reversal of removal, but do not tighten the fixed contact screw fully but just enough to allow the contact to slide stiffly.
10 With a socket spanner applied to the crankshaft pulley bolt turn the engine until the heel of the movable contact breaker arm is located exactly at the centre of a high point of the distributor cam. Using a screwdriver in the adjustment slots, move the fixed arm until, using feeler gauges, the points gap is 0.015 in (0.38 mm). Tighten the locking screw.
11 Check the ignition timing by one of the two methods recommended (test bulb or stroboscope). If necessary, any adjustment of the distributor will have to be carried out by loosening the clamp plate pinch bolt and turning the distributor body, as no vernier screw adjuster is fitted.
12 Refit the rotor arm and distributor cap.

4   Lucas 43D4 and 45D4 distributors - removal and refitting

1   The procedure is similar to that given in Chapter 4, Section 6, except that the LT lead must be detached at the coil end.

5   Lucas 43D4 and 45D4 distributors - dismantling, inspection and reassembly

1   Remove the distributor cap, rotor arm and felt lubrication pad.
2   On type 45D4 units remove the vacuum unit screws (17) (Fig. 13.25). (Note the two baseplate prongs which locate beneath one screw). Disengage the vacuum unit link from the moving plate pin and remove the vacuum unit.

3 Push back the LT lead (6) and rubber sleeve (26) into the centre of the distributor.

4 Remove the baseplate wedge screw (29) and then, using a small screwdriver, prise the expanded segment (28) of the fixed baseplate (9) inwards so that the complete baseplate/contact breaker assembly can be lifted from the distributor body.

5 Refer to Fig. 13.25 and drive out the drive dog securing pin (23). Pull off the dog and thrust washer.

6 The shaft, complete with centrifugal advance mechanism, can now be withdrawn through the distributor body. Retain the 'O' ring (1).

7 If the centrifugal advance mechanism is worn, it should be renewed as a complete shaft/advance mechanism assembly. Any servicing should be limited to renewal of the springs if they have stretched or broken.

8 Check the shaft for side movement in the bearings. If evident, then the complete distributor should be renewed on an exchange basis.

9 Reassembly is a reversal of dismantling, but the following points should be observed. Smear all friction surfaces of internal components with a Molybdenum type grease before assembly. Insert the baseplate assembly into its approximate position in the distributor body so that the two prongs are located either side of the hole through which the vacuum unit securing screw passes. On type 45D4 distributors, connect and screw the vacuum unit into position, and then snap the baseplate into position in the body, ensuring that it is pressed down against the ledge inside the body so that the chamfered edges will engage the undercut in the body side. Should there be any tendency for the baseplate not to be a tight fit in its groove, then renew the baseplate. Fit and tighten the securing screw. Later distributors have a second screw fitted for additional security, and also the baseplate has two lugs by which the plate is secured to the body by the two screws. See Fig. 13.28.

10 Fit the thrust washer (raised side of pips towards dog) and the drive dog, noting particularly the alignment of the large and small segments in relation to the electrode of the rotor arm (Fig. 13.25).

11 Fit the pin which secures the dog to the shaft and stake the holes at both ends. Should a new shaft be fitted, these are supplied undrilled and should be drilled to accept the pin using a 3/16 in (4.76 mm) twist drill. Use the dog as a guide to position the hole and press down on the cam end of the shaft whilst drilling, to compress the dog and washer against the shank. Where a new thrust washer is installed, assemble the drive dog and washer and pin and then tap the end face of the drive dog to slightly compress and flatten the 'pips' on the thrust washer to provide the specified shaft endfloat of between 0.010 and 0.020 in (0.2540 and 0.5080 mm).

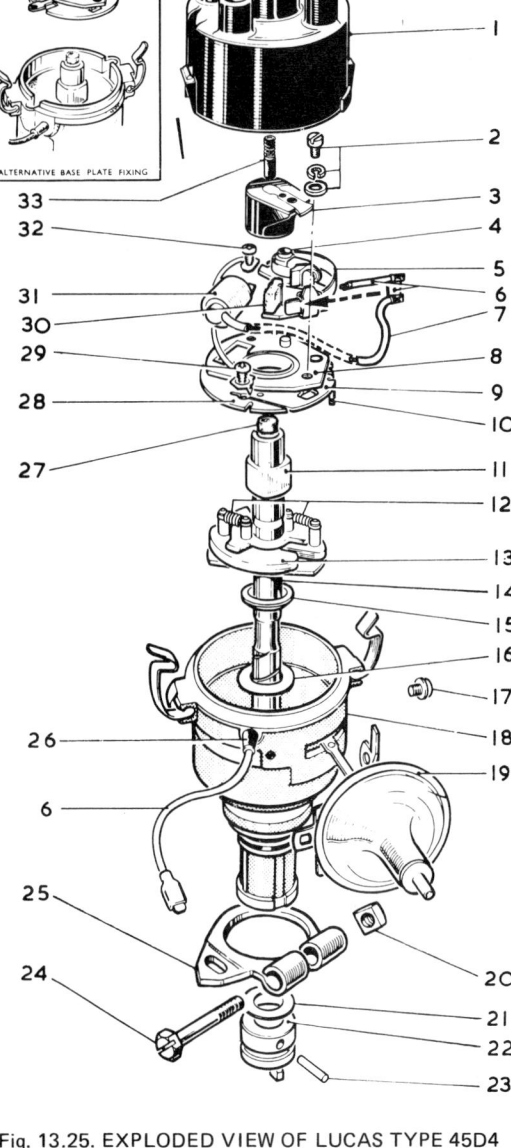

Fig. 13.25. EXPLODED VIEW OF LUCAS TYPE 45D4 DISTRIBUTOR (TYPE 43D4 IS SIMILAR EXCEPT THAT A BLANKING PLATE IS FITTED IN PLACE OF THE VACUUM ADVANCE CAPSULE) (Inset) Alternative baseplate fixing

1	Cap	17	Vacuum capsule or blanking plate screws
2	Contact securing screw	18	Body
3	Rotor	19	Vacuum capsule
4	Pivot post	20	Pinch bolt nut
5	Movable contact arm	21	Thrust washer
6	LT lead and terminal plate	22	Driving dog
7	Condenser (capacitor) lead	23	Pin
8	Movable baseplate	24	Pinch bolt
9	Fixed baseplate	25	Clamp plate
10	Baseplate locating prongs	26	Insulating sleeve
11	Cam	27	Felt lubricating pad
12	Centrifugal advance springs	28	Baseplate expanding section
13	Centrifugal advance mechanism	29	Wedge screw
14	Shaft	30	Cam lubricating wick
15	Nylon washer	31	Capacitor (condenser)
16	Steel washer	32	Retaining screw
		33	Carbon brush

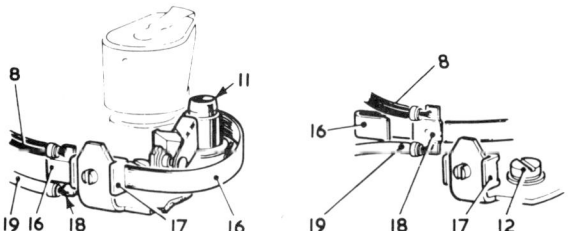

Fig. 13.26. DETAILS OF LT TERMINAL ON TYPE 45D4 OR 43D4 DISTRIBUTORS

8 LT lead
11 Pivot post
12 Fixed contact locking screw
16 Moving contact spring arm
17 Insulator
18 LT connecting plate
19 Capacitor lead

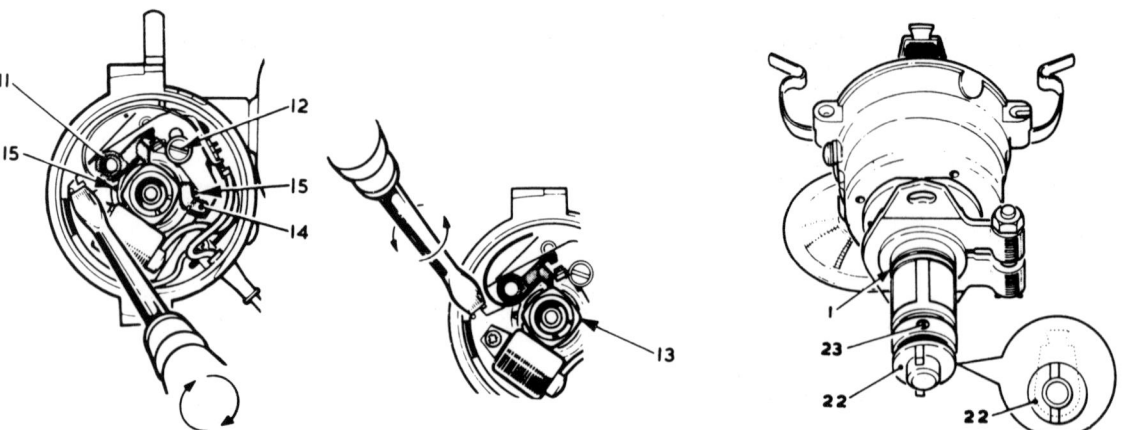

Fig. 13.28. LOCATION OF DRIVING DOG RELATIVE TO
ROTOR ARM (LUCAS TYPE 45D4 AND 43D4 DISTRIBUTORS)
1   'O' ring seal
22 Driving dog
23 Pin

Fig. 13.27. CONTACT BREAKER GAP ADJUSTMENT
(LUCAS TYPE 45D4 DISTRIBUTOR)
11 Pivot   13 Cam
12 Fixed contact locking   14 Felt lubricating wick
    screw   15 Lubrication holes

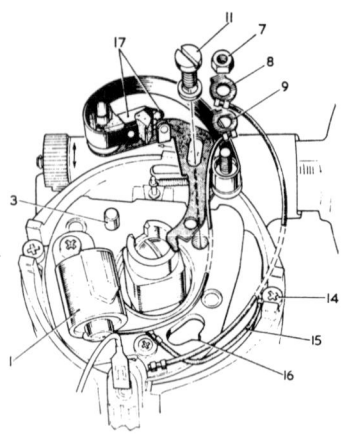

Fig. 13.29. THE ONE-PIECE CONTACT SET USED ON LATER
DISTRIBUTORS
1   Capacitor   11 Terminal pillar
3   Moving contact pivot   14 Contact breaker plate fixing
7   Nut   screw
8   LT lead   15 Contact breaker earth lead
9   Capacitor lead   16 Screwdriver adjustment slot
                               17 One-piece contact set

6   Lucas 23D4 - maintenance, dismantling and ignition timing

1   Apart from the fact that no vacuum unit is fitted, this
distributor is similar to the 25D4 unit which is described in
Chapter 4.

7   Ducellier distributor - description and operation

Certain models within the Hunter range have this distributor
fitted in place of the more normally found Lucas unit. The
Ducellier distributor, however, has a few unusual features not to
be found on the other distributor, namely:

a) *A floating driving dog.*
b) *Balanced rotor arm.*
c) *Springloaded slipper to bias the distributor shaft and
provide a light brake to reduce oscillation at low engine
speeds.*

d) *Adjustments that provide fine control of the dwell angle,
dwell variation with increase of speed, primary and
secondary centrifugal advance curves and the commencement of vacuum advance.*

The vacuum advance pull rod operates a pivoted arm that
slides the moving contact point across the domed fixed contact
(Fig. 3.30a). Consequently, sparking is not confined to one part
of the points and the usual pitting is virtually eliminated. The
points are also self-cleaning throughout their service life. This
action is due to the movement of the moving contact point
across the face of the fixed contact point.

Every throttle opening position, when the engine is running,
will change the degree of vacuum in the manifold and advance
capsule. This, in turn, will move the capsule pull rod and turn
the arm on its pivot, moving the heel towards the cam on the
spindle and sliding the moving contact point across the face of
the fixed contact point. The arm of the lever alters the angle of
the contact breaker arm, bringing the heel closer to the cam,
advancing the ignition timing and reducing the dwell angle. The
height and contour of the fixed contact point will increase the
gap and dwell angle in direct proportion once the lever arm is
correctly set.

The operating end of the lever arm has a cam which can be
adjusted to compensate for manufacturing tolerances of the arm
and points assembly. The dwell angle should not change by more
than -2° once set.

A serrated cam (Fig. 13.30b) can be adjusted to set the tension
of the vacuum capsule return spring, thus providing a means of
correctly setting the commencement of the vacuum advance.

8   Ducellier distributor - maintenance

1   Keep the inside and outside of the distributor cap clean by
wiping with a soft cloth, also the HT leads, the plug caps and
exteriors of the plugs and finally the coil. Any trouble
experienced from dampness on these components and therefore
making easy starting a problem, can be remedied by the use of a
water-proof sealant, liberally sprayed over the ignition
components.

Every 5,000 miles (8,000 km) or 5 months
2   Lubricate the distributor. Release the spring clips, remove the
cap and rotor arm and apply two drops of engine oil to the
contact breaker pivot and to the felt pad in the spindle. Lightly
grease the distributor cam. Refit the rotor arm and cap.

9 Ducellier distributor - contact breaker points - removal and refitting

1 Remove the cap and rotor.
2 Disconnect the LT lead at the connector.
3 Pull the condenser lead from the LT insulator and pull the insulator from the distributor body.
4 Remove the clip and insulating washer from the moving contact pivot post.
5 Press the terminal end of the contact breaker spring towards the spindle and remove it from the insulator on the fixed post. Lift out the moving contact and LT lead assembly.
6 Remove the fixed contact securing screw and lift away the contact.
7 Installation is the reverse of the removal sequence, but remember to lubricate the various parts as described in Section 8, paragraph 2.

10 Ducellier distributor - contact breaker points - clean and adjust

The contact breaker points must not be cleaned with an abrasive when worn, but renewed, as the contour of the domed contact is critical to ensure the correct dwell angle. If the surfaces show signs of burning the points must again be renewed and no attempt must be made to redress them. Clean the points with a soft cloth only.
1 To adjust the points using feeler gauges is never a very accurate method and it is recommended that a dwell angle meter be used. The dwell angle indicates the period that the points are closed.
2 Connect the dwell meter according to the manufacturer's instructions. Switch on the ignition and crank the engine with the starter motor. Note the reading, which should be between 55 - 57°.
3 If the reading is not within the limits specified, slacken the fixed contact point plate screw and move as necessary to obtain the correct reading. Tighten the screw and recheck the adjustment.
4 Refit the rotor and cap, start the engine, disconnect the vacuum pipe from the distributor and set the idle speed to 1500 - 2000 rpm. The dwell angle reading should be within the limits specified previously, if not, it is likely that a mechanical fault exists within the distributor and must be traced and remedied. Reconnect the vacuum pipe and remove the dwell meter.

11 Ducellier distributor - removal and refitting

1 Turn the crankshaft so that the TDC timing mark on the crankshaft pulley is adjacent to the pointer on the timing case.
2 Remove the cap and note if the rotor arm is pointing to number 1 or 4 electrode.
3 Disconnect the LT lead at the connector and the vacuum pipe from the distributor.
4 Remove the bolt securing the clamp plate to the mounting bracket and lift away the distributor.
5 Note the position of the slots in the driving shaft.
6 Installation is a reverse of the removal procedure but the following points must be noted.

a) *It is important that the driving dog is in correct engagement with the slots. A combination of wear on the driving surfaces could easily result in the distributor becoming 180° out, resulting in wrong timing.*

7 Start the engine and reset the ignition if necessary.

12 Ducellier distributor - dismantling, examination and reassembly

1 Remove the distributor as described in Section 11.
2 Remove the rotor and contact breakers as described in Section 9.
3 Remove the securing screw and lift off the condenser.
4 Prise out the lubricating felt pad from the spindle.
5 Remove the clip from the 'D' shaped post, if available, use tool number 15518Q to release the spring tension. Rotate the tool in a clockwise direction.
6 Remove the vacuum unit securing screw and the cap clip. Tilt the vacuum unit so as to disengage the serrated cam and vacuum pull rod from the 'D' shaped post. Lift away the vacuum unit and the serrated cam, noting its position.
7 Remove the remaining base plate screw and the second cap clip. Pull the slipper away from the spindle and lift the base plate out of the body. Remove the arm from the plate.
8 Remove the circlips from the centrifugal weight posts. Disconnect the springs from the cam plate, taking care not to overstretch them. Note the relationship of the dog drive offset and rotor slot. Remove the cam securing screw and washers and lift the cam from the spindle. Unhook the springs from the fixed post. Remove the circlips from the pivots and lift off the balance weights.
9 Further dismantling is not recommended unless the driving dog is to be renewed. Renewing the spindle alone would not be an economical repair as it is more than likely for the body to be worn also.
10 If dismantling further, lift the end of the coil that surrounds the driving dog pin and wind the spring off. Clamp the dog in a vice and drive out the pin. Remove the dog, shims and washer.
11 Remove any burrs on the shaft before removing the shaft assembly from the body. Remove the thrust washer and 'O' ring.
12 Check for cracks or tracking in the distributor cap or on the rotor arm. Slight burning of the segments within the cap or on the edge of the rotor arm electrode is acceptable. The carbon brush should have free movement within its housing and the length protruding from the cap should not be less than 5/32 in (4 mm). If below this figure, renew the brush.
13 Check the spindle for scoring on the bearing surfaces. Place the spindle in the body and check for side play. None should be present. Now check for endfloat which must not exceed 0.008 in (0.2 mm). Measure the endfloat by placing two equal thickness feeler gauges opposite each other between the dog drive and the shims under the body. Excessive endfloat can be eliminated by removing the dog drive and placing thicker shims between the body and the dog.
14 Reassembly can commence once all components have been checked and renewed where necessary.
15 Lubricate the upper part of the spindle and the weight pivots with grease. Fit the weights and circlips. Place the cam assembly over the slots and engage the slots with the balance weight posts. If the spindle is already installed in the body, with the driving dog fitted, align the rotor slot with the dog as shown in Fig. 13.28.
16 Fit the advance springs, taking care that they are not overstretched. Note that the closed end of the primary (weaker) spring and the oval end of the secondary (stronger) spring are attached to the fixed posts.
17 Fit the circlips to the balance weight posts and refit the cam securing screw with spring and plain washers.
18 Lubricate the lower end of the distributor shaft and the bushes in the body with engine oil, ensuring that it is between the bushes. Place the thick thrust washer on the shaft, insert the shaft into the body, and place the lower washers (thin thrust washer with a steel shim either side) on the lower part, followed by the driving dog.
19 Align the dog and rotor as shown in Fig. 13.28. Drive in the pin, making sure that it is free in the dog to provide the 'floating dog' characteristic. Check that the shaft is free to rotate.

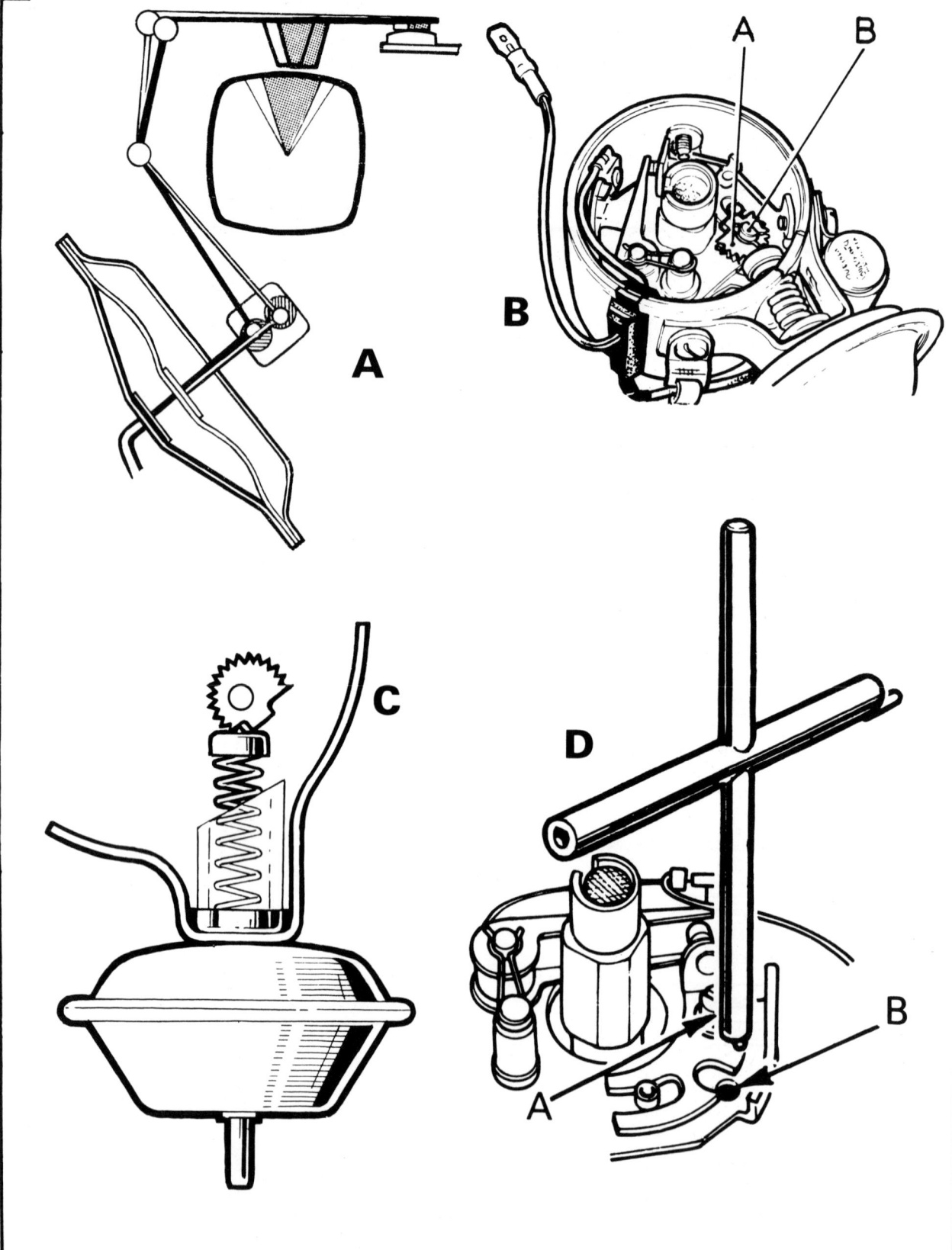

Fig. 13. 30. DETAILS OF THE DUCELLIER DISTRIBUTOR

A Movement of contact breaker arm with operation of the
   vacuum pull rod
B Details of distributor baseplate
   a) serrated cam, b) D post

C Position of serrated cam on pull rod
D Use of special tool to adjust dwell angle
   a) locking screw, b) hole for eccentric on special tool

20 Refit the coil spring in the groove by winding it over the dog.

21 Fit the slipper, with the step uppermost, and spring into the groove in the base plate. Align the base plate lugs with the securing screw holes, depress the slipper and fit the base plate into the body.

22 Lubricate the lever arm pivot with engine oil and place the lever arm in position, engaging the cam with the aperture in the base plate. Lubricate the 'D' shaped post with engine oil.

23 Fit the serrated cam over the pull rod of the vacuum capsule with the cam in the minimum tension position, serrated teeth to the left as viewed from above and the hole offset toward the vacuum unit (see Fig. 13.30c).

24 Align the long edge of the dust cover and the long arm of the vacuum unit. Insert the pull rod and cam through the hole in the body and engage them with the 'D' shaped post on the lever arm.

25 Fit the vacuum unit securing screws, together with the condenser and second cap clip and tighten the screws.

26 Refit the fixed contact to the base plate and lightly tighten the securing screw. Lubricate the moving contact pivot with engine oil. Fit the moving contact onto the post and engage the spring with the insulator. Fit the insulating washer and spring clip.

27 Refit the LT insulator into the distributor and insert the condenser lead. Fit the clip to the 'D' shaped post.

28 Soak the felt pad in engine oil, squeeze out the excess and fit to the top of the shaft.

29 Before the final adjustment can take place refitted to the engine using the dwell meter, some preliminary adjustments must be made. Rotate the 'D' shaped post until the moving contact point is central upon the fixed contact. Turn the serrated cam anti-clockwise six clicks from the installed position, and adjust the points gap to 0.016 in (0.4 mm).

30 Refit the distributor to the engine and adjust, if necessary, to obtain the correct dwell angle as described in Section 10. As the distributor has been completely stripped, it will be necessary to check the mechanical efficiency of the distributor.

31 With the engine running, the dwell meter connected and the vacuum pipe disconnected, increase the engine speed to 2,000 rpm and note the dwell angle. It should be within the limits described in Section 10. Any reading outside of these figures indicates a mechanical fault within the distributor.

32 To check for dwell variation with vacuum advance, reconnect the vacuum pipe and accelerate the engine quickly from idling speed to 2,000 rpm, release the throttle and note the dwell angle reading. It must not exceed a $+ 0^O - 2^O$ variation, if it does, rotate the 'D' post in very small amounts to obtain the correct setting.

33 Finally, recheck the dwell angle as described in Section 10.

5 Clutch

1 Laycock clutch - general description

1 The Laycock clutch fitted to some models differs from the Borg and Beck clutch in the manner by which the diaphragm is coupled to the pressure plate.

2 With Borg and Beck clutches, drive is transmitted via straps which are rivetted to the pressure plate and clipped to the diaphragm. The pressure plate on the Laycock clutch has lugs which locate through a driving plate and which houses the diaphragm.

3 In all other respects the clutch and actuating mechanism are similar.

2 Laycock clutch - removal, inspection, renovation and replacement

1 The procedure for removal, inspection, renovation and replacement is similar to that detailed in Chapter 5.

6A Manual gearbox

1 Gearbox - general note

1 On some gearboxes, the 3rd/4th selector fork has been modified (see Fig. 13.33). This does not affect the assembly procedure.

2 With the modified 3rd/4th selector fork, a modified oil shield (splash plate) is fitted beneath the gearbox top cover. This does not affect the assembly procedure, but the 3rd/4th selector fork can only be used with the appropriate type of oil shield and vice versa.

2 Mainshaft assembly - removal

Modifications were carried out to later type gearboxes and the details are as follows.

1 Remove the top cover, overdrive or rear cover, front cover assembly and selectors as described in Chapter 6.

2 Remove the speedo drive wheel or, on overdrive models, the pump drive cam. On earlier cars, this entails removing two circlips, wheel and key. Later cars have a modified mainshaft and speedo wheel together with a retaining ring, which supersedes the two circlips and key. The overdrive pump cam is unchanged.

3 To remove the speedo wheel on later model gearboxes, tap the wheel and retaining ring forwards, using a piece of tubing as a drift, until it reaches the narrow portion of the mainshaft. Remove the retaining ring from the speedo wheel and then separately remove the wheel and retaining ring from the mainshaft.

4 To refit the later type speedo wheel, note the register at one end of the internal bore of the wheel. Fit the retaining ring, followed by the wheel, with the register facing rearwards, over the splines of the mainshaft. Refit the retaining ring into the bore of the wheel until it contacts the register mark. Drive on the wheel assembly using the tubing again as a drift.

6B Overdrive

2 Type D overdrive - general description

1 The overdrive unit is attached to the extension on the rear of the gearbox by eight studs and nuts, and takes the form of a hydraulically operated epicylic gear. Overdrive operates on third and fourth speeds to provide fast cruising at lower engine revolutions. The overdrive 'IN—OUT' switch on the left of the steering wheel actuates a solenoid attached to the side of the overdrive unit. In turn the solenoid operates a valve which opens the hydraulic circuit which pushes the cone clutch into contact with the annulus when overdrive is engaged.

2 Attached to the end of the extended gearbox mainshaft are the inner components of a unidirectional clutch. The hydraulic pressure which enables the overdrive clutch to be engaged is provided by a hydraulic pump operated by an eccentric cam on the front of the mainshaft.

3 Behind the cam is a steady bearing with a plain phosphor-bronze bush carried in the main housing. Next to this is the sun wheel of the epicyclic gear which is carried on a Clevite bush. The planet carrier and unidirectional clutch come next and are mounted on splines cut in the mainshaft. The smaller diameter portion of the end of the mainshaft turns in a needle roller bearing fitted inside the larger diameter output shaft.

4 Two roller bearings mounted in the rear of the overdrive casing support the output shaft. A ball bearing housed in a flanged ring is held to the cone clutch member. A bolt at each of the four corners of the flange passes through one of the four clutch return springs by which the ring, together with the clutch cone, is held against the annulus.

5 The pressure of the springs prevents free-wheeling on overrun, and they are also strong enough to handle reverse torque. Also attached to the bolts are two bridge pieces which rest against two hydraulic operating pistons working in cylinders

cast in the main casing.

6 The sun wheel and pinions are case hardened and the annulus heat treated. The pinions have needle roller bearings and run on case hardened pins. The gearteeth are helical. The outer ring of the unidirectional clutch is pressed into the annulus. The clutch is of the caged roller type and is loaded by a round wire lock type spring.

7 The overdrive unit works in the following way. Under normal running conditions with the overdrive switched out the cone clutch is held against the centre annulus by the four clutch return springs, so locking the sun wheel to the annulus. In this way the complete gear train rotates together as a solid unit giving direct drive.

8 On switching in the electrically operated solenoid, the centre rod moves inwards, operating the linkage mechanism which lifts a tube, so raising the ball valve off its seating against the pressure of the spring which normally holds the ball in place.

9 With the ball valve lifted, oil, under pressure, is free to travel along the drillings in the casing to the two operating cylinders. The pistons are pushed forward against the two bridge pieces which move the clutch cone into contact with the cast iron brake ring sandwiched between the main and tail casings. This brings the sun wheel to rest and allows the annulus to overrun the unidirectional clutch and so give an increased speed to the output shaft.

10 When the overdrive is switched out the rod in the centre of the solenoid moves outwards, allowing the valve tube to drop and the ball valve to return to its seat. Oil from the two cylinders is then free to return through the centre of the tube to the bottom of the overdrive casing. To ensure direct drive is re-engaged smoothly, the cylinders are emptied slowly because of a small restrictor jet in the base of the valve tube. The oil is then free to flow round in open circuit.

11 The oil for the hydraulic system is supplied by a pump which is pressed into the main housing and held by a grub screw. The pump supplies oil through a non-return valve to a relief valve, in which a piston moves back against a compression spring, until the correct pressure is obtained when a hole in the relief valve is uncovered. Excess oil from the relief valve is then led through drilled passages to an annular groove in the mainshaft steady bush. Radial holes in the shaft feed oil, through axial drillings, to the needle roller bearings, thrust washers and unidirectional clutch.

12 The overdrive is normally a very reliable unit and trouble is usually due to either the solenoid sticking, a fault in the hydraulic system due to dirt or insufficient oil, or incorrect solenoid operating lever adjustment.

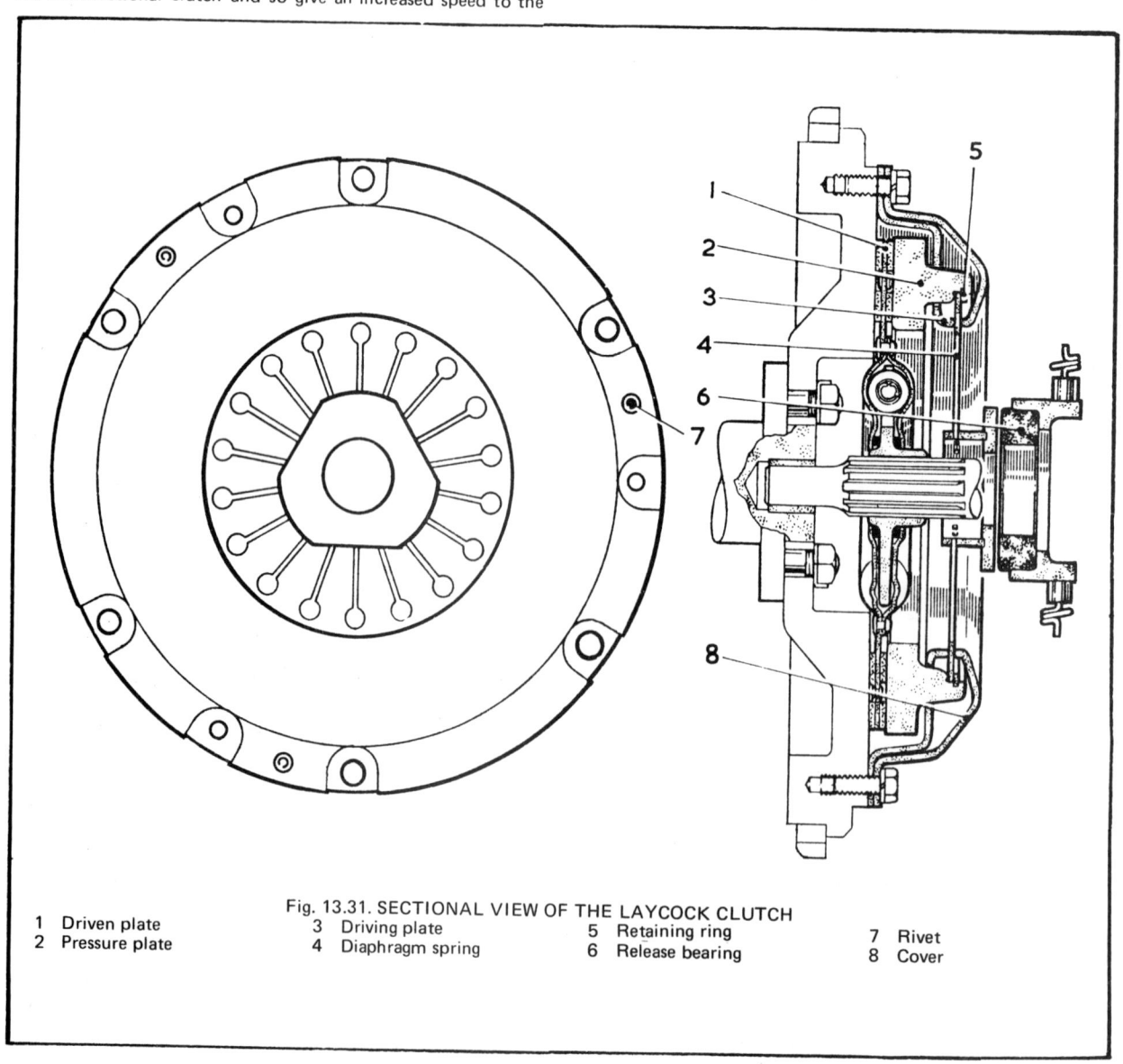

Fig. 13.31. SECTIONAL VIEW OF THE LAYCOCK CLUTCH

| 1 Driven plate | 3 Driving plate | 5 Retaining ring | 7 Rivet |
| 2 Pressure plate | 4 Diaphragm spring | 6 Release bearing | 8 Cover |

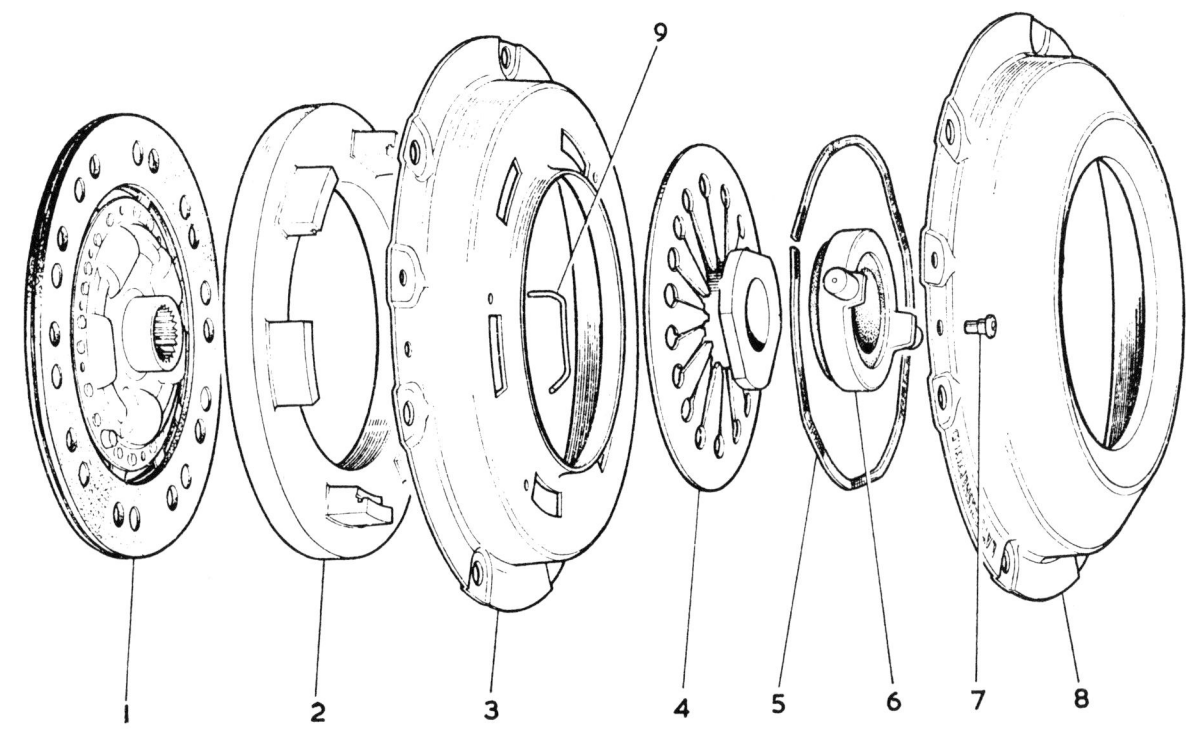

Fig. 13.32. EXPLODED VIEW OF THE LAYCOCK CLUTCH

1 Driven plate	3 Driving plate	5 Retaining ring
2 Pressure plate	4 Diaphragm spring	6 Release bearing

7 Rivet
8 Cover
9 Spring clip

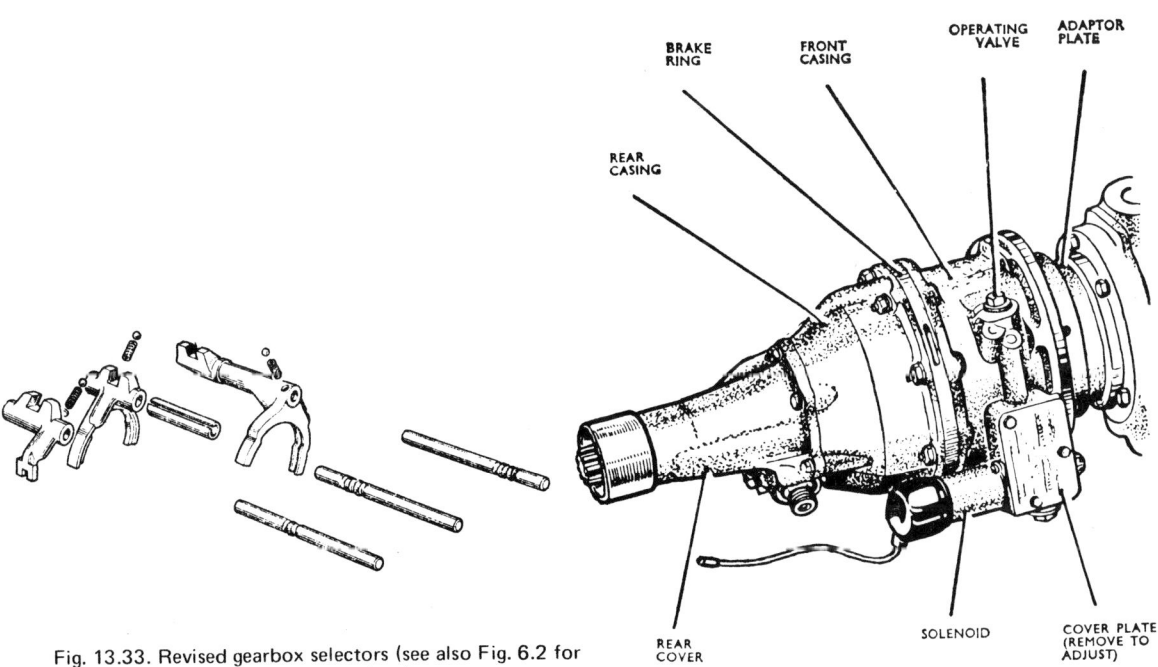

Fig. 13.33. Revised gearbox selectors (see also Fig. 6.2 for comparison)

BRAKE RING
FRONT CASING
OPERATING VALVE
ADAPTOR PLATE
REAR CASING
REAR COVER
SOLENOID
COVER PLATE (REMOVE TO ADJUST)

Fig. 13.34. General view of the type D overdrive unit

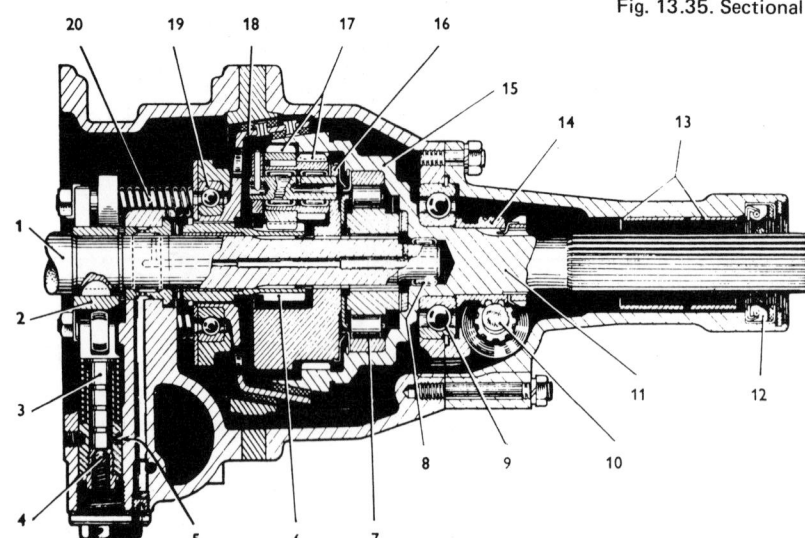

Fig. 13.35. Sectional view of the type D overdrive unit

1 Input shaft
2 Pump cam
3 Oil pump
4 Pump valve
5 Pump inlet
6 Sunwheel
7 Unidirectional clutch
  (splined to input shaft)
8 Spigot bearing
9 Rear bearing
10 Speedometer pinion
11 Output shaft (integral with
   annulus)
12 Oil seal
13 Support bushes
14 Speedometer wheel
15 Annulus
16 Planet carrier
17 Planet wheel
18 Cone clutch
19 Clutch thrust bearing
20 Clutch spring

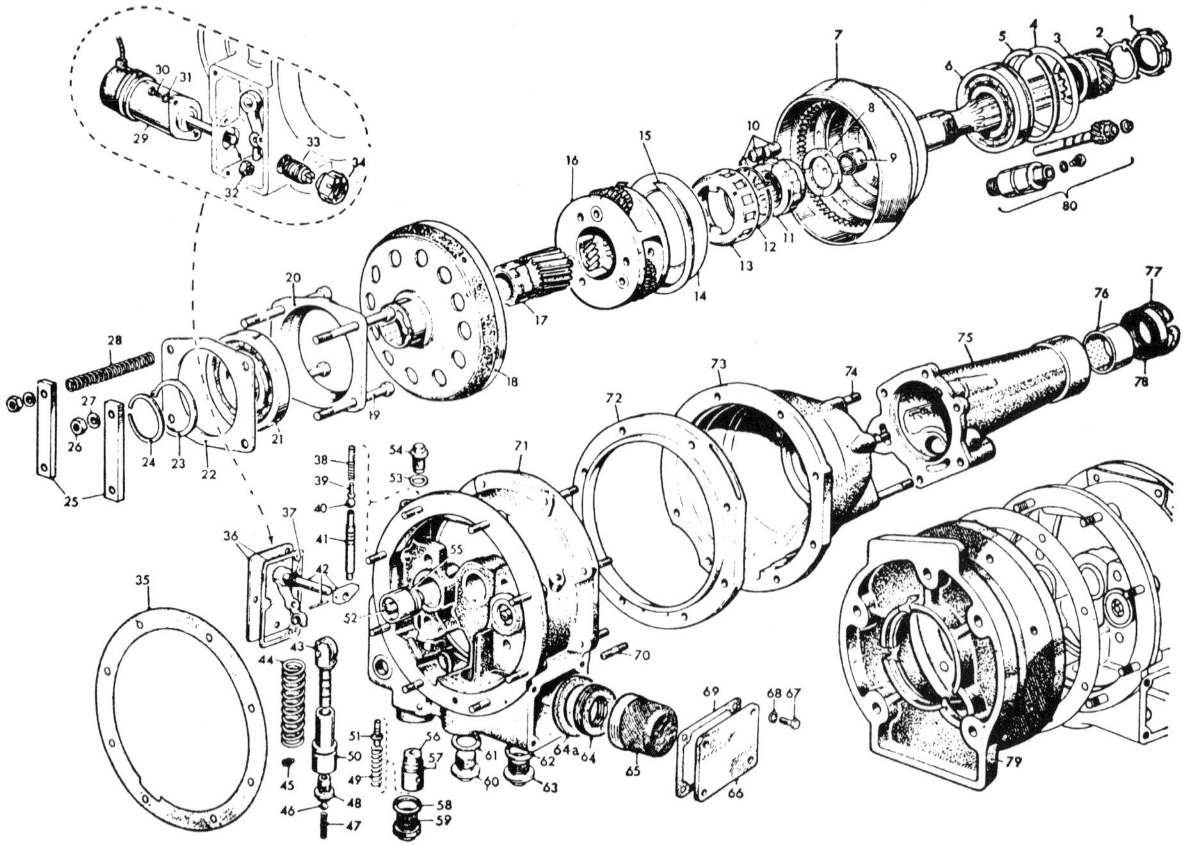

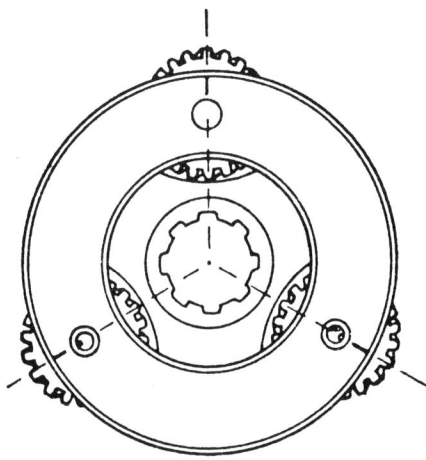

Fig. 13.37. Aligning the planet gearwheels on the type D overdrive unit

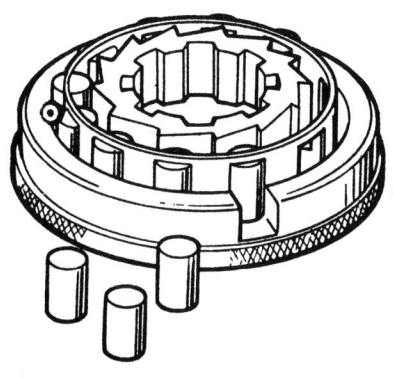

Fig. 13.38. Assembling the uni-directional clutch using tool L178 or L178A

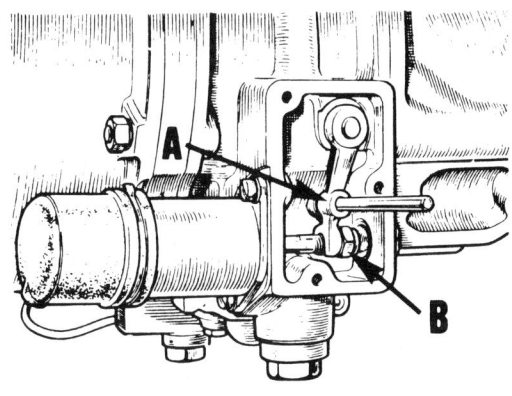

Fig. 13.39. Checking the adjustment of the operating plunger

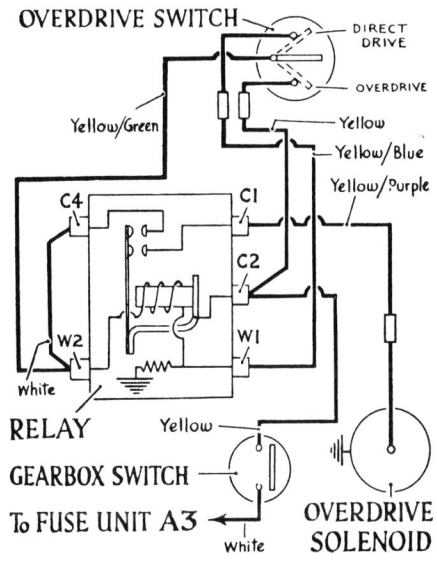

Fig. 13.40. Type D overdrive circuit diagram

Fig. 13.36. EXPLODED VIEW OF THE TYPE D OVERDRIVE UNIT

1	Locknut	28	Spring	55	Piston ring (rubber)
2	Tabwasher	29	Solenoid	56	Relief valve body
3	Speedometer wheel	30	Set screw	57	Rubber ring
4	Shim	31	Washer	58	Washer
5	Circlip	32	Nut - solenoid to valve lever	59	Plug
6	Rear bearing	33	Stop pad) solenoid and valve	60	Cover plug
7	Annulus	34	Locknut) lever adjustment	61	Washer
8	Thrust washer	35	Joint ring	62	Washer
9	Mainshaft bearing	36	Valve lever cover	63	Drain plug
10	Rollers)	37	Sealing ring-operating shaft	64	Ring magnets
11	Ratchet) free	38	Spring)	64a	Sealing ring
12	Circlip)	39	Plunger) Operating valve	65	Filter
13	Roller cage)	40	Ball)	66	Filter cover plate
14	Retaining plate	41	Operating valve	67	Set screw
15	Circlip	42	Operating lever assembly	68	Washer
16	Planet carrier with wheels	43	Plunger	69	Filter cover plate joint
17	Sunwheel	44	Spring	70	Stud - front to rear casing
18	Clutch cone	45	Pump body retaining screw	71	Front casing
19	Bolt	46	Ball	72	Brake ring
20	Bearing housing	47	Spring	73	Rear casing
21	Bearing	48	Valve body	74	Stud - rear casing to rear cover
22	Retainer plate	49	Spring	75	Rear cover
23	Circlip	50	Pump body	76	Bush
24	Snap ring)	51	Plunger	77	Circlip
25	Bridge plates) Clutch	52	Operating piston	78	Rear oil seal
26	Nut) release	53	Washer	79	Gearbox adaptor
27	Tab washer)	54	Plug	80	Speedometer drive assembly

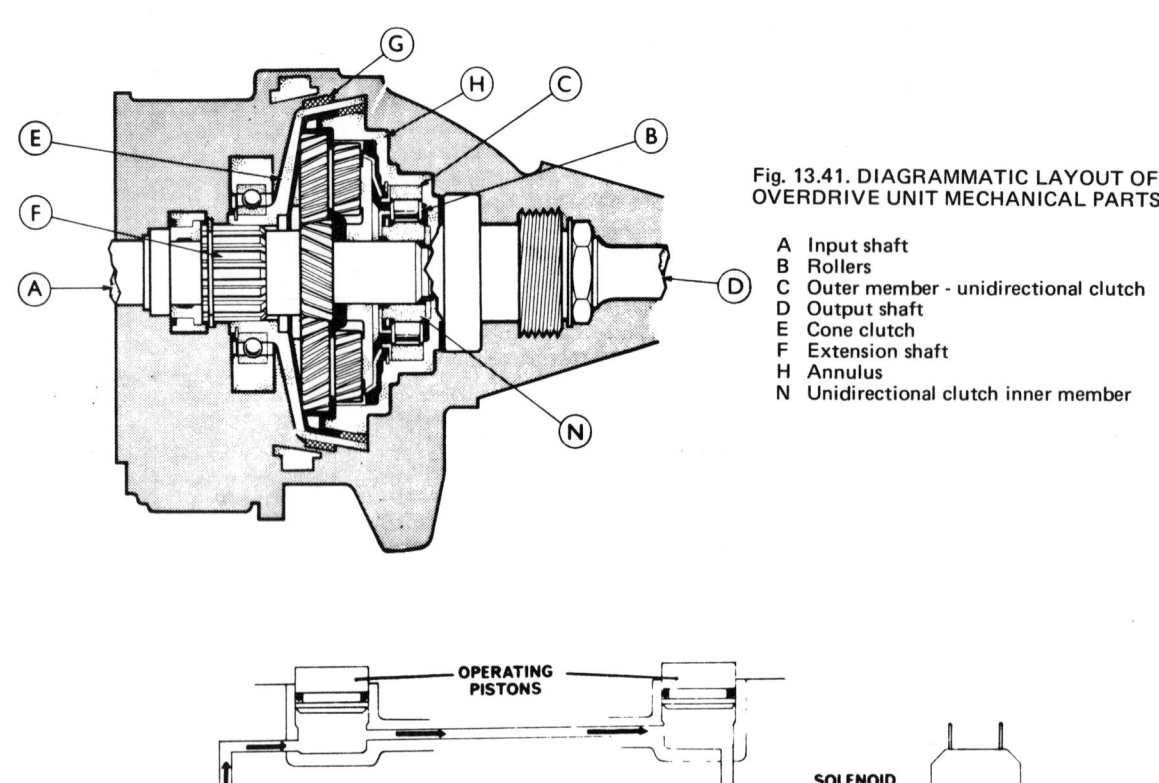

Fig. 13.41. DIAGRAMMATIC LAYOUT OF OVERDRIVE UNIT MECHANICAL PARTS

A   Input shaft
B   Rollers
C   Outer member - unidirectional clutch
D   Output shaft
E   Cone clutch
F   Extension shaft
H   Annulus
N   Unidirectional clutch inner member

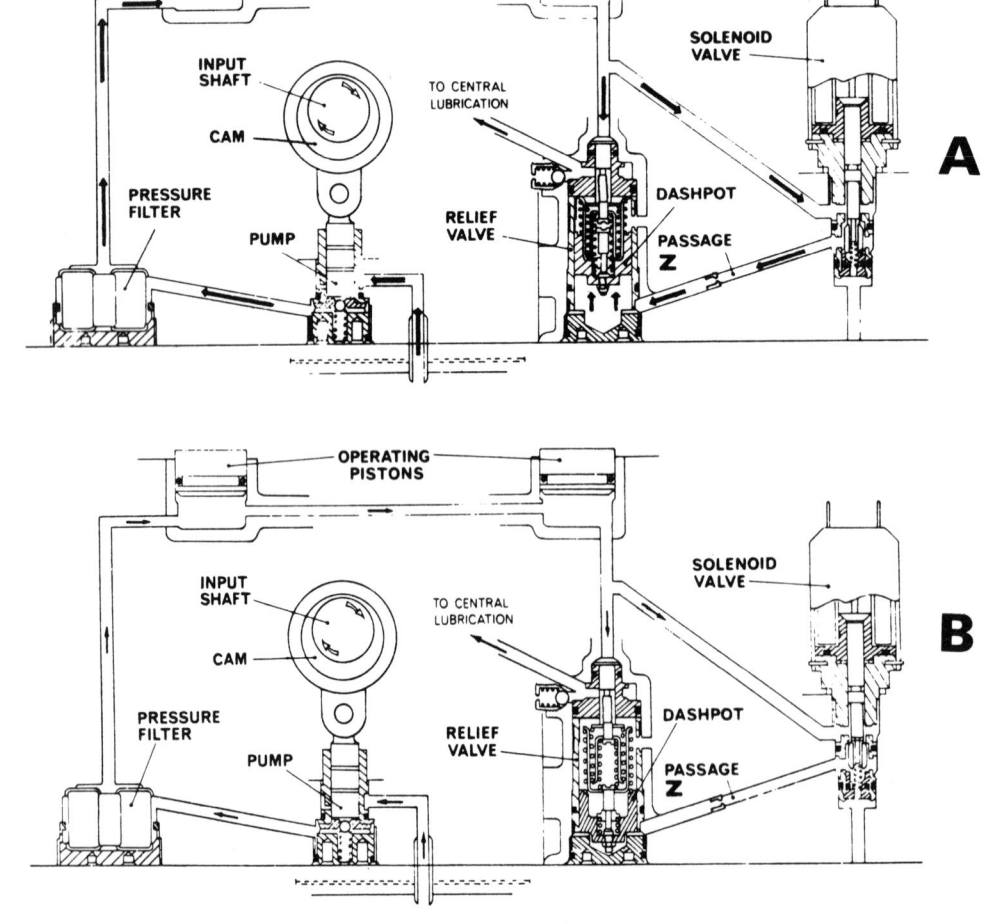

Fig. 13.42. TYPE J OVERDRIVE HYDRAULIC CIRCUIT
A Overdrive   B Direct drive

3 Type D overdrive - removal and refitting

1 It is not necessary to remove the overdrive from the car in order to attend to the following: the hydraulic lever setting; the relief valve; the non-return valve; the solenoid and the operating valve.

2 The overdrive unit can be removed from the car as a separate item if the gearbox is not requiring attention.

3 Remove the gearbox top cover and remote control assembly as described in Chapter 6, Section 4, paragraph 2. **Note:** carry out the operation in paragraph 4 first, if a pit is to be used.

4 Place the car over a pit or raise it on axle stands to provide the maximum possible working space beneath.

5 Drain the oil from the overdrive unit and gearbox.

6 Remove the propeller shaft. Refer to Chapter 7 or the Propeller Shaft Section of this Chapter, as appropriate.

7 Unscrew the speedometer drive from the overdrive rear cover.

8 Disconnect the snap connectors to the overdrive solenoid.

9 Refer to the procedure given in Section 3 of Chapter 6, and lower the gearbox sufficiently to allow eventual withdrawal of the overdrive. **Note:** there is no intention of removing the gearbox unless specifically required.

10 Remove the eight nuts from the overdrive/gearbox retaining studs then carefully pull the overdrive off the end of the mainshaft.

11 To mate the overdrive and gearbox, start by placing the overdrive in an upright position and then line up the splines of the clutch and planet carrier by eye, turning them anticlockwise only, with the aid of a long thin screwdriver.

12 Under normal circumstances, if everything is in line, the gearbox mainshaft should enter the overdrive easily. If trouble is experienced, do not try and force the components together but separate them and re-align the components. Place the gearbox in top gear while refitting.

13 As the mainshaft is fed into the overdrive gently, rotate the input shaft to and fro to help 'feed-in' the mainshaft into the splines. At the same time make certain that the lowest portion of the cam on the mainshaft will rest against the pump. Also take care, as the gearbox extension and overdrive come together, that the end of the mainshaft enters into the needle roller bearing in the tail shaft.

14 The remainder of the replacement procedure is a straightforward reversal of the removal sequence.

4 Type D overdrive - dismantling, overhaul and reassembly

1 All numbers in brackets in this Section refer to Fig. 13.36. Unscrew the operating valve plug (54) and take out the spring (38), plunger (39) and ball (40).

2 Undo the nuts (26) from off the bolts (19), then remove the two bridge pieces (25). If wished, the two operating pistons (52) can now be pulled out of their cylinders in the main casing assembly (71).

3 Cut the locking wire (if fitted) on the non-return relief valve plug (59); undo the plug and remove the spring (47) and ball (46). The non-return valve body (48) can then be unscrewed from the pump body (50). Undo the grub screw (45) and pull the pump body (50) from the casing (71).

4 Undo the eight nuts and spring washers a turn at a time from the studs (70) which hold the main casing assembly (71) to the rear casing (73). As the nuts are undone the pressure of the springs (28) will gradually be released. Take off the main casing (71) together with the brake ring (72) and pull the four clutch springs (28) off their guide bolts (19). Remove the clutch (18) together with the sun wheel assembly (17).

5 It is likely that the brake ring (72) will stick to the casing (71). To separate the ring, gently tap it on its flange with a soft faced hammer.

6 To free the sun wheel (17) from the centre of the clutch assembly, (18) release the circlip (24) on the splined end of the sun wheel and push out the sun wheel (17).

7 Remove the large circlip (23) with a pair of circlip pliers, and pull the bearing housing (20), complete with thrust bearing (21), off the clutch assembly (18).

8 Lift out the planet carrier (16) from the annulus (7). Removal of the unidirectional roller clutch is not recommended, unless the rollers are thought to be chipped or worn, but if it is wished to do so, take off the circlip and brass retaining washer in front of the clutch.

9 As the inner member (11) is removed, the roller bearings (10) will fall out. Gather them together carefully. On no account should the outer bearing ring be removed as it is expanded into the annulus.

10 If it is wished to renew the roller bearing (9) in the centre of the annulus (7), carefully lever it out or use an extractor if available.

11 To remove the combined output shaft and annulus (7) from the rear casing, first undo the locking screw to free the speedometer pinion and bush (80), then remove the tailshaft casing (75) from the rear casing (73) by undoing the six retaining nuts. When sliding off the tailshaft casing take care not to damage the oil seal (78) and bush (76).

12 Remove any shims (4) between the tailshaft cover and the annulus main bearing (6). Remove the circlip (5) from round the bearing (6) and remove the annulus (7) and bearing (6) by driving them forward into the rear casing (73).

13 To remove the rear bearing (6), knock back the lockwasher (2), undo the locknut (1) and slide off the speedometer drive gear (3) and the bearing (6).

14 Thoroughly clean all component parts and then examine them carefully. Check that the oil pump plunger and pin are not worn and that the spring has not contracted. Examine the 'O' rings from the operating pistons and renew them if worn, or if they are becoming hard, and check that the cylinder bores are free from score marks and wear. Check the ball bearings for roughness when turned and for looseness between the inner and outer races. Examine the splines for burrs and wear, and the rollers of the clutch for chips and flat spots.

15 Renew the clutch linings if they are burnt or worn, and carefully examine the main and rear casings for cracks or other damage. Renew the steady bush if it is worn, and examine the gear teeth for cracks, chips and general wear. Examine the sealing balls for ridges which will prevent them seating properly and check the free length of the springs.

16 Assembly of the unit can commence after any damaged or worn parts have been exchanged and new gaskets and seals obtained. Start by fitting the rear bearing (6) with its circlip groove to the rear over the output shaft. Drive the bearing with a piece of pipe into its correct position against the locating shoulder behind the annulus.

17 Fit the speedometer gear (3), the lockwasher (2) and the locknut (1). Now fit the annulus assembly (7) into the rear casing (73) and fit the circlip (5) into its groove in the bearing (6).

18 The bearing (6) is located at the rear of the tailshaft cover (75) and a shim or shims (4) is fitted into the recess in the cover to ensure a snug fit with a correct endfloat of the output shaft of 0.005 to 0.010 in (0.127 to 0.254 mm).

19 If it was necessary to fit a new bearing, note that four different thicknesses of shim are available. Shims can be obtained in the following sizes:

    0.090 in (2.28 mm); 0.095 in (2.41 mm);
    0.100 in (2.54 mm) and 0.105 in (2.67 mm)

20 Refit the tailshaft cover (75) and secure it with the six nuts. Insert the speedometer drive and pinion (80) and secure it with its washer and locking screw.

21 Reassemble the components of the unidirectional clutch, holding the rollers (10) in place in the cage (13) with grease prior to fitting the inner member (11). Ensure that the circlip (12) is fitted in such a way that it pushes the rollers up the ramp on the inner member (11). Do not omit to replace the thrust bearing (8). Finally, fit the retaining plate (14) and circlip (15) in place.

This job will be simplified if tool number L178 is available. See Fig. 13.44.

22 Turn each of the planet gearwheels so that the line etched on one tooth of each of the gearwheels lines up with one of the three corresponding lines on the periphery of the planet carrier (see Fig. 13.37). Insert the sun wheel (17) into the carrier to keep the planet gearwheels in the correct positions, and carefully fit the complete sun wheel and carrier assembly to the annulus. When fitted, the sun wheel can be withdrawn. Note that the sun wheel can now be inserted or removed as frequently as required, but if the planet carrier is removed from the annulus, the carrier gearwheels will have to be reset as described at the beginning of the paragraph.

23 Slide the splined end of the sun wheel (17) into the centre of the clutch assembly and secure the sun wheel with the circlip (24). If the thrust bearing was removed for renewal, press the new bearing (21) into its housing (20). Insert the four bolts (19) into the housing, threaded ends facing forwards, and fit the bearing and housing assembly over the centre of the clutch assembly (18). Lock the bearing and housing in place on the clutch with the bearing retaining circlip (23) which fits in a groove on the clutch.

24 Carefully fit the clutch and sun wheel assembly to the planet carrier in the annulus. Refit the retainer plate (22) and clutch springs (28) over the bolts (19).

25 Coat the mating faces of the main casing (71) and rear casing (73) with jointing compound, and offer up the rear casing to the brake ring and front casing. Slide the four bolts (19) through their holes in the main casing and replace and tighten down a turn at a time, the nuts and washers which hold the casings together.

26 Fit the rubber 'O' rings (55) to the two operating pistons (52) and with the pistons generously lubricated with oil, slide them into their cylinders in the housing, so the spigoted ends face the front of the overdrive assembly. Slip the two bridge pieces (25) over the ends of the four bolts (19) and refit the nuts and washers (26, 27) and tighten them down.

27 Replace the oil pump body, smaller end first, into the centre hole at the bottom of the casing, making sure that the oil inlet faces the rear. Gently tap it into position until the groove lines up with the grub screw hole. Fit and tighten the grub screw.

28 Refit the component parts of the relief valve, operating valve, and non-return valve in the order shown in Fig. 13.36, and do up the three plugs. Do not fit the operating lever cover plate until adjusted (see next Section) after fitting the unit to the car.

5 Type D overdrive operating lever - adjustment

1 If the overdrive does not engage, or will not release when it is switched out, providing the solenoid is not at fault, the trouble is likely to be that the operating lever is out of adjustment. Adjustment can be made without removing the overdrive.

2 Undo the three bolts and washers holding the solenoid cover plate in position, to give access to the operating lever and solenoid plunger.

3 Procure a short length of mild steel rod of 3/16 in (4.76 mm) diameter. Switch the ignition on, put the car in top gear, and flick the actuating switch to the overdrive position.

4 If the rod can now be passed through the hole 'A' in the operating arm (see Fig. 13.39) into the hole in the casing, adjustment is correct.

5 If the solenoid does not move the arm far enough for the rod to be inserted, or if it moves the arm too far, hold the solenoid plunger from turning by means of the two flats machined on its shank, and pressing the plunger tightly into the solenoid, screw the self locking nut 'B' (Fig. 13.39) in or out until the test rod can be pushed fully home into the hole in the casing.

6 Operate the switch several times, checking with the test rod to ensure adjustment is correct. Measure the current consumed by the solenoid which, with the operating arm correctly set, should be 2 amps. If a reading of about 17 amps is obtained this shows that the solenoid plunger is not moving sufficiently to switch to the holding coil from the operating coil. If very fine adjustment will not remedy this condition, fit a new solenoid and plunger.

6 Type D overdrive relief valve, non-return valve and operating valve - removal, inspection and replacement

1 Access to the relief and non-return valves located in the bottom of the overdrive is gained after removing the engine steady rod and bracket from the rear crossmember. Drain the oil from the gearbox and overdrive.

2 Cut through the locking wire, unscrew the plugs and remove and clean the components. Note that the valve cap and non-return valve body are unscrewed from the pump, and that the relief valve body is removed with circlip pliers.

3 Examine the seatings for pits or chips, and the balls for wear and ridges. The steel ball in the non-return valve is very hard and if the ball is undamaged and the seating is suspect tap the ball firmly into its seat with a soft metal drift.

4 Reassembly is a straightforward reversal of the removal sequence. Do not omit to fit the copper washer on the relief valve between the cap and main casing, and hold the non-return valve ball to its spring with petroleum jelly during refitment.

5 Access to the operating valve can only be gained after removing the remote control assembly from inside the car. Undo the plug and check that the ball is lifted 1/32 in (0.79 mm) when the solenoid is actuated. Failure to move points to a fault in the solenoid or operating arm.

6 The ball can be removed with a magnet and the valve with a piece of 1/8 in (3.1 mm) wire. Check the ball and seat and clean out the small hole in the side of the valve tube. Check if the oil pump is working by jacking the rear of the car off the ground and placing the car in top gear. Engage overdrive and with the engine running, watch and see if oil is being pumped into the valve chamber. Replacement is a reversal of the removal procedure.

7 Type D overdrive - routine maintenance

1 With regard to topping up the oil level and renewal of the oil, the same service intervals and procedures apply as for the manual gearbox (see Chapter 6.).

2 When the oil is to be renewed, the filter unit must be removed and cleaned. To do this unscrew the four retaining bolts then take off the cover plate and gasket. Clean the filter in paraffin and dry thoroughly, before reassembling. Ensure the three magnetic rings are fitted into the filter, followed by the large diameter sealing ring. This is to be fitted with its rubber face towards the filter.

8 Type D overdrive - fault finding chart

Symptom	Possible cause
Overdrive will not engage	Solenoid faulty. Selector mechanism requires adjustment.

	Oil level in unit tol low.
	Relief valve faulty.
	Internal hydraulic leakage.
	Operating valve faulty.
	Non-return valve faulty.
	Hydraulic pump faulty.
	Damaged gears, bearings or moving parts.
Overdrive will not release	Wiring fault.
Note: If this occurs immediate attention is required to preclude damage	Selector mechanism requires adjustment.
	Restrictor jet blocked in operating valve.
Do **not** select reverse gear	Clutch sticking.
	Solenoid stop incorrectly adjusted.
	Damaged internal parts.
Overdrive clutch slipping	Oil level in unit too low.
	Selector mechanism requires adjustment.
	Internal hydraulic leakage.
	Foreign matter in valves.
	Clutch linings worn or carbonised.
Free wheeling on overrun or clutch slipping in reverse	Selector mechanism requires adjustment.
	Clutch linings worn or carbonised.
	Restrictor jet blocked in operating valve.
	Clutch springs broken.
	Solenoid stop incorrectly adjusted.

9   Type J overdrive - general description

1   The type J overdrive unit takes the form of a hydraulically operated epicyclic gear which operates on third and top gears to provide fast cruising at lower engine revolutions. The overdrive is engaged or disengaged by a driver controlled switch which controls an electric solenoid mounted on the overdrive unit. A further switch called an inhibitor switch is included in the electrical circuit to prevent accidental engagement of overdrive in reverse, first or second gears.

The overdrive unit is designed to be engaged or disengaged, when engine power is being transmitted through the power line and also, without the use of the clutch pedal at any throttle opening or road speed. It is important that the overdrive is not disengaged at high road speeds as this will cause excessively high engine speeds.

It will be seen from Fig. 13.41 that the overdrive gears are epicyclic and comprise a central sun wheel which is in mesh with three planet wheels. These three gears are also in mesh with an internally toothed annulus. The planet carrier is splined to the input shaft which is, in fact, the mainshaft of the manual gearbox. The annulus is an integral part of the output shaft.

When the overdrive is disengaged the engine torque is transmitted from the input shaft (A) (Fig. 13.41) to the inner member of an unidirectional clutch (N) and then onto the outer member of the clutch (C), via rollers (B), which are driven up inclined faces, and wedge or lock the inner and outer members. The outer member of the clutch (C) forms part of the combined annulus (H) and the output shaft (D). Thus, as the gear train is not operative, the drive is direct through the overdrive unit.

Mounted on the externally splined extension shaft (Γ) of the sun gear is a cone clutch (E) and this is pressed onto the annulus by a number of springs which press against the overdrive unit casing. The spring pressure is transmitted to the clutch member by a thrust ring and ball bearing, so causing the inner friction lining of the cone clutch to be in contact with the outer cone of the annulus (H) and rotate with the annulus whilst the springs and thrust ring remain stationary.

As the sun wheel is splined to the clutch member, the whole gear train is locked together so permitting over-run and engine torque in reverse gear to be transmitted through the overdrive unit. Also, an additional load is imparted to the clutch during over-run and reverse conditions by the sun wheel, which, due to the special helix angle of the gear teeth, thrusts rearwards and has for its reaction member the cone clutch.

When the overdrive unit is engaged, the cone clutch takes up a new position, whereby it is no longer in contact with the annulus, but has moved forward, so that its outer friction lining is in contact with the brake ring which is part of the overdrive unit casing. The sun wheel to which the clutch is attached is now held still. The planet carrier rotates with the input shaft (A) and the three planet wheels are caused to rotate about their own axis and drive the annulus at a greater speed than the input shaft. This is made possible because the unidirectional clutch outer member can over run the inner member. Hydraulic pressure generated by a pump in the overdrive unit acts on two pistons when a little valve is opened and moves the cone clutch in a forward direction. The little valve is controlled by the solenoid which is operated by the driver using an electric switch. This hydraulic pressure is sufficient to overcome the spring pressure that holds the clutch member onto the annulus, and cause the clutch to engage with the brake ring and hold the sunwheel at rest. As the overdrive unit is attached to the rear of the gearbox, it is able to share the oil in the gearbox. The cam operated plunger pump draws the oil from the overdrive oil sump and, via drillings, passes it to the two operating piston chambers, the ball type operating valve and the pressure relief valve. Oil is also passed to various other parts of the overdrive unit for lubrication purposes.

When the driver moves the overdrive switch to the 'engaged' position, current passes to the solenoid and causes the operating valve to close. Pressure built up in the hydraulic system causes the two pistons to move against the action of the springs which hold the sliding member onto the annulus. Therefore, the sliding member is moved into contact with the brake ring.

Oil is then continued to be pumped into the hydraulic operating system, so compressing the modulator springs that are inside the pistons, resulting in a cushioning effect by the progressive application of the load between the sliding member and the brake ring. As the sunwheel is now in a locked condition and the planet gears are free to revolve, the overdrive condition is in existence. Any further delivery of oil will open the pressure relief valve which will allow oil to pass to the various components for lubrication purposes and then return to the overdrive oil sump.

When the driver moves the overdrive switch to the 'disengaged' position, current will cease to flow to the solenoid and the operating valve ball will be unseated by hydraulic pressure, so uncovering the exhaust port. The spring load on the sliding member will force oil to pass from the piston chambers whilst, at the same time, oil will continue to be pumped into the circuit, and, with the two circuits connected, allowing mixing of the two oil flows, causing action against each other, will control the movement of the sliding member. The sliding member is, therefore, disengaged from the brake ring and this time engaged with the annulus at a controlled rate. The oil flow will then pass through the exhaust port and provide lubrication for the various internal parts.

10 Type J overdrive - removal and refitting

1 Before beginning the sequence to remove the overdrive unit it is necessary to drive the vehicle and engage overdrive and then disengage with the clutch depressed. This will release the spline loading between the planet carrier and unidirectional clutch which can make removal difficult.

2 The procedure for removal of the type J overdrive is similar to that for the type D overdrive previously described, but in addition it is recommended that the battery earth lead is temporarily removed.

3 When refitting the overdrive, first rotate the gearbox mainshaft until the cam is at its lowest point which will coincide with the pump strap when the two units are fitted together.

4 Check that the planet carrier retaining clip is in position on the mainshaft and then, to prevent the mainshaft rotating, select first or reverse gear.

5 Fit a new gasket to the front face of the overdrive unit using a non-setting gasket cement.

6 Rotate the overdrive output shaft clockwise whilst applying slight forward pressure until the splines engage as the unit is being offered up to the gearbox. Ensure that the pump strap slides onto the cam smoothly; do not use excessive force.

7 Should it be found that the overdrive unit will not push fully home onto the adaptor plate face but a gap of about 5/8 inch (16 mm) exists, it is an indication that the planet carrier and unidirectional clutch splines have become misaligned. Remove the overdrive unit again and rotate the inner member of the unidirectional clutch in an anti clockwise direction, using a long shaft screwdriver.

8 Replace the eight nuts that secure the overdrive unit to the adaptor plate and tighten in a diagonal manner.

9 The remainder of the replacement procedure is the reverse of the removal procedure.

11 Type J overdrive - dismantling, overhaul and reassembly

Note: Before dismantling the overdrive unit it must be appreciated that special tools are required for certain operations. These are:-

Tool L354A, dowelled plug spanner. A tool of this type is not difficult to make but beware of using a drift to attempt to remove the plugs if the tool is not available since irreparable damage can occur.

Tool L178 or 178A, for assembling unidirectional clutch. It may be possible to dispense with this tool if the clutch rollers are held in position with grease during assembly.

Tool L401A. Removing tool for relief valve body and dashpot sleeve. It is not envisaged that this tool will be readily made.

1 Refer to Fig. 13.43 which shows all the components of the overdrive unit.

2 Using a screwdriver or small chisel, bend back the tab washers that lock the four nuts securing the operating piston bridge pieces and undo the four nuts. Lift away the four nuts and tab washers followed by the two bridge pieces.

3 Undo and remove the six nuts that secure the main casing to the rear casing in a progressive manner as these two parts will be

under the influence of the clutch return spring pressure. Note the position of the copper washers which fit on the two studs at the top of the casing.

4 The main casing complete with brake ring can now be separated from the rear casing. 5

5 Lift out the sliding member assembly complete with the sunwheel followed by the planet carrier assembly. This should be done with care as it is easy to accidentally damage the oil catcher which is located under the planet carrier assembly.

6 To dismantle the main casing and brake ring, first tap the brake ring from its spigot in the main casing using a suitable drift.

7 Using a pair of pliers carefully remove the two operating pistons.

8 Undo and remove the six bolts and spring washers securing the sump to the main casing. Lift away the sump, gasket and suction filler.

9 To remove the relief valve and dashpot assembly a special tool is now necessary. It has a part number of L354A. Remove the relief valve and then withdraw the dashpot piston complete with its component springs and cap, followed by the residual pressure spring. It should be noted that this spring is the only loose spring in the general assembly.

10 The relief valve piston assembly can now be withdrawn, by pulling down carefully, using a pair of pliers.

11 A further special tool is required to remove the relief valve. Using tool number L401A inserted into the now exposed relief valve bore, withdraw the relief valve together with the dashpot sleeve. Take great care not to damage these parts during removal.

12 Using tool number L354S, undo and remove the pump plug taking care not to lose the non-return valve spring and ball bearing.

13 The pump valve seat can now be withdrawn. The pump body will be held in position by its 'O' ring, so, to remove this, hook a piece of wire into the inlet port and draw the assembly downwards.

14 To remove the pressure filter use tool number L401A and unscrew the pressure filter base plug. The filter element will be released with the plug. Note the aluminium washer which locates on the shoulder in the filter bore.

15 Using an 1 inch (25 mm) A/F open ended spanner, unscrew the solenoid control valve. Do not use a wrench on the cylindrical body as it will be irreparably damaged.

16 With a screwdriver, carefully remove the circlip from the sunwheel extension and lift out the sunwheel.

17 Again, using a screwdriver, remove the circlip from its groove on the cone clutch hub and tap the clutch from the thrust ring bearing with a soft-faced hammer.

18 If necessary, the bearing may be removed from its housing using a vice and suitable packing. It will be necessary to remove the larger circlip which retains it before removal commences.

19 Using a screwdriver, remove the circlip which retains the unidirectional clutch. Lift away the oil thrower.

20 Place tool number L178A over the now exposed unidirectional clutch and lift the inner member, complete with rollers, into the special tool. Lift away the bronze thrust washer.

21 Withdraw the speedometer driven gear and bearing.

22 To remove the annulus first drive a centre punch into the welch plug located at the top of the rear casing and lever it out.

23 Using a pair of circlip pliers expand the circlip which secures the annulus bearing.

24 Place the rear casing vertically over supports and with a light blow from a soft-faced mallet on the end of the annulus, drive the annulus complete with bearing downwards from the rear casing.

25 Undo and remove the nut that secures the speedometer driving gear and with the aid of a universal puller withdraw the ball race.

26 The overdrive unit is now fully dismantled and may be inspected for wear.

27 Inspect the teeth and cone surface of the annulus for wear. Check that the unidirectional clutch rollers are not chipped and

that the inner and outer members are free from damage.

28 Examine the spring and cage for distortion. Check that the lubrication port at the rear of the annulus is clear.

29 Inspect the rear casing bush and oil seal for wear or damage.

30 Examine the clutch linings on the sliding member for signs of excessive wear or overheating. Should there be signs of these conditions the whole sliding member assembly must be renewed. It is not possible to fit new linings as these are precision machined after bonding.

31 Make sure that the ball race rotates smoothly as this can be a source of noise when the car is running in direct gear.

32 Inspect the clutch return springs for any signs of distortion, damage or loss of springiness.

33 Check the sunwheel teeth for signs of wear or damage.

34 Inspect the main casing for cracks or damage. Examine the operating cylinder bores for scores or wear. Check the operating pistons for wear and replace the sealing rings if there are any signs of damage.

35 Check the pump plunger assembly and ensure that the strap is a good fit on the mainshaft cam and that there is no excess play between the plunger and strap.

36 Should the pump plunger assembly be worn or damaged, this must be replaced as a complete assembly.

37 With the non-return valve assembly clean, inspect the ball and valve seat and also the 'O' rings for signs of damage.

38 Check the relief valve and dashpot assembly for wear. The pistons must move freely in their respective housings. Ensure that the rings are in good order.

39 Do not dismantle the dashpot and relief valve piston assemblies otherwise the pre-determined spring pressures will be disturbed.

40 Finally, examine the 'O' rings on the solenoid valve for damage, which, if evident, should be renewed, together with the sealing washers.

41 Clean the sump filter in petrol and if any particles are stuck in the gauze, rub with an old toothbrush. Wipe the magnetic plug free of any metallic particles.

42 Reassembly of the unit can commence after any damaged or worn parts have been renewed and new gaskets and seals obtained. Do not use jointing compound during assembly.

43 Fit a new annulus ball race and then position the speedometer driving gear so that the plain portion is facing the ball race. Secure with the nut and a new locking washer. Tighten the nut to a torque wrench setting of 50 to 60 lb f ft (6.910 to 8.28 kg f m).

44 Place the ball race circlip in the rear casing and expand using a pair of circlip pliers.

45 Press the annulus through the circlip and into the casing until the bearing is fully home and the circlip is located in its groove. This must be done carefully so that the rear bush and oil seal are not damaged.

46 Fit a new welch plug and secure by striking lightly in the centre with a suitable size flat-faced punch.

47 Next, position the spring and inner member of the uni-direction clutch in the cage, locating the spring so that the cage is spring loaded in an anticlockwise direction when viewed from the front.

48 Place this assembly onto tool L178A with the open side of the cage uppermost and feed the clutch in, in a clockwise direction, until all the rollers are in place. Refit the bronze thrust washer in the recess in the annulus.

49 Transfer the unidirectional clutch assembly from the special tool into its outer member in the annulus.

50 Re-fit the oil thrower and secure with the circlip. Check that the clutch rotates in an anticlockwise direction only.

51 To assemble the clutch sliding member assembly fit the ball race into its housing and secure with the large circlip.

52 Place this assembly onto the hub of the cone clutch and fit the circlip into its groove.

53 Insert the sunwheel into the hub and refit the circlip onto the sunwheel extension.

54 Lightly smear the operating pistons with oil and refit to the main casing.

55 Place a new gasket into the main casing and fit the brake ring, ensuring it is fully home on its spigot location.

56 Before refitting the relief valve and dashpot assembly, ensure that all component parts are clean and lightly oiled. Insert the relief body in the bore, and, using the relief valve outer sleeve, push it fully home. **Note:** The end with the 'O' ring is nearest to the outside of the casing.

57 Next, place the relief valve spring and piston assembly into the dashpot cup taking care that the ends of the residual pressure spring are correctly located.

58 Place these parts in the relief valve outer sleeve whilst at the same time engaging the relief valve piston in its housing.

59 Finally, fit the base plug and tighten flush with the housing to a torque wrench setting of 16 lb f ft (2.2 kg f m).

60 Place the pump non-return valve spring in the non-return valve plug and then place the ball on the spring.

61 The non-return seat can now be located on the ball and the complete assembly screwed into the main casing using tool L354A. Tighten to a torque wrench setting of 16 lb f ft (2.2 kg f m).

62 Refit the pressure filter and new aluminium washer. Tighten the plug to a torque wrench setting of 16 lb f ft (2.2 kg f m).

63 Refit the overdrive sump, suction filter and gasket and secure with the six bolts and spring washers.

64 Refit the solenoid control valve and tighten firmly, using an open-ended spanner.

65 Mount the rear casing assembly vertically in a bench vice and insert the planet carrier assembly. The gears may be meshed in any position.

66 Place the sliding member assembly, complete with clutch non-return springs, onto the cone of the annulus, at the same time engaging the sunwheel with the planet gears. Fit the brake ring into its spigot in the tail casing using a new joint washer on both sides.

67 Position the main casing assembly onto the thrust housing pins, at the same time entering the studs in the brake ring.

68 Fit the two operating piston bridge pieces and secure with the four nuts and new tab washers.

69 Fit the six nuts which secure the rear and main casing assemblies, ensuring that the two copper washers are correctly located on the two top studs. It will be observed that as the nuts are tightened the clutch return spring pressure will be felt.

12 Type J overdrive solenoid control valve - removal and refitting

1 The solenoid and operating valve are a self-contained factory sealed unit.

2 Disconnect the two terminals at the rear of the solenoid, noting which way round the cables are fitted.

3 Using a 1 inch (25 mm) A/F open-ended spanner, unscrew the assembly. Do not use a wrench around the cylindrical body of the solenoid valve otherwise it will be severely damaged.

4 To test the solenoid, connect into a circuit using a 12 volt battery and ammeter. The solenoid should require approximately 2 amps.

5 Check that the plunger in the valve moves forwards when the solenoid is energised and is returned to its direct drive position by spring pressure when de-energised.

6 It should be noted that this type of solenoid does not operate with a 'click' as observed in other types of overdrive.

7 Inspect the 'O' rings on the solenoid valve for damage and, if necessary, renew them together with the sealing washer.

8 If it is necessary to clean the operating valve, immerse, this part of the solenoid valve only, in paraffin until the valve is clean.

9 If the solenoid proves to be faulty it should be renewed as a complete unit.

10 Refitting is the reverse sequence to removal.

13 Type J overdrive relief valve and dashpot assembly - removal and refitting

1 For this a special tool, L354A, is necessary to remove the relief valve plug. If the vehicle has been used recently, take care to avoid burns from hot oil which will be released.
2 Undo and remove the six bolts and spring washers securing the overdrive sump oil gauze filter. Lift away the sump joint washer and gauze filter.
3 Lift out the dashpot piston complete with its component springs and cup followed by the residual pressure spring.
4 The relief valve piston assembly may now be withdrawn by carefully pulling down with a pair of pliers. The components are shown in Fig. 13.45.
5 Another special tool is required, part number L401A, which should be inserted into the now exposed relief valve bore. Withdraw the relief valve, together with the dashpot sleeve, taking extreme care not to damage the valve bore.
6 Do not attempt to dismantle the dashpot and relief valve piston assemblies, otherwise the predetermined spring pressures will be disturbed.
7 Inspect the pistons and ensure that they move freely in their respective housings. Make sure the 'O' rings are not damaged.
8 Before assembly make sure all components are clean and lightly oiled.
9 Insert the relief body in the bore and, using the relief valve outer sleeve, push fully home.
10 It should be noted that the end with the 'O' ring is nearest the outside of the main casing.
11 Next, position the relief valve spring and piston into the dashpot cut taking care that both ends of the residual pressure spring are correctly located. Carefully position these components in the relief valve outer sleeve, at the same time, engaging the relief valve piston in its housing. Fit the base plug and tighten flush with the main housing to a torque wrench setting of 16 lb f ft (2.2 kg f m).
12 Refit the filter, gasket and sump and secure with the six bolts and spring washers.

14 Type J overdrive pump non-return valve - removal and refitting

1 For removal a special tool, L354A, is necessary to remove the pump plug. If the vehicle has been used recently, take care to avoid burns from hot oil which will be released.
2 Undo and remove the six bolts and spring washers securing the overdrive sump and gauze filter. Lift away the sump, joint washer and gauze filter.
3 Using tool L354A, remove the pump plug taking care not to lose the non-return spring and ball. The pump valve seat can now be lifted away.
4 The pump body will be held in position by its 'O' ring. Should it be necessary to remove this, rotate the propeller shaft until the pump plunger is at the top of its stroke.
5 Next, carefully withdraw the pump body by hooking a piece of wire into the now exposed inlet port.
6 Carefully clean and then inspect the non-return valve ball and valve seat and make sure that the 'O' rings are not damaged. Fit new 'O' rings if necessary.
7 To refit the non-return valve assembly, first place the spring in the non-return valve plug, then position the ball on the spring.
8 The non-return valve seat can now be located on the ball and the complete assembly screwed into the main case using tool L354A. Tighten to a torque wrench setting of 16 lb f ft (2.2 kg f m).
9 Refit the suction filter, sump gasket and sump and secure with the six bolts and spring washers.

15 Type J overdrive pressure filter - removal and refitting

1 For removal a special tool, L354A, is necessary to remove the pump plug. If the vehicle has been used recently, take care to avoid burns from hot oil which will be released.
2 Undo and remove the six bolts and spring washers securing the overdrive sump and gauze filter. Lift away the sump, joint washer and gauze filter.
3 Using tool L354A, remove the pressure filter base plug.
4 The filter element will come away with the plug. Note the aluminium washer which locates on the shoulder in the filter bore.
5 Remove any dirt and thoroughly wash the element in petrol or paraffin.
6 Refitting is the reverse sequence to removal. Always fit a new aluminium washer. Tighten the plug to a torque wrench setting of 16 lb f ft (2.2 kg f m).

16 Type J overdrive - fault finding chart

Symptom	Possible cause
Overdrive will not engage	Low oil level. Electrical wiring fault. Solenoid faulty. Filters blocked. Pump non-return valve faulty. Sticking piston in relief valve. Control orifice between solenoid and dashpot blocked. (To remove any blockage, compressed air only should be used; do not probe the orifice with wire).
Overdrive will not release **Note**: If this occurs immediate attention is required to preclude damage, do **not** select reverse gear	Closed circuit in electrical system. Solenoid control valve plunger seized. Sticking piston in relief valve. Control orifice between solenoid and dashpot blocked. (To remove any blockage, compressed air only should be used; do not probe the orifice with wire). Cone clutch sticking (tap brake ring with a soft-faced mallet).
Overdrive clutch slipping	Clutch faulty. See items listed under 'Overdrive will not engage' also.

Overdrive disengagement slow and/or free-wheeling on overrun and/or reverse gear slipping

Sticking piston in relief valve.
Solenoid sticking.
Control orifice between solenoid and dashpot blocked (to remove any blockage, compressed air only should be used; do not probe the orifice with wire).

17 Type J overdrive - routine maintenance

1 With regard to topping-up the oil level and renewal of the oil, the same service intervals and procedures apply as for the manual

gearbox (see Chapter 6).

2 When the oil is to be renewed, the pressure and sump filters should be cleaned as detailed in the Type J overdrive - dismantling, overhaul and reassembly Section.

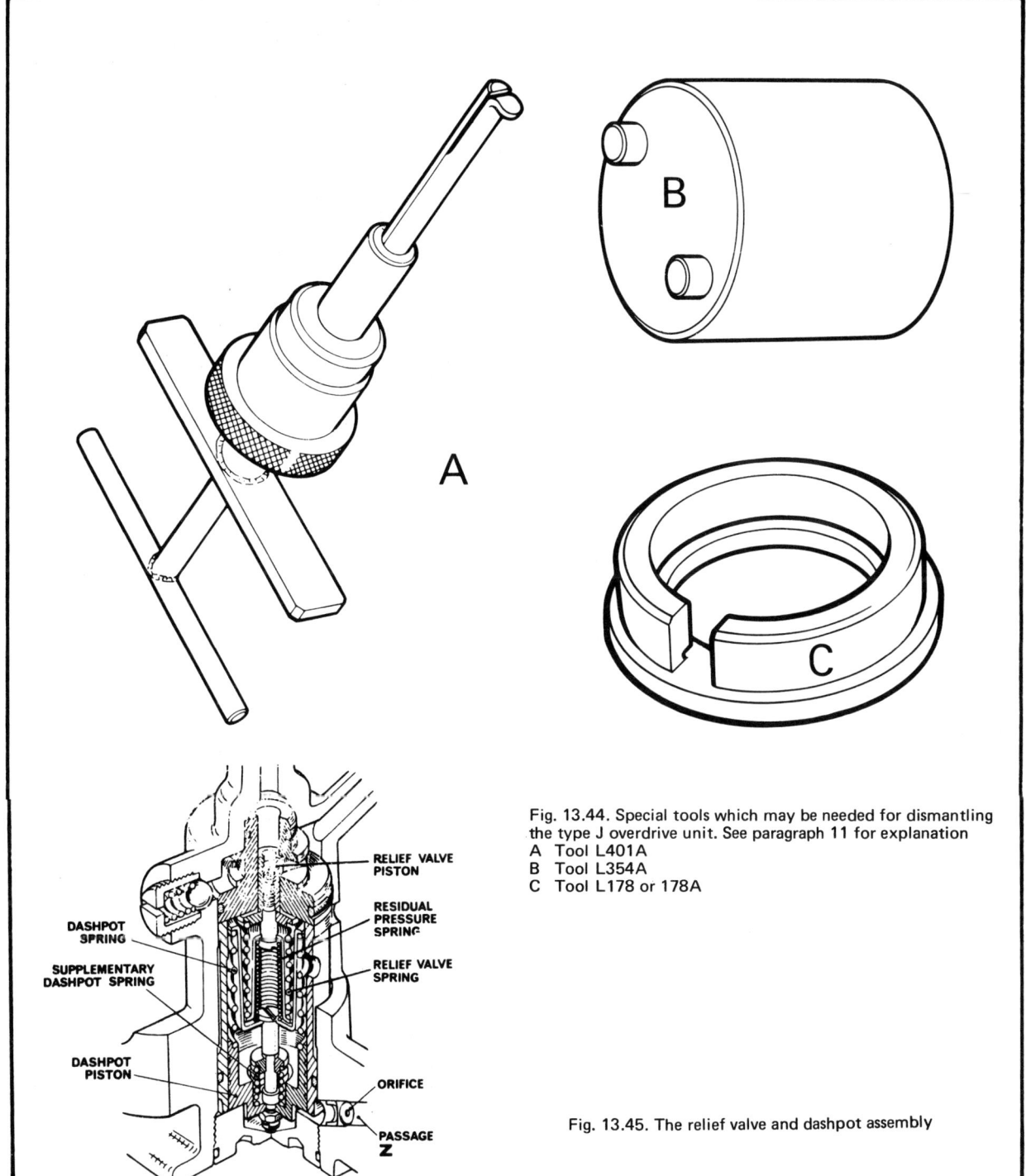

Fig. 13.44. Special tools which may be needed for dismantling the type J overdrive unit. See paragraph 11 for explanation
A Tool L401A
B Tool L354A
C Tool L178 or 178A

RELIEF VALVE PISTON

RESIDUAL PRESSURE SPRING

RELIEF VALVE SPRING

DASHPOT SPRING

SUPPLEMENTARY DASHPOT SPRING

DASHPOT PISTON

ORIFICE

PASSAGE Z

Fig. 13.45. The relief valve and dashpot assembly

Fig. 13.43. EXPLODED VIEW OF THE TYPE J OVERDRIVE UNIT

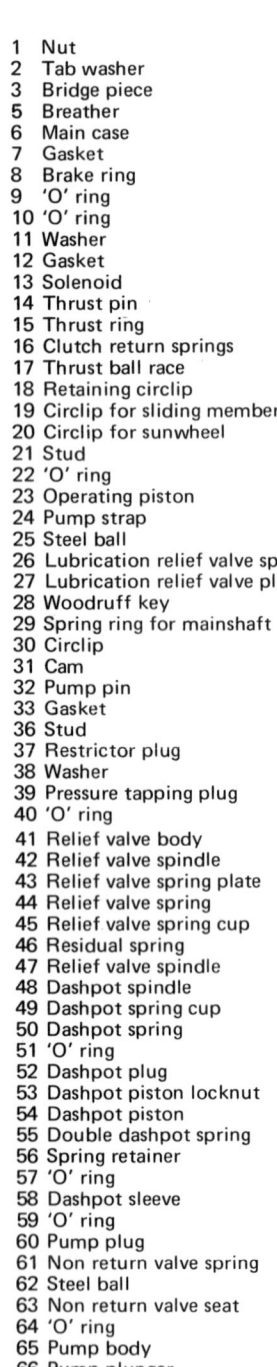

1 Nut
2 Tab washer
3 Bridge piece
5 Breather
6 Main case
7 Gasket
8 Brake ring
9 'O' ring
10 'O' ring
11 Washer
12 Gasket
13 Solenoid
14 Thrust pin
15 Thrust ring
16 Clutch return springs
17 Thrust ball race
18 Retaining circlip
19 Circlip for sliding member
20 Circlip for sunwheel
21 Stud
22 'O' ring
23 Operating piston
24 Pump strap
25 Steel ball
26 Lubrication relief valve spring
27 Lubrication relief valve plug
28 Woodruff key
29 Spring ring for mainshaft
30 Circlip
31 Cam
32 Pump pin
33 Gasket
36 Stud
37 Restrictor plug
38 Washer
39 Pressure tapping plug
40 'O' ring
41 Relief valve body
42 Relief valve spindle
43 Relief valve spring plate
44 Relief valve spring
45 Relief valve spring cup
46 Residual spring
47 Relief valve spindle
48 Dashpot spindle
49 Dashpot spring cup
50 Dashpot spring
51 'O' ring
52 Dashpot plug
53 Dashpot piston locknut
54 Dashpot piston
55 Double dashpot spring
56 Spring retainer
57 'O' ring
58 Dashpot sleeve
59 'O' ring
60 Pump plug
61 Non return valve spring
62 Steel ball
63 Non return valve seat
64 'O' ring
65 Pump body
66 Pump plunger
67 Packing washer
68 Pressure filter
69 Pressure filter washer
70 Pressure filter plug
71 Name plate
72 Securing screws
73 Planet carrier assembly

74 Sunwheel
75 Clutch sliding member
76 Sump filter
77 Sump gasket
78 Sump gasket
79 Sump
80 Sump setscrews
81 Shakeproof washer
82 Annulus
83 Restrictor plug
84 Mainshaft support bush
85 Thrust washer
86 Oil thrower

87 Circlip
88 Free wheel assembly
89 Stud
90 Shakeproof washer
91 Nut
92 Rear case
93 Oil seal
94 Bearing bush
95 Speedo driven gear
96 'O' ring
97 Speedo bearing
99 Setscrew
101 Oil seal

102 Stud
103 Weir
104 Locking nut
106 Speedo driving gear
107 Annulus ball race circlip
108 Annulus front ball race
109 Welch washer

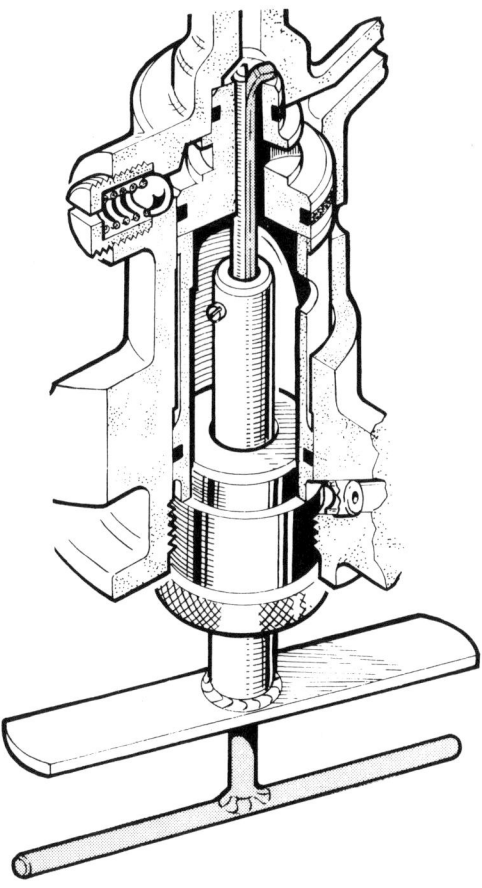

Fig. 13.46. Using tool L401A to remove the relief valve and dashpot body (sectional view)

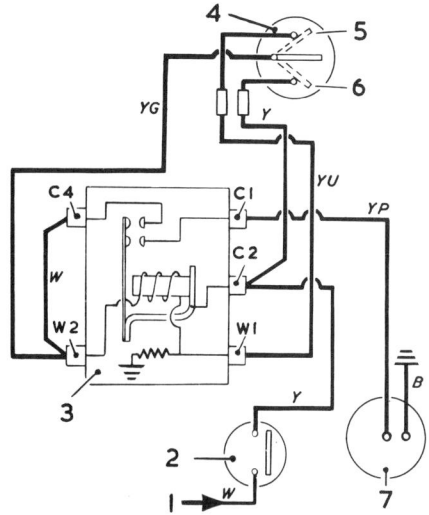

Fig. 13.47. WIRING DIAGRAM FOR THE TYPE J OVERDRIVE UNIT

1 Supply wire from fuse box	5 Direct drive
2 Isolator (gearbox) switch	6 Overdrive
3 Relay	7 Overdrive solenoid
4 Overdrive (column) switch	

Wire colour code

B	Black	U	Blue
G	Green	W	White
P	Purple	Y	Yellow

6C Automatic transmission

18 Automatic transmission - general description

1   An optional fitment on models in the Hunter range is the Borg Warner automatic transmission. Until 1974, this was the Model 35 three-speed transmission which has been used on a wide range of British cars, but for 1974 models the Model 45 four-speed unit was made available.

2   The automatic transmission comprises two main components, namely, a three-element hydrokinetic torque converter capable of torque multiplication at an infinitely variable ratio between 2.0 : 1 or 2.3 : 1 (according to the application), and a torque/speed responsive, hydraulically operated planetary gearbox.

3   The Model 35 gearbox comprises a planetary gearset providing three forward gears and one reverse; the Model 45 is similar in operating principle but provides four forwards gears and one reverse.

4   Early Model 35 transmission use a selector with five positions, these being L, D, N, R and P. Later Model 35 transmission use a selector with six positions, these being 1, 2, D, N, R and P.

5   Model 45 transmissions use a selector with six positions, these being 2/1, 3, D, N, R and P.

6   Due to the complexity of the automatic transmission unit, if any malfunction is suspected, or if overhaul is required, the job should be entrusted to a Chrysler dealer or automatic transmission specialist. The contents of the following Sections are for general guidance and for servicing information.

19 Automatic transmission - fluid level

Model 35 transmission

1   Run the car for about 5 miles (8 km), then select 'P' and

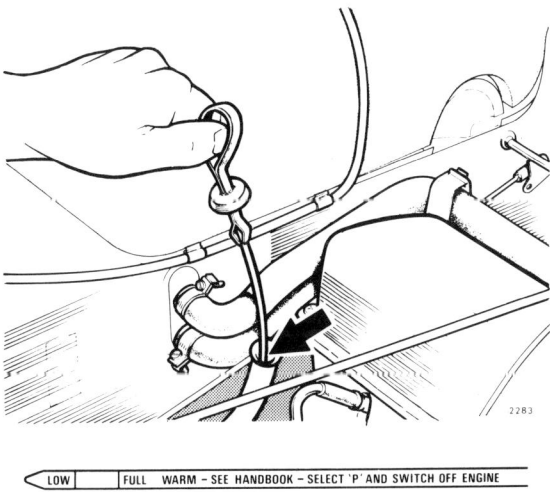

Fig. 13.48. Checking the automatic transmission fluid level

allow the engine to idle for about two minutes.

2 With the engine still idling and 'P' selected, remove the transmission fluid dipstick, wipe it clean and then re-insert it in the dipstick/filler tube.

3 Withdraw the dipstick again, check the fluid level and, if necessary, top-up to the 'HIGH' mark. Do not overfill.

4 If it becomes necessary to check the level with the transmission cold, the fluid level should be 3/8 inch (9.5 mm) below the 'HIGH' mark with the engine idling and 'P' selected. At the first opportunity the level should be re-checked when hot.

Model 45 transmission

5 Run the engine at a fast idle for about five minutes, select each driving range in turn, then switch off the engine with 'P' still selected.

6 Remove the transmission fluid dipstick, wipe it clean and re-insert it.

7 Withdraw the dipstick again after approximately 30 seconds, check the fluid level and, if necessary, top-up to the 'FULL' mark on the dipstick. If the procedure was started with a cold engine, the 'WARM' side of the dipstick should be used. If the procedure was started with a hot engine (having run at least 5 miles - 8 km) the 'HOT' side of the dipstick should be used.

20 Downshift cable - adjustment

Note: The following procedure is given as a guide to adjustment only, and is not suitable where a replacement downshift cable has been fitted (because the cable stop is not crimped in position), where an existing cable stop is loose or damaged, or where a replacement engine, carburettor or transmission has been installed. In any of these instances, adjustment should be made by a Chrysler dealer, since transmission pressure checks will have to be made.

1 Adjust the outer cable so that the stop is 0.03 to 0.06 in (0.76 to 1.55 mm) clear of the abutment for Model 35 transmission or 0.01 to 0.02 in (0.25 to 0.50 mm) for Model 45 transmissions.

2 Adjustment is by slackening the locknut(s) at the abutment bracket and repositioning the outer cable.

21 Accelerator pedal linkage - full throttle adjustment

1 This adjustment should be set so that when the accelerator pedal is depressed to within 1 inch (25 mm) of the floor covering, the downshift valve cam passes over the hard spot (detent). The carburettor butterfly should be 7/8 open at this point.

2 When the accelerator pedal is depressed to the forced throttle position on Model 45 transmissions, there must be 1.75 in (44 mm) travel of the downshift cable. If this is not occurring, do not alter the downshift cable setting, but check the throttle linkage and cable settings.

22 Selector lever linkage - adjustment

Model 35, cable operated, early type

1 Disconnect the cable at the transmission end from beneath the car.

2 Place the selector lever at 'N', and the transmission lever in the 'N' position (move it fully forward to 'P' then back two clicks to 'N').

3 Set the adjuster at the lower end of the cable to the mid position, then adjust the upper end so that the cable can be connected to the transmission lever (see Fig. 13.54A).

4 Check the operation of the lever in all its positions.

Model 35, rod operated, early type

5 Remove the cover plate on the right-hand side of the floor tunnel for access to the adjustment nuts.

6 Referring to Fig. 13.54, check, that if the lever (5) has a nut (6) at its lower end, this nut is tight.

7 Disconnect the adjustable rod (4) from the lever (5) and put the lever to the 'D' position (move it fully backwards to 'P' then forward three clicks to 'D').

8 Put the selector lever (1) at 'D', then adjust the rod (4) so that when it is reconnected to the transmission lever, the centre of the pin (2) is central in the slot of the lever (3) into which the pin engages, when the selector lever (1) is moved to the right. The rod adjustment (4) has a right- and left-hand thread.

9 Support the rod and tighten the locknuts. Move the selector lever to 'L' to reach the rear locknut.

10 Check the operation of the lever in all its positions.

Model 35, rod operated, later type

11 Referring to Fig. 13.55, loosen the nut (1).

12 Move the lever (3) at the front end of the connecting rod (2) fully rearwards to the 'P' position, then forward three clicks to 'D'.

13 Hold the selector lever fully backwards in 'D' and tighten the nut (1).

14 Check the operation of the lever in all its positions.

Model 35, cable operated, later type

15 Referring to Fig. 13.56, place the selector lever (5) at 'D', then remove the clevis (2) from the lever (1).

16 Slacken the cable clamp bolts (3), then move the lever (1) fully forwards to 'P' and then three clicks backwards to 'D'.

17 Reconnect the clevis, then push the outer cable forward to take up any cable slackness. Tighten the clamp bolts to position the clamp in the elongated holes.

Model 45

18 Place the selector lever at 'P', then loosen the self-locking nuts securing the transmission lever to the selector rod.

19 Move the external lever on the transmission fully rearwards into its detent, then support the rod lightly and tighten the self-locking nut.

20 Check the operation of the lever in all its positions, and ensure that the key start only occurs with the selector lever in 'N' or 'P'.

23 Starter inhibitor/reverse light switch - replacement

Model 35

1 Remove the existing switch by unscrewing, after removing the electrical connections. (Note the terminal numbers and refer to the table at the end of this section, to ensure that they are replaced correctly, since different types of switch have been used. The latest type of switch can be used to replace the earlier types, whether mounted vertically or horizontally).

2 Select 'P', then ensure that the washer is on the replacement switch. Apply a little non-setting gasket sealant on the switch screw threads, then screw the switch into the transmission. Use a spanner of about 4 in (10 cm) in length and tighten until **just** tight to avoid stripping the switch threads.

3 Fit the electrical leads and check that the engine will only start with 'N' or 'P' selected. Also check that the reverse lights operate with 'R' selected.

Wiring connections - inhibitor

Early switch	Terminals 1 and 2 (adjacent)
Later switch, vertical or horizontal mounting	Terminals 1 and 3 (opposite)

Wiring connections - reverse light

Early switch	Terminals 3 and 4 (adjacent)

*Later switch, vertical or
horizontal mounting*   *Terminals 2 and 4 (opposite)*

Model 45

4 Identify the switch wires, then remove them from the switch.
5 Remove the single retaining screw, then slide the switch off the cross-shaft.
6 Refitting is the reverse of the removal procedure.

---

24 Automatic transmission - removal and refitting

Model 35

1 Disconnect the battery, then drain sufficient water from the cooling system to permit removal of the top hose.
2 If necessary, remove the air cleaner, rocker cover and distributor cap.
3 Remove the throttle operating shaft from the carburettor and its bearing.
4 If necessary, disconnect the brake servo hose from the manifold.
5 Disconnect the downshift cable clevis from its yoke on the cable end by removing the nut at its attachment position.
6 Disconnect and plug the fuel feed pipe.
7 Disconnect the transmission filler tube at its cylinder head end.
8 Where applicable, remove the body tunnel cover plate and undo the filler tube nut. Pull the tube out of the transmission case.
9 Disconnect the starter motor heavy lead and, where applicable, the oil gauge feed pipe.
10 Using a suitable attachment bracket and lifting tackle, take the weight of the engine at the rear lifting eye.
11 From beneath the car, drain the transmission fluid, but beware of scalding if the fluid is hot.
12 Disconnect the exhaust pipe(s) and remove the exhaust system as necessary for access purposes.
13 Disconnect the starter inhibitor switch wires and the speedometer cable.
14 Remove the propeller shaft (refer to Chapter 7, Section 3).
15 Disconnect the transmission selector linkage.
16 Undo and remove the gearbox rear mounting rubbers and the crossmember.
17 Lower the engine to give access to the transmission filler tube nut (where not previously removed), then remove the filler tube.
18 If the torque converter is to be removed (as well as the transmission), disconnect the two stay bars from the bellhousing to the sump (where applicable).
19 Commencing with the two bottom bolts, remove all six bolts from the gearbox to converter housing, using a suitable cranked spanner.
20 With a container beneath the transmission to catch spilt fluid, withdraw the gearbox rearwards and downwards.
21 To remove the converter housing, disconnect and remove the starter motor.
22 Remove the bottom front cover plate, and the stay brackets to the cylinder block (where applicable).
23 Remove the retaining bolts and lift away the housing.
24 The converter can be removed, after removal of the housing, by taking out the four special bolts. On engines with aluminium sumps, a special spanner will be required unless the sump is removed (Fig. 13.59)..
25 Refitting the transmission is essentially the reverse procedure to removal, but the following points should be noted.

a) *Special washers are used beneath the leads of the special bolts retaining the torque converter to the engine drive plate. Consult your Chrysler dealer for replacement parts. Do not use ordinary bolts and washers, and ensure that the replacements are correctly torque tightened.*
b) *To ensure correct engagement of the oil pump drive, rotate the converter so that the drive fingers on the hub*

will be in the 9 o'clock and 3 o'clock positions. The slots in the oil pump driving gear are rotated to a similar position by using a screwdriver or similar tool.
c) *Fill the transmission with new fluid on completion, then check the level*

Model 45

26 Disconnect the battery, then drain sufficient water from the cooling system to permit removal of the top hose.
27 Loosen the exhaust manifold flange nuts.
28 Remove the plenum chamber drain hose.
29 Disconnect the inner and outer downshift cables at the carburettor.
30 From beneath the car, remove the propeller shaft (refer to Chapter 7, Section 3).
31 Remove the sump stiffener brackets (where applicable) and the dirt shield.
32 On twin carburettor models, loosen the exhaust down pipe/exhaust pipe joint.
33 Remove the transmission guard plate.
34 Using a suitable separator, disconnect the steering tie-rod at the drop arm and idle arm. Lift the ball pins free and allow the tie-rod to hang from the outer balljoints.
35 Place a suitable container in position, loosen the oil filler tube union nut and drain the oil.
36 Disconnect and plug the oil cooler lines at the transmision.
37 Disconnect the selector lever linkage, noting whether the rod is inside or outside the lever.
38 Disconnect the speedometer cable and inhibitor switch wiring, noting the wire colours.
39 Using a suitable adapter and jack, take the weight of the transmission at the sump flanges only, **not** on the sump pan.
40 Whilst turning the crankshaft as necessary, remove the torque converter to drive plate bolts.
41 Remove the rear engine crossmember, noting the position of the insulating rubbers and sleeves as the bolts are removed.
42 Lower the jack until it is just supporting the weight of the transmission, then remove the bolts and nuts securing the torque converter housing to the engine and starter motor. Leave the starter bolts in position.
43 Remove the transmission filler tube, then move the transmission and torque converter away from the engine, whilst ensuring that the torque converter does not separate from the transmission.
44 Refitting is essentially the reverse of removal, but the following points should be noted:

a) *Suitably jack-up the front end of the engine to facilitate alignment with the transmission.*
b) *Special washers are used beneath the heads of the special bolts retaining the torque converter to the engine drive plate. Consult your Chrysler dealer for replacement parts. Do not use ordinary bolts and washers, and ensure that replacements are correctly torque tightened.*
c) *When refitting the filler tube, loosely attach the bracket to the converter housing, then align the tube in its seat in the sump and tighten the union nut. Do not strain the tube when tightening.*
d) *Ensure that the thick spacers are fitted between the rear engine mounting and transmission.*
e) *Adjust the selector linkage and downshift cable.*
f) *Fill the transmission with fresh oil and check the oil level.*

---

25 Automatic transmission - fault finding

1 Fault finding on automatic transmissions is not easily translated into do-it-yourself terms and will inevitably require the use of special knowledge and equipment for rectification.
2 In the event of troubles occurring it is best to consult a Chrysler agent or an automatic transmission specialist.

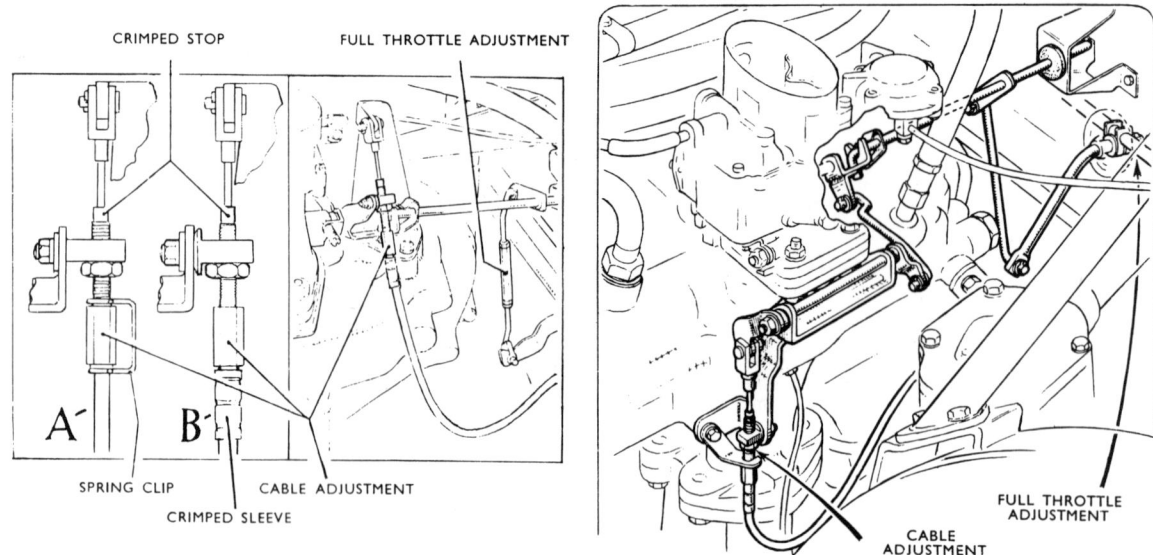

CRIMPED STOP   FULL THROTTLE ADJUSTMENT

SPRING CLIP   CABLE ADJUSTMENT

CRIMPED SLEEVE

FULL THROTTLE ADJUSTMENT

CABLE ADJUSTMENT

Fig. 13.49. Early (A) and later (B) BW35 downshift cables

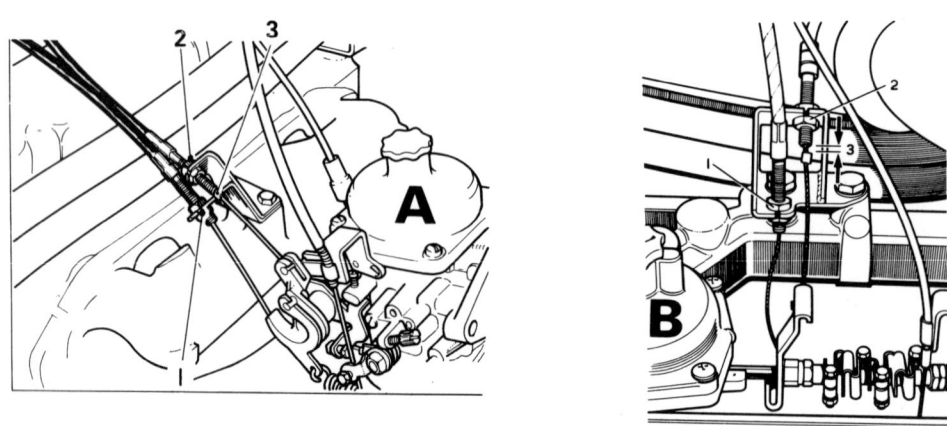

Fig. 13.51. Downshift cable adjustment, BW45

A   Single carburettor
B   Twin carburettors
1   Throttle cable adjustment
2   Downshift cable adjustment
3   Clearance at crimped stop

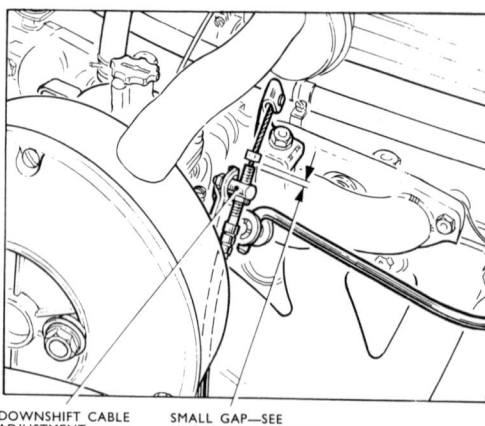

DOWNSHIFT CABLE
ADJUSTMENT

SMALL GAP—SEE
UNDER ADJUSTMENT

Fig. 13.50. Downshift cable adjustment, BW35

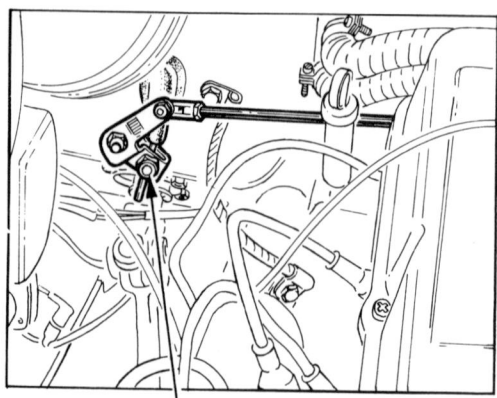

FULL THROTTLE ADJUSTMENT

Fig. 13.52. Throttle cable adjustment, BW35

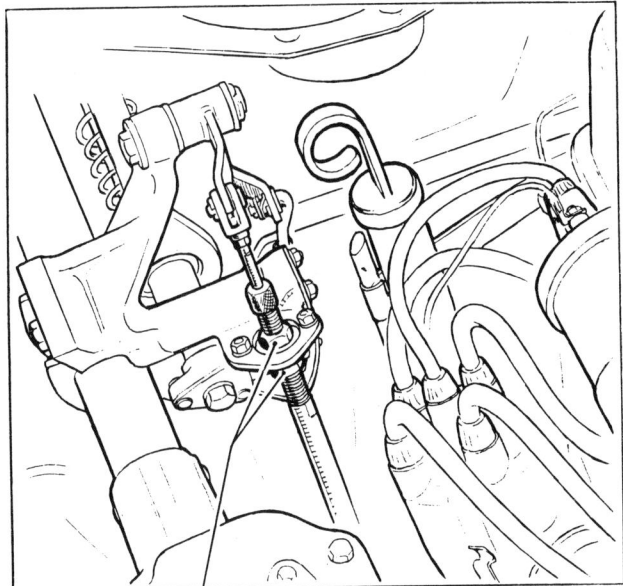

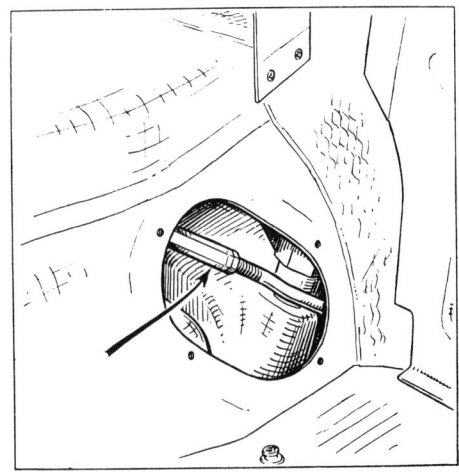

Fig. 13.53. Selector cable adjustment, early BW35 cable operated type

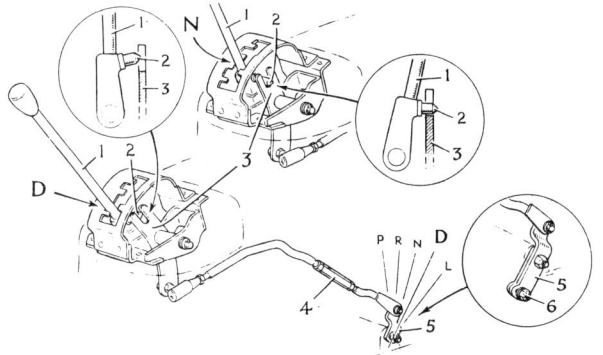

Fig. 13.54A. Selector linkage adjustment, early BW35 rod operated type

Fig. 13.54B. Component parts of linkage
Refer to the text for the captions

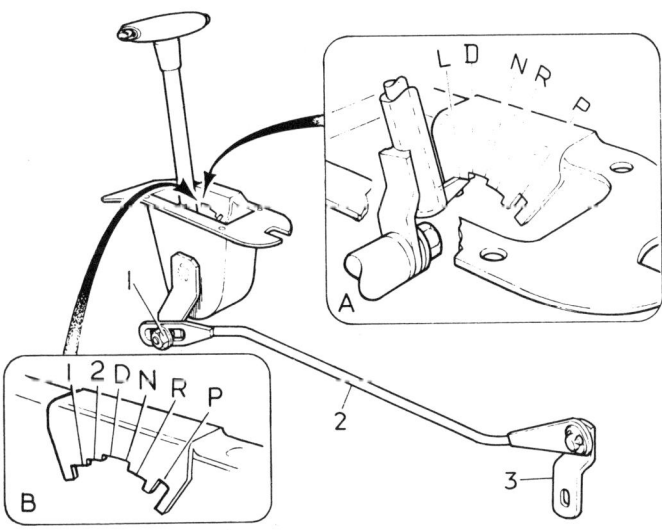

Fig. 13.55. Selector linkage adjustment, later BW35 rod operated type
Refer to the text for the captions

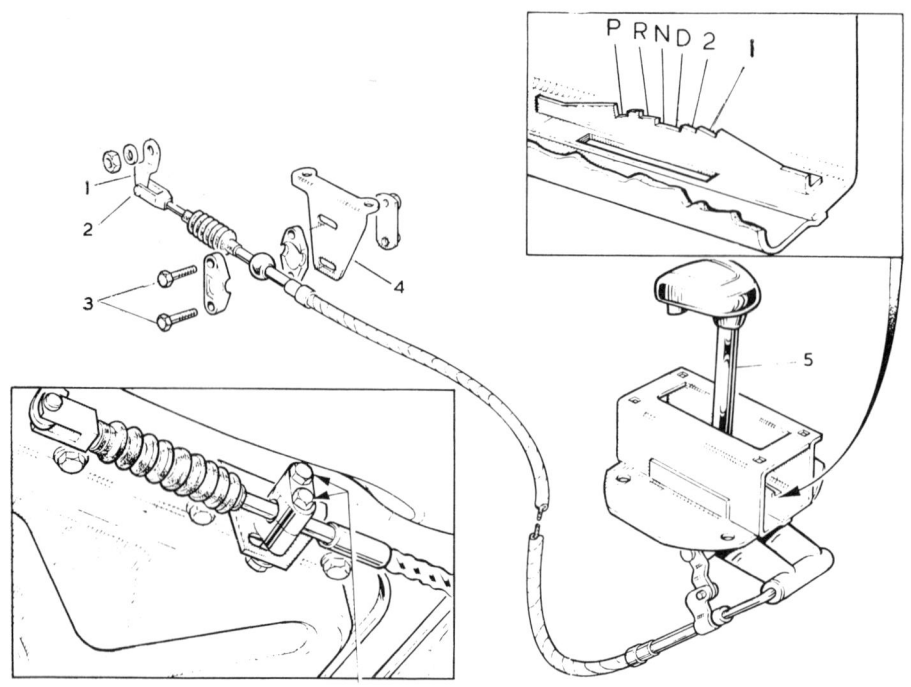

3 CABLE CLAMP FIXING BOLTS

Fig. 13.56. Selector linkage adjustment, later BW35 cable operated type
Refer to the text for the captions

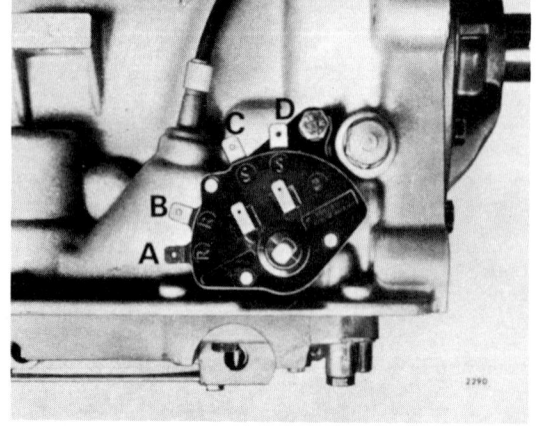

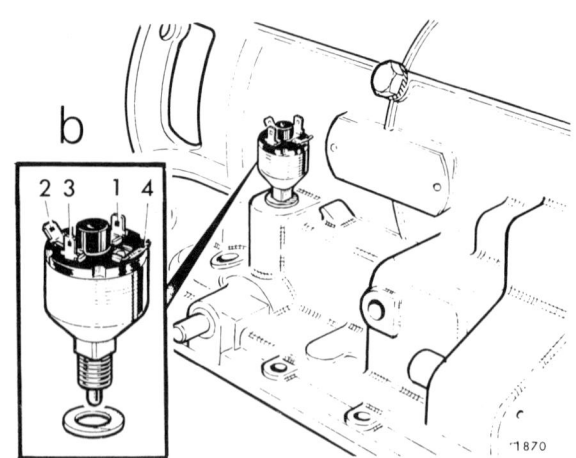

Fig. 13.58. Types of starter inhibitor switches

Refer to the text for the captions
A Starter inhibitor switch, horizontal types - BW35
B Starter inhibitor switch, vertical types - BW35
C Starter inhibitor switch - BW45

A   Green
B   Green/Brown
C   White/Red
D   White/Red

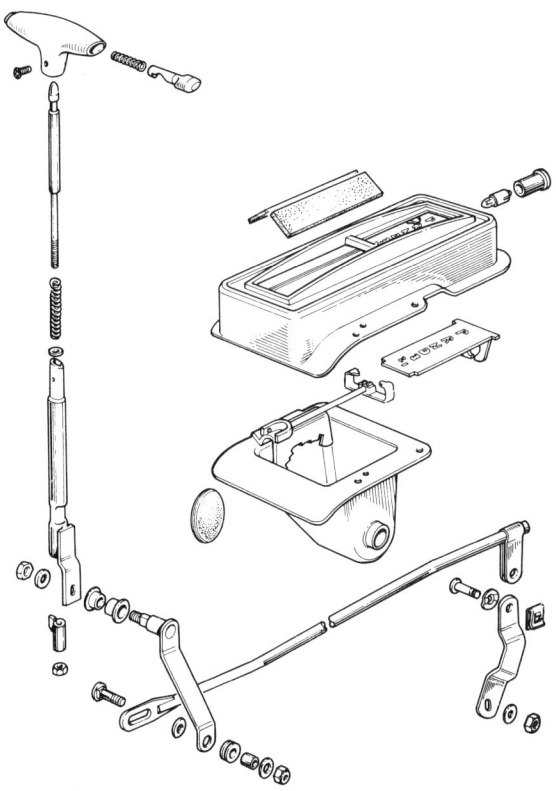

Fig. 13.57. BW45 selector linkage

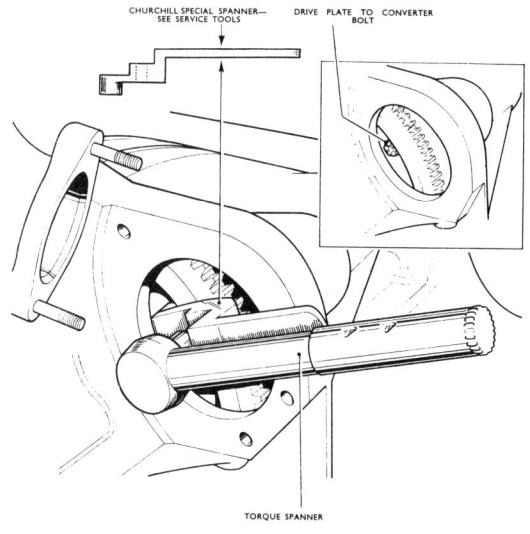

Fig. 13.59. Using the special spanner and a torque wrench on the converter/drive plate bolts. The tool illustrated is Churchill part no. RG523

7   Propeller shaft and universal joints

1   Two piece propeller shaft - removal and refitting

1   As the two piece shaft with its centre bearing is rather an unwieldy object, it is better to remove the rear portion of the shaft first.

2   Jack-up the rear of the car, or position the rear of the car over a pit or ramp.

3   If the rear wheels are off the ground, place the car in gear and put the handbrake on, to ensure that the propeller shaft does not turn when an attempt is made to loosen the four nuts securing the propeller shaft to the rear axle.

4   The propeller shaft is carefully balanced to fine limits and it is important for it to be replaced in exactly the same position as it was prior to removal. Scratch a mark on the propeller shaft and rear axle flanges, also on the flanges at the front end of the rear portion, to ensure accurate mating when the time comes to reassemble.

5   Unscrew the four self-locking nuts, bolts and securing washers which hold the flanges together at either end, and lower the rear portion from the car.

6   Place a can or tray under the rear of the gearbox or overdrive extension to catch any oil that may leak out when the front of the propeller shaft is drawn out.

7   Undo the bolts holding the centre bearing assembly to its mounting bracket and draw it to the rear, complete with the front portion of the propeller shaft.

8   Replacement of the propeller shaft is a reversal of the above procedure. Make sure that the mating marks made on the rear portion line up correctly.

2   Two piece propeller shaft centre bearing - removal and refitting

1   Mark the coupling and the front half of the propeller shaft to ensure the shaft goes onto the same splines in the rear coupling on reassembly.

2   Undo the self-locking nut holding the front portion of the propeller shaft in the rear coupling, then withdraw the shaft and remove the water shield from the front of the bearing housing and the dust seal from the rear.

3   Remove the circlips from their grooves in the bearing housing from either side of the bearing; then press out the bearing.

4   To replace the bearing, fit one of the circlips in its groove, press the bearing up to it, then fit the other circlip to lock it in position. Both sides of the bearing should now be packed with a waterproof sealing compound.

5   Reassembly from now on is a direct reversal of the removal procedure.

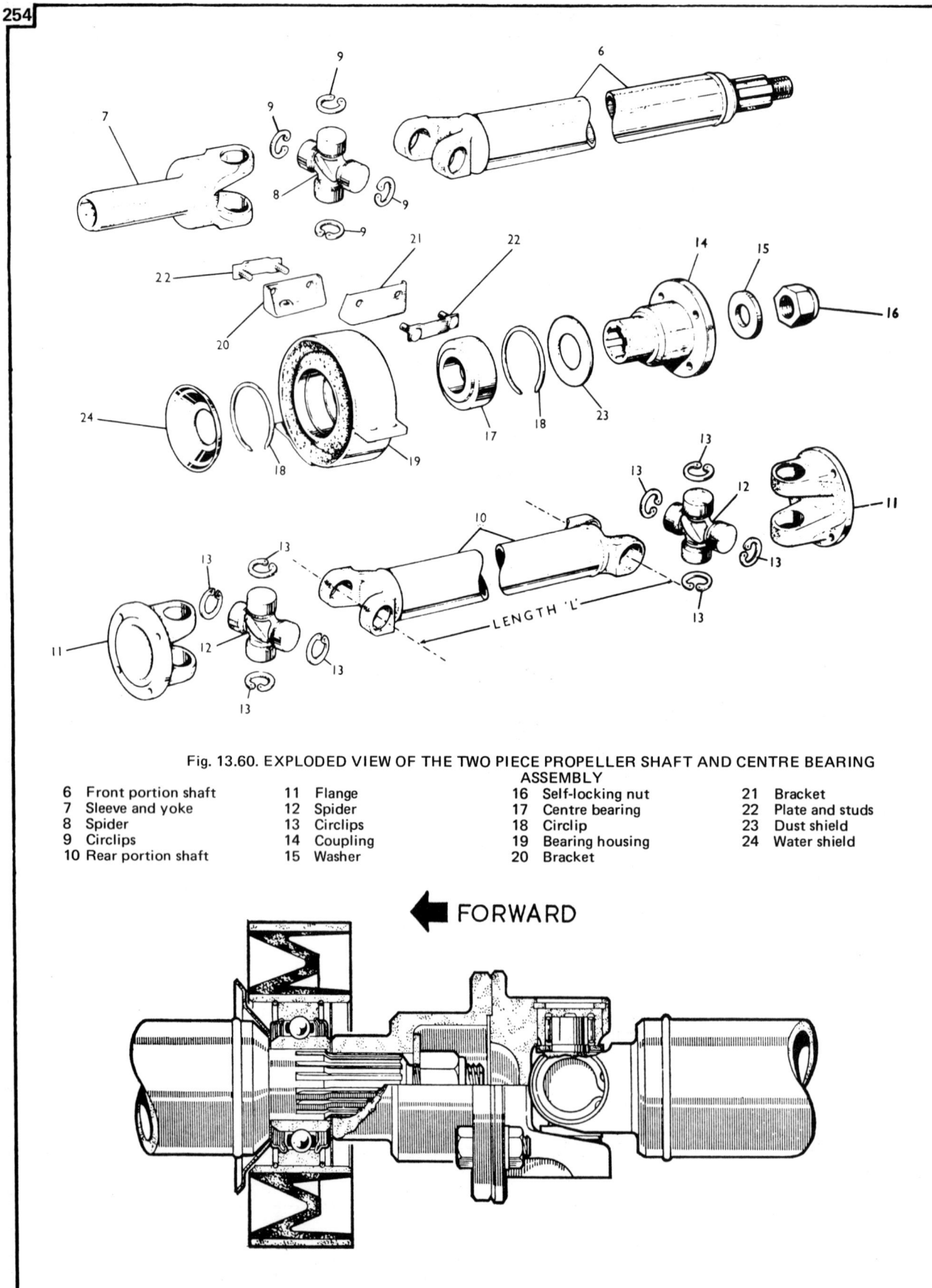

Fig. 13.60. EXPLODED VIEW OF THE TWO PIECE PROPELLER SHAFT AND CENTRE BEARING ASSEMBLY

6	Front portion shaft	11	Flange	16	Self-locking nut	21	Bracket
7	Sleeve and yoke	12	Spider	17	Centre bearing	22	Plate and studs
8	Spider	13	Circlips	18	Circlip	23	Dust shield
9	Circlips	14	Coupling	19	Bearing housing	24	Water shield
10	Rear portion shaft	15	Washer	20	Bracket		

◀ FORWARD

Fig. 13.61. Cutaway view of the centre bearing assembly

8 Electrical system

1 Lucas 16AC, 15ACR and 16ACR alternators - general information

1 These alternators are similar in design to the 10AC alternator described in Chapter 10, except that a field isolating relay is no longer required, due to a modified arrangement for the field supply diodes. The earlier 8 pole rotor and stator have been superseded by 12 pole equivalent, and on the 15ACR and 16ACR versions there is a built-in electronic voltage regulator unit. The 16ACR is similar to the 15ACR alternator except for a higher nominal dc output.

2 With regard to maintenance, precautions, removal and replacement, reference should be made to the appropriate Sections in Chapter 10.

2 Lucas 16AC alternator - testing in the car

1 Before testing the alternator in the event of malfunction, check the fan belt tension and adjust if necessary (Section 10 of Chapter 2).

2 Check that all connections in the charging circuit are tight, clean and undamaged.

3 Disconnect the battery earth lead temporarily.

4 If no ammeter is fitted to the car, disconnect the alternator main output lead from the positive (+) terminal, then connect a moving coil ammeter capable of reading up to 60 amps dc between the disconnected output lead and the alternator positive (+) terminal.

5 Disconnect the 'F' and negative (—) terminal leads from the 8TR regulator unit, then join, using a jumper lead, the leads (not the terminals) together.

6 Reconnect the battery earth lead.

7 Switch the headlamps on with main beam selected, turn on the ignition and check that the warning lamp illuminates.

8 Start the engine and check that the warning lamp extinguishes at 800 rpm (approximately) as engine speed slowly increases.

9 Increase engine speed to approximately 3100 rpm and check that the current is not less than 25 amps.

10 If the requirements of paragraphs 8 and 9 are not satisfied a fault in the alternator is indicated.

11 If the requirements of paragraphs 8 and 9 are satisfied, but the charging system is faulty, first check through the wiring. If this is satisfactory a faulty voltage regulator is indicated.

12 Rectification of alternator faults (with the exception of attention to the bushes and slip rings), or voltage regulator faults, are best entrusted to a car electrical specialist due to the possibility of further damage being caused during investigation or renewal of components.

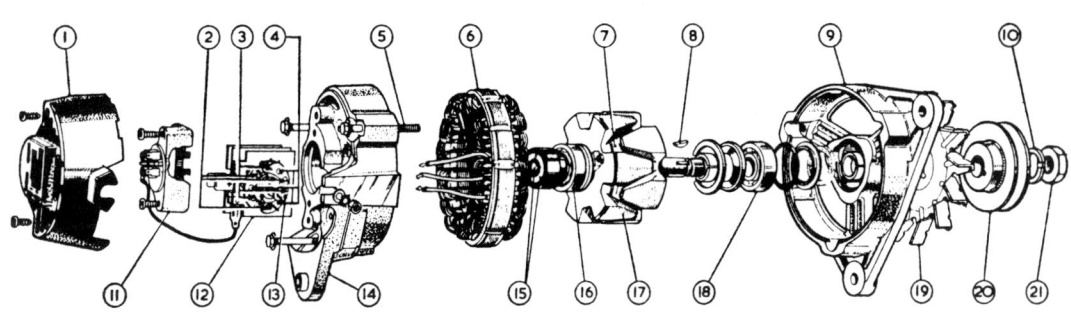

Fig. 13.62. EXPLODED VIEW OF TYPE 16AC ALTERNATOR

1 Cover	6 Stator	11 Brush box moulding	16 Slip ring bearing
2 Live side output diodes	7 Field winding	12 Rectifier pack	17 Rotor
3 Earth side output diodes	8 Shaft key	13 Rectifier assembly bolt	18 Drive end bearing
4 Field diodes	9 Drive end bracket	14 Slip ring end bracket	19 Fan
5 Through bolts	10 Spring washer	15 Slip rings	20 Pulley
			21 Nut

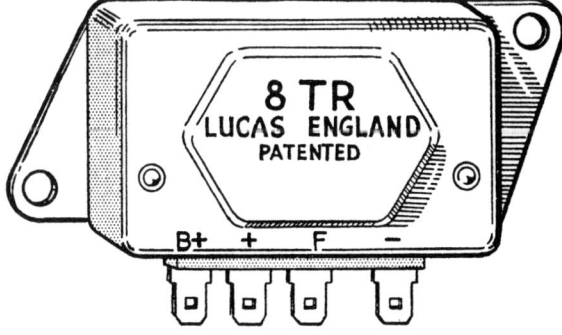

Fig. 13.63. The 8TR regulator used with 16AC alternators

3 Lucas 15ACR and 16ACR alternators - testing in the car

Alternator output

1 With the engine switched off, disconnect the battery earth lead.

2 Remove the two screws retaining the moulded end cover, then take off the cover.

3 Link the green inner brush lead (F) and black earth lead (—).

4 Connect a test circuit as shown inside the dotted lines of Fig. 13.65, taking great care that polarities are correct, then reconnect the battery earth lead. Proceed to the checks in paragraphs 5 and 6 without delay, since the variable resistor must not be connected for longer than absolutely necessary; also ensure that the resistor is initially set to give maximum resistance or it may become permanently damaged.

5 Switch the ignition on, check that the warning lamp is illuminated, then start the engine and increase the speed to approximately 800 rpm. The lamp should now be extinguished.

6 Increase the engine speed to approximately 3200 rpm, adjust the variable resistor to give a voltmeter reading of 14 volts and check that the current is approximately equal to the rated alternator output given in the Specifications.

7 Switch off the engine and disconnect the variable resistance without delay.

8 If the requirements of paragraphs 5 and 6 are not satisfied, a fault in the alternator is indicated. Apart from attention to brushes and slip rings, alternator faults are best left to a car electrical specialist to rectify and preclude the possibility of further damage being caused during investigation or renewal of components.

Regulator test

1 If the requirements of paragraphs 5 and 6 of the alternator output test are satisfied but there is still a fault in the charging circuit, use the same test circuit but remove the variable resistor and the bridging link between (F) and (−).

2 Run the engine up to approximately 3200 rpm and check that when a current of 10 amps is recorded, the voltmeter reading is in the region of 13.6 to 14.4 volts. Any appreciable deviation from this value indicates that the regulator is at fault and requires specialist attention.

3 On completion, disconnect the battery earth lead, remove the test circuitry, then reconnect the battery earth lead.

4 Lucas 16AC, 15ACR and 16ACR alternators - servicing

1 Servicing, other than renewal of the brushes, is not recommended. The major components should normally last the life of the unit; in the event of failure a factory exchange replacement should be obtained.

2 To renew the brushes, remove the two cover screws and withdraw the moulded cover.

3 Unsolder the three stator connections to the rectifier assembly noting carefully the order of connection. Take great care that the diodes are not overheated or permanent damage will result. See also paragraph 9 of this Section.

4 On 16AC alternators, withdraw the two brush moulding securing screws and slacken the nut on the rectifier screws and slacken the nut on the rectifier assembly bolt. The brush moulding and rectifier can now be withdrawn together, complete with the cable which links them.

5 On 15ACR or 16ACR alternators, pull off the brush wire, earth wire and suppressor wire (if fitted) from the Lucas terminals on the rectifier. Slacken the nut on the rectifier assembly bolt and withdraw the rectifier, then remove the brush moulding securing screws. Unscrew the bolt securing the regulator to the end bracket, then withdraw the brush box and regulator complete with the cable which links them.

6 Inspect the brushes which should protrude 0.2 inch (5 mm) beyond the brush box moulding when in a free position. Renew if worn to, or below this amount, and do not lose the leaf spring fitted at the side of the inner brush.

7 Should a brush stick, then clean it with petrol or lightly rub with a smooth file.

8 The surfaces of the slip rings should be clean and smooth. If necessary, clean with a petrol moistened cloth. If there is evidence of burning, use only very fine glasspaper to clean (not emery).

9 Reassembly is the reverse of the removal procedure, but for the soldering operation it is important to use only M grade 45/55 tin-lead solder. To prevent overheating of the rectifier diodes, the pins should be lightly gripped with a pair of long nosed pliers to act as a heat sink whilst soldering. This operation should be carried out as quickly as possible. Also take care that the pins are not bent since this will damage the hesmetric seal.

5 Delco Remy DN460 alternator - general information

1 The DN460 alternator is a 14 pole machine which, although considerably different with respect to design, functions in a similar manner to the Lucas 15ACR and 16ACR models.

2 With regard to precautions, removal and replacement, reference should be made to the appropriate Sections of Chapter 10.

3 The manufacturers do not recommend any periodic maintenance.

4 It is recommended that in the event of the alternator requiring repair, the job should be carried out by a car electrical specialist.

6 Delco Remy DN460 alternator - testing in the car

Faulty warning light operation

1 If the warning light is on when the ignition is switched off, a faulty rectifier bridge is indicated and the alternator should be passed to a car electrical specialist for repair. This condition will also give an undercharged battery.

2 If the warning light is off when the ignition is switched on (engine not running), this will lead to an undercharged battery. To trace the fault, disconnect the 'IND' terminal from the alternator and temporarily earth it. If the light fails to illuminate when the ignition is switched on, check the switch, light and associated leads for continuity.

3 If the light illuminates as paragraph 2, reconnect the 'IND' lead, then use a screwdriver, as shown in Fig. 13.67, to earth the field winding.

4 If the light is now extinguished, check the wiring connection between the 'IND' alternator terminal and the wiring harness. If these are satisfactory, a fault in the brushes, slip rings or field windings is indicated. If the light is still illuminated, a fault in the regulator unit is indicated.

Undercharged battery

1 This condition may be accompanied by erroneous warning light indications and, where evident, it is important to ascertain that all wiring connections are clean and tight, and that the fan belt is correctly adjusted (see Chapter 2, Section 10).

2 To check the alternator, switch on the ignition (engine not running) and connect a dc voltmeter, capable of registering 12 volts, between the alternator positive (+) and earth, then between the alternator 'IND' terminal and earth. A zero reading indicates a fault in the alternator.

Overcharged battery

1 In cases where an overcharged battery is evident, as indicated by excessive usage of distilled water, a faulty alternator is indicated.

7 Starter motor - removal and refitting

1 In addition to the information given in Chapter 10 for the removal of the starter motor, it will be necessary on some models to temporarily remove the air cleaner for access purposes (refer to Chapter 3 if necessary).

2 Where a pre-engaged starter motor is fitted, it is also necessary to disconnect the cables from the solenoid.

3 On Holbay engined models, when removing the starter motor, its front end should be moved towards the air cleaner and not directly backwards.

4 Refitting is a reversal of the removal procedure.

8 Lucas M35J starter motor - general description

1 The Lucas M35J starter motor is of the inertia type, and has a series-wound, four-pole, four-brush motor with an extended shaft which carries a conventional inertia drive.

2 The armature shaft rotates in two porous bronze bushes. A squared extension of the shaft protrudes to enable the shaft to be rotated to clear any jamming between the inertia drive and engine flywheel ring gear. The armature features a face-type moulded commutator.

3 A plastic brush box is riveted to the commutator end bracket. It holds four wedge-shaped brushes and captive coil springs. The brushes are keyed to ensure correct fitting.

4 The field winding is a continuously wound strip with no joints. One end is attached to two brush flexibles, while the other is attached to a single flexible which is earthed to the yoke.

5 The yoke is windowless and has no through-bolts. The commutator end bracket is secured by four screws which align with tappings in the yoke. The drive end bracket is attached by two slot-headed bolts which screw into tappings provided in the armature shaft.

3 It is most important that the drive gear is completely free from oil, grease and dirt. With the drive gear removed, clean all parts thoroughly in paraffin. Under no circumstances oil the drive components. Lubrication of the drive components could easily cause the pinion to stick.

4 Reassembly of the starter motor drive is the reverse sequence to dismantling. Use a press or the large valve spring compressor to compress the spring and retainer sufficiently to allow a new circlip to be fitted to its groove on the shaft.

10 Lucas M35J starter motor - dismantling, overhaul and reassembly

Should it be necessary to dismantle the starter motor

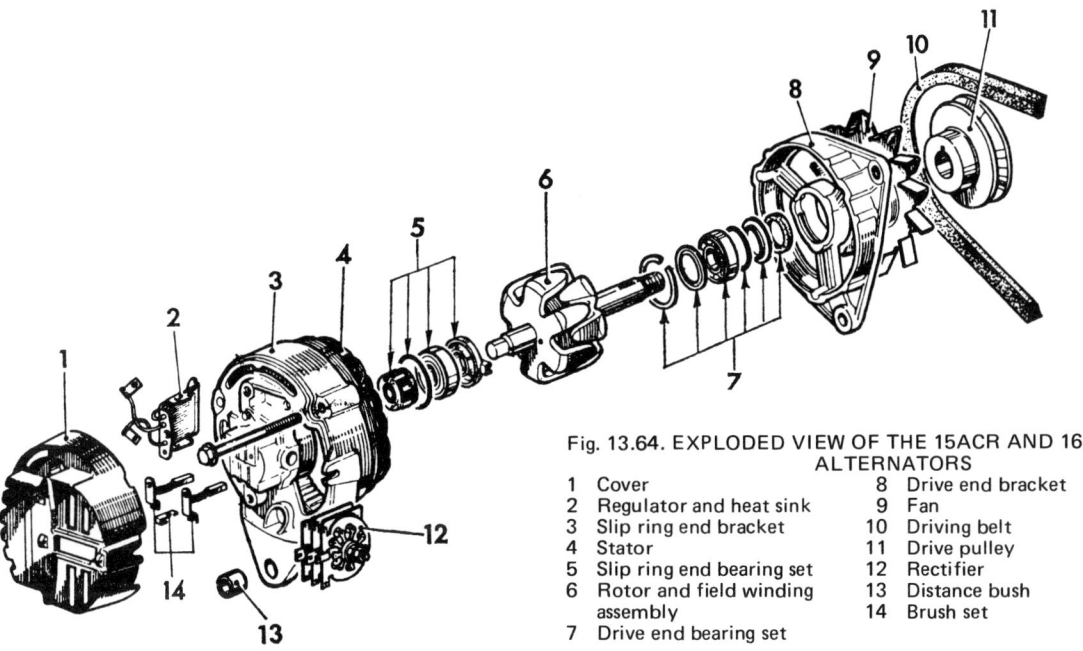

Fig. 13.64. EXPLODED VIEW OF THE 15ACR AND 16ACR ALTERNATORS

1	Cover	8	Drive end bracket
2	Regulator and heat sink	9	Fan
3	Slip ring end bracket	10	Driving belt
4	Stator	11	Drive pulley
5	Slip ring end bearing set	12	Rectifier
6	Rotor and field winding assembly	13	Distance bush
7	Drive end bearing set	14	Brush set

end faces of two of the pole-shoes.

6 The principle of operation of the inertia type starter motor is as follows: When the ignition switch is turned, current flows from the battery to the starter motor solenoid switch which causes it to become energized. Its internal plunger moves inwards and closes an internal switch so allowing full starting current to flow from the battery to the starter motor. This creates a powerful magnetic field to be induced into the field coils which causes the armature to rotate.

7 Mounted on helical splines is the drive pinion which, because of the sudden rotation of the armature, is thrown forwards along the armature shaft and so into engagement with the flywheel ring gear. The engine crankshaft will then be rotated until the engine starts to operate on its own and, at this point, the drive pinion is thrown out of mesh with the flywheel ring gear.

9 Lucas M35J starter motor inertia drive - removal and refitting

1 To dismantle the starter motor drive, first use a press or large valve spring compressor to push the retainer clear of the circlip which can then be removed. Lift away the retainer and main spring.

2 Slide off the remaining parts with a rotary action of the

completely, the following operations will facilitate overhaul. Bear in mind, though, that it may be more economical in terms of money plus time, to purchase an exchange unit.

The other factor that may mitigate against overhaul is the need for special tools and test gear.

1 To strip the starter, remove the two bolts holding the drive end bracket to the yoke, and take off that bracket, withdrawing the armature. Remove the thrust washer from the brush end of the armature.

2 Undo the four small bolts holding on the commutator end bracket. Pull the bracket aside. Note the way the flexible cable from the field windings to the brushes is fitted. Then undo these brushes.

3 To separate the armature from the drive end bracket and inertia drive, remove the inertia drive, and slide the drive end bracket from the shaft.

4 Inspect the laminations for score marks. These may indicate a bent shaft, worn bearings or a loose pole shoe.

5 Clean the commutator with a petrol moistened cloth. If the commutator is in good condition, it will be smooth and free from pits or burned spots.

6 If necessary, polish the commutator with fine glass-paper. If the commutator is badly scored it will need skimming. Mount the armature in a lathe and rotate at high speed. Using a very sharp tool, take a light cut. Polish with fine glass-paper. Do not cut below the minimum skimming thickness of 0.080 in (2.05 mm). Do not undercut insulators between segments.

7 Inspect the porous bronze bearing bushes for wear and renew as necessary. To renew the commutator end bracket bush, drill out the two rivets and discard the plate and felt seal. Screw a ½ in (12.70 mm) tap squarely into the bush and withdraw. Prepare the porous bronze bush by immersing it in thin engine oil for 24 hours. Using a highly polished, shouldered mandrel suitably dimensioned, and a suitable press, fit the bush. Do not ream the bush after fitting or its porosity may be impaired. Assemble the brush box, felt seal and plate. Secure with two rivets.

8 To renew the drive end bracket bush, remove the inertia drive, and slide the drive end bracket from the shaft. Support the bracket and press out the bush. Prepare the porous bronze bush by immersing it in thin engine oil for 24 hours. Using a highly polished, shouldered, mandrel suitably dimensioned, and a suitable press, fit the bush. Do not ream the bush after fitting or its porosity may be impaired.

9 The brushes should be renewed if worn down to a length of 0.375 in (9.5 mm).

10 The commutator end bracket brushes are supplied attached to a new terminal post. Withdraw the two brushes from the brush box. Withdraw the terminal post and remove the insulation piece. Reverse to assemble. Retain the longer flexible under the clip.

11 The field winding brushes are supplied attached to a common flexible. Cut old flexibles 0.250 in (6 mm) from the joint. Solder the new flexible to the ends of the old flexible. Do not attempt to solder direct to the field winding strip as the strip may be produced from aluminium.

12 Check the field winding insulation from the yoke as follows. Drill out the rivet at the earth connection. Apply the normal 110 volt ac test-lamp circuit to the field winding and yoke. Do not attempt to disconnect the flexible from the field windings strip as the strip may be produced from aluminium.

13 To renew the field winding, drill out the rivet at the earth connection. Using a wheel-operated screwdriver, slacken the four pole-shoe screws. Remove two diametrically opposite screws and pole-shoes. Slacken the remaining two screws sufficient to allow the field winding to be withdrawn from the yoke. Reverse to assemble.

14 Assembly is the reverse of dismantling.

   a) *Insert the two field winding brushes into the brush box with the flexibles positioned as shown in Fig. 13.70.*
   b) *Position the commutator end bracket and secure it with four BA bolts.*
   c) *Fit the thrust washer.*
   d) *Insert the drive end bracket, armature and inertia drive. assembly complete into the yoke.*
   e) *Fit the two drive end bracket bolts and spring washers.*

11 Lucas M35J PE starter motor - general description

1 The M35J PE starter motor comprises the motor part of the M35J starter previously described and a pre-engagement drive pinion mechanism. When the device is energised, a solenoid mounted on the motor body energises and actuates the drive pinion into engagement in the flywheel ring gear. To allow for the possibility of overrun, the pinion drive is transmitted through a oneway roller clutch.

12 Lucas M35J PE starter motor - dismantling, overhaul and reassembly

1 It will be necessary to dismantle the starter motor if checks indicate that failure to turn the engine is due to faults with it. After some time the brushes will also wear sufficiently to warrant renewal.

2 The solenoid may be removed after detaching the short connecting cable from the other main terminal and removing the two securing nuts. If this is all that needs replacing, a new one

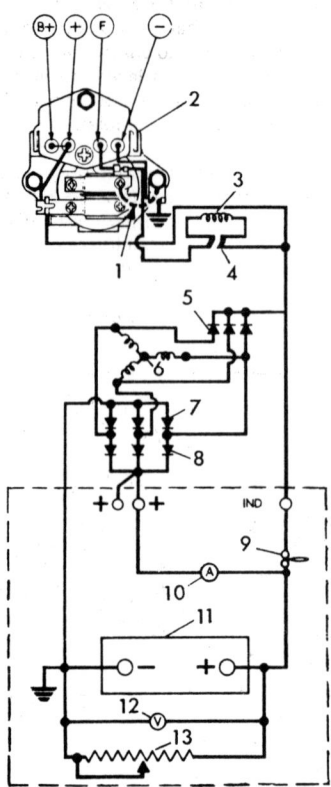

Fig. 13.65. TEST CIRCUIT FOR 15ACR AND 16ACR ALTERNATORS

1   Link bridging 'F' and '–ve' terminals
2   Voltage regulator
3   Exciter field winding
4   Slip rings
5   Exciter field diodes
6   Stator winding
7   Earth side output diodes (3)
8   Live side output diodes (3)
9   12 volt 2-2W bulb
10 0-40 or 0-60 ammeter
11 Car battery
12 0-20 voltmeter
13 0-15 ohm 35 amp rated variable resistor

can be fitted over the existing plunger now.

3 To dismantle the motor further, remove the short bolts, or through bolts, which hold the commutator end bracket with the brush gear to the main yoke. Also remove the split pin, washers and shims from the end of the shaft. The end bracket may then be carefully removed. Do not lose the thrust washer which is located over the end of the shaft inside.

4 Next, remove the bolts holding the drive end cover in position (if necessary) and the end cover complete with armature and shaft may be drawn out of the yoke.

5 Take off the pivot pin retaining ring and then push out the pin.

6 To take the drive pinion and clutch assembly off the armature shaft, it will be necessary to drive the thrust collar down the shaft with a piece of suitable tube and then remove the circlip which is exposed. If the driving gear assembly is worn the whole unit should be renewed: To check that the roller clutch is in good condition it should lock and take up the drive in one direction immediately it is turned. When turned in the opposite direction it should rotate smoothly and evenly. The whole clutch unit should also slide easily without excessive play along the splines of the armature shaft.

7 Examination of the motor is similar to that given in the Section for the M35J starter motor previously.

8 Assembly is a procedure that must be carried out in sequence with attention to several points to ensure that it is correct.

9 First assemble the engagement lever to the solenoid plunger so that the chamfered corner faces the solenoid. Then, make sure that the retaining plate is correct, relative to the lever (Fig. 13.71).

10 Next, fit the drive pinion and clutch assembly on the armature shaft, fit the engagement lever fork to the clutch, and assemble the whole lot together to the drive end cover. Then, fit a new lever pivot pin and a new retaining ring.

11 Replace the yoke, and then lightly screw up the end cover bolts (if fitted).

12 Next, place the thrust washer over the commutator end of the shaft, fit all the brushes into their appropriate holders in the end cover and replace the end cover onto the shaft. Both end covers have locating pips to ensure they are fitted correctly to the yoke.

13 Replace the through bolts or end cover bolts as appropriate and tighten them up at both ends.

14 Replace the thrust washer and shims to the end of the shaft, install a split pin, and then measure the endfloat gap between the thrust washer and the end cover with a feeler gauge. It should be no more than 0.010 in (0.25 mm). Additional shims should be added to reduce the endfloat as required.

15 Next, replace the rubber pad between the drive end bracket (under the solenoid plunger housing) and the yoke, and refit the solenoid. Reconnect the short cable to the solenoid terminal.

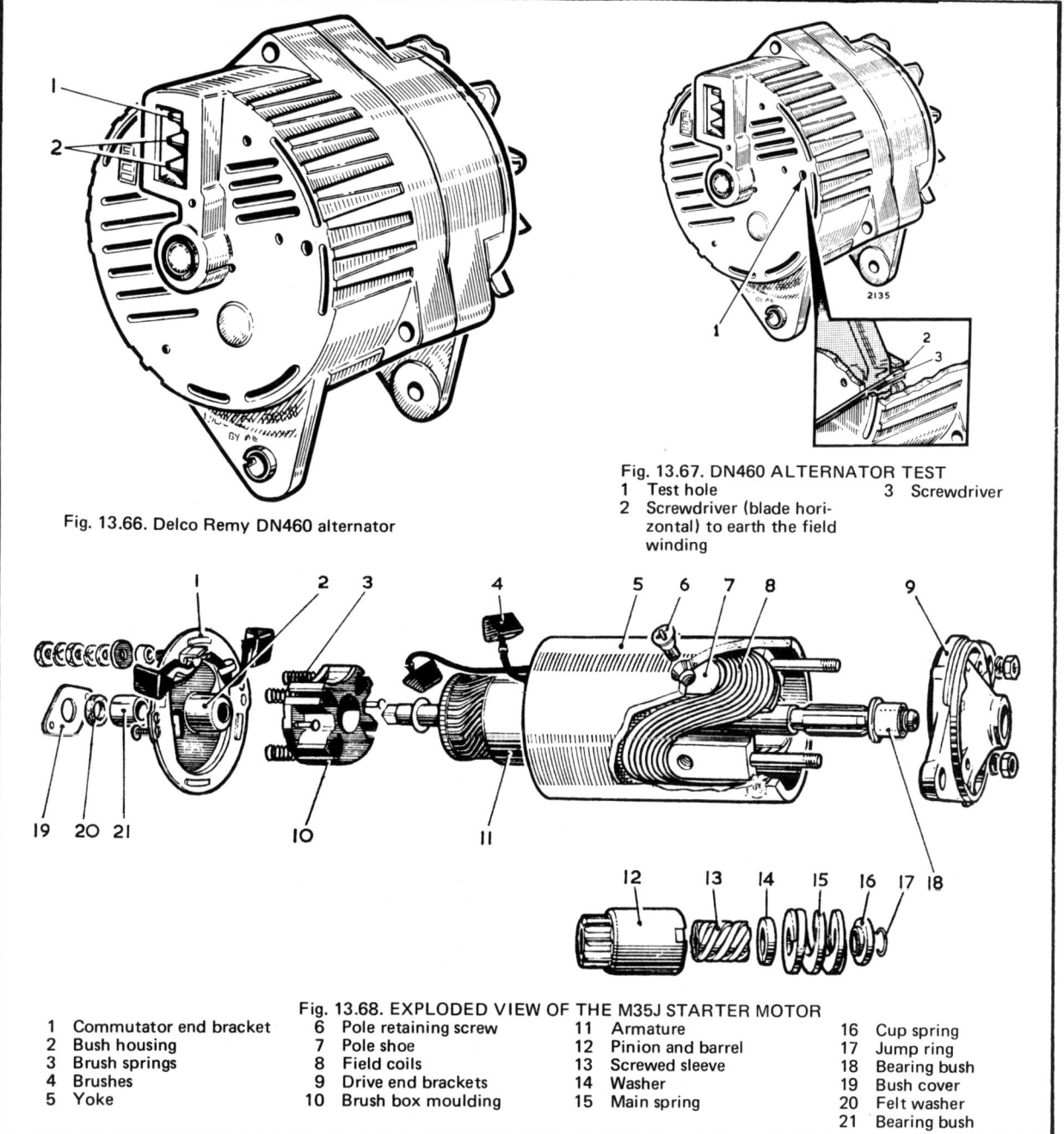

Fig. 13.66. Delco Remy DN460 alternator

Fig. 13.67. DN460 ALTERNATOR TEST
1 Test hole
2 Screwdriver (blade horizontal) to earth the field winding
3 Screwdriver

Fig. 13.68. EXPLODED VIEW OF THE M35J STARTER MOTOR

1	Commutator end bracket	6	Pole retaining screw	11	Armature
2	Bush housing	7	Pole shoe	12	Pinion and barrel
3	Brush springs	8	Field coils	13	Screwed sleeve
4	Brushes	9	Drive end brackets	14	Washer
5	Yoke	10	Brush box moulding	15	Main spring
				16	Cup spring
				17	Jump ring
				18	Bearing bush
				19	Bush cover
				20	Felt washer
				21	Bearing bush

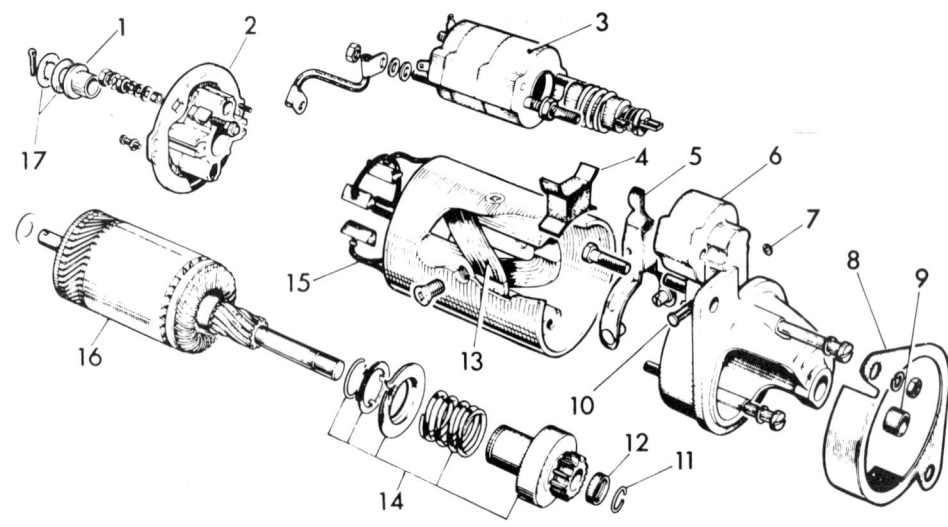

Fig. 13.69. EXPLODED VIEW OF THE M35J PE STARTER MOTOR

1	Bush commutator end	6	Drive end bracket	11	Jump ring	16	Armature
2	Commutator end bracket	7	Pivot pin retainer	12	Thrust collar	17	Thrust washer -
3	Solenoid	8	Dust cover	13	Field coil set		shim set
4	Grommet	9	Bush - drive end	14	Drive - roller clutch assy.		
5	Engagement lever	10	Pivot pin	15	Brush set		

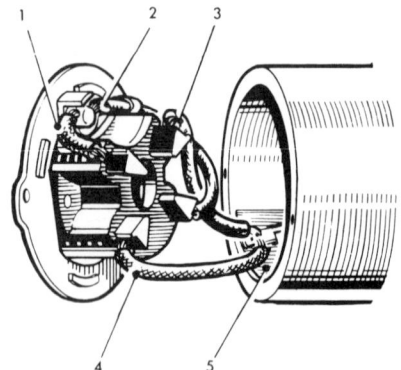

Fig. 13.70. BRUSH LEAD TERMINATIONS ON THE M35J
PE STARTER MOTOR

1 Short brush - flexible, commutator end bracket
2 Long brush - flexible, commutator end bracket
3 Long brush - flexible, field winding
4 Short brush - flexible, field winding
5 Yoke insulator - field connection joint

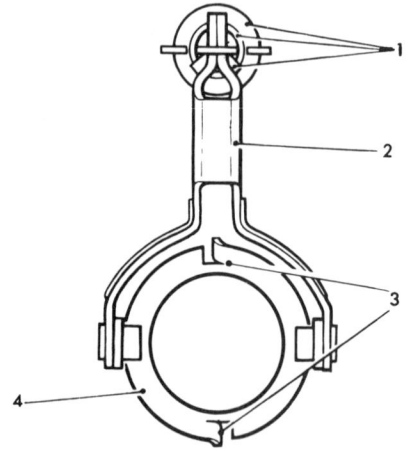

Fig. 13.71. CORRECT ASSEMBLY OF ENGAGEMENT
LEVER AND SOLENOID PLUNGER

1 Plunger, 'lost motion' spring   3 Drive engagement lever
   and retaining plate   4 Locking shoulders
2 Drive operating plate

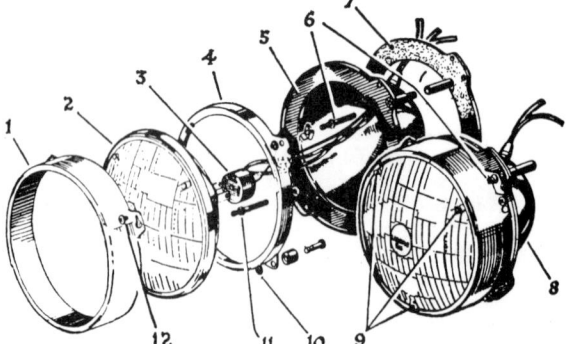

Fig. 13.72. F575 DUAL HEADLAMPS

1	Front rim	7	Sealing gasket
2	Light unit (2A)	8	Lamp body
3	Cable adaptor	9	Aiming pads
4	Seating rim	10	Retaining ring
5	Lamp body	11	Beam adjustment screw
6	Beam adjustment screw		(horizontal)
	(vertical)	12	Rim retaining screw

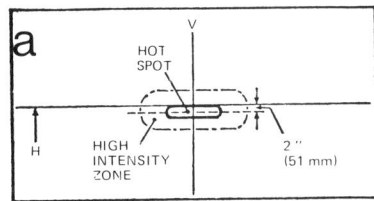 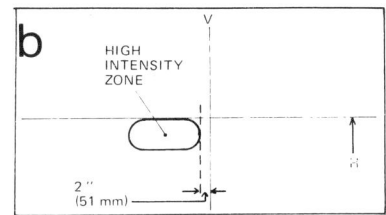 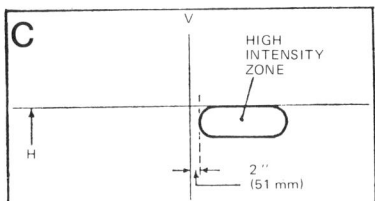

Fig. 13.73. BEAM ALIGNMENT

A Inner lamps   C Outer lamps, left-hand   H Height of headlamp centre above ground
B Outer lamps, right-hand drive   drive   V Vertical line through headlamp centre

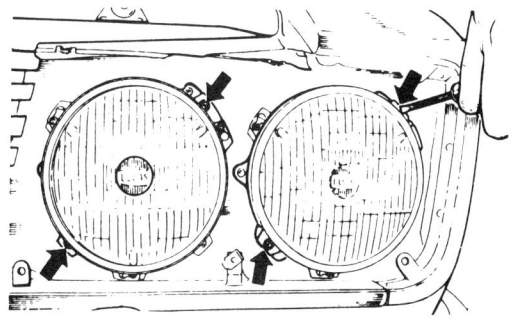

Fig. 13.74. Beam adjusting screws (arrowed)

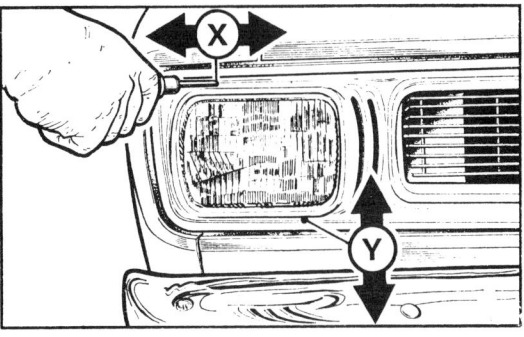

Fig. 13.75. 4FR HEADLAMP ADJUSTING SCREWS
X Horizontal   Y Vertical

13 Dual headlights - adjustment, removal and refitting

1   Dual circular 5¾ in (128 mm) Lucas sealed beam units are
fitted to certain models, whilst some others have similar
assemblies with replaceable pre-focus bulbs.

Lucas unit - removal and installation
2   Remove the securing screws and headlamp finisher.
3   Loosen the three screws securing the unit and rim and turn
the unit anticlockwise to align the large keyhole slots with the
screw heads.
4   Lift the unit clear and detach the wiring connector. Where
the bulb is of the replaceable type, the holder may be unclipped
and the bulb removed.
5   Do not attempt to clean the reflective surface on units fitted
with a bulb.
6   Installation is a reverse of the removal sequence.

Marchal unit - removal and installation
7   Remove the securing screws and headlamp finisher.
8   The unit is retained by three ball ends that 'snap' into
recesses in the shell. Withdraw the light unit by forcing it out of
the shell with finger and thumb pressure applied at the two
adjusting screws.
9   Disconnect the wiring plug and remove the rubber plug from
the bulb. Remove the bulb retaining springs, and lift out the
bulb.
10 Installation is a reverse of the removal procedure, but care
must be taken not to touch the glass envelope of the bulb when
replacing into the unit.
11 Beam adjustment should normally be performed with the
proper optical equipment, but a good guide can be obtained by
using the alignment diagrams 10.22, 13.73A, B, C. Each of
the lamps should be masked while checking the alignment of the
other lamp opposite.

14 Lucas 4FR rectangular headlights - adjustment, removal and refitting

1   These units are similar to the 2FR rectangular units referred
to in Chapter 10, Section 32, except that they are retained by
four screws which are accessible once the grille has been
removed. When the headlights are withdrawn, care should be
taken not to lose the four rubber anti-rattle pads.

15 Cibie rectangular headlights - adjustment, removal and refitting

This headlight is fixed to the shell in exactly the same way as
the Marchal unit, fitted to the four headlamp model. Refer to
Section 13, paragraph 8 after removing the screws and radiator
grille.

16 Later models - stop-tail and rear flasher bulbs renewal

Bulb renewal on later models has to be performed from inside the luggage compartment.
1   Remove the four plastic thimbles.
2   Take off the plastic cover (if fitted) on Deluxe, Super, GL
and GLS models or release the press studs securing the covering
on the inside of the panel on Sceptre models. This will expose
the rear lamp assembly bulb holders.
3   The two lamp holders are clipped in position and can be
removed by a straight pull. The cables need not be disconnected
when changing bulbs.
4   Refitting is a reverse of the removal procedure, but ensure
that the wiring is located through the cut-outs in the cover and
the four thimbles are pushed fully home.

17 Instrument panel and instruments - removal and refitting   ıt

1 The details given in Section 36 of Chapter 10, are also applicable to Hillman GT models.
2 The details given in Section 37 of Chapter 10 are also applicable to Sceptre, Hunter de-luxe, Super, Gl and GT models, until the introduction of the modified layout described later in this section.

Later type instrument panel
1 To remove the later type instrument panel, first disconnect the battery earth lead.
2 Disconnect the choke cable at the carburettor(s).
3 Remove the screws which secure the steering column control, and the U-clip which is inside.
4 Remove the steering column clamp bolts and allow the column to drop down a little.
5 Slacken the clamp screws for the steering column switch(es) and point the switch levers downwards.
6 Depress the heater control knob spring clips; remove the knobs.
7 *GT and GLS models:* Remove the two screws which retain the auxiliary instrument panel, draw the panel forwards, then disconnect the brown/white lead to the lighting switch and the oil pressure gauge pipe. Draw the panel further forward, mark the relative lead positions for when refitting is required, then disconnect the leads and remove the panel completely.
8 *DL, Super and GL models:* Remove the two screws which retain the centre panel. Pull the panel forward, then push the switches out from the rear. Turn them through 90° and then back through the aperture in the panel. If a radio is fitted, this must now be removed, then the panel can be withdrawn.
9 *All models:* Remove the two screws which retain the heater control bracket to the top and bottom rails.
10 Detach the heater control, then pass it through the fascia complete with the wires.
11 Depress the speedometer outer cable retaining button and withdraw the inner and outer cables.
12 Remove the speedometer trip cable after unscrewing the knurled nut.
13 Noting the pipe locations, disconnect the screenwasher pipes from the pump (if fitted).
14 Disconnect the four harness connections at the rear of the fascia and the harness connection(s) from the column switch(es).
15 Where hazard and heated rear window switches are fitted, disconnect the harness leads.
16 Mark the leads to the windscreen wiper motor, then disconnect them.
17 Disconnect the snap connector in the glove box light lead.
18 Remove the face level vent heater hoses.
19 Ease off the draught seals from the door aperture adjacent to the sides of the instrument panel.
20 Remove the nuts and washers from below the panel that are located at either side of the radio speaker grille.
21 Remove one screw at each end of the panel and the four screws attaching the panel to the bottom fascia rail.
22 Carefully lift the panel to permit the long screws at the sides of the speaker grille to clear the top rail, then pull the panel backwards and clear of the fascia.
23 Refitting the panel is essentially a reversal of the removal procedure, but ensure that the contact surfaces at the rear of the panel, and at the front of the fascia rails, and the securing screws, are clean, since they provide the earth return for the voltage stabilizer and instrument lighting. Do not overtighten the nuts on the top rail for fear of distorting the instrument panel. Check, that when the steering column cowl is being fitted, it does not impede the operation of the column switches.

18 Flasher unit type 8FL - fault tracing and rectification

1 To remove the 8FL flasher unit it can simply be pulled from its spring clip beneath the steering column.
2 If the flasher fails to operate or works very slowly, first examine the front and rear bulbs for broken filaments. If these bulbs are satisfactory, then check the fascia warning bulb and renew if necessary.
3 Check the flasher circuit connections after reference to the appropriate circuit diagram.
4 Check fuse cartridge number 1.
5 Switch on the ignition and check the current is reaching the flasher unit by connecting a voltmeter between unit B, X or + terminal and earth.
6 Assuming that current is reaching the flasher unit but the flashers are still inoperative, connect the two unit terminals together and operate the flasher switch. If the flasher warning light comes on, then the flasher unit is faulty and must be renewed.

19 Hazard warning flasher unit type 9FL - fault tracing and rectification

1 The 9FL hazard warning flasher unit is a heavy duty version of the 8FL direction indicator flasher unit.
2 In the event of malfunction of the system it can be checked as described for the 8FL flasher unit in the previous Section. The fuse, however, may be an in-line fuse in the lead to the flasher unit.

20 Electrical windscreen washer - maintenance and testing

1 On some later models, a sealed motor and pump assembly is located in an external pocket of the plastic fluid container.
2 Maintenance of the assembly is limited to occasional removal of the container from the car, removal of the pump from the external pocket, disconnecting the plastic inlet pipe from the pump body and swilling the container in warm water. At the same time, check that the pipes are not blocked.
3 If the unit fails to operate, check the wiring and fuse. If this is satisfactory, rig up a temporary lead between the right-hand (negative) motor terminal and earth. If the pump fails to operate when the ignition is switched on, the unit is faulty and must be renewed.

21 Fuse units

With the introduction of the Series 4 and 5 models, the three fuse unit made way for one with eight fuses. These are housed in a plastic holder mounted on the bulkhead. In-line fuses, provided for the heated rear window and hazard warning lights, are located close to the steering column.
The eight fuses comprise:

Fuse No	Colour/ Rating	Circuits protected
1	Red 16A	*Ignition controlled: Horn, stop lamp, petrol gauge, water temperature gauge, screenwiper, blower*
2	White 8A	*Cigar lighter, interior lamps, clock*
3	White 8A	*Right-hand side lamp, tail lamp, boot lamp and fascia illumination*
4	White 8A	*Left-hand side lamp, tail lamp and number plate*
5	Red 16A	*Right-hand headlamp main beam*
6	Red 16A	*Left-hand headlamp main beam*
7	White 8A	*Right-hand dipped beam*
8	White 8A	*Left-hand dipped beam*

The two in-line fuses comprise:

In Line Fuse 15A	*Heated rear window (12 amp continuous)*
In Line Fuse 8A	*Hazard warning system*

Series 6 fuses have been altered slightly from those of the Series 4 and 5 as follows:

Fuse No	Colour/ Rating	Circuits protected
1	*White 8A*	*Ignition controlled: Horn, stop lamp, fuel gauge, water temperature gauge, screen wash, reverse lights, screen wiper, turn indicators, voltmeter (Sceptre only)*
2	*White 8A*	*Cigar lighter, interior light, clock, boot lamp*
3	*White 8A*	*Right-hand sidelamp, tail lamp, fascia lamps, rear fog lamps*
4	*White 8A*	*Left-hand sidelamp, tail lamp, number plate*
5	*Red 16A*	*Heated backlight*
6	*White 8A*	*Heater fan motor, voltmeter (Voltmeter to Fuse 1 on Sceptre)*
7	*White 8A*	*Right-hand dipped beam*
8	*White 8A*	*Left-hand dipped beam*

The in-line fuses comprise:

In-line Fuse 15A	*Hazard warning*

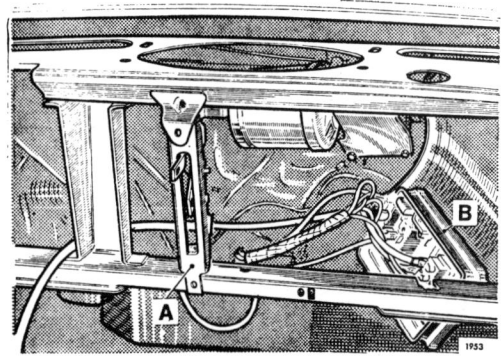

Fig. 13.77. THE HEATER CONTROL AND SWITCH PANEL
A Heater control   B Switch panel

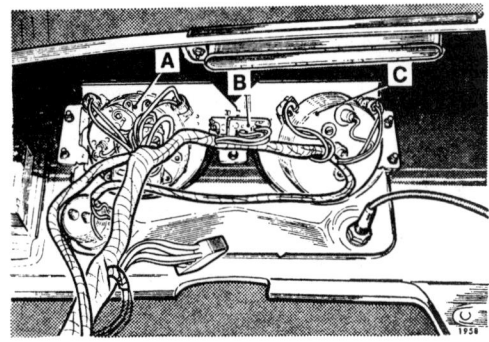

Fig. 13.78. REAR VIEW OF INSTRUMENT PANEL
A Instrument cluster   B Voltage stabiliser
C Speedometer

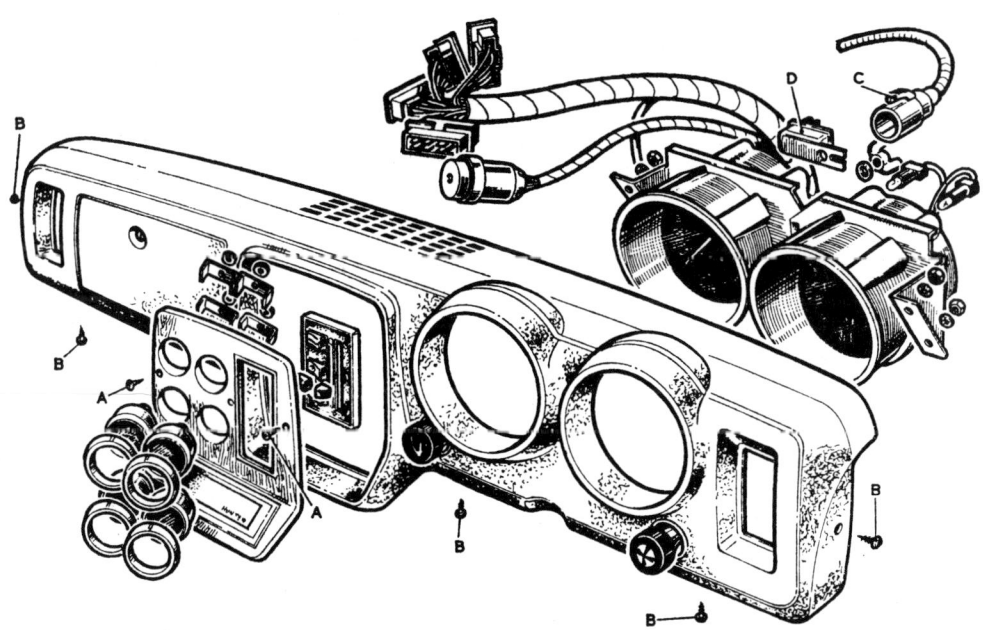

Fig. 13.76. LATER TYPE INSTRUMENT PANEL (GLS AND GT ILLUSTRATED)

A Fixing screws   B Fixing screws   C Button, outer speedometer cable   D Voltage stabiliser

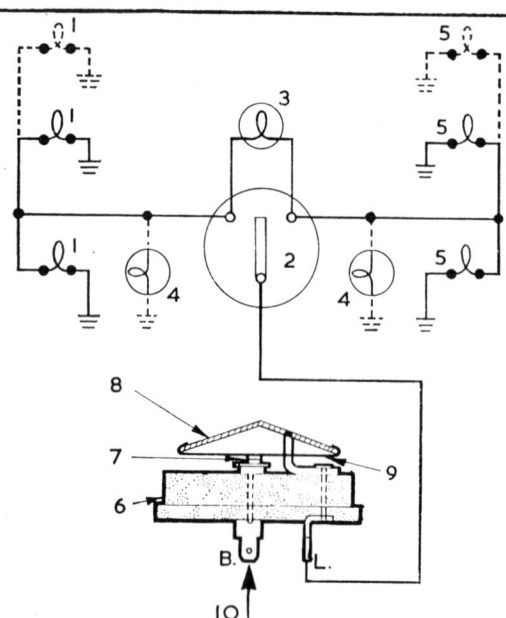

Fig. 13.79. 8FR FLASHER UNIT CIRCUIT DIAGRAM

1 Direction indicator lamps (left-hand)
2 Direction indicator switch
3 Pilot warning lamp
4 Alternative connection for two pilot warning lamps
5 Direction indicator lamps (right-hand)
6 Base moulding
7 Contacts
8 Vane
9 Metal ribbon
10 Supply terminal

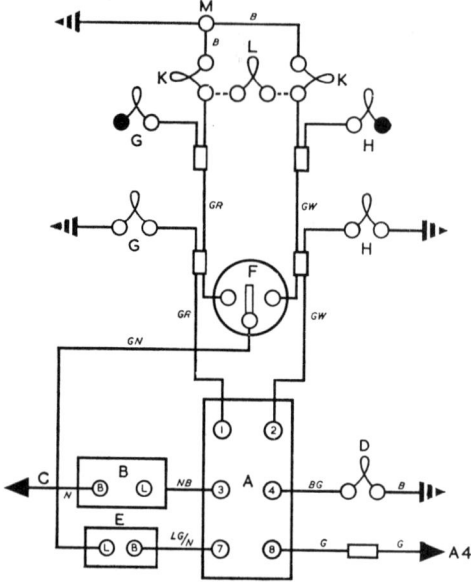

Fig. 13.80. 9FR HAZARD FLASHER UNIT CIRCUIT DIAGRAM

A Hazard warning switch
B Hazard flasher unit, warning
C Supply wire from ignition or lighting switch
D Hazard warning light
E Flasher unit, direction indicator
F Switch, direction indicator
G Direction indicator lamps, left-hand
H Direction indicator lamps, right-hand
K Warning lamps, direction indicator
L Warning lamp, direction indicator, alternative
M Earth connection, plug and socket

Wiring colour code:
N — Brown
G — Green
LG — Light green
R — Red
W — White
B — Black

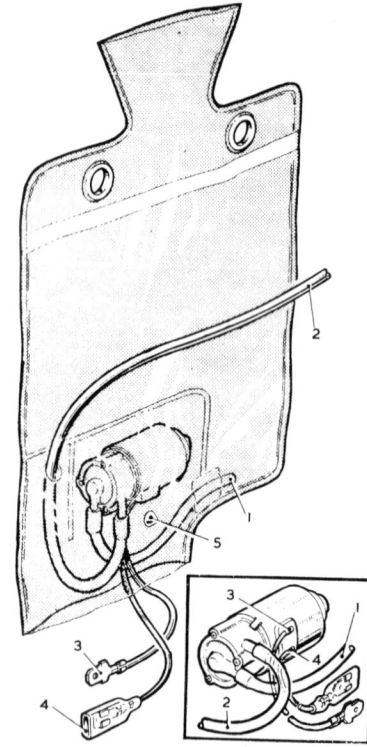

Fig. 13.81. ELECTRIC WINDSCREEN WASHER PUMP AND CONTAINER

1 Plastic pipe, pump inlet
2 Plastic pipe, pump outlet
3 Motor supply wire and terminal, coloured
4 Motor earth wire and terminal, black
5 Flap retaining stud, pump pocket

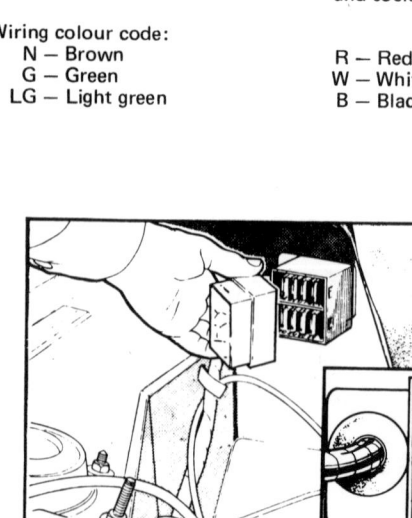

Fig. 13.82. Later type fuse block with eight fuses

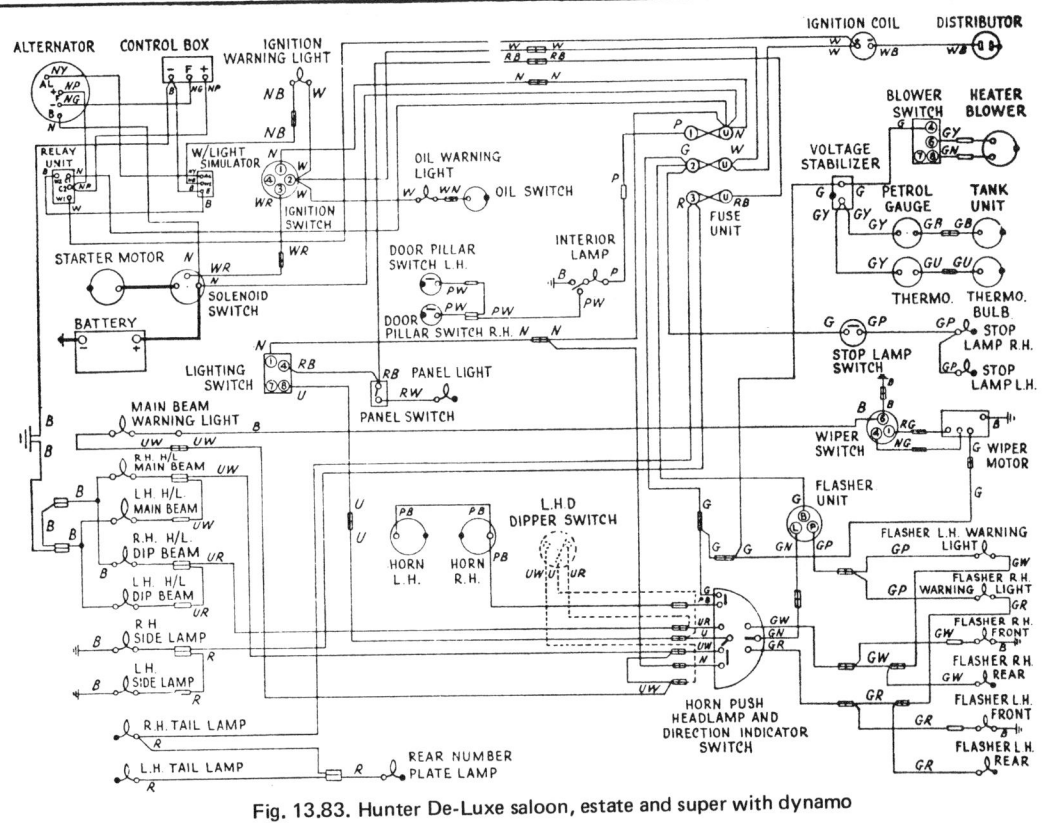

Fig. 13.83. Hunter De-Luxe saloon, estate and super with dynamo

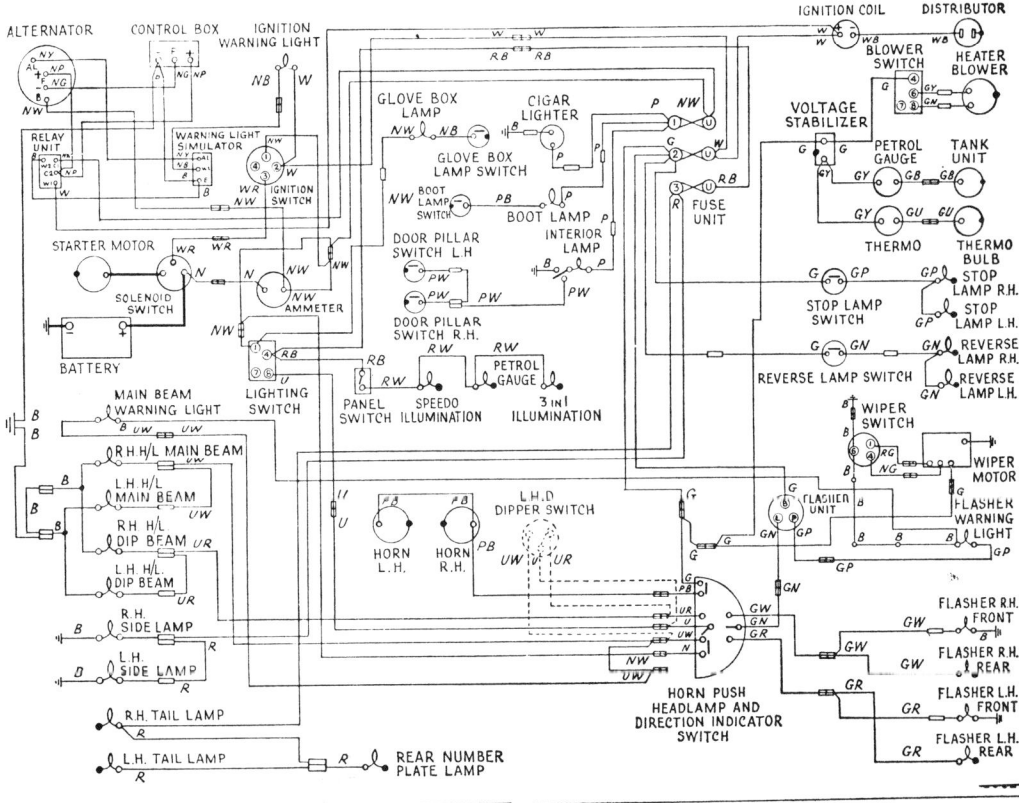

COLOUR CODE				ABBREVIATIONS
R	RED	N	BROWN	R.H. = RIGHT-HAND
Y	YELLOW	P	PURPLE	L.H = LEFT-HAND
G	GREEN	W	WHITE	L.H.D = LEFT-HAND DRIVE
U	BLUE	B	BLACK	H/L = HEADLAMP

SYMBOLS

– – – – –	ALTERNATIVE WIRING FOR LEFT-HAND DRIVE MODELS
––○–○––	SNAP CONNECTOR
––▭–▭––	PLUG AND SOCKET CONNECTOR
––B––○	EARTH THROUGH CABLE
––B–◖	EARTH THROUGH UNIT

Fig. 13.84. Hunter GL saloon and estate

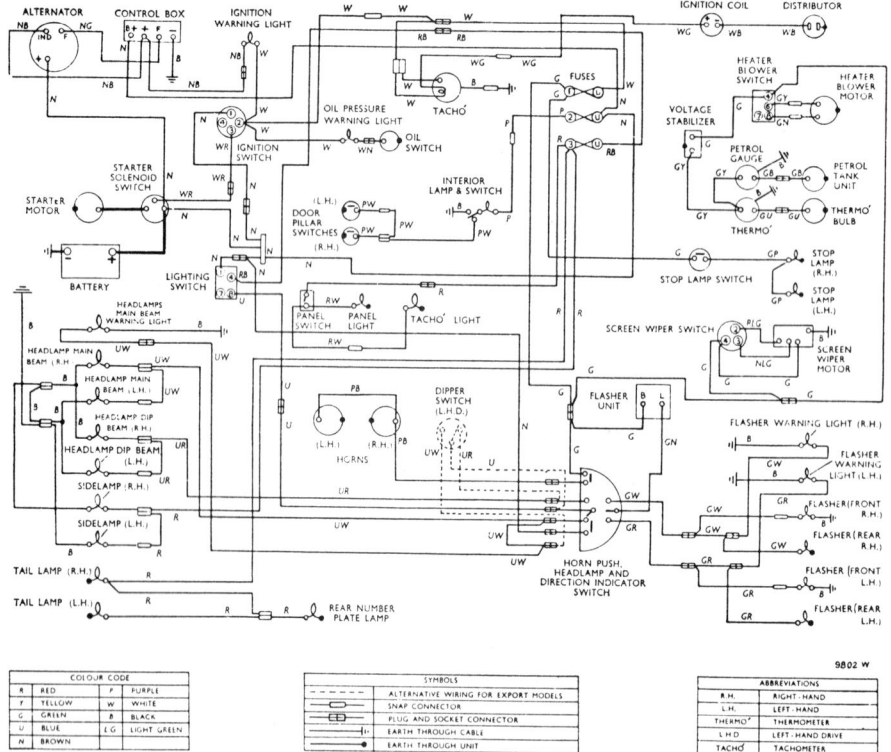

Fig. 13.85. Hillman GT with 16AC alternator

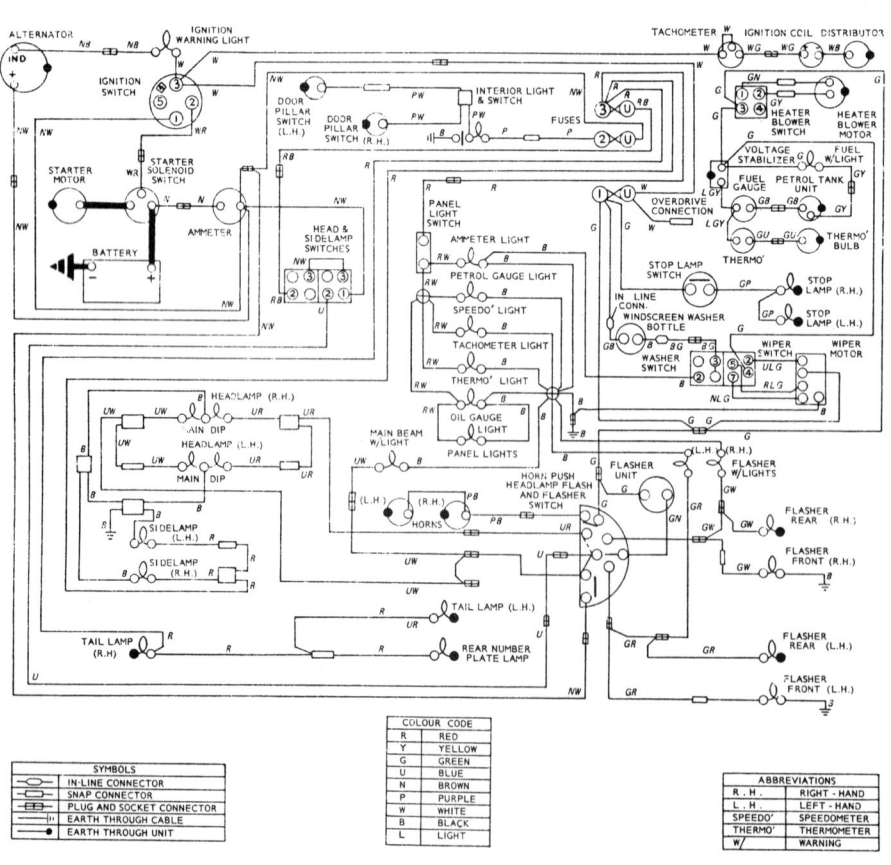

Fig. 13.86. Hillman GT

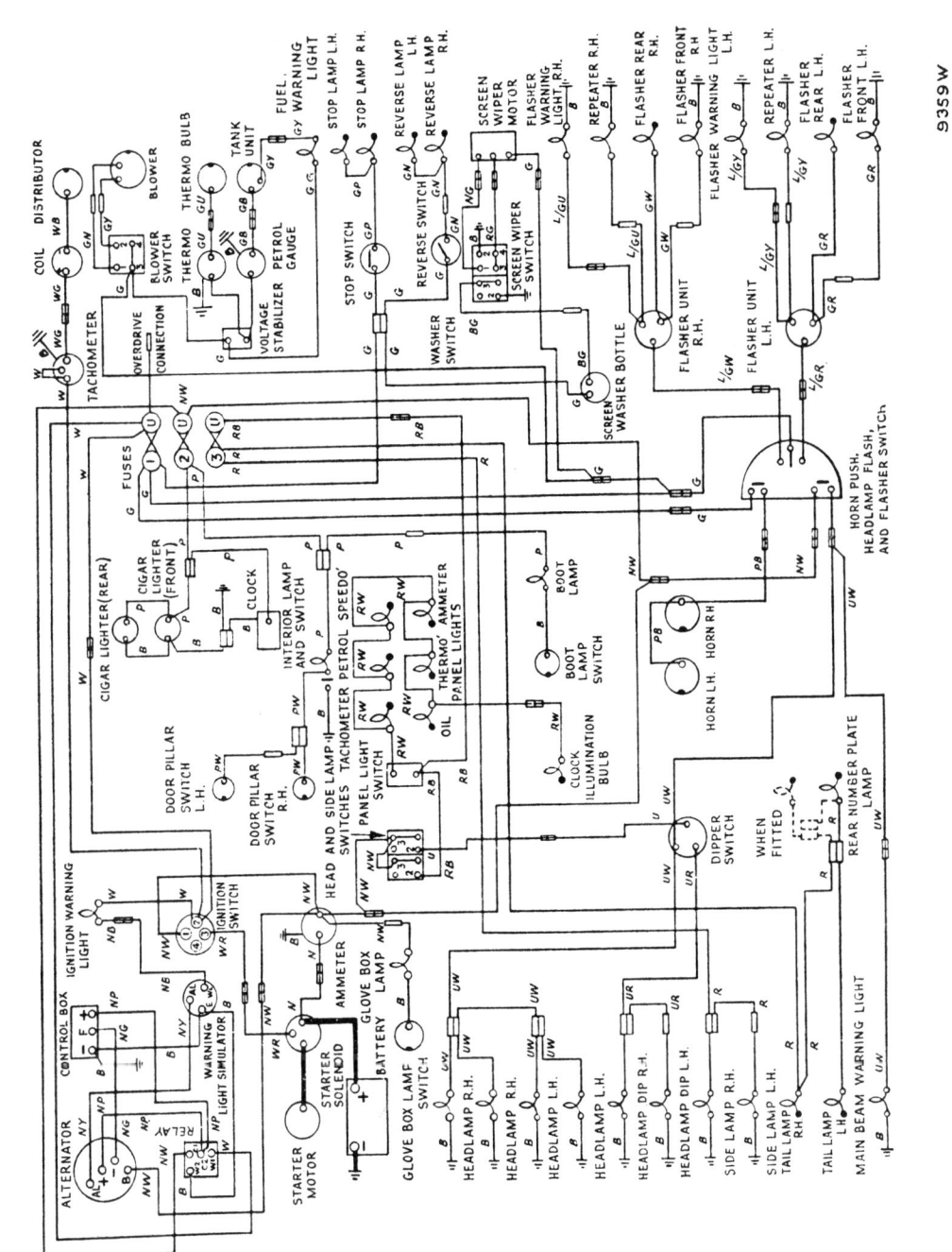

Fig. 13.87. Sceptre with 10AC alternator

9359w

ABBREVIATIONS

R.H.	RIGHT-HAND
L.H.	LEFT-HAND
THERMO'	THERMOMETER
SPEEDO'	SPEEDOMETER

SYMBOLS

– – – –	ADDITIONAL WIRING (EXPORT MODELS)
	SNAP CONNECTOR
	PLUG AND SOCKET CONNECTOR
—B—	EARTH THROUGH CABLE
—•|	EARTH THROUGH UNIT

COLOUR CODE

R	RED	N	BROWN
Y	YELLOW	P	PURPLE
G	GREEN	W	WHITE
U	BLUE	B	BLACK
L/G	LIGHT GREEN		

268

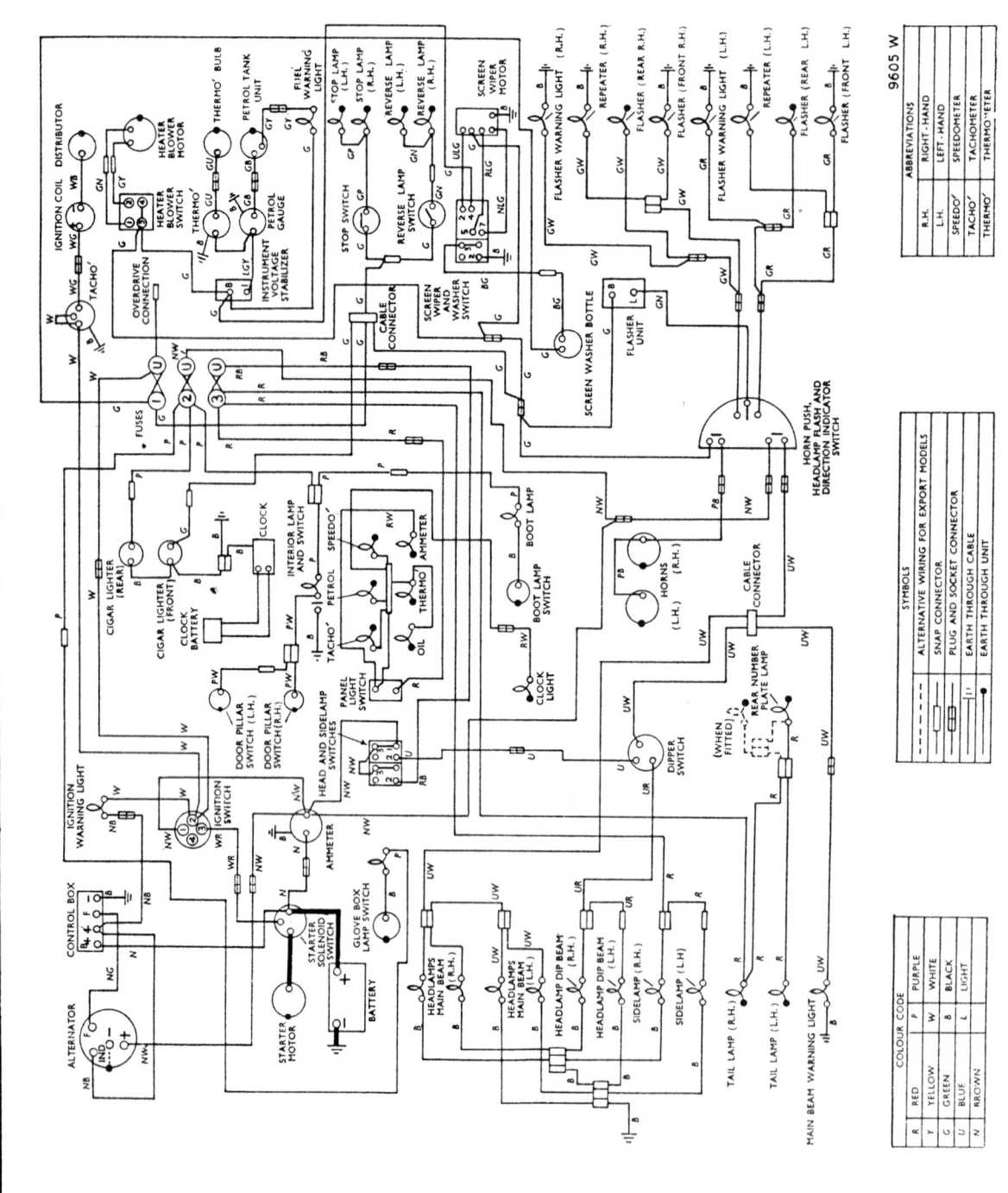

Fig. 13.88. Sceptre with 16AC alternator

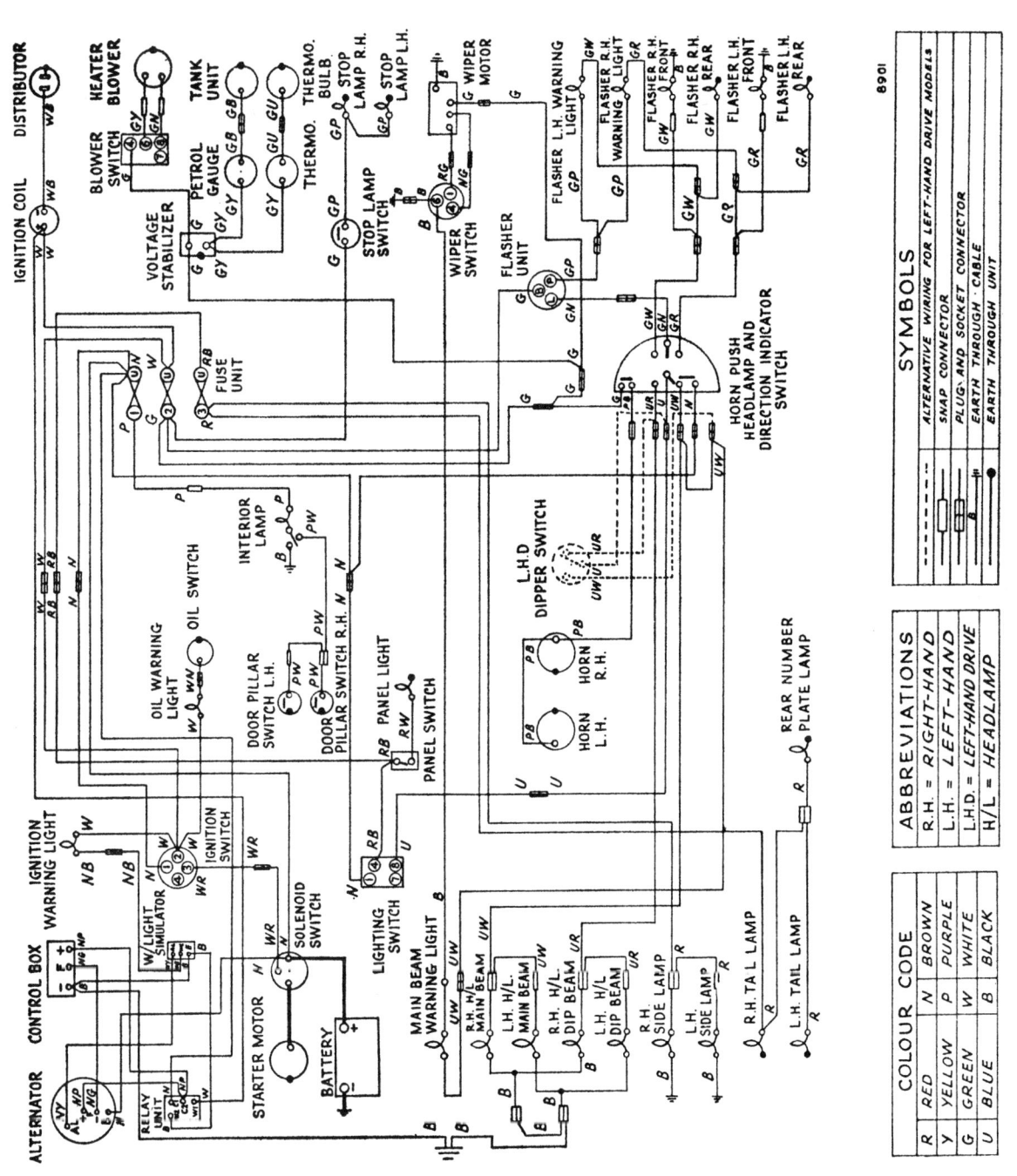

Fig. 13.89. Hunter with 10AC alternator

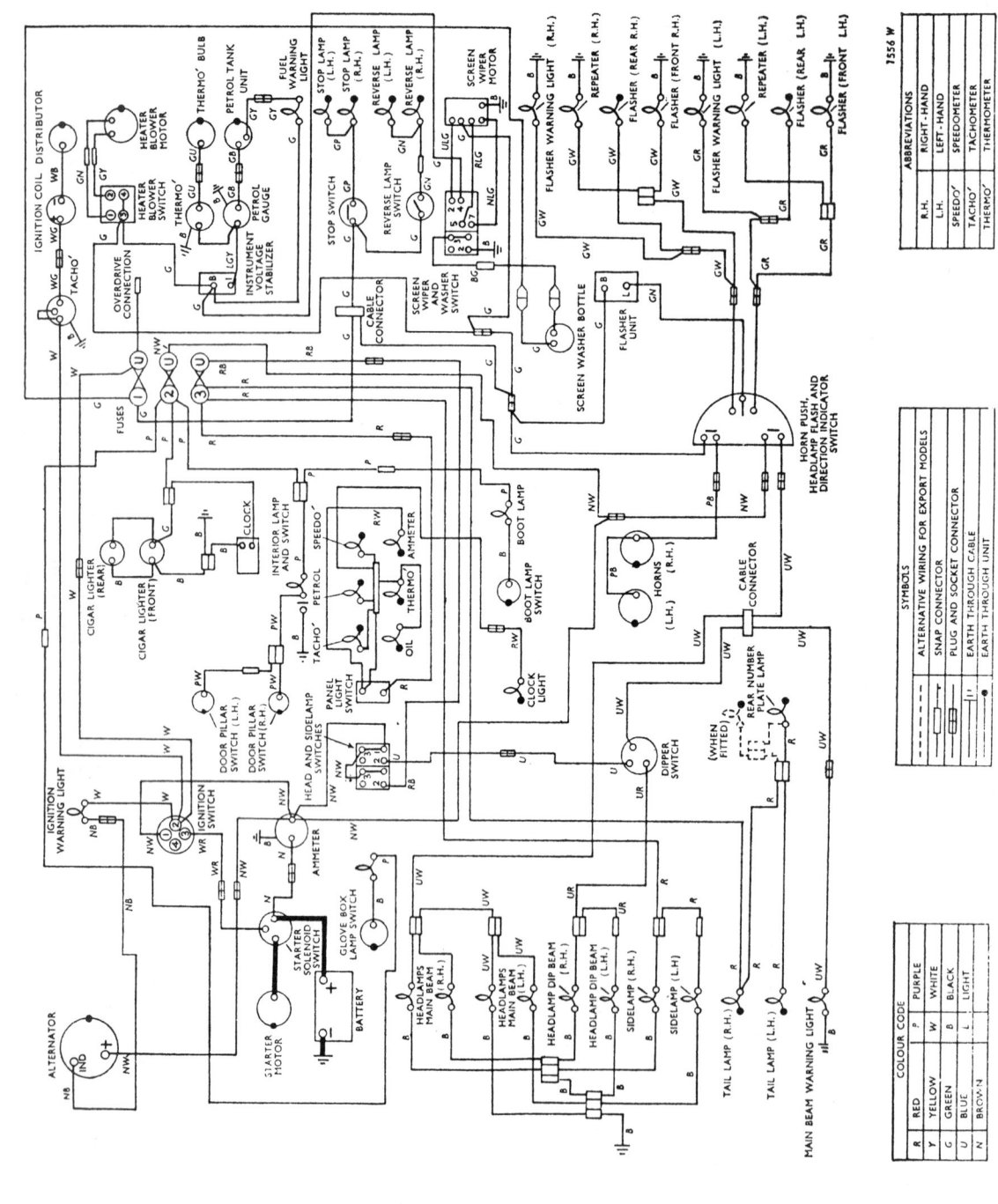

Fig. 13.90. Sceptre with 16ACR alternator

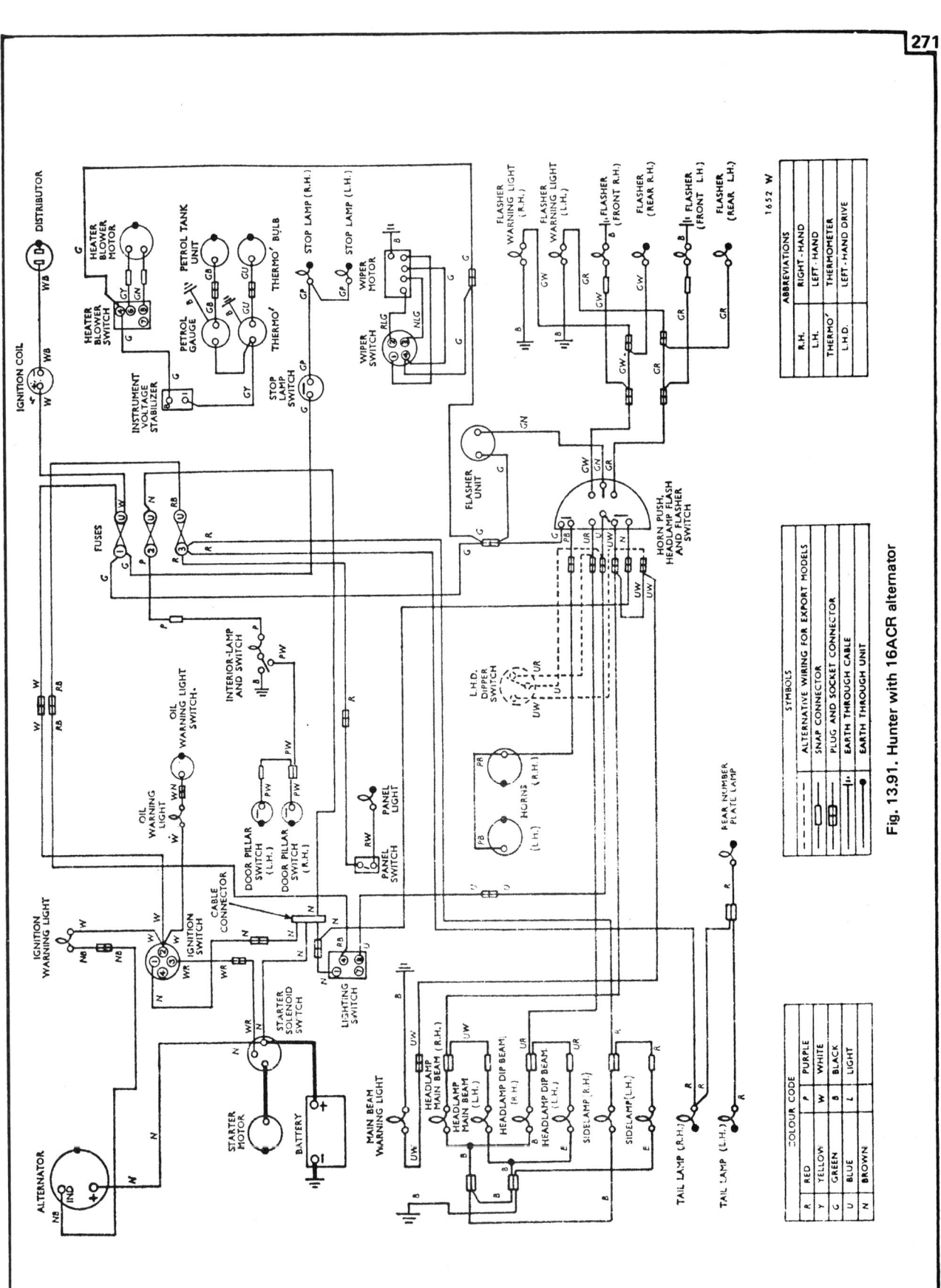

Fig. 13.91. Hunter with 16ACR alternator

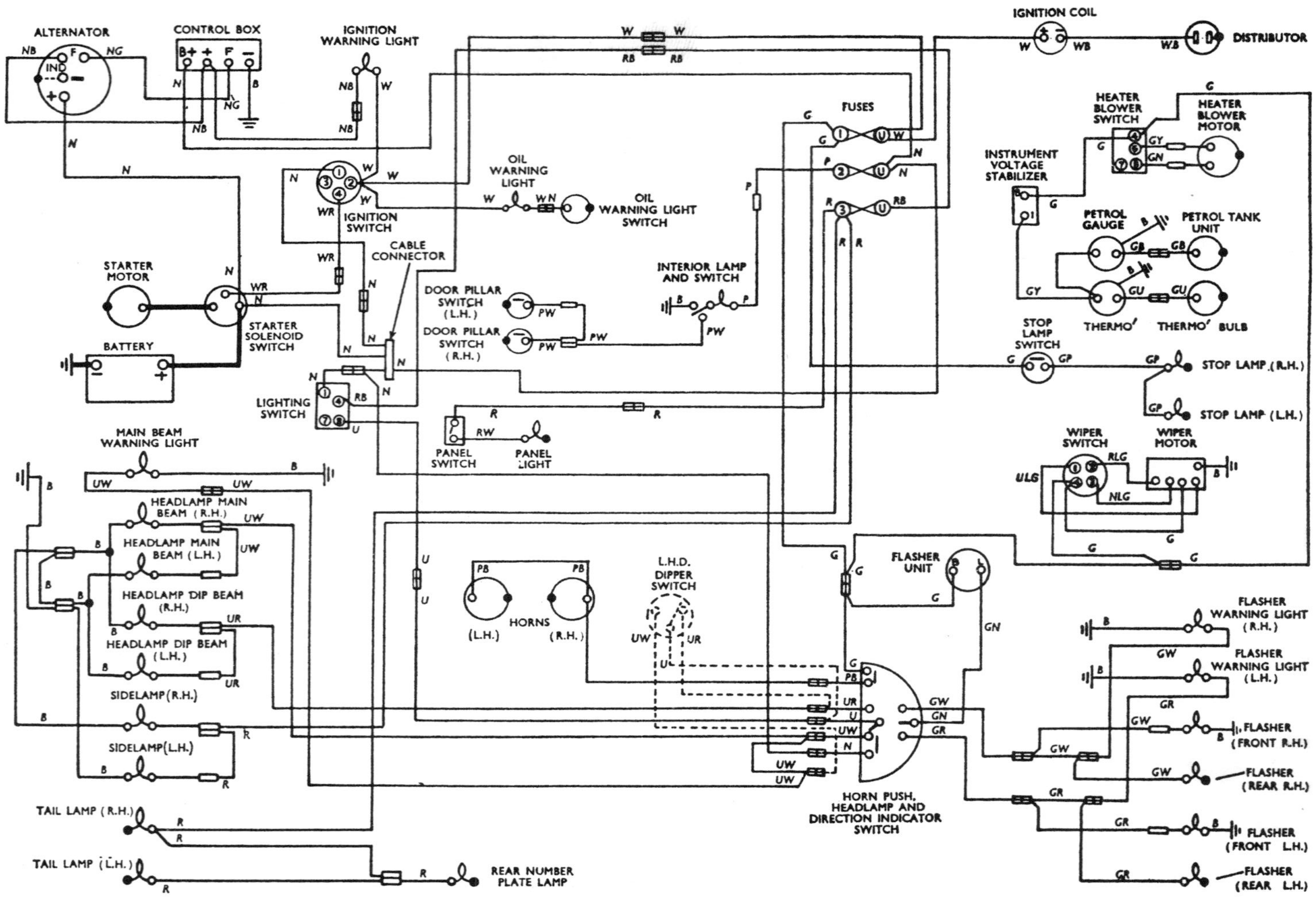

Fig. 13.92. Hunter with alternator

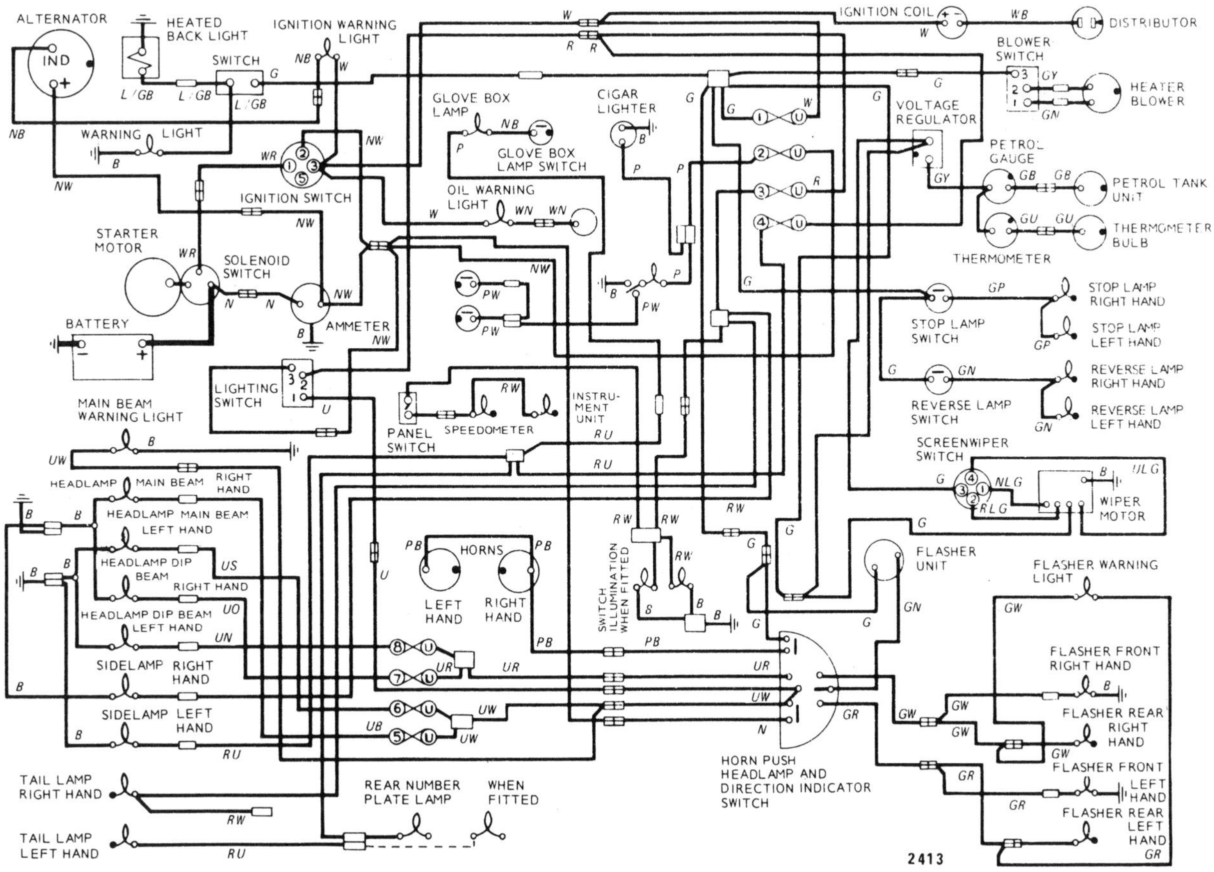

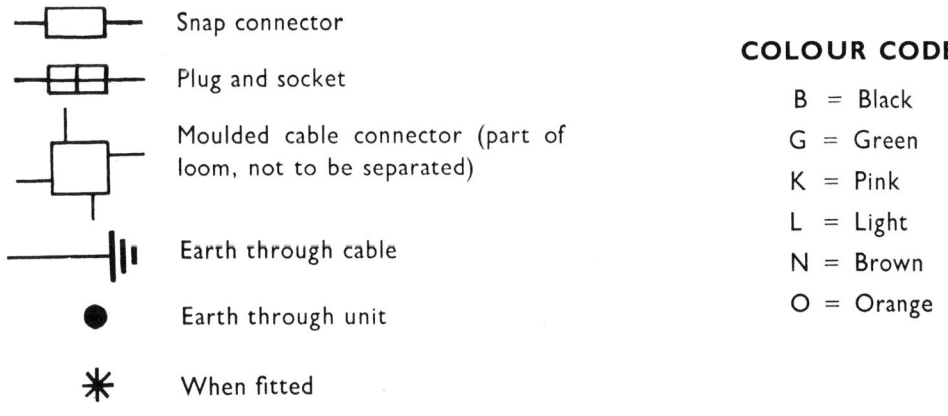

Fig. 13.93. Hunter GL saloon and estate

KEY TO SYMBOLS

▭	Snap connector
▭	Plug and socket
▢	Moulded cable connector (part of loom, not to be separated)
⏚	Earth through cable
●	Earth through unit
✳	When fitted

COLOUR CODE

B = Black

G = Green

K = Pink

L = Light

N = Brown

O = Orange

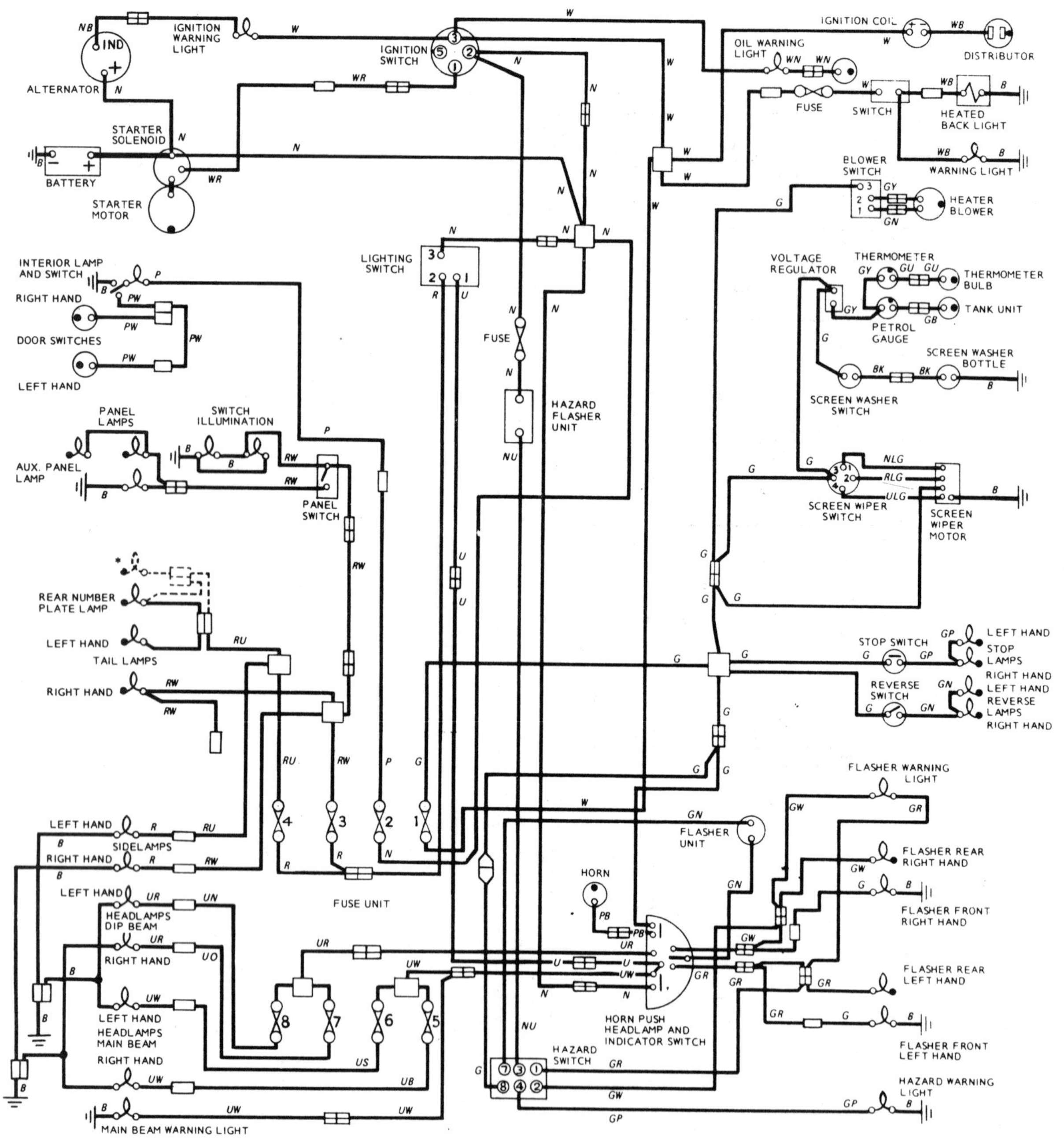

Fig. 13.94. Hunter De-Luxe saloon and estate. For Colour Code and Key to Symbols see page 273

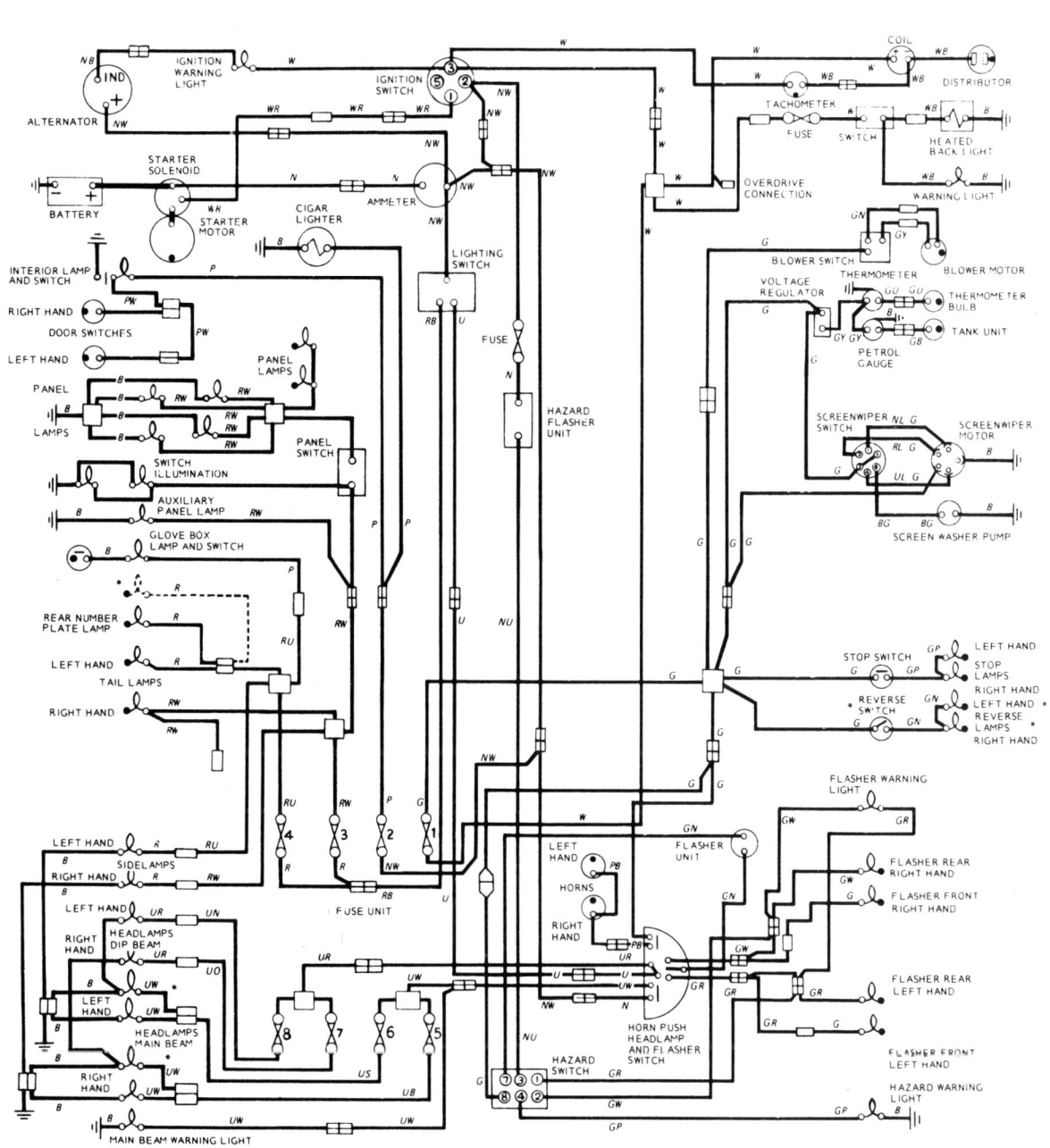

Fig. 13.95. Hunter GLS and GT. For Colour Code and Key to Symbols see page 273

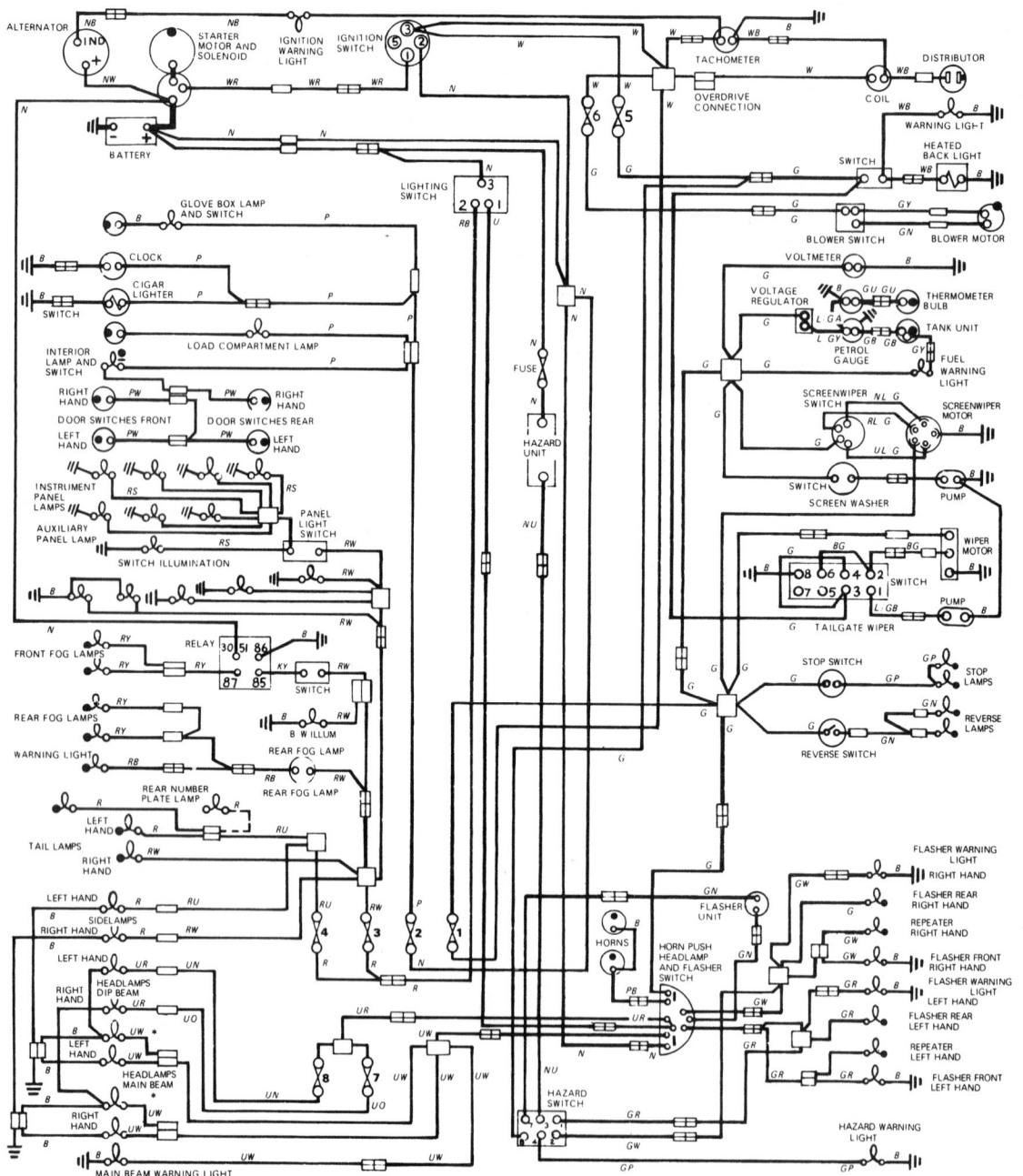

Fig. 13.96. Sceptre saloon and estate. For Colour Code and Key to Symbols see page 273

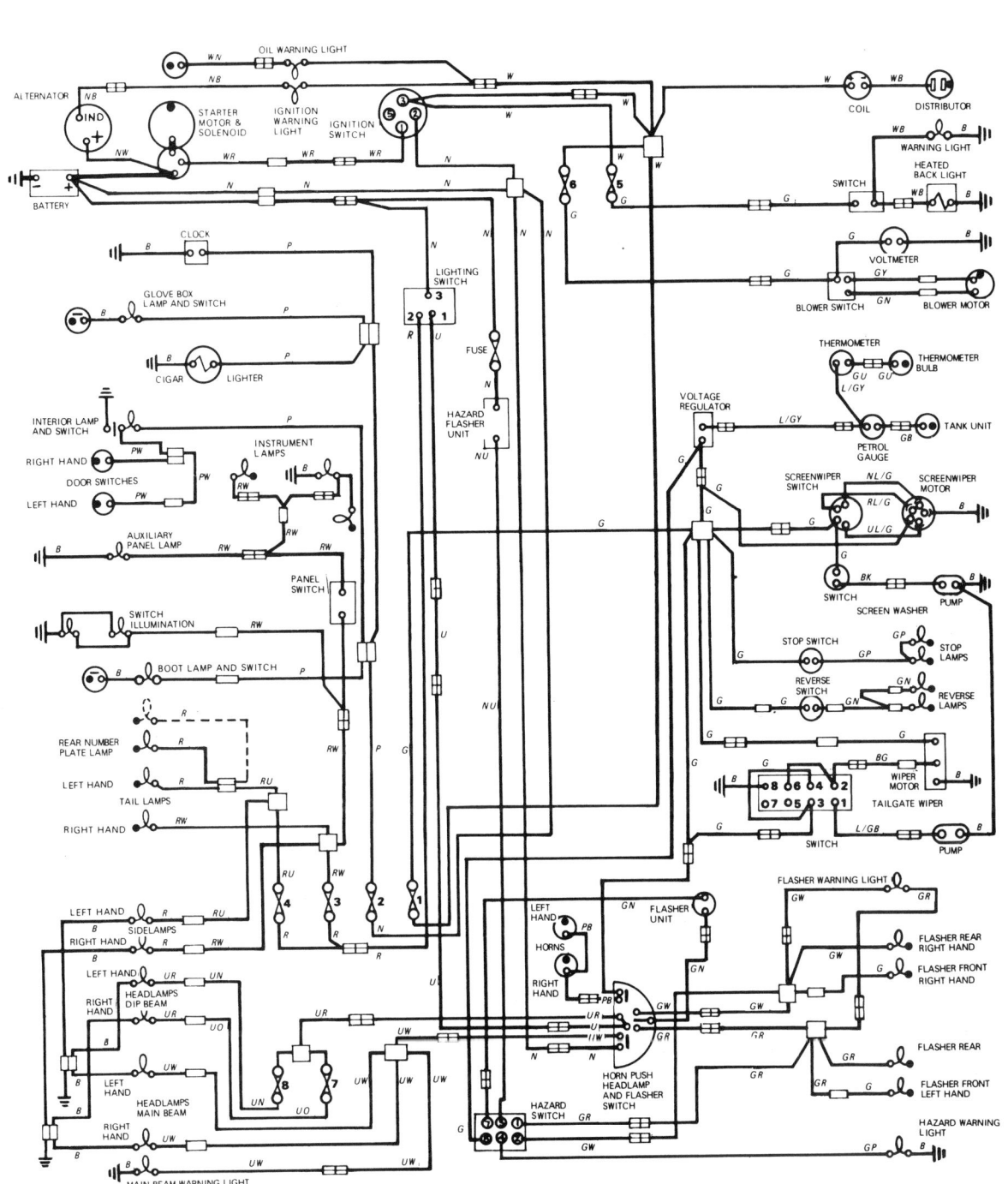

Fig. 13.97. Hunter GL saloon, estate and super. For Colour Code and Key to Symbols see page 273

9 Suspension, dampers, steering

1 Spring wedges - general note

1 Most early cars had a wedge fitted between the spring and axle pad, fitted so that the thick end of the wedge was to the front.
2 Early Vogue and Hunter models without wedges should only have them fitted in cases where axle and transmission vibration occurs.
3 For cars with single propeller shafts, the use of wedges was discontinued from the following serial numbers onwards.

Minx	*B 011001229*
Hunter	*B 051008444*
Gazelle	*B 711000270*
Vogue	*B 7510002748*

4 For cars with two-piece propeller shafts, the same part number spring wedge was re-introduced but fitted with the thin end to the front.

2 Steering wheel with adjustable steering unit - removal and refitting

1 Carefully prise off the steering wheel hub cap using a screwdriver in the slot under the cap outer edge.
2 Unscrew the nut and washer securing the hand control nut to the inner squared expander bolt adjusting nut.
3 Carefully withdraw the hand control unit.
4 Unscrew the three crosshead screws which retain the circular pressure plate: withdraw the plate.
5 Undo and remove the inner squared expander bolt adjusting nut.
6 Set the roadwheels to the straight ahead position.
7 Loosen the large nut securing the steering wheel to the splined inner column extension.
8 Rock the steering wheel a little from side to side to loosen it on its splines, then remove the steering wheel nut and pull off the wheel.
9 Refitting is a reversal of the removal procedure, but particular attention should be paid to the following points:

　　a) *The inner column should be set to its lowest position and the nylon circlip fitted to the top expander bolt.*
　　b) *Ensure that the roadwheels are in the straight ahead position.*
　　c) *Align the spokes of the steering wheel as it is being fitted.*

3 Burman adjustable steering gear - removal and refitting

1 The procedure for removal of the adjustable steering gear is similar to that for the conventional steering gear as described in Section 12 of Chapter 11, with the exception of the removal of the steering wheel which is described in the preceding paragraph.

4 Steering gear with column lock - removal and refitting

1 Initially, remove the steering lock as described in the following Section, then follow the procedure for the conventional steering gear.

5 Steering lock and ignition switch - removal and refitting

1 To remove the switch only, remove the battery earth lead, then apply thumb pressure to lever off the plastic ring on the back of the unit. The switch can then be carefully withdrawn from its location by pulling on the cables.
2 To remove the complete lock and switch, first remove the battery earth lead.
3 Withdraw the gaiter from the rear of the switch, then disconnect the cables.
4 Remove the front parcel tray, then take off the steering column cowling. Disconnect the steering column supporting brackets.
5 Loosen the bolts which retain the steering unit to the car frame, then remove them all **except** for one.
6 Lower the top end of the column to gain access to the steering lock fixing bolts.
7 Using a sharp centre punch, mark the centre of the domed head of the shear head bolts, then drill out the bolts to a depth of 1/8 in (3 mm) using a ¼ in (7 mm) drill.
8 Remove the slot headed screws from the fixing clamp and withdraw the unit from the column.
9 Using suitable grips, unscrew the bolt shanks remaining in the body of the unit.
10 To refit the lock unit, set to the park position with the locking plunger disengaged.
11 With the clamp removed, fit the unit to the column ensuring that the spigot registers squarely in the location hole.
12 Secure the unit to the column by fitting the clamp, fixing screws and bolts, taking care not to shear the heads of the special bolts at this stage.
13 Check the operation of the lock and, if satisfactory, tighten the shear head bolts fully.
14 Install the steering column in its original position then refit the parcel tray.
15 Reconnect the wires to the rear of the switch, then refit the rubber gaiter.
16 Reconnect the battery earth lead.

6 Front strut replacement damper cartridge - fitting

1 Replacement strut damper cartridges are available through normal motor vehicle factors. The cartridges are oil filled, sealed and self-priming but their operation should be checked before installation. When the cartridge is being used to replace an early type damper, they must be fitted to both sides of the car.
2 To fit a replacement damper cartridge, follow the instructions given in Chapter 11, Section 8, paragraphs 1 to 10.
3 Clean the strut internally and externally.
4 Insert the replacement cartridge into the strut.
5 Fit a new securing nut to the top of the strut, ensuring that it engages correctly with the threads in the strut.
6 Tighten the nut as far as possible using the wrench CS 0015.
7 Stake over the top edge of the strut into the slot in the nut.
8 Continue with the assembly operations as described in Chapter 11, Section 8, paragraphs 10f to 10i.

10 Bodywork and Underframe.

1 Front grille, twin headlamp models - removal and refitting

1 The grille can be detached by removing the retaining screws arrowed in white (see page 194). The black arrows indicate the screws which retain the headlamp finisher panel.

2 Directional air diffusers - removal and refitting

1 Take off the outer fascia panel after removing the retaining screws.
2 Press the clips which retain the diffusers against the body of the vent from behind the fascia, then withdraw the vent from

the front. Take great care with this operation since the clips can readily be damaged and thus render the unit unfit for further service.

3 Replacement is a straightforward reversal of the removal procedure.

3 Fascia crash roll - removal and refitting

1 From beneath the fascia, remove the two nuts (A in Fig. 13.103), then unscrew the two self-tapping screws (B) from the inner ends of the grilles over the heater vents.

2 Insert a thin piece of plastic or card between the A-post trim and each end of the roll, then remove the latter upwards and outwards, taking care that the windscreen weatherstrip is not damaged.

3 Replacement is a reversal of the removal procedure.

4 Seat belts

1 The illustrations show the different types of seat belt and fittings which have been used on models in the range.

5 Rear embellisher assembly (later models) - removal and refitting

1 From inside the luggage compartment gently pull back the trim on the rear quarter panel on both sides of the compartment, exposing three nuts and bolts per side which secure the corner chrome moulding to the top of the rear wings. Remove the nuts, plain washers and water sealing washers and lift off the top corner moulding.

2 Remove one nut and washer and one self-tapping screw from just below the moulding points and lift off the corner embellisher.

3 Remove the three screws which secure the boot lid lock to the inner side of the rear panel and remove.

4 Release the circular spring from the rear of the boot lock barrel, also the washer securing the lock shaft. Separate the lock barrel and the lock shaft before removing the barrel and draw the lock barrel forward clear of the panel.

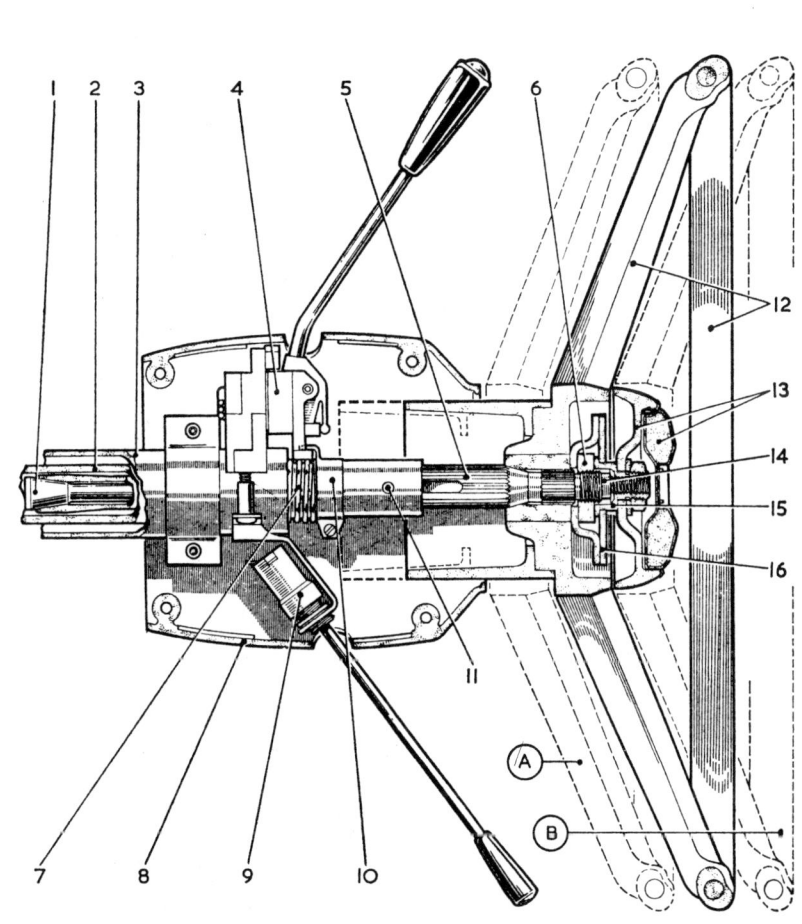

Fig. 13.98. SECTIONAL VIEW OF THE UPPER SECTION OF THE ADJUSTABLE COLUMN

1	Expander bolt	6	Steering wheel nut	10	Indicator striker	15	Expander bolt adjusting nut
2	Inner column	7	Bearing spring	11	Dowel	16	Circular pressure plate
3	Outer column	8	Column cowl	12	Steering wheel	A	Lowest position of steering wheel
4	Direction indicator switch	9	Overdrive switch (where fitted)	13	Hand control and cap	B	Highest position of steering wheel
5	Splined extension			14	Nylon circlip		

5 Remove three self-tapping screws from along the top of the embellisher. From inside the boot remove four self-tapping screws, one at each end of the panel, one in the centre, and one just left of the centre line.

6 Lower the petrol filler flap and from inside the panel, remove two nuts located just below the filler neck. Do not remove the screws as these are held by double nuts. Now pull forward the whole embellisher and petrol filler flap compartment clear of the vehicle.

7 Refitting is a reverse of the removal procedure.

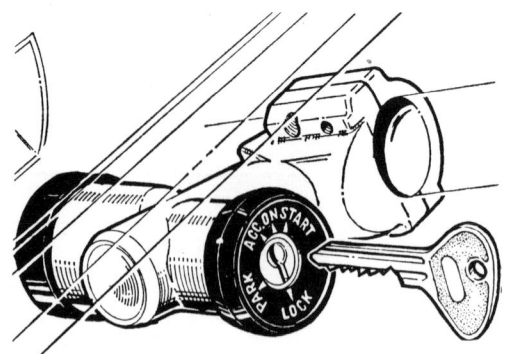

Fig. 13.99. Steering lock and ignition switch

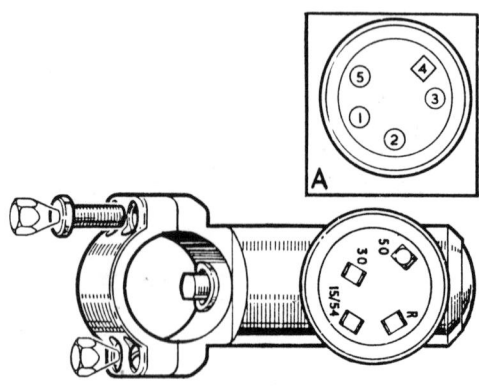

Fig. 13.100. Rear view of steering lock and ignition switch showing terminals and shear head bolts (inset A shows alternative terminal markings)

Terminal		Connection to	Cable colour
50	1	Starter sol.	white/red
30	2	Battery	brown (without ammeter) brown/white (with ammeter)
15/54	3	Fuse 1	white
—	4	Buzzer	black/brown
R	5	Accessories	green

Fig. 13.101. Lead colours on the steering lock and ignition switch

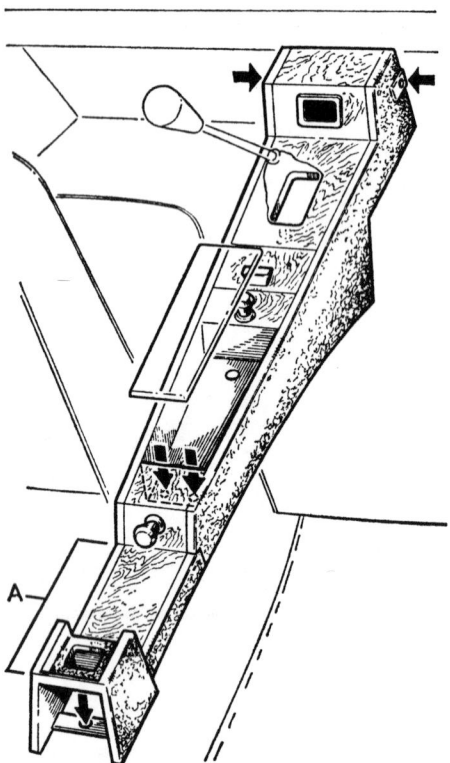

Fig. 13.102. Centre console fixing screws. 'A' Sceptre only

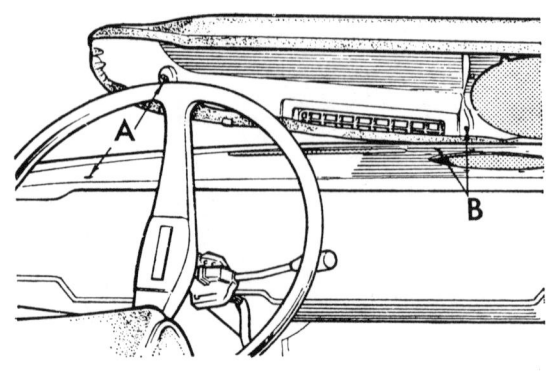

Fig. 13.103. FACIA CRASH ROLL REMOVAL
A   Crash roll nuts   B   Screw locations

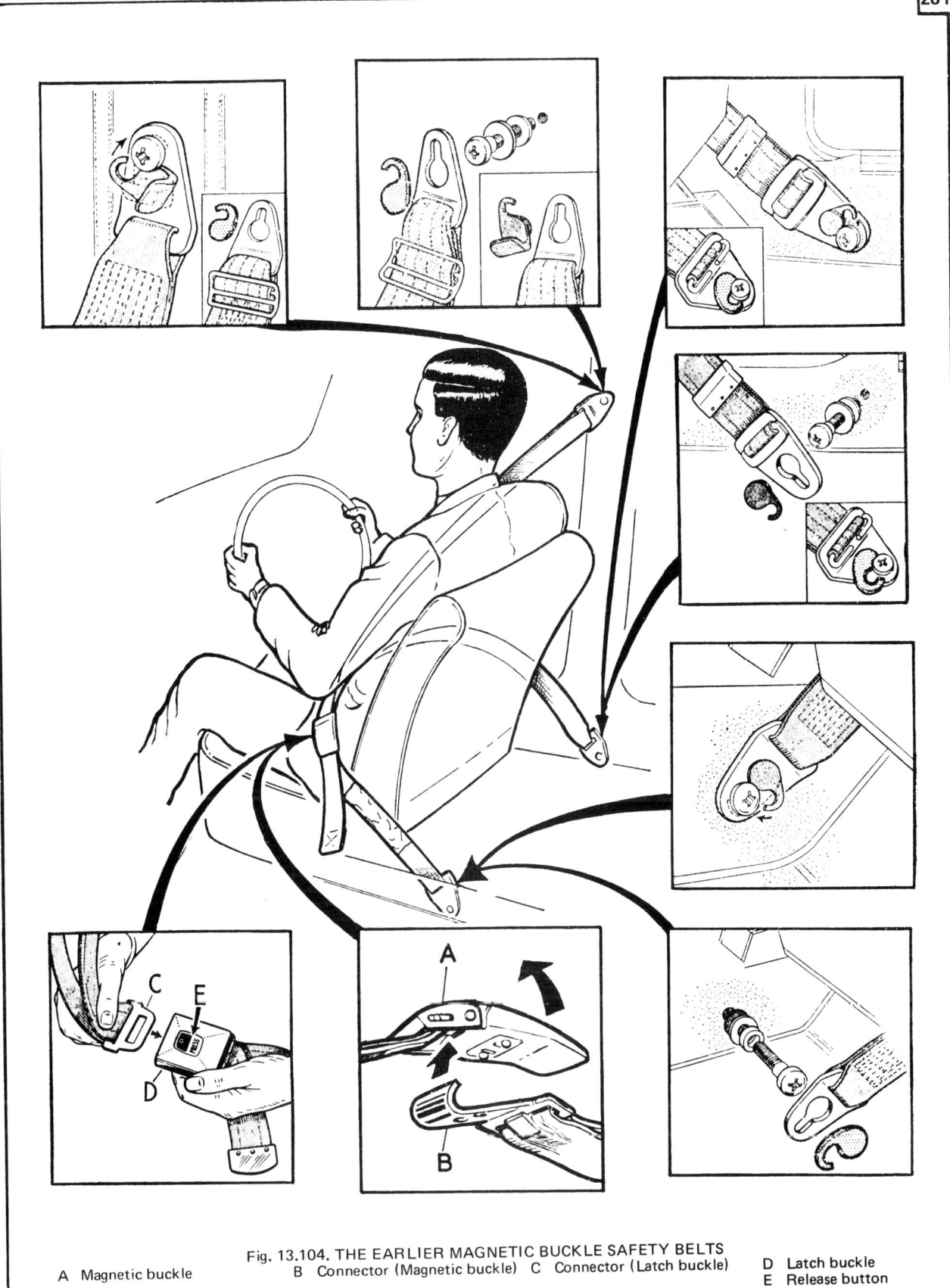

Fig. 13.104. THE EARLIER MAGNETIC BUCKLE SAFETY BELTS

A Magnetic buckle
B Connector (Magnetic buckle) C Connector (Latch buckle)
D Latch buckle
E Release button

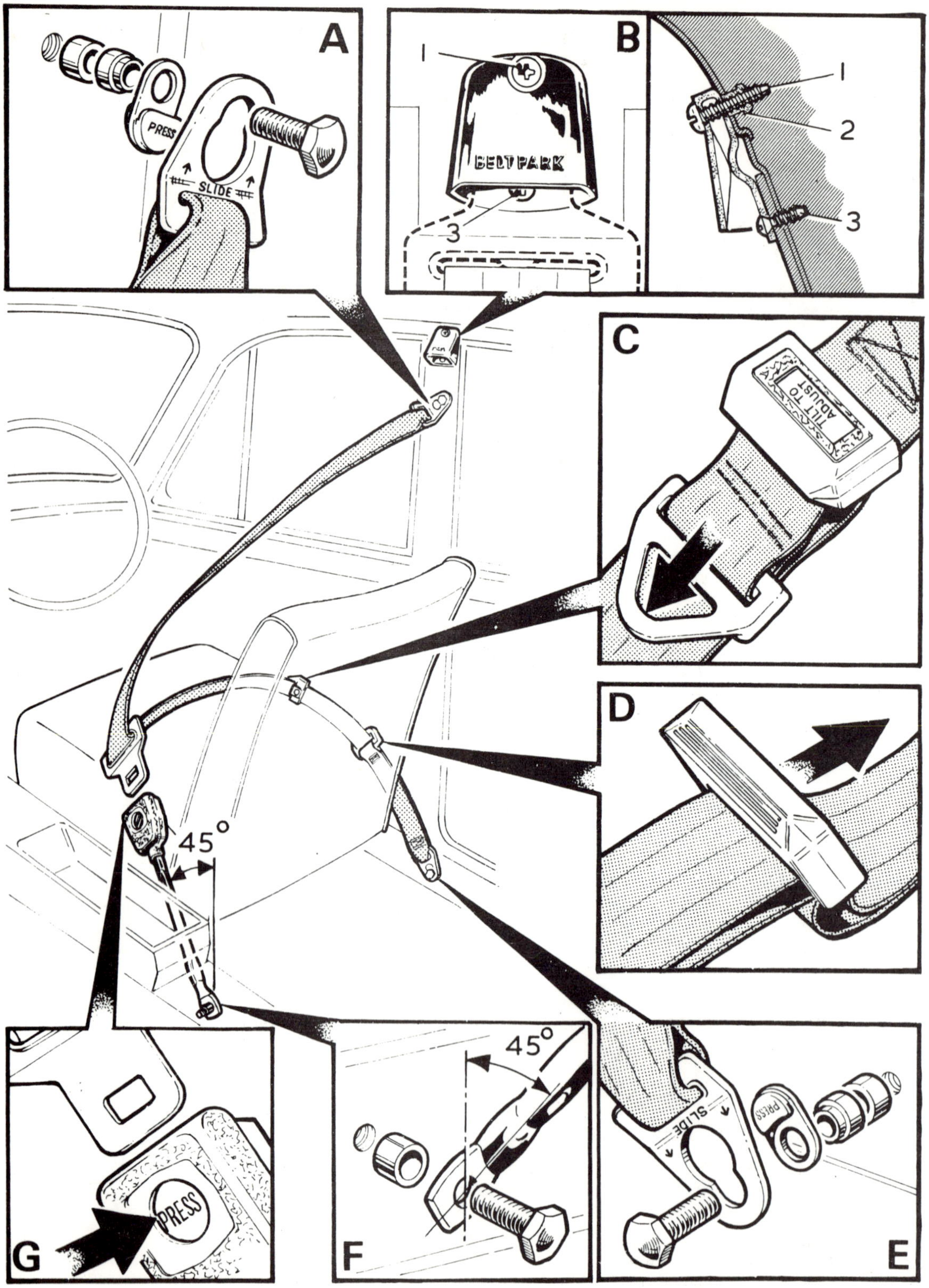

Fig. 13.105. KANGOL ONE-HANDED SAFETY BELTS

A	Pillar anchorage	D	Adjuster	G	Locking assembly	3	Small screw
B	Stowage fixing	E	Lower outer anchorage	1	Large screw		
C	Adjuster	F	Tunnel anchorage	2	Insert		

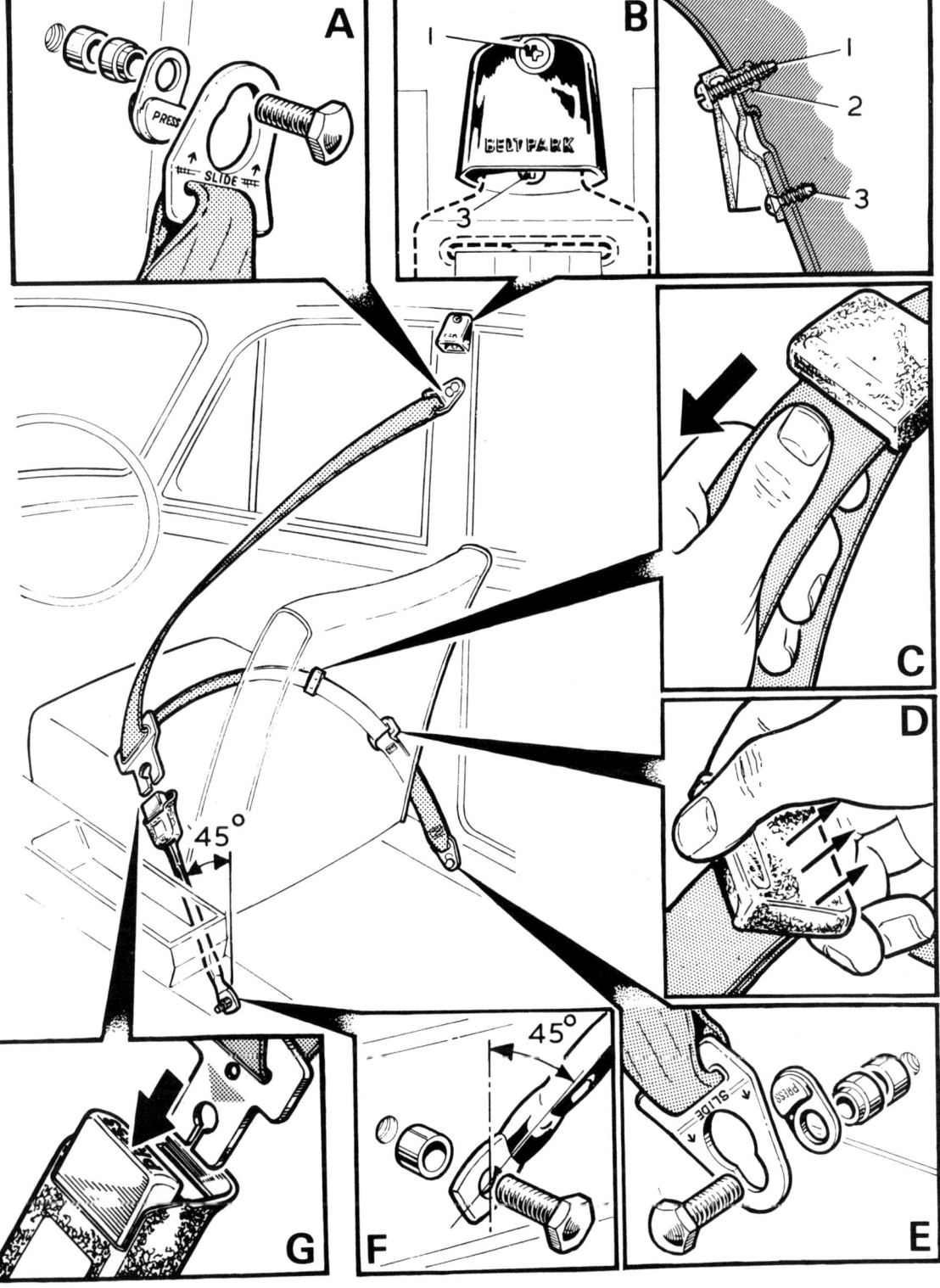

Fig. 13.106. BRITAX ONE-HANDED SAFETY BELTS. SEE
FIG. 13.105 FOR KEY

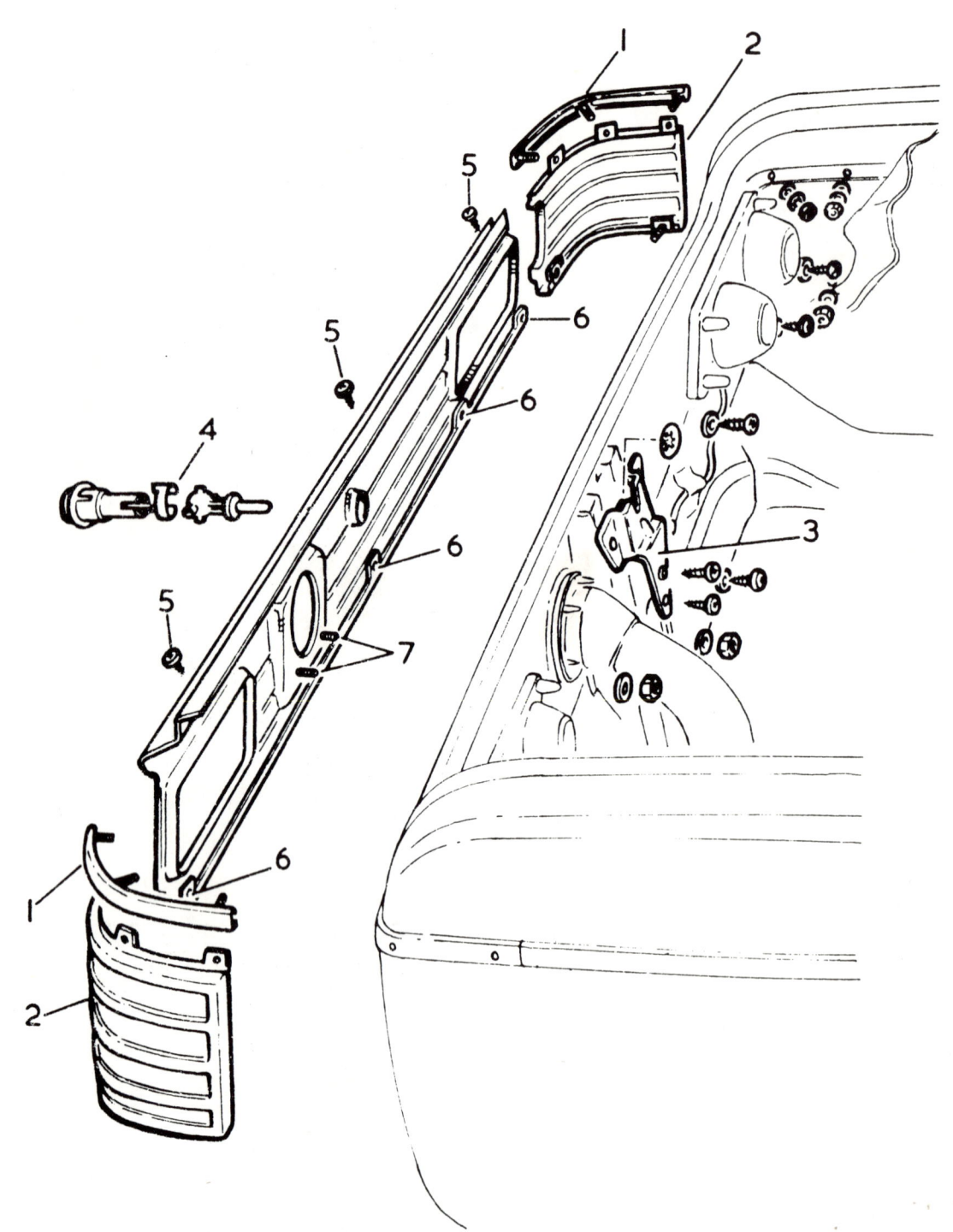

Fig. 13.107. EXPLODED VIEW OF REAR EMBELLISHER ASSEMBLY

| 1 Moulding | 3 Boot lock | 5 Screw | 7 Studs |
| 2 Embellisher | 4 Circular spring | 6 Screw | |

Index

Printed by
Haynes Publishing Group
Sparkford Yeovil Somerset
England